KU-236-632

WITHDRAWN FROM
THE LIBRARY
UNIVERSITY OF
WINCHESTER

REFERENCE

KA 0365425 7

THE IDEA OF LABOUR LAW

The Idea
of Labour Law

EDITORS: GUY DAVIDOV & BRIAN LANGILLE

OXFORD

UNIVERSITY PRESS

UNIVERSITY OF WINCHESTER
LIBRARY

OXFORD

UNIVERSITY PRESS

Great Clarendon Street, Oxford OX2 6DP

Oxford University Press is a department of the University of Oxford.
It furthers the University's objective of excellence in research, scholarship,
and education by publishing worldwide in

Oxford New York

Auckland Cape Town Dar es Salaam Hong Kong Karachi
Kuala Lumpur Madrid Melbourne Mexico City Nairobi
New Delhi Shanghai Taipei Toronto

With offices in

Argentina Austria Brazil Chile Czech Republic France Greece
Guatemala Hungary Italy Japan Poland Portugal Singapore
South Korea Switzerland Thailand Turkey Ukraine Vietnam

Oxford is a registered trade mark of Oxford University Press
in the UK and in certain other countries

Published in the United States
by Oxford University Press Inc., New York

© The several contributors, 2011

The moral rights of the authors have been asserted
Database right Oxford University Press (maker)

Crown copyright material is reproduced under Class Licence
Number C01P0000148 with the permission of OPSI
and the Queen's Printer for Scotland

First published 2011

All rights reserved. No part of this publication may be reproduced,
stored in a retrieval system, or transmitted, in any form or by any means,
without the prior permission in writing of Oxford University Press,
or as expressly permitted by law, or under terms agreed with the appropriate
reprographics rights organization. Enquiries concerning reproduction
outside the scope of the above should be sent to the Rights Department,
Oxford University Press, at the address above

You must not circulate this book in any other binding or cover
and you must impose the same condition on any acquirer

British Library Cataloguing in Publication Data

Data available

Library of Congress Cataloging in Publication Data

Library of Congress Control Number: 2011928002

Typeset by SPI Publisher Services, Pondicherry, India
Printed in Great Britain
on acid-free paper by
CPI Antony Rowe, Chippenham, Wiltshire

ISBN 978–0–19–969361–0

1 3 5 7 9 10 8 6 4 2

UNIVERSITY OF WINCHESTER

03654257   344.01
DAV

Table of Contents

List of Abbreviations xi

Introduction 1
Guy Davidov and Brian Langille

PART I THE IDEA OF LABOUR LAW IN HISTORICAL CONTEXT

1. **Labour Law After Labour** 13
   Harry Arthurs
   A. Introduction 13
   B. What is labour law for? A brief history of the question 13
   C. What is labour law? 15
   D. Conclusion: labour law 'after labour' 28

2. **Factors Influencing the Making and Transformation of Labour Law in Europe** 30
   Bob Hepple
   A. Introduction 30
   B. Changing purposes of labour law 31
   C. Indicators of comparative development 34
   D. Economic developments and policies 36
   E. The changing nature of the state 37
   F. The character of the employers and labour movements and the growing influence of civil society 39
   G. Ideology 40
   H. The future 41

3. **Re-Inventing Labour Law?** 43
   Manfred Weiss
   A. Introduction 43
   B. Need for adaptation 46
   C. Conclusion 56

4. **Hugo Sinzheimer and the Constitutional Function of Labour Law** 57
   Ruth Dukes
   A. Introduction 57
   B. Sinzheimer's conception of the economic constitution 58
   C. The constitutional function of labour law 61
   D. The constitutional function of labour law today 65
   E. Conclusion 67

5. **Global Conceptualizations and Local Constructions of the Idea of Labour Law**   69
Adrián Goldin
   A. The idea of labour law: one or many?   69
   B. On the evolution of 'particular ideas' on labour law   72
   C. Conclusion   87

6. **The Idea of the Idea of Labour Law: A Parable**   88
Alan Hyde

PART II NORMATIVE FOUNDATIONS OF THE IDEA OF LABOUR LAW

7. **Labour Law's Theory of Justice**   101
Brian Langille
   A. Labour law's identity crisis   101
   B. Labour law has always had, and will always have, a theory of justice   102
   C. Labour law's traditional theory of justice   104
   D. Anxiety   107
   E. Therapy   109
   F. A new normativity   111
   G. New ideas, but old anxieties   115

8. **Labour as a 'Fictive Commodity': Radically Reconceptualizing Labour Law**   120
Judy Fudge
   A. Introduction   120
   B. Labour law's past   121
   C. Competing accounts of labour law   124
   D. Expanding the boundaries of, and justifications for, labour law   129
   E. Conclusion: a different imaginary   135

9. **Theories of Rights as Justifications for Labour Law**   137
Hugh Collins
   A. Are labour rights human rights?   140
   B. Fundamental rights in liberal theories of justice   144
   C. Conclusion   153

10. **The Contribution of Labour Law to Economic and Human Development**   156
Simon Deakin
   A. Introduction: law, growth, and development   156
   B. Theoretical perspectives on the relationship of labour law to labour markets   158

C. An illustration of the developmental functions of labour
  law regulation: social insurance systems 164
D. The operation of labour law regulation in developing
  and transition systems 167
E. Labour law and human development 171
F. Conclusion 173

PART III NORMATIVE FOUNDATIONS AND
LEGAL IDEAS: RETHINKING EXISTING
STRUCTURES

11. **Re-Matching Labour Laws with Their Purpose** 179
Guy Davidov
A. Introduction 179
B. Problems of application – bilateral employment relations 181
C. Problems of application – multiple employers 187
D. Conclusion 188

12. **The Legal Characterization of Personal Work Relations
  and the Idea of Labour Law** 190
Mark Freedland and Nicola Kountouris
A. Introduction 190
B. The idea of legal characterization 192
C. A descriptive taxonomy and a critical taxonomy of PWRs 194
D. The critical analysis of PWRs – the role of the personal work profile 197
E. Legal characterization as regulatory technique 202
F. Conclusion 206

13. **Ideas of Labour Law – A View from the South** 209
Paul Benjamin
A. Introduction: 1979 209
B. Towards more secure employment 211
C. Judicial responses 214
D. Employer responses 217
E. Conclusion 220

14. **Informal Employment and the Challenges for Labour Law** 223
Kamala Sankaran
A. From the contract of employment to informal employment 223
B. Labour – from employment, to work, to activity? 227
C. Duality of an employer and employee 230
D. Dealing with poverty and deprivation: is labour law the answer? 232

15. **The Impossibility of Work Law** 234
Noah D Zatz
A. Introduction 234
B. Taking nonmarket work seriously 234

C. Against homogeneous work regulation   244
D. Conclusion: channeling as a possible way forward   253

16. **Using Procurement Law to Enforce Labour Standards**   256
    Catherine Barnard
    A. Introduction   256
    B. Labour law and the public procurement rules   257
    C. The implications of *Commission v Germany (occupational
        pensions)* for social clauses   264
    D. Public procurement, the Posted Workers Directive, and
        labour standards   267
    E. Procurement outside the scope of the General Directive 269
    F. Conclusions   271

17. **Labor Activism in Local Politics: From CBAs to 'CBAs'**   273
    Katherine Stone and Scott Cummings
    A. Introduction   273
    B. The local as an alternative site of labor activism   275
    C. Local labor initiatives: the Los Angeles experience   277
    D. Local labor activism beyond Los Angeles   285
    E. Is local labor activism the new front of labor law?   286
    F. Concluding observations   291

                PART IV NEW LABOUR LAW IDEAS:
              RETHINKING EXISTING BOUNDARIES

18. **The Broad Idea of Labour Law: Industrial Policy, Labour
    Market Regulation, and Decent Work**   295
    John Howe
    A. Introduction   295
    B. Time and place: the historical and cultural contingency
        of traditional labour law   297
    C. Labour law as labour market regulation and the role
        of industrial policy: 'new protection' and the foundations
        of Australian labour law   303
    D. The new industrial policy as labour law   308
    E. Conclusion   313

19. **The Third Function of Labour Law: Distributing Labour
    Market Opportunities among Workers**   315
    Guy Mundlak
    A. Introducing two functions of labour law, and then a third 315
    B. The problem of intra-labour distribution   317
    C. Who speaks for 'labour'?   325
    D. Conclusion – 'Proletarier aller Länder, vereinigt euch!' 328

20. **Beyond Collective Bargaining: Modern Unions as Agents of Social Solidarity** 329
Gillian Lester
   A. Unions and the civic sphere 330
   B. The crisis of labor and the idea of social solidarity 334

21. **From Conflict to Regulation: The Transformative Function of Labour Law** 344
Julia López, Consuelo Chacartegui, and César G Cantón
   A. Conflict and regulation: the transformation of labour law through conflict 344
   B. Invisibility of rights (in international instruments of regulation) and the invisibility of conflict at the national level 348
   C. Self-regulation instruments: a corporate culture of denial of conflict 355
   D. Transforming the regulation of social rights through conflict as a manifestation of solidarity 358

PART V NEW IDEAS OF LABOUR LAW FROM AN INTERNATIONAL PERSPECTIVE

22. **Out of the Shadows? The Non-Binding Multilateral Framework on Migration (2006) and Prospects for Using International Labour Regulation to Forge Global Labour Market Membership** 365
Leah F Vosko
   A. Citizenship boundaries in international labour regulations on migration for employment: an historical perspective 368
   B. The Multilateral Framework on Migration: expanding citizenship boundaries through international labour regulation? 377
   C. Fostering global labour market membership 380

23. **Flexible Bureaucracies in Labor Market Regulation** 385
Michael J Piore
   A. The problem: the need for flexibility in a regulatory framework 385
   B. A note about analytical ambition 386
   C. Two models of labor market regulation 388
   D. Managing the Franco-Latin model: work inspectors as street-level bureaucrats 389
   E. A scientific foundation for labor inspection 395
   F. The moral foundations of labor standards 400
   G. Conclusions: globalization 403

24. **Collective Exit Strategies: New Ideas in Transnational Labour Law** 405
Silvana Sciarra
   A. A short preface on transnational juridification 405
   B. A war of messages and measures 408

C. Beyond the state: consensual strategies at a global level   413
D. Concluding remarks   418

25. Emancipation in the Idea of Labour Law   420
Adelle Blackett
A. Introduction   420
B. Commoditization   421
C. Emancipation   431
D. Conclusion   435

Index   437

List of Abbreviations

ACAS	Advisory, Conciliation and Arbitration Service
ACFTU	All-China Federation of Trade Unions
ADR	alternative dispute resolution
AFL	American Federation of Labor
AMRC	Asia Monitor Resource Center
ATA	American Trucking Association
BRU	Bus Riders' Union
CBA	Collective Bargaining Agreement, Community Benefits Agreement
CCMA	Commission for Conciliation, Mediation and Arbitration
CHIRLA	Coalition for Humane Immigrant Rights of Los Angeles
CIO	Congress of Industrial Organization
CLUE	Clergy and Laity United for Economic Justice
CoC	code of conduct
CSR	corporate social responsibility
CUP	conditional use permit
ECHR	European Convention on Human Rights
ECJ	European Court of Justice
ECtHR	European Court of Human Rights
ETI	Ethical Trade Initiative
EU	European Union
EWC	European Works Council
FAAA	Federal Aviation Administrative Authorization Act
FLA	Fair Labor Association
GDP	gross domestic product
GFC	global financial crisis
GLA	Greater London Authority
GPA	Agreement on Government Procurement
GRI	Global Reporting Initiative
GWC	Garment Worker Center
HDI	Human Development Index
HERE	Hotel Employees and Restaurant Union
HPWS	high-performance work systems
ICFTU	International Confederation of Free Trade Unions
ICMM	International Council on Mining and Metals
IFBWW	International Federation of Building and Wood Workers
ILO	International Labour Organization
IMF	International Monetary Fund
ITUC	International Trade Union Confederation
LAANE	Los Angeles Alliance for the New Economy
LAX	Los Angeles Airport
LMR	labour market regulation
MEAT	most economically advantageous tender

MFM	Multilateral Framework on Migration
MNE	multinational enterprise
MRBW	We Make the Road by Walking
NDLON	National Day Labor Organizing Network
NFM	Non-Binding Multilateral Framework on Migration
NGO	non-governmental organization
OECD	Organisation for Economic Co-operation and Development
OGC	Office of Government Commerce
PWD	Posted Workers Directive
SAJE	Strategic Actions for a Just Economy
SEIU	Service Employees International Union
SEWA	Self-Employed Women's Association
TFEU	Treaty on the Functioning of the European Union
TIDC	Tourism Industry Development Council
TNC	transnational companies
UCL	University College London
UCLA	University of California, Los Angeles
UFCW	United Food and Commercial Workers Union
UK	United Kingdom
UN	United Nations
UNITE	Union of Needle Trades, Industrial and Textile Employees
UPS	United Parcel Service
USA	United States of America
WRAP	Worldwide Responsible Accredited Production
WTO	World Trade Organization

Introduction

Understanding Labour Law: A Timeless Idea, a Timed-Out Idea, or an Idea Whose Time has Now Come?

*Guy Davidov and Brian Langille**

Labour law is widely considered to be in crisis, at least by scholars of the field. This crisis has an obvious external dimension – labour law is attacked for impeding efficiency, flexibility and development; vilified for reducing employment and for favouring already well-placed employees over less fortunate ones; and discredited for failing to cover the most vulnerable workers and workers in the 'informal sector'. These are just some of the external challenges to labour law. But there is also an internal challenge, as labour lawyers themselves increasingly question whether their discipline is conceptually coherent, relevant to the new empirical realities of the world of work, and normatively salient in the world as we now know it. The goal of this book is to respond to such fundamental challenges by asking the most fundamental questions: What is labour law for? How can it be justified? And what are the normative premises on which reforms should be based? There has been growing interest in such questions in recent years.[1] The current book seeks to take this body of scholarship seriously and take it forward. Its aim is to provide, if

* This book is the result of a workshop we held at St Catharine's College, Cambridge in April 2010. We wish to express our deep gratitude to the Inter-University Research Centre on Globalization and Work (CRIMT) for generously supporting this conference.

[1] See H Collins, 'Justifications and Techniques of Legal Regulation of the Employment Relation' in H Collins et al (eds), *Legal Regulation of the Employment Relation* (Kluwer, 2000) 3; A Supiot, *Beyond Employment: Changes in Work and the Future of Labour Law in Europe* (Oxford University Press, 2001); B Langille, 'Labour Law's Back Pages' in G Davidov and B Langille (eds), *Boundaries and Frontiers of Labour Law: Goals and Means in the Regulation of Work* (Hart Publishing, 2006), 13; A Hyde, 'What is Labour Law?' in Davidov and Langille, ibid 37; Christopher Arup et al (eds), *Labour Law and Labour Market Regulation: Essays on the Construction, Constitution and Regulation of Labour Markets* (Federation Press, 2006); G Davidov, 'The (Changing?) Idea of Labour Law' (2007) 146 International Labour Review 311; R McCallum, 'In Defence of Labour Law' (Sydney Law School Research Paper No 07/20, available at <http://ssrn.com/abstract=985006>); S Deakin and W Njoya, 'The Legal Framework of Employment Relations' (CBR Working Paper No 349, September 2007, available at <http://www.cbr.cam.ac.uk/pdf/WP349.pdf>); H Spector, 'Philosophical Foundations of Labor Law' (2006) 33 Florida State University Law Review 1119; and R Dukes, 'Constitutionalizing Employment Relations: Sinzheimer, Kahn-Freund, and the Role of Labour Law' (2008) 35 Journal of Law and Society 341.

not answers which satisfy everyone, at least intellectually nourishing food for thought for those interested in understanding, explaining and interpreting labour laws – whether they are scholars, practitioners, judges, policy-makers or workers and employers.

The global economic crisis of 2008 brought these questions even more to the forefront. If nothing else it exposed the dangers of 'deregulation'. As a result it provided a moment for renewed interest around the world in rethinking unconstrained market ordering and in systems that secure less risky processes and more equitable outcomes. But neo-liberal thinkers and neo-classical economists have hardly surrendered intellectually and the debate over how best to govern labour markets continues – only with more urgency. This presents an opportunity for a rethinking of possible and different methods of market regulation. What role should labour law play (alongside other market institutions) in a sustainable and just version of capitalism? The crisis of labour law, both internal and external, which has been widely observed over the past years, has turned into an opportunity for reinvigoration and renewal. The basic notion informing this volume is that this opportunity to re-think labour law will be lost if we do not start from first principles – that is, if we do not focus our thinking on the very idea of labour law.

In an effort to take the opportunity presented by the crisis in labour law, and in the belief that it is only by starting with basic principles that this opportunity can be seized, 29 leading scholars form around the globe have contributed to this book. Each has a different approach; each touches upon a different aspect of the same problem. There are different ways to connect them and we have chosen one option for the structure of this book out of many which were possible and plausible. We elaborate upon that structure below. But we should note that one of the questions that continue to hover in the background throughout most of the book is whether the idea of labour law is constant or changing. Is it different in different countries? Should it change as circumstances change? Is it the same at the national and international level, or for developed and developing economies? Are we looking for new solutions to old problems? Or are perhaps the problems themselves new? Are we trying to provide a better understanding of an existing body of law, or are we searching for a new legal order? Otherwise put, is the idea of labour law a timeless one, an outdated one, or is labour law, better understood, a new idea whose time has now come?

Part I: The idea of labour law in historical context

It is most appropriate to start such inquiries by taking an historical perspective. **Harry Arthurs** argues in his chapter that labour law used to be concerned with 'labour' – as a class and a movement – which is now disappearing. He then puts forward three possible directions which labour law can take 'after labour': labour rights as a subset of human rights; facilitating the accumulation of human capital; and retaining the original idea – enabling workers to mobilize to seek justice in the workplace – but with new structures and forms of mobilization. This analysis is a prelude (and in some sense, a response) to many of the discussions that appear later in this book.

Like Arthurs, **Bob Hepple** also puts emphasis on the role of broad social and economic developments in shaping labour law. He argues that labour law is best understood as the outcome of struggles between different social groups and competing ideologies. He therefore prefers a descriptive analysis, which seeks to explain changes over time and variations between different legal systems by linking them to particular historical circumstances. Among the factors shaping the making and transformation of labour law, Hepple lists the level of economic development; the changing nature of the state; the character of the employers and labour movements and the growing influence of civil society; and ideology.

Manfred Weiss begins his contribution by putting forward the original idea of labour law as expressed mainly by Hugo Sinzheimer. He then argues that, even though realities in the workplace have changed dramatically, the core assumptions have not disappeared. There is no need for a new paradigm. There is, however, a need to adapt labour laws to new circumstances, and the chapter goes on to discuss a few examples, such as the need to find ways for collective representation of people in new (atypical) work forms; the need to create a closer link between labour law and social security law; and the need to strengthen transnational collective structures and other international standard-setting institutions.

A belief in a basic idea of labour law which has not changed is shared by **Ruth Dukes**, who also relies on the work of Sinzheimer (regarded as the founding father of German labour law). Searching for a core idea which can be generalized and remains valid today, she emphasizes the constitutional function of labour law, in the sense of its role in establishing a social and economic order while taking the humanity of the worker as a 'first reference point'. She then uses this framework to highlight the strains currently put on labour law from supra-national powers.

Adrián Goldin examines directly the question of whether there is a universal idea of labour law by using an historical but also a comparative methodology. He identifies the 'basic' idea of labour law, which is joined by 'particular ideas' adding specific and idiosyncratic elements. Goldin argues that, in the face of the past decades' changes, 'some legal systems have shown a bigger propensity to move away from that basic idea', while others have not. The chapter reviews some significant changes undergone in European labour law, but argues that there was no separation from the basic idea. In common-law countries Goldin finds some divergence from the basic idea, although more so among academics than in practice. And in Latin America, he sees no departing from the basic idea, and criticizes the inability to adapt and the 'freezing' of the traditional order.

The opening part of the book is concluded with the witty critique of **Alan Hyde**, who lists no less than 22 different 'ideas of labour law' that have been put forward over the years. He argues, however, that these lofty ideas have lost contact with what actually happens on the ground – at least in the United States. It is not only that labour unions have weakened dramatically. The fact that, for many years, no significant labour laws have been enacted by Congress or developed by the Labour Board, is equally discouraging for those who believe in the future of labour law.

Hyde concludes that labour law will continue only as a 'technical' branch of regulation; the idea of labour law can no longer realistically continue to provide a source of inspiration.

Part II: Normative foundations of the idea of labour law

The chapters constituting the next part of the book tackle directly the philosophical foundations of the field. **Brian Langille** starts by explaining why labour law *must* have a theory of justice. He then argues that labour law's 'traditional' theory of justice – based on the idea of inequality of bargaining power – is out of date. There is another (better) moral foundation that can justify labour law and at the same time help us to rethink the field – in much broader terms. Following Amartya Sen, Langille argues that our basic goal is 'real, substantive, human freedom – the real capacity to lead a life we have reason to value'. And labour law is needed to structure the creation and deployment of human capital – which is 'at the core of human freedom'. He goes on to provide a detailed response to some of the critiques of this idea.

Judy Fudge examines in her chapter some competing accounts of labour law, including ones that rely on Sen's idea of enhancing people's 'capabilities' to live the kinds of lives that they value.[2] She sees a number of strengths with this approach, but also a few important limitations. She then goes on to suggest a different basis for conceptualizing labour law: the idea that labour is not a commodity but rather a 'fictive commodity'. The unique problems associated with selling labour create 'regulatory dilemmas' – and the role of labour law is to address them. In this context Fudge uses the 'capabilities' approach but supplements it to argue against the exclusion of unpaid care work from the scope of labour law.

Hugh Collins has written before about two prominent strands of justifications for labour law: efficiency/welfare on the one hand and social justice/fair distribution on the other.[3] Aware of the difficulties with both types of justifications, he sets out on a journey, in his chapter, to examine whether some theory of rights can provide the basis for labour rights. He concludes that the case for including labour rights as universal human rights is weak. However, following John Rawls' liberal theory of justice – and rebutting Rawls' reasons for excluding social and economic rights – Collins argues that at least *some* labour rights can be justified as 'fundamental constitutional guarantees'.

In the final chapter of this part, **Simon Deakin** argues that labour law not only 'corrects' the market (when imperfections/failures are present) and 'limits' the

---

[2] Alongside Langille, she refers here especially to J Brown, S Deakin, and B Wilkinson, 'Capabilities, Social Rights and European Market Integration' in R Salais and R Villeneuve (eds), *Europe and the Politics of Capabilities* (Cambridge University Press, 2004) 205; and to S Deakin and F Wilkinson, *The Law of the Labour Market; Industrialization, Employment, and Legal Evolution* (Oxford University Press, 2005).

[3] Collins, above n 1.

market (when results are not socially acceptable), it also has a 'market constituting' role. That is, labour laws sometimes play an important role in stimulating development. This 'systemic' view can also explain how labour laws have developed over the years alongside other market institutions, and which processes are likely to create pressures to deregulate them. Deakin gives a number of examples from developing and transition systems, but he points out that this analysis is relevant to developed economies as well. Referring not only to economic development but also to human development, he concludes by connecting between his analysis and Sen's 'capabilities' approach.

Part III: Normative foundations and legal ideas: rethinking existing structures

In the next group of chapters, the authors discuss connections between the *goals* and *means* of labour law. In different ways, they consider what a particular understanding of labour law means for the scope or contents of this body of laws, or how legal techniques should be recast to better reflect the idea behind the field. **Guy Davidov** insists that the crisis of labour law is not the result of any change in our goals. It is rather a mismatch between some labour laws (legislation and case law) and these goals, created by changing realities. The idea of labour law can be articulated in different ways and at different levels of generalization.[4] After examining problems with the actual application of labour laws, as encountered by workers in many countries, Davidov argues that for purposes of determining the scope of labour law as well as updating labour laws in light of changing employment practises, it is useful to focus on the characteristics showing the vulnerability of employees vis-à-vis their employers – that is, on the factual situation that labour laws are designed to address.

Mark Freedland and Nicola Kountouris provide some new analytical tools that can assist in understanding and regulating the employment relationship. Focusing in general on 'personal work relations', they classify them into three groups: secure, autonomous, and precarious work. In order to classify particular relations into one of these groups, one should look at the 'personal work profile' of the worker in question. This perspective, they argue, helps to uncover elements that have been traditionally concealed by the binary employee/self-employed divide. The entire context (the work profile) should be taken into account, even aspects that have nothing to do with a specific employer. Freedland and Kountouris further explain that new kinds of personal work relations are being created all the time, but the law usually fails to recognize them. The implications of this 'phenomenon of fully or partly innominate personal work contracts or relations' are discussed in their chapter.

---

[4] He explored the idea of labour law itself in Davidov, above n 1.

The chapter by **Paul Benjamin** examines the operation of legal techniques and institutions vis-à-vis one of the goals of labour law: protection against unfair and arbitrary dismissals. This is an important reminder that the goals of labour law are often elusive in practice, so it is crucial to examine to what extent – and how – can they be materialized. Benjamin discusses the Commission for Conciliation, Mediation and Arbitration created in South Africa in 1995, which has been successful because of its focus on access to justice instead of the traditional model of rights enforced through conventional litigation. Judicial responses (which sometime have hindered the achievement of labour law's goals) and employer responses (which, as in many other countries, have looked for ways to evade the law) are also discussed.

Another developing economy perspective is offered by **Kamala Sankaran**, who writes from the point of view of India, where 93 per cent of the workforce is considered to be in 'informal' employment. Sankaran discusses the definitions of labour statisticians for 'informal work' and their relation to labour law, including the invisibility of unpaid domestic work on the one hand, and the inclusion of own-account workers who are also employers on the other. She then considers the implications for the future of labour law.

In recent years there have been increasing calls to broaden the scope of labour law to include other relationships involving work. Such calls are echoed and further developed in a number of chapters in this book. **Noah D Zatz** argues that replacing labour and employment law with a broader 'work law' is in fact impossible. Although he shares the view that nonmarket work should be taken more seriously, as an object of study and regulation, and provides a sophisticated critique of existing boundaries based on 'control' and 'exchange', Zatz goes on to argue against an homogenous system of work regulation. He shows how the multiplicity of work relations makes this unwarranted; 'different forms of work must be treated differently'. He nonetheless refuses to retreat to the problematic 'market' boundaries, introducing the idea of 'channelling' work into specific institutional forms as a possible solution.

One of the most salient aspects of the crisis of labour law is its inability in an increasing number of cases to deliver the necessary rights and entitlements to workers. While scholars look for solutions, innovations also emerge from the workers themselves (and their lawyers). The next two chapters discuss new legal means that are being used by workers (or others on their behalf) *outside* of what we traditionally considered labour law, in an attempt to secure the same goals. **Catherine Barnard** analyses the use of procurement law in this context. Can a government spending public money include a 'social clause' in tenders to ensure compliance with labour standards and/or the hiring of local workers? There has been pressure from the bottom up for such clauses. However, as Barnard shows, European Union law as well as international law put various obstacles on their inclusion. She concludes by considering the possibility that a *private* contractor, bowing to pressure from public opinion and relying on a commitment to corporate social responsibility, will demand a social clause from its subcontractors.

Barnard's focus is on Britain, but experiments rising from the bottom up are also flourishing in the United States. **Katherine Stone and Scott Cummings** discuss the use of Community Benefits Agreements as well as other local initiatives which 'have emerged in the vacuum where labour law has failed'. The new CBAs (which in practice often replace the now-uncommon Collective Bargaining Agreements bearing the same acronym) are negotiated between labour/community groups and developers, to secure (among other things) a certain level of labour standards. The authors analyse the legal and practical challenges faced by these local initiatives of labour and community alliances, and consider whether they can be seen as a new form of unionism, and whether they can offer an adequate substitute for traditional techniques.

Part IV: New labour law ideas: rethinking existing boundaries

The next group of chapters offer new ways of thinking about labour law. None of them aims to contradict or challenge the basic understanding of why labour law is needed. But they all suggest that there are additional aspects that have so far been neglected and should be considered as part of our understanding of the filed. **John Howe** argues that industrial policies (such as tariff protection or industry assistance) should be considered as part of labour law. This chapter has direct connections with the previous two chapters: it also shows how legal issues that appear to be outside the scope of labour law in fact have direct impact on labour standards. But here the focus is different. While the previous chapters discussed new means (legal techniques), Howe makes the point that a broader understanding of labour law should lead to a re-stating of our goals. As part of a 'labour market perspective' (which is broader than traditional labour law, and concerned not only with employees but also with other work arrangements, including unpaid work, as well as transitions between employment and unemployment), labour lawyers should be interested in the role and impact of industrial policies. This view, the chapter argues, recognizes that regulation of the employment relationship has multiple purposes that change over time and place. The idea is not to abandon the familiar 'protective' function of labour law, but rather to supplement it with a broader view that can also help explain why traditional labour law is ineffective.

Guy Mundlak argues that, alongside the 'traditional' functions of labour law, there is another, and often neglected, function: to distribute labour market opportunities among workers. Labour law is not only concerned with distribution between capital and labour, but also between the workers themselves (including those who *can* work but are unemployed). Different workers have different (and clashing) interests, and this chapter argues that these divisions should not be concealed. Rather, we should acknowledge them and 'make labour law accountable to the distributive impact it bears' – always asking ourselves which workers gain and which workers lose from any particular arrangement.

The chapter by **Gillian Lester** also uncovers a neglected part of labour law: labour unions' participation in the civic and political spheres, going beyond the immediate bargaining concerns of their members. Lester justifies this role and advocates its development; she argues that unions can restore their vitality by 'taking leadership in generating broader social solidarity'. She gives examples of two recent trends to support this point: the first is identity-based organizing (in the United States); the second, legal action by unions to enforce employment rights which is used strategically to encourage organizing. If this view of the function of labour unions is accepted, arguably some labour laws will have to change to support this function.

Unions are also the focus of the chapter by **Julia López, Consuelo Chacartegui, and César G Cantón**. Here too, the broader political role played by unions is justified. But while the previous chapter focused on solidarity, the current one is concerned with *conflict*. The authors do not see conflicts as a problem; rather, they celebrate their value in promoting transformation. They thus make the case for 'understanding labour law through the prism provided by strikes and other forms of conflict'. The right to strike (and protest) plays an important role, they argue, in allowing and encouraging divergences, which are healthy for democracy and for society. Conflict, which is often denied, should become more visible, and the right to strike should assume a more explicit and prominent role in labour law.

Part V: New ideas of labour law from an international perspective

The chapters constituting the final part of the book all take an international perspective, using it to explore the goals (and sometimes the means) of labour law. **Leah F Vosko** focuses on migrant workers and their exclusion (or *partial* exclusion) from the 'full range of labour protections', based on citizenship. She identifies four different phases in the development of international regulations concerning migrant workers, concluding with the Non-Binding Multilateral Framework on Migration (MFM) adopted by the ILO on 2006. Vosko finds a continued tension in the MFM between national sovereignty concerns and the need to protect migrant workers. She argues that these tensions highlight the need for 'global labour market membership'[5] to prevent the exclusion of migrant workers from protection due to citizenship boundaries. She puts forward five principles for international action in this regard, that can be seen as routes to achieve the goals of labour law in this context.

The chapter by **Michael Piore** offers an economist's perspective on the future of labour law following the recent financial crisis. He sees renewed interest in enforcing labour standards, which in many countries brought about increased resources to labour inspection. Piore compares the approaches of the United States and France to labour inspection, and argues that – contrary to common beliefs about the rigidity of European systems – the French system is considerably more flexible and able to adjust to variations in economic and social conditions. The fact that inspectors in France – and in other countries that adopted similar systems – hold considerable power and discretion is seen as an advantage by Piore. He uses various

---

[5] A concept she developed in LF Vosko, *Managing the Margins: Gender, Citizenship and the International Regulation of Precarious Employment* (Oxford University Press, 2010).

strands of socio-economic literature to analyse the work of inspectors. He concludes that the perceived conflict between regulation and flexibility is to a large extent artificial, because as we can learn from the French – using the example of labour inspection – a system of labour market regulation has the potential to include the needed flexibility within it.

Silvana Sciarra also situates her chapter in the context of responding to the recent financial crisis. Rising economic uncertainties – resulting not only from the current crisis but also from long-term processes of globalization – put pressure on traditional (national) labour laws and on accepted hierarchies of legal sources. Sciarra describes some innovative forms of standard-setting at the European level – in particular transnational collective strategies – that mix private and public actors. Special attention is given to agreements signed by European Works Councils. The chapter discusses the relations between such new instruments and the nation state, raising in particular the problem of legitimacy. This chapter as well is useful in analysing new means (in this case, transnational) to achieve the goals of labour law.

In the final chapter of the book, **Adelle Blackett** challenges the common view of labour law, which she sees as being concerned only with developed economies, including boundaries defined 'as after the formation of mature capitalism, in individual nation states of the North, and outside of the domestic household'. Blackett builds instead 'on the experiences of the overwhelming majority of workers who have remained outside of the story of the paradigmatic worker', and offers an alternative narrative, which starts from the idea of *emancipation*. Her story of labour law centres on workers' resistance to commoditization and their struggle for citizenship at work. Like the opening chapters of the book, this chapter takes an historical perspective, but from a global/development angle. Blackett's analysis sheds light on the distributive aspects of labour law beyond borders, arguing that this is – and should be – a necessary part of the story.

The future of the idea of labour law

Roughly a century has passed since the emergence of modern labour law, yet the very idea of the field is still being debated. This is not necessarily a problem. Indeed, perhaps the problem has been that the idea of labour law has not been questioned and examined sufficiently in the past. The 'traditional' story of labour law was important, but in retrospect, always incomplete. The same is true for the traditional economic critique of the field. The chapters of this book show that there is still a reason to treat labour law as an independent and coherent field of law – but it is necessary to continually rethink the goals and means of this field.

Some of the contributors to this book argue that the idea of labour law is unchanged, and offer their own articulation for it, or examine the implications (notably the need to change the law to respond to new realities). Others believe that the idea of labour law should itself be broadened in different ways to respond to new needs. Yet others offer an entirely new way of thinking about the idea of the field. This is not a book that aims to provide an authoritative conclusion to a problem. Rather, the cumulative effort of the contributors puts forward a rich variety of new ways to think about labour law. These in turn will help thinking about reforms in labour market regulation, about new interpretations to existing laws, about the constitutionality of labour laws, and more.

PART I

THE IDEA OF LABOUR LAW IN HISTORICAL CONTEXT

1

Labour Law After Labour

*Harry Arthurs**

A. Introduction

'What is labour law for?' is a question with a past. I therefore begin by sketching out its history. It has a present too, whose most striking feature – I argue – may well be the end of 'labour'. And of course it has a future: what will labour law look like 'after labour'? I address all three questions largely from a North American perspective, but with reference to experience in the United Kingdom and Europe.

B. What is labour law for? A brief history of the question

In Anglo-American countries, at various times, labour law has aspired to make it possible for workers to conform to the tenets of Christian morality,[1] to confer on them a sense of membership in 'one nation',[2] to prevent them from destroying 'that property which is the source of their own support and comfort in life',[3] to wean them from materialism[4] or radical ideologies,[5] to give them a stake in the success of the enterprise and/or the capitalist system,[6] to restore their capacity to consume and hence their incentives and opportunities to produce,[7] to enable

---

* Osgoode Hall Law School, York University, Toronto. I am grateful for the research assistance of Ian Medcalf and for the helpful critique of participants in the workshop on *What Is Labour Law For?* (Cambridge, April 2010) and in several seminars at which earlier versions of this essay were presented.

[1] See DC Somervell, *English Thought in the Nineteenth Century* (Methuen & Co Ltd, 1947) 82–3.

[2] 'One nation' conservatism – the antecedent of today's Red Toryism – takes its name and inspiration from Benjamin Disraeli's 1845 novel *Sybil, or the Two Nations* (Oxford University Press, 1981).

[3] *Springhead Spinning Co* v *Riley*, LR 6 Eq 551 (1868) 562–3.

[4] Pope Leo XVIII, 'Rerum Novarum' (Encyclical of Pope Leo XII on Capital and Labour 1891) <http://www.vatican.va/holy_father/leo_xiii/encyclicals/documents/hf_l-xiii_enc_15051891_rerum-novarum_en.html>.

[5] KE Klare, 'Judicial Deradicalization of the Wagner Act and the Origins of Modern Legal Consciousness, 1937–1941' (1977–1978) 62 Minn L Rev 265, 267.

[6] See, eg, KE Klare, 'Labor Law as Ideology: Toward a New Historiography of Collective Bargaining Law' (1980–1981) 4 Indus Rel LJ 450, 458–9.

[7] The National Labor Relations Act, 29 USC §§ 151 (1935) begins with a Congressional finding that: 'The inequality of bargaining power between employees...and employers...substantially

them to claim in the workplace the constitutional guarantees provided by liberal democracies to all citizens in the larger polity,[8] to enlist their support for the national war effort[9] and ongoing projects of nation building,[10] to legitimate and reinforce the 'web of rule' they help to spin in every workplace,[11] to create a system of counter-vailing power which facilitates the operation of labour markets and improves their outcomes,[12] and to incorporate workers into enterprise-level structures designed to manage their discontent,[13] broker compromise amongst them,[14] and implement workplace practices that contribute to productivity and profitability.[15]

Understandably, therefore, the substantive content of labour law has changed over time. In the early years of the industrial revolution, it sought to protect the most vulnerable workers against physical and moral brutality,[16] then to ensure that they worked in safe and salubrious conditions[17] and ultimately to require that they be paid enough to meet 'the normal needs of the average employee regarded as a human being living in a civilized community'.[18] However, from the end of the 19th century, and through much of the 20th, labour law was largely focussed on collective issues. In one version, labour laws permitted, protected or promoted concerted worker action;[19] in another they sought to regulate, and if possible resolve, union–management conflict;[20] and in a third, they ideally operated by way of 'abstention' so that employer and worker representatives could institute a regime of 'collective laissez faire'.[21]

---

burdens and affects the flow of commerce, and tends to aggravate recurrent business depressions, by depressing wage rates and the purchasing power of wage earners.'

[8] See, eg, WM Leiserson, 'Constitutional Government in American Industries' (1922) 12 Amer Econ Rev 56, 61 ff; H Shulman, 'Reason, Contract, and Law in Labor Relations' (1955) 68 Harv LR 999, 1002 ff; and M Derber, *The American Idea of Industrial Democracy, 1865–1965* (University of Illinois Press, 1970). For extensive critiques see K Stone, 'The Post-War Paradigm in American Labor Law' (1981) 90 Yale LJ 1509, 1514–15; and J Fudge, 'After Industrial Citizenship: Market Citizenship or Citizenship at Work?' (2005) 60 Indus Rel / Rel Indus 631.

[9] See J Fudge and E Tucker, *Labour Before the Law: The Regulation of Workers' Collective Action in Canada, 1900–1948* (Oxford University Press Canada, 2001) 251–2.

[10] D Beland and A Lecours, 'Nationalism and Social Policy in Canada and Quebec' in N McEwen and L Moreno (eds), *The Territorial Politics of Welfare* (Routledge, 2005) 189, 196–7.

[11] J Dunlop, *The Industrial Relations System* (Southern Illinois University Press, 1958) 7–18.

[12] JK Galbraith, *American Capitalism: The Concept of Countervailing Power* (Houghton Mifflin, 1952) 137–8.

[13] C Wright Mills, *The New Men of Power: America's Labor Leaders* (Harcourt, Brace, 1948) 9.

[14] A Cox, 'Rights under a Labor Agreement' (1956) 19 Harv LR 601, 626–7; G Mundlak, 'The Third Function of Labour Law: Distributing Labour Market Opportunities Among Workers' (this volume).

[15] R Freeman and J Medoff, 'The Two Faces of Unionism' (1979) 57 The Public Interest 69, 79–80; and for a less positive view see R Freeman, 'What Do Unions Do?' (2005) 26 J Lab Res 641, 657.

[16] EP Thompson, *The Making of the English Working Class* (Pelican Books, 1977) ch 10.

[17] H Arthurs, *Without the Law: Administrative Justice and Legal Pluralism in Nineteenth-Century England* (University of Toronto Press, 1985) ch 4.

[18] *Ex Parte H v McKay* (1907) 2 CAR 1 per Higgins CJ (Commonwealth Court of Conciliation and Arbitration).

[19] Trade Disputes Act 1906 (UK) XLIV 246 f 6 Edward VII c 47 (permitted); Norris Laguardia Act 29 USCA § 101 et seq (1932) (protected); National Labor Relations Act 29 USC §§ 151–69, §151 (1935) (promoted).

[20] Industrial Disputes Investigation Act, SC 1907, ch 20.

[21] O Kahn-Freund, *Labour and the Law* (Hamlyn Lectures, Stevens for the Hamlyn Trust, London 1972).

However, this focus on collective bargaining and economic conflict left many questions unresolved. First: how to integrate collective bargaining outcomes with macro-economic policies? In the early postwar period, most advanced economies relied on Keynesian measures to promote economic expansion and full employ-ment, thereby creating a positive environment for collective bargaining; latterly, they adopted monetarist policies often in tandem with the deregulation of labour markets and restrictions on union power. Second: how to address labour market issues that collective bargaining could not resolve because they affected workers before or after entering employment? States either left such problems unresolved, or intervened to train workers, deploy them across the economy, and insure them – more or less – against illness, redundancy, and retirement. And third: how to protect workers in non-union workplaces? Again the answers varied: the extension of collective agreements to cover non-union workers; the adoption of employment standards and anti-discrimination legislation; enhanced protection of job tenure and against arbitrary dismissal; the establishment of arrangements designed to ensure worker participation in corporate governance. But neither the questions nor the answers much interested labour law scholars and practitioners whose focus, as noted, was on collective relations, primarily at the workplace level.

This impressionistic sketch of two centuries of labour law development might suggest that 'labour law' is a legal field with arbitrary but variable boundaries and no inherent content or purpose. However, many of us who teach, practice, and administer labour law want to believe in its distinctiveness, coherence, and even (here opinions differ) its functional and conceptual autonomy.[22] Hence the ques-tion posed in the next section of this chapter: 'What is labour law?'

C. What is labour law?

1. Is labour law *law*?

Law is usually understood to emanate from legislatures, to be administered by state officials, interpreted by state judges, and enforced by the state's coercive power. However, in many accounts of the origins and operation of labour law, labour and management are said to play a significant role in its enactment and adminis-tration.[23] Indeed, this role has sometimes been described as 'constitutional'.[24] Moreover, even when labour laws are enacted by the state, they are often inter-preted and applied by specialized public, private or hybrid agencies and tribunals,

---

[22] See, eg, Lord Wedderburn, 'Labour Law: From Here to Autonomy' (1987) 16 Indus Law J 1; Lord Wedderburn, 'Labour Law: Autonomy from the Common Law' (1987–1988) 9 Comp Lab LJ 219; and D Howarth, 'The Autonomy of Labour Law: A Response to Prof Wedderburn' (1988) 17 Ind LJ 1.

[23] H Arthurs, 'Landscape and Memory: Labour Law, Legal Pluralism and Globalization' in T Wilthagen (ed), *Advancing Theory in Labour Law in a Global Context* (North Holland Press, 1997) 21; and H Arthurs, 'Who's Afraid of Globalization? The Transformation of Canadian Labour Law' in J Craig and M Lynk (eds), *Globalization and the Future of Labour Law* (Cambridge University Press, 2005) 51.

[24] R Dukes, 'Constitutionalizing Employment Relations: Sinzheimer, Kahn-Freund and the Role of Labour Law' (2008) 35 J L Soc 341.

staffed by non-legal experts including labour and management representatives. These bodies do not simply adjudicate; they use other strategies – rule-making, education, inspection, mediation, negotiation – to secure compliance and reinforce relationships. And when they do adjudicate, they typically employ evidentiary and interpretative rules, modes of reasoning, and remedial powers that diverge from the curial model.[25] Finally, the labour law that actually regulates workplace relations often differs from state law partly because the state concedes the parties considerable latitude in defining their relationship, partly because it lacks the capacity to enforce its law in countless workplaces, and partly because of the irrepressible tendency of workplaces to generate their own indigenous law that is sometimes explicit (contracts, collective agreements, standard operating procedures), sometimes implicit (customs, usages, and patterns of behaviour imbricated in routines of work)[26] – but always powerful. Hence the apparent paradox of 'labour law without the state'.[27]

To sum up, labour law is different from other legal fields because it is so often promulgated through non-legal (ie political, social, and cultural) processes, expressed in the form of 'non-legal' (ie non-state) norms and administered through 'non-legal' (ie non-curial) forums operating with 'non-legal' processes (ie those not normally employed by conventional courts). Indeed, labour law – as it functions in actual workplaces – has often been used by legal scholars not only to challenge the hegemonic claims of state law and legal institutions, but also to initiate alternative approaches to law such as legal pluralism, reflexive law, and critical theory.[28] Seen from this perspective, labour law is neither non-law nor a mutant form of law, but law incarnate, an experiment in social ordering that reveals the true nature of the legal system in general.

2. What makes law *labour* law?

Labour law is labour law because within a particular configuration of historical circumstances we choose to apply that particular taxonomic label to a body of rules, a cluster of professional practices, and a field of scholarship.[29] In postwar North America, labour law, as noted, was generally understood to refer to the law of collective labour relations. It was distinguished from 'employment law' (individual employment contracts and statutory labour standards) and from other legal sub-fields (such as workers' compensation, health and safety, and pension law) that

---

[25] H Arthurs, 'Developing Industrial Citizenship: A Challenge for Canada's Second Century' (1967) 45 Can Bar Rev 786.

[26] H Arthurs, 'Understanding Labour Law: The Debate Over "Industrial Pluralism"' (1985) 38 Current Legal Problems 83.

[27] H Arthurs, 'Labour Law without the State?' (1996) 46 U Tor LJ 1.

[28] Arthurs (n 23); R Rogowski, 'The Concept of Reflexive Labour Law: Its Theoretical Background and Possible Applications' in J Priban and D Nelken (eds), *Law's New Boundaries: The Consequences of Legal Autopoiesis* (Ashgate, 2001); and K Klare, 'Critical Theory and Labor Relations Law' in D Kairys (ed), *The Politics of Law* (Pantheon Books, 1982).

[29] The taxonomic task, begun in the 1930s, has been long and difficult. J Goldberg, *Development of a Universal Law Classification: A Retrospective on Library of Congress Class K* (2003) 35 Cataloguing and Classification Quarterly 355.

affected workers' rights, wealth, power, and dignity no less than collective labour law. This narrow definition of labour law owed much, I suspect, to its emergence in leading law schools and law firms during the period when the Wagner Act seemed to be ushering in a new era of protections for American workers.[30] However, it had unfortunate consequences.

It led to the dismissal of other aspects of labour law as suboptimal alternatives to collective bargaining; deprived them of the academic critique and professional attention they deserved; disadvantaged important worker populations they were meant to protect;[31] discouraged international comparisons amongst models of collective bargaining[32] and between collective bargaining and other regimes of labour market regulation; and delayed the development of integrated theorizing in the field.[33] But most seriously, given the long – arguably terminal – decline of North American trade unionism, it exposed labour law in Canada, and especially the United States, to the charge that 'after labour' it has become dysfunctional, politically irrelevant and intellectually ossified.[34]

The collective bargaining focus of labour law, however, is encoded in what Brian Langille calls its 'constituting narrative'.[35] Here is how, at some level, we understand labour law: Wealth and power are asymmetrically distributed in our society; since workers possess less of both than employers, they are inherently disadvantaged; disadvantage generates injustice, injustice resistance, and resistance social unrest. Hence, states must intervene in the employment relation. This they may do in various ways: by redistributing wealth through taxation and transfer payments, by detaching power from wealth by mandating workers' participation in enterprise and workplace governance, or by nullifying the advantages enjoyed by employers by encouraging countervailing worker power in the form of unions. Or they may leave asymmetries of wealth and power undisturbed but place outer limits on their use by enforcing minimum labour standards, or palliate inevitable injustices through social programs, or forbid worker resistance and suppress unrest. Any of these forms of state intervention might be called 'labour law', but all stem from the same 'constituting narrative'.

A slightly different constituting narrative might have produced a different understanding of the field. If we were to look beyond the workplace to asymmetries of wealth and power in other economic relationships (lenders/borrowers, landlords/tenants, agribusiness/farmers)[36] and beyond conventional union strategies (strikes and picketing) to other modes of resistance (voting, demonstrations, boycotts,

---

[30] See generally L Cooper, 'Teaching ADR in the Workplace Once and Again: A Pedagogic History' (2003) 53 J Legal Ed 1; and D Beatty, *Labour Law in a Nutshell: The Influence of a Casebook* (1996) 75 Can B Rev 35.

[31] J Fudge, *Labour Law's Little Sister* (Canadian Centre for Policy Alternatives, 1991).

[32] See, eg, B Aaron and KVW Stone (eds), *Rethinking Comparative Labor Law: Bridging the Past and the Future* (Vandeplas Publishing, 2007).

[33] For an early effort at integration see B Langille, 'Labour Law is a Subset of Employment Law' (1981) 31 U Toronto LJ 200.

[34] C Estlund, 'The Ossification of American Labor Law' (2002) 102 Col L Rev 1537.

[35] B Langille, 'Labour Law's Back Pages' in G Davidov and B Langille (eds), *Boundaries and Frontiers of Labour Law* (Hart Publishing, 2006) 13.

[36] A Hyde, 'What is Labor Law?' in Davidov and Langille, above n 35, 37.

petitions, cultural representation, consumer cooperatives) 'labour law' might have been subsumed into 'the law of unequal economic relations' or 'social law', a term widely used in Europe. However, this did not happen because it seemed neither natural to scholars nor useful to practitioners to shape the boundaries of a legal field around the meta-structures of social ordering such as state, markets, class or culture.

This choice has impaired the vision of labour law by obscuring important facts: that market dynamics are often a more powerful determinant of decent labour standards than regulatory legislation; that states shape labour markets and the relations of market actors as effectively by trade, fiscal, monetary, immigration, social welfare, and education policies as by labour laws; and that enterprise-specific, ethnic, and popular cultures can reinforce or undermine indigenous systems of workplace normativity no less powerfully than legislation. Instead, labour law has focussed on one site of interaction (the workplace), one set of actors (unions, workers, and employers), and one set of responses (conflict and negotiation). This has simplified the organization of materials for research and teaching (legal rules and decisions about workplace relations), determined the shape of professional practice (union-side or employer-side law firms), and encouraged the growth of sub-specialisms (wrongful dismissal, sexual harassment, disability law). But it has curtailed the explanatory power, practical efficacy and moral force of labour law.

3. Who *is labour law for?*

Whatever its substantive content, we can at least be sure that labour law is about 'labour', that it operates in the context of 'employment', that it is designed to protect 'workers'. As Richard Mitchell concludes in his insightful review of labour law's travails – a review hardly less lugubrious than my own – '[o]ur loyalty is surely to *labour* as a class, not to "labour law"'.[37] However, members of that class themselves exhibit diminishing loyalty to it. In recent decades in most affluent democracies, unions have steadily lost members, economic power, political influence, and cultural salience[38] – except ironically those that represent privileged workers who need protection least.[39] Labour-friendly political parties have experienced similar reversals, and have had to reinvent themselves by abandoning their historic links to unions, disavowing their traditional aim of eliminating inequality, and appealing to a broader cross-section of the electorate.[40]

Some studies suggest that these setbacks for labour's industrial and political wings are cyclical or context-specific,[41] or attributable to bad laws or unfortunate

---

[37] R Mitchell, 'Where Are We Going in Labour Law? Some Thoughts on a Field of Scholarship and Policy in Process of Change', Workplace and Corporate Law Research Group, Working Paper No 16 Monash University (March 2010); online: <http://ssrn.com/abstract=1615196>.

[38] See, eg, M Hechter, 'From Class to Culture' (2004) 110 Am J of Soc 400.

[39] Eg athletes, professionals, academics, and public servants.

[40] Perhaps the most dramatic example was the re-branding of the UK Labour Party as 'New Labour' under Tony Blair in 1996.

[41] J Godard, 'The Exceptional Decline of the American Labor Movement' (2009–10) 63 Indus and Lab Rel Rev 82.

organizational arrangements.[42] However, a significant body of literature ascribes them to the disappearance of labour as a social class[43] and of class as a prime determinant of political and social affairs.[44] Social status, some propose, has displaced class as a prime determinant of workers' attitudes and actions.[45] When they self-identify, Americans in particular state their family status, occupation, religion, domicile, gender, and age in priority to their class.[46] Similar trends appear to prevail even in the UK where until fairly recently labour's industrial and political wings had deep roots in a robust proletarian culture.[47]

Explanations of the cause of labour's 'disappearance' vary, as do estimates of its extent and consequences. The American working class (or at least its white component) has supposedly been transmogrified into a new mass upper middle class – better educated, more affluent, increasingly distanced from manual work – with new interests, values, and voting habits.[48] (Ironically, some argue, these improvements in workers' lives owe much to unions[49] and to labour-backed parties that built the welfare state.)[50] By contrast, many studies suggest that by any objective standard, in the Anglo-American democracies, class distinctions have persisted, and indeed grown,[51] and that they continue to influence workers' political alignment[52] and propensity for collective action.[53] However, as even these studies acknowledge, the traditional agendas of both labour parties and unions no longer fully encompass the interests or express the concerns of their members, who now have their own 'second agenda' that includes such issues as religion, taxation, and lifestyle.

Labour's diminished capacity for electoral and social mobilization augurs ill for workers' interests. Right-wing parties tend to pursue economic policies harmful to

---

[42] RB Freeman and J Rodgers, *What Workers Want* (Russell Sage, 1999); and RB Freeman, 'Do Workers Still Want Unions? More Than Ever' (2007) 23 Economic Policy Institute Briefing Paper, 9–10; online: <http://www.sharedprosperity.org/bp182.html>.

[43] M Crain and K Matheny, 'Labor's Identity Crisis' (2001) 89 Cal L Rev 1767.

[44] M Hechter, 'From Class to Culture' (2004) 110 Am J Soc 400; and P Achterberg, 'Class Voting in the New Political Culture: Economic, Cultural and Environmental Voting in 20 Western Countries' (2006) 21 Intl Soc 237.

[45] J Scott, 'Social Class and Statification in Late Modernity' (2002) 45 Social Class & Stratification in Late Modernity 23.

[46] TW Smith, 'Social Identity and Socio-Demographic Structure' (2007) 19 Int J Public Opinion Res 380.

[47] E Hobsbawm, *Workers* (Pantheon Books, 1984).

[48] R Teixeira and A Abramowitz, 'The Decline of the White Working Class and the Rise of a Mass Upper Middle Class' in R Teixera (ed), *Red, Blue & Purple America: The Future of Election Demographics* (The Brookings Institution, 2008).

[49] M Hechter, 'From Class to Culture' (2004) 110 Am J Soc 400.

[50] W Korpi and J Palme, 'New Politics and Class Politics in the Context of Austerity and Globalization: Welfare State Regress in 18 Countries 1975–1995' (2003) 97 Am Pol Sci Rev 425.

[51] P Gottschalk and T Smeeding, 'Empirical Evidence on Income Inequality in Industrialized Countries' 154 (Luxembourg Income Study Working Paper Series, Luxembourg, 1999), online: <http://www.lisproject.org/publications/liswps/154.pdf>.

[52] JVD Waal, P Achterberg, and D Houtman, 'Class is Not Dead – It has Been Buried Alive: Class Voting and Cultural Voting in Postwar Western Societies' (2007) 35 Politics & Society 403.

[53] D Brady, 'Institutional, Economic, or Solidaristic? Assessing Explanations for Unionization Across Affluent Democracies' (2007) 34 Work and Occupations 67.

workers: they reduce the redistributive effects of the tax system, retrench the welfare state, weaken protective labour laws, and restrict the activities and influence of unions.[54] Nonetheless workers vote for them in significant numbers not so much because of false consciousness as because these parties support their 'second agenda'.[55]

The disappearance of labour as a movement and class, and the disinclination of workers to identify themselves as such, seem to have been widely recognized and, indeed, to have become self-reinforcing. Three examples: Governments in many countries have dissolved their labour ministries and redistributed their functions to economic ministries or ministries concerned with social protection to whose primary mandates labour issues become subordinate.[56] Large Wall Street law firms which formerly provided labour law representation to corporate clients no longer find it profitable to do so.[57] Consequently, labour issues figure even less prominently in the calculus of corporate obligation and self-interest than they once did. And media organizations that used to employ a specialist labour reporter no longer do,[58] with unfortunate consequences for the quantity and quality of reportage and ultimately, the extent of public understanding of labour issues.[59] Labour, then, has become marginalized as a subject of public policy making, as a concern of corporate advisors and decision makers, and as a topic familiar to ordinary citizens.

If labour's identity is dissolving, if class generally matters less, if workers' issues have fallen off the public policy agenda, the familiar 'constituting narrative' of labour law ceases to constitute. Without labour solidarity, collective bargaining legislation becomes inoperable; without public support and government engagement, labour standards legislation becomes more difficult to implement; and without effective class mobilization, the prospects for worker-friendly labour market policies, legislation and administration diminish considerably.

But a new, optimistic narrative may be emerging – notably (and oddly) in the domain of legal discourse. To cite one example, Canada's Supreme Court has affirmed that employment provides workers not only with 'a means of financial support and, as importantly, a contributory role in society' but also with a sense of 'identity, self-worth and emotional well-being'.[60] Countless legal-scholarly and

---

[54] D Brady and KT Leicht, 'Party to Inequality: Right Party Power and Income Inequality in Affluent Western Democracies' (2008) 26 Research in Social Stratification and Mobility 77.

[55] M Trotman, 'AFL-CIO Poll Shows Union Households Boosted Brown' *The Wall Street Journal* (22 January 2010) <http://online.wsj.com/article/SB1000142405274870442320457501769090022 6982.html>.

[56] H Arthurs, 'What Immortal Hand or Eye? – Who Will Redraw the Boundaries of Labour Law?' in Davidov and Langille, above n 35, 373.

[57] H Arthurs, 'The Role of Global Law Firms in Constructing or Obstructing a Transnational Regime of Labour Law' in R Appelbaum, W Felstiner, and V Gessner (eds), *Rules and Networks: The Legal Culture of Global Business Transactions* (Hart Publishing, 2001) 273.

[58] D Meister, 'Labor and the Media' <http://www.dickmeister.com/id65.html>; and P Wilby, 'Why Labour Reporters Aren't Working' *The Guardian* (5 March 2007) <http://www.guardian.co. uk/media/2007/mar/05/mondaymediasection.politicsandthemedia>.

[59] J Lloyd, 'A Gap in the Picket Line', *The Guardian* (16 February 2009) <http://www.guardian. co .uk/media/2009/Feb/16/newspaper-reporting-labour-news>.

[60] *Reference Re Public Service Employee Relations Act (Alta)*, [1987] 1 SCR 313 at para 91, Dickson CJC dissenting; affirmed *Health Services and Support – Facilities Subsector Bargaining Assn v British Columbia*, 2007 SCC 27, [2007] 2 SCR 39.

judicial pronouncements, in Canada, in other countries and at the international level, make the same point; indeed, it seems self-evident. If, then, 'employment' is invested with such social and economic significance, surely the continued importance of labour law ought to be assured.

However, the future of 'employment' as a descriptor of work relations may itself be in question. A recent study suggests that fewer and fewer workers, barely 60 per cent of Canada's workforce, are now party to a relatively long-lasting full-time standard employment relationship.[61] Moreover, some standard 'employees' do not receive a full measure of employment rights because they do not meet statutory criteria of entitlement,[62] others because they work in remote workplaces beyond the reach of labour inspectors or union organizers, and still others because their employers are small and struggling or powerful and aggressively hostile to unionization and regulation. As for the 40 per cent of the workers in non-standard employment – those who work part-time (20 per cent), on short-term contracts, casually or through labour market intermediaries (10 per cent) or are self-employed (10 per cent) – a significant number are partially or entirely denied coverage under labour legislation or, if covered, face practical obstacles to claiming their rights. Clearly the Supreme Court's views have neither influenced recent labour market trends nor improved statutory coverage nor softened the hearts of recalcitrant employers.

Moreover, the rise of non-standard employment has not only cost millions of workers their rights, benefits, and sense of 'identity and self-worth'. By widening the gulf and shifting the numerical balance between workers still protected by labour law and those who are not, it may also have contributed to a new political dynamic in which have-not workers acquiesce in or support efforts to strip the haves of their advantages.

Finally, it is important to note a radical shift in the spatial relations of labour law's intended beneficiaries. Labour law used to be for people who worked in close physical proximity to each other in a mine, mill, shop or office or at least had periodic contact at a union hiring hall or company despatch office. Even in large, complex enterprises, where workers no longer inhabited the same physical space, they at least shared psychic proximity based on their membership in the same organization. Proximity fostered solidarity; it enabled workers to develop personal ties, identify potential leaders, reflect on their common fate, and respond collectively to a shared sense of grievance. In North America, workers with a 'community of interest' were included in a 'unit appropriate for collective bargaining',[63] often

---

[61] LF Vosko, N Zukewich, and C Copeland, 'Precarious Jobs: A New Typology of Employment' (October 2003) 4 Perspectives 16, 19.

[62] Eg, in Ontario, managerial and professional employees are denied coverage altogether under labour statutes; see, eg, Ontario Labour Relations Act (OLRA) SO 1995, ch 1, s 1(2). Civil servants, hospital employees, teachers, police, and firefighters are subject to special legislation that limits or denies their right to strike; see, eg, OLRA, s 3(d) (e) (g); Hospital Labour Disputes Arbitration Act RSO 1990, ch H14 (as amended); Crown Employees Collective Bargaining Act, 1993 SO 1993, ch 38 (as amended); and Education Act, RSO 1990, ch E2, Part X1 (as amended).

[63] See OLRA s 1(1) for definition of 'bargaining unit'; the 'community of interest' requirement is commonly read into the legislation by labour relations boards in both Canada and the United States.

defined by its physical location. And collective agreements – won through industrial action undertaken 'in combination or in concert or in accordance with a common understanding'[64] – gave workers the experience of working under rules they had collectively negotiated[65] and could enforce through grievance procedures they collectively controlled.[66]

To be sure, proximity and solidarity had their dark side: 'others' who were not physically or psychologically proximate, and therefore not perceived to share a community of interest, did not qualify for solidarity, and risked being marginalized and having their interests ignored.[67] But today labour law is often 'for' people with little or no proximity, whose interests are (rightly or wrongly) perceived to conflict, and whose solidarity therefore cannot be sustained. This loss of proximity is attributable to many factors including the outsourcing and relocation of work to remote locations, the re-engineering of workplaces and processes but, above all, to globalization.

Globalization has expanded the world supply of labour, created a transnational labour market, and facilitated the development of global supply chains whose links to the core enterprise are often obscure and sometimes covert. Consequently even workers who in fact work for the same ultimate employer often do not even know of each other's existence, let alone share common experiences, cultures, customs, languages, or legal frameworks. Worse: they frequently perceive each other not as co-workers, but rather as competitors for available work. In these ways, globalization not only abolishes proximity in employment but radically undermines labour solidarity.

To sum up: who can labour law possibly be for 'after labour': in a world in which 'labour' as a sociological descriptor and political force has become anachronistic, in which 'workers' no longer answer to that name, and in which 'employment' has become so conceptually indeterminate and functionally attenuated that it no longer constitutes a stable platform for the protection of rights or the projection of entitlements?

4. What is labour law for 'after labour'?

If the ultimate underlying rationale for labour law has been so inconstant; if it is directed to an increasingly heterogeneous and widely dispersed labour force populated by individuals who seem no longer to share a common working class identity or occupational affinity; if it depends on a labour movement that has become incapable of effective industrial or political action; if it is designed to regulate an obsolete paradigm of employment; if its substantive content is in question, its boundaries contested and its intellectual coherence given up for dead – if in all these

---

[64] See OLRA s 1(1) for definition of 'strike'.
[65] See OLRA ss 1(1), 55, 56 for definition of 'collective agreement'.
[66] See OLRA s 48.
[67] D Bernstein and T Leonard, 'Excluding Unfit Workers: Social Control versus Social Justice in the Age of Economic Reform' (2009) 72 Law & Contemp Prob 177.

respects we are living in an era 'after labour' – is it still worth asking 'what is labour law for?'

This, I would argue, is indeed the right moment for such a question precisely because we are confronting what Daniel Rodgers calls 'the intellectual economy of catastrophe':

Crises [he says, speaking of the Great Depression]...sustained long enough...can bring the established structure of responses into deep discredit...By eroding the conventional wisdom, extended crises may create room into which innovations may flow. [However]...the paradox of crisis politics is that at the moment when the conventional wisdom unravels, just when new programmatic ideas are most urgently needed, novel ones are hardest to find...One of the most important consequences of crises, in consequence, is that they ratchet up the value of policy ideas that are waiting in the wings, already formed though not yet politically enactable.[68]

At a time when we are confronting the worst economic crisis since the 1930s, what innovative 'policy ideas' about labour law are 'waiting in the wings'? What 'new programmatic ideas' about labour law are available to replace the 'established structure' which has, indeed, fallen into 'deep discredit'? Three broad approaches have emerged, each offering a different answer to the question: 'What is labour law for?'

a. Labour law should be embedded in, and help to advance, a regime of fundamental and universal human rights

As is well known, labour rights and human rights have historically developed in parallel, because of their different (though related) intellectual and ideological origins and because states, international bodies, social actors and scholars have been unable or unwilling to integrate them into a single discourse.[69] However, integration is attracting increasing support.[70] Workers might benefit considerably if labour law were embedded in a framework of rights that is fundamental, not merely statutory or contractual; universal, not merely class-based and parochial; and principled, not merely pecuniary. Having shed their old class affiliations and identities, workers would be able to form new alliances with other rights-seekers, to assert new identities as 'citizens' and to initiate new discursive and legal strategies. Finally, couching labour rights as human rights would enable its architects to avoid national exceptionalism and to construct transnational regimes of labour law. Conversely, human rights regimes and advocacy groups would profit from closer integration with labour law and its clientele. Integration would redirect human rights

---

[68] D Rodgers, *Atlantic Crossing: Social Politics in a Progressive Age* (Belknap Press of Harvard University Press, 1998) 413–16.

[69] The roots of the debate are nicely exposed by Hugh Collins in 'Theories of Rights as Justifications for Labour Law' (this volume).

[70] RJ Adams, 'From Statutory Right to Human Right: The Evolution and Current Status of Collective Bargaining' (2008) 12 Just Labour: A Canadian Journal of Work & Society 48; V Leary, 'The Paradox of Workers' Rights as Human Rights' in LA Compa and SF Diamond (eds), *Human Rights, Labor Rights, and International Trade* (University of Pennsylvania Press, 1996); and J Gross (ed), *Workers Rights and Human Rights* (Cornell University Press, 2003).

analysis towards collective or social rights and away from what is often de-politicized individualism, force liberal legalism to address substantive as well as adjectival rights, and facilitate the mobilization of a mass movement for human rights.

But for all the attractions of labour law reconceptualized, and hopefully reinforced, as a branch of human rights law, it would be a very different kind of labour law. It would be de-coupled from employment, de-emphasize worker agency, delegitimate extra-legal self-help initiatives and, increasingly, direct disputing parties to courts that lack historical legitimacy in the labour field as well as institutional capacity to deal with its quotidian tasks. In short it would lack the historical, contextual and functional specificity of labour law as we now know it. Conceivably these concerns might be overcome if human rights law were to function according to Teubnerian logic, reflexively, by influencing the decision-making processes of workplaces, enterprises, labour markets and other semi-autonomous legal fields.[71] But this would be a very different kind of human rights law from the one now dispensed by constitutional courts and their transnational counterparts.

If labour law were to develop along these lines, then, it would be 'for' the transcendent purpose of erasing the line between the rights we enjoy as citizens of a democratic polity and those we are effectively denied as citizens employed in workplaces characterized by asymmetries of wealth and power. But there are strong reasons to be sceptical about the capacity of constitutions to deliver on their promises in general,[72] and in particular about the prospects for a rights-based, litigation-led regime of labour law.[73]

b. Labour law should empower workers by facilitating their accumulation of human capital and the realization of their human capacities

When the current crisis passes (some say it already has, others that it will linger and recur) we will still be left with some version of capitalism. Indeed, it seems to be widely accepted that while there are many varieties of capitalism,[74] there are presently no credible alternatives to it. Labour law should therefore ensure that workers accumulate the human capital that will enable them both to fully realize their individual capacities and to contribute to and share in the success of capitalism. To oversimplify, labour law should abandon its traditional mission of protecting workers in favour of enhancing their capacities and endowing them with human capital.[75] Naturally, there will be disagreement over how to do this, and

[71] G Teubner, 'Societal Constitutionalism: Alternatives to State-Centred Constitutional Theory?' in C Joerges, IJ Sand, and G Teubner (eds), *Transnational Governance and Constitutionalism* (Hart Publishing, 2004).

[72] H Arthurs and B Arnold, 'Does the Charter Matter?' (2005) 11 Rev Constit Stud 37.

[73] H Arthurs, 'The Constitutionalization of Employment Relations: Multiple Models, Pernicious Problems' (2010) 14 Soc & Leg Stud 403.

[74] PA Hall and D Soskice (eds), *Varieties of Capitalism: The Institutional Foundations of Comparative Advantage* (Oxford University Press, 2001).

[75] See, eg, B Langille, 'Labour Policy in Canada – New Platform, New Paradigm' (2002) 28 Can Pub Pol 134; and for a more critical view AD Frazer, 'Reconceiving Labour Law: The Labour Market Regulation Project' (2008) 8 Macquarie LJ 21.

whether such an approach should complement, rather than displace, traditional protective labour laws. But all versions of the human capital and capacities approach envisage that workers and employers will co-exist in a collaborative, rather than an adversarial, relationship.

Collaboration between workers and employers may be a necessary condition for the success of a human capital- or capacity-based labour law system; but it is not sufficient. As some proponents acknowledge, collaboration between the social partners and the state is essential, but difficult to achieve in liberal market economies. Consider recent developments in North America. The 'psychological contract' that once underpinned unionized industrial employment has been unilaterally rewritten by employers;[76] job tenure has been truncated;[77] there are fewer standard jobs and more non-standard jobs;[78] labour's share of GDP has shrunk and income inequality grown;[79] employer-provided pensions and benefits are available to fewer workers, while the universal state-provided social safety net has shrunk significantly.[80] These developments reveal structural, not merely cyclical, impediments to a human capital strategy. North American capitalism rejoices in 'creative destruction', is driven by next-quarter results and is disinclined to long-term investment, in human capital or otherwise. Moreover, its industrial relations systems are atomistic. Their primary sites are the workplace and enterprise; sectoral, bilateral or tripartite institutions are rare, *ad hoc*, and often unstable; and employer unilateralism is the default position.

Nonetheless, some employers – whether to forestall unionization or in the spirit of enlightened self-interest – have internalized the premise that workers must be consulted about changes in working conditions or operating procedures; and some have bound themselves to observe codes of conduct or adhere to ISO performance standards.[81] Indeed, some have initiated so-called high-performance work systems (HPWS) under which they pay their employees well; provide them with training and other opportunities to enhance their human capital; set them challenges and entrust them with responsibilities; and accommodate the personal, family and civic dimensions of their lives.[82] In return these firms expect that employees ('associates'

---

[76] K Stone, *From Widgets to Digits: Employment Regulation for the Changing Workplace* (Cambridge University Press, 2004).

[77] Stone, above n 76, 74 ff.

[78] AL Kalleberg, BF Reskin, and K Hudson, 'Bad Jobs in America: Standard and Nonstandard Employment Relations and Job Quality in the United States' (2000) 61 Am Sociological Rev 256.

[79] SM Jacoby, 'Finance and Labor: Perspectives on Risk, Inequality, and Democracy' (2008–9) 30 Comp Lab Law & Pol 17, 28; and R Morissette and X Zhang, 'Revisiting Wealth Inequality' (2007) 18 Perspectives on Labour and Income 6.

[80] D Brady and KT Leicht, 'Party to Inequality: Right Party Power and Income Inequality in Affluent Western Democracies' (2008) 26 Research in Social Stratification and Mobility 77. For a recent Canadian example see L Osberg, 'Canada's Declining Social Safety Net: EI Reform and the 2009 Budget' (John Deutsch Institute – Queen's University, Ottawa May 2009) online: <http:// myweb.dal .ca/osberg/classification/conference%20papers/Canadas%20declining%20social%20safety %20net%20text%20May%207.pdf>.

[81] H Arthurs, 'Private Ordering and Workers Rights in the Global Economy: Corporate Codes of Conduct as a Regime of Labour Market Regulation' in J Conaghan, K Klare, and M Fischl (eds), *Labour Law in an Era of Globalization: Transformative Practices and Possibilities* (Oxford University Press, 2004) 471.

[82] See generally P Kumar, *Rethinking High-Performance Work Systems* (IRC Press, 2000).

or 'partners') will devote their loyalty, skill, energy, and imagination to the enterprise with corresponding gains in productivity and profitability. Indeed, even some relatively militant unions have been persuaded to experiment with so-called 'value added' or 'mutual gains' approaches to bargaining, an approach which should also be congenial to human capital development and capacity building.[83] However, neither of these related initiatives seems to be an unequivocal success. On the contrary: studies indicate that HPWS initiatives are often associated with layoffs and downsizing; that once implemented they may generate stress for employees and disempower them;[84] and that many unions view the human capital approach as a strategy to dissuade workers from organizing – a suspicion fuelled by the use of the HPWS vernacular (words like 'empowerment') precisely for that purpose.[85] Of course, specific initiatives such as HPWS cannot be equated with the profound normative, attitudinal and behavioural shifts contemplated by the human capital and 'capacities' approaches. But they do signal that it will not be easy for employers, workers or unions to make the necessary adjustments.

A final difficulty: many elements of a human capital strategy cannot be accomplished within the employment nexus or on the basis of contractual arrangements. They require state action either by way of universal provision (health insurance and pensions), or specific programs to ameliorate labour market risks (unemployment insurance, workers' compensation, job-finding) or cooperative ventures with employers and unions at the sectoral or enterprise level (skills training, youth employment, redundancy payments).[86] Hence, such strategies seem less likely to succeed in North America than in the coordinated market economies of Western Europe, where labour markets are managed more purposefully, the quality of working life and the preservation of social solidarity are matters of public policy, and workers are generally assured a voice in workplace governance.

This is hardly a surprising conclusion. Labour law is to a significant extent path-dependent; it takes its purpose, form and content from the larger political economy in which it originates and operates. Predictably, a labour law system that is 'for' promoting human capital, reducing conflict, furthering collaboration and achieving an equitable sharing of enterprise gains is more likely to achieve its purposes in a political economy that shares those goals than in one that does not.[87]

---

[83] For a review of the literature see B Nissen, 'What are Scholars Telling the US Labor Movement to Do?' (2003) 44 Lab Hist 157.

[84] Kumar, above n 82; J Godard and J Delaney, 'Reflections on the "High Performance" Paradigm's Implications for Industrial Relations as a Field' (1999–2000) 53 Indus & Lab Rel Rev 482; P Cappelli and D Neumark, 'Do High Performance Work System Practices Improve Establishment-Level Outcomes?' (2001) 54 Indus & Lab Rel Rev 737; and B Harley, 'Employee Responses to High Performance Work System Practices' (2002) 44 J Indus Rel 418.

[85] Wal-Mart's use of these terms is notorious. See, eg, N Lichtenstein, 'How Wal-Mart Fights Unions' (2007–8) 92 Minn L Rev 1462.

[86] See especially Alain Supiot, *Beyond Employment: Changes in Work and the Future of Labour Law in Europe* (Oxford University Press, 2001).

[87] B Langille, 'What is International Labour Law For?' (2009) 3 Law & Ethics Hum Rights 46, 53 ff.

c. The purpose of labour law should remain unchanged: to enable workers to mobilize to seek justice in the workplace and the labour market

In Rodgers' 'intellectual economy of catastrophe', the idea that labour law exists to enable workers to mobilize is hardly 'innovative'; indeed, it has been centre stage for decades, rather than 'waiting in the wings'. However, if justice is not handed down to workers from on high by benevolent judges or enlightened employers, mobilization remains their only recourse. That said, assuming that 'after labour' there will be little political pressure to revise the structures of enterprise governance, the architecture of labour markets or the fundamental assumptions of capitalism, a new approach to mobilization is clearly needed.

This new approach implies greatly enlarged ambitions for labour law. In response to innovative forms of worker mobilization, labour law scholarship will have to extend its reach to all policy domains that influence work relations or labour market outcomes; to all normative regimes whether domestic or transnational, formal or informal, that justify the ends and limit the means of concerted action by workers and other citizens; to all labour market participants whether or not they qualify technically as 'employees' under labour legislation or economically as potential 'clients' of labour lawyers; and ultimately to all non-participants whose activities impinge on the dynamic of labour markets including unemployed workers, workers in the informal sector, and workers engaged in the non-waged tasks of social reproduction.

In practical terms, any attempt to reinvigorate worker mobilization 'after labour' – after unions – will require the formation of new workplace collectivities. Such collectivities already exist both in the English-speaking world and on the continent. Works councils (with or without union participation) are widely recognized in Europe.[88] Workplace committees are mandated by statute in some North American jurisdictions to deal with specific issues such as health and safety and pension fund administration.[89] Non-union workplace associations may now have memberships that equal or exceed those of unions.[90] Caucuses, networks and web-based virtual organizations have emerged to give workers 'voice' and economic leverage in certain enterprises and sectors.[91] However, all of these alternative forms of workplace organization have serious shortcomings. To the extent that they proliferate in the absence of unions, they are sometimes rightly suspected of siphoning off support for collective bargaining. To the extent that they do not see themselves

---

[88] M Whittall, H Knudsen, and F Huijgen (eds), *Towards a European Labour Identity: The Case of the European Works Council* (Routledge, 2007).

[89] H Arthurs, 'Reconciling Differences Differently: Reflections on Labor Law and Worker Voice After Collective Bargaining' (2007) 28 Comp Lab L and Pol'y J 167.

[90] I extrapolate from a 1996 survey: SM Lipset and N Meltz, 'Estimates of Non-Union Employee Representation in the United States and Canada: How Different Are the Two Countries?' in B Kaufman and D Taras (eds), *Nonunion Employee Representation* (ME Sharpe, 2000).

[91] See, eg, A Hyde, *Working in Silicon Valley: Economic and Legal Analysis of a High-Velocity Labor Market* (ME Sharpe, 2003) esp ch 9, 'Employee Representation: Networks, Ethnic Organizations, New Unions'.

UNIVERSITY OF WINCHESTER
LIBRARY

as engaged in an ongoing power struggle with employers, they are likely to be co-opted. To the extent that they lack formal status, structure, powers or resources, they will probably have a short shelf life.[92] And most crucially, to the extent that they do not reach beyond the workplace to recruit new supporters, they will likely enjoy no more power or influence that unions once did.

On the other hand, if workers do renew their appetite for more robust forms of collective representation, are unions in a position to respond? In America some unions have been attempting to reinvent themselves and their approach to collective bargaining. They have experimented with new strategies, such as 'social' or 'civic' unionism, built on broad-based coalitions – workers, the unemployed, members of ethnic, religious, consumer, student, human rights and anti-poverty groups – rather than on traditional craft- or workplace-specific 'bargaining units'.[93] Some have worked with local civic movements to address labour market issues such as racial discrimination, safety hazards or failure to pay a 'living wage'.[94] And some have organized consumer and investor boycotts of domestic or offshore employers suspected of egregious workplace practices.[95] These campaigns have sometimes produced gains: they have helped workers to unionize, or augmented their bargaining power; they have improved working conditions for unorganized, minority, immigrant, women, and low-skill workers; they have sensitized the public to labour market issues and reduced hostility to unions; they have introduced unions to the potential advantages of domestic and international alliances; and most importantly, they have inspired some unions to articulate a vision of social justice.[96] But these gains, impressive as they may be in given circumstances, have been for the most part local and ephemeral. They have – so far – neither fundamentally altered labour market structures, nor reawakened class consciousness, nor reinvigorated the labour movement as a whole, nor laid the foundations for a new party of the centre-left committed to justice for working people.

D. Conclusion: labour law 'after labour'

All three visions of what labour law might be for 'after labour' suggest that it will have to be integrated into a larger project, whether of constitutionalized human rights, of collaborative and productive capitalism or of bottom-up civic democracy and social protest. One way or another, then, 'labour' seems destined to be

---

[92] See generally D Taras, 'Reconciling Differences Differently: Employee Voice in Public Policy-making and Workplace Governance' (2007) 28 Comp Lab L & Pol J 167.

[93] See, eg, R Milkman and K Voss (eds), *Rebuilding Labor: Organizing and Organizers in the New Union Movement* (Cornell University ILR Press, 2004); and D Reynolds (ed), *Partnerships for Change: Union and Community Groups Build Coalitions for Social Justice* (ME Sharpe, 2004).

[94] See, eg, RB Freeman, 'Fighting For Other Folks' Wages: The Logic And Illogic Of Living Wage Campaigns' (2004) 44 Indus Rel 14; and K Stone and S Cummings, 'Labour Activism in Local Politics: From CBAs to "CBAs" and Beyond' (this volume).

[95] See, eg, Clean Clothes Campaign <http://www.cleanclothes.org>.

[96] See, eg, G Lester, 'Beyond Collective Bargaining: Modern Unions as Agents of Social Solidarity' (this volume).

subsumed into larger and more general socio-economic categories, and downtrodden members of the working class to be reincarnated as rights-bearing middle-class citizens. If this is so, labour law itself is likely to evolve into a broader, more inclusive and perhaps more efficacious regime of social ordering, field of intellectual inquiry and domain of professional practice.

But there are dangers.

Workers – its intended beneficiaries – will continue to experience a loss of identity, solidarity and agency but their expectations of justice in the workplace and the labour market may have to be adjusted to accommodate the claims of their new allies and 'relevant others'. Understandably, too, workers will hesitate to exchange their old, familiar, if tattered, rights for new forms of protection whose efficacy is untested and whose provenance is, frankly, suspect. Important labour market actors – unions and employers – will find it difficult to slough off their old adversarial attitudes and to abandon the legal rules, institutions, and processes designed to resolve their differences. Social democratic and labour parties – for so long the 'natural' proponents of worker-friendly labour laws – will have to rethink their position in order to retain the confidence of new constellations of supporters. And not least, labour law intellectuals, policy makers and practitioners, having sunk their intellectual and social capital in the existing system, are unlikely to want to liquidate their investment at a loss.

Moreover, in each of these three new, possible instantiations, labour law may well lose some of its unique character. If it does, if labour law 'after labour' is so transformed that it no longer advances justice in labour markets, it will lack legitimacy. If its connection to quotidian workplace relations becomes so attenuated that it no longer regulates them closely, it is unlikely to be efficacious. And if it becomes so intellectually diffuse that – after decades of increasingly ambitious, methodologically varied, and cosmopolitan scholarship – the discursive community of labour lawyers dissolves, then we will be unable to help much during the current 'intellectual economy of catastrophe'.

Still, for all their possible shortcomings, these three new approaches represent not only the best approximation of what labour law is likely to look like 'after labour' but also a significant advance over what it looks like today.

2

Factors Influencing the Making and Transformation of Labour Law in Europe

Bob Hepple*

'The struggle of man against power, is the struggle of memory against forgetting.'
Milon Kundera

A. Introduction

When Mahatma Gandhi was asked 'What do you think of Western Civilization?', he is said to have replied: 'It would be a good idea.' A system of labour law which guaranteed 'decent work' for all and upheld the human rights of workers would also be a good idea.

The temptation for labour law scholars is to focus their energies on developing an ideal theory of labour rights or social justice. But any theory is sterile unless we first try to understand why real employers, workers, politicians, and judges act as they do in practice. Labour law is not an exercise in applied ethics. It is the outcome of struggles between different social actors and ideologies, of power relationships. Labour laws are used by people to pursue their own goals, and sometimes they need rights such as to a minimum wage or to freedom of association simply in order to survive.

It was this approach to the subject, rather than one based on abstract conceptions of rights and justice, that led seven European scholars, including myself, to establish the European Comparative Labour Law group in 1978 leading to the publication in 1986 of *The Making of Labour Law in Europe: A Comparative Study of Nine Countries up to 1945.*[1] Twenty years later the group was reconstituted with three of the original authors and six newcomers to produce *The Transformation of Labour*

---

* Emeritus Master of Clare College and Emeritus Professor of Law, University of Cambridge. This chapter includes extensive extracts from B Hepple (ed), *The Making of Labour Law in Europe: A Comparison of Nine Countries up to 1945* (Mansell, 1986, reprinted Hart Publishing, 2009) ch 1, and B Hepple and B Veneziani (eds), *The Transformation of Labour Law in Europe: A Comparative Study of 15 Countries 1945–2004* (Hart Publishing, 2009) ch 1.

[1] B Hepple (ed), *The Making of Labour Law in Europe: A Comparison of Nine Countries up to 1945* (Mansell, 1986, reprinted Hart Publishing, 2009) ch 1.

Law in Europe: A Comparative Study of 15 Countries 1945–2004, published in 2009.[2] The aim of these books, which distinguish them from other comparative studies, is to describe and analyse labour law as part of an historical process – as a motion picture rather than still photographs – and to explain the processes by which convergences and differences developed between the labour laws on the countries that were members of the EEC in 1980, in the case of the first volume, and of the EU on 30 April 2004 (before the accession of the former communist countries), in the second volume.

Comparative legal history requires both *diachronous* order, examining development in stages or periods, and *synchronous* order, that is a cross-evaluation between countries and their institutions in the same period. Within these orders, we discuss developments thematically in relation to specific aspects of labour law, such as labour market regulation, the employment relationship, equality at work, wage labour and social security, collective labour relations, workers' representation at plant and company level, and enforcement of labour law. There is no single grand theory, such as one that claims that all national systems follow the same process of development. One must agree with Karl Klare[3] that the law regulating work cannot be fitted into a single overarching paradigm. The thematic approach reveals that the development of labour law in general, and specific features of it, are the product of a variety of factors which are neither 'natural' nor 'necessary'. So, in *Making* we found very specific explanations for why the work (pass) book and police supervision were significant features of the labour market in continental Europe but not in the British Isles, why in some countries the eight-hour day was achieved by collective bargaining, and in others by legislation, and why workers' participation took the form of shop stewards in Britain and Denmark, but works councils in Germany. In *Transformation*, we offered explanations linked to particular historical circumstances as to why some countries, such as France, regulated working time by legislation, while others such as Britain and Denmark left this to collective or individual agreement, why some countries were slower than others in adapting the contract of employment to economic and technological changes, why some countries adopted anti-discrimination and equal pay laws before others, why some adopted universal social security benefits and others work-related insurance, why 'positive' rights to collective bargaining and to strike were embraced in some countries but not in others, and why juridification has been more apparent in some systems than in others.

B. Changing purposes of labour law

The origin of modern conceptions of labour law was a response to what German scholars at the end of the 19th century characterized as the 'social question' – a set

---

[2] B Hepple and B Veneziani (eds), *The Transformation of Labour Law in Europe: A Comparative Study of 15 Countries 1945–2004* (Hart Publishing, 2009) ch 1.
[3] K Klare, 'The Horizons of Transformative Labour Law and Employment Law' in J Conaghan, M Fischl, and K Klare (eds), *Labour Law in the Era of Globalization* (Oxford University Press, 2002) 3.

of 'problems resulting from industrialization, including the degradation of women and children, poverty, unemployment, and strikes as well as the legal treatment of trade unions and collective agreements'. Some groups of scholars in Germany were liberal, others conservative. All had connections with the bureaucracy and shared the ideology that these problems required state action. They tended to the view that pure police measures were counter-productive, and they wanted to promote the development of a 'works constitution' and to accommodate trade unions and collective agreements. The legal recognition of social and labour rights in the Weimar constitution (1919) owed its inspiration to the social-democratic politician and lawyer Hugo Sinzheimer. It is to him, according to Kahn-Freund, that we owe the conception of labour law as a unified independent legal discipline.[4] In an article in 1910 Sinzheimer justified labour law as a separate discipline on several grounds including the importance of the subject matter, the special nature of the subject containing elements of both public and private law, the special treatment which labour law needs, not limited to dogmatic statements but concerned with legal policy, the need for an interdisciplinary approach including sociology, social policy and business organization, and the unity of the goal – 'the guardian of human beings in an age of almost unrestrained materialism'. The specific features of the conception of labour law were that: (1) labour law is created not only by the state but also by autonomous groups, in particular trade unions and employers; (2) the contract of employment is 'emancipated' from the nexus of property law; and (3) the autonomous contract rests upon the subordination or dependence of the individual worker to the enterprise.

The post-war period saw the consolidation and final breakthrough of labour law as a separate legal discipline in all European countries. The starting point of most scholars in the period before the 1980s continued to be the inequality between the supplier and purchaser of labour-power. Labour law was seen as serving primarily a social and not an economic function, providing institutions and processes, mainly collective, that created a fair balance between employers and workers.

Paradoxically, no sooner had labour law established itself in this way than its boundaries and rationale began to be seriously questioned. One challenge was the inability of traditional labour laws to protect the rapidly increasing number of workers in new work relationships that could not readily be defined as 'subordinate' or 'dependent' labour. A second challenge came, mainly after the 1970s as the post-war consensus broke down, from liberal and neo-liberal theories that tended to ignore the inequitable distribution of wealth and power in society. Some scholars argued that it is no longer appropriate to focus on the 'protective' features of labour law. They suggested that the subject should be reconceptualized around its advantages and disadvantages to employers, the economy and society at large.[5] Their starting point was regulatory theory. For example, Collins remarked that:

---

[4] O Kahn-Freund, *Labour Law and Politics in the Weimar Republic* (Blackwell, 1981) 75.
[5] G Davidov and B Langille, *Boundaries and Frontiers of Labour Law* (Hart Publishing, 2006) 3–4.

The regulatory agenda for the traditional field of labour law commences with a disarmingly naïve question: Why regulate the employment relation? . . . Why should we exclude ordinary market principles such as the general law of contract and property from employment relations in favour of special rules?[6]

He said that there is a 'heavy burden of proof' on advocates of employment rights to 'establish the superiority of regulation over ordinary market rules', and that 'the special regulation must be demonstrated to be efficient in the sense that its costs do not outweigh the potential benefits or improvements'.[7] Not surprisingly, in view of the presumption in favour of private law rules, regulatory theory was used to justify deregulation of the employment relationship. 'Deregulation' was not infrequently portrayed as an absence of regulation; in fact, it meant leaving regulation to ordinary market rules, to the private law of property and contract.

Alternative versions of regulatory theory were also applied to labour law from the late 1980s onwards. In these versions, special regulation of the employment relationship could be justified on two grounds. The first is market failure, that is where there is a significant deviation between the ideal outcomes which would result from perfect competition and the actual operation of the labour market. So when the labour-power of some is undervalued, this leads to productive inefficiency, hampers innovation, and encourages short-term strategies and destructive competition. Only employment rights (for example to a minimum wage, equal pay for women and men, etc) can correct this market failure. The second justification for regulation is to correct unacceptable distributive outcomes – for example, regulation may be necessary to enable those who wish to enter the labour market to do so, by providing better education, training, and child care. But, even in this version of regulatory theory, there remains a presumption against regulation unless it can be shown that it will not harm those whom it was designed to help: for example, increasing job security of workers is justifiable only if this leads to better selection and training, and monitoring of performance of workers which outweighs the risk that the employer will hire fewer workers. Some advocates of this version of market regulation argue that labour market institutions which encourage 'high trust' or co-operation lead to superior economic performance. This leads them to support more legal provision for information, consultation, and other forms of workers' participation in the enterprise.[8]

Another variant of regulatory theory that has been influential since the 1980s regards 'competitivity' of the enterprise and 'flexibility' of work practices as of central importance in the context of globalization. The liberalization of trade and investment within the EU, by removing barriers on the free movement of capital, goods, services, and labour, is said to throw the labour law and welfare systems of

---

[6] H Collins, 'Justification and Legal Techniques of Legal Regulation of the Employment Relationship' in H Collins, P Davies, and R Rideout (eds), *Legal Regulation of the Employment Relation* (Kluwer and Institute of Advanced Legal Studies, 2000) 4.

[7] Ibid.

[8] S Deakin and F Wilkinson, 'Labour Law and Economic Theory' in Collins, Davies, and Rideout, above n 6, 56–61.

the Member States into competition with each other. This leads to a process of market selection by which states adopt the most efficient forms of regulation. Countries with low labour costs attract investment; this in turn leads to greater demands for wages, higher wages, and improved working and living conditions. This kind of argument has frequently been used against harmonization of labour laws and the setting of minimum standards.

Even those who reject some or all of these regulatory approaches have sought to shift the traditional focus on the 'protective' purposes of labour law (which implies that this is given by a paternalistic state to vulnerable individuals or groups) towards an emphasis on 'rights' to decent conditions of work, fair pay, job security, participation in trade unions, collective bargaining, and so on. Rights, rather than 'protection', are increasingly seen as a means of redressing the inequality in bargaining power between employer and worker. In this labour movements have won allies in the human rights movement since the Second World War; sometimes it has been the human rights movement which has been ahead of trade unions in pressing for change, such as in respect of equality for ethnic minorities and migrants at work. A distinctive feature of rights discourse in the employment context in recent decades has been the individualization of these claims: it is the individual, not the collective group, that becomes the subject of labour law, as seen for example in the rights under Article 11 (freedom of association) of the European Convention on Human Rights (ECHR).

C. Indicators of comparative development

A traditional approach in comparative legal studies is to divide legal systems into just a few large groups of 'legal families'.[9] There are different views as to the criteria that should be used to distinguish between these families: should it be the historical sources of law, the general structure of systems, their legal techniques, their substance or their ideology, or a combination of these factors? The approach which we favoured in *Making*[10] was to concentrate on the substance of labour laws over time, having due regard to factors which had shaped that substance, such as economic and social development, the changing nature of the state, the character of employers' and labour movements, and ideology. We suggested a number of indicators by which to measure the comparative development of labour laws in different European countries. These ranged from the earliest forms of law, such as the protection of children, young persons and women, up to measures to promote self-regulation by workers' and employers' organizations and to facilitate workers' participation at plant and enterprise level and the integration of workers' representatives in the administration of the economy and of the state. By 1945, these

---

[9] K Zweigert and H Kötz, *An Introduction to Comparative Law*, 3rd edn, trans T Weir (Clarendon Press, 1998) 63.

[10] Hepple, above n 1, 11–12.

indicators had been reached, in different forms, in nearly all the nine countries studied, and the process continued after the Second World War.

The 'transformation' of labour laws since 1945 involves not simply changes in form, but of substance. The distinction may be made between 'path dependence', when changes follow the path of previous laws and policies, and so are generally changes in form, and 'path departure', when a juncture is reached at which substantively different laws and policies begin to be followed. It is possible to draw up another list of indicators of the comparative extent of 'transformation' of labour laws since 1945, in the sense of 'path departures'. Among these are the following:

- the classification within the sphere of labour law of personal work contracts beyond the classic model of subordinate employment relationships
- the regulation of new forms of personal work contracts such as part-time, fixed-term, and agency work
- the privatization of employment services, and the legitimation of temporary work agencies
- individual rights against unfair dismissal, and for payment of compensation in the event of redundancy
- protection of acquired rights of workers on the transfer of undertakings
- mandatory information and consultation with workers' representatives in the event of collective (economic) dismissals and transfers of undertakings
- active labour market policies to promote high levels of employment, particularly for vulnerable groups such as women, young persons, ethnic minorities, older workers, and disabled persons
- laws against discrimination in employment on grounds of sex and sexual orientation, race and religion, age and disability, and positive duties to promote equality of opportunity
- enforceable social welfare rights in cases of important needs; means-tested social assistance in cases of poverty or unemployment; access to charge-free health care at least in severe cases financed by the community or by insurance; and provision for old-age benefits above the level of social assistance
- the 'containment' of freedom of association, the right to collective bargaining and the right to strike
- rights of workers' representatives at plant and enterprise level to information and consultation on management decisions affecting employment, and some rights to co-determination on social matters
- 'social dialogue' between employers' organizations and trade unions at European, national, and sectoral levels
- individualized and juridified procedures for the enforcement of labour laws.

This list of indicators of 'transformation' is not exhaustive but, in similar fashion to the earlier indicators of 'making', provides a guide to the extent of 'transformation' in each labour law system. In seeking explanations for the transformations that have occurred, the contributors to the two volumes have considered a number of factors, including socio-economic developments and policies, the changing nature of the state, the character of workers' movements and civil society, and ideology. This approach does not exclude the relevance of other factors such as legal techniques: for example, in explaining the development of the concept of the contract of employment, the differences between the legal methods of civil law systems, and the common law ones are very important. However, the practical effect of our approach is to make historical comparisons specific, rather than to fit labour law systems into traditional families such as Romanistic, Germanic, and Anglo-American. The comparative substance of labour laws cuts across these categories.

D. Economic developments and policies

The connection between labour laws and economic development is obvious. Here one may simply note that while the 'making' of labour law was the product of the industrial revolution, of the shift from an agrarian handicraft economy, to one in which machine manufacture in mills, mines and factories (including the Fordist system of production) dominated, 'transformation' has been the outcome of the shift to a post-Fordist service-based and information-technology-based society. The 'new' systems of labour law have been a response to global competition and the decentralization and fragmentation of work and the workforce. But, as we found in respect of 'making',[11] there is no mechanical connection between an economic 'base' and a 'superstructure' of labour law. The 'timing of changes in legal institutions can and does materially affect the pace and character of economic development',[12] but equally the transformations in labour laws may come well after the economic changes. Several contributors point to the paradox that the golden age of labour legislation and the welfare state occurred in most countries in the 1970s and 1980s, when the period of economic growth had already slowed down or ended, and there was stagflation and slump. The deep explanation for this may lie in the contradiction between political freedom and economic subordination and inequality of wealth and power.[13] Demands for greater job security and welfare came from enfranchized workers including women who demanded equal treatment in the labour market. These demands had to be met by democratically elected governments, as the price for continuing economic subordination, even when they had become less affordable.

[11] Hepple, above n 1, 14–15.
[12] D Landes, *The Unbound Prometheus: Technological Change and Industrial Developments in Western Europe from 1730 to the Present* (Cambridge University Press, 1969) 199.
[13] M Desai, *Marx's Revenge: The Resurgence of Capitalism and the Death of Statist Socialism* (Verso, 2005) 310.

E. The changing nature of the state

This kind of interaction between political democracy and economic subordination is underlined when one considers the changing nature of the state since the Second World War. The form of state under which labour law was 'made' was liberal constitutionalism (with some notable exceptions, such as the German Empire before 1914), characterized by the active promotion of *laissez-faire*, which meant giving almost uncontrolled power to property owners, particularly the owners of capital. Moreover, the 'public' sphere of the state and the private sphere of economic life (civil society) were separated. Key to the 'making' of labour law was the participation by workers in the 'public' sphere in order to improve their situation in the economic sphere. This led, even before the Second World War (for example in the Weimar Republic), to the recognition of some social 'rights' of citizenship: labour laws, instead of being the 'gift' of an enlightened ruling class, became the 'rights' of workers and their collective organizations who could exercise pressure on the state.[14]

This process was accelerated, after 1945, by the building of neo-corporatist social democratic welfare states, which were based on steady economic growth, and rising levels of employment until the 1970s. Under the welfare state there was a trade-off between economic dependence and social rights. In return for continuing to be subject to hierarchical management organization, it was understood that there would be a guarantee of job and income security.[15] The dominant task of the state in relation to labour relations, which remained relatively stable, was to maintain 'balanced' industrial pluralism. The 'principal purpose of labour law' was seen, in Kahn-Freund's words, in 1972, as being 'to regulate, to support, and to restrain the power of management and the power of organized labour'.[16] The welfare state aimed to provide the institutions and processes, mainly collective, that created a 'fair' balance between employers and workers. The focus was on subordinated workers within the employment relationship and not on the wider labour market. 'Rights' were of increasing importance in order to end the distinction in liberal states between the 'private' sphere of economic life and the 'public' sphere of what was now directly controlled by the state. The new rights, such as the 'right to work', were different from the rights of the individual proclaimed in the French Revolution and in most liberal constitutions. 'They were claims on the state to provide work and economic security and to recognize the collective interests of workers through the rights to organize, to bargain collectively, and to strike.'[17] However, not all democratic states created legal 'rights', for example the British approach 'was to defend social and organizational "rights" won through industrial

---

[14] Hepple, above n 1, 15–22.
[15] A Supiot, *Beyond Employment: Changes in Work and the Future of Labour Law in Europe* (Oxford University Press, 2001) 151–55.
[16] O Kahn-Freund, *Labour and the Law* (Stevens, 1972) 5.
[17] B Hepple, *Labour Laws and Global Trade* (Hart Publishing, 2005) 259.

struggle, using the law on a pragmatic basis only when voluntary means were inadequate',[18] although from the 1960s onwards there was also a growing 'floor of rights' for individual employees in Britain. Moreover, in all the western democracies the desire to emphasize the priority of political rights and freedoms, in contrast to the communist countries' claims that their workers had greater job security and social protection, led to artificial distinctions between political and socio-economic rights.

When the post-war welfare state consensus broke down in the 1980s, the character of European states became increasingly 'deregulatory' based on neo-liberal theories (see above). Britain took the lead in this, under the Thatcher (Conservative) government elected in 1979. The downsizing of the British state in controlling the economy began with the deregulation of capital movements, so removing 'a basic building block for the state's control over the economy'.[19] One consequence of this was that the state could no longer run large deficits, and economists ceased to believe that such deficits could achieve full employment. State intervention in the economy and welfare spending declined and this was accompanied by privatization and the breaking of collective union power through legal restrictions and by crushing strikes such as that of the miners in 1984. By contrast, the French socialists (led by Mitterand), who came to power in 1981, followed aggressive Keynesian policies, increasing public expenditure and the budget deficit, in response to the crisis of profitability and rising unemployment. At the same time, they strengthened labour laws (such as *lois Auroux*). This 'competition' between the French welfare state and the British neo-liberal one was 'won' by Britain whose economy began to revive, while that of France declined, and the new measures had to be severely modified after 1983. This was not a true competition because of the many differences in starting points, but Thatcher's success (and that of Reagan in the United States) led the continental states to become increasingly neo-liberal in respect of the labour market the late 1980s and 1990s. Italy, after experiencing a new burst of pro-worker legislation in the early 1990s, moved by the turn of the century to greater privatization and individualization. The Nordic countries, however, managed to retain strong collective organization as the basis of labour law, while modifying labour legislation which was regarded as being too restrictive, or made the legislative open to deviation by collective agreement.[20] In Germany, too, deregulation never became mainstream, and the collective labour law framework was left largely untouched, but flexibility was introduced by opening up collective agreements to plant agreements, and, after 1998, by attempts to 'reform' the social security system.

In fact, most states did not go as far as the neo-liberal advocates of de-collectivization and deregulation of employment rights would have liked. For example, all states maintained their laws against unfair dismissal and for compensation in the

---

[18] Ibid.
[19] Desai, above n 13, 298.
[20] O Hasselbalch, 'The Roots – the History of Nordic Labour Law' in P Wahlgren (ed), *Stability and Change in Nordic Labour Law* (Stockholm Institute for Scandanavian Law, 2002) 34.

event of redundancy. Most striking of all was the enactment of comprehensive anti-discrimination legislation, partly in response to the changes in the changes in the labour market (feminization, migration, ageing population, etc) but also due to the pressure of feminist and other human rights movements. Towards the end of the 1990s, most European states came to espouse the ideas of 'fundamental human rights' – including labour rights – although some, like Britain, were more reluctant than others to do so. The states were increasingly characterized by 'rights-based' regulation of the labour market. Two consequences of this were the growing individualization of employment rights and disputes-settlement procedures, and the juridification of labour relations. Human resource managers and trade union officials turned increasingly to their lawyers.

F. The character of the employers and labour movements and the growing influence of civil society

In the 'making' of labour law, before the Second World War, the relationship between the trade unions and political parties was a crucial factor.[21] The depoliticization of most European trade unions and the weakening of their links with communist, socialist, and liberal parties after the war reduced their direct influence on labour legislation. France, Italy, Spain, and Portugal were exceptions. The end of the Cold War in 1989 narrowed the ideological and political gap. European unions were able to join in a single confederation (ETUC). Trade unions in most countries continued to exert pressure, and were particularly successful in periods of neo-corporatist cooperation, such as the social dialogues in Austria, Belgium, and the Netherlands which effectively gave law-making powers to the social partners, and the 'social contract' between the Labour government and TUC in Britain in the 1970s which promised wage restraint in return for employment protection legislation. In the former dictatorships – Spain, Portugal, and Greece – the contribution of trade unions to the struggle for democracy was rewarded by extensive modern legislation supporting trade unions and the right to collective bargaining and to strike.

The decline in union membership was reflected in the increasing number of mergers and a concentration into a few relatively large organizations. Their weakness, in the wake of changes in the labour market, from the 1980s onwards made unions more reliant than ever before on the 'method of legislation', in particular EC legislation was favoured as a means of counteracting 'social dumping' resulting from globalization. The new forms of legislation gave a role to trade unions to negotiate derogations from statutory standards. This was a recognition of their weakness rather than their strength because they were put on the defensive against employers' demands for greater 'flexibility'. The character of employers' organizations also changed, including the ending of the divisions between 'economic' and 'social' bodies. Decentralization of collective bargaining meant a loss of central organizational control, although in some

---

[21] Hepple, above n 1, 22–6.

such as Germany, local agreements continued to be integrated into national and sectoral arrangements.

Perhaps the most significant change has been the growing importance of civil society organizations and action. For example, the rise of the feminist movement had a direct impact on anti-discrimination legislation and family-friendly policies, as did activists seeking rights for ethnic minorities and migrants, disabled people, homosexuals, and older workers. The students' and workers' demonstrations around May 1968 in France and elsewhere produced changes in cultural attitudes, and also on issues such as workers' representation on plant and enterprise level.

G. Ideology

In the 'making' of labour law, no single ideology predominated; the law was the outcome of struggles between conflicting ideologies, including the ideologies of the market and self-help, of state-help, socialism, and social Christianity, and of patriarchy.[22] In the period after 1945, new or recast ideologies became important. The most significant clash was between the supporters of liberal capitalist democracy and the supporters of one or other form of democratic socialism or social democracy. Confessional divisions based on Christianity declined. Soviet-style socialism had only a very limited appeal in the western countries, apart from France and Italy in the early post-war years, and by the 1980s had become widely discredited both ideologically and in practice. There was a revival of feminist ideas and a new landscape of human rights. To many in the labour and socialist movements in Europe, who remembered the Great Depression, Keynesian economics had solved the problems of unemployment and had pointed the way to steady economic growth, on the basis of which workers could get a larger share of income and better conditions, and public expenditure could expand the welfare state. This could ensure a harmonious equilibrium between capital and labour within a framework of labour laws that enhanced collective organization as a countervailing force to the power of capital.

This ideology came under increasing criticism, both academically and politically, as economic crisis reappeared in the late 1970s. There was a revival of 19th-century liberal ideology. This, as Desai points out, is somewhat misleadingly labelled neo-liberalism.[23] We need to distinguish, in his view, between 'mere conservatism' (such as that of the World Bank and the transnational corporations), which retains a large role for the state, trade unions, and workers' protection, and 'liberalism' or 'libertarianism', which takes the view that the state and other agencies cannot control civil society and the economy and should not try to do so; it rests on an almost unquestioning belief in the power of markets and the profit-motive. This liberal ideology – espoused especially by Mrs Thatcher's government in Britain – was reflected in the work of Hayek, who argued that trade unions used labour law

---

[22] Hepple, above n 1, 26–30.
[23] Desai, above n 13, 297–8.

to cartelize the market, so that in the British context they had to be stripped of their 'special privileges' which protected them from the operation of the ordinary law of obligations.[24] In relation to individual rights, such as against unfair dismissal and discrimination, Epstein of the University of Chicago claimed that such legislation interferes with the efficient incentive structures provided by the law of contracts.[25] Political parties and social partners in European countries varied in their addiction to these ideas.

As prosperity and stability began to return to Europe in the late 1990s, the ideology of the 'Third Way' began to permeate labour law policy. This took many forms, but, as Fredman explains, had several common themes.[26] First, it rejected the liberal faith in free markets and hostility to the state; but, its supporters also rejected the traditional social democratic state, arguing for a new 'balance' between the individual and the state within a competitive market economy. Second, the idea of individual responsibility (what in an earlier age might have been called 'self-help') was given renewed importance. While rejecting the complete 'hollowing out' of the welfare state, supporters of the 'Third Way' emphasized that individuals should take primary responsibility for themselves. Third, equality of opportunity is a central tenet. Finally, the 'Third Way' stressed the importance of social inclusion, active citizenship, and democracy. At the time our story ends, this was an influential ideology of labour law in most European countries. But this will not, as some have forecast, be 'the end of ideology' in shaping labour law.

H. The future

There are two underlying socio-economic factors that bring into question the very survival of the labour and social law systems of regulated capitalism as they have developed in Europe since 1945, and more particularly since 1990 in the face of globalization. The first is the pace of technological change. The traditional social models in most of continental Europe have been coordinated market economies, dependent on low labour turnover, strong job security, workers' participation, social security, and the protection of income. These models were a source of comparative institutional advantage at the time of stable Fordist production systems with long-term investment, the development of in-firm skills, and incremental technical innovation. They have, however, proved to be less well placed when radical innovation is required in a highly competitive globalized market. The more 'flexible' British model, although not as liberal as the American and Japanese ones and itself constrained by regulation in some areas by the EU, appears to have given better opportunities to develop new technologies in rapidly changing industries

---

[24] F Hayek, *Law, Legislation and Liberty* (Routledge, 1980) 89–90.
[25] R Epstein, 'In Defense of Contract at Will' (1984) 51 University of Chicago L Rev 947, and *Forbidden Grounds: The Case Against Employment Discrimination Law* (Harvard University Press, 1995).
[26] S Fredman, 'The Ideology of New Labour Law' in C Barnard, S Deakin, and G Morris, *The Future of Labour Law; Liber Amicorum Sir Bob Hepple* (Hart Publishing, 2004) 10–18.

such as biotechnology and information technology. This is because firms wanting to develop new products can hire and fire workers with relative ease, using non-standard forms of employment relationship, and placing a premium on transferable industry skills, with relatively little involvement of workers' representatives.[27] The Nordic countries have moved furthest in providing a mix of social protection and labour market reforms, that are believed to be necessary to improve productive efficiency, while maintaining collective workers' participation. The other European countries will have to make more progress in the same direction if their labour law systems are to adapt to new technologies and to become more effective in facing global competitition.

The second question mark which hung over the future of European social and labour models in 2004, and approached a tragic climax in 2008–10, was whether the traditional bank-based financial system could survive the growing competition from new markets in securities.[28] Banks were increasingly under pressure to provide quick profits and were becoming less willing to finance long-term corporate investments and the development of human resources including on-job training. This threatened to make it harder for firms to offer employment security and other forms of labour protection. The collapse of the global banking system, as later events have shown, not only results in mass unemployment but also deeply threatens the gains of labour over the period since the Second World War.

As a general proposition, we continue to take the view that labour legislation is the outcome of struggle between different social groups, and of competing ideologies. As Abrams said: 'What any particular group of people gets is not just a matter of what they choose, but whether they can force or persuade other groups to let them have.'[29] In other words, in the future as in the past, the crucial element in both the making and the transformation of labour law will be the power of capital, and the countervailing power of organized labour and civil society – workers, consumers, and active citizens.

---

[27] Hepple, above n 17, 252–3.
[28] Foreseen by B Eichengreen, *The European Economy since 1945* (Princeton University Press, 2007) 419–23.
[29] P Abrams, *Historical Sociology* (Open Books, 1982) 15.

3

Re-Inventing Labour Law?

Manfred Weiss

A. Introduction

1. The notion of 'labour law'

The notion of 'labour law' needs explanation. In some contexts (for example in the USA) it is understood as merely referring to collective labour relations, in others (for example in Continental Europe) it is taken for granted that it covers both individual as well as collective labour law. This terminological difference is not only of semantic interest. It indicates totally different approaches to labour law. In the context of the USA labour law and employment law are understood as two legal disciplines only loosely interconnected.[1] This implies to an increasing extent that labour law is disappearing from the curricula of the law schools whereas employment law is taught as a separate entity. Such a separation would be unthinkable in Continental Europe where the two parts are conceived as closely interrelated parts of an overarching entity. This terminological and at the same time conceptual difference shows how much labour law is embedded in the cultural, legal, and political traditions of respective countries. This different perception goes much further and is also reflected in the structural appearance of the laws of different countries.

Therefore, I have my doubts whether there is a universal approach to labour law. It rather seems to me that due to the different connotations of labour law in different regions of the world it is necessary to clarify from which angle the idea of labour law is approached. In my case it should be clear that my perspective is embedded into the experience and the context of Continental Europe.

2. Reasons and goals

The history of labour law has been told very often.[2] In the 19th century it became evident that the competition between individual employees at the labour market

---

[1] See T Kohler, 'Restatement – Technique and Tradition in the United States' (2009) IJCLIR 469 at 470.
[2] See the excellent introduction by B Hepple in B Hepple (ed), *The Making of Labour in Europe* (Mansell Publishing, 1986) 6 ff.

was a race to the bottom and that only collectivization of employees combined with protective legislation could prevent this destiny. Therefore, the interplay between collective self-regulation and legislative intervention from the very beginning characterized labour law. The main goal always has been to compensate the inequality of the bargaining power.[3] However, there were in particular four more insights which became a driving force for labour law regulation. They all were brilliantly analysed by Hugo Sinzheimer, the most prominent founding father of German labour law. First, the object of transaction in an employment relationship is not a commodity but the human being as such.[4] Or as, later on, the Philadelphia Declaration of the International Labour Organization (ILO) listed as its first principle: 'Labour is not a commodity.' This insight is of utmost importance because it makes perfectly clear that the labour market is not a market as any other, and therefore cannot follow the same rules as other markets do. Second, personal dependency is the basic problem of labour law.[5] Third, human dignity may be endangered by the employment relationship and, therefore, one of the main goals of labour law is the fight for human dignity.[6] This already at a very early stage expresses the goal of the ILO's present decent work agenda. It should be stressed that the three above-mentioned factors – labour not being a commodity, personal dependency as a characteristic feature of the employment relationship, and the endangering of human dignity – are closely linked to each other. They are the three core aspects of the same phenomenon. And they explain why the employment contract is not just a contract among others: it establishes a relationship *sui generis.*[7] Fourth, Sinzheimer stressed that labour law cannot be perceived as merely law for the employment relationship but has to cover all the needs and risks which have to be met in an employee's life, including the law on creation of job opportunities. In other words: Sinzheimer understood social security law in its broadest sense as also being an inseparable part of labour law.[8] The traditional distinction between public law and private law no longer played a role in this comprehensive understanding of labour law as an autonomous legal discipline. It has to be admitted, however, that unfortunately Sinzheimer's concept of labour law as including social security law has not succeeded even in Germany. This is still reflected in the universities' curricula. In spite of Sinzheimer's suggestions, labour law is still conceived as an annex of private law and social security as part of public law, an evident and dangerous perversion of the idea of the founding fathers.

To sum up: According to the original idea as expressed mainly by Sinzheimer, the goal of labour law first of all is the protection of the employees' (including the unemployed) material needs, of their health and safety as well as of human dignity.

---

[3] O Kahn-Freund, *Arbeit und Recht* (Bund Verlag, 1979) 7.

[4] H Sinzheimer, 'Das Wesen des Arbeitsrechts' (1927) in H Sinzheimer, *Arbeitsrecht und Rechtssoziologie*, vol 1 (Bund Verlag, 1976) 108 ff at 110.

[5] Ibid, 112.

[6] Ibid, 111.

[7] For a different view see G Mundlak, 'Generic or Sui generis Law of Employment Contract' (2000) IJCLIR 309.

[8] Sinzheimer, above n 4, 110.

There is another aspect of labour law which in the course of history has become more and more important: the active involvement of employees in management's decision making. This, admittedly, is not a universal feature of labour law. It is most developed in Europe, and there are big differences between different countries, even if due to the legislative activities of the European Union (EU) it is becoming more and more a common European phenomenon.

3. Changed reality

Labour law is a product of industrialization. It has been developed in view of a social and economic reality which is no longer the reality of today. The main point of reference for the development of labour law was the Fordist model.[9] The workplace was embedded in a factory of manufacturing industry, a more or less large unit, where employees – mainly blue-collar and only to a small extent white-collar – did not work in splendid isolation but as a collective entity. This, by the way, was the reason why in particular in Germany very early the employment contract was no longer conceived as a merely individual relationship between employee and employer but as an element of the collective relationship between the employer and the workforce. The workforce was relatively homogeneous, as were the employees' interests. (Of course, there always have been exceptions. Therefore, special groups from the very beginning needed different treatment, for example, home-workers.) The prototype of this workforce was the male employee in an undetermined full-time employment relationship. This male employee was regularly functioning as 'breadwinner', responsible for the family's budget. Continuity and stability were a characteristic feature of employment. The enterprise was characterized by a clear structure of hierarchies. It was easy to define subordination and the employer's power to command and control as criteria for the employment relationship and thereby at the same time as a reference point for labour law. Homogeneous interests of the workforce as well as the experience of being part of the collective were ideal preconditions for unionization. Thereby protection by collective bargaining could be organized without serious problems. Labour law was focusing on the domestic labour market. Globalization was not a real issue.

In our post-industrial era practically everything of this scenario has disappeared. The factory as a location where employees cooperate with each other is eroding to an increasing extent. Outsourcing, networking, sub-contracting, teleworking, and similar dislocating strategies are on the agenda. The enterprise often is turned into a merely virtual entity. Vertical structures are replaced by flat hierarchies. Manufacturing is becoming an ever-smaller part of the economy; the service sector is increasing. Owing to technological changes, work organization has changed dramatically. The workforce is no longer homogeneous, it is fragmented and segmented into core groups and marginal groups, less traditional employment and more and more new forms of work. The number of part-time jobs, of fixed-

---

[9] For a good description of this reality see S Simitis, 'Hat das Arbeitsrecht noch eine Zukunft?' in S Simitis, *Arbeitsrecht – Unwaegbarkeiten und Dilemmata* (Bund Verlag, 2005) 366 ff.

term contracts as well as of temporary agency workers is significantly increasing. There are increasing numbers of economically dependent self-employed. The labour market is no longer male-dominated; feminization of the labour market has become an important feature. The male 'breadwinner' model belongs to the past. Balance of work and family obligations, thereby, has become a serious problem. Globalization puts pressure on the national economies. Relocation of production to other countries is on the agenda. New communication technologies allow for dividing the process of production and providing services between different countries all over the globe.

These very sketchy and admittedly superficial and simplistic observations may be sufficient to illustrate that the reality of work has changed dramatically. This leads to the question whether and how far the traditional concept of labour law is still appropriate to cope with this new reality of work, whether smaller or bigger adaptations may be sufficient or whether a total change of paradigm, a re-invention of labour law, is needed.

B. Need for adaptation

1. Disappearance of the original assumptions?

Evidently the 'social question' is no longer as burning as it was in the 19th century. And it is taken for granted that at least on average the economic situation of employees has significantly improved. The question, however, is whether this has any impact on the legitimacy of labour law. As indicated above, labour law was based on the assumptions that there is a need to compensate the bargaining power of the employees, that labour is not a commodity, that employees are personally dependent and that the employee's human dignity has to be protected. These assumptions have remained to be as valid as ever.

Even if the category of subordination may no longer be applied in such a simplistic manner as before and has to be substituted by all kind of criteria and tests, the asymmetric structure of bargaining power has remained. Employees – whether in traditional employment relationships or in new forms of employment relationship – are personally dependent of their employers, even if it has become more difficult in many cases to find out who is the employer.[10] And, of course, the assumption that labour is not a commodity has lost nothing of its validity. In view of the possibilities of new technologies there is an ever-increasing danger to intrude into the employee's privacy, thereby attacking and destroying the employees' human dignity, to just mention one aspect where protection is badly needed.

In short: in spite of the dramatic changes in work reality, there is no reason to question the need for labour law as such. As far as the core assumptions are concerned on which labour law is based, I see no need for a change of paradigm.

---

[10] For details of the analysis see B Veneziani in B Hepple and B Veneziani (eds), *The Transformation of Labour Law in Europe* (Hart Publishing, 2009) 99 ff.

This, of course, does not mean that the structure of the field can remain as it is. It may have to be adapted to the new circumstances. Whether and in what way this is necessary and possible is now to be discussed by taking some selected examples.

2. Diversity of interests within the workforce

Traditional labour law has been focusing on full-time employment for an indefinite period. Other forms of work were considered to be atypical. Only recently they have been brought under the roof of labour law. In Europe this strategy was pushed by Directives on part-time work,[11] on fixed-term contracts,[12] and on temporary agency work.[13] However, this strategy is based on equal treatment with full-time employees on an indefinite contract. In the case of temporary agency employees, even this attempt failed.

Equal treatment is not sufficient. It ignores that employees in new forms of work are in a different situation. To just give an example: if there is a system of protection against unfair dismissal this is useless for the employee in a fixed-term contract if the contract comes to an end. Or if it remains possible to reduce part-time work to minimal hours, equal treatment is not very helpful for an employee who wants to make a living by this kind of employment. Instead of merely insisting on the principle of equal treatment, labour law has to react to the needs of people in new forms of work by providing tailor-made regulations which by necessity will be different from those for people in traditional employment. These rules have to be based on the insight that people in new forms of work are more vulnerable than those in traditional employment and, therefore, need more and not less protection.[14]

Here the real dilemma starts. Whereas in spite of the decline of trade unions – which is in Continental Europe much less dramatic than elsewhere – for traditional employment it still is possible to be protected by collective self-regulation, this is much more difficult for people in new forms of work. Their unionization rate not only is marginal, it also is extremely difficult for traditional trade unions to integrate their specific interests into a bargaining strategy. Their focus still is on traditional employment. Bargaining for employees who do not belong to the core group of trade union members leads to difficult problems of representativity. In short: satisfying collective representation of interests for people in new work forms cannot be provided by traditional trade union and bargaining structures. Whether alternative forms of representation can be organized is an open question.

Diversity of interests and erosion of the factory model also put a question mark behind the functioning of systems of workers' participation. The reality on which these systems – for example the works council system in Germany – are built, is a workplace where a collective of employees with more or less homogeneous interests

---

[11] Directive 97/81/EC of 15 December 1997, OJ 1998, L 14/9.
[12] Directive 99/70/EC of 28 June 1999, OJ 1999, L 175/43.
[13] Directive 08/104/EC of 19 November 2008, OJ 2008, L 327/9.
[14] In this sense see also N Smit and E Fourie, 'Extending Protection to Atypical Workers, Including Workers in the Informal Economy in Developing Countries' (2010) IJCLIR 43.

is present. Again the representation of core groups is no problem. However, for people in new forms of work it is problematic. For example the works council in a temporary work agency is almost not accessible for the temporary workers who are never there but in the users' companies. And why should a works council in the user company care for temporary workers who are there only for a limited time? The question is whether and how such systems of workers' participation can be restructured in order to integrate the whole diversity of interests of the workforce. In Germany a modest attempt in this direction was made by giving women seats in the works council according to their proportion in the workforce of the respective establishment. But what about the integration of part-timers, of those on fixed-term contracts, of teleworkers, or of migrant workers, all of them with different interests? Is this possible at all? Would the strength of a representative body composed of such diverse groups be as strong to defend and promote employees' interests as before? Again, open questions remain.

3. Extending the scope of application?

Whether it is still appropriate to limit the scope of application of labour law to the employment relationship in a strict sense, has been the topic of a widespread and intensive discussion for quite a time.[15] The demarcation line between employment and self-employment has become very difficult to draw. To an increasing extent there are persons labelled as being self-employed but in reality being employees. They of course are to be included into the scope of application of labour law, even if it might be difficult to exactly identify their status. Problematic are those who undoubtedly are self-employed but economically in a similar position as employees.[16] Therefore, in many countries a specific category was invented for the economically independent self-employed. In Germany they are called 'employee-like persons'. However, only some rules of labour law are applied on them. The reason is very simple: if they are only economically but not personally dependent, their situation remains to be essentially different from employees.

Extending the scope of the full amount of labour law application on economically dependent self-employed might lead to de-legitimacy of labour law. Therefore one has to be cautious. In my view more empirical evidence is needed to allow for a reliable assessment of similarities and differences, before taking such a far-reaching step. However, it might be recommendable to establish basic principles which govern such economically dependent self-employed as well as employees.[17] This then would allow the elaboration of tailor-made protective schemes, taking full account of the specific situation of this group. It has to be kept in mind that

---

[15] See, eg, the articles collected in G Davidov and B Langille, *Boundaries and Frontiers of Labour Law* (Cambridge University Press, 2006); and A Supiot, *Beyond Employment – Changes in Work and the Future of Labour Law in Europe* (Oxford University Press, 2001).

[16] M Freedland, 'Application of Labour and Employment Law Beyond the Contract of Employment' (2007) International Labour Review 146.

[17] See Simitis, above n 9, 392.

collectivization of this group is particularly difficult and rather unrealistic. Therefore, legislation has to be the predominant protection tool in this context.

De-legitimacy of labour law definitely would be the result if one would follow the suggestions of those who plead for inclusion of all relationships which are characterized by inequality of bargaining power.[18] In my view these suggestions ignore not only the specific character of the employment relationship as indicated above but also the interrelationship of individual and collective mechanisms as means of protection. The changes of the employment reality as sketched above force labour law to be adapted to the new employment reality. But labour law is not to be misunderstood as a tool to compensate the position of the weaker party everywhere. There are different subsystems in society for which legal progress has developed specific instruments which are shaped according to the needs within the respective subsystem, be it family law, consumer protection law or whatever. This progress is not to be reversed but has to be adapted to changes of reality. For labour law this means that it has to respond to the new realities in the area of employment in its broadest sense but not to expand in overarching categories for all the miseries of the world. Then it would lose its function.

4. Closer link between labour law and social security law

In spite of Sinzheimer's warning and as already mentioned above, labour law and social security law too seldom are seen as the two sides of the same medal. This has to be changed. Such a change is more urgent than ever. The modern world of work is characterized by instability of employment. To remain in the same job until retirement has become a rare exception. In an employee's biography mobility between different jobs has become the normal situation. A satisfying legal response to such a challenge cannot be given exclusively by traditional instruments of labour law, as for example job security. It needs a close interaction between rules of labour law and social security law. The latter has to care for decent conditions in the periods of transition and for facilitating possibilities of re-employment, including training and retraining. This in essence is meant by the often misinterpreted notion of 'flexicurity'. Or to take another example: if part-time work is to be made attractive in order to facilitate compatibility of family and work responsibilities for men and women, traditional labour law alone cannot resolve the problem. The situation of the part-timer is not only shaped by the working conditions regulated by labour law but to at least the same extent of coverage of social security law, be it unemployment benefits, health insurance, or retirement pension. In short and without offering more examples: Sinzheimer's request for conceiving social security law as integral part of labour law finally has to be met.

---

[18] For such an approach see A Hyde, 'What is Labour Law?' in Davidov and Langille, above n 15, 37 ff.

5. Human dignity and fundamental rights

Sinzheimer's request to maintain human dignity is based on the assumption that the employee is not to be treated as an object but as a bearer of fundamental rights. Fundamental rights have to be fully implemented within the employment relationship. This not only refers to the so-called fundamental social rights but to all the fundamental rights human beings enjoy in modern society. These rights are embedded in national constitutions as well as in international and supranational charters. In the European context there are two important regimes. One is the European Convention on Human Rights as developed in the context of the Council of Europe.[19] It has gained importance by the case law of the European Court of Human Rights. There is in addition the Charter of Fundamental Rights of the European Union. It has become legally binding by integration into the Lisbon Treaty, which came into force on 1 December 2009. This Charter contains a whole chapter of fundamental social rights (the right to collective bargaining; the right to strike; the right to information and consultation; the right to working conditions which respect his or her health, safety and dignity; the right to protection against unfair dismissal, etc). It particularly reacts to challenges of modern society by guaranteeing the right to integrity of the person, respect for private and family life, the right to protection of personal data, or the right to education and to have access to vocational and continuing training, to just give a few examples. Of course the right of non-discrimination in its broadest sense is guaranteed as well as freedom of thought, conscience and religion or freedom of expression and information. Labour law has to make sure that all these fundamental rights are fully respected in the employment relationship. The method of horizontal application of fundamental rights is to be applied everywhere. Much still remains to be done in this respect. The controversies in the course of the transposition of European Union Directives on anti-discrimination[20] have shown the opposition particularly of those who consider strict anti-discrimination rules as endangering business interests. The opposition of business so far has succeeded in preventing a Directive on protection of personal data in employment. Such opposition of course is to be overcome. Fundamental values expressed by fundamental rights cannot be pushed aside by business interests or economic considerations.

6. From shareholder to stakeholder capitalism

If the employee is not to be treated as a mere object it is also necessary that the democratic structure of modern society is reflected in the employment relationship. Therefore, it is necessary that the employee is not merely an object of management's

---

[19] For a brief description of its structure see L Betten, *International Labour Law* (Kluwer, 1993) 36 ff.
[20] Directive 2000/43/EC of 29 June 2000, OJ 2000, L 180/22 and Directive 2000/78/EC of 27 November 2000, OJ 2000, L 303/16; see for further information M Weiss, 'Unfair Discrimination Law – Developments at European Level' (with special reference to the new German Act on Equal Treatment) in O Dupper and C Garbers (eds), *Equality in the Workplace* (YUTA, 2009) 63 ff.

decision making but participating – either directly or by representatives – in the decision-making process. Employee involvement in management's decision making is becoming more and more important. Even if its driving force is the idea of workplace democracy it should be seen that employees' involvement in management's decision making has also advantages for the respective companies and for the economy as a whole. The legitimacy of management's decision making is increased, implementation of decisions is facilitated and conflicts are absorbed. The permanent dialogue between management and employees or their representatives helps to build up trust and confidence on both sides. The need to justify the planned decisions towards employees or their representatives evidently leads to more careful and, therefore, better decision making. Since employees and their representatives tend to favour long-term strategies, the stability of the companies is supported. There is lots of empirical evidence for these positive effects.[21] A good illustration of the success of such participation schemes may be the way the present economic crisis has been managed in Germany. Germany, as is well known, has a highly developed system of employee involvement in management's decision making, not only via works councils but also via employees' representatives in company boards.[22] Based on the participation of employees' representatives, Germany has succeeded to manage the crisis without significant loss of jobs and without serious conflicts between the two sides of industry. In full agreement of both sides short-time work schemes were introduced to prevent lay offs, to mention only the most important instrument. At least partially the gain of free time was used for further training of the employees. Thereby, the companies after the crisis can count on their skilled workforce. Unilateral decision making by management never would have succeeded in introducing quietly and without conflict such mechanisms which after all for the employees meant a reduction in income (in spite of State subsidies). The joint crisis management has helped to rebuild trust and confidence in management which was seriously endangered by the crisis.

However, there are at least two serious challenges for establishing schemes of employee involvement. The one refers to the diversity of interests, already indicated above: it is difficult to represent all the different interests in bodies of workers' participation. And secondly it is – even in Germany – extremely difficult to include small and medium-sized companies in such a concept. Much remains to be done in this respect.

Schemes of employees' involvement in management's decision making suffer from another deficiency. The promotion of employees' interests is not necessarily in line with other legitimate interests of society as are, for example, environmental interests or consumer interests.[23] Therefore, there is a need to make sure that other interests are not ignored. Ways have to be found to meet this request. In some

---

[21] See also M Weiss, 'Employee Involvement in the European Community' in M Weiss and M Sewerynski, *Handbook on Employee Involvement in Europe* (Kluwer, 2005) 1 ff, 20.

[22] For details see M Weiss and M Schmidt, *Labour Law and Industrial Relations in Germany*, 4th edn (Kluwer, 2008) 222 ff.

[23] For this problem of particularized interest promotion see also Simitis, above n 9, 368.

countries representatives of public interest are integrated in schemes of workers' participation in order to fulfil this task.[24] Whether this is a satisfactory solution or whether other possibilities have to be envisaged is an open question.

The particularistic interest promotion, by the way, is not only a problem of schemes of workers' participation but also a problem of collective bargaining. However, in schemes of workers' participation it might be much easier to integrate other interests than in collective bargaining which is based on the very idea that a compromise between employers' interests and the collective interest of employees is to be achieved by way of bipolar negotiation.

7. The transnational dimension

a. Transnational legislation

To a bigger and bigger extent multinational enterprises (MNEs) play a role in the era of globalization. Relocation of production and services in other countries has become a normal pattern of global economy, as well as transnational division of labour in the production process or in providing services. In particular transnationally operating companies do have the possibility of 'forum shopping', thereby choosing the most convenient jurisdiction for their cases. Therefore, labour law no longer can be conceived as a national phenomenon but has to be put into the international context.

The international labour standards as developed by the ILO are to be seen as the universal basis of the international body of labour law. Of course they exceed by far the core fundamental rights as contained in the Declaration on Fundamental Principles and Rights at Work of 1998. The goals to be achieved are properly stated in the ILO's decent work agenda.[25] However, the ILO's approach of standard setting is not without problems. To only mention a few: first, many of the conventions are outdated and no longer feasible for the modern world of work. Second, a significant number of Member States are very hesitant in ratifying conventions. Third, it has to be stressed that ratification does not mean implementation. In many countries the administrative mechanisms for such implementation are simply not available. In addition the monitoring procedure by the ILO is relatively complicated but in the very end rather inefficient.[26] Not much progress has been made in this respect. The sanctioning mechanism is still based on the idea of 'mobilization of shame'. But it seems that 'shame' is not very widespread among those who do not live up to what they have ratified. Fourth, quite often ILO standards are shaped according to the needs and conditions of highly industrialized countries and not according to the situation of developing countries. Without going into further details, much has to be improved in the ILO's standard setting, the rules are to be adapted to the challenges of today's world of work and the enforcement machinery has to be strengthened significantly.

---

[24] Such as in the Netherlands.
[25] For an assessment see B Hepple, *Labour Laws and Global Trade* (Hart Publishing, 2005) 56 ff.
[26] Ibid 46 ff.

The situation is different if standard setting on a regional scale is envisaged. If Europe is taken into account a distinction has to be made between the Council of Europe and the EU. The European Social Charter developed in the context of the Council of Europe has the same problems of enforcement as the ILO. It also is based on the assumption of 'mobilization of shame'. This, however, is different in the context of the EU, a supranational entity with legislative and judicial powers. EU law has supremacy over national law. EU law already has shaped significantly important areas of labour law: anti-discrimination law, law on health and safety or law on new forms of employment, to take just some examples of the individual employment relationship, and promotion of information and consultation of workers' representatives on the collective side. However, the EU regulation of labour law is still very fragmentary. And in view of the heterogeneous interests of the 27 Member States it may well be doubted whether a comprehensive regulation on this level can be expected.

b. *Transnational collective structures*

Not only legislation but also workers' participation schemes and collective bargaining have to be internationalized. On the international level countervailing powers to MNEs are to be built up. National actors are unable to cope with transnational phenomena.[27] However, even in Europe collective bargaining is exclusively a matter of national policy. There have been attempts at coordination which have not turned out to be very successful. Nevertheless, there is a pattern on the European level which is not to be confused with collective bargaining, but which should not be underestimated: the social dialogue between the European confederations of both sides of industry. In the context of the social dialogue so-called voluntary framework agreements can be concluded. The inter-professional social dialogue has produced four such agreements in the last decade: on tele-work (2002), on stress at the workplace (2004), on harassment at the workplace (2006), and on violence at the workplace (2009).

The agreements voluntarily concluded are no more than an offer for the actors on the national scale to give them some guidance and to enrich their imagination. The national actors are supposed to reflect on the basis of the framework agreements. This implies that the European actors have no choice but to convince the national actors of the advantages of their proposals. Only close and continuous communication offers a chance of success. This form of vertical communication is of utmost importance for the growth of real European actors of both sides of industry: an important step towards a European collective bargaining system which then might deserve its name. The problems which arise in the context of the 37 sectoral social dialogues are essentially the same.[28]

---

[27] See A Seifert, 'Global Employee Information and Consultation Procedures in Worldwide Enterprises' (2008) IJCLIR 327 at 330.

[28] See B Keller, 'Social Dialogues at Sectoral Level – The Neglected Ingredient of European Industrial Relations' in B Keller and HW Platzer (eds), *Industrial Relations and European Integration* (Ashgate, 2003) 30 ff.

The development of trans-national workers' participation in Europe goes much further. As already indicated, its structure has been established by EU law. Most important in this context are the European Works Councils (EWCs).[29] EWCs were designed as a tool for information and consultation. However, in the meantime the system of EWCs has developed dynamics of its own and gone far beyond information and consultation towards negotiations, leading to agreements. These agreements refer to a whole variety of topics. The most spectacular agreements were concluded in the automobile industry. There several agreements were concluded in which rules for restructuring (including relocation) were established. The legal effect of all these agreements is still totally unclear. Nevertheless they have a factual impact. Since in this context the interaction between national and European actors is far more developed than in the context of the inter-professional and sectoral social dialogue, the EWC pattern might be somehow the forerunner for a system of European collective agreements, of course confined to the respective groups of undertakings. This development is not without risks. The danger might be that the focus is too much on big groups of undertakings, thereby neglecting other companies, in particular small and medium-sized enterprises. One of the difficult tasks in developing a European system of collective bargaining will be to find the right balance between big groups of transnationally operating undertakings and all the many other companies which are not linked to the EWC structure.

Without any legal base, the workforce of some MNEs (such as VW, Daimler, or Renault) has established world works councils whose powers should not be over-estimated. But they certainly are a step in the right direction.[30] And Framework Agreements between MNEs on the one side and world works councils or international trade unions are concluded to an increasing extent.[31]

In short and to make the point: there are rudimentary signs of developing trans-national collective schemes and agreements. This development has to be strengthened in the future.

c. Codes of conduct

In the 1970s the ILO and the Organisation for Economic Co-operation and Development (OECD) developed guidelines for MNEs which have been amended several times. These guidelines mainly recommend the MNEs to implement the ILO labour standards. And in 2000 the United Nations (UN) presented the 'global compact' programme. Undoubtedly these initiatives were an important input for the codes of conduct as developed by the companies themselves.

Most of these codes of conduct were developed in the last decade of the 20th century and in the first decade of the 21st century. The main driving force was

---

[29] Directive 94/45/EC of 22 September 1994, OJ 1994, L 254/64.
[30] See Seifert, above n 27, 340.
[31] See the comprehensive analysis by RC Drouin, 'Promoting Fundamental Labor Rights Through International Framework Agreements: Practical Outcomes and Present Challenges' (2010) Comparative Labor Law & Policy Journal 591 ff.

consumer-protecting non-governmental organizations (NGOs) which, in the countries of origin of the MNEs, not only have turned consumers' attention to the MNEs' violations of the above-mentioned guidelines of the ILO and the OECD but which also have succeeded in organizing consumer boycotts which proved to be extremely efficient. This has led to a sensitivity of the public in the industrialized countries. Therefore, in order not to lose consumers in the markets of their home countries, MNEs presented codes of conduct which go far beyond the patterns of the guidelines of the ILO and the OECD. This wave of self-obligation started in the textile and sportswear industries. In the meantime it covers almost all branches of economic activity.

The codes of the different MNEs are by no means homogeneous. There are big differences between them. Even more significant are the differences between different branches of activity. Not only the content of the codes is differing from code to code but also the genesis of these codes. Originally most codes were unilaterally established by the companies. However, to an increasing extent there is a new generation of codes called 'multi-stakeholder' initiatives. Companies, international trade unions, human rights groups, and community and development organizations participate in formulating such a code of conduct. These multi-stakeholder codes also contain provisions on monitoring, verification, certification of supplier factories, enforcement mechanisms, and transparency.[32]

Many of the codes only cover the relationship between the multinational enterprises and their employees. However, to an increasing extent sub-contractors as well as the whole supply chain and sometimes even clients are included. Normally such codes require that in case of violations these either have to be corrected or the business relationship has to be stopped. The latter, of course, is a very ambiguous sanction since it may lead the employees of the sub-contractor or the client to the loss of their job and, thereby, to a further worsening of their situation.

All these codes are legally non-binding. They again are 'soft law'. There is only a moral obligation of the multinational enterprises to respect them. In case of unilaterally developed codes the companies are very much interested in internal conflict resolution. Therefore, in these cases the outside observers do not learn anything about possible violations. However, many companies want to make perfectly clear that they are not interested in hiding violations and, therefore, have decided to be exposed at regular intervals to so-called 'external monitoring'. This pattern applies to all 'multi-stakeholder' codes of the new generation. Such monitoring procedures prove to be quite efficient. In case of negotiated codes it depends on the strength and vigilance of the partner with whom the code was established whether and how far the public can be mobilized and thereby put pressure on the company's management. In this respect, up to now the NGOs have proved to be much more efficient then trade unions. In short and to make the

---

[32] For an assessment see I Mamic, *Implementing Codes of Conduct. How Businesses Manage Social Performance in Global Supply Chains* (Greenleaf Publishing, 2004); and more specifically for one branch of activity C Adam, F Beaujolin, and M Combermale, *Codes of Conduct Implementation and Monitoring in the Garment Industry Supply Chain* (Fondation des Droits de l'Homme au Travail, 2005).

UNIVERSITY OF WINCHESTER
LIBRARY

point: even if the codes are not legally binding and even if there are still deficiencies in implementing them, to a bigger and bigger extent the external pressure in case of violation can no longer be ignored. The future development of such codes very much depends on the activities of trade unions, media, and NGOs.

C. Conclusion

Labour law does not need to be reinvented; there is no need for a new paradigm. Labour law still has its unique function in the context of employment in its broadest sense. The interrelationship between individual and collective instruments has to be maintained and further developed. Labour law should not be mixed with law for other subsystems of society which all do have their specific patterns of regulation. Labour law is not to be misunderstood as an overarching category for all cases in societies where the needs of weaker parties are to be met.

However, there is an urgent need for adaptation to new circumstances. Far-reaching legislative re-regulation is the predominant tool to be envisaged. It is also necessary to restructure and further develop the mechanisms of collective self-regulation and employees' involvement in management's decision making. In particular it is necessary to develop labour law on an international scale. The international institutions for standard setting are to be significantly strengthened. In the attempt to transnationalize labour law, the most promising strategy is a public–private policy mix as well as a combination between 'hard law' and 'soft law'.

4

Hugo Sinzheimer and the Constitutional Function of Labour Law

Ruth Dukes[*]

A. Introduction

Inherent in any attempt to redefine labour law – as a tool for labour market regulation; as a means of 'regulating for competitiveness'; or, post financial crisis, as some as yet undefined, less market-centric alternative – is a rejection of old ways of thinking about the subject. Often the 'old', or 'traditional', ways are discussed in a shorthand form with reference to the 'inequalities of bargaining power' paradigm, or to state intervention to further employee-protective aims: fair terms and conditions, equality of treatment, some measure of wealth redistribution. Such shorthand referencing carries with it a danger that the old paradigms might be over-simplified or caricatured; that significant links might be undone, the constitutive blurred with the incidental; and that, as a result, the whole might be rejected too hastily.

My aim, in this chapter, is to return to the traditional conception of labour law as presented in the work of the Weimar scholar, Hugo Sinzheimer.[1] Through a close reading of Sinzheimer's prescriptions for the creation of an economic or labour constitution, I attempt to identify those elements which are capable of generalization: those elements which are true of the regulation of work relations in all types of capitalist economy. This exercise is motivated by a belief that while much of Sinzheimer's writing has become outdated, there is a generalizable core that is still valid today. To begin, as he did, with a recognition of the humanity of the worker, to move from that recognition to a concern with securing respect for human dignity and liberty in the context of working relations, cannot be dismissed as anachronistic without abandoning much wider aspirations to constitute free and equal societies. In line with the themes of the workshop, a second aim of the chapter is to consider how the generalizable elements of Sinzheimer's conception of

---

[*] School of Law, University of Glasgow.

[1] I build here on earlier work: R Dukes, 'Constitutionalizing Employment Relations: Sinzheimer, Kahn-Freund and the Role of Labour Law' (2008) 35 Journal of Law and Society 341; R Dukes, 'Otto Kahn-Freund and Collective Laissez-Faire: An Edifice Without a Keystone?' (2009) 72 MLR 220; and R Dukes, 'The Origins of the German System of Worker Representation' (2005) 19 Historical Studies in Industrial Relations 31.

labour law might be re-specified for current economic conditions. Though it is not possible within the confines of a short chapter to consider this second question fully, I attempt, at least, to provide an indication of the potential benefits and difficulties involved.

B. Sinzheimer's conception of the economic constitution

Hugo Sinzheimer (1875–1945) was a legal scholar and politician whose work had a direct and highly significant influence on the labour law and constitution of the Weimar Republic. Today, he is widely regarded as the founding father of German labour law.[2] In his academic writings, he developed several of the ideas which came to underpin labour legislation in Germany and beyond. In his role as a parliamentary representative, in 1919 and 1920, he was personally involved in drafting parts of the Weimar Constitution. Having failed in a bid to become the Minister of Labour of the new Republic in 1919, he worked as the Professor of Labour Law and the Sociology of Law at the University of Frankfurt until 1933. As a Jew, he was stripped of his chair in that year and moved to the Netherlands, where he continued to work until 1940 at the Universities of Amsterdam and Leiden. Following the German invasion of Holland, he spent the remainder of the war in hiding, surviving only barely to die of exhaustion some weeks after VJ Day.

Given the lasting influence of Sinzheimer's work on German labour law, both during the Weimar Republic and in the decades since the Second World War, the greater part of his writing remains easily accessible to readers today. In order to understand it fully, of course, one must have reference to the period in which it was written – a time of enormous social, economic, and political upheaval. In particular, Sinzheimer's work on labour law is best read as an integral element of wider efforts to establish a new social democratic state following German defeat in the imperialist First World War, and the November Revolution that followed. It is imbued, even as late as the 1930s, with the sense of a search for a new type of justice; with a belief in the capacity of the people to construct a better and fairer way of life.

The detail of Sinzheimer's writing, too, must be read with reference to the peculiarities of German industrial relations at the time. In the immediate aftermath of the war, for example, one of the questions which most occupied him was the 'question of the workers' councils'. By reason of the central role played by workers' and soldiers' councils in the revolution, they retained initially a great deal of political strength, such that it was unclear, for some years, whether the councils or the trade unions should assume the role of the principal representatives of workers within the new Republic. It remained unsettled, too, what the role of the workers' representatives should be. While calls were made from the left for the institution of a new form of democracy based on representation through councils,

---

[2] A biography describes him as such: K Kubo, *Hugo Sinzheimer – Vater des deutschen Arbeitsrechts* (CH Beck, 1985). For further biographical detail in English see O Kahn-Freund, 'Hugo Sinzheimer' in R Lewis and J Clark (eds), *Labour Law and Politics in the Weimar Republic* (Blackwell, 1981).

the belief elsewhere was that any significant political role for the councils and/or the unions should be excluded as inimical to parliamentary democracy. This was a matter on which Sinzheimer himself underwent a change of opinion as the years wore on. Having advocated the assumption of a limited political role by the workers' councils, he came to believe that they should function in the economic sphere only, in a capacity subsidiary to the trade unions.[3] The latter view was given legislative support in the Works Councils Act of 1920 and came, with time, to form the basis for the German 'dual channel' system of worker representation still in place today.

For the most part, Sinzheimer's beliefs and proposals for the regulation of working relations remained constant over the years, so that it is possible, without too much disregard to detail, to present his work on labour law as a unified whole. The starting point for this work was the recognition of the worker as a human being – *die Arbeit ist also der Mensch selbst* – and the characterization of the working relationship as one of subordination. According to Sinzheimer, the source of the subordination of the worker lay with the employer's ownership of the means of production.[4] In order to live and work, the worker was absolutely reliant on the employer (on 'Property'), 'since Property contains the means of living and working'.[5] Having agreed to perform work in exchange for wages, the worker remained under the control of the employer whose 'right of command' was inherent in the ownership of capital.[6] In liberal democracies, this domination of the worker by 'Property' was obscured by the notion of freedom of contract, which posited free agreements between legal persons, each the bearer of legal rights and legal capacity. In social democracies, the subordination of the worker was recognized, and steps taken to make the worker truly free by imposing limits on the exercise of the social power inherent in private property. This was the primary task of labour law: to free the worker and thereby to effect his transformation, in law, from legal person to human being.[7]

That said, it is important to emphasize that for Sinzheimer the role of labour law was not exhausted with fulfilment of the task of securing freedom for workers from abuses of employer power. It was not exhausted by rules directed at securing fair wages and working hours, and at providing social insurance against periods of sickness or unemployment.[8] Labour law was best understood more widely as a tool to be employed in the process of democratizing the economy. This process was central to the achievement of a truly democratic society. Without economic democracy, as a supplement to political democracy, the vast majority of the people remained unfree, subject to the control of a minority wielding economic power. Moreover, economic democracy, like political democracy, had two sides to it. Political democracy aimed not only at guaranteeing individual rights of freedom

---

[3] HA Winkler, *Von der Revolution zur Stabilisierung: Arbeiter und Arbeiterbewegung in der Weimarer Republik, 1918 bis 1924* (JHW Dietz, 1984) 236.

[4] See in particular 'Die Demokratisierung des Arbeitsverhältnisses' in H Sinzheimer, *Arbeitsrecht und Rechtssoziologie* (Europäische Verlagsanstalt, 1976).

[5] Ibid 117.

[6] Ibid.

[7] Ibid 124–5.

[8] Ibid 118–23.

vis-à-vis political power, but also at seizing political power from private hands and transferring it instead to a 'public community' (*öffentliches Gemeinwesen*), in which all citizens participated in the creation of a political common-will. The same went for economic democracy. On the one hand, it involved the emancipation of individuals *vis-à-vis* the bearers of economic power; and, on the other, it was directed at transferring such power from private persons to a 'community of the economy', in which all economic actors could participate in the creation of an economic common-will. In an economic democracy, workers should be *free from* employer efforts to dictate the social and economic conditions of their existence and, at the same time, *free to* participate in the formation of those conditions.

The means of achieving economic democracy lay with the institution of an economic constitution (or labour constitution) alongside the already existing political constitution. Just as the constitutionalization of state power had brought to citizens political equality and freedom from subordination at the hands of the state, so the constitutionalization of economic power would bring equality in the economic sphere, freeing workers from their subordination to the power of Property. Just as the political constitution allowed for political power to be wielded collectively through a parliament representative of all, so the economic constitution would allow for economic power to be wielded collectively through an economic community representative of all. Specifically, the economic constitution would involve the institution of an order based on the joint action of organizations representative of employers and workers. Through the creation of such an order, employers' and workers' organizations would work together, as equals, to govern the economy, regulating working relations and production. Matters which previously had fallen within the employer's sole prerogative would now be decided in community with labour;[9] and the exercise of labour power would be rendered conditional on the participation of the will of organized labour.[10]

The notion of autonomy and autonomous law was thus central to Sinzheimer's conception of constitutionalization. It was fundamental to the idea of economic democracy that *all* economic actors should be free to participate in regulation of the economy. Just as the state created law by means of legislation, so the 'autonomous class organizations' that existed within the economic sphere should be free to make law by reason of their 'spontaneous law-creating powers'.[11] Critically, however, the intention behind constitutionalization was not to afford the collective economic actors *absolute* freedom of action. Individual liberalism should not simply be replaced with collective liberalism (or as we might otherwise put it, collective *laissez-faire!*).[12] Because the economy was a matter of public concern, the ultimate goal of the constitution had to lie with furtherance of the general public interest. 'Collective liberalism', Sinzheimer noted, was informed by the same belief as

---

[9] H Sinzheimer, *Grundzüge des Arbeitsrechts*, 2nd edn (Verlag von Gustav Fischer, 1927) 207–13.

[10] H Sinzheimer, 'Die Reform des Schlichtungswesens' in Sinzheimer, above n 4.

[11] Kahn-Freund, above n 2, 80.

[12] 'Reform des Schlichtungswesens', above n 10, 243. The similarities, at a descriptive level, between Sinzheimer's depiction of 'kollektive Liberalismus' and Kahn-Freund's 'collective laissez-faire' are striking. See Dukes, 'Otto Kahn-Freund', above n 1.

individual liberalism, namely, that the public interest would best be served by the unmitigated emancipation of individuals. Where parties were free of every state obligation to reach agreement, the common interest would be furthered, as if automatically. State intervention in free collective bargaining could serve only to damage the community between labour and property.[13] According to Sinzheimer, experience had shown that this was not the case. A wholly free economy did not result in collective regulation by means of collective bargaining, but rather in the reassertion of employers' control through the 'free' negotiation of individual contracts of employment.[14] Where no means of defence were in place to protect the furtherance of the common interest, there was no guarantee that it would in fact be furthered.

It was vital, for this reason, that the state should assume the role of ultimate guarantor of the public interest.[15] The (social democratic) state's interest in the economy was not exhausted with the freeing of the collective economic actors. It had a direct interest in the social and economic conditions of existence of working people and, more widely, in the efficient functioning of the economy. It had an interest, too, in ensuring that economic decisions were not reached with reference solely to economic considerations: economic interests were not the only interests of the people, and the economy as life-sphere should not be isolated such that it functioned without reference to other life-spheres. In Sinzheimer's view, the terms of the economic constitution should allow for state intervention to further the various interests that it had in the economy. The state should be able, for example, to take and implement decisions where the 'economic community' was unable to do so; to intervene where industrial action threatened the public interest; and to protect individuals from harm at the hands of powerful economic actors. A balance had always to be struck, however, between the autonomy of the economic actors (fundamental to democracy), and state intervention in furtherance of the public interest. The state should not assume the task of regulating the economy, and collective actors should not be regarded as instruments of the state. Therein lay the path to totalitarianism.

C. The constitutional function of labour law

It is undoubtedly the case that the globalization of capital and the liberalization of markets have wrought significant changes on work and working relationships since the time when Sinzheimer lived and wrote. In the context of efforts to make sense of these changes and to consider the question of what labour law is, or ought to be, under conditions of globalization, I wish to argue that elements of his writing retain

---

[13] Ibid.
[14] 'Zur Frage der Reform des Schlichtungswesens' in Sinzheimer, above n 4.
[15] The role of the state is discussed at length in 'Zur Frage der Reform', above n 14; 'Reform des Schlichtungswesens', above n 10; H Sinzheimer, 'Eine Theorie des Sozialen Rechts' (1936) XVI Zeitschrift für öffentliches Recht 31.

their relevance and their utility. Specifically, I wish to argue for the continued usefulness of the idea of the constitutional function of labour law, echoing Sinzheimer's prescriptions for an economic constitution. As a first step, it might be helpful to clarify what Sinzheimer meant by the term 'constitution'; what I understand by it when used in application to labour relations. What is immediately clear is that Sinzheimer invoked the concept with reference to the role played by law in the regulation of labour relations, and not to signify that labour rights ought to be protected as fundamental within the Weimar Constitution.[16] Similarly, I refer to the 'constitutional function' rather than the 'constitutionalization' of labour law or labour rights, since my concern is not, or not exclusively, with the entrenchment of labour rights as fundamental rights.[17] Might this allow the objection to be raised, however, that by using the term 'constitution' other than in reference to the inclusion of labour rights within a bill of rights or similar text, we stretch its meaning to the point where it is merely metaphorical; synonymous with the legal recognition of worker rights?[18]

In order to explore this a little further, we might begin by considering a general definition of the term 'constitution', and the potential of that definition to fit with labour relations and labour law. Writing about the use of the concept 'constitution' in the context of globalization, 'beyond the nation state', Neil Walker provides a useful definition constructed around the characteristic functions of constitutions.[19] According to Walker, constitutions typically create or recognize a particular 'body politic', and provide an encompassing framework for and measure of the limits of that 'body politic'. They typically provide for the creation of norms and for the resolution of conflicts between norms, for example, by establishing a hierarchy among them. And they typically enjoy an entrenched status, a precedence over other system norms.

Sinzheimer's proposals for the democratization of the economy through the institution of an economic or labour constitution seem to me to fit rather well with this general definition. What was intended was that law ('state law', as he referred to it) should be used to institute, or recognize, a system of bi-partite regulation of the economy.[20] Law should be used to create or to recognize a system of workers' councils and bi-partite industrial councils, and to confirm the continued existence of the trade unions and employers' associations.[21] It should be used to endow these bodies with the capacity to legislate and to perform other administrative acts in regulation of the economy. And it should create the legal

---

[16] Though labour rights were in fact guaranteed within the terms of that constitution.

[17] Cf J Fudge, 'The New Discourse of Labour Rights: From Social to Fundamental Rights?' (2007) 29 Comparative Labour Law and Policy Journal 29; and J Fudge, 'Constitutionalizing Labour Rights in Europe' in T Campbell and K Ewing (eds), *Rescuing Human Rights*, forthcoming.

[18] H Arthurs, 'The Constitutionalization of Employment Relations: Multiple Models, Pernicious Problems' (2010) 19 Social & Legal Studies 403–22.

[19] N Walker, 'Beyond the Holistic Constitution', *School of Law Working Paper Series*, 2009/16 (SSRN, 2009).

[20] See, eg, H Sinzheimer, 'Das Rätesystem' and 'Rätebewegung und Gesellschaftsverfassung', both in Sinzheimer, above n 4.

[21] Art 165 Weimar Constitution.

framework within which regulation should proceed, assigning particular duties or spheres of influence to particular bodies, for example, and placing legal limits on the exercise of their powers. Whether issued in the form of legislation or provisions of the Constitution, the state law that fulfilled these functions should have the status of 'fundamental norms' – *Grundnormen*. The aim of the economic constitution was to allow for self-determination within the economic sphere *by virtue of state fundamental norms.*[22]

A similar analysis can be applied to the current German law regulating works councils, which bears the name 'works constitution law'. The Works Constitution Act can be understood to have a foundational quality, constituting actors ('works councils', 'electoral boards', 'economic committees', etc). It can be understood to provide an encompassing framework for those actors, endowing them with norm-creating and other powers, and establishing a hierarchy of norms, so that for example norms created collectively have precedence over individual contracts of employment, and collective agreements have precedence over works agreements. And the Act can even be understood to be entrenched, insofar as it takes precedence over autonomously created norms, and appears to enjoy a measure of permanency. (The Act has been in force, and amended only twice, substantially, since 1952.[23] While it would of course be possible, as a matter of law, to abolish or fundamentally amend it, politically this would be rather more difficult.)

It would seem, then, that in the context of German labour law the term 'constitution' is used not only metaphorically, but in a rather more literal sense. The question remains, however, whether the concept can meaningfully be applied to the role of labour law beyond Germany. What would it mean to apply it to a jurisdiction such as the UK, for example, where labour relations have never been governed by an encompassing legal framework similar to the Works Constitution Act;[24] where it was never attempted, in statute, to entrench certain norms, or to prioritize some above others? What did Sidney and Beatrice Webb have in mind when they described the legal recognition of collective bargaining and the gradual elaboration of a labour code as the concession of an industrial constitution to the working class?[25] What might it mean to talk about the constitutional function of labour law in application to the transnational sphere, beyond the nation state?

In my understanding, the Webbs meant something rather similar to Sinzheimer when they used the term constitution. Like him, they wished to refer to the role that law should play in emancipating workers and giving them control over their working lives. Just as the political constitution had served to limit the power of the king over his subjects, constituting the people as citizens rather than subjects, so the industrial constitution would serve to limit the power of employers over workers, constituting them as something other than commodities – as 'human beings', as

---

[22] Sinzheimer, 'Das Rätesystem', above n 20, 327.

[23] Since 1789, the median duration of constitutions is a mere 17 years, and their average life span less than half that: Arthurs, above n 18.

[24] Except, perhaps, the short-lived and catastrophically unsuccessful Industrial Relations Act of 1971.

[25] S and B Webb, *Industrial Democracy vol II* (Longman, 1897) 840–2.

Sinzhemer would have had it, or, perhaps, as 'labour citizens'.[26] Used in this somewhat looser sense, the idea of the constitutional function of labour law can meaningfully be applied in a variety of contexts. Returning to the example of the UK: while it is true that there was never any all-encompassing legal framework in this country, there has been, for around a century, a set of laws which recognize the legality of trade unions, create freedom for the unions to bargain collectively and to take industrial action, and dictate that the normative terms of a collective agreement will usually be implied into the contracts of employment of union members. This would seem sufficient, at least, to fulfil the central constitutional function of constituting labour as something other than a commodity; of allowing workers, through the trade unions, to participate in the creation and enforcement of the norms which govern their working lives.

Might this, then, be one key sense in which the term 'constitution' could be useful in thinking about the aims of labour and the means to be used to achieve those aims? Referring to the labour constitution, or to the constitutional function of labour law, reminds us of the work that labour law ought to be doing – in nation states or at the supranational or international level – to fulfil the function of constituting labour as something other than a commodity. That harm is done to working people when their labour is treated as a commodity is an idea familiar from a wide range of authors, from Karl Marx to Karl Polanyi.[27] And the imperative of action to prevent the commodification of labour has, of course, been enshrined in Article 1 of the International Labour Organization's (ILO) Declaration of Philadelphia since 1944.

In addition to the goal of the emancipation of labour, the idea of the constitutional function of labour law implies a particular means of achieving that goal, namely the exercise of democratic control over the economic sphere. Time and again, Sinzheimer highlighted the dangers involved in allowing regulation of the economy to proceed entirely freely, guided only by economic considerations. As Emilios Christodoulidis has noted:

The economic constitution was conceived [by Sinzheimer] along the lines of a genuinely constitutional dialogue and in the context of a political economy... It is this marked emphasis on the irreducibly political nature of the economic constitution that underlies and drives its interpretation and realisation.[28]

Without democratic control, the economy collapses into its market form. All that remains 'entrenched' in terms of fundamental norms are the rules of market logic.[29] Labour is understood as a commodity, low wages and poor working conditions are

---

[26] E Fraenkel, 'Zehn Jahre Betriebsrätegesetz' in T Ramm (ed), *Arbeitsrecht und Politik* (Luchterhand Verlag, 1966) 111; H Arthurs, *The New Economy and the Demise of Industrial Citizenship* (IRC Press, 1996) and J Gordon, 'Transnational Labor Citizenship' (2007) 80 Southern California Law Review 503.

[27] K Polanyi, *The Great Transformation: The Political and Economic Origins of Our Time*, 2nd edn (Beacon Press, 2002).

[28] E Christodoulidis, 'A Default Constitutionalism? A Disquieting Note on Europe's Many Constitutions' in K Tuori and S Sankari (eds), *The Many Constitutions of Europe* (Ashgate, 2010).

[29] Ibid.

understood as rational cost-cutting measures, and, on an international stage, as offering a country comparative advantage. The consequences of market performance are categorically separated from political deliberation or negotiation, and the political and social spheres are thereafter 'burdened with an impossible compensatory task, the means for the performance of which are no longer at their disposal'.[30] The idea of the constitutional function of labour law reminds us of this, emphasizing that there is nothing natural or inevitable about economies organized as free markets, and directing us to resist the logic of the market where that logic causes harm.

In parenthesis, it might be emphasized that there is no suggestion in Sinzheimer's work that the furtherance of justice must involve a pay-off in terms of decreased economic efficiency.[31] In the context of the economic destitution of Germany following the First World War, and the colossal suffering that resulted, the utmost importance was placed on the goals of *increasing* production and *improving* economic efficiency. The very aim behind the economic constitution was that all economic actors – workers and owners – should work together in furtherance of the common interest, defined by Sinzheimer, in terms of economic aims, as: the increase of productivity, the minimization of the costs of production, and the direction of production to meet the needs of the masses. Following the war and the revolution, he wrote, we can no longer afford the luxury of a liberal economy.[32] Though the economic constitution would certainly have involved the limitation of free market outcomes, and the subversion of market logic in terms of the characterization of labour as a commodity, it was not understood to involve a reduction of productive or economic efficiency. Limitation of the market in furtherance of the goal of justice was not equated, in other words, with the limitation of economic efficiency.

D. The constitutional function of labour law today

Building on Sinzheimer's work, I have argued that thinking about labour law in terms of its constitutional function allows for important lines of analysis. It provides us with a way of conceiving of the subject that is not focussed narrowly on the imbalance of power in individual employment relations. It highlights, instead, the importance of considering the contribution of labour law to the constitutional task of establishing a particular economic and social order; and it calls to mind the fact that the regulation of working relationships cannot usefully be considered in isolation from the broader constitutional context. Against those who argue for a labour law adapted to meet the needs of the market, the idea of the constitutional function of labour law allows us to maintain a critical edge; to resist the logic of the market where that logic causes harm, and to focus instead on conceptions

---

[30] Ibid.

[31] Cf the characterization of the 'old' or 'traditional' way of thinking about labour law in B Langille, 'What is International Labour Law For?' (2009) 3 Law & Ethics of Human Rights 47; and G Davidov, 'The Changing Idea of Labour Law' (2007) 146 International Labour Review 311.

[32] H Sinzheimer, 'Über die Formen und Bedeutung der Betriebsräte' (1919) in Sinzheimer, above n 4, 322; and 'Rätebewegung und Gesellschaftsverfassung' (1920) in Sinzheimer, above n 4, 357.

of the role and aims of labour law which take the humanity of the worker as the first reference point.

In attempting to apply the idea of the constitutional function of labour law to today's economic and constitutional orders, however, we encounter a number of difficulties. Christodoulidis' depiction of a free market economy insulated from political control, and a political and social sphere impotent to mitigate potentially harsh and unjust market outcomes, directs us to the first of these. His comments were made with reference to the European Union (EU), where in recent years the Court of Justice (ECJ) has held that European rules guaranteeing market freedoms must take precedence over national rules protecting fundamental labour rights, such as freedom of association.[33] As a matter of constitutional law, the reasoning of the ECJ can be traced to the original decision of the drafters of the Treaties of Rome to assign the task of creating a single market to the supranational institutions of the new Economic Community, and to leave responsibility for the guarantee and maintenance of social standards to the national institutions of the Member States. By reason of this division of labour, a Court decision reached some years later, that Community law must have precedence over Member State law, had the effect of instituting a constitutional prioritization of economic, market-creating aims above other (for example, social) aims.[34] Similar patterns of split-level competences and the constitutional prioritization of free market rules can be found in other jurisdictions.[35]

It follows from the nature of such constitutional frameworks that efforts to promote and to guarantee labour and other social rights are significantly handicapped. Again with reference to the EU, Fritz Scharpf has described the existence of a 'competency gap' between a Union without legislative competence to regulate social matters, and Member States prohibited from doing so in the myriad of ways judged to breach the 'fundamental freedoms' of the single market.[36] In fact the problem is more wide-ranging even than that. First and foremost, globalization has meant the globalization of capital and of markets. While centres of economic power and decision making have become increasingly supranational, representative and democratic structures have remained tied to particular localities. Where legislative competence to enact labour protective and other 'social law' measures exists only at the national level this is to some extent inevitable, since trade unions and other organizations will seek to lobby and influence decision making within national institutions. At the same time, however, economic policy decisions of huge importance will be taken above the national level (where labour's influence remains weak), potentially limiting the capacity of the national legislatures to act. What are the consequences of this for the idea of a global economic constitution? Unless and until effective mechanisms for the exercise of countervailing power can be instituted at the supranational level, what might supranational constitutionalization mean? Simply the

---

[33] Case C–341/05 *Laval v Svenska Byggnadsarbetareförbundet* [2007] ECR I–11767; Case C–438/05 *International Transport Workers Union v Viking* [2007] ECR I–10779; Case C–346/06 *Rüffert v Land Niedersachsen* [2008] ECR I–01989; and Case C–319/06 *Commission v Luxembourg* [2008] ECR I–04323.

[34] F Scharpf, 'Negative Integration and Positive Integration in the Political Economy of European Welfare States' in G Marks and others (eds), *Governance in the European Union* (Sage, 1996).

[35] See, eg, Harry Arthurs' discussion of the federal constitution of Canada: Arthurs, above n 18.

[36] Scharpf, above n 34, 15.

judicial protection of individual rights against more powerful economic opponents?[37] What of Sinzheimer's two-sided definition of democracy, as securing for individuals *freedom from* abusive treatment, and *freedom to* participate in the formation of the social and economic conditions of their existence?

A second related difficulty encountered in applying the idea of the constitutional function of labour law to current conditions lies with the question of who or what might do the work of constitutionalizing. It is true that, as used by Sinzheimer, the idea of constitutionalization acknowledges the existence of multiple state and non-state sources of normativity in labour law.[38] As was mentioned above, the term 'state law' was used to distinguish norms created by the legislature from norms created autonomously by social actors such as trade unions and employers' organizations: both were equally 'law'. But it is also the case that in Sinzheimer's prescriptions for the institution of an economic constitution, the role of the state was absolutely central. As the guarantor of the furtherance of the public interest, it fell to the state not only to facilitate the exercise of regulatory power by employers, trade unions, and works councils, but also to set the correct limits to the exercise of that power through the institution of the constitutional framework. In a globalized context, who or what could perform this role at the transnational level? Could constitutionalization be understood with Gunther Teubner as a spontaneous, stateless process?[39] If so, what could it mean, in the context of work, other than a reinforcement of already existing market relations and market powers? Could the ILO form the core of a market-correcting international labour law? Could international labour standards serve as a globally respected set of rules, 'entrenched' increasingly through recognition by a constellation of human rights adjudicators, trade unions, non-governmental organizations (NGOs), consumer groups, transnational companies (TNCs)?[40] Or are the barriers to such a global labour constitution insurmountable: the apparent universality of the flexibility leitmotiv; the diversification of working relations and fragmentation of the working classes; the asymmetry between global capital, on the one hand, and weakened trade unions and other democratic, representative institutions still tied to the national level, on the other?

E. Conclusion

The prospects for a global labour constitution akin to the national labour constitutions of the 20th century appear bleak. The idea of the constitutional function of labour law continues nonetheless to provide a useful basis for the critical analysis of

---

[37] F Rödl, 'Re-Thinking Employment Relations in Constitutional Terms' (2010) 19 Social & Legal Studies 241–6.

[38] Arthurs, above n 18.

[39] See, eg, G Teubner, 'Constitutionalising Polycontexturality', Social & Legal Studies, forthcoming; and G Teubner, 'Societal Constitutionalism: Alternatives to State-centred Constitutional theory?' in C Joerges, I-J Sand, and G Teubner (eds), *Transnational Governance and Constititionalism* (Hart Publishing, 2004) 3–28.

[40] B Hepple, *Labour Laws and Global Trade* (Hart Publishing, 2005).

labour law at the national and transnational levels. It acts to unsettle the notion of the market order as pre-ordained, and to remind us of the aspirations of labour law – 'labour is not a commodity' – as a benchmark for the shortcomings of current constitutional and economic arrangements. In drawing our attention, as labour lawyers, to the nature of these arrangements it invites us to re-think the constitutional function in terms of international institutions – the ILO, TNCs, NGOs, etc. At the same time, it directs us to think carefully before dismissing the potential of national institutions and the normative work that they might still do. Most importantly, perhaps, the idea of the constitutional function of labour law provides us with a means of holding on to long traditions of thought and action which understand labour law as a tool for the furtherance of economic and social justice.

5

Global Conceptualizations and Local Constructions of the Idea of Labour Law

*Adrián Goldin**

A. The idea of labour law: one or many?

1. Formulating an idea of labour law

From a comparative approach, we must pose some preliminary questions on addressing the topic: is it possible to formulate an idea of labour law of a (rather) universal reach? Has there, at least, ever been one, if it is the case that, nowadays, having undergone hypothetical alterations, there is no such thing any longer?

Finding an answer is not an easy task, indeed, and its obvious comparative dimension suggests it is only possible as the product of the concerted reflection of scholars coming from the most diverse legal experiences. As it has recently been said with overwhelming honesty, few of us know many legal orders in depth besides our own,[1] and even fewer manage to prevent considering other scholars' orders through the sieve of their own conceptions.[2]

At any rate, it seems to be obvious that any pretence of (relative) universality calls for the recognition of the *idea* of labour law in a very schematic and stylized conceptual dimension, for only such an approach may enable it to express such a wide-ranging transnational and intertemporal scope it is expected to have.

Aware as we may be of such severe restrictions, it might be, nonetheless, possible to try out a characterization of the *idea* of labour law, on the understanding that it will have just a hypothetical value. And that it may be justifiable as a mere starting point for a collective and comparative building task that may either let us address the idea in more rigorous terms, or, on the contrary, lead to the conclusion that there is no such idea, has never been, or else bears such a limited and elementary

---

* Full professor at the Universidad de San Andrés (Argentina). The author prepared this chapter as part of his activities as a resident fellow researcher in the Institut d'études avancées de Nantes (October – December 2009).

[1] X Blanc-Jouvan, 'Lessons from An Experiment in Comparative Labor Law (Reflections on the Comparative Labor Law Group)' (2007) 28-3 Comp Lab L & Policy J 407.

[2] H Arthurs, 'Compared to What? The UCLA Comparative Labor Law Project and the Future of Comparative Labor Law' (2007) 28-3 Comp Lab L & Policy J 591.

configuration that it renders any reflection on its hypothetical evolution a senseless purpose. In any case, I will call it the '*basic*' or '*original*' *idea* to distinguish it from *other ideas* that, although within its framework, bear the distinctive marks of the particular legal systems harbouring them and, hence, is lacking that purported quasi-*universality*.

From this modest perspective, labour law would be the branch of the legal order that deals with the provision of human labour within the framework of production and service processes organized by another (the job giver), to the benefit of the latter. In that relation the job giver is the holder of a scarce factor (capital), which is fundamental for the working of these processes which the providers need to join to obtain a consideration enabling them to satisfy their needs.

The main concern inspiring labour law has to do with the fact that that service, unlike others exchanged in product markets, is inseparable from the person providing it, and, in addition, with the connatural impossibility of postponing the needs that have to be satisfied with the consideration the provider receives. This inseparability prevents the original dispossession of the service the job giver is paying for, which calls for a certain degree of subjection (subordination) to substitute for that inaccessible dispossession.[3]

That group of conditions in the hands of by job givers – among them, capital ownership, organizational power, priority of their interests, economic dependency, subordination – generates a structural asymmetry of powers between both subjects of the relationship (job givers or employers; service providers or workers) expressed when it comes to both setting up the job conditions and managing the relation itself. That virtual one-sidedness (unilaterality) in the settlement of work conditions determines that the possible outcome, considering the commitment of the worker's body[4] and his or her economic dependency, may prove highly burdensome and offensive for his or her dignity, health, and sustenance conditions.

This asymmetry expressed above reveals the radical ineptitude of individual autonomy in the contract to produce balanced and optimal satisfactory conditions for both parties. Given that presupposition, a prevailing function of legal orders is to restrict the one-sidedness through regulatory sources – often different in nature, combination, and precedence – whose common trait is the impossibility of their being displaced by the exercise of individual autonomy.[5] Legal order fosters, or at least, acknowledges those sources.

In spite of their diversity, legal orders recognize inspiration and grounds in a group of common values that, due to their paradigmatic universality, and for the sake of brevity, may be identified among those inspiring the creation of the International Labour Organization (ILO) and its regulatory system and that are

---

[3] M Fabre-Magnan, 'Le contrat de travail défini par son objet' in A Supiot (ed), *Le travail en perspectives* (LGDJ, Collection Droit et Société, 1998) 101.

[4] A Supiot, *Le droit du travail* (Que sais-je, PUF, 2004).

[5] O Kahn-Freund, 'Trabajo y Derecho' (Colección Estudios Serie Relaciones Laborales, trans JM Galiana Moreno, Ministerio de Trabajo y Seguridad Social, 1987) has remarked that the main purpose of labour law had always been, and (he dared say) would always be, to serve as counterweight balancing the inequality in the negotiating power that is necessarily inherent to the work relation.

expressed – among many other sources – in the ILO constitution and, in particular, in the Declaration of Philadelphia there included. It does not seem inappropriate to consider that group of values as the grounds for that *basic or original idea of labour law* we intended to outline in these paragraphs.

2. The 'particular ideas' of labour law

If that 'basic idea' had the degree of purported universality we hypothesize herein, it should be admitted that its contents are part, in turn, of the different 'particular ideas' of labour law identifiable in every legal regime, system or experience. Those 'particular ideas', although informed by the alleged 'basic idea', would add their own specific and idiosyncratic elements, such as the dominant presence of one source or another, the different rule construction manners, the typology of techniques in use, the different ways of subject recognition, etc.

In the past decades, those 'particular ideas' of labour law and, of course, the *'basic idea'* informing and integrating them have been subjected to a series of challenges that have put them to the test: economy claims, dominant ideological paradigms, the clamour of market internationalization, new hard technologies and organizational work and production developments, new ways of hiring and including human labour, among others.[6] The main interest in this document lies in dissociating them (telling the 'basic idea' apart from the different 'particular ideas'), since the core of this chapter is the hypothesis that *in the face of those challenges, some legal systems have shown a bigger propensity to move away from that 'basic idea', whilst others, in spite of their having undergone significant changes, have stayed within its scope.* To put it in terms dear to convergence theories, in this case we are in front of a certain convergence of challenges, but not of reactions or answers.

Indeed, on undertaking the task of weighing how affected the idea of labour law, typical of every legal system taken into consideration, was (which, due to the restricted extent of this chapter, will only be hinted at), relevant indicators are not just the group of regulatory and institutional transformations present in them, *but mainly the academic developments conceived to interpret and follow them up.* It must be conceded, in fact, that the (basic) idea and the (particular) ideas of a certain branch of the law are only externalized in a fairly systematic way in scholars' constructions; and that, thus, the specific ideas of certain branches of the law (in our case, labour law), which result from such constructions, may reflect an evolution that is lacking (or at least, has not reflected yet) a correlation in patent institutional changes.

All of the above is meant to suggest the additional hypothesis that *in the last decades not only has the basic idea of labour law been affected in different dimensions or intensity in each of the various legal systems – which in the medium term might affect its original condition of extended universality – but especially that legal scholars' constructions have been inclined to stray from that historical idea, which might have also been determined, in turn, by the structure of the 'particular ideas' of their native legal systems.*

---

[6] A Bronstein, *International and Comparative Labour Law: Current Challenges* (ILO and Palgrave Macmillan, 2009) has thoroughly addressed those challenges.

Were this the case, it would be clear throughout the comparative task that some of those judgements would rightfully express certain tendencies present in certain systems or legal orders but that they would not always be able to account for others that evolve in a different way. Even though it sounds as a quite self-evident hypothesis, that in the course of the comparison keeps bringing out the deep institutional gaps separating constitutively different legal orders, to put it forward may well prove justifiable on carrying out such a task as proposed here, that originates from the assumption, although subjected to preliminary discussion, of the existence of a certain *(almost) universally shared basic or historical idea of labour law*. This perspective entails the formulation of the third hypothesis (a mere specification of the previous two) that *the legal origin – perhaps irrelevant to determine legal orders efficiency levels[7] – is indeed significant when it comes to defining their evolution paths and, particularly, those of their exponents' constructions.*

In view of the purpose of this chapter – the formulation and justification of merely descriptive hypotheses – I will omit, to the extent of my possibilities, my own critical appreciation of the transformation processes labour law has been undergoing, as well as of the theoretical constructions operating on those processes; I have already voiced it in many previous works and this is not the opportunity to go back to it.

To carry out the aforesaid proposal, the following section will ponder on the impact those 'challenges' (which, due to the need for brevity in this chapter, will not be examined here either) have had on the different legal experiences, each one of them expressing a 'particular idea' of labour law. In the last section, I will attempt to draw some conclusions.

B. On the evolution of 'particular ideas' on labour law

1. An imperfect sample

To test the consistency of the formulated hypotheses – their mere tenability as hypotheses, and in no way their scientific confirmation, which is beyond the reach of this chapter – we will go along a traditional divide: the one that distinguishes the continental legal system, or civil law, from the Anglo-Saxon system, or common law. They both might recognize themselves in that 'basic idea' of labour law, much as their respective 'particular ideas' may differ in a clear-cut way due to various distinguishing factors. Among the most noteworthy are their highly varied regulatory intensity, expressed in the so much dissimilar configuration of their respective source systems, and especially, in the role of the statutory law, dominant in the continental system, of lesser importance in the regulation of individual relationships in the common law legal systems.

I will also consider, by probably inappropriately assigning it the condition of a third 'particular idea', the labour laws in Latin America; it may prove useful to

---

[7] S Deakin and others, 'The Evolution of Labour Law: Calibrating and Comparing Regulatory Regimes' (2007) 146 (3–4) ILR 133.

illustrate one approach, among others from developing economies' perspectives, to the subject matter of this chapter. It must be noted, however, that this third 'particular idea' is far from being as independent from the other two as they are from each other. In fact, Latin American labour laws fall within the civil law legal system and, therefore, share many of its distinctive traits. They do not constitute, in consequence, three symmetrically independent legal experiences.

2. Examining the particular ideas

a. *Labour laws of the continental legal system*

i. Labour flexibility

In the last decades, labour laws of Western European countries enrolled in the civil law legal system *have been subject to repeated and extensive reforms*, many of which, undoubtedly, have been the product of recurring claims for adapting labour law to efficiency considerations.[8] There is an emphasis on the demands for the economic rationality of the laws. They are expected to take into account economic goals such as employment performance and the good functioning of labour markets. They are also expected to consider the companies' prosperity. These objectives did not form part of their initial programme.[9] It may, however, be said that that demand for efficiency operates under the figure of demands for an increase in *flexibility* in regulations and practices. It is, we might say, an economic approach tending to question the hypothetical excesses concerning the rigidity of labour regulations of state stock rather than their existence itself.[10]

If it is true that flexibility claims and techniques tend mostly to reduce the intensity of protection legal systems, in my view they do not involve a qualitative change in the logic of protection. On the contrary, it may be claimed that – at least to a certain extent – such mechanisms *constitute a characteristic feature of the protection system itself – they only make sense in relation to a legal protection regime as the one prevailing here – and, as a result, they qualify it in different degrees, but they do not alter its nature.*

Nor does the idea of 'flexicurity', core of the European discussion after the Lisbon summit, that included it as one element of the European Strategy of Employment, seem to enervate the *basic idea* of labour law in any substantial terms. Its flexibility component pressures towards weakening the intensity of employment rules, but not towards a significant change of the idea of protection.[11]

---

[8] S Sciarra, 'The evolution of labour law (1992–2003)' vol I: General Report for the European Commission, Employment & Social Affairs (June 2005).

[9] M Rodríguez Piñero, 'Derecho del Trabajo y Racionalidad' (2006) 5 Relaciones Laborales La Ley 1.

[10] Existence that from the logic of law and economics would thwart the freedom of the 'homo economicus', rational maximizer of their lives' goals (R Posner, *El Análisis Económico del Derecho* (1st edn, Fondo de Cultura Económica, México DF, 2000). Among European critical perspectives on law and economics, A Lyon-Caen (ed), 'L'évaluation du droit du travail: problèmes et méthodes', Institut International Pour les Etudes Comparatives – DARES Appel a Projets de recherche 2005 – L'analyse économique du droit du travail. Rapport final (vol I) Rapport de Synthèse, 11/04/2008.

[11] Rather than eliminated, contractual protection of labour law seems to be weakened, weakening which is said to be made up for with the strengthened presence of social security tools regarding

That condition (continuity of the logic of protection) is ratified by the Danish legal order itself – referent of this proposal – in which the counterpart of the high flexibility in redundancy and the accentuated functional flexibility is a still intense regulation of salaries and employment duration.[12]

ii. The sources of labour law

If it has ever been possible to speak of the stability of labour law sources (which they were and how they related to one another as opposed to their changing contents),[13] it should be admitted that such a condition of stability has nowadays been lost. In fact, the addition of new species is a generalized practice today, multiplying the type of relationships among them and assigning them new functions. In addition to traditional statutory regulations and collective bargaining agreements, other forms of international regulation are also embodied, rendering 'internormativity' matters notably more complex with unresolved hierarchy relations. Also, non-binding regulations – soft law expressions – appear at an international level, together with voluntary initiatives of highly diverse dimension, and there is a generalization of the imposition of procedural rules aiming at regulating the deciding actors' way of interaction rather than the decisions themselves.

New relations between the traditional sources – statutes and collective agreements – are set up and a certain weakening of the law in face of the collective agreement can be verified,[14] as is also the case with industry in relation to company agreements.[15] Furthermore, collective bargaining agreements are assigned competence that used to be within the purview of the statutory law.

The contents of those sources – in line with the referred trend towards labour flexibility – bear a lower protection intensity, but not a reduction in the density of the regulating machinery that, bent precisely on that flexibility aim, increases the bulk of regulations.

It is worth noting, nonetheless, that in spite of all those innovations notably qualifying the source system, in the continental area the law has not lost its condition of being the sphere of the *incalculable*[16] understood as pertaining matters transcending any individual assessment or utility and including those minima that are considered irreducible to ensure people's dignity.

---

earnings continuity, active labour market policies, lifelong learning, mechanisms ensuring employment compatibility with family life, and a broad health coverage system.

[12] Lyon-Caen, above n 10.

[13] G Lyon-Caen, 'L'Etat des sources du droit du travail (agitations et menaces)' (2001) Droit social Décembre 2001, 1031.

[14] Which Emmanuel Dockés, 'Le pouvoir dans les rapports de travail: Essor juridique d'une nuisance économique' (June 2004), Droit Social No 6 620 categorizes as one more sign of the dominant power of the employer, since in the shaping of the collective agreement the employer's vote equals that of all the workers, whilst in the law, from a democratic system logic, every individual has one vote.

[15] As pointed out by Sciarra, above n 8, traditionally, lower levels could only improve what was established in the upper ones. Now that logic is reversed, as is the case, for instance, in Germany, where the 'opening clauses' of the collective agreement enable its abolition at company level.

[16] A Supiot, *L'esprit de Philadelphie* (Éditions du Seuil, 2010).

So, it must be accepted that it is in this field of sources and their reciprocal relations where the most intense changes in the European scene are noted[17] – perhaps some alteration of the *particular ideas* of labour law – without this bringing about any alteration whatsoever in the *basic idea:* the individual autonomy is still framed within a regulatory mechanism tending to neutralize its substantial asymmetry. Neither does regulatory abundance resulting from labour flexibility advances deny the *basic idea* (although it certainly weakens the protective intensity of labour law); as stated above, those rules of 'labour flexibility' only make sense in relation to a work protection system that, although less intense, still is fully in force.

iii. Alteration in the criteria of identification of the subjects in the labour relation

If during a major part of the history of labour law only the subordinated workers constituted its main concern – there were others, but the subordinated workers field was vast and expansive enough and they embodied the most pressing social problem – nowadays that category seems to be contracting whereas the number of *economically dependent autonomous workers* has been acquiring increasing social relevance. This evocation is, naturally, by no means an attempt to go back to the aetiology of these phenomena, rather it is meant to reflect on the way in which legislation and continental literature have taken charge of them, with the purpose of establishing if that treatment implies decisive changes in the 'continental' idea of labour law and whether it, by extension, entails any relevant affectation on the basic idea of labour law.

It is evident that inequality – imbalance, asymmetry – that called for a particular treatment of subordination relations is far from having disappeared; more so, it persists in the traditional figure of subordination and extends, in turn, to other bonds of personal work, legally autonomous but economically dependent. We must recognize, in consequence, that if, at the personal work level, the space where the *inequality feature* settles expands, the technical protection tools, and whatever else is necessary to provide it with appropriate answers, must correlatively do so.[18]

Thus, there are few European legal scholars who propose leaving aside the classical employer–employee relationship – probably, as stated, in retreat, but still dominant[19] – there are rather theoretical constructions proposing the inclusion of economic indicia to the bundle of signs (the indicia test) used to verify the existence of an actual employer–employee relationship, the extension of protection to 'semi-dependent' or 'quasi-dependent' workers[20] and some legislative practices to assign a certain number of protection resources to economically dependent, autonomous

---

[17] Sciarra, above n 8.

[18] Rodríguez Piñero, above n 9.

[19] The General Director of the International Labour Organization points out that labour law evolution has not meant a global crisis of the previous model of labour recruiting. Even though the presence of more autonomous work is verified, *subordinated employment forms still prevail, and within them stable recruiting of undetermined duration, that the ILO report considers as the most beneficial for productivity:* investment in human capital and workers' welfare and motivation (OIT (2006) 'Tendencias de la legislación laboral', del informe del Director General a la 95 Conferencia 'Cambios en el mundo del trabajo').

[20] For some recent treatment of the issue see L Nogler, *The Concept of 'Subordinations' in European and Comparative Law* (University of Trento, 2009).

workers (such are the already traditional cases of Italian and German legislation and the more recent Spanish regime of *Trabajadores Autónomos Económicamente Dependientes* – 'Economically Dependent Autonomous Workers').[21]

In this way, labour law in the continental legal system shows tendencies of incorporation of 'quasi-dependent' workers, by no means implying that the traditional category of subordinated workers, still unquestionably presiding the centre of imputation of labour law,[22] may no longer be in force. If it is, thus, possible for the traditional formula which served as grounds for the application of the protection system (labour + legal-personal subordination) to be replaced by a broader one in the definition of the subjective field of labour law (labour + contractual inequality), so far that has not meant the abasement of the still-dominant category of subordination. At any rate, if that new formula may imply a certain alteration of the 'continental idea' of labour law, it does not entail, to the best of my judgement, moving away from the 'basic idea' we have attempted to outline in the first section of this document.

iv. Other issues: fundamental rights, capacities (capabilities?), a new relation with social security

From a different perspective, the courts' recognition of the fundamental rights of employees under an employment relationship that, for their own dimension, are not subjected to the debate on labour subordination and intensity of the individual labour relations, has reached noteworthy development. As far as this work is concerned, those personal rights express, among other phenomena, a new state of critical evolution in the employer's power of direction; if one of the objectives of labour law is to limit the power of direction, it may be said that remarkable progress has been made through this way.[23] From that perspective, this trend, so concisely stated, seems to go deep into the historical idea of labour law.

From another perspective, and to enable further comparison with the legal space of common law, it is to be noted that in the continental territory the idea of 'capabilities', product of Amartya Sen's workings,[24] does not seem to have found significant shelter in scholars' thought.[25]

Finally, and as apparent from previous paragraphs, a more intense relation between labour law and social security can indeed be perceived. In *flexicurity*

---

[21] For some brief examination of the Spanish experience see J Cabeza Pereiro, 'The Status of Self-Employed Workers in Spain' (2008) 147–1 ILR 9.

[22] Dockés, above n 14.

[23] At a time of growing disparity between regions and within countries, a person's fundamental rights may become the means to keep a minimum of social cohesion and solidarity in society (Christophe Vigneau, 'Labor Law between Changes and Continuity' (2004) 25–1 Comp Lab L & Policy J 129).

[24] See, in particular, Sen in *Commodities and Capabilities* (OUP, 1999) and *Desarrollo como libertad* (Planeta, 2000).

[25] Supiot draws close to it only to take distance in an explicit way; it is not, he states, a category-holding citizenship card in the continental tradition. He claims that this order of reflections is better supported by the idea of 'capacity' as soon as it is admitted to transcend its traditional spaces in legal science and it is nurtured by other contents. A Supiot, 'En guise de conclusión: la capacité, une notion à haut potential' in S Deakin and A Supiot (eds), *Capacitas* (Hart Publishing, 2009) 161 ff.

schemes, labour flexibility concessions in rules regulating contracts of employment seek their counterpart in the strengthening of social security tools that especially ensure the earnings continuity of workers subjected to a more unstable regulatory framework regarding redundancy and, thus, regarding their right to enjoy a legal guarantee of permanence. From a different axiological perspective – *that, rather than to predicate the correlative loss of protection intensity of the rules preventing unfair redundancy, seems to acknowledge their unrelenting weakening* – the theoretical proposal of the establishment of the *person's professional state*[26] implies the need to offer some treatment of transitions and mutations in a multiplicity of activity and inactivity situations that a regime belonging to the security area is in charge of integrating in a continuous sequence, ensuring in every one of them and their transitions, earnings continuity. In this way social security relates that continuity condition to the persons themselves, becoming detached from their occupational situation to ensure access to that protection.

In such schemes labour and social security law do not lose their reciprocal autonomous condition, but they relate more intimately, for this is required by the social protection needs in bonds that become changing and unstable such as links that have traditionally been part of labour law or that are being currently added due to the increasing presence of employment situations marked by inequality between the parts (although not subordinated in a strict sense), and still others that simply exceed labour law: freelance services, periods of unemployment or non-employment, of fulfilment of civic or family duties, etc. Novelty does not lie in the relation between both branches of the law, but in the intensity of the bond that lets us state, as in the past but with accented emphasis today, that, to a certain degree, *labour law is also what it is, depending on the type of relation it has with social security law, which it once made its main, if not only, access point.*

v. Provisional appraisal

In sum, it can be said that *reform in European labour laws has been frequent and extensive to the extent that it could be stated that traditional labour laws have been consigned to the world of legal-labour archaeology.*[27]

This superficial tour across the continental experience suggests, in sum, *that its own particular idea of labour law, or some of the particular ideas integrating it have undergone significant changes in some of its dimensions,* such as the intensity of its protection system (according to the claims for labour flexibility), the recognition of employed people's fundamental rights, the identification of its sources and their interrelations, the nature of its centre of imputation and its subject's configuration, its relations with social security, etc. In the same line is the contribution of

---

[26] Supiot has recently come back to that proposal in *L'esprit de Philadelphie* (Éditions du Seuil, 2010), which, as therein mentioned, has been included – under the form of professional social security – in the proposal of unions such as the French CGT. In the same line, Pascal Lokiec, 'Le travailleur et l'actif' (2009) Droit Social no 11 (numéro spécial) 1017 and before, Robert Salais, 'Liberté du travail et capacités: une perspective pour la construction européenne?' (1999) Droit Social no 5 467.
[27] F Valdes dal Re, 'El debate europeo sobre la "modernización del Derecho del trabajo" y las relaciones laborales triangulares' (2009) Relaciones Laborales No 3 año XXV 1.

experiences turning into regulatory proposals, such as *flexicurity* and others conceived by scholars, as the *professional state of persons*. It looks, though, as if none of those changes may actually constitute an essential separation from the basic idea or labour law, such as we have attempted to outline in the first lines of this document.

b. In Anglo-Saxon tradition countries

i. On their system of sources

While in countries drawing on the continental legal system one of the areas experiencing the biggest transformation was their source system and, in particular, the scheme of relations between the law and the collective agreement (one of the basic binary equations of continental labour network), few of that was verified in Anglo-Saxon tradition countries. In them, labour law, seen as the group of state rules regulating in an imperative way minimal work conditions, is less relevant[28] and, in terms of density, is far from being on a level with the ones in the continental legal tradition. The establishment of those conditions is up to the agreements between employers and trade unions, though subjected in each legal experience to its own local regime.

I think it is this source system configuration that enables, both from regulatory reality per se and from legal scholars' constructions, the most noteworthy separation from *particular ideas* of their respective labour laws and, a fortiori, from the *basic idea* that, in the stylized dimension we tried to picture in the first section, also shaped their legal orders. If, as perceptively marked, the law is the realm of the *incalculable* concerning matters that go beyond any individual estimate or utility[29] it is only understandable for its (the law's) absence to enable the most audacious separation; a legal order in which certain tools protecting a working person – operative translation of the *basic idea* – may be there or not (may be negotiated or not), is more likely to suffer radical alteration in its *original idea*.[30]

ii. Contract of employment and subordination

Theoretical constructions inspired on the insufficient capacity of the traditional concept of subordination to include the diverse expressions of labour relations respond to the same logic. They not only question its exclusiveness (that of the concept of subordination) to define the centre of imputation of labour law, but they also invalidate it as a parameter of separation or proximity from other kinds of personal work relations. Those constructions even propose to eliminate the concept of subordination as a qualifier for access to enjoying certain rights historically

---

[28] R Dukes, 'Constitutionalizing Employment Relations: Sinzheimer, Kahn-Freund, and the Role of Labour Law' (2008) 35–3 JLS, 341, 363.

[29] Supiot, above n 26.

[30] As the intervention of other regulatory forms, as considered by C Arup, 'Labour Law as Regulation: Promise and Pitfalls' (2001) 14 Australian Journal of Labour Law 230, or the establishment of the tendency towards labour law without state or with less state (which, on the other hand, is not new, since in these countries mediators, conciliators and other non-state organisms of conflict solving is generalized); private mediation is called in to ensure the enforcement of collective agreements, together with other non-state regulation forms (Arthurs, above n 2).

conceived to assist workers in maximum asymmetry situations present in human labour services.[31]

While in the continental dogma there seem to be certain movements tending to both conceptually broaden the idea of dependency, and to add further categories of workers whose legal-personal autonomy fails to hide a determining situation of contractual inferiority defined by a state of economic subjection, the aforementioned influential Anglo-Saxon literature proposes to abandon the traditional criterion of subordination and substitute it with wider-ranging categories including every expression of personal work.[32] Those authors invoke purposes such as including situations so far excluded from the employment contract paradigm, establishing a logic of continuity for contracts outside the labour protection system, enabling deeper and more successful legal experimentation for the recognition of contractual agreements tolerating greater degrees of autonomy on the part of the worker, revealing the inadequacy of the traditional concept of subordination to recognize it as mould or matrix to identify the categories reached by and excluded from the protection system, setting up a multidimensional framework of personal work to facilitate convergence between employment contracts regulation and that of other personal work contracts.

iii. On the theoretical construction of 'capabilities'

Amartya Sen's ideas, in particular the theoretical construction of 'capabilities', have certainly been welcome in legal Anglo-Saxon literature.[33] Especially, Deakin has

---

[31] M Freedland, *The Personal Employment Contract* (OUP, 2003); M Freedland, 'From the Contract of Employment to the Personal Work Nexus' (2006) 35–1 Industrial Law Journal, 1, 29; M Freedland, 'Developing the European Comparative Law of Personal Work Contracts' (2007) 28–3 Comp Lab L & Policy J 487; S Deakin and W Njoya, *The Legal Framework of Employment Relations* (Centre for Business Research, University of Cambridge, Working Paper No 349, September 2007); A Hyde, 'What is Labour Law?' in G Davidov and B Langille (eds), *Boundaries and Frontiers of Labour Law: Goals and Means in the Regulation of Work* (Hart Publishing, 2006); B Langille, 'Imagining Post "Geneva Consensus": Labour Law for Post "Washington consensus" Development', Rough Draft, 11 June 2009, prepared for the conference 'Regulating for Decent Work: Innovative Regulation as a response to Globalization' (ILO, 2009); and M Linder, 'Dependent and Independent Contractors in Recent US Labor Law: An ambiguous Dichotomy Rooted in Simulated Statutory Purposelessness' (2009) 21 Comp Lab L & Policy J 187. These authors' constructions differ from one another, and so do their respective conceptions of the path labour law should take – in some cases they are even contradictory; however, all of them coincide in calling into question the traditional idea of subordination and contract of employment, and that is what is worth pointing out here within the framework of the hypothesis constituting the object of this reflection. Up to now, the law does not seem to have come this far: the British figure of the 'worker' as a subject enabled to access some rights (its conceptualization in G Davidov, 'Who Is a Worker?' (2005) 34 Indus LJ 2005, 57 and of the *dependent contractor* in Canada, seem – *mutatis mutandis* – rather to recall the idea of the 'quasi-dependent' worker of the continental experience).

[32] Langille (see n 31) quoting Freedland states that the negative to 'open up' the centre of imputation of labour law derives from the fear of losing the justification of inequality in negotiating powers. We barely reach, he says, the quasi-dependent workers, precisely because in them that asymmetry of powers is indeed present. But the opportunity of 'capturing' autonomous workers is wasted, he says, in favour of that anachronistic obsession to preserve the idea of dependency.

[33] Among others, S Deakin, 'The "Capability" Concept and the Evolution of European Social Policy', ESRC Centre for Business Research, University of Cambridge, Working paper No 303, 2005 and, within the framework of quite a different proposal, Langille, above n 32.

attempted to project that conception on labour law, inspired in the idea that legal order requires the establishment of the necessary institutional preconditions to facilitate the development of individual capabilities enabling the deliberate and effective participation of individuals in market activities, a function which, to a certain extent, is embodied by the dominant state regulation in continental law.[34] It is claimed that, to that end, neither the assignment of legal or factual contractual capacities nor the acknowledgement of property rights are enough – pure neoclassical logic so far – but that it is necessary to endow workers with other forms of institutional support besides the collective action traditional ones, to improve their participation in markets operation.

From this point of view, summarized by Deakin, that of *capabilities* seems to be a practice in the making, that transcends the compelling rule – *but not necessarily excludes it* – and that, together with security mechanisms and social assistance or other public policies allows for the application of the necessary adjustments, with the purpose of strengthening the capacity of workers in the market.

iv. Law and economics

Last but not least, it is evident that law and economics, firmly mounted in the Anglo-Saxon world since the early 1960s, enables constructions inclined to separate their legal orders from that *basic and original idea* of labour law. If legal order is to be designed so as to eliminate the obstacles hindering private agreements,[35] the space left for a legal regime as labour law, which is originally based on the structural inequality of the negotiating powers and the consequent inadequacy of the autonomy of will, and, in consequence, of the contract regulating working conditions, is certainly smaller. It goes without saying that a legal system that has adopted this conception – the one of law and economics – is likely to be, as it in fact is, more prone to distance itself from *the original idea*.

c. In Latin America

i. Some common features

If there is something worth anticipating to our purpose in relation to labour law legislation in Latin American countries, it is that the whole of such legislation seems to be comfortably framed within the stylized '*basic idea*' of labour law we proposed in the first lines.

---

[34] It is from that logic that that author seems to be stating that if a contract law system encapsulated the capability approach (rather than the standard approach to the conceptualization of economic exchange) it 'would look very much like the kinds of contract law regime that are observed in European (and other) systems today – that is to say, regimes in which the classical principles of freedom of contract and *pacta sunt servanda* are supplemented by mandatory and default regulations of various kinds, mostly originated in legislation' (S Deakin, '*Capacitas*: Contract law, Capabilities and the Legal Foundations of the Market' in S Deakin and A Supiot (eds), *Capacitas* (Hart Publishing, 2009) 1).

[35] In that sense, Coase's theorem according to R Cooter and T Ulen, *Derecho y Economía* (Fondo de Cultura Economica, 1998); in the same sense, with special reference to Chilean law, J-L Ugarte, *El análisis economic del derecho; el derecho laboral y sus enemigos* (Fondo de Cultura Universiaria, 2001).

To that purpose, it is worth mentioning that labour laws in Latin America share common membership with the continental legal system; then, from that perspective, their *particular idea* of labour law stands out as clearly different from those answering to other legal heritages (for example, that of common law).

Due to this condition, legal orders of Latin American countries express rights grounded on the law as the first legal experience,[36] the idea of public social order, active state intervention, prevalence of imperative rule and a source system which is a mixture, in different dosages in every nation, of laws and collective conventions that, as a whole, constitute a complex system of techniques for the restriction of the autonomy of will.

Certainly, belonging to the continental system does not necessarily mean that those countries constitute expressions of the so-called 'European social model'. Due to various (historical, cultural, political) factors in the experience of the countries of the region, I hold the hypotheses that these rights express, in a different degree, a *weak* sense of belonging to the European social model. This circumstance, I dare say, has made them more sensitive to the neoclassical compulsions that were most energetically implanted in the 1990s, and therefore to their abrupt and disproportionate impact, the ensuing introduction of biased and inconsistent reforms, the ineptitude to start out a more rigorous process to react to the challenges aforementioned and even the tendency to subsequent restorations, anachronistic or deviated in some cases, produced in some countries as from the first years of the new millennium.

One other feature among the most singled out by literature is the *authenticity crisis*[37] or, in other words, the *gap ranging between the law and reality*[38] and the ensuing lack of effectiveness of these orders, in different degrees, of course, at two associated, but certainly distinguishable levels:

- the generalized presence of informal work, a certain tendency to establish rules that exceed the regional contexts or practices, and that, therefore, are not applied or at least, not always, or not fully applied;

- a certain tendency to establish rules that exceed the regional contexts or practices and that, therefore, are not applied or at least, not always, or not fully applied.

ii. Labour reforms in Latin America; the counter-reformation

These legal orders did not come out unscathed from the reform processes displayed in many of them in the 1990s.

To start with, a certain process of *institutional convergence* may be noticed in those legal orders, that, regarding individual work relations, has gone along the so-called *labour flexibility* path in several of its expressions, and regarding employment

---

[36] L Diez Picaso, *Experiencias jurídicas y teoria del derecho* (Ariel, 1973).

[37] M Deveali, *El derecho del trabajo en su aplicación y sus tendencias* (selected texts, annotated by JI Brito Peret, AO Goldin, and R Izquierdo) (Astrea, 1983).

[38] O Ermida Uriarte, 'Las relaciones de trabajo en América latina' (1990) Revista Andaluza de Trabajo y Bienestar Social; Temas Laborales, No 18.

collective relations has had labour union freedom conventions and the principles arising from them as their own – and rather different – *convergence point.* These convergence paths were driven in each of those areas by simultaneous political and ideological factors of quite different nature: in the first case, neoclassical thought, within the framework of exchange liberalization and the ensuing homogeneity in the contesting discourse of legal orders; democracy recovery and a more extended conception of a system of liberties, in the second.

But at the onset of the new millennium it had already become clear that those labour reforms, within the framework of their correlative economic ones, had not had a virtuous effect on the socio-labour situation nor on the labour markets in the region: high levels of unemployment, growing degrees of informality, precarious and insecure employment, work protection inapplicability, a fall in real salaries and social protection, a significant increase of poverty and inequality. Within that framework we can find a virtual suspension of the reform process of neoclassical inspiration and, in some, a tendency of reflux (counter-reformation?) of varied intensity.

It must be said, notwithstanding, that reform carried out in last decades – particularly the 1990s – *could not shake the structural grounds of social rights in Latin America,*[39] not even during the period when the deepest transformations were established. At any rate, the reforms were more related with the *protection intensity* than *with substantial transformations which might have given way to say, as was the case with European labour law, that their traditional versions were already part of the archaeology of social law.* As a result of the non-substantial characteristic of those reforms and, in some cases, of the posterior restoration of the preceding institutions, it is evident that the particular idea of those rights, although weakened, has not been dramatically changed and, a fortiori, that neither has it moved away from the basic idea.

iii. Further challenges and transformations
At any event, Latin American labour laws must face further challenges and transformations beyond the amendment trends of the 1990s, predominantly neoclassical.

The effects of market internationalization also affect labour laws in Latin American countries, although not in exactly the same way they operate in developed countries, and probably with more excruciating intensity. The latter may face

---

[39] E Córdova, 'The Challenge of Flexibility in Latin America' (1996) 17–2 Com Lab L & Policy J 314 points out that not even the Chilean military dictatorship, which reduced rights, deactivated state control – it went from control of law compliance to control of labour union and conflict – tried to decentralize labour union structure and collective bargaining and curtailed striking, succeeded in shaking the bases and foundations – the very idea – of labour law. In the same line, G Bensusan, 'La ditancia entre normas y hechos: instituciones laborales en América Latina' (2006) Revista de Trabajo (Buenos Aires) (año 2, núm 2 (nueva época) states that these reforms – those affecting Argentina, Brazil, Chile, and Mexico – 'did not manage to dramatically affect pre-existing rules'. From another perspective, but confirming the same idea, E Lora and C Pagés Serra, *La legislación laboral en el proceso de reformas estructurales de América Latina y el Caribe* (Banco Interamericano de Desarrollo (BID), 1996) bear a grudge against the lack of strength of labour reforms, this time in relation to those produced in other areas of public policies.

international competition, particularly concerning direct investment and facing investment offshoring trends, through the most varied tools of what are generally regarded as systemic competitiveness factors. The lack of those areas in developing nations, on the other hand, led them to make up for them with the preservation of low labour costs, often associated with the decline in protection standards. Thus, it is more complex to defend those standards in these countries[40] and their employment rights, affected by that pressure and the one of outsourcing that tend to disorganize them (F Valdes dal Re (2001), 'Descentralización productiva y desorganización del Derecho del Trabajo', Relaciones Laborales (Madrid) No 20 Año XVII Octubre 2001, 1); all of which requires the most creative reactions to 'reorganize' them, at the risk that, bereft of their immunological defence, these legal orders may come across insurmountable obstacles to guarantee their sustenance. It is from this perspective that the aforesaid immobility of the *particular ideas* in Latin American labour law – anachronistic restorations in some cases – may not be news to rejoice in, as it was neither the case, at that moment, of the boom of insubstantially deregulatory practices inspired by international credit organisms.

From another perspective, along the same line of the correlative process triggered in the European Union countries although in a certainly less trenchant fashion, there is also in Latin American countries an incipient tendency to extol the fundamental rights of a person at work, the specific ones recognized in the eight fundamental agreements of the ILO, and those others that belong to every person, when considered in the work environment.

Finally, it is worth mentioning that Latin American labour laws will have to redefine the issue concerning the determination of the existence of employer–employee relationships and consequently the complexity involved in the task of identifying individuals included within the protection range afforded by labour law. In any case, it must be borne in mind that while in industrialized economies factors prevail that are consequences of technological and organizational innovation (though other less sophisticated ones, such as informality and fraud, are also present to a lesser extent), in developing countries the subjective weakening process finds its most deeply rooted expressions in informality and other analogously primitive factors. Notwithstanding, in the latter, though to a lesser degree, other more modern and newer factors can also be recognized, especially in the more advanced technological areas.

iv. Provisional appraisal

Subsequent to such procedures, Latin American labour laws have not been subject to any further significant changes and, thus, they do not seem to have departed

---

[40] Thus, globalization pressure is not even and will produce negative effects, especially in developing countries, increasing segmentation (K Banks, 'The Impact of Globalization on Labour Standards. A Second Look at the Evidence' in JDR Craig and SM Lynk (eds), *Globalization and the Future of Labour Law* (Cambridge University Press, 2006) 77, 107); such a phenomenon tends to take place more through outsourcing than through direct investment; and these countries can certainly take part of a 'race to the bottom' (or, even worse, of a 'stay at the bottom'). Here there is a tendency to labour-intensive activity, low-skill producers, wide offer of unqualified workers with no market power whatsoever; easily movable production processes and, therefore, greater susceptibility to delocalization.

from the *basic idea* of labour law. However, we are not certain that this, as reflected in such jurisdictions, constitutes good news; that absent evolution may move local labour laws away from the most recent facts, contexts, and processes – new technologies, new organization of work and production, and the fluctuations of the global economy. Local labour laws may be unfit to solve not only the old deficiencies but the new challenges as well.

This thought suggests a new hypothesis: *the possibility of keeping the 'basic idea of labour law', seen as a value, depends on whether the 'particular ideas' of every legal order (or of every group) show a capacity for pliant adaptation. 'Freezing' traditional order, comfortable as it may seem to our labour legal scholars' eyes, may constitute a sign of necrosis allowing for mass questioning of the* basic idea.[41]

3. The *particular ideas* in comparative treatment

a. *On requirements from economy*

All the legal orders we have considered so far have been the object of steady claims of adequacy to efficiency and economic rationality considerations. But while in the common law area countries those claims have adjusted – with greater or lesser rigour – to the conception of *law and economics* and have not had to face a consistent legislative network, in the continental area countries, and also in those of Latin America, they have taken up the form of claims of labour flexibility that, in addition, have had to operate on legal extended and consistent regimes.

In consequence, the Anglo-Saxon legal scholars' constructions have not had to overcome insurmountable restrictions to the practice of contractual freedom, which may have paved the way for the choice some of them make to move away from that *basic and original idea* of labour law that rests upon the dominant technique of curtailing the individual autonomy.

As stated, in the remaining areas (continental Europe and Latin America) the same claims were projected in the shape of claims for flexibility of rules, which were not questioned as such, but for the rigidity of their texts. The highly numerous reforms that affected them would later derive in legal orders bearing lesser protection intensity, but not having given up their role of curtailing individual contracts, nor, therefore, their commitment to the *basic idea* outlined in the first section. Let us then say, once more, that labour flexibility mechanisms, also organized in a mighty legislative arsenal, are today but property and score of rules that are still imperative and that still impose restrictions (although of a lesser degree) to the practice of contractual freedom.

Labour law may be, as Hyde states, a 'failing paradigm'[42] or else a paradigm facing difficulty due to a change in the context requiring, in turn, a change and

---

[41] If we project such hypothesis by opposition, we may ask ourselves whether the fact that some legal scholars depart from the basic idea of labour law does not actually evidence the ineptitude of their own legal systems to adapt to changes (idea suggested by Guy Davidov in personal email correspondance, 26 May 2010).

[42] A Hyde, 'What is Labour Law?' in G Davidov and B Langille (eds), *Boundaries and Frontiers of Labour Law: Goals and Means in the Regulation of Work* (Hart Publishing, 2006).

adjustment of its tools. We could daringly say that American literature shows a certain shared perception of an exhausting paradigm, destiny that some seem to accept, while others gaze at it in dismay and determination of resistance.[43] In the continental area that perception has a noticeably smaller space. In Latin America, with rare exceptions, there have been fluxes and refluxes around labour law in relation to the degree of intensity of the protection institutions, without its *basic idea* having been seriously questioned in labour thought.

b. In relation to the system of sources

It goes without saying that at the very heart of that different impact of economic logic lies the radical difference in the source system. Even though in the continental area relations between sources are modified – in general, in favour of collective autonomy and to the detriment of the source of legal nature – and although non-binding rules are included into the system (soft law), it can still be said that the law is somewhat less vigorous, *sed lex...* and that soft law does not have the same dimension in the context of a legal order framed within the force of law and the constitutions regulating the labour action as in others where the former and the latter do not play a relevant role in that matter.

It is to be concluded, then, that from the system of sources point of view, the original idea of labour law is modified if the system gives up on the equating function of the compelling rules (autonomous and heteronomous) but not if, instead, what changes is internormativity modes, provided that work conditions and social level protection are not settled, as they used to, in relation to the free play of contractual freedom. From this perspective, the structure of the system of sources – more or less voluntarist – fosters the choice of different paths when the common challenges put the very continuity of legal orders to the question. Within the framework of the law and with constitutional support, legal systems adhering to continental views tend to evolve within the *basic and original idea of labour law*, whereas those legal orders of Anglo-Saxon extraction seem to have fewer restrictions to move away from that idea.

c. On the concept of dependency or labour subordination

The paths also divert as regards the inclusive aptitude of the traditional idea of *labour subordination*. In the continental experience, that 'challenge' tends to be overcome without recourse to dismantling the traditional concept – the narrative of the worker's determining contractual inferiority situation is not conceptually postponed – but rather by broadening the concept or by adding other categories susceptible to protection, whereas in Anglo-Saxon countries constructions suggesting the plain

---

[43] K Van Wezel Stone, 'A New Labor Law for a New World of Work: The Case for a Comparative-Transnational Approach' (2007) 28–3 Comp Lab L & Policy J 565; and H Arthurs, 'Who Is Afraid of Globalization?: Reflections on the Future of Labour Law', in Craig and Lynk, above n 40.

dismantling of the idea of subordination, or even, in their place, the construction of other ideas of wider inclusive range are in full bloom.

Thus, the less intense the legal source regulatory tissue, the less the caution confronting the opening up, or even the dissolution, of categories determining the object of a certain legal regime and, correlatively, the thicker that tissue is, the less is the propensity to accept such an opening up of those categories.

In that particular respect, we must add, as a conclusion, that not all evolution in the definition of the subjects of individual work relations implies a separation from the *basic and original idea* of labour law. Certainly not the one including categories of lessened dependency, insofar as it does not deprive the dominant category of compensatory limitation from the unevenness of the bargaining powers. What does imply separation from that idea, instead, are the recognition techniques not including that unevenness as the condition of legal order application.

d. *Theoretical constructions of capabilities or capacities*

The theoretical construction of capabilities appears as an intervention mechanism more required by some legal orders – those of the common law (legal system) – not provided for, by the law, with other institutional mechanisms to achieve their goals, especially in a context where the collective action tools seem to have been impoverished in a way the law is unable to make up for in these areas.

It is clear that this perspective may be invoked to accompany the performance of the legal rule, to stand in for it when it is missing and even to transcend it, or rather, simply to take its place and substitute for it. While the first options do not seem to necessarily lead to the desertion of the *basic idea* of labour law, basis of this reflection, the second clearly entails the separation from that idea.

e. *New spaces for social security*

Social security law seems to have also been assigned with new roles, when subordinated work, dominant before, loses that condition; when, at least, it loses its vocation to endure in time in relations marked by the condition of permanence. The relation turns, in consequence, unstable, it includes new profiles – for example, the various levels of 'quasi-dependency' – and enters in succession with instances of autonomous work, unemployment, training periods, etc. There, constructions tend to ensure earnings continuity, whose adherence to the field of social security seem highly pertinent. The aim of providing protection in transitions and interstices in no way implies separating from the basic idea of labour law; on the contrary, it contributes to enhance it, by supplementing a role that social security has been playing since the very beginning of the development of labour law.

Finally, it must be said that a labour law that keeps its basic scheme (with a function that cannot be delegated in whatever is related to the subject who is, more or less categorically, the employer), transfers or includes social security protection tools or tools from certain labour market active policies, may well be modifying its own 'particular idea', but not necessarily its *historical idea* (it is, of course, a matter of degree, since a massive transfer of its institutions would certainly mean a substantial change in that idea).

C. Conclusion

In their statutory dimension, historical European labour laws have undergone deep changes in their *particular ideas*; however, neither the resulting legal orders nor the legal scholars' constructions have drifted away from the *basic idea* of labour law. The idea of public order and, its derivation, the curtailment of individual autonomy and the principle of non-renounceability still have a predominant role. Labour flexibility tendencies are none other than property of the protection system and it should not be ruled out that, paradoxically, they may carry the virtue of contributing to the upkeep of the historical model. To summarize: more regulatory changes (logical ones, because of the prevailing role the law has been and still is bearing); less tendency to separate from the *basic idea*.

Labour laws in Latin America, of undeniable continental extraction, equally tend to operate within the framework of the historical idea of labour law; their *weak* affiliation to the European social model may probably contribute to explain the disproportionate impact – of biased and inconsistent reforms, anachronistic or deviated restorations – some of these legal orders have undergone in the last years.

In common law countries, whose legal orders are less structured around the law, and, as a result, tend to require fewer legal changes, legal scholars are noted to be more inclined to revise the '*basic idea*' of labour law. They show deeper sensitivity to economic reconceptualization, a certain disposition for the substitution of protection techniques, for the opening of the categories defining the centre of imputation of labour law, for the disposal of the concept of dependency (as referential mould or directly as category) and for the design of other, more inclusive categories. It is only natural for a legal order that does not take the law as its primary legal experience to have less qualms in moving away from that *historical idea*.

All of which allows us to maintain the initial hypothesis, now stated as follows: *the way of being of some 'particular ideas' of labour law may facilitate separation from the 'basic and original idea' of that branch of the law, which other 'particular ideas' are less prone to go through.* In any case, and as proposed at the outset of this chapter, we must admit that this is just a preliminary hypothesis; and that therefore, its scientific assessment requires further and deeper research.

UNIVERSITY OF WINCHESTER
LIBRARY

6

The Idea of the Idea of Labour Law: A Parable

*Alan Hyde**

The elders tell us of a golden age when labour law dwelled in mighty mansions in every nation's capital. Each mansion naturally reflected the styles and building materials of its country. But had you gone down to the basement in those years, you would have seen that they all rested on very similar foundations, with the same pillars sunk deep into the ground.

There were jobs, or sometimes crafts, in which working people lived most of their adult lives. They invested their youth and became strongly identified with their job or craft, and thus with the community of others who shared it. There were large enterprises, with profits that had to be distributed. The leading enterprises usually sold cars, steel, rubber, airplanes, ships, coal, electricity, and telephone services, in domestic markets, sheltered by barriers of space and often by tariffs or other trade restrictions, often as oligopolists. They faced little or no price competition, and could generally afford to pay for benefits for workers by raising prices without having to reduce the share of profits either going to managers or retained as corporate earnings. There were, of course, labour organizations of many types: unions, labour parties, works councils, guilds. Those labour organizations sometimes went out on strike, and this collective action became the prototype by which labour law imagined human solidarity, community, democracy, and political action and the relationship between thought and action.

And, in addition to this socio-economic system, there was labour law in the narrow sense, the output of specialized government officials. There were nearly always foundational statutes, sometimes part of the national constitution, amended periodically by the national legislature. There were specialized administrative officials, possibly labour courts or boards. While these statutes, orders, and decisions varied considerably, they all employed variations on a very limited set of techniques. They sometimes specified minimum or mandatory terms in individual contracts of employment. They specified how works councils or collective bargaining relations would be established and what kind of issues they might properly be

* Rutgers University School of Law, Newark NJ, USA.

concerned with. They provided formal and informal services for resolving disputes. They could order employers to pay fines or reinstate workers. However, the system was usually oriented more toward establishing, as normal, the industrial self-government by employers with works councils or labour unions. There was not much concern about sanctions for non-compliers.

Now it might seem that, on such a foundation – jobs, organizations, collective action, laws, and decisions – the labour law of that era had everything that it needed. Certainly it must seem that way to those of us living today. Curiously, however, there was always one thing more. In those days, they not only had labour law. They had the Idea of Labour Law.

Actually they had many Ideas of Labour Law. We cannot understand today exactly how these Ideas related to the daily activities of managers, employee representatives, and government officials. The Ideas seemed to tell the people in the system something about what was their ultimate goal. But there were always several Ideas, at best compatible, sometimes not.

So people in the system had their pick of stories to help them through their work every day. Some thought they were (1) building a more equal society in which there might be fewer very rich or poor people, and whatever income differences existed would not matter much. And they probably were building such an equal society, though the mechanisms were often indirect. For example, the worker organizations that derived privileges from labour law would then be strong participants in (2) social democratic coalitions that would enact progressive taxation and public benefits. Others thought they were (3) building socialism directly. We know now that they were not, that socialism was never built that way, but this was less clear to them. Others thought they were (4) reducing conflict. It is very hard to say with hindsight whether or not they were. Still others thought the Idea of Labour Law was more about (5) fairness and justice than about equality. Louis Brandeis in the USA, and Hugo Sinzheimer in Germany, thought labour law was about building (6) democracy – political democracy would be fragile unless there was also economic democracy at work.[1] Later it was said that labour law was about (7) representing worker interests in enterprise managerial structures. In every mansion, people with these different Ideas sometimes fought about them, but usually they were able to do their jobs and their different Ideas of Labour Law didn't seem to matter very much.

I've never been able to work out exactly where in the mansion people made the Idea of Labour Law. I don't think it was down in the basement with the foundation. (Although the people of that time argued about that, too. Some thought that

---

[1] On Sinzheimer, see Dukes, this volume. Brandeis famously testified before the US Commission on Industrial Relations (23 January 1915), in language still powerful despite its gendered usage: 'Unrest, to my mind, never can be removed – and fortunately never can be removed – by mere improvement of the physical and material condition of the workingman. If it were possible we should run great risk of improving their material condition and reducing their manhood. We must bear in mind all the time that, however much we may desire material improvement and we must desire it for the comfort of the individual, that the United States is a democracy, and that we must have, above all things, men. It is the development of manhood to which any industrial and social system should be directed.' Quoted in CW Summers et al, (2007) Legal Rights and Interests in the Workplace 44.

law was never part of the foundation – they sometimes called it 'superstructure' – and others thought that it was. It is hard to say now why they argued about this.) I've always imagined that the Idea of Labour Law was made by scholars in a tower, across the garden from the main mansion. Sometimes they came down from their tower, walked across the garden, and walked into the mansion. Sometimes they examined the labour law that lived in the mansion, and sometimes they even went down to the basement to check the foundation. But, most of the time, they lived in the tower.

Scholars sometimes noticed that there were things in other people's basements that weren't in theirs.[2] But I think the mid-1950s was the first time anyone noticed that something that actually had been in his own basement had gone missing. The first pillar to disappear was formal output of rules from government officials. Clyde Summers noticed that in his country, nobody was actually making any new labour law. The national legislature couldn't, and the administrative agency wouldn't.[3] We can now see what a clever observation this was. Congress made a few amendments to labour law in 1959,[4] shortly after Summers' article, but that turned out to be the last time that it enacted any labour law of any significance. But the point I want to make is that, whenever anything in the basement went missing, it just made the Idea of Labour Law more important. The Idea of Labour Law helps us see what is missing from the basement. Sometimes it helps us think of a replacement. Summers' country was missing labour law. That situation has only become worse, as we shall see. But it still had the Idea of Labour Law.

The next pillar of the foundation to begin to erode was the labour union. This time a lot of people began to notice in the 1960s that union membership wasn't growing much and was even shrinking in some places.[5] Strikes, too, began to decline everywhere, and with them so declined labour law's prototype of community and action. In the 1970s in the country I know best, there seemed to be a growing number of employers who openly stated that they would never bargain with labour unions, such as the textile company JP Stevens and Litton Industries.[6] Cooperative employers were still found in the basement, but in smaller proportion.

But while the foundation definitely needed repair, this was normal and not a crisis. Because, after all, we still had the Idea of Labour Law. We knew what was needed: some stronger sanctions against really recalcitrant employers; shortening the protracted election campaigns that had become a device for frustrating representation.[7]

---

[2] Eg O Kahn-Freund, *Labour Relations and the Law: A Comparative Study* (Stevens, 1965), or the work of Hugo Sinzheimer, discussed in Dukes, this volume.

[3] CW Summers, 'Politics, Policy Making, and the NLRB' (1954) 6 Syr L Rev 93.

[4] Labor-Management Reporting and Disclosure (Landrum-Griffin) Act of 1959, 73 Stat 519 (1959). One Title amended scattered sections of the National Labor Relations (Wagner) Act, codified at 29 USC ss 151–169; the rest of the 1959 Act is codified at 29 USC ss 401–531.

[5] Eg P Jacobs, *The State of the Unions* (Atheneum, 1963).

[6] Hearings before the Subcommittee on Labour Management Relations of the Committee on Education & Labour, US House of Representatives, 95th Cong, 1st Session, 9 August 1977 (on JP Stevens); and C Craypo, 'Collective Bargaining in the Conglomerate, Multinational Firm: Litton's Shutdown of Royal Typewriter' (1975) 29 Indust & Lab Rel Rev 3–25.

[7] C Becker, 'Democracy in the Workplace: Union Representation Elections and Federal Labour Law' (1993) 77 Minn L Rev 495.

Legislation to accomplish these reforms was introduced in Congress in 1977, a year of heavy Democratic Party majorities in both houses following the Watergate scandals and the election of President Jimmy Carter, but despite support from the executive and Congressional leaders, it was not enacted. So another pillar of the foundation, labour legislation, was also going missing.

The next year the scholar whom I know best entered teaching labour law. By this time, the role of the labour law scholar was clear. Obviously he or she could not say that labour law was dying. Who would hire or tenure such a scholar? And fate no longer permitted scholars in his country to develop labour law. New labour law was clearly out of the question by 1978. Congress wouldn't pass it. Labour boards wouldn't make it (and didn't read scholarship anyway). And the union movement was already too weak to bring about any legal change. Instead of developing labour law, the scholar could, however, indeed must, develop the Idea of Labour Law.

What a contrast was the Idea of Labour Law! For if labour law was ossified, the Idea of Labour Law was fresh, verdant, expanding! We have seen already that there were many Ideas of Labour Law. So many narratives of its supposed purpose: equality, socialism, conflict reduction, justice and fairness, community, democracy, supporting modern welfare states. Why not add to this list, the young scholar thought.

So each failure of labour law became a triumph of the Idea of Labour Law.

In fact, the problem of the Idea of Labour Law was precisely the problem of the disappearance of the foundations of labour law and, eventually, of labour law itself. All the blossoming Ideas of Labour Law were, at bottom, just ways of coping with the disappearance of the pillars: oligopolistic employers, unions, jobs, strikes, or new law.

The failure of the very mild 1977 reform legislation led this scholar to a new Idea of Labour Law. Labour law, he argued, was (8) the vehicle for symbolic concessions by elites to insurgent worker movements.[8] This explained why Western European countries like France, Italy, Sweden, the Netherlands, and West Germany had enacted new fundamental labour statutes in the decade before 1977. He put forward a broader Idea of Labour Law in the same article: (9) labour law was the source of signs and symbols through which working people understood their place in the political and social order.

Similarly, the accelerating decline in labour union density was definitely weakening labour law. But it was an opportunity for the Idea of Labour Law. New forms of worker organization would arise. Employees would be represented by racial, ethnic, or gender caucuses, or nonmajority unions, or worker centers, or immigrant rights groups. And just like that, we had less labour law, but more Idea of Labour Law. Labour law, in this Idea, did not have to be about labour unions. It could be about (10) facilitating new movements and organizations.[9]

---

[8] A Hyde, 'A Theory of Labour Legislation' (1990) 38 Buff L Rev 383.
[9] A Hyde, 'Employee Caucus: A Key Institution in the Emerging System of Employment Law' (1993) 69 Chi-Kent L Rev 149; 'Who Speaks for the Working Poor?: A Preliminary Look at the Emerging Tetralogy of Representation of Low-Wage Service Workers' (2004) 13 Cornell JL & Pub

The next time the scholar came down from the tower and went into the basement, the erosion was even more severe. Reduced trade barriers and increased global trade had become known as globalization. Fewer employers sold in sheltered domestic markets without price competition. Manufacturers of cars, steel, rubber, aircraft, ships, and telephone services now faced intense competition. They were not oligopolists and could not simply grant benefits, then raise prices; their wages were increasingly set in global competitive markets.[10] More of them were behaving like the recalcitrant employers who had already demonstrated in the 1970s that there were no effective sanctions against the employer who simply refused to recognize unions. A devastating blow to labour law, to be sure. But what a stimulus to the Idea of Labour Law! Scholars could imagine the Idea of Labour Law to be (11) global. This revived some old Ideas of Labour Law, such as (12) taking wages out of competition and (13) preventing races to the bottom.[11]

Globalizing the Idea of Labour Law led to new Ideas, too. The Idea of Labour Law was now (14) a good kind of economic development, such as (15) implementing Amartya Sen's ideas about human development.[12] Another new Idea of Labour Law was (16) to solve collective action problems among governments. On this view the Idea of Labour Law was implicit pacts among governments to achieve cooperative solutions to games where that cooperative solution would abort if any player defected.[13]

Each trip to the basement revealed the foundation crumbling at an alarmingly accelerated rate. Legislation was long gone. Administrative labour law was gone. Unions were mostly gone. Strikes were a memory. Employers who behaved like oligopolists were gone. And nation states were yielding to transnational structures.

On the next trip to the basement, the jobs, too, were gone. Not entirely. But they were definitely eroding. Decreasing percentages of the workforce would be attached for life to a job at a place that was the source of community and organization. Many more were unattached to the labour market at all.[14] Others changed jobs so rapidly that they barely had a relationship with any particular employer. Others, in rapidly increasing numbers, worked at one employer but were legally the employees of a temporary help agency or labour contractor. Not only did

---

Pol'y 599–614; 'New Institutions for Worker Representation in the United States: Theoretical Issues' (2006) 50 New York Law School L Rev 385–415; and *Working in Silicon Valley* ch 9 (ME Sharpe, Inc, 2003).

[10] M Bertrand, 'From the Invisible Handshake to the Invisible Hand?: How Import Competition Changes the Employment Relationship' (2004) 22(4) J Lab Econ 723 (correlation between import competition, and extent to which wages reflect market conditions, rather than arithmetic progression from starting wage).

[11] C Summers, 'The Battle in Seattle: Free Trade, Labor Rights, and Societal Values' (2001) 22 U Pa J Int'l Econ L 61; and K Van Wezel Stone, 'To the Yukon and Beyond: Local Laborers in a Global Labor Market' (1999) 3 J Small & Emerging Bus L 93.

[12] Langille, this volume. Labour law in its golden age was about collective, not individual, development, and reorienting it toward individual development is not easy.

[13] A Hyde, 'A Game-Theory Account and Defence of Transnational Labour Standards – Preliminary Look at the Problem' in JDR Craig and SM Lynk (eds), *Globalization and the Future of Labour Law* (CUP, 2006) 143–66.

[14] KE Klare, Toward New Strategies for Low-Wage Workers' (1995) 4 Boston U Pub Interest LJ 245.

they not know where their loyalties lay, they often didn't know for whom they worked.[15] Almost none of these individuals described in this paragraph had union representation, and many were on the margins of labour law.[16]

But, in the familiar pattern, while these trends were devastating for labour law, they were yet another opportunity for the Idea of Labour Law. Scholars just had to fashion a new Idea of Labour Law that was not linked to jobs as we knew them. This was not difficult. We already had so many Ideas of Labour Law. Another Idea or more could easily be created. One new Idea of Labour Law suggested (17) that it existed to serve these deracinated workers, though the details were very vague indeed.[17] Another said that the Idea of Labour Law was (18) to help these workers form new organizations, based in geographical communities and political action.[18] Or it was said that the Idea of Labour Law really had nothing to do with jobs. Its association with jobs was just a historical coincidence. The Idea of Labour Law, it was said this time, was (19) just a collection of regulatory techniques for intervening into any market, such as housing markets, where collective action problems produced suboptimal bargains.[19]

So many Ideas of Labour Law! Labour Law without legislation, or administration, or unions, or cooperative employers, or strikes, or jobs, or even labour markets! Ideas of Labour Law: aspirational, ethical, philosophical, evolutionary, political, game-theoretic, abstract. But, without its foundation, what else could the Idea of Labour Law be? Obviously it could only live at some very high distance from the ground. It had to be very abstract, idealized, simplified, like a game or economic model. And light, so light. Lighter than air, lighter than the sun.

Who could bring such an Idea into the basement? The basement was collapsing. Hardly anyone went there any more. The basement had become dangerous. Too dangerous for something as precious as the Idea of Labour Law.

The course in labour law had nothing to do with the radiant Ideas of Labour Law coming out of the tower. The course in labour law is a series of well-established scripts that can be mastered by unimaginative employer counsel to preserve employer privilege and avoid sharing any power. One day the students learn the script for scaring the workers, so they will vote against the union at a representation election, with complete legal impunity. Another day they learn how to go to the

---

[15] In the 1995 supplement to the Current Population Survey, 57 per cent of employees of temporary help agencies 'inaccurately' gave as their employer the client to which they had been referred. SN Houseman and AE Polivka, 'The Implications of Flexible Staffing Arrangements for Job Stability' in D Neumark (ed), *On the Job: Is Long Term Employment a Thing of the Past?* (Russell Sage Foundation, 2000) 427–62. The scare quotes around 'inaccurately' reflect a regulation of the US Department of Labor, rarely enforced in practice, that 'joint employment will ordinarily be found to exist when a temporary placement agency supplies employees to a second employer' 29 CFR s 825.106 (b)(1); the words 'ordinarily' and 'found' reflect the Swiftian irony associated with the US Department of Labor in its decadent period.

[16] G Davidov and B Langille (eds), *Boundaries and Frontiers of Labour Law: Goals and Means in the Regulation of Work* (Hart Publishing, 2006).

[17] A Hyde, *Working in Silicon Valley: Economic and Legal Analysis of a High-Velocity Labour Market* (ME Sharpe, 2003).

[18] K Van Wezel Stone, *From Widgets to Digits: Law and the Changing Workplace* (CUP, 2004).

[19] Hyde, 'What is Labour Law?' in Davidov and Langille (eds), above n 16, 37–61.

bargaining table, concede nothing, never sign an agreement, and never face legal liability. There is a similar script for every day of the course in labour law.

But up in the tower, the Idea of Labour Law grew increasingly baroque, mannered. Nothing tethered it any more. Nobody was really going to use the Idea of Labour Law to guide his or her own practice. Perhaps nobody ever did. The Idea of Labour Law became increasingly recondite, unrelated to the practice of legal officials, employers, or unions. Unrelated to earth, really. One Idea of Labour Law said that labour law was just about (20) reducing the transaction costs when employers and employee organizations bargained about redistributing surplus.[20] Another said that labour law (21) implemented the ethical philosophy of Kant.[21] Still other people said that the Idea of Labour Law was to implement (22) New Governance. Nobody ever figured out what was New Governance. It seems to have been some kind of mystery cult of legal scholars who, through some kind of law school yoga, had freed themselves from all moral and political commitments. Other people, who still had moral and political commitments, were too 'rigid' to join the 'flexible' yogis of New Governance.

In 2010 the scholar I know best was invited to a conference far from home on the Idea of Labour Law. Much as he wanted to see his friends again, he felt very weary. Have I not given them a new Idea of Labour Law every year or two? Have I not explained that the Idea of Labour Law is really to grant symbolic concessions to workers, and overcome collective action problems of workers, and coordinate governments in developing countries, and other ideas too? Well, let me see what new Idea of Labour Law I can produce. So he walked down from the tower, walked across the garden, and climbed into the basement to examine the foundation of labour law in his country.

> And this time, there was nothing.
> Really, really nothing.

There was literally no lawful National Labour Relations Board. I don't mean there was no effective board, none that did anything other than routine administration. Of course there wasn't. There had not been an effective Labour Board for as long as this scholar had lived. I mean there was literally no National Labour Relations Board. For 26 months from 2007 to 2010, there were only two members of what the statute required to be a five-member Board. The Supreme Court of the United States held that these two members could not issue legal decisions, so all of their purported decisions for over two years are of no effect.[22] Yet it is not easy to find any ill effects from his country's two years without a labour board.

Why were there only two members? During 2008 the Democratic Senate would not have confirmed any nominees of a Republican President in the last year of his term. In 2009, there was a Democratic President and Democratic Congress. The President sent three names to the Senate for ratification, the kind of package one expects from a Democratic administration (two union lawyers and one management lawyer). But the Senate had not ratified them.

---

[20] KG Dau-Schmidt, 'A Bargaining Analysis of American Labour Law' (1992) 91 Mich L Rev 419.
[21] H Spector, 'Philosophical Foundations of Labour Law' (2006) 33 Fla St L Rev 1119.
[22] *New Process Steel, LP v NLRB*, 130 S Ct 2635 (2010).

One of the President's nominees is a former professor of labour law, one of whose articles, already cited here, is the standard reference for understanding the law of union elections.[23] He is a lawyer for the Service Employees International Union (SEIU), usually described as its country's most dynamic and interesting union,[24] though often criticized from the left for coziness with employers and an autocratic internal structure.[25] The scholar thought that Becker was the best nominee to the National Labour Relations Board in its history. Few labour professionals would put him anywhere but among the top two or three. Two Democratic senators joined all the Republicans in refusing to permit a vote on his nomination. The President at first refused to appoint him during Congressional recess, a technique widely used in the past. So the stalemate continued. Finally the President made three recess appointments, restoring the Board to full strength, though it remains unlikely that Member Becker will ever be confirmed by the Senate, in which case his appointment will lapse at the end of 2010. Perhaps up in the tower the SEIU seemed too cozy with employers, but down on the ground it was not cozy enough.

There has been no labour legislation since 1959. Many had thought, however, that with large Democratic majorities in each house of Congress and a Democratic President, that there might be some. The proposed legislation was hardly a fundamental rethinking. It would have adopted two moderate reforms already part of labour law in some Canadian provinces and in some public sector labour law in the USA: requiring employers to recognize unions who sign up a majority of the workforce,[26] and mandatory arbitration of the first contract after union recognition, if the parties fail to agree.[27] The legislation is going nowhere.

The unions blame the President for this, as if it were his job to organize the public for the unions, instead of the other way around. There is not a single representative of the US labour movement who can make an effective television appearance or public speech. The union movement is so depleted of talent that its representatives could not even explain in friendly environments what the failed legislation would have done or why it was needed.[28]

---

[23] Becker, above n 7. See also C Becker, 'Better Than a Strike: Protecting New Forms of Collective Work Stoppages Under the National Labor Relations Act', (1994) 61 U Chi L Rev 351.

[24] See, eg, SH Lopez, *Reorganizing the Rust Belt: An Inside Study of the American Labour Movement* (University of California Press, 2004), discussing the SEIU's innovative organizing of nursing homes.

[25] S Early, *Purple Haze: Andy Stern, Anna Burger, and the Civil Wars in American Labor* (forthcoming); S Early, 'The Progressive Quandary About SEIU', 14 December 2009 <http://www.zcommunications.org/the-progressive-quandary-about-seiu-by-steve-early>.

[26] C Riddell, 'Union Certification Success under Voting versus Card-Check Procedures: Evidence from British Columbia 1978–1998' (2004) 57 Indus & Lab Rel Rev 493; and S Slinn, 'An Empirical Analysis of the Effect of the Change from Card-Check to Mandatory Vote Certification' (2004) 11 Canad Lab & Empl LJ 259.

[27] S Slinn and RW Hurd, 'Fairness and Opportunity for Choice: The Employee Free Choice Act and the Canadian Model' (2009) 15 Just Labour 104.

[28] I listened in horror in spring 2009 as a union representative, in the very friendly environment of a daily talk show on New York City's public radio affiliate, could not explain what the legislation would do, under gentle and supportive questioning from the show's very intelligent host, Brian Lehrer.

Labour unions have not entirely disappeared from the basement. But they continue to decline, and their character has changed. Only 6.9 per cent of the private sector workforce is represented by a labour union.[29] The union movement is increasingly dominated by unions representing public sector employees. These unions function largely as political lobbies for these employees, competing with public programs for public funds. In 2009, there were precisely five major strikes in the US, that is, strikes involving more than a thousand workers, the lowest figure ever recorded.[30]

The failure of labour legislation is nothing new, but the significance this time is the crushing of hope. The Congress elected in 2008 has the largest Democratic majorities in a lifetime, but has accomplished little, certainly no labour law reform. It has made clear that there will never be new labour legislation. We had two-fifths of a National Labour Relations Board. Perhaps we will also have two-fifths of a labour statute.

Peter Brook once described the structure of Shakespeare's great King Lear. Lear loses his kingdom, his power, his retinue. It appears that he has lost everything. But he still has his reason. Then he loses that, and it appears that he now really has lost everything. But he retains one thing: his hope of reconciliation with Cordelia. Then he loses that, and dies. Just so. If one has hope, one has not lost everything. Losing the hope of labour law reform is no small matter.

Well, thought our scholar, this is depressing. But, really, it is nothing new. And labour law, after all, is not what we are about. We are about the Idea of Labour Law, and the Idea of Labour Law can outlive the complete disappearance of jobs, unions, strikes, cooperative employers, legislation, and, now, specialized government officials. Are they, the scholar asked himself, paying you for nothing? What is happening with all those other institutions that you have already suggested might carry on labour law in different ways? Has there been a rebirth of alternative worker organizations, or global labour rights, or new organizations for workers with low attachment to the labour force or to particular employers? Not exactly. They poke along, sort of like labour law.

Well, this is a challenge, thought the scholar. How can I invent a new Idea of Labour Law when all the elements of the old foundation are definitively gone, never to return. For invent I must. If there are no constantly new Ideas of Labour Law, my professional life has no meaning or purpose.

No, he realized. I cannot keep doing this. I cannot keep inventing stories that explain how the Idea of Labour Law, like a Platonic form, can survive the disappearance of every one of its earthly manifestations. Labour law will continue as a technical branch of regulation, like securities or banking regulation. People will consult its rules before doing, or not doing things. But nobody will think to look to

---

[29] US Department of Labor, Union Members – 2010, USDL 11-0063 (21 January 2011), available at <http://stats.bls.gov/news.release/pdf/union2.pdf>.
[30] US Department of Labor, Major Work Stoppages in 2010 (8 February 2011), available at <http://www.bls.gov/news.release/wkstp.nr0.htm>.

labour law for inspirational values, any more than they expect to find these in securities or banking regulation.

We will have to be inspired by something else. Something must inspire us, even more utopian than was The Idea of Labour Law even in its golden age. We can take inspiration from freedom and equality and democracy and human development for their own sakes. But not, any more, from The Idea of Labour Law. This time, as a source of inspiration, it is really over.

PART II

NORMATIVE FOUNDATIONS OF THE IDEA OF LABOUR LAW

7

Labour Law's Theory of Justice

*Brian Langille**

A. Labour law's identity crisis

Many papers written about labour law these days, including many chapters in this volume, share much in common. This is because many labour lawyers agree with Harry Arthurs that labour lawyers and labour law face an identity crisis.[1] Whether or not we agree with Alan Hyde that 'this time ... it is really over'[2] many of us do agree that the idea of labour law is under a lot of stress. The crisis confronting labour law has three dimensions: (1) empirical (has the real world changed so much as to leave traditional labour law beside the point, inoperable, fading from view?); (2) conceptual (are our basic concepts of 'employee', 'employer', employment contracts, and so on, still viable and capable of organizing our thinking in a useful way?); and (3) normative (are the moral ideas which motivate our enterprise still salient, robust, and capable of rallying us to the continued defence of our subject?). We do not all agree, it seems, that we need to be in a state of real crisis. But, as I see it, we agree that that is the state we are in.

As a result labour lawyers face the questions of whether we should, can, and will re-think our discipline. To these questions we find a range of responses. While there is widespread agreement that there have been large changes in the empirical world of work there is no agreement on what this portends for the discipline of labour law and we can identify a number of positions: (1) there is no resulting normative crisis, and thus no need for a normative re-evaluation. Rather, we simply face the problem of developing new techniques (means) for applying old values (ends) to new empirical realities; (2) the problems are, again, not essentially normative but, rather, ones requiring conceptual innovation to ensure that labour law is not held hostage to old categories, old ways of thinking, and old ways of doing business, which may stand now as barriers to the achieving of labour law's normative goals; (3) the real problem is that we actually do need normative renovation and renewal. But among those taking this position there is no consensus

---

* Faculty of Law, University of Toronto.

[1] Arthurs, this volume.

[2] Hyde, this volume, 97.

about how that might be undertaken or achieved; (4) this sort of normative renewal is not so much required as thrust upon us and comes with a hefty price – at the expense of disciplinary coherence; (5) such 'ideal' or 'overarching' normative accounts of labour law are not possible; (6) we have had in fact many such accounts, but now the normative jig is up.

Cutting across this set of positions are other differences in intellectual approach and level of focus in addressing labour law's crisis: international, regional, or domestic law? Developed or developing state focus? Public or private institutional frameworks? Doctrinal/institutional or more abstract analysis? Pragmatic policy reform or purely theoretical conclusions? Comparative approach? Historical? Locating labour law within larger and longer time scale empirical, economic, political, and social narratives? Within differing and larger theoretical paradigms? And so on.

Where does that leave us and our discipline? It seems that it leaves us with an admixture of points of view about the nature of our problems, what to do about them, and whether we can, should and will do anything. This is not a terrible state to be in. A state of real disagreement is much better than a state of mere mutual incomprehension.

I have been of the view for some time that labour law requires a re-orientation at the basic empirical, conceptual, but most importantly, the normative level. Also that such a re-orientation is possible. I do not see our problems as 'merely' those of means (technique) or 'simply' conceptual reconfiguration or enlargement. I believe that labour law needs to expand its justificatory horizons and as a result liberate itself from its traditional empirical domain and conceptual categories. The normative question 'What is labour law for?' is basic. It will be answered one way or another, and labour law will have, one way or another, a constituting normative narrative. This narrative will inform and reveal the concepts which are central to labour law and describe the limits of labour law's empirical domain. The question is, simply, which narrative will it be?

But, is it possible to do more than simply put one's cards on the table at this stage? Is there something more which we can glean from what we know about our current state of disciplinary affairs, and our individual and varied reactions to it?

It seems to me that we can say something more. This something more will not dissolve all of our problems, nor will it result in a consensus about 'what is to be done'. But it may permit us to see something of a structural feature in what appears to be merely an unexplained and unhelpful scattering of viewpoints.

B. Labour law has always had, and will always have, a theory of justice

The basic idea is this: labour law faces, as always, two sets of questions: (1) What is labour law's domain/scope? With what part of the world as we know it is it concerned? How does it carve itself off from the rest of the legal world? How do we know what issues are labour law issues, what materials to read, what subject matters go on the syllabus? (2) Within that domain, what is labour law to do?

What is it for? Why does it exist? These are separate questions – of scope and content. But the issues I wish to confront, and which the chapters in this volume reveal are of concern to many, can be stated as follows: is there a relationship between the two issues of scope and content and, if so, what is it?

It seems to me that there is a profound, necessary and intimate link between these two sets of questions. Even stronger – they are the same questions in the sense that the answer to both turns on the answers to the same deep set of issues. These issues are, and must be, ones of deep normative exploration. On this view we simply cannot avoid normative inquiry. Labour law's jurisdiction is defined, as is its content, by labour law's morality. Labour needs, does have, and will have a 'theory of justice'.

Here one needs to confront the challenge which seems to be presented by Bob Hepple[3] who, at the beginning of his chapter, questions the usefulness, and urges us to resist the 'temptation' of, 'an ideal theory of labour rights'.[4] He writes:

The temptation for labour law scholars is to focus their energies on developing an ideal theory of labour rights or social justice. But any theory is sterile unless we first try to understand why real employers, workers, politicians and judges act as they do in practice. Labour law is not an exercise in applied ethics. It is the outcome of struggles between different social actors and ideologies, of power relationships. Labour laws are used by people to pursue their own goals, and sometimes they need rights such as to a minimum wage or to freedom of association simply in order to survive.[5]

What are we to make of that? At one level this looks like a perfectly reasonable call for labour lawyers to return to their concrete and pressing agenda and not be tempted to waste their time gassing around in the abstract with normative theory. And although I disagree, in the sense that a division of labour here between those inclined to such theory and those to practice is possible, fair enough. But there is a second claim here about theory itself. It is that any theory 'will be sterile' unless we understand 'why real employers, workers, politicians and judges act as they do in practice'. And in this latter regard we need to keep our eye on the truth that labour law is the 'outcome of struggles between different social actors and ideologies, of power relationships'. That claim appears to be true. And the claim that 'labour laws are used by people to pursue their own goals, and sometimes they need rights such as to a minimum wage or to freedom of association simply in order to survive' sounds more than merely a fair assessment. But the claim that 'any theory will be sterile' unless we remind ourselves of these truths seems to express a preference for a certain type of theorizing – of a sociological, empirical, causal kind which looks for explanations of how things came to be as they are. It does not allow much space for normative theorizing about how things should be. This is not the claim that there is no normative agenda implied here – rather, it is a claim about the role of normative theory. Indeed this is made plain by the blunter assertion that 'labour law is not an exercise in applied ethics'. That is a claim worth pushing on a bit.

---

[3] Hepple, this volume.
[4] Ibid 1.
[5] Ibid.

This is so because this claim simply seems to me to be wrong. Labour law has to be an exercise in ethics, applied and otherwise. Otherwise we have no way of knowing who the labour lawyers, as opposed to other sorts of lawyers, are, and what their concrete and pressing agenda would consist in. Without an account of our normative purposes we have no way of seeing our reality as divisible into and constituted by subject matters such as labour law. This is a point which is conceded in the paragraph quoted above – which depends implicitly upon, and appeals to, what must be an account of what labour law is, what rights are labour rights, and so on. This point Hepple also concedes, a little more explicitly, when he[6] returns to Sinzheimer to whom 'we owe the conception of labour law as a unified and independent legal discipline'.[7] At the core of Sinzheimer's contribution in this regard lies the 'unity of the goal' which is stated as 'the guardian of the human being in an age of almost unrestrained materialism'.[8] This is a very important point, to which I return below. The point here can be stated as follows: it is true that 'labour law is not an exercise in applied ethics' if we take this to mean that normative theorizing does not and cannot explain how labour law turns out at the level of legal and institutional detail in various places at various times. To do that we need more – as Hepple explains. Here it is true that there is 'no grand single theory'.[9] But the claim is false when we turn not to how things turned out in various historical circumstances, but what the thing called labour law, that turned out in those various ways, actually is. Here it is precisely and necessarily true that 'labour law is an exercise in applied ethics'. Without such an ethical account there is no conceptual coherence, nor even an identifiable empirical reality to agree with, dispute, or study – that is, no 'labour law'.

C. Labour law's traditional theory of justice

We have known instinctually, and since the beginning, that the question of the *content* of labour law is profoundly normative. We know the answer to the normative questions 'What is labour law for?' 'What is its mission?' Manfred Weiss has articulated this accepted and basic informing normative instinct of labour law, rightly drawing together the whole of what is variously called employment and labour law, writing as follows:

The history of labour law has been told very often. In the 19th century it became evident that the competition between individual employees at the labour market was a race to the bottom and that only collectivization of employees combined with protective legislation could prevent this destiny. Therefore, the interplay between collective self-regulation and

---

[6] Along with most others who think about this issue – see, eg, Dukes, this volume.
[7] Hepple, above n 3, 3.
[8] Ibid.
[9] Ibid 2. Also B Langille, 'Imagining Post Geneva Consensus Labour Law for Post Washington Consensus Development' (2010) 31 Comparative Labor Law and Policy Journal 523.

legislative intervention from the very beginning characterized labour law. The main goal always has been to compensate the inequality of the bargaining power.[10]

Weiss's citation is to Kahn-Freund. In Paul Davies and Mark Freedland's *Kahn-Freund's Labour and the Law* the point is forcefully expressed as follows:

The relationship between an employer and an isolated employee is typically a relationship between a bearer of power and one who is not a bearer of power ... The main object of labour law has always been, and we venture to say always will be, to be a countervailing force to counteract the inequality of bargaining power which is inherent and must be inherent in the employment relationship.[11]

I believe this idea to be basic to the received wisdom about our labour law. This idea of labour law coming to the aid of employees who do 'and must'[12] lack bargaining power is the moral foundation of the constituting narrative of labour law.[13] We do not have too many theories – we have one. (And in my view, the problem is that it is out of date.)

As Weiss rightly points out, there are other basic normative 'insights' which have long been associated with labour law's self-understanding. He identifies others including 'labour is not a commodity' and 'human dignity'.[14] The slogan 'labour is not a commodity' is basic to the articulation of the ILO's normative vision in particular and labour law's in general.[15] But like 'inequality of bargaining power' it stands in need of explication. They both make for good slogans, but need to be elaborated upon.[16] And we do have an accepted way of elaborating upon them and in concert. We see them both hitting a particular nerve and, this is a critical point, in a particular way. We have glued these two notions to one another.

It is vitally important to see the particular nerve which 'inequality of bargaining power' and 'labour is not a commodity' hit and how they are thus linked in our thinking. The nerve we see them both impinging upon is the nerve of market ordering. From a pro-market perspective the claim that 'labour is not a commodity' is simply empirically false.[17] And the deployment of the idea of 'inequality of bargaining power' is taken as an indicator of economic illiteracy.[18] But, as I have tried to explain elsewhere,[19] claims about 'inequality of bargaining power' or that

---

[10] Weiss, this volume, 1–2.
[11] 3rd edn (Stevens, 1983) 18. Cited by the Supreme Court of Canada in *Slaight Communications v Davidson* (1989) 59 DLR (4th) 416, per Dickson CJC at 424.
[12] Ibid.
[13] See B Langille, 'Labour Law's Back Pages' in G Davidov and B Langille (eds), *The Boundaries and Frontiers of Labour Law* (Hart Publishing, 2006) 13.
[14] Above n 10, 2.
[15] D Beatty, 'Labour is not a Commodity' in J Swan and BJ Reiter (eds), *Studies in Canadian Contract Law* (Butterworths, 1980) 313–55; and B Langille, 'Labour Law is not a Commodity' (1998) 19 The Industrial Law Journal (South Africa) 1002.
[16] The question of whether and in what way the addition of references to 'human dignity' aid in this elaboration is one which is of much current interest – this is why.
[17] 'Whatever its emotional appeal the assertion is misleading. Labor service is bought and sold daily.' A Alchain and W Allen, *University Economics*, 3rd edn (Wadsworth, 1972) 407 ff.
[18] Ibid.
[19] B Langille, 'Fair Trade is Free Trade's Destiny' in J Bhagwati and R Hudec (eds), *Fair Trade and Harmonization* (vol 2) (MIT, 1996) 231, 244–5.

'labour is not a commodity' are not empirically false because they are not empirical claims at all. They are normative claims. Talk of 'inequality of bargaining power' *is* a form of economic nonsense *if* intended to be a claim *within* market theory. But it is not intended as a claim within market theory, but is a remark external to, and about, market theory, which makes an important point about the limitations of market theory given its scant normative resources. (The assertion 'property is theft' works in the same way.)

These two claims have been joined in our minds. We see them as necessarily linked and in a compelling way. Their explications are in parallel and sound in the same critique.

Thus, seemingly instinctually, we have understood our rallying cries as urging a contrast between labour (not a commodity) and all things that are commodities (physical goods, raw materials, finished products) not in general, but when it comes to contracting about them. The urge has been to establish a set of constraints upon the market in labour just because labour is not a commodity. The logic here is: the set of rules we establish to regulate and structure contracting in markets for various commodities is taken as a given, as the default position, as the baseline. But we see that this set of 'normal' contract rules needs to be limited/regulated/constrained in various ways when the subject matter of the transaction is labour. When human bodies encounter the wheels of commerce some precautions are in order. This set of ideas and way of thinking is at least partially so easy to grasp because it fits with a number of familiar views about 'rights' in general and not just labour rights. This is sometimes expressed in the idea that rights are a sort of 'side constraint'[20] upon the actions of others and also in the idea of rights as 'trumps' whose very identifying marker is that they rule even in the teeth of the consequentialist conclusion that we would all be better off if they did not.[21] This is how the idea that 'labour is not a commodity' is bound up with, and limited to, the other of labour law's basic normative planks – the idea of 'inequality of bargaining power'. Labour markets, and our concerns for their impact upon human beings, would be another matter if we were all Premier League football players. But we are not. Our ideas of exploitation, subordination, dependence, and so on are fundamental to our understandings here. The normative engine of our rallying cry is fuelled by the reality of the labour market position of most workers. And the logic of labour law so fuelled is, again, the idea of a set of constraints on otherwise available market power. Both the logic of collective bargaining as a procedural device structuring a countervailing power in the process of bargaining, and the logic of employment legislation as simply removing certain issues from the bargaining process, are driven by this logic. This is why Weiss is right to see direct statutory intervention in the substance of the employment bargain as well as the procedure of collective bargaining as parts of a larger whole.[22] Taken as a whole they construct a body of 'consumer protection' for the vulnerable in the labour market. This body of law stands and speaks fairness, or

---

[20] R Nozick, *Anarchy State and Utopia* (Basic Books, 1974).
[21] R Dworkin, *Taking Rights Seriously* (Duckworth, 1978).
[22] Above n 10.

'decency',[23] to the superior bargaining power of capital. There is a compromise, a deal, a trade-off here which we need to make in the name of decency, in the name of our ideal that 'labour is not a commodity'.

These normative foundations of the content of labour law are intuitively and it seems attractively available. The problem is that this normative picture 'holds us captive'.[24] But the result is not simply that we are wedded to and driven to see the content of labour law in these terms – but that we are also driven to answer questions about the scope of labour law in a certain way. The two issues of scope and content are, as we have seen, bound together and when we lock onto this particular account of labour law's normativity we get a particular account not only of its content but its scope, that is, its 'jurisdiction' or 'domain'. It is a package deal. If this is our moral concern then these actors and events (people negotiating contracts regarding work) are, in the nature of things, the centre of our attention. And our central categories and concepts (employee, employer, contracts of employment, and so on) are thus thrust upon us.

The picture painted by this specific morality tale provides its own frame.

D. Anxiety

If this is so then there will be a real struggle for the soul of labour law if we either (1) attempt to expand beyond the traditional domain of regulating contract power in the negotiation of contracts for labour, whether individual or collective, or (2) suggest a new normative foundation for the enterprise. This cuts both ways. Efforts to find a broader normative basis for labour law will put stress upon our traditional understanding of the domain of labour law. So too, explicit efforts to expand the domain of labour law will put stress upon our basic normative account of why we do what we do.

It is this anxiety-inducing struggle which now describes the current state of play in our thinking about labour law. This is precisely the 'anxiety' which Mark Freedland has so acutely commented upon:

The anxiety . . . is one which has attended, in some degree, much of the recent debate about the personal scope of employment law. It is a fear that, as one extends the frontiers of labour law to include contracts or relationships formerly regarded as outside the territory, because they are more in the nature of business contracts or relationships with independent contractors, so one risks foregoing the normative claim for labour law to constitute an autonomous legal domain within which inequality of bargaining power between worker and employer may be taken for granted, and where protection of the worker against unfair exploitation is therefore a paramount and systemic rationale for law-making and for adjudication. This fear has, however, generally been a rather muted one, if only because the discussion has mainly concentrated upon modest or intermediate extensions of the personal scope of employment law, which can be envisaged as reaching out to working

---

[23] To use a word currently in vogue at the ILO and elsewhere.
[24] L Wittgenstein, *Philosophical Investigations* (Blackwell, 1958) para 115.

people who, although deemed independent, are, in reality, at least semi-dependent upon employing enterprises, and as vulnerable to exploitation as workers in the 'employee' category.

This muted anxiety becomes the more strident as we further extend the personal scope of employment law... It becomes hard to see how the normative edge of labour law can fail to be blunted... Two alternative particular dangers present themselves, Scylla and Charybdis or a rock and a hard place, between which it is hard to discern a path which can be steered. Either the worker-protective envelope of labour law will fail to 'stick' at the entrepreneurial margins... or, on the other hand, the inclusionary category will prevail but at the cost of a normatively crippling compromise with the economic and social neutrality of general private contract and commercial law.[25]

As usual in labour law matters, Freedland has hit the nail on the head and there are important questions which flow from his observations. But before the questions, note the structure of Freedland's remarks – their way of revealing our instinctive and shared pattern of thinking about labour law. Labour law has a 'paramount and systemic rationale' in the very idea of the 'protection of the worker against unfair exploitation'. Correct. If we think of, or are driven to by changes in the real work of work, expanding the scope of labour law beyond its traditional (employer/employee/contract negotiation, and so on) setting we encounter a dilemma – either the paramount rationale will lose its grip ('will not stick') or will be 'compromise[d]' by the norms of 'general private contract and commercial law'. When the rationale of constraining market power in the name of the inequality of its distribution is exhausted we are left with the only other logic in town – the idea of simply unconstrained market power. These are, on our received view, two sides of the same normative coin. Freedland's is a very important intervention. It sounds in our basic, classic, understanding of labour law. On this view our particular normative account scope and content are tied up in just this particular way. A particular morality gives a particular content, a particular jurisdictional boundary, a particular dilemma, and a particular anxiety for labour law.

And this particular dilemma is only available to us (if I can put it that way), only makes sense, only seems compelling, only induces the 'anxiety' Freedland describes, because of the way we have been brought up to think about labour law. Freedland is again correct because he knows what labour lawyers know. This is that, as described above, the essence of the normativity of labour law is that, in the name of its 'paramount and systemic rationale' of 'protection if the worker against unfair exploitation', constraints are placed upon the default position which is 'general contract and commercial law'. This is the normative box or, as Freedland has it, our rock and our hard place. It is labour law's normative 'Scylla and Charybdis'.[26]

---

[25] M Freedland, 'From the Contract of Employment to the Personal Work Nexus' (2006) 35 Ind LJ 1, 28–9.

[26] In the struggle structured by this dilemma we can identify a number of positions:

1. We can expand the domain without a normative recalibration. (Rejection of the dilemma.) (Manfred Weiss.)
2. You cannot expand the domain without giving up on the traditional normative goals for the traditional domain. (Noah Zatz.)

Labour law's normative account of itself also limits its world. When we venture beyond this world we have lost our bearings. Worse, we dilute and put at risk the power of our normative wellspring. Better to keep everything in its place and stay at home in labour law's familiar terrain. But for many that terrain is looking like a coastline under threat from climate change. Labour law may be going the way of the Maldives. This is an anxious time. We cannot stay at home but we cannot be at home anywhere else.

E. Therapy

Now let us turn to the questions posed by Freedland's account. The most important of these questions can be asked as follows: is it possible that a therapy exists for this normative 'anxiety' thrust upon us by changes in our familiar world (of long-term contracts of employment between employers and vulnerable workers which need to be regulated to avoid exploitation)? As we draw back our camera from its close-up on our familiar protagonists (employee–employer) performing their familiar drama (negotiating and living with contracts of employment) in order to take account of other and perhaps new actors playing different roles on our stage of the world of work, is it true that we are stuck between a normative rock and a normative hard place? Is it possible to draw back our normative lens as well and in a way which will permit us to see the illusion of a dilemma rather than its inevitability? Is it possible that labour law can find a new normative home? Or is Alan Hyde right in claiming that the theoretical pantry is now empty?[27]

The answer to that question depends, first, upon whether we can first *see* how this anxiety is visited upon us by our traditional approach. This requires being explicit about the picture which has 'held us captive'.[28] That picture is the one which we outlined above and which Freedland condenses into the obvious truths which we have just reviewed. But, if we see it, how is that picture not inevitable? How could we break free from it? That is the question. Here is one way of answering it.

The view of the world which drives us to the anxiety Freedland describes can be captured in the large with the following observation. We have reduced the power of

3. Any effort to expand beyond labour law's traditional domain also threatens, or weakens the traditional normative account with which it coheres. This causes anxiety. (Mark Freedland.)
4. Any effort to broaden the normative account of the content of labour law undermines, or threatens, the existing normative account and therefore should not be undertaken. (Guy Davidov.)
5. Agreement on the need for a new normative account – but disagreement about what it might be. (Judy Fudge, Adelle Blackette.)

[27] The most obvious answer must be 'no'. One way of getting at this is to observe that Hyde could have been writing 50 years ago as a professor of master and servant law, lamenting its passing and the termination of its normative line of credit. Ideas do come and go. So, too, the world changes. But there will always be productive activity and some set of rules governing it.

[28] Wittgenstein, above n 24.

the idea that 'labour is not a commodity' by tying it to, and seeing it intimately connected with, our other rallying cry of 'inequality of bargaining power'. The critical issue now is whether our understanding of our rallying cries, especially 'labour is not a commodity' can, should, and will, continue to be so understood. Can we liberate them from this point of view? That, in my view, is the question. And it is the question which many are struggling with. We have had a particular understanding of 'labour is not a commodity'. We need a new one.

At bottom, the idea is that 'inequality of bargaining power' has incarcerated our thinking about labour law and has held us hostage to a thin normative ideal. The rock and the hard place made inevitable by that thin ideal are part of a package deal we can and should decline. More positively, we can restart or normative engines by revisiting the idea that 'labour is not a commodity'.

Labour law's current understanding of the claim that 'labour is not a commodity' is too narrow. It places this claim in harness with the claim that labour law seeks to protect human beings who suffer from lack of bargaining power in the negotiation of terms and conditions of employment. As a result the project of labour law is to place constraints, both substantive and procedural, upon this process. This is our standard empirical, conceptual, and normative set-up.

It is true that collective bargaining is, by at least some, understood to give workers power so that they may negotiate better terms of their contract. In this sense, the current understanding of labour law approaches and touches a deeper idea. This is the idea of employees as agents or participants, and not merely recipients of the law's largesse. But this idea is both generated by, and limited to, the idea of a need for countervailing bargaining power against employers in the market for labour. It is true that the idea of 'inequality of bargaining power' leads to the idea of equalizing bargaining power with the result that workers become co-authors of contracts rather than recipients of them as written. This does introduce an important idea, but it is an idea for which the standard account has no defence or account, other than that just outlined. There is no normativity here other than the idea of equality in bargaining. But to the obvious question – 'why are we interested in that?' we have no response. In fact, once we get beyond inequality, labour law has exhausted its normative resources, has lost contact with 'its paramount and systemic rationale',[29] and as a result we encounter the 'anxiety' described by Freedland. If we run out of the fuel of inequality in bargaining power we have nothing left to say and thus have established real limits not only to our moral reasoning underpinning the content of labour law but to labour law itself.

We have constructed our normative world as a response to market ordering. But we have no account of the virtues or limits of market ordering – only about 'inequality' of the distribution of bargaining power within that account. Labour law is conceived of as a resistance movement inside that normative system. As a result we have no deeper account of why, if the resistance movement were successful, more equal labour markets, and their outcomes, are a good thing.

---

[29] Freedland, above n 25.

What this suggests is that labour law needs a more substantive normative ideal than the resources made available by the idea of equality operating in the bargaining context can provide. This morality cannot be merely an adjunct to market ordering's normativity, one insisting upon equality in the working of that normative ideal. It must be something more. 'Dignity' will not provide the required moral ammunition if it is understood as merely providing a set of reasons as to why humans must be protected when they meet the wheels of commerce. It will have to go deeper than that. It too will have to tell us something more about 'labour is not a commodity' than simply underwriting the sentiment behind our intuitive desire for more equality of bargaining power or outcomes in the labour market. It, or any other normative ideal, must tell us more – it must cut loose from a shallow and insecure mooring in inequality of power in the negotiation of contracts and tell us something positive about why that is a matter of concern. Only such a set of normative resources will reduce our 'anxiety' and enable us to enter the new world we see, structure the new concepts we need to engage it, and tell us why it is important to do so. It is true that labour law's jurisdiction and content are bound together by labour law's morality. Adjusting one alone is not possible. But that means that rethinking labour law is not a piecemeal empirical or conceptual enterprise. Labour law does not simply exist and exist waiting to be found, it must be normatively imagined.

F. A new normativity

In my view there is a broader, deeper morality which can be understood as underwriting in a more powerful and morally salient manner what we have known as labour law, but also allow/force us to see that labour law's remit/jurisdiction/scope/domain is much broader. A key to this new normativity lies is the distinction between workers as objects and workers as subjects. While some traditional defences of collective bargaining rights glimpse this distinction, they do so through the limiting lens of 'inequality of bargaining power'. 'Labour is not a commodity' does not limit itself, and should not be limited, to providing a rationale for limiting the market power of others – it gives us a broader and more positive reminder and rationale for labour law.

Here is a sketch of how we can make progress in this regard. As I have argued elsewhere, the best way to get at such a new normativity is through the work of Sen.[30] Sen's work is very rich and radical in its approach, starting with very basic

---

[30] B Langille, 'Seeking Post-Seattle Clarity – And Inspiration' in J Conaghan, M Fischl, and K Klare (eds), *Labour Law in An Era of Globalization* (Oxford University Press, 2002) 137–57; B Langille, 'Labour Policy in Canada – New Platform, New Paradigm' (2002) 28 Canadian Public Policy 133–42; B Langille, 'Re-Reading the 1919 ILO Constitution in Light of Recent Evidence on Foreign Direct Investment and Workers' Rights' (2003) 42 Columbia Journal of Transnational Law 101–13; B Langille, 'Core Labour Rights – The True Story' (2005) 16 European Journal of International Law 1–29; B Langille, 'Globalization and the Just Society: Core Labour Rights, the FTAA, and Development' in J Craig and M Lynk (eds), *Globalization and the Future of Labour Law* (Cambridge

questions about our true ends as opposed to our means for achieving them. His work has large implications for much of what labour lawyers, both domestic and international, have to worry about in these times.

If we could think clearly and from first principles then I take it that our starting point would be that the purpose of labour regulation is to improve the lives of the inhabitants of the world, insofar as work has something to do with it. And work has a lot to do with it. This is because, in Sen's formulation, our goal is real, substantive, human freedom – the real capacity to lead a life we have reason to value. Development, in Sen's terms, consists in the removal of barriers to human freedom so conceived. The reason that labour law has a lot to do with this enterprise is that there is an intimate connection and fundamental overlap of human freedom, on the one hand, and human capital, on the other. Human capital is here not thought of, as is common, solely in economic or instrumental terms (indirectly contributing to productivity and GDP growth) but also as an end in itself (directly contributing to a more fulfilling and freer life).[31] Labour law can be seen as that part of our law which structures the mobilization and deployment of human capital. Human capital is at the core of human freedom. Labour law is at its root no longer best conceived as law aimed at protecting employees against superior employer bargaining power in the negotiation of contracts of employment. That is a now an empirically limited and normatively thin account of the discipline. Rather, we can say that labour law is now best conceived of as that part of our law which structures (and thus either constrains or liberates) human capital creation and deployment. Education ('Education is the key to all the human capabilities'[32]) and, especially, early childhood development strategies, are critical to human capital creation. But so is the set of policies which govern the lives of human beings when they enter the workforce – whether as employees, independent producers, or under any other legal rubric or economic arrangement or relation of production. Human capital must not only be created, it must be utilized, effectively deployed: that is, in the best sense of the word, exploited. In the modern world of the 'knowledge-based economy' human capital will be as physical capital was to the industrial revolution. Getting human capital policy right will be critical to nations such as Canada and any other state attempting to structure a just and durable economy and society in the modern, and

University Press, 2006) 274–303; B Langille, 'Labour Law's Back Pages' in G Davidov and B Langille (eds), *The Boundaries and Frontiers of Labour Law* (Hart Publishing, 2006) 13–36; B Langille, 'The ILO Is Not a State, Its Members Are Not Firms' in G Politakis (ed), *Protecting Labour Rights as Humans Rights: Present and Future Of International Supervision* (ILO, 2007) 247–57; B Langille, 'The Future of ILO Law, and the ILO' in *The Future of International Law* (Proceedings of the American Association of International Law 101st Annual Meeting) (2007) 394–6; B Langille, 'What is International Labour Law For?' (2009) 3 Law and Ethics of Human Rights 47–82; B Langille, 'Putting International Labour Law on the (Right) Map' in A Blackett and C Levesque (eds), *Social Regionalism in a Global Economy* (Routledge, 2011) 290; and B Langille, 'Imagining Post Geneva Consensus Labour Law for Post Washington Consensus' (2010) 31 Comparative Labour Law and Policy Journal 523.

[31] On these points see A Sen, 'Human Capital and Human Capability' (1997) 25 World Development 1959; and A Sen, *Development as Freedom* (Knopf, 1999) 292–7.

[32] M Nussbaum, *Frontiers of Justice* (Belknap, 2006) 322.

'globalized', world. As a recent Canadian study put it: '... for the first time in human history, the logic of economic development and prosperity requires that we harness and develop our full human potential.'[33] Or as Alain Supiot recently re-stated what he called a 'simple idea' – 'there is no wealth other than human beings, and that an economy which ill-treats them has no future'.[34]

The law which governs these critical dimensions of our common life is labour law. That is a large category. It would include much that we now exclude. But although we have burst the bounds and the comforts of the old way of thinking, we also have the answer to, or perhaps relief from, Freedland's 'anxiety': we have not cast off and become adrift from our normative moorings for we have found deeper ones in the positive idea of human freedom.

The link between this conception of labour law and development, understood in Sen's terms as removing obstacles to human freedom, is deep and has yet to be fully explored. The agenda for labour law is not the complete agenda of human development – there will still be laws and agencies and agendas concerning health, trade, the environment, macroeconomic stability, and so on, at domestic, regional, international, and supranational levels. There will be overlap, as now, but also more powerful centres of gravity. Sen has addressed the issue of the connection between human capital and his foundational idea of human freedom which he views as 'closely related but distinct'.[35] His insight is that in recent times economic theory and public policy discussions have shifted from seeing capital accumulation in primarily physical terms and come to recognize 'human capital' as integrally involved.[36] He notes that there is no necessity to limit the idea of human capital to instrumental justifications, in practice that is how it is discussed. As a result, that idea has to be supplemented by the idea of human freedom which brings to bear intrinsic justifications. So, as Sen writes: '... if education makes a person more efficient in commodity production then this is clearly an enhancement of human capital. This can add to the value of production in the economy and also to the income of the person who has been educated. But even at the same level of income a person may benefit from education, in reading, communicating, arguing, in being able to choose in a more informed way, in being taken seriously by other, and so on.'[37] Thus the two concepts are closely related. As Sen puts it in *Development as Freedom*: 'If a person can become more productive through better education, better health, and so on, it is not unnatural to think expect that she can, through these means, also directly achieve more – and have the freedom to achieve more – in leading her life.'[38] The relationship between the two ideas is not, however, simply cumulative but integrative. This is because even though human capital is important

---

[33] R Florida and R Martin, *Ontario in the Creative Age* (Martin Prosperity Institute, 2009) 31.

[34] In an interview entitled 'Possible Europes', 57 New Left Review (May–June 2009).

[35] A Sen, 'Human Capital and Human Capability', above n 31. See also Sen, *Development as Freedom*, above n 31.

[36] In large and good company.

[37] Sen, 'Human Capital and Human Capability', above n 31.

[38] Sen, *Development as Freedom*, above n 31, 294.

for productivity and economic growth we need to know 'why economic growth is sought in the first place'.[39]

This is what must lie at the centre of a more robust account of what it means when we say 'labour is not a commodity'. We need the idea of 'human freedom to lead lives that people have reason to value and to enhance the choices they have' to do that. Or, more simply, 'human beings are not merely the means of production, but also the end of the exercise'.[40] So, to supplement our new thinking about the category of labour law we can say: its subject matter is the regulation of human capital deployment; its motivation is both the instrumental and intermediate end of productivity and the intrinsic and ultimate end of the maximizing of human freedom.[41]

The law which governs these critical dimensions of our common life is labour law.

This is an account which is much deeper and broader than the old received wisdom about the scope and purpose of labour law. Both the empirical/conceptual and the normative dimensions of labour law are radically altered on this view. If we see labour law as underwritten by the idea of human freedom we not only have a set of reasons for traditional labour law – but also for non-contractual approaches to work relations (informality, for example) and for other non-traditional labour law subjects (unpaid work, education, child care, and so on). That is, we have a way of thinking about a re-conceptualization of the field of labour law, a task which is forced upon us by changes in the organization of work, family, and other realities. It is not confined, as was the old account, to a story about employees, employers, and contracts of employment. It is about all dimensions of law which bear upon human capital deployment. We need new categories going beyond 'employee and employer'. We will need new 'platforms' going beyond contract, whether individual or collective, for the delivery of labour law. We will need new systems of representation for workers. And so on.

But even more fundamental is the change in our normative underpinning of labour law. Its morality is much more compelling and positive – not confined to preventing unfairness in negotiation of contracts. It covers all productive activity and places labour law, conceived as the law which regulates the deployment of human capital, at the centre of our policy agenda and central to achieving both our instrumental and intrinsic values.[42]

---

[39] Ibid 295.

[40] Ibid 296.

[41] Labour law has long been dogged, as has development theory, with the confusion caused by debates at cross purposes because sometimes based on means and instrumental outcomes, on the one hand, and sometimes on discussions of intrinsic ends on the other. On this account they go hand in hand with human freedom being both the end and the way there. Without the idea of human freedom development techniques will be inadequate and we will have no account of the worth of any outcomes of reform in any event.

[42] Such a view has the added bonus of letting us re-imagine international labour law – see Langille, 'What Is International Labour Law For?' above n 30.

G. New ideas, but old anxieties

But, if Freedland is right, the introduction of these ideas will be anxiety-inducing for labour lawyers, and doubly so. This is because this package of ideas accepts as true what Freedland has revealed – the necessary normative link between scope and content – and yet is prepared to face the challenge presented in confronting that truth.

There are some basic and predictable responses to this way of proceeding. Two of the most important are: first, there will be, Freedland predicts, a resistance to the new normative ideas and a defence of the old normative order. Second, there will be an attack on the adequacy of the new normative ideas. On this latter score, one of the most interesting lines of thinking can be best understood as the mapping of our old anxieties onto new ideas.[43]

1. Defending the received wisdom – 'They say that breaking up is hard to do'[44]

Defences of labour law's existing normative underpinning – that the idea is to protect workers in the negotiation of contracts against abuses caused by inequality of bargaining power and all in the name of decency, redistribution, avoidance of subjugation, etc – have a number of themes. Large among them is the idea of throwing the baby out with the bath water. That is, the new normative theory threatens the existing moral basis of labour law, with the result that the project of labour law will be undermined, and is therefore to be resisted.

This is a criticism made most forcefully by Guy Davidov. In his essay 'The (Changing?) Idea of Labour Law',[45] Davidov expresses disapproval of efforts to rethink labour law's normative underpinnings. He does not see them as an effort to revive what he himself calls our 'battered enterprise'.[46] Rather, Davidov accuses me, along with Alan Hyde, of treachery against our shared discipline of labour law. He alleges that we are involved in an 'attack' on labour law.[47] Moreover, in his view it is an insidious attack 'from within' the 'international community of labour lawyers'.[48] Even more provocatively, he accuses us of deception in our methods of attack, stating that although this attack is 'ostensibly from a supportive position'[49] it is not simply one that is 'likely to end up weakening'[50] labour law but that it is actually an 'attempt to undermine it'.[51] The basic idea is that any normative re-thinking by

---

[43] There are other responses as well – eg, the strategy of going down with the good ship labour law as we knew and loved her, abandoning all hope. See Hyde, this volume.
[44] Neil Sedaka.
[45] (2007) 146 International Labour Review 311.
[46] Ibid 319.
[47] Ibid 311.
[48] Ibid.
[49] Ibid.
[50] Ibid.
[51] Ibid 318.

labour lawyers is actually an 'inside job', in parallel with more familiar attacks upon labour law from outside by its enemies (such as conservative economists) and that all those who wish to remain true to labour law should be on guard against such insidious efforts.

There is much that could be said about this point of view but I think the most important point is as follows. The view Davidov attacks is not an attack on labour law but something quite different. It is that labour law's traditional account of itself rests on a normative foundation which is too narrow, too thin, and as a result, inadequate to labour law's destiny. Davidov insists that the argument is one which is against labour law's traditional view of workers as lacking power vis-à-vis employers and against the idea of 'redistribution' as labour law's concern. This is wrong. The real problem, in my view, is that Davidov believes that redistribution is the purpose, the 'end' of labour law. (He believes, as most labour lawyers do, that sometimes this comes at a price and sometimes not.) But redistribution is not a purpose, not a goal, not an 'end in itself'. The issue for labour law is, on the view Davidov resists, that it needs an answer to the question 'why is redistribution important?' There is no argument against redistribution. It is also not a position advocated by 'inequality of bargaining power' deniers. It is not a view which says that employers' and employees' interests always align and that 'the lion will lie down with the lamb'.[52] The idea is that the vital question is 'why is it important to care about such inequality?' And, unlike some labour lawyers, I not only believe that we have to ask that question, I believe there is a good answer to it. My only claim is that there is a set of larger and better reasons for having labour rights and labour standards. A labour law theory which contents itself with the idea that labour law's purpose is 'redistribution' is a labour law theory which does not have an adequate normative foundation at all because it stops short of an appeal to a compelling account of why these alleged purposes are important. This is what I take to be so radical about Sen's ideas. He really does take us back to a re-evaluation of our true ends – as opposed to our means for achieving them. Increasing efficiency, increasing GDP per capita, creating a labour code domestically or internationally, or 'redistribution', are not ends in themselves. We can, following Sen, see that they are means to our true ends which I find to be best expressed in Sen's notion of human freedom. The point of labour law's redistributive and other efforts is to advance the cause of 'human beings leading lives we have reason to value', to use one of Sen's formulations. It is this normative ideal which lets us know what labour law (at least smart and useful labour law) is for, and what a smart and useful labour law would look like. And why, to use Davidov's key word for expressing labour law's traditional normative self-understanding, 'redistribution' is important. Discussions of redressing imbalances of power in employment relations need real and better normative grounding. What I argue against is a view of labour law that believes it has, and needs, no good reason for thinking it is important. I think it is

---

[52] I am reminded of a remark by a senior American military officer, whose name I cannot recall: 'When the lion lies down with the lamb, I still want to be the lion.'

possible and necessary to have such a set of reasons. This is not a threat to labour law as we know it but a precondition to any decent future for the subject.

Redistributing power in the negotiation of employment contracts (procedurally and substantively), as important as that might have been and might be, is not an idea adequate to this task. Nor does an account of labour law which takes that as its purpose have the best available account of its own normative salience.

2. Mapping the old anxieties onto the new ideas

There is a second and very interesting package of related critiques which has a different focus than that of the first reaction. The focus here is not upon defending the status quo, but upon attacking the new idea. This critique is mounted in a number of specific ways, such as: 'The new normativity privileges procedural (civil and political) rights over substantive (economic and social) rights', 'freedom over capabilities', 'process over substance', 'the individual over the collective', and so on.[53] This is a critique which deserves a longer and more careful reply because some of the difficulty flows, it seems to me, simply from differing usages of words such as 'labour standards' and 'labour rights',[54] conflicting views on other issues, such as whether there are differences in the structure of political/civil as opposed to social/ economic rights, from conceptual confusions and disagreements regarding the nature of freedoms, on the one hand, and rights on the other, and regarding how best to understand 'collective rights', and so on. Here I wish to discuss what I see as an important feature of these objections taken as a set.

The idea is that there exists a real risk, and some evidence, of an inappropriate mapping onto Sen's ideas of the anxieties which were naturally visited upon us by labour law's traditional self-understanding. A simple way of capturing this point is that under the old view of what is important in the life of labour law there is a perfectly understandable and intuitive resistance on the part of labour lawyers to the idea of 'freedom'. That word worries labour lawyers because they see it as dangerous for reasons which the history of their discipline, as understood through the lens of the received and standard account of it, makes plain. On that story 'freedom' of contract, which favoured those with the bargaining power, that is, employers, was what labour law was to be a cure for – through procedural and substantive regulation of the labour bargain. Freedom is the problem on this view. Freedom is what labour law seeks to cure, not what it seeks to advance. Freedom is associated with the old common law of the contract of employment, with 'formal', that is, empty freedom, where equal liberty to bargain was sufficient without any inquiry into resource or power imbalances, with a cold, atomistic, neo-conservative or even

---

[53] See A Blackette, 'Situated Reflections on International Labour Law, Capabilities, and Decent Work: The Case of Centre Maraîcher Eugène Guinois' (2007) Revue Québécoise de Droit International 223; and J Fudge, 'The New Discourse of Labor Rights' (2007) 29 Comparative Labor Law and Policy Journal 29. See also P Alston, 'Core Labour Standards and the Transformation of the International Labour Rights Regime' (2004) 15 European Journal of International Law 457.

[54] For a discussion on this point see K Kolben, 'Labour Rights as Human Rights?' (2010) 50 Virginia Journal of International Law 250.

UNIVERSITY OF WINCHESTER
LIBRARY

libertarian view of the virtues of 'unregulated' (actually meaning regulated by a certain set of contract rules) labour market, with the very world that modern labour law seeks to escape. Labour law spent much of its early life dismantling that view of freedom. (And much of its recent life defending itself against a neo-conservative attack on its accomplishments in that regard.) It is difficult for labour lawyers to hear the word freedom without images of a 'free market' assault upon their discipline coming into their minds.

But this is, in my view, something which labour law needs desperately to straighten out. My view is that this is precisely what Sen is doing – taking us past this way of thinking. This is done in several ways. First, by clearly focusing upon something close to the hearts of labour lawyers – that is, concentrating not on formal freedom but on substantive freedom, which he expresses as the 'real capacity' to lead a life we have reason to value. As Sen famously puts it: 'Individual liberty is a quintessentially a social product.'[55] But there is more. Labour lawyers are very familiar with the distinction between real and formal freedom. This is basic to the idea of inequality of bargaining power. Sen's point goes much deeper. It is a point about real human freedom as an end in itself, and as a remarkable means to that end. On this view market ordering and economic opportunities are not understood as operating on some non-normative basis – but as sounding in the same deep set of ideas other sorts of freedoms. The labour market does not exist as an autonomous fact of life justified solely in instrumental terms, which is then resisted in the name of moral ideals of fairness and freedom. The 'labour market' and economic opportunities rest on the same normative foundation as 'labour law'. There is no residual non-normative, non-human-freedom, pro-market default position when the normativity of labour law 'runs out'. The same normative ideas underlie both our attachment to the labour market as an abstract ideal and our ideas about proper construction and 'regulation' of it.

But what we see in the writings of the critics is instead a mapping onto Sen of labour law's familiar dichotomous way of thinking which results in the argument that you have to choose which side of the great trade-off you are on – freedom or capability. This is seeing in Sen's ideas a replication of the great trade-off which labour law's traditional account of itself made inevitable, and upon which labour law made its choice and took its stand. So those relying upon Sen stand accused of privileging freedom. This is a serious, if understandable, error. But it is very disheartening for the future of labour law.

Sen articulates a view which enables us to overcome this unfortunate way of thinking. The key is that if we have a rich enough understanding of human freedom – one that allows us to see that human freedom (conceived of as the real capacity to lead lives we have reason to value) is both our true end, and a critically important dimension of the way there, then we see that capabilities are not at war with freedom and freedom is not the enemy of capabilities. Human freedom is real capability. We also see that human freedom turns out, just empirically and

---

[55] Sen, *Development as Freedom*, above n 31.

amazingly, to be the best way to itself. This is something labour law has known for a long time. It is why freedom of association is so basic. It is not only that workers who organize do better at enforcing other (substantive) rights. We must also remember that without such freedom of association of workers we would not have the panoply of either domestic legislation, or international law, to enforce in the first place. My sense is that because so many labour lawyers know in their hearts that the whole point of labour law is to rid us of, or at least constrain to some degree, the world of 'the free market' in labour they cannot quite get used to Sen's resurrection of the idea of human freedom, even though conceived very differently, and even though it is at the core of any understanding of the history of, and any viable future for, their discipline. Markets need to be understood and justified in terms of substantive freedom as well. We need a theory which explains why market activity and economic growth are desirable in the first place. This justification has to be undertaken in terms of advancing the cause of real human freedom. It makes no sense on Sen's view to ask whether political, economic, or social freedoms are conducive to, or hinder, development – they are constitutive of it. Any account, such as labour law's traditional account, which pits justice against markets (and posits a trade-off between the two) is thus missing a big point. It imagines a normative world in which the market stands outside the realm of moral justification and in opposition to our efforts to advance our normative cause. So Sen's is a much more radical view than labour law's traditions can comprehend or allow. It is expressed in the idea that 'individual freedom is a social commitment'. This, I suggest, may be the best way to get beyond our limited content and understanding of 'labour is not a commodity'.

It may actually be closer to Sinzheimer's original idea than we have been able to see. Kahn-Freund's essay about Sinzheimer's writings and ideas about labour law notes his view that the project of labour law was to get beyond mere formal equality of the employer and employee in law to the fact of dependency. But beyond this now familiar and basic labour law idea we find the following: 'Sinzheimer's whole work is dominated by the motif of freedom'. So, '. . . additional legal obligations in the employment relationship would contribute to the emancipation of the working human being'. Finally: 'His whole work is a call to the emancipation of man.'[56]

The working out of these connections at any level of credible detail remains to be done in the future. But the task of articulating a more robust conception of labour law's animating spirit, its theory of justice, and thus both a better account of both its scope and content, is not avoidable, merely difficult.

---

[56] See O Kahn-Freund, 'Hugo Sinzheimer, 1875–1945' in *Labour Law and Politics of the Weimar Republic* (Blackwell Publishing, 1981) 73 at 103–4. See Dukes, this volume.

8

Labour as a 'Fictive Commodity': Radically Reconceptualizing Labour Law

*Judy Fudge**

All revolutions are the sheerest fantasy until they happen; then they become historical inevitabilities.

David Mitchell, *Cloud Atlas* (Sceptre. 2004) 342

A. Introduction

Concerns about the future of labour law, which were raised in the mid-1990s, have more recently taken the form of laments about its ossification and dirges over its death. However, unlike the stages of death described by Elisabeth Kübler-Ross in her 1969 book, *On Death and Dying*, not all labour law scholars have progressed through denial, anger, bargaining, and depression to acceptance. While all would agree that the basic pillars that supported labour law and enabled it to flourish after the Second World War – the nation state, the vertically integrated firm, the standard employment relationship, the male breadwinner and female housewife gender contract, industrial unions, and social democracy – have either weakened or been transformed, revitalizing the discipline, instead of eulogizing it, is now at the top of scholarly agenda. The problem is that there is no consensus about the conceptual and normative foundations needed to move the project of labour law forward.

In this chapter, I want to consider the way forward for labour law, but to do so I will first reflect on its past. My goal is to historicize[1] what Anglo-common law scholars have accepted as labour law's narrative – to recontextualize and re-interpret the dominant story of labour law in light of categories and problems that percolated beneath its surface in order to offer a different account, one that treats labour as a

* Judy Fudge, Professor and Lansdowne Chair in Law, University of Victoria. I would like to thank the Social Science and Humanities Research Council for awarding me the Bora Laskin National Fellowship in Human Rights in 2009, which gave me the opportunity to think about labour law from a fresh perspective, and Guy Davidov and Brian Langille for inviting me to 'The Idea of Labour Law' Workshop (Cambridge, 7–8 April 2010) and the workshop participants for a lively exchange of ideas.

[1] Nancy Fraser, 'Mapping the Feminist Imagination: From Redistribution to Recognition to Representation' (2005) 13(3) Constellations 295–307, 295.

'fictive commodity'.[2] In historicizing the dominant narrative, I will divide it into two periods: the golden years that emerged out of the rubble of the Second World War, and labour law's decline, which coincided with, and was provoked by, the embrace of neo-classical economic labour market policies and anti-welfare state politics in the late 1970s. By distinguishing the internal story told by labour lawyers from the external perspective that focuses on labour law's broader function, my goal is to unearth its subordinate goals, lest we forget the plurality of labour law's objectives during both its rise and decline. After historicizing labour law's narrative, I will briefly review one of the major contemporary contenders to replace it, an account that sees the function of labour law as regulating the labour market. I will use this account as a jumping-off point for developing a reinvigorated conceptual and normative account of labour law. My goal is to sketch both an alternative conception of labour law based on the understanding of labour as a fictive commodity and the normative argument for such a reconceptualization.[3]

B. Labour law's past

Much of the discussion of the role or purpose of labour law is remarkably ahistorical.[4] Scholarship on master and servant law demonstrates how late, well into the 20th century, contract displaced status, paternalism, and direct coercion as the dominant legal paradigm for regulating labour.[5] The use of coercive master and servant law as part of the creation of a labour market substantiates Karl Polanyi's claim that 'regulation and markets . . . grew up together. The self-regulating market was unknown; indeed the emergence of the idea of self-regulation was a complete reversal of the trend of development.'[6] This iterative and dynamic development between regulation and labour markets presents what Jamie Peck identifies as an analytic problem: . . . in concrete research it is difficult to distinguish the *object* of regulation (a labor market problem of some kind or other here termed a regulatory dilemma) from the *means* of regulation (particular institutional responses).'[7] This analytic problem plagues the contemporary debate about the role of labour law; a specific form of regulation at a particular moment in time has come to be seen as *the* form, rather than *a* form, of labour law.

---

[2] According to Karl Polanyi, commodities are produced for sale on the market. Thus labour, land, and money are 'fictive commodities' because they are not produced for sale on the market. K Polanyi, *The Great Transformation: Origins of Our Time* (Victor Gollancz, 1944) ch 6.

[3] The purpose of this chapter is conceptual and normative, and, as such, does not prescribe specific policies. However, in the penultimate section and conclusion I gesture towards some policies that would be compatible with the reconceptualization of labour law that I propose.

[4] As Michael Quinlan noted, 'often debates about the role or purpose of labour law are conducted within a narrow time frame'. M Quinlan, 'Contextual Factors Shaping the Purpose of Labour Law: A Comparative Historical Perspective' in C Arup et al (eds), *Labour Law and Labour Market Regulation* (Federation Press, 2006) 22.

[5] D Hay and P Craven (eds), *Masters, Servants, and Magistrates in Britain and the Empire, 1562–1955* (University of North Carolina Press, 2004); and S Deakin and F Wilkinson, *The Law of the Labour Market: Industrialization, Employment, and Legal Evolution* (Oxford University Press, 2005).

[6] Polanyi, above n 2, 74.

[7] J Peck, *Workplace: The Social Regulation of Labour Markets* (The Guilford Press, 1996) 26.

The prevailing (and dominant) understanding of labour is linked to the political economy of hegemonic countries – Western Europe, the United States, and white-settler former British colonies such as Canada – from 1930 to today. The Second World War marked the turning point for labour law; according to Bob Hepple and Bruno Veneziani, 'the post-war period saw the consolidation and final break-through of labour law as a separate legal discipline in all European countries'.[8] This was also true of the United States and Canada.[9] The previous paradigm – master and servant law – was clearly supplanted, and the contract of employment emerged after the Second World War as the primary platform for delivering the entitlements of industrial citizenship.[10] However, as Hepple and Veneziani also note, 'the labour laws of European countries were transformed almost beyond recognition in the 60 years following the end of the Second World War'.[11]

Labour law's conceptual and normative narrative can be broken into two periods – the golden years, from 1944 to the mid-1970s, when the maxim 'labour is not a commodity' was in ascendance, and from the late 1970s to today, when claims that labour was a distinctive subject of legal regulation went into decline. However, in reconstructing the narrative, it is important to identify the *dominant* and *contrapuntal* themes in order to trace both continuity and change in goals and techniques.

1. Labour law's golden years: labour is not a commodity

The maxim 'labour is not a commodity', which was adopted by the ILO at the Philadelphia Convention in 1944, symbolized the new approach to labour law, one that emphasized the complex bundle of restraints on freedom to contract.[12] Normatively, labour law was animated by the grand ideals of social democracy – social justice, equality, and human rights. Conceptually, contract was minimized and the new status of industrial citizenship, which was to be attained through autonomous collective bargaining, was given pride of place.[13] After the Second World War, labour law's primary purpose was conceived as addressing the power imbalance between employees and employers,[14] and thus it had an explicit redis-tributive goal. However, Ruth Dukes has reminded us of an earlier constitutional function of labour law, endorsed by the English Fabians Beatrice and Sydney Webb in the 1890s and the German social democrat Hugo Sinzheimer following the First World War, which was to facilitate the participation of collectivized labour in the

---

[8] B Hepple and B Veneziana, 'Introduction' in Hepple and Veneziana (eds), *The Transformation of Labour Law in Europe* (Hart Publishing, 2009) 13.

[9] B Laskin, *A Selection of Cases and Materials on Labour Law* (Toronto, 1947) Introduction.

[10] B Langille, 'Labour Policy in Canada – New Platform, New Paradigm' (2002) 28 Canadian Public Policy 133–42; Deakin and Wilkinson, above n 5; and J Fudge, 'After Industrial Citizenship: Market Citizenship or Citizenship at Work?' (2005) 60(4) Relations Industrielles 631–56.

[11] Hepple and Veneziana, above n 8, 1.

[12] G Rodgers et al, *The ILO and the Quest for Social Justice* (ILO, 2009) 7.

[13] H Arthurs, 'Developing Industrial Citizenship: A Challenge for Canada's Second Century' (1967) XLV Canadian Bar Review 786–830.

[14] O Kahn-Freund, *Labour and the Law* (2nd edn, Stevens, 1972) 6.

management of the economy.[15] Bringing the 'rule of law' to the workplace, protecting vulnerable workers, and mediating industrial conflict were all recognized within the panoply of labour law's goals. And just as the dominant narrative of labour law acknowledged a variety of objectives, it also deployed two general techniques to achieve those objectives – the provision of procedures to facilitate collective bargaining and the imposition of minimum substantive standards. Collective bargaining was generally the preferred technique for limiting the commodification of labour law and it resulted, especially in Canada and the United States, in semi-autonomous legal subsystems with their own norms, institutions, and personnel, the goal of which was to keep the common law and the ordinary courts out of labour–capital relations. In these countries, labour law came to be seen exclusively in terms of the law regulating collective labour relations, minimum employment standards were regarded as labour law's little sister, and the contract of employment was virtually ignored.

However, the narrative about labour law that emphasized the goal of redressing the inequality between employees and employers was always counterpoised by a strong, albeit background, narrative. As Hugh Collins explains, 'employment law addresses the paradox encapsulated in the slogan "labour is not a commodity". It regulates employment relations for two principal purposes: to ensure that they function successfully as market transactions, and at the same time, to protect workers against the economic logic of the commodification of labour.'[16] Labour law, even during its golden period, was concerned with *production* and *protection*. Labour law guarded managerial prerogatives and employees were legally, not only economically, subordinate to their employers. These features of labour law – its commitment to hierarchy and to the protection of the prerogatives of private property – marked the continuity between employment and master and servant law, and, along with labour law's protective dimension, served to distinguish it from commercial law.

The protective and redistributive goals of labour law were always in tension with its productive goal. In their introduction to the third edition of Otto Kahn-Freund's *Labour and the Law*, Paul Davies and Mark Freedland suggested 'there is some scope for a re-casting of the conceptual framework of labour law'.[17] From a governmental perspective a central concern throughout the post-war years was the control of inflation.[18] From the very inception of collective bargaining legislation, Canadian governments shared this concern. Canada's narrow workplace-based collective bargaining regime and family allowances were designed to dampen wages in order to control inflation.[19] From a macro-economic perspective, labour

---

[15] The Fabian Society is a British democratic socialist movement, founded in 1854, that adopted a reformist agenda to social change and improvement. R Dukes, 'Constitutionalising Employment Relations: Sinzheimer, Kahn-Freund and the Role of Labour Law' (2008) 35 JLS 341.

[16] H Collins, *Employment Law* (Oxford University Press, 2003) 5.

[17] P Davies and M Freedland, *Kahn-Freund's Labour and the Law* (3rd edn, Stevens, 1983) 3.

[18] P Davies and M Freedland, *Towards a Flexible Labour Market: Labour Legislation and Regulation Since the 1990s* (Oxford University Press, 2007) 3–5.

[19] J Fudge and E Tucker, *Labour Before the Law: The Regulation of Workers' Collective Action in Canada, 1900 to 1948* (Oxford University Press, 2001).

law is what Harry Glasbeek called a 'mechanism of adjustment'.[20] This broader perspective not only allows us to see the variety of strategies and goals of labour law,[21] it also emphasizes the continuity, as much as the rupture, between the halcyon days of labour law and its current decline.

2. Regulating for flexibility

From a labour lawyer's perspective, the most important shift in the discipline has been away from collective bargaining towards individualization, whether in the form of the contract of employment, human rights and anti-discrimination law, or employment standards. The embrace of active labour market policies, especially workfare, has marked an equally profound transformation in the goals of labour market regulation. In official accounts of labour law, redistribution and protection have given way to competition and flexibility. Forms of work outside of the standard employment relationship have proliferated and the scope of collective bargaining has contracted in most developed economies. These empirical changes have resulted in a conceptual and normative crisis in labour law, and a concomitant loss of prestige.[22]

Labour law's crisis both reflects and is part of a broader conceptual and normative shift within society and the academy. In economics, the neo-classical vision of Friedrich Von Hayek and Milton Friedman eclipsed the institutional approach of John Maynard Keynes and John Kenneth Galbraith, and social democracy was dislodged by neo-liberalism and the third way in politics. In the academy, work and class gave way to identity and social movements in sociology, and in political science and political theory recognition and identity trumped redistribution as the prevailing normative discourse. The predominant normative concern shifted away from redistribution from capital to labour to promoting horizontal equity within the workforce. At the same time, vertical inequality increased to levels not seen since before the Second World War in the dominant developed countries.[23]

C. Competing accounts of labour law

In light of the conceptual and normative crises of labour law, a number of alternatives have been offered. Many of these go beyond the contract of employment as the fulcrum of regulation and redressing inequality in bargaining power as the key justification for regulation. My aim is not to provide a definitive account of the range of different approaches; instead, I want to identify key themes in a particular strand of the conceptual and normative revitalization of labour law that

---

[20] H Glasbeek, 'Labour Relations Policy and Law as Mechanisms of Adjustment' (1987) 25 Osgoode Hall Law Journal 179.

[21] Davies and Freedland (above n 17) 6.

[22] C Estlund, 'The Death of Labor Law?' (2006) 2 Annual Review of Law and Social Science 6.1–6.19.

[23] M Lynk, 'Labour Law and the New Inequality' (2009) 59 UNBLJ 14–47.

moves beyond employment as a conceptual basis and inequality of bargaining power between employees and employers as a normative foundation.

In constructing an alternative narrative for labour law, both Hugh Collins and Alan Hyde have emphasized labour law's function of addressing market failures such as: (1) information asymmetry; (2) inelasticity in labour supply; (3) collective action problems; (4) overcoming low trust, opportunism, and sub-optimum investment in human capital; (5) high transaction costs; and (6) externalities.[24] Regulation that addresses these market failures and promotes efficiency includes laws permitting workers to form organizations and bargain as a group, the creation of consultative institutions, minimum terms of employment (such as minimum wage), restrictions on child labour, ground rules for collective conflict, default terms for employment contracts (such as minimum notice provisions and implied duties), health and safety rules, and notice requirements in the case of economic dismissals.[25] It also extends beyond the confines of the employment contract. However, refashioning the goal of labour law as responding to labour market failures assumes that the neoclassical model of the labour market is accurate, and that market failures are aberrations and not systemic. If, as I shall argue in the next section, the neoclassical model of the labour market is mistaken, then there is little reason to adopt it as the basis for regulating labour.

Expanding the scope of labour law beyond employment is an explicit commitment of Richard Mitchell and Christopher Arup, who are of the view that the discipline of labour law should be reformulated as the law of labour market regulation.[26] They propose to recast the discipline as the construction and governance of labour markets,[27] which they recognize would dismantle disciplinary boundaries between what have hitherto been considered distinctive areas of law, such as immigration law on the supply side and company law on the demand side. They acknowledge that disciplinary line drawing has 'a normative or "ideological" dimension to it'.[28] However, they disavow the need for a grand narrative for labour law, and accept that labour laws might contain a multiplicity of purposes.

There is widespread agreement that labour law needs to be broadened to encompass the law of labour market regulation, but precisely where to draw the line is contentious. Commenting on Mitchell and Arup's suggestion to focus on labour market regulation, Simon Deakin claims that for the *'legal discipline* of labour law to be redefined... requires corresponding changes to its conceptual foundation lest the field fold back into private law or merge with company law and

---

[24] H Collins, 'Justifications and Techniques of Legal Regulation of the Employment Relation' in H Collins, P Davies, and R Rideout (eds), *Legal Regulation of the Employment Relation* (Kluwer International, 2000) 3; A Hyde, 'What is Labour Law?' in G Davidov and B Langille (eds), *Boundaries and Frontiers of Labour Law* (Hart Publishing, 2006) 37. While both Collins and Hyde agree over the importance of values, such as respect for human rights and human dignity, they believe that these norms do not supply an adequate foundation for labour law.

[25] Ibid.

[26] R Mitchell and C Arup, 'Labour Law and Labour Market Regulation' in C Arup et al (eds), *Labour Law and Labour Market Regulation* (Federation Press, 2006) 3.

[27] Ibid 17.

[28] Ibid 5.

thereby lose the doctrinal reference points for the application of protective labour standards'.[29]

In *Beyond Employment*, Alain Supiot offers a new conceptual foundation for labour law, based on labour force membership status, which would displace employment as the basis for inclusion under the umbrella of social protection.[30] He grounds labour force membership status in work, which he distinguishes from activity since work 'results from an obligation, whether voluntarily undertaken or compulsorily imposed'.[31] Supiot develops a typology consisting of four concentric circles of labour and social protection, moving from the smallest circle, employment, which hinges on dependency and provides the highest degree of protection, to occupational activity, followed by rights based on unpaid care work, to the largest circle, universal social rights, which provides the least amount of protection. Labour market membership status would be supported by a new type of social right, described as social drawing rights, that would be activated by the establishment of a sufficient reserve and the decision of the individual reserve holder to make use of it. These rights would be publicly supported and would be based on an individual's participation in socially valuable work. The goal of labour force membership status is to provide individuals with real freedom of choice in relationship to labour market participation by combining flexibility with security.

Several labour law scholars have relied on the work of economist and philosopher Amartya Sen to provide a normative basis for a broad understanding of labour law as the law regulating labour market relations.[32] In *Development as Freedom*, Sen's basic proposition is that we should evaluate development in terms of 'the expansion of the "capabilities" of people to live the kinds of lives that they value – and have reason to value',[33] which is his definition of freedom. For Sen, freedom includes both well-being, an individual's own advantage in terms of valuable states of being, but also agency, the different ways that individuals act and exercise their choice to achieve valuable states.

A capability is a type of freedom to achieve a number of different things a person may value being or doing, and the actual beings or doings are human functionings. Capabilities are the powers people have as human beings and opportunities that people have to nurture and exercise their capacities. Central to the conception of

---

[29] S Deakin, 'A New Paradigm for Labour Law' (2007) 31 Melbourne University Law Review 1161–73, 1169. In 1989, Hugh Collins noted that such an expansive view of labour law, the legislation of labour markets, risked the loss of the disciplinary vocational centre, 'Labour Law as a Vocation' (1989) 105 LQR 468.

[30] A Supiot, *Beyond Employment: Changes in Work and the Future of Labour Law in Europe* (Oxford University Press, 2001) 55.

[31] Ibid 54.

[32] B Langille, 'Globalization and The Just Society: Core Labour Rights, the FTAA, and Development' in P Craig and M Lynk (eds), *Globalization and the Future of Labour Law* (Cambridge University Press, 2006) 274–303; J Brown, S Deakin, and B Wilkinson, 'Capabilities, Social Rights and European Market Integration' in R Salais and R Villeneuve (eds), *Europe and the Politics of Capabilities* (Cambridge University Press, 2004) 205; Deakin and Wilkinson, above n 5, 343 citing Supiot.

[33] A Sen, *Development as Freedom* (Anchor, 1999) 18. For an earlier discussion of capabilities and labour law see J Fudge, 'The New Discourse of Labour Rights: From Social to Fundamental Rights?' (2007) 29(1) Comparative Labour Law and Policy Journal 29–66.

capabilities is the idea of conversion factors, which include personal characteristics, such as an individual's metabolism or biological sex, societal characteristics that could include social norms, legal rules, and public policies (such as norms that result in social discrimination or gender stereotyping, or legal interventions to offset these phenomena), and environmental characteristics that could refer to climate, physical surroundings, technological infrastructure, and legal-political institutions.[34]

Sen's concept of capabilities provides a framework for debating which labour and social rights ought to be considered fundamental rather than offering a justification for a particular set of rights.[35] The appeal of the capabilities approach to labour lawyers is that it links the normative ground of social rights (human freedom) directly to the welfare goal (market efficiency) by providing both a metric and a substantive value and, thus, responds to the prevailing concern that social rights conflict with the market.[36]

Jude Brown, Simon Deakin, and Frank Wilkinson 'explore the potential for linking the economic notion of capabilities to the juridical conception of social rights'.[37] The idea they pursue 'is that social rights be understood as part of the process of "institutionalizing capabilities", that is to say, as providing mechanisms for extending the range of choice of alternative functions on the part of individuals'.[38] Social rights operate as conversion factors that seek to enhance the real choices for individuals. They identify two categories of social rights: '(1) social rights as immediate claims to resources (financial benefits such as welfare payments) and (2) social rights as particular forms of procedural or institutionalized interaction (such as rules governing workplace relations, collective bargaining and corporate governance).'[39] The first category of social rights, such as sick and maternity pay, can be seen as claims to commodities that can be converted by individuals into functionings. The second category of social rights is social conversion factors, such as collective bargaining and trade unions. These procedural rights are the means by which institutional environments can be shaped to ensure that all individuals can convert their endowments into a range of possible functionings and achieve further capabilities.[40]

Deakin and Wilkinson emphasize the market-creating role of social rights, and they are critical of the general equilibrium framework of neoclassical labour market economics.[41] Following Karl Polanyi, they regard the labour market as an instituted process, and they view the price mechanism as simply one among several methods of coordination. According to them, 'the capability concept could provide us with a guiding principle for a neo-Fabian agenda of labour market reform, one which

---

[34] Brown, Deakin, and Wilkinson, above n 32, 209.
[35] Deakin and Wilkinson, above n 5, 351.
[36] Brown, Deakin, and Wilkinson, above n 32.
[37] Ibid 205.
[38] Ibid 210.
[39] Ibid 211.
[40] Ibid 212–13.
[41] Deakin and Wilkinson, above n 5, 278.

would seek to recreate, under modern conditions, the institutional basis for reconciling individual freedom with the market order'.[42]

There are several strengths of this approach to revitalizing labour law. First, it broadens the scope of discipline beyond work relations in the enterprise to the labour market more generally. Second, it provides a conceptual basis – a legal evolutionary approach to the employment relationship – for the law of the labour market. Third, it provides a normative framework, capabilities, which allows for a plurality of goals, of which efficiency is but one. Fourth, it is based upon a model of the labour market that better reflects social reality than the neoclassical model. Fifth, it recognizes that workers' and employers' interests often conflict.[43]

Although I consider this to be the most promising account of a new law of the labour market, I have a few reservations. First, although Deakin and Wilkinson are critical of the neo-classical model of the labour market, and they adopt an institutional approach, since their primary concern is to show how social rights are compatible with the market there is a danger that they concede too much to the orthodox model of the labour market. As part of their neo-Fabian revival they seek to renew the 'political project of democratic emancipation on which labour law was first constructed';[44] however, their emphasis on the 'constitutional' function of labour law is subordinate rather than dominant in their reconstruction.[45] Second, the legal evolution approach, while a very sophisticated and nuanced account of law, tends to place too much emphasis on the consistency and coherence of juridical concepts. As Deakin and Wilkinson note, the legitimacy of the legal system depends, to a great extent, on its self-portrayal as an autonomous system that is separate and distinct from the economic and political systems.[46] However, not only at the level of 'low' law does this distinction tend to break down; at the level of high law *ex post*, rather than *ex ante*, rationalizations contain the conflicts between legal values and concepts. The legal evolution approach tends to diminish the extent of conflict within the legal system and the degree to which legal forms are stretched in order to 'adapt' to new substantive values.[47]

Third, while there is much to recommend in Sen's idea of capabilities as a normative basis for a law of the labour market, it has some limitations.[48]

---

[42] Ibid 353.

[43] According to Antonella Picchio, Smith thought that conflict was avoidable because increased labour productivity satisfies both capital's need for profit and labour's demand for increased standards of living; *Social Reproduction: The Political Economy of the Labour Market* (Cambridge University Press, 1992) 133.

[44] Deakin and Wilkinson, above n 5, 35.

[45] Dukes (above n 15).

[46] Deakin and Wilkinson, above n 5, 27.

[47] Ibid 26–35.

[48] It is important not to ask Sen's concept of capabilities to carry too much weight; it does not provide a complete theory of social justice. Sen is very clear to acknowledge that although the idea of capability has considerable merit in the assessment of the opportunity aspect of freedom, it cannot possibly deal adequately with the process aspect of freedom, since capabilities are characteristics of individual advantages, and they fall short of telling us about fairness or equity in the processes involved, or about the freedom of citizens to invoke and utilize procedures that are equitable. A Sen, *The Idea of Justice* (Harvard University Press, 2009).

The benefit of the capabilities approach is that it rests upon a positive conception of freedom, it is committed to ethical individualism, it is pluralistic, it is context-specific, and it emphasizes agency.[49] However, Sen emphasizes individual responsibility, and he employs a choice-centred view of responsibility.[50] He also concentrates too much on adaptive preferences, and does not devote enough attention to social relations of exploitation.[51] Moreover, justice cannot be defined simply by the satisfaction of individual preferences; it is also a matter of obligation, as the example of care work makes so clear.[52]

In the following section, I will explore the idea of labour as a 'fictive' commodity in order to suggest a different basis for conceptualizing the role of labour law. Once the conceptual task is complete, I will draw upon the work of feminist political theorists to supplement Sen's conception of capabilities to provide a normative basis for the role of law in governing the labour market.

D. Expanding the boundaries of, and justifications for, labour law

1. Labour as a 'fictive' commodity

It is easy enough to make models on stated assumptions. The difficulty is to find the assumptions that are relevant to reality.[53]

Labour is at the same time 'the most fundamental and the most inherently problematic of categories'.[54] Political economists and sociologists have long described labour as a 'fictive commodity'.[55] It is neither produced as a commodity, nor is its production governed by an assessment of its realization on the market. Labour cannot physically be separated from its owner. The propertyless owner derives no utility from consuming labour, and, therefore, must enter into a wage

---

[49] Ingrid Robeyns distinguishes between ethical and ontological individualism; see 'Sen's Capability Approach and Gender Inequality: Selecting Relevant Capabilities' in B Aggarwal, J Humphries, and I Robeyns (eds), *Amartya Sen's Work and Ideas: A Gender Perspective* (Routledge, 2005) 63.

[50] JM Alexander, *Capabilities and Social Justice: The Political Philosophy of Amartya Sen and Martha Nussbaum* (Ashgate, 2008) 112; Deakin specifically identifies the difficulty or danger that Sen's approach to capabilities, which focuses exclusively on the individual and the real, or effective, choices that are available to each person, poses to both the right to collective action and the principal institutions of the welfare state: collective bargaining, social insurance, and progressive taxation; S Deakin, 'Social Rights in a Globalized Economy' in P Alston (ed), *Labour Rights as Human Rights* (Oxford University Press, 2005) 25, 59.

[51] E Anderson, 'What is the Point of Equality?' (1999) 109 Ethics 287, 336; and I Robeyns, 'Is Nancy Fraser's Critique of Theories of Distributive Justice Justified?' in K Olsen (ed), *Adding Insult to Injury: Nancy Fraser Debates her Critics* (Verso, 2008) 190.

[52] S Fredman, *Human Rights Transformed: Positive Rights and Positive Duties* (Oxford University Press, 2008) 16.

[53] J Robinson, *Economic Heresies, Some Old-Fashioned Questions in Economic Theory* (Basic Books, 1971) 141–2 quoted in D Lampen Thomson, *Adam Smith's Daughters* (Exhibition Press, 1973) 128.

[54] Peck, above n 7, 23 quoting F Block, *Postindustrial Possibilities: A Critique of Economic Discourse* (University of California, 1990) 75.

[55] Peck, above n 7; K Marx, *Capital* (Penguin, 1981) (trans D Fernbach); Polanyi, above n 2; C Offe, *Disorganized Capitalism* (Polity Press, 1985) ch 1; Picchio, above n 43; and J Howe, *Regulation for Job Protection* (The Federation Press, 2008) ch 2.

contract in order to subsist above a very low minimum level. Although allocated through the market and institutionally treated as a commodity, labour power is embodied in human beings who are born, cared for, and tended in a network of social relations that operate outside the direct discipline of the market. And unlike other commodities, human beings have the capacity to act individually and collectively to resist the dull compulsion of supply and demand. Thus, there are profound differences between labour power and other commodities.

Peck identifies four social processes that illuminate the social character of labour.[56] First, there is the problem of incorporating labour into the labour market. The market does not govern the supply of labour; instead families determine the quality and quantity of labour, albeit influenced by state policies, and by the state directly though immigration policies. Second, labour is not allocated by price, but matched by institutions. The same social groups suffer disadvantage on account of ascribed rather than achieved characteristics.[57] Gender and racial ideologies relating to appropriate roles and traits, employer strategies to enhance profits, along with norms and customs give rise to labour institutions such as job labelling, labour market segments, internal labour markets, and glass ceilings which perpetuate discrimination against women and certain racial groups.[58] Third, the problem of labour control is endemic. Labour is only partially commodified; human beings sell their capacity to work, not themselves. Thus, cooperation on the part of workers is essential to the success of any enterprise, and this cooperation is based upon a blend of coercion and consent. Moreover, since it is an indeterminate contract, social norms, not bargains, determine much of the content of the employment relationship. Fourth, there is the fundamental question of the reproduction of labour.

It is important briefly to elaborate upon the concept of social reproduction since this process is ignored even in many institutional analyses of the labour market. Social reproduction refers to the social processes and labour that go into the daily and generational maintenance of the population. It also involves the reproduction of bodies and minds located in historical times and geographic spaces.[59] It 'includes the provision of material resources (food, clothing, housing, transport) and the training of individual capabilities necessary for interaction in the social context of a particular time and place'.[60] Social reproduction is typically organized by families in households and by the state through health, education, welfare, and immigration policies. It can also be organized through the market and through voluntary organizations such as churches. Although Polanyi, for example, understood that labour was an instituted process, according to Lourdes Benería, his analysis of the social construction of markets has important gender-related consequences that

---

[56] Peck, above n 7.

[57] Ibid 30.

[58] R Tarling and F Wilkinson, 'Economic Functioning; Self Sufficiency and Full Employment' in J Michie and J Grieve-Smith (eds), *Full Employment Without Inflation* (Oxford University Press, 1995).

[59] A Picchio, 'A Macroeconomic Approach to an Extended Standard of Living' in A Picchio (ed), *Unpaid Work and the Economy: A Gender Analysis of the Standards of Living* (Routledge, 2003) 1.

[60] Ibid 2.

he did not take into consideration.[61] He, like William Beveridge, treated the traditional gendered division of labour – male breadwinner and female unpaid caregiver – as natural, and both were inattentive to unequal relations within the household.[62]

Traditional accounts of work and labour law have ignored all of the unpaid domestic work, overwhelmingly performed by women, that is involved in maintaining living spaces, buying, and transforming the commodities used in the family, supplementing the services provided to family members by the public and private sectors, caring for people, and managing social and personal relationships. Neoclassical, as well as many institutional, economists fail to recognize the socially valuable labour that goes into the processes of social reproduction, which, in turn, contributes to and compounds the gender blindness of labour law and policy. Not only does the neo-classical model deny the huge productive contribution that women make through their socially necessary, although unpaid, labour, it ignores the link between production and social reproduction.

Each of Peck's four social processes identified above pose regulatory dilemmas and the nature of these dilemmas changes over time.[63] The concept of market failure does not capture the systematic nature of the contradictions. It suggests, for example, that the inelasticity of labour supply – the fact that labour is not produced for sale on the market – is a question of adjustment.[64] The neo-classical model treats these contradictions as temporary; however, the problem is that the contradictions are systemic, whereas the institutional resolution is only temporary. If the labour market is understood as an instituted process, then regulation is necessary to constitute it, and not simply to adjust it. However, the specific form that regulation takes at a specific place in time depends on the social, political, and cultural context as well as the balance of power between men, women, workers, employers, and different segments in the labour market.[65]

The role of labour law and policy should be to address the different aspects of the 'regulatory dilemmas' that arise when labour is sold. Where the line is drawn about what constitutes labour law, as opposed to social or corporate law, is normative and ideological, and not conceptual. Traditionally, labour law has primarily addressed the problems of labour control and labour allocation by providing collective bargaining legislation, direct minimum standards, and anti-discrimination law. Regulatory dilemmas relating to labour supply and social reproduction have fallen outside of the traditional scope of labour law.

By treating a key component of social reproduction, women's unpaid domestic work, as either family law or social law, conflicts between men and women are

---

[61] L Benería, *Gender Development and Globalization* (Routledge, 2003) 74.
[62] The economist Antonella Picchio criticizes the neo-classical model of the household as firm because it is based on the denial of the specific nature of labour as a commodity, in particular on the specificity of its process of reproduction and its political implications. Picchio, above n 43, 107.
[63] Peck, above n 7, 24.
[64] See, eg, Hyde, above n 24.
[65] Peck, above n 7, 25–6. See also E Tucker, 'Renorming Labour Law: Can We Escape Labour Law's Recurring Regulatory Dilemmas' (2010) 39 Industrial Law Journal 99.

ignored, and the huge amount of care labour that is required to achieve and maintain social reproduction is obscured. Labour law's continued focus upon a model worker who is unencumbered with care responsibilities and the current emphasis on employment policy to increase women's employment rate by requiring everyone, including carers, to engage in paid employment, simply reinforces gendered labour market segmentation because it is not possible fully to commodify care. While it is possible (assuming sufficient income) to purchase the necessary services to fulfil many domestic responsibilities, economist Jean Gardiner has argued that 'those aspects of domestic provision that entail the giving of care are particularly resistant to commodification as the relations of exchange are not susceptible to monetary evaluation'.[66] Social needs are very complex and there is an important affective dimension of care. Care is more than a task; it is embedded in personal relationships of love and obligation, and is a crucial part of the process of identity formation.[67]

Care work is essential for social reproduction, which is a crucial process in instituting a market for labour. Treating care as work, that is, as a socially necessary activity that is a matter of obligation and initiative, rather than women's natural role, results in a profound reconceptualization of labour law. There is no *a priori* conceptual reason why such work should fall outside the boundaries of labour law, and, as I will explain in the next section, there are good normative reasons for including it.

2. Democratic equality, collective capabilities, and caretaking norms

In developing a normative justification for a radically expanded conception of labour law I will build on Sen's notions of capabilities in three ways. First, I will identify and describe a normative goal – Elizabeth Anderson's idea of democratic equality – to supplement Sen's conception of capabilities.[68] I have chosen to focus on Anderson's account of democratic equality because she endorses Sen's idea that egalitarians 'should seek equality for all in the space of capabilities'.[69] Second, I will discuss the need to counter what Peter Evans characterizes as Sen's 'classic liberal exaltation of the individual and implicit acceptance of individual (as opposed to social) preferences as exogenous'.[70] Third, I will expand on Sen's conception of capabilities to incorporate a relational understanding of the individual in which 'long periods of dependency are a normal and inevitable part of everyone's life cycle'.[71]

---

[66] L McDowell, 'Father and Ford Revisited: Gender, Class and Employment Change in the New Millennium' (2001) 26 Trans Inst Br Geogr NS: 448–64, 460, referring to J Gardiner, *Gender, Care and Economics* (Macmillan, 1997).

[67] J Lewis and S Giullari, 'The Adult Worker Model Family, Gender Equality and Care: The Search for New Policy Principles and Problems of a Capabilities Approach' (2005) 34(1) Economy and Society 76–104, 86.

[68] Anderson, above n 51.

[69] Ibid 316.

[70] P Evans, 'Collective Capabilities, Culture, and Amartya Sen's Development as Freedom' (2001) 37 Comparative International Development 54, 56.

[71] Anderson, above n 51, 311.

Elizabeth Anderson offers a political understanding of equality which she calls 'democratic equality', the goal of which is to overcome social relations of oppression and exploitation.[72] Her relational theory of equality aims to further what Nancy Fraser helpfully termed equality of recognition (status) and redistribution.[73] Anderson, like Fraser, provides a radical democratic interpretation of the norm of equal respect for and equal autonomy of all human beings, the goal of which is to abolish forms of social relationship in which some people dominate, exploit, marginalize, demean, or inflict violence on others.[74] Democratic egalitarians seek to live together in a democratic community, as opposed to a hierarchical one, and they are 'fundamentally concerned with the relationships within which goods are distributed and not only the distributions of the goods themselves'.[75] While Anderson agrees with Sen that capabilities are the space or metric for understanding equality, she, unlike him, believes that it is important to specify which capabilities a society has an obligation to equalize.

Sen refuses to provide a list of capabilities that a society must equalize because he believes that it is important that societies determine which capabilities are critical through a process of democratic deliberation.[76] Sen's commitment to political debate and discussion in setting the goals of development is a welcome counter to economists who are critical of social choice.[77] However, according to Evans, despite the radical character of his critique of the real-income framework and welfare economics, 'Sen continues to be a good Manchester liberal'.[78] The problem is that Sen focuses exclusively on individuals and their relationship to the social context and fails to appreciate the significance of collectivities as the bridge between the two.[79]

Sen rejects the notion of collective capabilities, and he does not explore the relationship between individuals and collectivities.[80] However, as Evans notes, 'gaining the freedom to do things we have reason to value is rarely something we can accomplish as individuals'.[81] Organized collectivities, such as unions, women's groups, and political parties are fundamental to people's ability to choose lives they have reason to value. Not only do such organized collectivities provide an arena for formulating shared values and preferences, they are essential for pursuing them in

---

[72] Ibid 288.

[73] N Fraser, *Justice Interruptus: Critical Reflections on the 'Postsocialist' Condition* (Routledge, 1997).

[74] Anderson, above n 51, 313. Fraser's ultimate goal is participate parity, which has three dimensions: recognition (status), redistribution, and representation. For Fraser, like Anderson, justice is about dismantling obstacles to parity that are institutionalized in unjust social arrangements; see N Fraser, *Scales of Justice: Reimagining Political Space in a Globalizing World* (Columbia University Press, 2009).

[75] Anderson, above n 51, 314.

[76] Sen, above n 33.

[77] See Evans' discussion of Kenneth Arrow and Sen, above n 70, 44.

[78] Evans, above n 70, 56.

[79] Ibid.

[80] S Feldman and P Gellert, 'The Seductive Quality of Central Human Capabilities: Sociological Insights into Nussbaum and Sen's Disagreement' (2006) 35(3) Economy and Society 423–52, 427; and Evans, above n 70, 56. For Sen's most recent discussion of the relationship between capabilities and collectivities see Sen, above n 48, 245–7.

[81] Evans, above n 70, 56.

the face of powerful opposition. Collective organizations are crucial for giving meaning to deliberative democracy, and a necessary compliment to electoral institutions and civil and political rights. In order to achieve development as freedom, public policy must recognize and support collective organizations.[82]

Although Sen is clear about the need for open communication and arguments in order to have informed and unregimented formation of values, he does not 'pursue the question of how distribution of economic power over cultural processes in the modern economy might undermine the processes he advocates'.[83] Evans suggests that 'the increasing concentration over the production of culture, information, and preferences in the modern economy constitutes an impediment to the kind of deliberative preference formation that is essential to the expansion of capabilities'.[84] Collective capabilities provide an important counterweight to more thoroughly marketized economic relations and how they distort preferences and values.[85]

Elizabeth Anderson, like other feminists who build upon Sen's conception of capabilities, insists on the need to specify capabilities. She emphasizes the need for an expansive conception of the social conditions of freedom, which includes private relations of domination, even those entered into by consent or contract, as violations of individual freedom.[86]

The capabilities approach need not be limited to behaviour in the paid labour market, and it can, and should, encompass people's beings and doings in market and non-market contexts. It is important to recognize that individuals are socially embedded and dependent upon others for large periods of their life cycle. In elaborating their list of capabilities, Anderson, Robeyns, and Benería emphasize care work, which is an essential component of the process of social reproduction.[87] It is also important, as I have argued in the preceding section, not to confuse the economy with the market sector; dependent caretakers are part of the system of production and they engage in household production, producing workers of the future, and discharging the obligations everyone has to dependants. It is an indispensable condition of the continuation of human society that many adults devote a great deal of their time to such caretaking however poorly such work may be remunerated in the market.[88]

---

[82] Feldman and Gellert, above n 80, 444 argue that the space for democratic deliberation requires greater specification than Sen provides. They also suggest that his lack of attention to inequalities amongst collectivities and the challenges such inequalities pose to democratic deliberation leads Sen to be naïve about the conditions of democratic deliberation.

[83] Evans, above n 70, 57.

[84] Ibid 58, 59.

[85] For a discussion of distorted preferences in the context of union recognition see A Bogg, *The Democratic Aspects of Trade Union Recognition* (Hart Publishing, 2009).

[86] Anderson, above n 51, 315; Robeyns, above n 49; and L Benería, 'The Crisis of Care, International Migration, and Public Policy' (2008) 14(3) Feminist Economics 1–21. Unlike Martha Nussbaum (*Women and Human Development: The Capabilities Approach* (Cambridge University Press, 2000)), who favours a universal list of capabilities, these authors regard the list of capabilities as the outcome of a deliberative process and, as such, subject to revision and variation.

[87] Robeyns' list of capabilities is drawn for women in developed economies, specifically Europe. Benería adopts her methodology for determining a list of capabilities for women in developing economies in South America.

[88] Anderson, above n 51, 324.

According to Anderson, democratic equality entails that no one should be reduced to an inferior status because they fulfil obligations to care for others.[89] However, as long as participating in paid employment provides greater status than performing socially necessary, but undervalued, care work, full equality may not be attainable simply through redistribution. 'Equality may require a change in social norms, by which men as well as women would be required to share in caretaking responsibilities.'[90] Such a change in norms would likely require a profound reconfiguration of the prevailing working-time regime, which is rooted in the standard employment relationship and male-breadwinner and female-caregiver sexual division of labour.[91] It would also require public support for, and recognition of, the social significance of care.[92]

Moreover, changing gendered social norms regarding caretaking is especially important once the demands of justice are considered outside of a narrow Westphalian frame.[93] Public policies in developed countries that emphasize increasing women's employment rates without simultaneously stressing the obligations of men to engage in care activities are likely to perpetuate global care chains in which women from poor countries migrate to richer countries to perform care work.[94] While women's decisions to migrate can increase their financial autonomy and increase their financial contribution to their household through remittances, their absorption into the care markets of the North reinforces the gendered nature of care. Thus, not only do global care chains illustrate the ways in which unequal resources are distributed globally,[95] they also reveal the gendered nature of this inequality.

E. Conclusion: a different imaginary

I have argued for a new imaginary for labour law, one that is designed to address the regulatory dilemmas that result from the fact that labour is a

---

[89] Ibid 325.

[90] Anderson, above n 51, 324 citing Fraser, above n 73.

[91] For a discussion of the need both for men to take on more care responsibilities in order to further women's equality and for redesigned working-time and leave policies to support and inculcate more equitable care-giving norms see J Fudge, 'Working-time Regimes, Flexibility, and Work-Life Balance: Gender Equality and Families' in C Krull and J Sempruch (eds), *Demystifying the Family/Work Conflict: Challenges and Possibilities* (University of British Columbia Press, 2011) and 'The New Duel-Earner Gender Contract: Work-life Balance or Working-time Flexibility?' in J Conaghan and K Rittich (eds), *Labour Law, Work and Family: Critical and Comparative Perspectives* (Oxford University Press, 2005) 261–88. See also S Lee and D McCann, 'Working time Capability: Towards Realizing Individual Choice' in J-Y Boulin et al (eds), *Decent Working Time: New Trends, New Issues* (ILO, 2006).

[92] Such support for, and recognition of, care would likely run counter to employment activation policies such as workfare for women and might require care activation policies for men.

[93] Fraser, above n 74. Labour law has adopted a nation state frame. For a caution against using the nation state as the exclusive frame see A Wimmer and G Schiller, 'Methodological Nationalism and Beyond: Nation-State Building, Migration and the Social Sciences' (2002) 2(4) Global Networks 301–34.

[94] J Fudge, 'Global Care Chains: Transnational Migrant Care Workers', paper prepared for the International Association of Law Schools Conference on Labour Law and Labour Market in the New World Economy, Milan, 20–22 May 2010.

[95] S Hassim, 'Global Constraints on Gender Equality in Care Work' (2008) 36(3) Politics & Society 388–402, 397.

fictive commodity.[96] Instead of addressing only two (allocation and control) of the four social processes involved in the construction, maintenance, and reproduction of a market for labour that have been the traditional focus of labour law, I have argued that labour law should also address the problems of incorporating labour into the market and the reproduction of labour.[97] Disciplinary boundaries are both ideological and conceptual, and there are compelling ideological and conceptual reasons for expanding the scope of labour law to include all of the regulatory dilemmas that any attempt to govern the labour market must confront. In societies that value paid employment as the primary path to 'citizenship', treating unpaid care work, the socially necessary labour predominantly performed by women, as a matter of social or family law, and not labour law, reinforces the idea that such work is not only a woman's natural role, but also that in the social hierarchy it is of lower value than paid employment. It also helps to explain why public welfare provides a lower living standard than does employment. Excluding unpaid care work from the scope of labour law is an example of what Anderson characterizes as a 'perfect reproduction of Poor Law thinking, including its sexism and its conflation of responsible work with market wage-earning'.[98] Broadening the scope of labour law to include all of the regulatory dilemmas inherent in governing the labour market allows us to address power relationships in households, workplaces, and society at large.

The normative basis for this reconceptualization of labour law is the achievement of democratic equality through the space of capabilities. Although the capabilities approach typically is located within a liberal framework, it offers valuable resources for a critique of the liberal conception of justice.[99] I have argued that it is both possible and desirable to supplement Sen's account in order to appreciate the need for collective capabilities, to address private power within the market and the household, and to adopt a relational understanding of the individual as dependent upon the obligations of others for care. Care work demonstrates that justice is not simply a matter of individual choice but also a matter of social obligation.[100] It also demonstrates the need to revise our conception of labour law in order better to capture the 'fictive' nature of labour's commodity status, and to recognize that employing labour is an instituted process and not a simple exchange.

---

[96] A new imaginary would require us to go beyond analogizing household and familial relations to employment and put a greater emphasis on public provision and social responsibility. For this reason, I would support basic income strategies over 'wages for housework' policies.

[97] In this chapter, I have not addressed the need to consider justice claims beyond the nation state. For a compelling argument for the need to do so, see Fraser, above n 7. Nor does this chapter respond to Adelle Blackett's challenge (this volume) to refigure labour law in an inclusive way that is attentive to labour before and beyond the market. However, my intuition is that an historical and global approach to the labour market as an instituted process can meet this challenge.

[98] Anderson, above n 51, 311–12 (footnote omitted).

[99] Alexander, above n 50, 1.

[100] Anderson, above n 51, 325; and Alexander, above n 50, 112.

9

Theories of Rights as Justifications for Labour Law

Hugh Collins*

An investigation of the idea of labour law calls for a theory. Such a theory must address the moral, political, and legal force of labour law. Ideally, the theory should justify the existence and weight of such typical rules and principles of labour law as minimum wages, safety regulations, maximum hours of work, the outlawing of discrimination against particular groups, and the recognition of a trade union for the purposes of collective bargaining. Given the general commitment in liberal societies to respect for freedom of the individual and a free market, labour law requires a theory of why such mandatory constraints should exist.

There is no shortage of theories of this kind.[1] Historically, it is possible to detect two predominant strands of justification. One strand appeals to efficiency or welfare considerations, in order to justify rules that address market failures caused by transaction costs and asymmetric information, problems arising in the governance of contracts of employment such as coercion and opportunism, and more generally the desirability of promoting productive efficiency and competitiveness through a well-coordinated and flexible division of labour. From this perspective, labour law addresses the idiosyncratic problems that arise in relation to contracts of employment through a mixture of special contract law and market regulation. The other predominant strand of justification for labour law appeals to considerations of a fair distribution of wealth, power, and other goods in a society. On this view, the principal aim of labour law is to steer towards a particular conception of social justice, such as a more egalitarian society, and the norms of labour law are required primarily for the instrumental purpose of securing that goal. This second strand of justification tends to support the practice of collective bargaining and the imposition of basic labour standards such as a minimum wage, because these interventions in the labour market are calculated to improve the position of poorer and weaker members of the society. In diverse combinations and variations, most labour lawyers have either explicitly or implicitly traditionally relied on these two kinds of competing and to some extent antagonistic justifications – efficiency and social justice – to explain the normative foundations of labour law.

---

* London School of Economics.

[1] Eg H Spector, 'Philosophical Foundations of Labor Law' (2006) 33 Florida State University Law Review 119.

Yet these justifications for labour law are evidently vulnerable to critiques that question whether the goals justify the means used in labour law. In brief, the problem is that the efficiency-based justifications for labour law can be deployed in ways that propose the dismantling of most of the special rules for employment. At the same time, the social justice justifications for labour law have been challenged both on the ground that they lack merit and for the reason that, even if they possess some worthwhile aims, these goals should be pursued through other, less intrusive, governmental measures involving taxation and expenditure on welfare, leaving the market free to maximize the wealth of a society as a whole. Combining this two-pronged critique of traditional justifications for labour law, it seems possible, as in the example of Richard Epstein,[2] to justify the elimination of labour law altogether and to replace it with a general freedom of contract regime. One can, of course, take issue with this sort of conclusion. Using a different economic analysis and a more complex conception of social justice than welfare maximization, one can produce a different outcome that justifies quite an elaborate labour law system. For instance, a combination of an appreciation of the persistence of certain kinds of market failures in the labour market combined with the insights of behavioural economics that individuals do not make rational assessments of risks in contracting can lead to justifications for fairly detailed mandatory protections for workers. Even such efficiency-based theories remain vulnerable to the further charge from the New Right of excessive paternalism: employers and workers are adults and should be permitted to fashion their contracts according to their preferences, whether or not they invariably reach the most efficient outcomes. It is better, on this anti-paternalist view, to permit the market to experiment, than to attempt to regulate these arrangements on the basis of imperfect information. Such challenges to the existence of labour law based upon considerations of efficiency and welfare are not merely theoretical.

Legal regimes steer markets or capitalist societies through many legal measures designed to protect their economic institutions and mechanisms. Not only does the law vindicate private property rights and contractual agreements, it also ensures that the competitive market cannot be subverted by participants through anti-competitive measures. In many countries such as the United Kingdom and the United States, labour law was initially conceived in order to create an exception to competition rules against cartels and interference with business by unlawful means. In the European Union, however, though strong rules in the Treaties protect the operations of the competitive single market against obstructions to free trade, there is no exemption for organized labour, a topic, indeed, which is technically outside the competence of European Union (EU) laws.[3] Recent decisions of the Court of Justice reveal how this absence of strong protections for organized labour at European level may lead to legal restrictions on industrial action and collective bargaining that affects

---

[2] RA Epstein, *Forbidden Grounds: The Case Against Employment Discrimination Laws* (Harvard University Press, 1992); RA Epstein, 'In Defense of the Contract at Will' (1984) 51 University of Chicago Law Review 947; and RA Epstein, 'A Common Law for Labor Relations: A Critique of the New Deal Labor Legislation' (1983) 92 Yale LJ 1357.
[3] Treaty on the Functioning of the European Union, Art 153(5).

cross-border trade.[4] The lesson one draws from this history must be that collective labour law can only survive with strong laws that create a secure exception to the economic constitution that protects a market economy.

These challenges to the existence of labour law share a common perspective: considerations of efficiency and wealth maximization undermine mandatory employment standards and protections for organized labour. In response to such challenges, it is tempting to seek a theory of labour law that forecloses the discussions of efficiency and welfare by an appeal to an overriding value that justifies labour law. One sort of theory that holds out such a promise of foreclosure is a strong theory of rights. This special weight attributed to rights in some theories of politics and justice, sometimes described, following Dworkin, as 'rights as trumps',[5] views appeals to rights as a form of exclusionary reason, in the sense used by Raz.[6] Once a fundamental right is at stake, it tends to exclude from consideration or at least override any other policies or principles, except, probably, appeals to other rights. If labour law could be justified on the basis of fundamental rights possessing this special weight, its foundations would be much more secure. Not all theories of rights deliver the required degree of foreclosure: for instance, if rights are presented as important for the achievement of a particular goal, such as maximizing utility, individual well-being, or achieving 'capacities and functionings' for individuals (following Sen and Nussbaum),[7] it is always possible to argue that the rights, and the labour laws derived from them, should be discarded or modified in so far as the goal can be achieved more successfully by other means. Among theories of rights, only rights regarded as having pre-emptive force provide a theoretical basis for labour law that can securely withstand attacks that promote other values and goals which may argue against regulation of the labour market and the workplace.

Recognizing this potential trumping power of rights, in recent years many labour activists and lawyers,[8] though by no means all,[9] have been drawn towards the

---

[4] Eg Case C–438/05, *The International Transport Workers' Federation and The Finnish Seamen's Union v Viking Line ABP and OU Viking Line Esti* [2007] ECR I–10779; and ACL Davies, 'One Step Forward, Two Steps Back? The *Viking* and *Laval* Cases in the ECJ' (2008) 37 ILJ 126.

[5] R Dworkin, *Taking Rights Seriously* (Harvard University Press, 1977) Introduction and ch 12.

[6] J Raz, *Practical Reason and Norms* (Hutchinson, 1975); Raz does not himself attribute such a strong force to rights, though they have 'peremptory force, expressed in the fact that they are sufficient to hold people to be bound by duties'. J Raz, *The Morality of Freedom* (Oxford University Press, 1986) 192.

[7] MC Nussbaum, 'Human Rights Theory: Capabilities and Human Rights' (1997) 66 Fordham L Rev 273; S Deakin and F Wilkinson, *The Law of the Labour Market* (Oxford University Press, 2005) 342–53; and R West, 'Rights, Capabilities, and the Good Society' (2000–01) 69 Fordham L Rev 1901.

[8] RJ Adams, 'From Statutory Right to Human Right: The Evolution and Current Status of Collective Bargaining' (2008) 12 Just Labour: A Canadian Journal of Work and Society 48; L Compa, 'Labor's New Opening to International Human Rights Standards' (2008, March) 11(1) WorkingUSA 99; L Compa, 'Solidarity And Human Rights: A Response to Youngdahl' (2009) 18(1) New Labor Forum 38; J Fudge, 'The New Discourse of Labor Rights: From Social to Fundamental Rights?' (2007) 29 Comparative Labor Law and Policy J 29; and RJ Adams, 'On the Convergence of Labour Rights and Human Rights' (2001) 56 Industrial Relations/Relations Industrielles 199. More general discussions of this trend: P Alston (ed), *Labour Rights as Human Rights* (Oxford University Press, 2005); B Hepple, *Rights at Work* (Sweet & Maxwell, 2005); and L Compa and S Diamond (eds), *Human Rights, Labor Rights, and International Trade* (University of Pennsylvania Press, 1996).

[9] J Youngdahl, 'Solidarity First: Labor Rights are Not the Same as Human Rights' (2009) 18 New Labor Forum 31; H Arthurs, 'Who's Afraid of Globalization? Reflection on the Future of Labour Law'

articulation of the interests of workers and organized labour through the language of rights. Labour rights may be claimed as internationally protected human rights, or there may be calls for the constitutionalization of social and economic rights as well as civil and political liberties. In Europe, scholars speak of the rebalancing of the 'Economic Constitution' in the Treaties to secure a 'Social Europe'.[10] However expressed, the central idea seems to be the same: labour law should be grounded in fundamental rights that possess peremptory or constitutional force within the legal order.

Yet are labour rights really 'human rights' or some other kind of 'fundamental rights' with exclusionary force? What theory of rights justifies such a special status for labour rights? In addressing these questions, this paper searches for a justification for labour law that grounds this body of rules not by reference to welfare or social justice but rather on the imperative to vindicate fundamental rights. Added to this agenda will be the further question, if theories of rights can provide such a justification for labour law, what would be the content of these rules, their scope of application, and their degree of protection for collective organizations of workers? In response to these questions, the argument in this chapter concludes that the case for inclusion of labour rights as universal human rights appears weak. In contrast, it is argued that in a liberal political order the case for constitutionalizing labour rights is much stronger, at least with regard to certain fundamental rights such as the right to work.

A. Are labour rights human rights?

The modern idea of human rights, building on historical antecedents in natural law theory, proclaims that all human beings should be accorded certain fundamental rights by virtue of their humanity. These human rights are universal and imperative, with a special moral weight that normally overrides other considerations. Governments must always observe human rights. This conception of human rights clearly possesses the necessary attribute of peremptory force, but can a justification for labour law rest on this idea of universal human rights?

Some international declarations of human rights appear to secure a key place for labour laws. Articles 23 and 24 of *The Universal Declaration of Human Rights* (1948) are perhaps the pivotal measure in this respect:

---

in JDR Craig and SM Lynk (eds), *Globalization and the Future of Labour Law* (Cambridge University Press, 2006) 51, 64; RP McIntyre, *Are Worker Rights Human Rights?* (University of Michigan Press, 2008); and TJ Bartkiw, 'Proceed with Caution, or Stop Wherever Possible? Ongoing Paradoxes in Legalized Labour Politics', available at SSRN: <http://ssrn.com/abstract=1513361>.

[10] ME Streit and W Mussler, 'The Economic Constitution of the European Community – From Rome to Maastrict' in F Snyder (ed), *Constitutional Dimensions of European Economic Integration* (Kluwer Law International, 1996) 109; W Sauter, 'The Economic Constitution of the European Union' (1998) 4 Columbia J of European Law 27; and C Joerges, 'What is Left of the European Economic Constitution? – a Melancholic Polemic' EUI Working Papers Law No 2004/13 (EUI, 2004).

Article 23

(1) Everyone has the right to work, to free choice of employment, to just and favourable conditions of work and to protection against unemployment.

(2) Everyone, without any discrimination, has the right to equal pay for equal work.

(3) Everyone who works has the right to just and favourable remuneration ensuring for himself and his family an existence worthy of human dignity, and supplemented, if necessary, by other means of social protection.

(4) Everyone has the right to form and to join trade unions for the protection of his interests.

Article 24

(1) Everyone has the right to rest and leisure, including reasonable limitation of working hours and periodic holiday with pay.

To these provisions might be added other Articles such as the right to be free from slavery,[11] the right to non-discrimination and equal protection of the law,[12] the right to freedom of association,[13] and the right to social security.[14] This hallowed declaration undeniably supports a basic framework of labour law on the ground that these principles represent inalienable and universal human rights. When the two main Articles dealing with labour law were elaborated into four Articles of the UN Covenant of Economic, Social and Cultural Rights,[15] these declarations of universal human rights plainly provided a solid grounding for the principal elements of a labour law system. For those who worry that labour law cannot any longer rely securely upon its traditional justifications, this route of linking the justification for labour law to the protection of universal human rights is surely extremely tempting.

The uncertain and controversial basis of human rights themselves presents a potential problem in seeking help from this direction. In a sceptical age, the idea that there are natural rights or rights to which every human being is entitled, regardless of their personal identity and geographical location, can be dismissed as at best wishful thinking and at worst a grand delusion that functions as a distraction from more important material issues such as hunger and homelessness. Human rights discourse has its detractors with respect to its mystical or irrational foundations in natural law, its indeterminacy in producing practical normative guidance, and its tendency to emphasize the individual at the expense of recognizing the importance of social institutions and collective solidarity. It is, of course, possible for supporters of human rights as a foundational political discourse to respond to these detractors with attractive and persuasive arguments. For instance, human rights discourse certainly places respect for the dignity and autonomy of the

---

[11] Article 5.
[12] Article 7.
[13] Article 20.
[14] Article 22.
[15] Articles 6–9.

individual at the core of its framework, and this Kantian framework of treating individuals as ends rather than means offers an attractive starting-point for theories of how government can provide effective coordination of society whilst not becoming an oppressive system of domination. The opening phrase of the *Universal Declaration* reminds us of how respect for the dignity of the individual through rights provides a foundation for freedom, justice, and peace.[16] Furthermore, the inclusion of social and economic rights as well as civil and political rights in that Declaration and other charters and conventions reveals that invocations of human rights need not be confined to a narrow (though nonetheless vital) agenda of securing individual liberty and dignity, but can be used to argue in favour of conditions of material social justice such as adequate housing, health care, and food. The strength of these arguments in favour of the universal human rights discourse has elevated it to one of the most potent normative arguments in contemporary politics, especially, but not exclusively, in international relations.

If one accepts the general framework of belief represented by universal human rights discourse, the question that arises in this context of thinking about the foundations of labour law is whether universal human rights might provide grounding for the normative values espoused by labour law. Are labour rights really the same kind of right as the rights that are central to universal human rights discourse? When one compares, for instance, the rights to dignity and freedom and the right not to be tortured with (say) the right to just remuneration and a paid holiday, we seem to be considering different kinds of rights. Whereas the former present an urgent and weighty moral claim, applicable to every person, in every country, the latter do not seem to present such a compelling moral imperative. Labour rights are important, but the interests they protect do not appear to many people as compelling as, for instance, liberty, security, and subsistence.[17] As Waldron argues,[18] some period of rest from work is important to prevent exhaustion from becoming life-threatening, but a day of rest or an upper restriction on hours of work for this purpose would surely suffice, so this justification would not extend to a paid holiday. Nor do labour rights invariably apply to everyone or universally, but normally only those in paid employment or in employment-like relationships. Furthermore, it seems likely that what will be regarded as fair pay and a reasonable holiday must depend to a considerable extent on what the relevant society can afford, whereas respect for dignity and liberty seems to require observance of minimum standards below which no government should be permitted to operate. Finally, universal human rights are often conceived as timeless fundamental needs, whereas it seems possible that labour rights may evolve according to the system of production, the forms of work,

---

[16] 'Whereas recognition of the inherent dignity and of the equal and inalienable rights of all members of the human family is the foundation of freedom, justice and peace in the world…'

[17] M Risse, 'A Right to Work? A Right to Leisure? Labor Rights as Human Rights' (2009) 3(1) Law & Ethics of Human Rights 1, 8.

[18] J Waldron, *Liberal Rights* (Cambridge University Press, 1993) 12–13. Waldron effectively concedes this point by admitting that 'periodic holidays with pay represents a particular culture-bound conception' of the underlying interest in substantial respite from work.

and the division of labour.[19] These four contrasts between universal human rights and labour rights with respect to the moral weight of the claims, their universal applicability, the strictness of the standards, and their variability over time, create a significant doubt whether labour rights are properly classified as universal human rights.

It is puzzling, therefore, how these apparently different sort of rights came to be inserted in the *Universal Declaration*. How did this happen? The best explanation seems to be that the labour rights in the *Universal Declaration* were adapted from the Versailles Treaty that had concluded the First World War.[20] That Treaty, which gave birth to the International Labour Office (later International Labour Organization (ILO)),[21] was not merely concerned with a cessation of war, but sought to address the causes of war that were perceived to lie in aggressive economic competition between states in an increasingly global economy. One of the elements of this solution was to try to ensure social justice for workers by establishing minimum labour standards in binding international law, so that economic competition would not create intolerable economic hardship for ordinary working people and provoke a downward spiral of regulatory competition.[22] The outcome of these deliberations was the creation of international labour standards through the International Labour Office that set both minimum mandatory standards and also protected the collective organization of workers for the purpose of collective bargaining. The Versailles Treaty stated that the priorities for minimum standards should include: freedom of association, an adequate wage, a maximum 48-hour week, minimum rest periods, equal pay for women, abolition of child labour, and fair treatment of migrant workers.[23] At the end of the Second World War, in response to the outrages committed by totalitarian governments, the *Universal Declaration* emphasized concerns about dignity and freedom of the individual, but it also included the earlier declarations that were still regarded as relevant, including the provisions on international labour standards. These standards were, however, reformulated into the new language of universal rights. Whereas the Treaty of Versailles only described freedom of association for workers and employers as a right, the *Universal Declaration of Human Rights* reformulated all these priorities for international labour standards in terms of rights. This historical explanation reveals that, at least in their origins, international labour rights were not regarded as universal human rights, but rather as standards concerned to address problems of social justice or welfare caused by international regulatory competition and the globalization of markets.

---

[19] J Nickel, *Making Sense of Human Rights* (2nd edn, Blackwell, 2007) 128; P Macklem, 'Labor Law beyond Borders' (2002) 5 Journal of International Economic Law 605, 617; and T Pogge, *World Poverty and Human Rights* (Polity, 2002) 54.

[20] Risse, above n 17.

[21] Article 387.

[22] Part XIII, Section 1, Recitals: 'Whereas also the failure of any nation to adopt humane conditions of labour is an obstacle in the way of other nations which desire to improve the conditions in their own countries.'

[23] Article 427.

This historical explanation of the origins of the idea of universal labour rights does not lead to a normative conclusion that there are not and should not be international labour rights. But it does lend support to the view, based on the contrasts between most universal human rights and labour rights, that the latter are not compelling candidates for presence in the pantheon of the former. If so, the plan to use the discourse of universal human rights to provide fresh secure foundations for labour law begins to look flawed. If we cannot seriously maintain that labour rights (or at least most of them) qualify as universal human rights, we cannot in good faith invoke universal human rights as the basis for the justification of labour law.

Yet we should notice that the above argument against using universal human rights as a foundation for labour law makes one important presupposition.[24] It relies on a particular definition of universal human rights that stresses how human rights are universal, natural, inalienable, and possessed by human beings simply by virtue of their humanity or 'personhood'.[25] This view of universal human rights has its origins in ideas of natural law: the content of human rights must be discoverable by reason or rational intuition about human nature; they represent a pre-political moral foundation for all human societies.[26] Governments that systematically ignore or deny those rights can therefore be regarded as immoral and illegitimate regimes, not deserving of obedience on the part of their citizens and not secure in their sovereign powers from interference by the international community. Human rights discourse has been used in international law and international relations to justify interference in the internal affairs of sovereign states. For this purpose, it is essential to promote a narrow but extremely morally compelling account of rights, so that enforcement measures including war may be justified. For the purpose of justifying the need for labour law as a system of entrenched rights in every market economy, however, a non-universalistic, time-bound, less absolute and slightly less morally compelling, though still forceful constitutional type of right may prove viable.

B. Fundamental rights in liberal theories of justice

Theories of fundamental rights provide a key ingredient in liberal theories of justice. The idea of rights is employed to protect the liberty of the individual both against the state and other citizens. In his *A Theory of Justice*,[27] John Rawls provides a modern sophisticated interpretation of a liberal theory of justice. In brief,

---

[24] Charles R Beitz, 'Human Rights and The Law of Peoples' in DK Chatterjee (ed), *The Ethics of Assistance: Morality and the Distant Needy* (Cambridge University Press, 2004) 193.

[25] J Griffin, *On Human Rights* (Oxford University Press, 2008).

[26] The shift in language from natural rights to human rights avoids ontological questions about their existence by accepting that rights may merely rest upon a deep moral and political commitment (not 'nature' or 'God'), and simultaneously stresses the responsibility of states and governments as the principal addressees of rights: Pogge, above n 19, 57.

[27] (Oxford University Press, 1972). Although the main ideas of Rawls' theory are presented in that book, a subsequent book modified and explained many details, so this later work is used extensively here as well: J Rawls, *Political Liberalism* (Columbia University Press, 1993).

he asks the following question: what are the minimum conditions in terms of rules and political institutions that a reasonable person, who is ignorant of what goals and preferences he or she may have and how successful in achieving them he or she will prove to be (a condition known as the 'veil of ignorance'), would set before agreeing to become a member of a society that had the power of coercion over its citizens? One condition, for instance, might be a requirement that all important decisions should be taken democratically or at least through some representative democratic process. Another condition that a reasonable person would probably require is that punitive coercion should not be exercised without a fair trial in accordance with the law. This line of reasoning quickly builds up support for the view that a democratic political system governed by the rule of law would be the conditions set by the reasonable person. Rawls uses this method of argument to insist that the reasonable person would in fact demand that the political arrangements should include some inalienable and inviolable individual rights. Without following all the intricacies of Rawls' arguments, is it possible to use this method of philosophical reasoning about the basic conditions of justice in a society in order to construct essential or fundamental labour rights, which in turn would provide the theoretical foundation for a system of labour law?

It is important to understand that Rawls' method in *A Theory of Justice* does not produce a blueprint for an ideal society, the goal towards which we should be aiming. He is merely concerned to articulate what kind of insurance or minimum guarantees that a rational person would demand before willingly submitting himself or herself to a political association with the power of coercion. He argues that these guarantees would comprise firm protection for some individual rights and a fairly rudimentary criterion for steering the economy towards a pattern of welfare distribution that protects to some extent the position of the least well off. These are the two principles of justice that he argues would emerge from rational deliberation.

(a) Each person has an equal right to a fully adequate scheme of equal basic liberties which is compatible with a similar scheme of liberties for all.

(b) Social and economic inequalities are to satisfy two conditions. First, they must be attached to offices and positions open to all under conditions of fair equality of opportunity; and second, they must be to the greatest benefit of the least advantaged members of society.[28]

Rawls acknowledges that the model he produces may not be suitable for all societies, though it should be applicable to all developed societies.

Can we use this method of justification for fundamental rights as a philosophical grounding for protection of fundamental labour rights that would provide the basic principles on which labour law might be constructed? These rights would not be the same as universal human rights, owed to every individual simply by virtue of being a human. This method necessarily confines the rights to those who have

---

[28] *Political Liberalism*, above n 27, 291.

(hypothetically) consented to becoming a member of a community. The purpose of fundamental rights or 'equal basic liberties' in Rawls' scheme is to provide essential guarantees for the individual against the potential misuse of power by the state. These rights are intended to provide an inviolable protection for the individual, even when the state may be pursuing beneficent purposes such as seeking to improve the welfare of society as a whole. The rights place constraints on the pursuit of welfare goals (as well as less attractive goals such as oppression, discrimination, and terror). The rights define certain basic interests of individuals, which they will not rationally wish to jeopardize, even in return for the benefits of membership of an ordered society. Most importantly, the rights represent a special group of individual interests that are so important that they should always (subject perhaps to wartime conditions, national emergencies, and the like) trump countervailing considerations such as welfare and social justice.

Readers familiar with Rawls' works will be aware that he does not reach the conclusion that fundamental labour rights would be agreed during the hypothetical bargain between reasonable people. But that is beside the point here, because the aim is to use Rawls' philosophical method rather than adopt his precise conclusions, and Rawls himself invites a continuing dialogue to refine his conclusions. Nevertheless, it is worth noticing how close Rawls comes to providing foundations for the subject of labour law, and why, ultimately, he does not do so.

1. The argument for fundamental rights

Assuming (behind the veil of ignorance) that the rational person does not know whether he will be an employer, a worker, or unemployed, but he or she knows that in a market economy most people earn the necessary income to support themselves and their families by taking a job, and that workers spend a large proportion of their time in the workplace and forge many of their social relations and opportunities through their experience in the workplace, what protective guarantees would the rational person insist upon? Rawls argues at length for the view that a rational person would conclude that everyone is very strongly committed to certain individual interests, which he names 'primary goods'. He identifies five kinds of primary goods, which are, in summary: (1) civil and political liberties such as freedom of thought; (2) freedom of movement and free choice of occupation against a background of diverse opportunities; (3) powers and prerogatives of offices and positions of responsibility; (4) income and wealth; (5) the social bases of self-respect, so that the basic institutions protect the citizens in developing a sense of their own worth as persons and enable them to advance their aims and ends with self-confidence.[29]

---

[29] *Political Liberalism*, above n 27, 308–9. This list of primary goods omits some undoubted primary goods such as subsistence and security: H Shue, *Basic Rights: Subsistence, Affluence, and US Foreign Policy* (Princeton University Press, 1980). Rawls seems to presuppose that these basic conditions will be met in a just society with a certain level of economic development, though security interests may be covered to some extent by the civil liberties protected under the first principle of justice, and subsistence could be met by the Difference Principle.

Each of these primary goods has considerable bearing on the workplace and labour law, some more obviously than others. Item (2) amounts to what is often meant by the idea of the right to work. Item (4) is similarly closely approximate to the right to fair remuneration. The other primary goods in Rawls' list can also without difficulty be related to the workplace. Accepting that the workplace necessarily involves constraints on freedom and some kind of hierarchical organization for the purposes of efficient coordination, it is not difficult to anticipate that some civil liberties under (1) such as privacy and freedom of association may need protection, that fair treatment in the workplace provides an institutional basis for self-respect under (5),[30] and that under (3), though Rawls has primarily in mind the powers and responsibilities of government, this interest in good government can be applied to the exercise of power by managers. Given the importance of employment in the lives of most people, this close coincidence between the primary goods defined by Rawls and important interests of workers is hardly surprising. It is the next step in Rawls' argument that proves more troubling for the task undertaken here.

He draws his famous distinction between the 'right' and the 'good', and argues for the priority of the right in a scheme of justice. His assumption here, which is characteristic of liberal political theories that value liberty or individual freedom highly, is that citizens have different, incommensurable, and to some extent irreconcilable conceptions of 'the good', or what it is to have a good life, though they should, after reasonable discussion, Rawls believes, accept what he terms the primary goods as basic ingredients for their diverse plans. This reasoning leads to his two principles of justice: in the first principle of justice, the basic liberties viewed as primary goods in (1) above are given priority over all other interests or primary goods. They are protected as rights, whereas other interests take second place, in the second principle of justice. Civil and political rights, which include the right to own personal property, deserve this priority over other interests, according to Rawls, because they guarantee the freedom or capacity necessary to pursue differing conceptions of the good. Freedom of thought or conscience, for instance, is necessary for individuals to develop their own ideas about how to live their lives, rather than to have their plans dictated for them by a particular religion or political ideology. In turn, freedom of thought or conscience needs to be secured in practice by other key rights such as freedom of speech, freedom of association, and freedom of religion. The priority of the civil and political rights is justified because they are essential guarantees of a liberal society, one in which each person can define their own goals and pursue them, capacities which Rawls regards as fundamental moral requirements for a just political system. To secure that priority for civil and political rights, these rights are given priority over the other primary goods. In this sense, the rights are trumps over other welfare and egalitarian policies, which are contained in the second principle of justice, known (in its second phrase) as the Difference Principle.

---

[30] Cf Hepple, above n 82: 'Our rights at work are "precious jewels" that give us a sense of identity, self-worth and emotional well-being and so enable us to contribute to society.'

2. The expansion of fundamental rights to include labour rights

Although these arguments seem highly persuasive ones for providing secure protection for civil and political liberties, the question arises why other primary goods should not also receive an equivalent measure of protection in the basic scheme of justice. Rawls' response to that question is, primarily, that the second principle of justice does provide a significant measure of protection of those interests in other primary goods, with its emphasis on fair equality of opportunity, and the requirement that social and economic equalities should be tolerated only if they are to the greatest benefit of the least advantaged. He then argues that to go any further in the protection of primary goods by giving them a guarantee framed as a right would be 'either irrational or superfluous or socially divisive'.[31] Rawls' argument at this point is essentially that guarantees of other primary goods would lead to inefficiency in markets (which would be irrational to choose), or would be superfluous because of the second principle of justice, which secures adequately or at least as fairly as possible the other primary goods (social justice), or it would be socially divisive because it would lead to competing claims being raised about needs that are essential for particular life plans or conceptions of the good to be pursued.

Let us test this argument against a particular proposal. Suppose, for instance, it was argued that the right not to be unjustly dismissed by an employer should be elevated to the status of a protected right like a civil and political liberty.[32] This right could be justified by reference to a number of the primary goods, perhaps even all of them. For instance, the right might defend workers against interference with their civil liberties by employers, or it might protect workers against being treated with little respect in the workplace. Would the introduction of such a right be irrational, superfluous, or socially divisive?

It would be irrational, according to Rawls, if the right led to inefficiency, such as the undesirable effects of lowering wages and/or levels of employment because the right imposes costs on employers. We return thus to the allegation of inefficiency and harm to welfare made by neo-classical economics against all labour rights. Although simple assumptions about the cost of legally protected rights for workers are open to question on empirical grounds, even if there is a problem with labour rights regarding the creation of inefficiency, that point seems a strange argument for Rawls to rely upon. His principles of justice are deliberately constructed to provide an alternative to welfare maximization or efficiency, in order to protect the freedom of the individual to pursue his or her own conception of the good life. To achieve that freedom adequately requires individual access to the other primary goods, even if that causes some inefficiency. Rights to the benefits of the other primary goods, which might include the right to protection against unjust dismissal, can only be

---

[31] *Political Liberalism*, above n 27, 329.

[32] It is important to note at this point that Rawls does not rule out the possibility that such a law might be chosen by the democratic process as a way of securing primary goods. The question here is whether the right should be elevated to the equivalent status as civil liberties in Rawls' scheme, so that the existence of the right is non-negotiable, a fundamental condition of membership in a just society.

avoided if those goods are secured adequately by the second principle of justice. So this first point collapses into the second claim that rights protecting other primary goods would be superfluous.

Would a right to protection against unjust dismissal be superfluous in view of the second principle of justice? Under the second principle of justice, it seems possible that legislation might be enacted to protect certain interests of workers. Certainly the fair equality of opportunity requirement would mandate anti-discrimination laws. But the implications of the requirement for ensuring that inequalities are arranged in order to maximize the position of the least well off seem to be unclear with respect to many labour rights. This principle could be interpreted to justify a generous social security system funded through taxation rather than to regulate the workplace directly. On that interpretation,[33] workers would not require protection against unjust dismissal, because if they became unemployed as a result of a dismissal, the social security system would provide for their needs. If that interpretation of the second principle of justice is correct, it reveals (in my opinion) how inadequate the principle is in securing the primary goods. It seems to view a job as merely a means to the end of securing an income. Whilst that may be true for some workers, most people attach more significance to their jobs. The job helps to achieve other primary goods such as self-respect, and can be a way of developing other capacities through dialogue and social interaction.[34]

Finally, Rawls argues that to extend the range of protected rights beyond civil and political liberties would be divisive and could not be agreed in the original position. His concern here is that a more detailed scheme of rights would have distributive consequences, so that rational people would (correctly) perceive that claims for rights were really just claims for superior resources, which would inevitably provoke irreconcilable disagreements. He seems to overlook this problem of distributive consequences in his defence of civil and political liberties, which of course involve costs as well.[35] So the fact that there are distributive consequences should not be regarded as a decisive reason for rejecting candidates for rights. The question rather should be whether there are significant distributive consequences, which are likely to provide noticeably unequal or inequitable shares to some people. Civil and political liberties have moderate costs associated with them, and do not lead to unequal shares.[36] Similar arguments may be made about a right not to be unjustly dismissed: the costs to business and the legal system should be modest, and everyone is potentially an employee who would benefit from the protection. Other labour rights, however, such as a minimum wage or equal pay for men and women,

---

[33] This interpretation of limiting the Difference Principle to taxation and welfare provision has been challenged, eg: AT Kronman, 'Contract Law and Distributive Justice' (1980) 89 Yale Law J 472; and KA Kordana and DH Tabachnick, 'Rawls and Contract Law' (2005) 73 Geo Wash L Rev 598.

[34] CL Estlund, 'Working Together: The Workplace, Civil Society, and the Law' (2000) 89 Georgia LJ 1; and A Bogg, *The Democratic Aspects of Trade Union Recognition* (Hart Publishing, 2009).

[35] S Holmes and C Sunstein, *The Cost of Rights: Why Liberty Depends on Taxes* (WW Norton, 1999).

[36] Do accused criminals benefit disproportionately from the institutions associated with the Rule of law? In practice, yes, but presumably everyone is vulnerable to false accusations, so we all benefit from constraints upon such practices.

would more clearly engage Rawls's objection to the inclusion of divisive issues among the protected rights.

These rebuttals to Rawls's argument against social and economic rights do not secure the case for including some labour rights in the privileged group of values under the first principle of justice. More work needs to be done to demonstrate that, in order to secure some or all of the primary goods identified by Rawls, some further rights need to be added, and in particular that some of those rights should be key labour rights. Even so, we can feel reasonably confident that, given the centrality of work in the achievement of primary goods, some special protections for workers might be found to be necessary. It is not difficult, for instance, to see how the primary goods (2) and (4) could be used to justify some version of a 'right to work' that included the liberty to choose an occupation (subject to the capacity to do the job) and the right to be paid (in cash or its equivalent) for the work.[37]

3. The content of the fundamental labour rights

Without exploring in any further detail how Rawls's method might be employed to justify at least some labour rights becoming fundamental constitutional guarantees, enough has been said, I hope, to explain at least the potential of this method for providing foundations for a system of labour law. Before leaving this investigation, however, it is necessary to highlight a probable implication of this method for grounding labour law in fundamental individual rights. This implication is that the fundamental rights seem more likely to secure individual employment rights than rights to collective bargaining and to strike.

To understand why this is so, recall that Rawls's method requires one to ask what guarantees an individual would require before accepting subjection to a state under the circumstance that the individual is ignorant of his or her lot in life. Even behind this veil of ignorance, it seems plausible that an individual would be concerned about enjoying a right to work, given how important work can be for income, meaning, and a sense of self-worth. Furthermore, it seems likely that the rights produced by Rawls' mode of reasoning about a hypothetical contract would emphasize the significance of civil liberties in the workplace, though this concern has not, at least historically, been at the forefront of issues addressed by labour law. If the rational person is worried, for instance, about the protection of privacy from surveillance by the government, so too would that person be concerned about similar intrusions by other powerful actors such as employers. This concern for civil liberties could extend to freedom of association, including the freedom to join a trade union, provided that it was recognized that trade unions function not just to

---

[37] As in Art 6, International Covenant on Social, Economic and Cultural Rights: 'The States Parties to the present Covenant recognize the right to work, which includes the right of everyone to the opportunity to gain his living by work which he freely chooses or accepts, and will take appropriate steps to safeguard this right.' On the meaning of the right to work: Bob Hepple, 'A Right to Work?' (1981) 10 ILJ 65; G Mundlak, 'The Right to Work: Reflexive Linking of Human Rights and Labour Policy' (2007) 146 International Labour Review 3–4; and J Nickel, 'Is There a Human Right to Employment?' (1978–1979) X Philosophical Forum 149.

serve the economic interests of workers but also to provide a voice for workers in the political process. But behind the veil of ignorance, the individual would not know whether his or her interests might be served or hampered by collective bargaining, or indeed whether or not his or her political beliefs might be favourable or hostile to trade unions. Under these conditions, it seems improbable that all reasonable people would agree to the necessity of having a fundamental guarantee that protects collective bargaining and the right to take industrial action. Instead, these questions would be left to be settled subsequently through the agreed democratic legislative process. If that line of reasoning is correct, this strategy of grounding labour law in fundamental rights would only serve the purpose of guaranteeing some aspects of labour law, particularly those relating to the individual interests of all workers, rather than providing a justification for the necessity of guaranteeing the right to collective bargaining as a constitutional right.

4. Dignity

So far we have concentrated our attention on a particular strand in liberal theories of justice and fundamental rights. Rawls awards paramount place to individual liberty or freedom. Other liberal theorists, whilst also emphasizing liberty, attach greater weight to closely related values such as individual 'autonomy' and 'dignity'. The idea of autonomy is often understood to include not only the negative liberty of freedom from constraints, but also positive freedom to be able to choose a worthwhile and satisfying life.[38] Similarly, the concept of dignity extends beyond freedom of the individual to the opportunity to live a life with respect. A particular attraction of the idea of dignity, complex though it seems on closer investigation,[39] is that it can be regarded as a modern statement of the slogan 'labour is not a commodity', which itself has often been regarded as the guiding thread of justifications for labour law. The significance for our purposes of these other liberal theories is that they seem to offer a greater potential to justify labour rights as fundamental rights.

The emphasis on individual dignity, for instance, leads authors to stress the importance of satisfying the basic material needs of individuals, such as food, shelter, and health care. To ensure this fundamental requirement of justice, these liberal theorists often argue that as well as civil and political liberties, fundamental rights should include social and economic rights, without which civil liberties would be worth little and individual dignity would not be secured. Jeremy Waldron, for instance, makes this argument in two ways.

His first argument is that the protection of civil liberties is not much use to someone who is dying of hunger, suffering from untreated debilitating disease, or who has no shelter or security. Basic needs such as subsistence, shelter, clothing, and health have to be met if the civil liberties so cherished by liberals are to be worth

---

[38] Raz, *The Morality of Freedom* (above n 6).
[39] C McCrudden, 'Human Dignity and Judicial Interpretation of Human Rights' (2008) 19 European J of International Law 655.

UNIVERSITY OF WINCHESTER
LIBRARY

having at all.[40] 'If we truly respect human agency as an end in itself, we must follow that end where it leads and, in the circumstances of human life, that may well require us to attend to the needs of persons whose ability to function as agents is imperilled by poverty or disease or by the fear of those predicaments.'[41] On this general point, there is probably no disagreement with Rawls, who tries to address the problem through his second principle of justice. Waldron seems to conclude from this argument, however, that at least some social and economic rights should be guaranteed, in order to prevent the level of destitution that would deny individuals any dignity at all (that is, undermine their civil liberties). What Waldron does not explain fully is why these needs have to be or should be satisfied by the establishment of rights in the strong sense. Presumably his point is that if civil liberties have to be protected as rights, necessary conditions for the enjoyment of those rights must also be defended as rights.

Waldron's second argument more directly addresses this issue of the priority of socio-economic claims. The argument now is that 'any moral theory of individual dignity' is plainly inadequate if it does not take issues such as death, disease, malnutrition, and economic despair into account.[42] He argues that the best way to express this moral imperative to address basic human needs in political discourse is to give the claims of the needy the strong claim provided by the language of rights. These rights in Waldron's analysis are addressed to the state, which is under a correlative duty to coordinate efforts to meet these needs through progressive taxation, the institutions of the welfare state, and other regulation. He correctly observes that this framework necessitates the weakening of the priority attached to respect for private property in most liberal theories, so that any right to peaceful enjoyment of possessions must be qualified by the need to satisfy basic social and economic rights through taxation and redistribution.[43] Furthermore, because social and economic rights make demands for scarce resources, these rights cannot have quite the same peremptory force that might be attributed to some civil and political liberties. Nevertheless, Waldron concludes that in a society concerned deeply about the dignity and autonomy of individuals, ultimately social and economic rights are just the other side of the coin from civil and political liberties.

Although Waldron makes a compelling case for the recognition of some social and economic rights in a liberal political theory based upon autonomy and dignity, his arguments may not extend so far as to encompass most labour rights, but may be confined to claims that relieve destitution or provide a social minimum standard of living or satisfy urgent moral demands for food, shelter, and perhaps health care and education.[44] Indeed, given the scarcity of resources, there would have to be

---

[40]   Cf H Shue, *Basic Rights: Subsistence, Affluence, and US Foreign Policy* (Princeton University Press, 1980) 19: 'Rights are basic in the sense used here only if enjoyment of them is essential to the enjoyment of all other rights.' It is not clear, however, how any right could satisfy such a stringent test: T Pogge, 'Shue on Rights and Duties' in CR Beitz and RE Goodin (eds), *Global Basic Rights* (Oxford University Press, 2009) 113, 122.

[41]   Waldron, above n 18, 8.
[42]   Waldron, above n 18, 11.
[43]   Waldron, above n 18, 18–22.
[44]   Nickel, above n 19, 139.

trade-offs between these social and economic rights, and some, such as the right to a paid holiday, might not be achievable at all (whilst meeting other basic needs). Even worse than this conclusion for our project seeking a justification for labour law, if we concentrate our attention on basic material needs, such as food, shelter, and clothing, as Waldron tends to do to make his argument rhetorically powerful, it is unclear that the issues addressed by labour law regarding the labour market and the workplace are really necessary features of imperative social rights at all. Although it is true that most people are likely to satisfy their basic needs of this kind through paid employment, it does not follow that it is necessary for there to be labour rights or that to address those needs the state would have to regulate employment. A government could instead simply say that if the labour market failed to satisfy basic needs or social rights, the welfare state would do so through the provision of income or free services. This problem is essentially the same as the one identified in Rawls' work: the Difference Principle can be satisfied by taxation and welfare benefits, without the insertion of individual or collective labour rights into the basic constitution of society. In short, there is a distinct possibility that this route for justifying labour law by means of providing a compelling philosophical argument for social and economic rights would end up providing no justification at all for labour rights and a labour law system based upon it.

C. Conclusion

Before trying to state a conclusion to be drawn from these philosophical reflections, it is perhaps helpful to restate the nature of the enquiry conducted here and to point out the issues that have not been addressed. The question posed has been a narrow one. In view of the challenges to the existence of labour law emanating from theories of welfare and efficiency, is it possible to identify firm philosophical grounds for justifying the need for a labour system in a theory of fundamental or constitutional rights?

An answer to that question does not address in any detail a host of other questions that might be asked about labour law and rights. Using human rights as a strategic rhetoric may serve labour activists well in some instances, even if we conclude that the philosophical grounding of labour rights as human rights is poor or non-existent. Similarly, employment lawyers may find that they can succeed in advancing certain kinds of claims by invoking the rights contained in Bills of Rights and other legally binding conventions. Again, any weakness of philosophical underpinnings for labour rights should not deter lawyers from adopting these legal strategies to serve worthwhile ends. Nor do any doubts about the strength of claims for labour rights prevent us from trying to describe and analyse existing labour laws from the perspective of individual and group rights. On the contrary, there is good reason to believe that such a description may provide great insights into the central issues of the subject. Nor should the discussion cast any doubt on the validity of the strategy of using politics and the law to require states to achieve a social minimum for their citizens, as described in a charter of social and economic rights. Finally, it is worth observing that in so far as ideas of labour rights have been linked to concerns to prevent detrimental effects on workers resulting from the intensification of competition between economies, the problem remains and is probably worsening, so that the case for seeking agreement on and enforcement of core labour standards remains as compelling as ever.[45]

The purpose of this chapter has been far narrower than the important issues raised in the previous paragraph. The enquiry has been about the justifications for a distinct scheme of legal regulation known as labour law. If (and this is a big 'if') the traditional justifications for labour law in terms of welfare or social justice have ceased to be convincing, is it possible to articulate a plausible case for the need for labour law based on a doctrine of fundamental rights? This doctrine would employ rights as powerful exclusionary reasons, so that the rights would override other considerations, in particular concerns about efficiency. To do the job assigned to them in this philosophical enquiry, the rights would have to possess this strong or urgent quality, but at the same time they would have to be sufficiently concrete to provide credible foundations for a body of law that resembles current labour law systems. None of the theories we have considered quite match up to these demands.

A doctrine of universal human rights, based upon natural law ideas, satisfies the test of possessing the quality of a moral imperative, but it was argued above that the sorts of labour rights that might provide the foundation for a labour law system do not share a similar moral imperative force. The inclusion of labour rights in political proclamations of universal human rights was explained as a method for addressing problems arising from globalization of the economic system, not as a coherent articulation of any philosophical doctrine regarding universal human rights with a suitably strong moral imperative force.

A more promising line of argument turned out to be an adaptation of the philosophical methods used in liberal political theory. The central idea in liberalism of identifying fundamental interests of individuals, such as freedom and dignity, and guaranteeing them through a strong legal framework, seems to have the potential of justifying some fundamental labour rights. Running counter to that potential, however, was a willingness in liberal theories to relegate the task of defending basic economic interests, such as those addressed by the right to work, through welfare measures funded from general taxation rather than constitutionalizing labour rights along with civil liberties. Rawls' theory was criticized in this respect, because even though he recognized the significance of work to individuals in his list of primary goods, his two principles of justice only partly respond to this urgent demand by providing a justification for anti-discrimination laws. Some labour rights, such as a right to work, might also have to be included in a coherent restatement of liberal principles of justice in order to provide sufficient guarantees of the primary goods. From a core right, such as the right to work, it should be possible to derive support for other fundamental rights, such as general protection

---

[45] Arthurs, above n 9, 51; and K Banks, 'The Impact of Globalization on Labour Standards' in Craig and Lynk, above n 9, 77.

against discrimination on grounds unrelated to job performance and protection against unjust dismissal. Furthermore, the need to protect civil liberties against oppression by employers would also have to be included in a coherent liberal theory of justice. But the individualistic approach of liberal political theory does not readily embrace collective or group rights, so the elevation of solidarity rights, such as the right to strike, to constitutional status might not be warranted within this theoretical framework.

10

The Contribution of Labour Law to Economic and Human Development

*Simon Deakin**

A. Introduction: law, growth, and development

For the past two decades the debate over law and development has been dominated by the view, generally referred to as the 'Washington consensus', that countries should adapt their institutions to a global template based on constitutional guarantees for private property, a minimalist state, and the liberalization of trade and capital flows.[1] In the context of labour law, the Washington consensus proceeded on the basis that 'laws created to protect workers often hurt them'.[2] This approach was used in numerous countries to resist calls for the extension of labour laws and to initiate programmes of deregulation. The economic growth generated by the policies of the Washington consensus was uneven in its impact across countries and regions[3] and unequal in terms of its distributional effects.[4] Since the financial crisis of 2008, this growth has stalled, particularly in the so-called advanced industrial economies, and poverty and unemployment have risen sharply in more or less all countries.[5]

* This chapter draws on a longer paper written as part of a report to the ILO in 2010 (S Marshall (ed), *Promoting Decent Work: The Role of Labour Law*, report to DIALOGUE section, ILO (2010)). I am grateful to Shelley Marshall, Corinne Vargha, and Colin Fenwick for feedback on that work and for permission to republish part of it here. I would also like to thank participants at the 'Idea of Labour Law' workshop in Cambridge in April 2010 for comments.

[1] See H-J Chang, 'Understanding the Relationship between Institutions and Economic Development – Some Key Issues' in H-J Chang (ed), *Institutional Change and Economic Development* (United Nations University Press, 2007) 20.

[2] World Bank, *Doing Business 2009* (International Bank for Reconstruction and Development, 2008) 19.

[3] J Stiglitz, *Globalisation and its Discontents* (Allen Lane, 2002).

[4] AB Atkinson, T Piketty, and E Saez, 'Top Incomes in the Long Run of History', NBER Working Paper No 15408 (2009). The rise in inequality over the past 30 years has been driven by an increase in the shares of the top 5 per cent, 1 per cent, and even 0.1 per cent of the income distribution. This trend is particularly marked in the USA, UK, India, and China, but is not found in Japan or most of mainland Europe, suggesting that national institutional differences, including those derived from labour law, have an impact on inequality rates, which are therefore not simply the consequence of globalization.

[5] See IMF/ILO, *The Challenges of Growth, Employment and Social Cohesion*, Discussion Document, Joint ILO–IMF conference in cooperation with the office of the Prime Minister of Norway, Oslo, August 2010 (<http://www.osloconference2010.org/discussionpaper.pdf>).

Thus the time is right for a reappraisal of the developmental model which has informed economic policy and institutional reform, labour law reform included, since the early 1990s.

This chapter will seek to show that labour law has an important contribution to make to development, broadly understood as a process of modernization involving the emergence of market relations within a polity organized around an effectively managed and democratically accountable state.[6] Theoretical perspectives and empirical evidence will be called in aid to explain how labour law assists economic growth by underpinning and facilitating the operation of labour markets in various ways. The contribution of labour law rules to a broader developmental agenda, centred on the strengthening of democratic institutions and respect for human rights,[7] will also be addressed. It will be argued that labour law rules can be seen as one of a number of means for advancing human capabilities, whether understood in a generic sense as the substantive freedoms individuals have to achieve desired social and economic goals,[8] or more specifically as a set of 'functional capabilities', ranging from bodily integrity to social affiliation, which it is the role of institutions to promote.[9]

The relationship between development in the narrow sense of economic growth, and the wider set of goals associated with the concept of human development is a complex one. Labour law rules, and labour market institutions more generally, can be understood as offsetting some of the more dislocating effects of rapid economic development, and hence of constraining economic growth in the interests of a set of more broadly defined developmental goals. But the idea of a trade-off should not be pushed too far. In many contexts, growth and development complement each other. One of the principal functions of labour law is to reconcile the two, so that, as far as possible, economic growth is rendered compatible with human development in the wider sense of that term.[10]

Part of the approach taken to defining law and development in this chapter is the idea that development is a continuing process, which affects all countries which have undergone or are undergoing the transition to a market-based economic system. To view development this way has a number of implications. The first is that the law and development debate is just as much concerned with analysing and understanding the process by which markets and legal systems emerged alongside one another in those countries which were the first to experience industrialization, as it is about the present-day context of countries which are at a different stage of

[6] J Stiglitz, 'Towards a New Paradigm for Development', 9th Raúl Prebisch Lecture, UNCTAD, 19 October 1998 (<http://www.unctad.org/en/docs/prebisch9th.en.pdf>).
[7] K Kolben, 'Labour Regulation, Human Capacities and Industrial Citizenship' in S Marshall (ed), *Promoting Decent Work: The Role of Labour Law*, report to DIALOGUE section, ILO (2010).
[8] A Sen, *Development as Freedom* (Oxford University Press, 1999) 86.
[9] M Nussbaum, *Women and Human Development: The Capabilities Approach* (Cambridge University Press, 2000) 75.
[10] S Deakin and F Wilkinson, *The Law of the Labour Market: Industrialisation, Employment, and Legal Evolution* (Oxford University Press, 2005) 353.

that process. Second, it serves as a reminder that many developmental goals have not been met in the so-called advanced market economies. These are countries which have very far from succeeded in combining economic growth with social cohesion. Indeed, since the neoliberal policy turn of the 1980s, they have all, in varying degrees, achieved growth only by allowing unemployment to rise and inequality to return to levels last experienced in the early decades of the 20th century.[11] If this represents a model of development, it is one which is radically incomplete, and which shows signs of regressing. Third, and relatedly, the approach adopted here implies a rejection of the idea that the experience of North America and Western Europe necessarily provides a model for other systems to follow. This is not to say that countries undergoing development do not face certain common constraints or problems, in the context of which particular functional solutions may have general validity. The institution of wage labour may, in that sense, be more or less universal to societies undergoing the transition from a traditional economy to one based on a market-orientated division of labour. However, the ways in which systems respond to the emergence of wage labour may differ considerably from one country to another, and in particular may be shaped by local conditions in such a way as to limit the effectiveness of institutions when transplanted to different contexts. The association of 'best practice' with the institutions of those countries which have historically had higher living standards than others, or which, at a given time, are experiencing more rapid economic growth, may turn out to be mistaken.

To address the issues set out above requires, in the first place, a reconsideration of the concepts used to describe the relationship between labour law and labour markets. This is set out in section B below, which contrasts the neoclassical and new institutional approaches which have tended to predominate in recent analyses, with a systemic view which sees labour law rules as coevolving with market-based forms of economic relations. Section C provides an empirical illustration of the systemic approach, using the example of the historical development of social insurance systems. Section D considers aspects of the experience of labour law in developing and transition economies, and section E surveys evidence on the relationship between labour law and measures of human development. Section F concludes.

B. Theoretical perspectives on the relationship of labour law to labour markets

Within contemporary social and economic theory three distinct positions on the role of labour law with relation to labour markets can be identified, which may be characterized respectively as *neoclassical*, *new-institutional*, and *systemic*.

---

[11] Atkinson, Piketty, and Saez, 'Top Incomes', above n 4.

1. Neoclassical approaches

The neoclassical view sees labour law regulation as an external intervention in, or interference with, the market. As such, it is liable to distort the operation of supply and demand. The result will be to reduce economic growth in various ways.[12] This is the standard neoclassical view of, for example, minimum wage regulation. If employers are legally prohibited from providing jobs at wages which they can afford to pay, and workers, conversely, are prevented from offering to work under such conditions, market prices (here, wages) cannot operate to allocate resources to alternative uses as they normally would. The result is a deadweight loss to society, which is expressed in higher unemployment for workers, reduced profitability for firms, or some combination of the two, with further knock-on effects impacting negatively on economic development.[13]

The basic claim of the neoclassical approach is that autonomous decision-making by individual agents (workers and employers) can lead to an outcome which is in the interests of society as a whole. Regulation is seen as the expression of sectional, collective interests.[14] Labour laws enacted with a redistributive end in mind can be seen as involving a trade-off between equity and efficiency. Thus countries which maintain extensive labour law regulations are effectively making a choice which implies lower growth and reduced development, in favour of certain social goals such as a more egalitarian income distribution.

The view that labour regulation has a *market-limiting* function is not confined to neoclassical economics. Non-economic justifications for labour law which view protective legislation as 'decommodifying' labour relations take a similar position but, more or less explicitly, view the trade-off between efficiency and equity which this involves in a different, more positive light.[15]

However, neoclassical theory cautions that the trade-offs involved in regulation are likely to be complex, and that the belief that labour law necessarily promotes fairer outcomes may be misguided. Labour law rules, it is suggested, tend to benefit some workers (for example, those in stable employment) at the expense of others (the unemployed and excluded who cannot find work). Thus there is an ethical case, as well as one based on efficiency, for deregulation, which will help the poorest and most vulnerable in society by assisting their reintegration into the labour market.

2. New institutionalist approaches

Neoclassical models of the kind just described are based on the assumption that, in general, markets tend to self-adjust. Thus, in the absence of labour law regulation,

---

[12] For an overview of these arguments, see B Kaufman, 'Labor Law and Employment Regulation: Institutional and Neoclassical Perspectives' in K Dau-Schmidt, S Harris, and O Lobel (eds), *Labor and Employment Law and Economics* (Edward Elgar, 2009) 3–14.

[13] The classic statement of this position is by G Stigler, 'The Economics of Minimum Wage Legislation' (1946) 36(3) American Economic Review 358–65.

[14] R Posner, 'Some Economics of Labor Law' (1984) 51 University of Chicago Law Review 988–1004.

[15] A Okun, *Equality and Efficiency: The Big Tradeoff* (Brookings Institution, 1975) 10–17.

the labour market is in equilibrium. This position is challenged by new-institution-alist perspectives which view unregulated labour markets as affected by imperfections of various kinds, including transaction costs, information asymmetries and externalities. The presence of imperfections can give rise to an efficiency-based case for intervention.[16]

A relevant example is again provided by minimum wage regulation. Where employers are able to act as monopsonists (that is, as 'monopoly buyers'), they have the power to depress wages below the market-clearing rate. As wages are then 'artificially' low, workers have less incentive to offer their labour to employers and so labour supply is reduced. Minimum wage legislation, by restoring wages to a level closer to the market-clearing rate, can bring about a simultaneous increase in both wages and employment. The surplus which employers were previously able to capture by virtue of their monopsony power absorbs the extra costs of employing additional workers. Society as a whole is better off because resources are now being more efficiently allocated.[17]

The monopsony-based case for the minimum wage illustrates the 'market-correcting' role of labour law; that is, its use as a mechanism for correcting the effects of market failures. However, the same example highlights some potential problems with this approach. The first is that the nature and extent of supposed market failures or imperfections need to be carefully identified. Neoclassical economics accepts, in principle, the validity of regulation in situations of monopsony, but doubts that the phenomenon of employer power is widespread in practice.[18] A new institutionalist response might be that the case of monopsony should be understood as part of a wider problem of asymmetric information in labour markets. For markets to self-correct, economic agents must be well informed not just about prevailing prices but also about alternative trading possibilities. Employer power may result not simply from the absence of competition between potential buyers of labour services, but also from the limited information available to workers concerning alternative employment opportunities.[19]

Information asymmetries can be invoked to explain other forms of labour law regulation, such as unfair dismissal legislation.[20] In principle, employers might contract to offer job security guarantees in order to induce workers to invest in firm-specific skills. Prior to the hiring, however, workers may find it difficult to judge whether employers' commitments to long-term, stable employment are serious. Thus employers may not offer, and/or workers may not be prepared to accept, contractual arrangements which would otherwise be in their mutual interest. Unfair dismissal legislation makes the employer's commitment to job security more credible, thereby promoting efficient contracting.

---

[16] Stiglitz, 'New Paradigm', above n 6.
[17] A Manning, *Monopsony in Motion: Imperfect Competition in Labor Markets* (Princeton University Press, 2003) 15–16.
[18] Kaufman, 'Labor Law and Employment Regulation', above n 12, 17–18.
[19] Manning, *Monopsony*, above n 17, 132.
[20] See DI Levine, 'Just-Cause Employment Policies in the Presence of Worker Adverse Selection' (1991) 9(3) Journal of Labor Economics 294–305.

The basic claim of new institutionalist approaches is that autonomous decision making by economic agents may lead to societally beneficial outcomes, but only under certain conditions, and that regulation may be needed to bring these outcomes about or to adjust for their absence. To the extent that markets are not perfectly competitive, relevant information concerning prices and quality is not costlessly available, and the factors of production are not completely mobile, there is scope for intervention on efficiency grounds. The suggestion that labour law regulations act upon markets which are already at the equilibrium point is seen as implausible.[21] To this extent, new institutionalist perspectives offer a refutation of neoclassical arguments for deregulation.

However, it is more difficult to show the converse, namely that labour law regulations can be justified on efficiency grounds using the new institutionalist approach. The problem lies in knowing what the hypothetical equilibrium point would look like in practice. For example, it seems unlikely that minimum wage laws can accurately mimic the market clearing wage, or that unfair dismissal laws precisely reproduce the terms of hypothetically perfect employment contracts. Realistically, labour law regulations can only be regarded as offering approximate solutions for the effects of market failure. They *may* lead to improvements the resource allocation function of markets and, more generally, to societal well-being, but they may not do so in a consistent way across different market contexts.

A further dimension to this argument is the possibility that solutions to market failures can be expected to emerge on the basis of private ordering, making legal solutions unnecessary. Private solutions to information asymmetries may emerge, for example, in the form of 'signalling'.[22] Firms with the capacity to offer secure and rewarding employment may find ways to signal this to employees by absorbing certain costs (for example, by setting up occupational benefit schemes) which their less productive rivals may be unable to meet. More productive employees, conversely, can signal their potential value to employers by being willing to undertake firm-specific training at their own expense in the form of reduced wages in the early years of employment. Thus contractual practices can emerge 'spontaneously' in such a way as to address the problem of asymmetric information.[23] Norms based on a particular firm or industry's practices are more likely to be attuned to parties' needs than solutions imposed by statute.[24] This is not, in itself, a particularly strong objection to labour law regulation, much of which has the objective of creating an appropriate environment for private ordering rather than imposing particular distributional outcomes.[25] However, it suggests that the choice of regulatory mechanism can be expected to have efficiency implications.

---

[21] Ibid 58.
[22] G Akerlof, 'Labor Contracts as a Partial Gift Exchange' (1982) 97 Quarterly Journal of Economics 543–69.
[23] M Spence, 'Job Market Signaling' (1973) 87 Quarterly Journal of Economics 355–74.
[24] Kaufman, 'Labor Law and Employment Regulation', above n 12, 43–4.
[25] See Kolben, 'Labour Regulation', above n 7.

3. Systemic approaches

New institutionalist approaches use abstract economic-theoretical insights to generate a potential case for the efficiency-enhancing effects of labour law rules in a relatively narrow range of contexts. Approaches which are informed by new institutional economics but which, at the same time, take an empirically informed, comparative and historical view of the development of economic institutions, see labour law as having a more far-ranging, 'market-constituting' role. These theories view labour markets institutions not as exogenous variables acting on a largely self-constituting labour market, but as endogenous governance mechanisms which emerge out of particular economic and political contexts.[26] Thus the relationship between institutions and markets is one of systemic interaction.

According to this perspective, labour law rules are seen as evolved or emergent solutions to coordination problems in particular market contexts.[27] These solutions are based on distributional compromises which are often contingent in nature; the arrangements they embody are not necessarily optimal and may not be particularly stable.[28] However, they are capable of contributing to economic growth and to development more generally in a number of ways.

The basic insight here is that rational economic behaviour in market settings depends on an institutional framework, part of which is legal in nature. Institutions assist market-based exchange by identifying property rights and stabilizing contractual expectations, but also by providing solutions to coordination problems arising from the presence of transaction costs and externalities, which would otherwise tend to limit the scope of markets. While the economic institutions which perform these functions originate and operate beyond the legal system, they are underpinned by the legal order in various ways. The legal and economic systems have coevolved, in the sense of developing in parallel with each other in particular national or regional contexts. More specifically, the principal institutions of labour law – the individual employment relationship, collective bargaining and social insurance – have evolved in parallel with the emergence of labour markets in market economies.[29] Labour law institutions serve certain functional ends which are specific to societies in which labour markets are established – that is to say, societies in which a significant proportion of the adult population is engaged in waged or salaried labour of some kind.

This perspective on labour law is not confined to the more developed economies. For example, there is a long tradition of labour law regulation in Latin America,

---

[26] See J Howe, R Johnstone, and R Mitchell, 'Constituting and Regulating the Labour Market for Social and Economic Purposes' in C Arup, P Gahan, J Howe, R Johnstone, R Mitchell, and A O'Donnell (eds), *Labour Law and Labour Market Regulation* (Federation Press, 2006) 311.

[27] A Hyde, 'What is Labour Law?' in G Davidov and B Langille (eds), *Boundaries and Frontiers of Labour Law* (Hart Publishing, 2006).

[28] S Deakin and P Sarkar, 'Assessing the Long-run Economic Impact of Labour Law Systems: A Theoretical Reappraisal and Analysis of New Time Series Data' (2008) 39 Industrial Relations Journal 453–87, 455.

[29] Deakin and Wilkinson, *The Law of the Labour Market*, above n 10.

which saw the emergence of mature forms of collective bargaining and social insurance in the middle decades of the 20th century. These arrangements were put into question in the period of neoliberal ascendancy which began in the 1970s, but there has been a more recent switch in policy which has seen a renewed emphasis on collective wage determination and solidaristic forms of social security.[30] In India, substantial labour law reforms were introduced in the immediate post-colonial period of the 1940s and again in the 1970s. The liberalization of the economy which began in the 1980s and intensified in the following decades has not seen a fundamental change in the structure of these laws.[31] There has recently been a major recodification and extension of labour legislation in China, and labour law reform is currently a live issue in a number of other East Asian countries.[32] In South Africa, labour law reforms played a central role in the transition from apartheid to a democratic political order which recognized a place for social rights in legal and constitutional discourse.[33] In the former communist systems of Central and Eastern Europe, the transition to a market system has been accompanied by attempts to install social security systems to deal with the economic and social risks which arose from the ending of centralized control of the economy.[34]

The universality of labour law strongly suggests that it has a functional relationship of some kind to the spread of market economies and of democratic political institutions, but the fit is not exact. The relevance of western conceptions of labour law to developing countries are often questioned on grounds which include the limited coverage of labour law norms in those countries and problems over enforcement, both of which are associated with the phenomenon of labour informality.[35] To argue that there is a fundamental difference of kind (as opposed to one of degree) between the contexts of developed and developing countries, however, is to overstate the case. Problems of the incomplete coverage of labour law, and of gaps between the formal law and its operation in practice, are present in many developed country contexts. Moreover, the persistence, in developing country contexts, of traditional forms of support for social risks (including family structures and access to the land) means that the issue of labour law coverage often takes on a different significance in those contexts. Labour law mechanisms may have direct relevance only for a minority of the workforce in most developing country contexts, but this does not reduce their importance for those who do not have access to the land or to familial arrangements for the pooling of social risks.

---

[30] L Fraile, 'Lessons from Latin America's Neoliberal Experiment: An Overview of Labour and Social Policies since the 1980s' (2010) 148 International Labour Review 215–33.

[31] S Deakin, P Lele, and M Siems, 'The Evolution of Labour Law: Calibrating and Comparing Regulatory Regimes' (2007) 146 International Labour Review 133–62, 148–9.

[32] See World Bank, *Doing Business 2009*, above n 2, 7.

[33] See P Benjamin, 'Beyond "Lean" Social Democracy: Labour Law and the Challenge of Social Protection' (2006) 60 Transformation 32–57.

[34] C Spieser, 'Post-1989 Poland as a Laboratory for the Politics and Policies of Labour Market Adjustment', paper presented to ESRC Seminar *East Meets West*, 6 November, British Academy, London.

[35] See K Sankaran, 'Labour Market Regulation and the Right to Development' in S Marshall (ed), *Promoting Decent Work*, above n 7.

C. An illustration of the developmental functions of labour law regulation: social insurance systems

The evolution of social insurance offers an illustration of the developmental functions performed by labour law regulation.[36] Social insurance systems provide a degree of protection for workers and households against the social risks inherent in participation in a labour market: in particular, the risk of loss of income through sickness, unemployment, and old age.[37] In pre-modern societies, these risks were channelled through other means, such as access to the land or to extended family structures. Early forms of social insurance developed in western European countries (in particular, Britain, Germany, France, and the Low Countries) through the institution of the poor law prior to industrialization. Poor law systems were more coercive than the social insurance schemes which succeeded them, and provided only partial mitigation of social risks at a time when most individuals and households were not completely dependent on wage labour for subsistence.[38] The displacement of the poor law by comprehensive systems of social insurance took place alongside and in response to the erosion of traditional alternatives to wage labour. It was also a consequence of the extension of the democratic franchise in Western European and North American systems in the course of the 19th and early 20th centuries, and the resulting pressure from working class political parties for social reform and in particular for the mitigation of the disciplinary aspects of the poor law and its equivalents.[39] This is the sense in which social insurance systems, democratic politics, and modern labour markets can be said to have coevolved: they each developed incrementally in response to changes in the other.

This is not equivalent to saying that without institutions of social insurance, industrial development could not have occurred in Western Europe. That is a proposition which, by its nature, is impossible to verify or refute through empirical evidence. Nor can we assume that, without social insurance, industrialization would be impossible in other contexts. Nevertheless, the strong functional continuity which can be observed, from a historical perspective, between social protection and the growth of labour markets suggests that these trends have complemented one another, and that they might be interrelated in other contexts, including those of developing and transition economies.

Social insurance systems have various market-correcting functions. In the absence of state intervention, private schemes for unemployment compensation, for

---

[36] See generally P Köhler and H Zacher (eds), *The Evolution of Social Insurance, 1881 to 1981: Studies of Germany, France, Great Britain, Austria, and Switzerland* (St Martin's Press, 1982); P Baldwin, *The Politics of Social Solidarity: Class Bases of the European Welfare State 1875–1975* (Cambridge University Press, 1990); G Esping-Andersen, *Social Foundations of Post-Industrial Economies* (Oxford University Press, 1999); and Deakin and Wilkinson, *The Law of the Labour Market*, above n 10, ch 3.

[37] Baldwin, *Politics of Social Solidarity* (above n 36) 1.

[38] C Lis and H Soly, *Poverty and Capitalism in Pre-industrial Europe* (Harvester Press, 1979).

[39] Deakin and Wilkinson, *The Law of the Labour Market*, above n 10, 149–75.

example, would tend to insure only workers at low risk of losing their jobs. Systems based on purely private ordering result in under-insurance, the costs of which fall upon the state in the form of residual welfare expenditure, or directly on the more vulnerable workers. There is thus a strong case for social insurance on the grounds of cost-effectiveness as well social cohesion. Social insurance schemes typically bring about a pooling of risks, by bringing all employers and employees in a given industry or country within their scope.[40] They tend to begin as industry-level schemes, normally set up by trade unions but often involving employers as well, and develop into regional or national systems which allow for economies of scale to be captured and, by virtue of their greater scope, promote worker mobility across industries and occupations.[41] Social insurance schemes, their 'decommodifying' effect notwithstanding, thereby contribute directly to the extension of labour markets.

Social insurance schemes also have a market-constituting role. In an economic environment of transition to industrialization, which created a need for wage labour, social insurance schemes offered workers an incentive to operate in the formal (and capitalist) labour market, instead of operating as 'own account' or 'semi-dependent' workers in the informal sector, as farm labourers or as tradesmen in guilds.[42] By providing sources of income which offered an alternative to wages, such as unemployment compensation and retirement pensions, social insurance systems could be said to have contributed to the 'decommodification' of labour in the sense of 'removing it from the orbit of the market', as Karl Polanyi put it in *The Great Transformation*.[43] Yet the same social insurance rules can also be said to have promoted the institution of waged labour, and hence to have performed a 'constitutive' role with regard to labour market relations. The mechanisms through which social insurance mitigated the risks inherent in labour market participation simultaneously normalized the practice of waged labour. Thus conditions attached to the receipt of out-of-work benefits reinforced the duty of members of the active labour force to make themselves available for employment. The risks which social insurance protected against are mostly confined to those affecting employees as a group as opposed to the self-employed. By partitioning the labour force in this way, the first social insurance systems of Western Europe identified the limits of what was conventionally understood as waged employment and thereby defined, in an institutional sense, the boundaries of the labour market. The model they established spread to other developed countries, including those of North America, Australia, and New Zealand, as well as to Latin America and east Asia in the course of the 20th century. The considerable diversity which exists with regard to modes of financing and the structure of benefits provided by such schemes, and their

[40] Esping-Andersen, *Social Foundations of Post-Industrial Economies*, above n 36, 48.
[41] Ibid 22.
[42] Deakin and Wilkinson, *The Law of the Labour Market*, above n 10, 114–15.
[43] K Polanyi, *The Great Transformation: The Political and Economic Origins of our Time* (Beacon Press, 1944) 177.

widely differing degrees of success as income replacement mechanisms, does not detract from their near universal presence in market economies.

Social insurance schemes can be understood as combining efficiency and equity rationales in a way which is characteristic of many labour law institutions. While they correct for various kinds of market failures, and are thereby capable of making a net positive contribution to economic growth and hence to societal well-being, they are also based on distributional compromises which reflect the different degrees of influence of interest groups, particularly at the time of their formation, and they unavoidably benefit certain interests at the expense of others. Depending on precisely how they are framed – from the point of view of how contribution and benefit levels are defined and the extent of their coverage, for example – they can have more or less of a redistributive effect in favour of groups who would otherwise be most exposed to risk. They may, at the same time, create new forms of disadvantage, as, for example, in the treatment historically provided for married women who, in many systems, paid higher contribution rates while in employment and also received lower, 'derivative' benefits based on their marital status.[44] Thus in so far as social insurance schemes combine efficiency and equity rationales, they do so in practice in ways which are often contingent, incomplete, and contestable.

More generally, social insurance schemes very well illustrate the *systemic* nature of labour law rules. Labour law rules are systemic in the sense of working well in particular contexts or environments, within which certain institutions operate in a complementary way to one another. They may fail to operate as intended when these conditions are absent or when the environment changes. Social insurance schemes work well when other institutional mechanisms are in place to ensure a degree of employment stability. Thus they emerged, in the late 19th century, at the same time as efforts at decasualization through the introduction of labour exchanges and with the extension of collective bargaining and minimum wage legislation to previously unorganized trades or industries. They come under pressure, conversely, during periods of prolonged high unemployment in the inter-war period, and their financial stability is currently being threatened in some countries by the growth of precarious work.[45] They have created problems of their own in the form of new moral hazards, causing employers to become more disposed to making workers redundant during downturns[46] and providing governments with opportunities to divert social insurance funds to other ends, both trends which destabilize schemes financially.[47]

Deregulation of labour law, by removing the floor of rights to wages and conditions of employment and limiting employment rights to a core of full-time, 'permanent' workers, puts pressure on social insurance systems, by simultaneously narrowing the contribution base and producing new classes of claimant, including

[44] Esping-Andersen, *Social Foundations of Postindustrial Economies*, above n 36, 50.
[45] Deakin and Wilkinson, *The Law of the Labour Market*, above n 10, 162–3 and 175–95.
[46] G Schmid, 'Transitional Labour Markets and Flexicurity: Managing Social Risks over the Lifecourse', CES Working Paper No 2009.75 (Centre d'Economie de la Sorbonne, 2009).
[47] Deakin and Wilkinson, *The Law of the Labour Market*, above n 10, 187–92.

the working poor.[48] For this reason deregulation in collective and individual labour law tends to occur along with the erosion of social insurance systems and their displacement by systems of social protection based on means-testing, and by the payment of social security benefits (through the tax system) to low-paid workers, as a means of bringing household income up to the level previously provided by collectively guaranteed minimum rates of pay.[49]

The functionality of social insurance schemes in the past is no guarantee of their continued viability under changing market and political conditions. Yet it is also possible that social insurance schemes, again in common with other labour law institutions, are capable of adjusting to new circumstances, as testified by the more recent integration of married women workers into a number of schemes through the use of techniques such as contribution credits. The adaptation of social insurance schemes in the context of the 'flexicurity' model also illustrates the scope for innovation in forms of social protection. In national systems which have successfully combined job mobility with a high level of social protection, 'protective' labour law measures appear to operate in a way which is complementary to those which are more clearly 'facilitative'. Thus in Denmark and Sweden, in addition to high levels of expenditure on active labour market policy and generous unemployment compensation, sector-level collective bargaining operates in such a way as to take wages out of competition, and unions have the legal right to enforce industry-level terms and conditions through industrial action. The effective enforcement of labour standards within the market is complementary to the extensive out-of-market support which these systems provide to the unemployed and job seekers.[50]

D. The operation of labour law regulation in developing and transition systems

1. The feasibility of the diffusion of labour law norms

The emergence of the core institutions of labour law – the institution of the contract of employment, collective bargaining, and social insurance – took place alongside the growth of modern labour markets in the economies of industrialized nation states in the period roughly from the last quarter of the 19th century to the middle of the 20th. This functional continuity between labour law and industrialization need not imply that modern labour law institutions are a necessary precondition of economic development in other countries. It does, however, suggest that labour law institutions are capable of contributing to economic growth and social cohesion in emerging and transitional economies. In particular, they may

---

[48] ILO, *Global Employment Trends: January 2009* (ILO, 2009) 20.
[49] Deakin and Wilkinson, *The Law of the Labour Market*, above n 10, 197–9.
[50] C McLaughlin, 'The Productivity-Enhancing Impacts of the Minimum Wage: Lessons from Denmark and New Zealand' (2009) 47 British Journal of Industrial Relations 327–48.

be able to assist the growth and extension of labour markets in those countries. Nevertheless, the adaptation of labour law mechanisms to developing country contexts is not straightforward.

In developing countries, where normally a minority of the active working population is engaged in wage labour, or where wage labour is still supplemented by access to the land or the support of extended family structures, social protection mechanisms (including social insurance) may only have limited relevance. Similarly, labour law regulations which assume the existence of stable employment, such as employment protection legislation, may only be applicable to a small proportion of the labour force. Thus the simple transplantation, without more, of the labour law systems of developed systems into developing country contexts could lead to a severe mismatch between regulatory mechanisms and the social and economic environments in which they were intended to function.

In western societies, the regulatory mechanisms of labour law developed incrementally, as traditional forms of subsistence were gradually eroded by the rise of modern industry and by urbanization, and wage labour took their place.[51] The incremental, endogenous growth of labour law institutions, which helped ensure their durability in the countries in which they originated, cannot be reproduced in the *same form* in developing country contexts. However, the principle that regulatory mechanisms are most likely to work well when they are matched to local conditions and are able to adapt to the particular growth path of particular national economies is relevant to developing country contexts.

Labour law systems depend on the presence of additional external conditions for their successful operation. These include democratic forms of governance and a functioning state apparatus. Yet, a case can also be made for viewing labour law as a means of promoting democracy and an effective state.[52] A similar logic applies here as in the case of institutions supporting the extension of labour markets: the mechanism is one of parallel development rather than linear causation. Furthermore, it should not be assumed that economic conditions in developing and transition countries are inherently unsuited to labour law reforms.

These themes will be illustrated by two case studies, from developing and transition systems.

2. Case study 1: Labour law reforms in Latin America

In the first half of the 20th century, more or less all Latin American states adopted labour law and social insurance systems which were extensive by the standards then prevailing in Europe and North America. This trend, coupled with the strategy of import-substitution industrialization, led to a steady increase in the workers covered by formal employment arrangements and participating in social insurance schemes.[53] In the 1970s and 1980s these policies were abandoned and most states

---

[51] Baldwin, *Politics of Social Solidarity*, above n 36.
[52] Kolben, 'Labour Regulation', above n 7.
[53] Fraile, 'Lessons from Latin America's Neoliberal Experiment', above n 30.

instead pursued policies based on macroeconomic discipline and 'structural re-forms', including labour law flexibility, deregulation, and privatization. As in Europe during this period, labour law regulation by no means disappeared during the period of neoliberal policy ascendancy. This can be attributed to the continuing influence of organized labour interest groups, but it also suggests a continuing functional role for certain types of labour law regulation, even in liberalized economies. At the same time, labour flexibility increased through the promotion of atypical forms of work, particularly temporary and fixed-term work. Collective bargaining was decentralized in most systems and coverage rates fell. In respect of social security law, changes were more far-reaching. Social insurance schemes were eroded away and replaced by privatized pension arrangements in several countries.

A recent assessment of this period suggests that it did not lead to the expected economic gains. Economic growth was weak: GDP grew at an average of 1 per cent per year between 1990 and 2003, better than the negative growth (0.8 per cent) of the 1980s, but worse than the 2.8 per cent during period of import substitution industrialization from 1960 to 1980. In the same period from 1990 to 2003, economies in East Asia and Pacific grew at an average annual rate of 6.4 per cent and those in south Asia grew at 3.3 per cent. The poverty rate was 48.3 per cent in 1990 and 44 per cent by 2002, but had been 40.5 per cent in 1980. The standard measure of income inequality, the Gini coefficient, increased to 0.514 for the region as a whole, considerably above the international average.[54]

Nor did labour market performance improve during this period. Trade liberal-ization did not lead to an increase in the demand for labour as had been predicted. The employment rate for the region declined from 54.5 to 52.3 per cent, while the labour market participation rate rose from 57.7 to 59.1 per cent between 1990 and 2003. There was not only growing unemployment but also a deterioration in job quality. Six out of ten new jobs were in the informal economy; only five out of ten workers in new employment were participating in social security schemes. Labour market flexibility did not increase formality; informality increased alongside atypi-cal work. Job tenure declined, but the formal and informal sectors were not sharply segmented as there was evidence of high worker mobility between the two, suggesting that the change was not structurally linked to the characteristics of workers or their skill levels but to prevailing employer practices and the legal framework which tolerated or encouraged job instability. There was an increase in wage flexibility which was accompanied by a large fall in the proportion of wages in national income.[55]

Since 2000, however, a turn in social policy away from neoliberalism has seen the rise of the minimum wage in Argentina, Uruguay, Chile, and Brazil; restoration of industry-level bargaining in Argentina and Uruguay; restriction of the use of temporary contracts in Argentina and Bolivia; regulation of subcontracting in Chile and Uruguay; enhancing labour inspection and enforcement in Brazil, Argentina, and Chile; and the introduction of a basic universal pension in Chile.

[54] Ibid 216.
[55] Ibid 225.

In most countries, there has been a reversal of the trend towards informality, with rising coverage of labour law and social security legislation. For example, in Brazil the coverage rate, which had fallen from 50.3 to 44.9 per cent between 1980 and 2002, had risen again to 54.7 per cent by 2009. Labour's share of national income also saw a rise across the region after 2003.[56]

The Latin American experience suggests, first, that it is mistaken to view the core institutions of labour law regulation as necessarily bound up with Western European or North American practice. Labour law in Latin America is not just of long standing, but is durable and adaptable. Second, the ebb and flow of labour legislation is correlated to the success or failure of democratic political institutions. Labour law has been more stable during periods of the extension and consolidation of the democratic franchise. Third, employment informality is not a phenomenon which can be understood independently of political trends and regulatory mechanisms. Much of the rise in informality since the 1980s is a consequence of deregulatory labour law initiatives, and has been shown to be reversible when policy shifts.

3. Case study 2: Social insurance and labour law in Poland

In the early 1990s, Poland inherited a 'state of entitlements' which combined direct management of the economy with elements of universalistic and contribution-based social insurance, particularly with regard to retirement pensions. In the transition from communism, hiring and firing through the employment contract were reintroduced at the same time as economic 'shock therapy' was being delivered through privatization and deregulation. Direct state control of collective bargaining gave way to collective wage determination based on national-level tripartism, leading to the introduction of a minimum wage. The Labour Code was amended in several steps, in the direction of greater flexibility, in particular through the use of fixed-term employment. Unemployment rose from 6 per cent in 1990 to 20 per cent by 2000 and fell back to 10 per cent by 2008; by that stage the employment rate was 51 per cent (just below that in 1990). A generous, contribution-based unemployment compensation scheme was introduced in 1991, but was overly generous (it set levels between the minimum and average wage) and badly designed (there was no previous employment condition), and had to be cut back. Coverage was 79 per cent in 1991 and the replacement rate was 34 per cent. By 2007 coverage was 14 per cent and the replacement rate was 20 per cent.[57] The evolution of the system has been from a short-lived universalistic welfare state, incorporating elements of former entitlements, to a contribution-based model, and then to a residual one based on stricter eligibility rules, means testing, and low levels of benefit. There has been a fragmentation of social protection and

---

[56] M Pochmann, 'What Brazil Learned from Labour Flexibilization in the Late 1990s' (2010) 148 International Labour Review 269–82.

[57] Spieser, 'Post-1989 Poland as a Laboratory', above n 34.

growing segmentation of the labour force into 'insiders' with job security and 'outsiders' in atypical work.[58]

The experience of transition systems such as Poland since the early 1990s emphasizes the sense in which the defining feature of a market-based welfare state system is the pooling and allocation of risks. In communist systems, direct state control of the economy and the maintenance of full employment by administrative action removed the need for this kind of risk pooling. The move to a market economy created a need for labour law institutions, but the transition process exacerbates the difficulty of building effective political coalitions of the kind which are prepared to support solidaristic solutions.

E. Labour law and human development

The association made by the Washington consensus between development and growth has been challenged in the past decade by approaches which seek to make the case for policy to be driven by a wider set of developmental goals, summed up in the notion of 'human development'. The 'capability approach' advanced by Amartya Sen[59] does not necessarily see either the extension of markets or the economic growth which can result from this process in negative terms, but it does see them both as means to a greater end, which Sen describes as the enhancement of individual capabilities. Sen suggests that capabilities should be understood in terms of the degree of substantive freedom that individuals have, in a given physical, environmental, or societal context, to achieve certain states or goals which he calls 'functionings'. Functionings, thought of in this sense as ends which individuals have reason to value, are subjectively defined, although these are not simply the exogenously given preferences of neoclassical economic theory; Sen's account recognizes that external factors, including the possibility of public reasoning or deliberation over social values, play a role in framing notions of functionings and capabilities.[60] Thus ideas, for example, of what an acceptable level of income from waged employment would be, can be expected to differ from one societal setting to another.

Martha Nussbaum's account of capabilities differs from Sen's in stating a set of objectively defined developmental goals which policy should, at a minimum, aim to fulfil.[61] These include 'life', 'bodily health', 'bodily integrity', 'play', the 'ability to control one's environment', and 'affiliation'. This list can be understood as deriving from observation and experience concerning the basic conditions for human well-being in all societies, while at the same time being consistent with the approach to defining fundamental rights set out in legal texts such as the UN Declaration on

---

[58] C Spieser, 'Labour Market Policies in Post-Communist Poland: Explaining the Peaceful Institutionalisation of Unemployment (2007) 21 Politique Européenne 97–132, 108.

[59] Sen, *Development as Freedom*, above n 8, and *The Idea of Justice* (Allen Lane, 2009).

[60] See *The Idea of Justice*, above n 59, ch 11.

[61] Nussbaum, *Women and Human Development*, above n 9.

Human Rights and the International Covenant on Economic, Social and Cultural Rights. Nussbaum is more explicit than Sen in arguing that institutions of a given society or polity should be framed in such a way as to ensure that a minimum, threshold level of well-being, in terms of the basic developmental goals which she describes, is achievable for all citizens.

Despite the differences between them, there are complementarities in the approaches of Sen and Nussbaum and both can be drawn on in applying capability theory to labour law.[62] Nussbaum's developmental goals appear to be directed towards the case of less developed economies rather than to the more fully industrialized ones in which labour law systems tend to be found. It should not, however, be too readily assumed that even these more developed countries have met Nussbaum's conditions for supplying a threshold level of capabilities for all their citizens. Sen's more relativistic account is helpful in providing a basis for adjusting the content of the capability concept to the differences in cross-national levels of development. A capability-based perspective does not require, or even advocate, the simple transplantation of labour market institutions which have developed over decades or centuries, in the context of Western Europe and North America, to other systems. Equally clearly, it would not regard differences in levels of economic development across systems as providing a justification for a global levelling-down of labour laws, as this would negatively impact the capacity of the industrialized economies to meet developmental goals which are consistent with their particular stage of development.

If, as this chapter has argued, labour law norms and associated institutions play a role in constituting the conditions within which labour markets can emerge and then be stabilized, they would directly contribute to the enhancement of individual capabilities in the sense of market access identified by Sen. He has argued that individuals have reason to value certain of the freedoms which labour markets supply, which include freedom from bonded labour and, particularly in the case of women, freedom to work outside the home.[63] Developing Sen's argument, it can be suggested that labour market access, in the sense he refers to, is not simply a consequence of the legal recognition of contract as the foundation of the employment relationship. It also requires the presence of institutions which provide alternatives to more traditional forms of risk allocation (social security law as an alternative to the family and access to the land) and which seek to remove non-legal barriers to market access in the form of social discrimination (equal treatment law).[64]

More generally, labour law rules which have an egalitarian or solidaristic orientation are both cause and consequence of effective democratic institutions which ensure a voice in the political process for groups most exposed to social and economic risks. This implies a role for labour law in not just mitigating the effect

---

[62] See Kolben, 'Labour Regulation, above n 7.

[63] Sen, *Development as Freedom*, above n 7, 113–14.

[64] S Deakin, 'Capacitas: Contract Law, Capabilities, and the Legal Foundations of the Market' in S Deakin and A Supiot (eds), *Capacitas: Contract Law and the Institutional Foundations of a Market Economy* (Hart Publishing, 2009).

of social risks, but in establishing the conditions for effective deliberation in and beyond the workplace, through support for trade unions and other autonomous worker organizations and for the principle of freedom of association in the context of collective bargaining and the right to strike.[65]

Empirical research has a role to play in clarifying the relationship between labour law and developmental outcomes. While the link between labour law economic growth is, as we have seen, both complex and contested, there is less doubt over the positive relationship between strong labour laws and active trade unions, on the one hand, and income equality on the other.[66] In addition, cross-national studies have found a degree of correlation between solidaristic labour law mechanisms, in particular those of social security law, and higher scores on the Human Development Index (HDI).[67] The HDI attempts to provide an alternative measure of development to that of GDP by including, alongside economic indicators, data on a range of health and educational outcomes, such as mortality and literacy rates, so the existence of this statistical link is suggestive of the possible role that labour law rules can play in addressing a broadly defined developmental agenda.

F. Conclusion

This chapter has argued that labour law can contribute to both economic and human development in a number of ways. Development can be understood as a process of modernization involving the emergence of a market-based division of labour, the conditions for which are maintained and guaranteed by an effective state apparatus which includes a legal system. These conditions are not restricted to those identified by the Washington consensus, that is to say, private property, price stability, and trade openness. Labour law systems underpin one of the principal mechanisms of economic and societal coordination in a developed or developing country context, namely the labour market.

In relation to the labour market, labour law mechanisms (broadly defined to include social security law) have a 'market-constituting' role in addition to 'correcting' market outcomes (where they lead to negative externalities) and 'limiting' the market in the interests of a broader conception of individual and societal well-being. Distinguishing between these three functions can be helpful in identifying how labour law contributes to economic and social goals. The market-constituting role tends to get underplayed by critiques of labour law which mistakenly view the market as self-equilibrating. More generally, a 'systemic' conception of labour market institutions is useful in understanding how labour can facilitate development. Labour law rules have coevolved – that is, developed in parallel – with certain

---

[65] Kolben, 'Labour Regulation, above n 7.

[66] R Freeman, 'Labour Market Institutions without Blinders: the Debate over Flexibility and Labour Market Performance', NBER Working Paper No 11286 (2007).

[67] B Ahlering and S Deakin, 'Labour Regulation, Corporate Governance and Legal Origin: A Case of Institutional Complementarity?' (2007) 41 Law and Society Review 865–98. The same study finds an inverse (negative) relationship between the HDI and the strength of creditor protection laws.

economic and political institutions. For example, certain norms on the contract of employment and worker representation grew up alongside developments outside the law in the form of the business enterprise and collective bargaining. The growth of democracy (or, to be more precise, universal suffrage) is also associated with the emergence of labour law rules (because democratic political structures helped to create the coalitions which pressed for labour law reforms).

Thus the answer to the question of how labour law can facilitate development depends on the state of economic and political development in the particular context that is being considered. A certain level of economic development is probably a necessary precondition for a functioning labour law system. However, there is also evidence that certain types of labour law rules can be effective in stimulating development and do not depend on the prior existence of mature economic institutions. Social insurance systems are an example of this: early forms of social insurance developed alongside and, in some cases, preceded industrialization in Western Europe.

The efficiency-based case against labour law regulation which informed the Washington consensus is not as strong as is generally supposed. It rests upon a view of markets as self-equilibrating which, whatever its value as a heuristic model, is remote from the historical conditions under which labour markets emerged in industrial societies, and from the societal contexts in which they currently operate. Labour law systems embody solutions to coordination problems which are capable of promoting economic growth and development in various ways. At the same time, these solutions are based on contingent distributional compromises. As such, they are constantly open to challenge. The operation of labour law rules can also be undermined by shifts in economic and political environments. Thus the question of whether labour law rules help or hinder economic development, or human development in a broader sense, cannot be considered without a close consideration of the contexts in which they operate.

While empirical work is making some progress in establishing the nature of the links between labour law institutions and the achievement of certain social and economic goals, difficult questions remain, particularly in understanding the channels though which labour law systems influence the process of development. Labour law rules can be thought of as advancing development by putting in place a set of enabling conditions which make labour markets possible (the 'market-constituting' and 'correcting' functions), but also by reversing market outcomes in situations where they produce extreme or persistent inequalities (the 'market-limiting' function). The possibility of tension between these approaches clearly exists, and there is no consensus on how far they can be reconciled. Arguably, the embedding of markets in an institutional framework which makes the values of democracy and human dignity non-negotiable should serve to render economic growth more sustainable over the longer term, but whether this is the case remains an open question, both empirically and theoretically.

A pragmatic response to this issue might be to think of labour law as involving a never-ending search for solutions which, at best, are space- and time-specific. The solutions arrived at may be contingent and temporary, but they work well enough in certain contexts. A more pessimistic view is that labour law institutions are, deep down, incompatible with the operation of a market-based economic system. This is not just the view of the many present-day neoliberal critics of labour law. At the inception of the post-1945 welfare state, some of its most prominent theorists, including Michal Kalecki and Karl Polanyi, worried that the neutralization of unemployment as a disciplinary device, through a combination of social legislation and a macroeconomic policy aimed at full employment, would eventually prove impossible to maintain within a market economy.[68] In the late 1960s, the neoclassical economic argument that labour law rules push up the 'natural rate' of unemployment began to come into vogue.[69] It has more recently found its juridical counterpart in the claim that social legislation 'distorts competition' within the economic space of transnational trading regimes.[70] There is no sign of an early resolution to these debates. They will probably continue, in various economic and legal settings, as long as there are labour law systems, that is to say, as long as there are labour markets in the form we currently know them.

[68] M Kalecki, 'Political Aspects of Full Employment' (1943) 14 Political Quarterly 322–31. Kalecki, noting that 'unemployment is an integral part of the "normal" capitalist system' (326) and that 'under a regime of permanent full employment, the "sack" would cease to play its role as a disciplinary measure' (ibid), predicted that an alliance of business leaders and financial interests would oppose full employment policy notwithstanding the economic growth it was likely to induce. Whereas 'one of the important functions of fascism, as typified by the Nazi system, was to remove capitalist objections to full employment' (ibid), through authoritarian rule, in a capitalist democracy the best that could be expected was a cyclical movement from boom to slump, as the restoration of full employment would create the political conditions for its own undermining. Kalecki thought that if 'capitalism can adjust itself to full employment, a fundamental reform will have been incorporated in it. If not, it will show itself an outmoded system which must be scrapped' (330). Polanyi took the view that the restriction of property rights through social legislation meant 'the functioning of the market system' (*The Great Transformation*, above n 43, 234), and, via his theory of a 'double movement' between regulation and deregulation, arrived at the same conclusion as Kalecki on the implausibility of a lasting solution to poverty and unemployment in a market-based economy.

[69] M Friedman, 'The Role of Monetary Policy' (1968) 58 American Economic Review 1–17. In 1943 Kalecki had written that in a situation of full employment, 'a powerful alliance is likely to be formed between big business and rentier interests, and they would probably find more than one economist to declare that the situation was manifestly unsound. The pressure of all these forces, and in particular of big business – as a rule influential in government departments – would most probably induce the government to return to the orthodox policy of cutting down the budget deficit'. 'Political Aspects of Full Employment', above n 68, 327.

[70] Case C–438/05 *ITF v Viking Line ABP* [2007] ECR I–10779; and Case C–341/05 *Laval v Svenska Byggnadsarbetareförbundet* [2007] ECR I–11767.

PART III

NORMATIVE FOUNDATIONS AND LEGAL IDEAS: RETHINKING EXISTING STRUCTURES

11

Re-Matching Labour Laws with Their Purpose

*Guy Davidov**

A. Introduction

Why do we need labour laws?[1] The question is important for a number of different reasons. One is the need to defend this body of laws, which many consider to be an unwarranted intervention in 'free' markets. Another is the need to update and improve such laws in light of changing employment structures and labour market realities. Some laws are becoming outdated; others no longer cover many workers. This requires us to consider changes in the law, and before making changes it is imperative to remind ourselves (or rethink) what should be the goal of such laws. A third reason for the inquiry is the need to interpret existing labour laws. Questions of interpretation always arise in the application of legislation, especially so in the context of labour law, given frequent changes in employment practices that were not foreseen by the legislature and are often designed explicitly to evade the law.

An inquiry into the purpose of labour laws can be performed at different levels of abstraction. At the most general level (let us call it for ease of reference level 1), we can list the broad values that labour laws are designed to promote, such as human dignity, individual autonomy, equality, democracy, voice, and so on. At this level, recent debates have centred on whether labour laws can promote efficiency (even though traditionally they were considered to be impediments to efficiency),[2] and whether redistribution – traditionally considered to be one of the main goals of

---

* Elias Lieberman Chair in Labour Law, Hebrew University of Jerusalem.

[1] I use the term 'labour law' in this chapter in the broad sense, including what North Americans call employment law and workplace discrimination law. On the other hand, I refer only to labour legislation and judge-made laws – not to standards created by the parties themselves, laws that indirectly affect workers, and governmental policies affecting the labour market (cf Arthurs, this volume; and Howe, this volume).

[2] See, eg: H Collins, 'Justifications and Techniques of Legal Regulation of the Employment Relation' in H Collins, P Davies, and RW Rideout (eds), *Legal Regulation of the Employment Relation* (Kluwer Law International, 2000) 3; S Deakin and F Wilkinson, 'Labour Law and Economic Theory: A Reappraisal' in Collins, Davies, and Rideout, above, 29; and BE Kaufman, 'Labor Law and Employment Regulation: Neoclassical and Institutional Perspectives' in KG Dau-Schmidt, S Harris, and O Lobel (eds), *Labor and Employment Law and Economics* (Edward Elgar, 2009) 3.

labour law – is still a legitimate and viable goal.[3] Somewhat more specifically (level 2), one can explain the need for intensely regulating labour markets by reference to some broad characteristic of such markets, whether it be inequality of bargaining power,[4] or the prevalence of market failures,[5] or the existence of obstacles to the realization of human capital.[6] At this level the goal of labour law is articulated generally as addressing the perceived problem. Still more specifically, the need for labour law can be explained by pointing out the unique characteristics of employment relationships that put the employee in a vulnerable position (level 3). I have argued that the employment relationship is characterized by democratic deficits (subordination, in a broad sense) and by dependency on a specific employer (inability to spread risks – both economic and for the fulfilment of social and psychological needs).[7] At this level, the idea of labour law can be articulated as to minimize these vulnerabilities and prevent unwanted outcomes resulting from them.

Yet more specifically, the inquiry can focus on concrete results that society finds unacceptable (level 4). At this level, attention is shifted from the grand project to specific pieces of legislation. Thus, for example, we can try to explain why legislatures prohibit compensation that is too low – why society deems wages below a certain minimum unacceptable. The answer usually relies on general values or on the characteristics of employment relations – thus bringing us back to the higher levels of abstraction. For example, minimum wage laws are justified (and can be explained) as tools of redistribution and because they are needed to protect the human dignity of employees;[8] collective bargaining laws promote workplace democracy, redistribution and efficiency;[9] and 'just cause' dismissals laws are needed to prevent unnecessary injuries to the social/psychological well-being of workers who depend on a particular relationship for such purposes, and to ensure a fair 'price' in terms of security in return for workers' submission to a democratically deficient regime.[10] These are just examples and obviously others may have different views about the goals of these specific laws. My point here is simply that each piece of legislation has its own purposes, which correspond with the general values that

---

[3] See B Langille, 'Labour Law's Back Pages' in G Davidov and B Langille (eds), *Boundaries and Frontiers of Labour Law: Goals and Means in the Regulation of Work* (Hart Publishing, 2006) 13; A Hyde, 'What is Labour Law?' in Davidov and Langille, above, 37; and G Davidov, 'The (Changing?) Idea of Labour Law' (2007) 146 Int Lab Rev 311.

[4] P Davies and M Freedland, *Kahn-Freund's Labour and the Law* (3rd edn, Stevens, 1983) 18. For an attempt to explain this contested concept see G Davidov, 'The Reports of My Death are Greatly Exaggerated: "Employee" as a Viable (Though Overly-Used) Legal Concept' in Davidov and Langille, above n 3, 133.

[5] Hyde, above n 3.

[6] Langille, above n 3, 34.

[7] G Davidov, 'The Three Axes of Employment Relationships: A Characterization of Workers in Need of Protection' (2002) 52 U Toronto LJ 357.

[8] G Davidov, 'A Purposive Interpretation of the National Minimum Wage Act' (2009) 72 MLR 581.

[9] G Davidov, 'Collective Bargaining Law: Purpose and Scope' (2004) 20 Int J Comp Lab L & Ind Rel 81.

[10] G Davidov, 'In Defence of (Efficiently Administered) "Just Cause" Dismissal Laws' (2007) 23 Int J Comp Lab L & Ind Rel 117.

labour laws are aimed to protect and promote, or with the vulnerabilities that characterize employment relations in general.

Wherein, then, lies the crisis of labour law? Did our goals change, at any of those levels? I see no reason to believe that they have changed as a descriptive matter, nor any reason to argue that they should change. Workers are in need of protection in their relations vis-à-vis employers just as before (if not more). The 'free' market does not produce acceptable practices in the labour context any more than it used to. The crisis is not with our goals, but with the mismatch between some labour laws (legislation and case law) and these goals, created by changing realities.[11]

In the current chapter I would like to look at the project of labour law as a whole (rather than consider specific regulations), and take a 'bottom-up' approach that starts from examining problems with the actual *application* of labour laws, as encountered by workers in many countries. For the most part these are well-known problems. My aim in reciting them here is to show that for purposes of determining the scope of labour law as well as updating labour laws in light of changing employment practices, it is useful to focus on the characteristics showing the vulnerability of employees vis-à-vis their employers (that is, level 3). At least for these purposes, then, I argue in favour of a functional view of the idea of labour law. It is not that the ultimate goals (level 1) and the general deficiencies of labour markets (level 2) are not important or incorrect. They are simply less useful when one is trying to address actual problems that are so prevalent, concerning the growing irrelevance of labour law for so many workers around the world. For such purposes we should look more directly at the factual situation (specific vulnerabilities) that labour laws are designed to address. Then we can try to ensure that our labour laws are indeed covering the workers within this factual situation.

Parts B and C discuss problems with bilateral and multiple employment relations, respectively. In each context, I will show how a clear view of the vulnerabilities characterizing employment (and justifying the regulation of employment relations) can provide solutions for the mismatch between current labour laws and the workers who need them.

B. Problems of application – bilateral employment relations

For an easy presentation of the problems (and solutions) I will use the following denotations:

---

[11] On the changes in employment practices and labour market realities, see, eg: KVW Stone, *From Widgets to Digits: Employment Regulation for the Changing Workplace* (Cambridge University Press, 2004); and H Arthurs, 'Fairness at Work: Federal Labour Standards for the 21st Century' (2006) <http://www.hrsdc.gc.ca/eng/labour/employment_standards/fls/pdf/final_report.pdf.>. On the mismatch with current labour laws, see also: International Labour Office, *Report V(1): The Employment Relationship* (2005) 15 ('growing divergence between the law and the reality of the employment relationship'); N Countouris, *The Changing Law of the Employment Relationship: Comparative Analyses in the European Context* (Ashgate, 2007); and KVW Stone, 'A Labor Law For the Digital Era: The Future of Labor and Employment Law in the United States' in Dau-Schmidt, Harris, and Lobel, above n 2, 689.

- Employer = E
- Worker = W
- Characteristics of the relationship as they are learned from a written contract (if such a contract exists) = CC1, CC2, CC3, etc
- Characteristics of the relationship in real life, as an empirical matter = CE1, CE2, CE3, etc
- Characteristics that *should* trigger the application of labour laws, as a normative matter = CN1, CN2, CN3, etc.

It is widely accepted in principle that although entrance into employment relations is voluntary, the legal status is not a matter of choice. Labour laws apply to those considered to be 'employees' and 'employers' by law – not by self-declaration or contractual stipulations.[12] Accordingly, in 'traditional' employment relations, there is presumably a full match between the CCs, the CEs and the CNs. The lists of indicia developed by courts as identifying employment relations (control, no risk of loss and chance of profit, etc) are supposed to be CNs – based on normative considerations. For the factory worker directly employed by the manufacturer, these same characteristics correspond to the contract and they also represent his actual situation. The problems begin when there are discrepancies between CCs, CEs, and CNs, or a mismatch between the CNs developed by courts and normative considerations. Such phenomena are not new, but they are becoming ever more frequent. Below I discuss some of the common problems.

Problem 1: Courts consider W to be an 'employee' if (and only if) she has the characteristics of 'traditional' employees. One reason for the exclusion of workers from labour laws, even when they appear to *need* the protection of such laws from a purposive point of view, is the use of indicia detached from their normative foundations. Most commonly, the problem is using CNs that are based on 'traditional' CEs rather than real normative considerations. Thus, for example, in some countries (such as the US) the location of the work is a relevant indicator of employment. If you work at your employer's offices you are likely to be considered an employee, but if you are required to work from your own home, this is seen as an indication *against* employee status (and thus, you are more likely to stay outside of labour law's protection). However, those working outside of the employer's premises are not less vulnerable in their relationship vis-à-vis the employer. The location of the work cannot justify their exclusion.

The problem is that some courts mistakenly infer their indicia from paradigmatic (or 'traditional') employment relations. Working on E's premises is a common characteristic of 'traditional' employment – that is, traditionally it has often been the case that CE1 = working on the employer's premises. It does not mean that this should be a characteristic justifying the application of labour law as a *normative* matter. But courts sometimes make this mistaken move (CE1→CN1).[13] The solution is simple: the distinction between CNs and CEs must be maintained.

---

[12] See ILO Recommendation No 198 Concerning the Employment Relationship (2006), para 9.

[13] The US 'common law test' includes a number of additional indicia that are questionable from a normative perspective (ie, it is not clear why they should be seen as *justifying* the application of labour laws): the skill required, the method of payment, the provision of employee benefits, and the tax

Tests and indicia (CNs) should be based on a *purposive* analysis: CNs should be designed to include the workers that labour laws are aimed to protect.

The most recent attempt to articulate tests for the existence of an employment relationship comes from the USA – a tentative draft of a Restatement of Employment Law was approved by the American Law Institute on May 2009.[14] The main CN offered in this document is that 'the employer precludes the individual from rendering the services as part of an independent business'.[15] In my view, such a negative formulation blurs the connection with the *purpose* of the distinction. It is preferable to focus on characteristics that *exist* in the relationship, rather than missing from it, to ensure a more direct association with the need of protection.

Problem 2: Employers evading labour laws by sidestepping specific CNs, without necessarily changing the true nature of the relationship. A second example of a mismatch between labour laws and their purposes is found in judgments that allow employers to sidestep specific CNs without changing the true nature of the relationship. Consider, for example, the ownership of expensive equipment. In many countries this is seen as an indicator of being an independent contractor, and this seems reasonable, because ownership of the means of production does suggest less dependency on the employer (and as a result, less need of labour law's protection). So assume that CN2 = W is working with E's equipment. But in order to sidestep this CN, and evade employers' responsibilities, E demands that W will buy the equipment (for example, a truck), using a loan from E. As a result, both contractually and (on the face of it) empirically, W owns the equipment (CC2 = CE2 = W owns the equipment) – and the lack of fit with CN2 excludes W from the scope of labour law.

As a matter of fact, however, if W is otherwise in a position of vulnerability justifying the application of labour laws, the formal ownership of equipment does not change this vulnerability. If the payments are actually made by the employer, this is sophisticated evasion rather than a real change of labour market realities. The solution, in my view, is to articulate tests at a high level of generalization, with more specific indicia used only to assist. I would define CN1 as democratic deficits and CN2 as dependency. The indicia commonly used by courts can be useful, to the extent that they correspond with these two ultimate tests.[16] Thus, for example, working with E's tools is helpful to identifying dependency, so it can be seen as CN2.1 – but it must remain subordinate to the higher goal (CN2). So although in

---

treatment of the hired party. For the American test see, eg, *Nationwide Mutual Insurance Co v Darden*, 503 US 318 (1992) (US Supreme Court).

[14] Restatement (Third) of Employment Law (draft of 3 April 2009), available at <http://lawprofessors.typepad.com/files/restatement.pdf>. There is strong objection to this draft from a large number of American labour law scholars. See, eg: DR Nolan, TJ St Antoine, JE Slater, and A Goldman, 'Working Group on Chapter 1 of the Proposed Restatement of Employment Law: Existence of Employment Relationship' (2009) 13 Employee Rights and Employment Policy J 43; A Hyde, 'Response to Working Group on Chapter 1 of The Proposed Restatement of Employment Law: On Purposeless Restatement' (2009) 13 Employee Rights and Employment Policy J 87; and MW Finkin, 'A Consumer Warning for the Restatement of Employment Law: Read Carefully Before Applying' (2009) 70 Louisiana L Rev 193.

[15] Ibid, section 1.01(1)(c).

[16] For further elaboration see Davidov, above n 7.

most cases, CN2.1 is one of the characteristics pointing to the existence of CN2, and as a result, the absence of CN2.1 is usually one of the characteristics supporting the exclusion from labour laws, judges must ensure that it has not been detached from the ultimate normative considerations. In the above-mentioned example CN2.1 is absent, but because the equipment was bought with a loan from E, there is still a high degree of dependency in W's relationship with E (that is, CN2 exists) – and this justifies the inclusion of W within the scope of labour law.

Problem 3: Employers evading labour laws by sham appearances. In some countries (notably the UK), employers commonly insert contractual stipulations that do not represent the true nature of the relationship. This discrepancy between CCs and CEs, if not exposed by the courts, is an easy way to evade employers' responsibilities. Consider, for example, the 'zero-hours contract' (no commitment on either side – work is contingent on interest of both parties each day). Assume that CC1 = zero-hours contract, but in practice CE1 = W has no other employer, working many hours every day only for E.[17] Or, to take another example, assume that CC1 = W performs work for E as a volunteer, without payment, but CE1 = there is payment in kind for work (for example, accommodation).[18] In both cases, the exclusion of W from the scope of labour law is based on the mismatch between CC1 and CE1.

The solution is simple: determination of 'employee' status must be based on the true nature of the relationship – on CEs rather than CCs. And in countries that have a (refutable) presumption that CC = CE, judges must remember that E has an interest in misrepresenting the relationship, and therefore treat CCs with scepticism.

Problem 4: Labour laws based on the assumption of 'traditional' employment relationships exclude non-traditional work arrangements. The previous problems have all been concerned with total exclusion from the scope of labour law. But quite often workers in atypical relations are considered 'employees', and therefore subject in principle to labour laws, yet they do not fully enjoy these laws.[19] Thus, for example, laws that include a threshold of 12 months in employment, or a threshold of a certain number of working hours per week, exclude temporary employees and part-time employees, respectively. In theory, it could be that such exclusions are normatively justified. But often they result simply from the fact that laws were based on a 'traditional' view of the paradigmatic employee, and have not been updated in light of changing employment practices.

Consider, for example, a piece of legislation that limits its scope by CN1 = minimum 12 months in employment.[20] It may have been based on the assumption that almost all employees continue to work for longer periods, and the idea was to

---

[17] See, eg, *O'Kelly v Trusthouse Forte plc* [1983] ICR 728 (UK Court of Appeal).

[18] See *Best v St Austell China Clay Museum Ltd* [2004] UKEAT 0924_03_1106 (11 June 2004) (UK Employment Appeal Tribunal).

[19] See, eg: KVW Stone, 'Legal Protections for Atypical Employees: Employment Law for Workers without Workplaces and Employees without Employers' (2006) 27 Berkeley J Emp & Lab L 251; Countouris, above n 11; and LF Vosko, *Managing the Margins: Gender, Citizenship, and the International Regulation of Precarious Employment* (Oxford University Press, 2010).

[20] See, eg, the Israeli Severance Pay Act of 1963 (every employee is entitled to a severance payment when dismissed, with the exception of dismissals within the first 12 months of employment).

start a certain entitlement only after a 'trial period'. But today many workers are employed on a temporary basis and are being replaced before reaching the 12-months threshold, without any fault of their own – whether in order to avoid paying such entitlements, or for other managerial reasons. As a result, CN1 has been separated from its normative foundations. The law should be amended to prevent the situation in which many employees cannot enjoy the legislation for no apparent justification.

A similar problem occurs when the law neglects to provide a certain entitlement, on the assumption that it is not needed – an assumption based on 'traditional' employment relations. Consider, for example, people working on an hourly basis, that is, getting paid a certain salary for each hour of actual work, rather than a monthly salary. This method of employment is used by employers to avoid paying for non-work periods (whether because of slow business, public holidays or any other reason), thus shifting this risk to the employee. In a system based on the assumption that employees earn a monthly salary, the legislature will not bother providing an entitlement for payment with respect to public holidays (for example). But when many employees are employed on an hourly basis, the law must be updated to provide a solution for such non-work periods.

More broadly, the connection between some entitlements and ongoing employment has proved to be problematic. Our need for pensions and health care (for example) exists whether or not we work for the same employer and without interruptions. It has perhaps been convenient in the past to use the employment relationship as a vehicle for the delivery of such rights, relying on the prevalence of long-term relations with the same employer. But from a normative point of view, workers who move frequently from one employer to another, or experience periods of unemployment, should enjoy an entitlement to pensions and health care as well.[21] The law should be adapted to reflect the shift to atypical employment, based on an examination of the *purpose* of each entitlement and whether there is any normative reason to tie this entitlement to long-term or uninterrupted employment. As far as health care is concerned (for example), it does not appear to be based on the vulnerabilities characterizing employment, so the entire tie to employment (not to mention long-term and uninterrupted employment) cannot be justified.

Problem 5: Some workers should be 'employees' for the purpose of some labour laws and 'independent contractors' for the purpose of others. Yet another reason for the exclusion of many workers from the scope of protection is the fact that they are characterized only by *some* of the characteristics of employees, and at the same time display some characteristics of independent contractors. Thus, if CN1 = democratic deficits and CN2 = economic dependency, there are cases in which the relationship between E and W is characterized by CN2 but not CN1. For example, this is often the situation with regard to workers considered by their employers to be 'freelancers'.

---

[21] See generally A Supiot, *Beyond Employment: Changes in Work and the Future of Labour Law in Europe* (Oxford University Press, 2001); Stone, above n 19; and Vosko, above n 19.

In many legal systems such workers are excluded from the entire corpus of labour law because of the lack of subordination. But the existence of dependency justifies the application of at least *some* labour laws. It is clear that working time laws (for example) should not apply, because there is no subordination and the worker controls his own time. Arguably, however, collective bargaining laws (for example) should apply, to counteract economic dependency.

The solution, already adopted in a growing number of countries, is to add an intermediate category ('dependent contractors' or 'employee-like'). Such an additional category should *not* be seen as a general solution for 'grey areas' or difficult cases. Rather, it is only suitable for those who have some *specific* characteristics of employment that justify *specific* labour laws, but also some characteristics of independence.[22]

Problem 6: The broad discretion left by the tests is causing more evasion by employers. The tests and indicia developed by different courts around the world to determine who is an 'employee' are very similar. Although there are obviously variations, as well as significant differences in the way these tests are applied, the basic structure is similar. And one common feature is the fact that tests are based on terms that are open to broad judicial discretion. This in turn is used (or abused) by employers trying to evade labour laws. Knowing that most workers will not sue – either for lack of knowledge, lack of resources, or fear of reprisals – employers can rely on any uncertainty to ignore labour laws without taking the risk of criminal charges or punitive damages.

One solution to this problem is to use more concrete and determinate definitions (for example, anyone working more than a certain hours per week and earning less than a certain amount is an employee).[23] But this can be manipulated by employers working around such definitions. Moreover, such definitions are not capable of dealing with changing employment practices. Another solution proposed by some labour law scholars is to dissolve the legal distinction between 'employees' and 'independent contractors' altogether, and extend labour law protections to all those selling their capacity to work.[24] But this seems to ignore the fact that there are real differences between the two groups (at least when comparing the 'core' of those groups).[25] Thus, for example, a lawyer working as a sole practitioner, with numerous clients, will be considered an employee of each of those clients, according to this view. Can we really apply working time laws, for example, on such a relationship?

Such proposals focus on specific CNs that are used in some countries and cause the exclusion of atypical work relations. Judy Fudge, for example, has attacked the

---

[22] See G Davidov, 'Who is a Worker?' (2005) 34 Ind LJ 57.

[23] For a recent example see the Spanish intermediate group of 'economically dependent self-employed workers', introduced in 2007, which has been defined mainly by income of 75 per cent or more from the same client. See J Cabeza Pereiro, 'The Status of Self-Employed Workers in Spain' (2008) 147 Int Lab Rev 91.

[24] M Linder, *The Employment Relationship in Anglo-American Law: A Historical Perspective* (Greenwood Press, 1989) 239–41; J Fudge, 'Fragmenting Work and Fragmenting Organizations: The Contract of Employment and the Scope of Labour Regulation' (2006) 44 Osgoode Hall LJ 609; see also RR Carlson, 'Why the Law Still Can't Tell an Employee When it Sees One and How It Ought to Stop Trying' (2001) 22 Berkeley J Emp & Lab L 295.

[25] Davidov, above n 4.

'deeply rooted ideology . . . that independent contractors are entrepreneurs who are able to self-insure and who take profits for risk. The empirical evidence demonstrates that there is no necessary correlation between forms of employment and the rewards that workers enjoy and the risks that they bear'.[26] Fudge appears to admit that risks (for example) are relevant as a CN. The empirical evidence mentioned only reflects the fact that this CN is not used or not enforced properly. The solution: tests should be articulated at a high level of generalization, reflecting the ultimate goals of labour laws, to minimize evasion and cover atypical employment.

C. Problems of application – multiple employers

Employers have been evading labour laws by manipulations concerning the definition of 'employee' for many years. But courts and legislatures have stepped up attempts to counter such evasions (even if often half-heartedly or inefficiently), so employers have turned their attention to manipulating the definition of 'employer'. In this part I briefly discuss evasion by way of triangular and quadrangular employment relations.

Problem 7: Triangular employment. Assume that we have an additional employer (legal or factual) – either a temporary employment agency or a subcontractor – denoted as E1. The relationship between E, E1, and W is usually structured this way: between E1 and W there are CCs (a contract) and there are CEs (characteristics of the real relationship); between E and W there are no CCs (no contract), but there are CEs. The question is which relationship is truly (rather than contractually) characterized by W's need of labour law's protection – otherwise put, which set of CEs = CNs?

Some cases seem to suggest an easy solution. Thus, for example, when E1 is only a funnel for transferring wages, and W's subordination and actual dependency are vis-à-vis E (the user), it is quite obvious that E should be considered the legal employer.[27] On the other hand, in the case of a supply chain, when E buys a product from E1, and W's subordination and actual dependency are vis-à-vis E1 (the subcontractor), E1 should be considered the legal employer.[28]

More difficult are cases of mixed characteristics. Assume that we have four normative characteristics justifying labour laws (CN1–CN4). What if the relationship between W and E is characterized by CN1 and CN2, while the relationship between W and E1 is characterized by CN3 and CN4? One possibility is a solution of split employers: E will be the employer for purpose of some laws, while E1 will be the employer for purpose of others.[29] Another possibility, which I find preferable, is a solution of joint employers: both E and E1 will be responsible jointly

---

[26] Fudge, above n 24, 35.

[27] G Davidov, 'Joint Employers Status in Triangular Employment Relationships' (2004) 42 BJIR 727.

[28] Indeed, attempts in the USA and Canada to argue that the ultimate buyer of the product is a 'joint employer' – when there was no relationship whatsoever between the buyer and the workers – have been rightfully rejected. See *Lian v J Crew Group Inc* (2001) 54 OR (3d) 239 (Ontario Superior Court of Justice); and *Doe v Wal-Mart*, 9th Cir, judgment of 10 July 2009 (US Court of Appeals).

[29] S Deakin, 'The Changing Concept of the "Employer" in British Labour Law' (2001) 30 Ind LJ 72.

and severally. This will ensure that they allocate responsibilities between them, without being able to argue that the other party is responsible.[30]

Problem 8: Quadrangular employment. Employers using the triangular model have realized that a direct and continuous relationship with the workers formally employed by E1 could result in direct legal responsibility for them towards those workers. Most recently they have responded (at least in Israel) by adding an additional intermediary, in an attempt to further distance themselves from the workers – at least at the level of appearances. Thus, for example, janitors at Israeli universities are sometimes employed by a subcontractor (E2) who is engaged by a contractor (E1) who is engaged in turn by the university in a contract for supplying cleaning services.

Such further distancing of W from E at the formal level should not obscure the legal situation. The addition of E2 does not necessarily change the true nature of the relationship. The question is still where the CNs are – and it could very well be that they are vis-à-vis E. If this is the case – if the vulnerabilities that justify employment regulations are in fact vis-à-vis the 'client' (E) – then E should bear responsibility as the legal employer.

D. Conclusion

I started this chapter by asking why we need labour laws. My first aim was to show that before answering such a question we must ask what the purpose of this inquiry is. There are different possible answers, at different levels of abstraction/generality. In my view the main problem faced by labour law today is the mismatch between labour laws, as they are applied, and our goals. Not because the goals have changed, but because new employment practices – sometimes designed especially to evade labour laws, at other times resulting from new management techniques and changing labour market realities – have caused such a mismatch. As a result, labour laws are increasingly becoming irrelevant for many workers around the globe, who find themselves excluded (completely or partially) from the protection of such laws.

I have argued that for the purpose of addressing this crisis, the most relevant and useful articulation of the idea of labour law is at the level of describing the unique characteristics of employment relations that justify protective regulations. My own view, which I have put forward elsewhere in detail, is that there are two basic vulnerabilities suffered by employees – democratic deficits and dependency – that explain the need to intervene and provide various protections. To show how this level of abstraction is useful for addressing our mismatch crisis, I have listed eight common problems with the application of labour laws. By focusing on the

---

[30] Davidov, above n 27; and Fudge, above n 24, 644. Another approach is to argue that employers within the same 'network' should be required to treat their employees equally – see H Collins, 'Multi-Segmented Workforces, Comparative Fairness, and the Capital Boundary Obstacle' in G Davidov and B Langille (eds), *Boundaries and Frontiers of Labour Law: Goals and Means in the Regulation of Work* (Hart Publishing, 2006) 317.

existence of the characteristics that justify protection we can move towards a solution to such problems.

Thus, when courts set up tests that are based on 'traditional' employment patterns, such tests are detached from their normative foundations – and the solution is to use tests that are tied to the need of protection (ultimately, democratic deficits and dependency). Similarly, when courts are using specific indicia as tests for the application of labour laws, employers sometimes sidestep them and evade such laws even though the workers are still in a position of vulnerability. The solution is to remember that indicia are only proxies (at best) and should not replace the ultimate tests that have a normative basis. Also, when employers draft contracts that do not represent the real nature of the relationship, courts must ignore such sham appearances and ask whether the characteristics that justify protection appear in the real-life arrangements. Finally, when employers turn to the use of intermediaries (such as temporary employment agencies or subcontractors), courts must ask which relationship presents the vulnerabilities justifying protection. In many cases, notwithstanding the formal legal arrangement, it is the ultimate 'client' that will have to bear responsibility.

There are also mismatch problems that demand action from legislatures. Thus, there are laws that are based on the 'traditional' paradigm of employment, failing to provide adequate protection to people working part-time, on a temporary arrangement etc. Assuming that such a partial exclusion is not based on any normative justifications, these laws should be updated to fully cover new work arrangements. Also, when workers exhibit only *some* characteristics of employment, which can justify only *some* labour laws, the solution is to create an intermediate category, to capture workers who suffer only from some of the common vulnerabilities. Such an intermediate category must be based on the existence of certain normative justifications (most likely dependency) but the lack of others. Finally, there have been suggestions that legislatures should abolish the distinction between employees and independent contractors and extend the protection of labour law to both groups. The same focus on the characteristics that justify protection is useful in analysing such proposals as well. I have argued that there are observable differences between working people that justify the application of labour laws only to some of them – those suffering from specific vulnerabilities vis-à-vis their employers.

People who work for others often do so within a relationship characterized by democratic deficits and dependency. This has been the case in the past and has not changed. The goal of labour law is to provide protection to these people, by minimizing such vulnerabilities or preventing unwanted outcomes resulting from them. This has been the case in the past and has not changed either. To be sure, we have witnessed major changes in employment practices in recent years. This new reality requires an effort both from courts and from legislatures to re-match labour laws with their purpose. Obviously this is not easy politically, but at least we should be clear about what is required. Problems of mismatch can be solved by focusing attention to the *purpose* of labour laws, specifically to the level of the concrete vulnerabilities justifying protective intervention.

12

The Legal Characterization of Personal Work Relations and the Idea of Labour Law

Mark Freedland* and Nicola Kountouris**

A. Introduction

The present chapter reflects on the 'changing idea of labour law' from the analytical perspective of the legal construction of personal work relations, a perspective that has formed the object of our recent and current research interests. This has become a project of identifying the 'personal work relation' as a large and overarching analytical category for the theoretical understanding and normative development of labour law within European legal systems.[1] Part of that project has consisted in developing the idea of the 'personal work nexus' as a way of understanding and analysing the internal legal construction of 'personal work relations'.[2] We have also tried to show how those two analytical concepts between them enable us to transcend some difficult and unsatisfactory boundaries or dichotomies which have constrained the understanding and taxonomy of the forms in which work in the labour market is legally constructed.

The most obtrusive of these boundaries or dichotomies has been between the contract of employment and the personal contract for services; but we have also used these concepts to transcend the boundaries between both those contract types and other or further types of personal work contract.[3] Moreover, we have used the same analysis to challenge the more subtle dichotomy between personal work contracts and personal work relationships. We have also proposed and tried to develop a methodology for handling and making use of those two analytical concepts as instruments of comparative labour law as between European legal systems.[4]

---

* Professor of Employment Law, University of Oxford.
** Lecturer in Law, UCL Faculty of Laws.

[1] A project due to be completed by the publication of a work jointly authored between us on *The Legal Construction of Personal Work Relations* (Oxford University Press, forthcoming).

[2] MR Freedland, 'From the Contract of Employment to the Personal Work Nexus' (2006) 35(1) Industrial Law Journal 1.

[3] MR Freedland, 'Application of Labour and Employment Law Beyond the Contract of Employment' (2006) 145(4) International Labour Review 3.

[4] MR Freedland and N Kountouris, 'Towards a Comparative Theory of the Contractual Construction of Personal Work Relations in Europe' (2008) 37(1) Industrial Law Journal 49.

We believe that our analysis of the legal construction of personal work relations, and our challenge to unsatisfactory boundaries and dichotomies, might be usefully developed and pursued by the taking of some further analytical steps, and by the introduction of some further analytical concepts which would encapsulate those steps. We bring these steps and concepts together under the heading – itself a kind of analytical concept – of the 'legal characterization of personal work relations'.

In the first section of this chapter, we set out our notion of legal characterization of personal work relations; we present it as a particular way of thinking about what is normally regarded as the classification or taxonomy of personal work relations, or as the determining of the personal scope of labour law or labour laws; and we explain that it combines elements of descriptive classification of personal work relations with elements of prescriptive regulation of those relations. We are convinced, and we have suggested elsewhere, that the determination of the scope of labour law and, therefore, the taxonomy of personal work relations, are inextricably linked to the 'idea of labour law' and the rationales underpinning the discipline itself.

In the second section, we suggest a method of descriptive classification of personal work relations into three loose groupings, those of secure, autonomous, and precarious work; and we consider the ways in which the evolutions of the labour market, and of course of labour market regulation, produce certain dynamics of movement between and around these different groupings. Again, we suggest, an analysis of these dynamics can give us a further set of elements for identifying ways and directions in which the idea of labour law may have to evolve in order to realize a set of prescriptive regulatory objectives, a point to which we return in the fourth section of this chapter.

In the third section, we suggest that, in order fully to understand and make use of this method of descriptive classification, we need to take a further analytical step. This consists of identifying a further analytical element in the legal construction of personal work relations which we identify by the terminology of the 'personal work profile' of each worker. We advance and seek to deploy the idea of the personal work profile not as a status or relationship in and of itself, but as a technique of analysis for understanding in what sense and to what extent particular personal work relations should be regarded as secure, autonomous, or freestanding, or precarious – and for better understanding the ways in which the existing legal categories of personal work relations are articulated and applied. We argue that, seen through the lens of the personal work profile, personal work relations, and working lives at large, appear as far more multi-faceted and multi-dimensional than the traditional binary divide suggests. From the personal work profile perspective, elements that are traditionally concealed behind the normative implications and underpinnings of the employee/self-employed distinction, acquire a clearly visible dimension that casts a new light on the concepts of security, precariousness, and autonomy in employment or work. For instance the vexed question of work or employment under multiple contracts, or the issue of work or employment by a primary carer for a disabled dependant, acquire a distinct normative dimension typically obscured by the binary divide and the regulatory rationales – or ideas of labour law – normally attached to it.

In the fourth section, we begin to suggest ways in which, thus embellished with the notion of the personal work profile, our method of descriptive classification of personal work relations might contribute to the prescriptive regulation of those relations. We advance the idea that there are emergent new forms of personal work relation, often fully or partly innominate; and we suggest that this might represent a particular way of thinking about the roles of *jus cogens* and *jus dispositivum* in the legal construction of personal work relations.

In the Conclusion to this chapter we give a preliminary indication of the ways in which this scheme of analysis might play a part in the development of EU labour/ employment law. For this purpose we introduce the normative idea of 'personality in work', as a combination of the values of dignity, capability, and stability in personal work relations.

B. The idea of legal characterization

We begin this chapter by explaining what we mean by 'legal characterization' of personal work relations, a term that we see as an aspect or dimension of the 'legal construction' of personal work relations. By 'legal construction' of personal work relations we mean the whole process of ascribing legal form and structure to personal work relations, and of determining what legal norms or legally recognized norms (for example, valid contractual terms) apply to those personal work relations. There is a major aspect of that whole process which is normally thought of as the taxonomy or classification of personal work relations, carried out for the purpose of determining whether a particular norm or set of norms applies to a particular personal work relation. (For example, under English law we classify a personal work relation as being or not being a contract of employment in order to know whether or not the law of unfair dismissal applies to it.) This aspect is also thought of as being the determining of the 'personal scope' of labour law or of any particular law or set of laws which might be applicable to personal work relations.

However, we believe that the taxonomy or classification of personal work relations cannot satisfactorily be separated out from the rest of the process of legal construction of personal work relations as a distinctive or self-contained element in the process. And in fact we believe that much trouble and confusion comes about from trying to regard 'taxonomy' or the determination of 'personal scope' as a self-contained activity. We think it is preferable to think about 'taxonomy' or the determination of 'personal scope' as itself being part of a very complex activity which we identify as the 'legal characterization' of personal work relations. That is to say, we identify as the 'legal characterization' of personal work relations a complex activity which is a combination of taxonomy with regulation. The element of regulation consists of ordaining that a certain norm or set of norms applies to a particular personal work relation or set of personal work relations. The element of taxonomy consists of providing and applying the category which identifies that personal work relation or set of personal work relations. These two activities are integrally linked to each other; they combine into a complex activity which applies a certain legal normative framework to any particular personal work relation within any particular legal system. This combined activity thereby assigns a certain legal *character* to any particular personal work relation; hence our choice of the terminology of 'legal characterization' to designate this complex activity.

The very idea of 'legal characterization', as we have thus articulated it, serves to demonstrate how intimately the legal categories of personal work relations are bound up with particular sets of norms in particular legal systems at particular moments in time. The idea of 'legal characterization' reminds us that when we invoke and deploy a notion such as 'the contract of employment', we are identifying a certain set of personal work relations which are subject to a certain legal regime and which derive a certain legal character from that regime. So it will be apparent that our idea of 'legal characterization' depicts an activity which is very contingent upon the particular legal and practical context in which it takes place, and very dependent on the path by which that context was created. In the remainder of this chapter, we try to develop the idea of 'legal characterization' and to think about ways of illuminating the activity which it depicts. We begin by distinguishing between two different modes in which 'legal characterization' may take place.

Legal characterization may take place in a purely descriptive mode; or it may take place in a purely prescriptive one. It is in a purely descriptive mode where it classifies personal work relations with regard to an existing set of norms simply as a matter of applying existing legal systems, and with no aim of altering the ways in which personal work relations are regulated. It is in a purely prescriptive mode where it proposes a classification for personal work relations with regard to a set of norms in a way that consciously overrides existing legal systems and does imply fundamental alteration to the ways in which those systems are regulated. In this purely prescriptive mode, legal characterization involves both re-classification and re-regulation of personal work relations.

We can envisage a spectrum between these modes of legal characterization, so that the modes of description and prescription are combined in varying degrees. This is true of the legal characterization which is carried out in various senses by the various actors in the legal construction of personal work relations – legislators, judges, legal policy makers, and theorists. Generally speaking, each of these legal actors seeks to find a single mode of legal characterization in which to operate. Judges will tend to operate in a largely or entirely descriptive mode, legal policy makers and theorists will tend to choose a more prescriptive mode. Legislators may at times follow the contours of existing legal constructions of personal work relations, may at times fundamentally modify those constructions. But of late, the participants in the discussion about the role of taxonomy in labour law have been beset with uncertainty about what is the right mode of legal characterization in which to operate – in particular, as to whether to operate entirely in descriptive mode, or in gently prescriptive mode, or in strongly prescriptive mode. The discourses both of policy makers and theorists display great ambiguity in this respect.

We believe that it may be helpful consciously to think about and engage in the legal characterization of personal work relations in two distinct modes. On the one

UNIVERSITY OF WINCHESTER
LIBRARY

hand, we might, in largely descriptive mode, analyse existing legal practice to see what the trends and possibilities are, to some extent singling out the trends and possibilities which we would regard as ameliorative. On the other hand, we might, in a much more prescriptive mode, also present a consciously critical scheme of legal characterization which would have more radical implications for the ways in which personal work relations are regulated. We proceed in the next section to offer analyses in each of those two modes.

C. A descriptive taxonomy and a critical taxonomy of PWRs

Our method of legal characterization is therefore based upon two parallel taxonomies of personal work relations – a largely descriptive one and a critical one. We start with the largely descriptive one. Although largely descriptive rather than radically critical or strongly innovative, this analysis is not a static one; it depicts the taxonomies of personal work relations in European national legal systems as being in various states of flux. These states of flux are between binary and tri-partite taxonomies of personal work relations. Binary taxonomies are those which distinguish simply between employment and self-employment, or between dependent and independent work. Such taxonomies remain in place, albeit not without some difficulties, in legal systems such as the French one. Tri-partite taxonomies are those which distinguish between employment, employment-like work, and self-employment, or between dependent, semi-dependent, and independent work. European national labour law systems generally started with a binary taxonomy, and some have remained in that state (though having tended to enlarge the employment category). Other national labour law systems – such as that of the UK – are moving towards using mixtures of binary and tri-partite taxonomies, binary for some purposes and tri-partite for others. There is a noticeable centrifugal drive away from the pure binary divide and towards more complex and fragmented taxonomies. Even in France – a legal system where, until a few years ago, the notion of economic dependence was dismissed as '*trop imprécise*'[5] – the 2008 *Antonmattei-Sciberras rapport* reopened the academic and policy debate by advocating '*la création... d'un statut du travailleur économiquement dépendant*'.[6] There is no doubt, however, that the most significant advance in that sense has been produced by the widely commented upon[7] 2007 Spanish *Ley 20/2007, de 11 de julio, del*

---

[5] J Pélissier, A Supiot, and A Jeammaud, *Droit du travail* (Dalloz, 2000) 151.

[6] PH Antonmattei and JC Sciberras, *Le travailleur économiquement dépendant: quelle protection?* Rapport au Ministre du Travail, des Relations sociales, de la Famille et de la Solidarité (November 2008) 22. Cf also PH Antonmattei and JC Sciberras, 'Le travailleur économiquement dépendant, quelle protection?' (2009) Droit Social 221.

[7] JR Mercader Uguina and A de la Puebla Pinilla, 'Comentario a la Ley 20/2007, de 11 de julio, del Estatuto del Trabajo Autónomo' (2007) 20 Relacione Laborales 99; F Valdès Dal-Ré and O Leclerc, 'Les nouvelles frontières du travail indépendant. A propos du statut du travail autonome espagnol' (2008) RDT, 296; J and Cabeza Pereiro, 'The Status of Self-employed Workers in Spain' (2008) ILR 91.

Estatuto del Trabajo Autónomo, introducing and regulating the contractual category of '*trabajo autónomo económicamente dependiente*'.[8]

Reformist arguments in these states of flux generally concentrate on modifying these taxonomies by pressing either for enlargement of the employment category within a binary taxonomy, or for greater use of tri-partite taxonomy, or both. Rather than taking up a particular position within that debate, we prefer to advance a separate critical taxonomy which sits above existing descriptive taxonomies and aims to provide a basis for the critical evaluations of the working of the descriptive taxonomies, and for regulation on the basis of those evaluations. Our critical taxonomy is not intended to function as a taxonomy which could be used directly to provide a new set of legal categories. That might be terminally disruptive of an already very complex and fragile set of existing legal taxonomies. Instead, our critical taxonomy is advanced as possibly providing ways of adapting and adjusting the formulation and application of existing categories. We have, as it were, temporarily freed ourselves of the responsibility for creating a legal taxonomy in order to obtain a critical perspective upon existing legal taxonomies.

From that critical perspective, we advance a different taxonomy which consists not of hard legal categories, but rather of typologies which we regard as 'soft' ones in two senses. They are soft in the sense that they are loose socio-economic descriptors rather than legal terms of art, and also in the further sense that they describe transient locations in a rapidly changing or fluctuating world of personal work arrangements or relations. With those explanations or caveats, we advance the following tri-partite set of 'soft typologies' for personal work relations: we suggest that it is useful to make a critical analysis of personal work relations which distinguishes between them according to whether they are relations of 'secure work', 'autonomous or freestanding work', or 'precarious work'.

We advance this tri-partite taxonomy as one which is quite different in nature from existing bi-partite or tri-partite legal taxonomies in that, whereas existing taxonomies, whether bi-partite or tri-partite, assume or assert that there is a spectrum or axis from 'dependence' to 'independence', this taxonomy denies the existence of a single spectrum or axis (or even a double axis), preferring to see these as more elaborately (and loosely) differentiated kinds of personal work relation. We believe that this analysis, although it gives rise only to 'soft' typologies, nevertheless allows us to identify certain dynamics of development in the practice of personal work relations, which tend to be obscured by existing legal taxonomies. The general perception seems to be, from within existing legal taxonomies, that there is a dynamic from dependent towards apparently independent personal work relations, and that conceptions of dependent or semi-dependent employment should be advanced to keep pace with that dynamic. A further perception is that 'precarious'

---

[8] Article 12 of Ley 20/2007, de 11 de julio, del Estatuto del Trabajo Autónomo <http://www.boe.es/boe/dias/2007/07/12/pdfs/A29964-29978.pdf>. 2009, de 29 de febrero. Cf Mercader Uguina and/2009, de 29 de febrero. Cf Mercader Uguina and de la Puebla Pinilla, above n 7; Valdès Dal-Ré and Leclerc, above n 7; Cabeza Pereiro, above n 7; and J Fudge, 'A Canadian Perspective on the Scope of Employment Standards, Labor Rights, and Social Protection: The Good, the Bad, and the Ugly' (2010) 31 CLLPJ 253.

forms of employment or work are a closed, or at least a nominate legal category of 'atypical', or casual contracts.

We suggest that there is a rather more complex set of dynamics which can better be understood by using our set of three soft typologies. The most significant of these dynamics are those whereby both secure personal work relations and autonomous or free-standing personal work relations are tending to metamorphose into precarious work relations (probably reversing a much earlier set of dynamics whereby both autonomous or free-standing and precarious personal work relations tended to metamorphose into secure ones). There is hardly a type of job or profession that is being spared by this type of dynamic. At risk of sounding self-referential we feel the need to point out that, at the start of the 2010–2011 academic year, a British private higher education institution, which is part of the US corporation Kaplan Inc, announced a number of vacancies for 'Law Lecturers (Freelance)'. There are also some further dynamics whereby some personal work relations may metamorphose into other kinds of relation or state, which are not personal work relations at all. Some personal work relations, especially autonomous or freestanding ones, may metamorphose into non-personal work arrangements whereby the working person operates within a corporate commercial framework rather than within a personal work relation. Some personal work relations, especially precarious ones, may metamorphose into work arrangements which are so informal or non-obligational that they fail to come within the framework of legally recognized personal work relations. British current affairs provide us with a newly emerging example of these particular trends. The Coalition Government 'Big Society' policy, seeking inter alia to 'give communities the right to bid to take over local state-run services'[9] as well as 'give public sector workers a new right to form employee-owned co-operatives and bid to take over the services they deliver [and] become their own boss',[10] is likely to accelerate the transformation of secure forms of employment into precarious work relations, and give centre stage to non-personal work relations and to voluntary arrangements of explicitly non-obligational character.

We argue that it is the complexity of these dynamics, and the difficulty of reconciling them with essentially single-spectrum legal taxonomies, that has created great difficulties for the analysis and policy-making of labour law. We also argue that precarious work is not a particular category of atypical or casual work contracts or relations, but rather an increasingly broad and loose area of (de)regulation in which a growing number of work relations – including and in particular work relationships previously seen as 'secure' – emerge. In the next section, we suggest how certain other techniques of analysis may be helpful in understanding how personal work relations evolve and function – and how the legal construction of them may in certain ways malfunction – under the impulse of these dynamics.

---

[9] Cabinet Office, *Building Big Society* (May 2010) 1.
[10] Ibid 2.

D. The critical analysis of PWRs – the role of the personal work profile

In previously published work, we have advanced and developed a technique of analysis of personal work relations which, by using the idea of the personal work nexus, starts to get behind or underneath existing legal constructions of personal work relations and therefore to identify ways in which existing legal constructions sometimes fail to respond to the underlying dynamics which are revealed by our critical analysis of 'soft typologies' and the movements between them. We now introduce another such technique of analysis, which seeks to advance further down that path by invoking and using the idea of the 'personal work profile'. This serves to place the personal work nexus analysis in the larger context of the whole work situation and work-related situation within which each personal work relation operates.

Our starting point for the idea of the personal work profile is our perception that personal work relations cannot satisfactorily be understood, classified, or regulated in isolation from the overall personal work situation of the worker in question. That personal work situation may be that the worker simply has one personal work relation through his working life. But that is a rarity; much more common is the personal work situation in which the worker has more than one personal work relation occurring concurrently or sequentially, and where the one or more personal work relations are combined or interspersed with states which can be thought of work-related such as those of being in unpaid work – for instance as a carer for a dependant, or being an unemployed jobseeker, or being on long-term sickness absence, or even being retired from work. We suggest that it is useful to conceive of such personal work situations as constituting the personal work profile of each working person, made up primarily of one or more personal work relations and secondarily of one or more work-related states.

These additional dimensions of work are hardly receiving the attention they deserve, partly because of a lack of analytical tools necessary to see them as essentially linked to the personal work situation of a given worker. A good example of the current analytical shortcomings can be drawn from the way the European Court of Justice approached the personal work situation of Ms Christelle Deliège, in Cases C–51/96 and C–191/97.[11] Ms Deliège was a high-ranking and decorated Belgian judoka, with a grudge against her national sports federation for allegedly failing to select her for a number of international judo competitions, and ultimately depriving her of the possibility of joining the 1996 Belgian Olympic team competing in Atlanta. The reference to the ECJ focused on a number of legal questions that we need not address for the purposes of our analysis and argument. But it also raised the question of Ms Deliège's employment status, a question which received a rather inconclusive answer. Ms Deliège argued that she was a professional or at least

---

[11] Case C–51/96, *Christelle Deliège* [2000] ECR I–2549.

semi-professional judoka.[12] The Judo Federation, a number of governments, and the Commission argued that judo was an amateur sport, and that the case fell outside the scope of EU law and the Court's jurisdiction.[13] The Court took the different view that, in Ms Deliège's case, judo constituted an 'economic activity' and possibly amounted to a 'provision of services' covered by what was then Article 59 of the EC Treaty, mainly on the basis that athletes, 'by participating in the competition, enable the organizer to put on a sports event which the public may attend, which television broadcasters may retransmit and which may be of interest to advertisers and sponsors'.[14] On this basis the Court concluded that Ms Deliège's activity was indirectly falling under Article 59, without directly deciding on her employment status.

As labour lawyers, we do feel a certain degree of dissatisfaction with this type of conclusion, as indeed we would do with any suggestion that athletes at the level of Ms Deliège could be seen as amateurs, simply because they do not take part in prize-fighting competitions (say, as professional boxers would do), or they are not employed by a team (as professional footballers would do). These are the sort of complex work relationships that the notions of personal work nexus, of personal work profile, and of personal work situation may well help clarify and bring together. These professional athletes may well not be professional athletes in the sense of being employed under a contract of employment by a particular team, or their respective sports federations or boards. They may also not be professionals in the sense of performing in competition in direct exchange for an economic remuneration or prize. They are, however, remunerated, and the nature and volume of their remuneration is directly linked to their athletic performance. In Ms Deliège's case, the Court had been advised that she 'had received, by reason of her sporting achievements, grants from the Belgian French-speaking Community and from the Belgian Inter-Federal and Olympic Committee and that she has been sponsored by a banking institution and a motor-car manufacturer'.[15] There was, in our view, a direct personal work nexus between Ms Deliège and her grant-awarding bodies and sponsors, which very much depended on her performance, and on her national sports federation granting her the necessary opportunities to perform.

Indeed her personal work profile could have been even more complex than this, without the Court, or any national court of law, necessarily taking notice of it. She could have had a contract of employment, or some other personal work contract or personal work relation, as a physical education teacher in a local school, possibly part-remunerated by the national Ministry of Education, or by the national Sports Council. On top of that, she could have been a judo instructor in a local club, being paid a small mat fee by her students before each training session. Her personal work situation could have been further enriched by her being, or becoming, a visually impaired athlete. Or by converting to Islam and seeking to wear a hijab in training

---

[12] Ibid para 6.
[13] Ibid paras 6, 23, 25.
[14] Ibid para 57.
[15] Ibid para 51.

and competitions. Or by being the primary carer for a disabled person. Admittedly, some of these personal circumstances may well be caught by recent anti-discrimination legislation, but on a piecemeal basis. These circumstances should cast the role of her national sports federation (and possibly of other entities too) under a completely different light, and – we would argue – possibly trigger a series of positive duties in respect of her right not to be subject to any sort of unjustified discriminatory or capricious treatment, something that we would associate with the notion of 'dignity', and with her being accorded the career progression opportunities and 'capabilities' she deserves, as well as some degree of protection in respect of the stability of her athletic and work activity, at least as long as she continued to perform satisfactorily in high-level competitions. None of these considerations appeared to influence the Court's reasoning and one would struggle to find a comparable approach to the analysis of complex personal work relations in the domestic arena.

It is only in exceptional cases that the law, and legal interpreters, dare to venture outside the strict confines of the binary divide, and of bilateral contractual relations, to assess the broader context in which the latter are actually performed. In *Coleman v Attridge Law* the Court of Justice effectively recognized that domestic work performed as the primary carer of a disabled dependant may well cast important normative effect over the personal work relation of the carer,[16] a concept known as discrimination by association. The French Cour de Cassation has established a fairly resilient jurisprudential line of reasoning imposing important restrictions on the operation of mobility clauses which, because of the scope or actual application, may infringe Article 8 of the European Convention on Human Rights.[17] But these are limited, albeit important, departures from what is otherwise a very narrow approach to the analysis of complex personal work relations and to the application of employment protection legislation. In the early 1990s the Italian Constitutional Court deemed the *clausole elastiche* to be unconstitutional as, by rendering the working shifts of part-time workers amenable to unilateral variations by the employer at relatively short notice, these contractual clauses had the consequence of rendering their working lives unpredictable, and made it impossible for a part-time worker 'to program other activities through which he may integrate the income obtained from his part-time work', and thus attain an overall income 'sufficient for him and his family to obtain a free and dignified existence',[18] as required by Article 36 of the Italian Constitution. But, again, these decisions where the law and legal interpreter look beyond the narrow confines of the bilateral contractual relationship put before them, are a rarity even in Continental systems, let alone in the far less cohesive, common-law-based, labour law regimes.

Before concluding this section, it is important for us to be clear about how the conception of the personal work profile relates to that of *statut professionnel* – best translated as 'membership of the labour force' or 'labour force membership' – which

---

[16] Case C–303/06, *Coleman v Attridge Law* [2008] ECR I–5603.
[17] Cour de cassation (Soc), Decision No 96-40755 of 12 January 1999.
[18] Corte Costituzionale, Sentenza 4 maggio 1992, n 210, GU 20/05/1992.

has been identified as an analytical concept in existing labour law scholarship, in particular by Alain Supiot and his colleagues in the 'Beyond Employment' project.[19] Our conceptions of the personal work situation and the personal work profile are, in descriptive terms, quite similar to those of the *statut professionnel* or labour force membership. However, the way in which we seek to develop and deploy the idea of the personal work profile is different from the way in which the idea of the *statut professionnel* / labour force membership is developed and deployed by Supiot and his colleagues. They advance the idea of the *statut professionnel*/labour force membership as a kind of over-arching personal status for the working person involving responsibilities both for employers and for the state as guarantor of social security and regulator of the labour market, and, by the same token, correlative rights for the working person – identified as 'social drawing rights'.

We regard that as a very important basis for the design, on a strategic level, of labour law, social security law, and employment policy. However, we envisage the personal work profile as an analytical concept with a more limited function. We advance and seek to deploy the idea of the personal work profile not as a status or relationship in and of itself, but as a technique of analysis for understanding in what sense and to what extent particular personal work relations should be regarded as secure, autonomous or freestanding, or precarious – and for better understanding the ways in which the existing legal categories of personal work relations are articulated and applied.

We suggest that the idea of the personal work profile can be used as an analytical technique for that purpose in two main ways. At one level, which we could regard as that of detailed technical analysis, we can use the idea of the personal work profile to illuminate the ways in which a particular working person may be engaged or involved in a multiplicity of personal work relations or work-related states, and to show how those personal work relations and work-related states may have implications for each other. Thus, as exemplified in the hypothetical example discussed in the previous paragraphs, within a personal work profile there might be two or more personal work relations which, while remaining sufficiently separate as not to fuse together into a single complex personal work relation, might nevertheless have normative implications for each other – as for instance where the employer in personal work relation 1 has to take account, for the purposes of working time regulation, of the hours which the worker works for another employer in a separate personal work relation 2, or where both employers ought to be obliged to render the shifts of the two personal work relations as predictable as possible, in order to allow the worker to combine the two salaries and thus derive a decent income and a dignified living standard.

Thus again, within a personal work profile there might be a work-related state which has normative implications for the primary personal work relation in which the worker is engaged – as for instance where being in the work-related state of carer for a disabled relative transforms the primary personal work relation into one where there is a right to 'flexible working'. However, we also suggest that the idea of the

---

[19] A Supiot, with others, *Beyond Employment – Changes in Work and the Future of Labour Law in Europe* (Oxford University Press, 2001) 24.

personal work profile can be used as an analytical technique to question existing legal constructions of personal work relations at an altogether deeper level. We suggest that the idea of the personal work profile can be used to illuminate the way in which existing legal constructions of personal work relations tend, in a way which can be unsatisfactory and problematical, to characterize the personal work relation, and indeed the whole personal work situation of a working person, from within the confines and perspective of a single personal work relation, when in fact the opposite should be the case – that is to say, each personal work relation should be characterized in the context of the personal work profile as a whole.

Thus it is very noticeable that in many European legal systems, the taxonomy system for personal work relations – whether it is a binary or a tri-partite one – is very often, one might say typically, applied with reference to a single personal work relation or indeed personal work contract. The working person is classified as an 'employee' or a 'worker' or an 'independent contractor' by reference to one particular personal work relation or personal work contract. This classification of working persons themselves, *ratione personae*, rather than of their personal work relations, may itself be problematical in some important general ways – historically at least, it could amount to very questionable assignments of lowly status as 'servants' or 'workmen'. However, this way of taxonomizing (and thereby regulating) personal work relations gives rise to a more specific analytical problem: it fosters the illusion that this taxonomy can satisfactorily be effected, indeed can satisfactorily exist, at the level of each particular personal work relation or personal work contract, when in fact such taxonomies, in so far as they are sustainable at all, can only meaningfully be operated on the basis of the personal work profile as a whole.

Thus we suggest that the binary divide between 'employment' and 'self-employment', or between 'dependent employment' and 'independent contracting', itself evolved primarily as a distinction between personal work profiles which involved one personal work relation with one employer over a significant time period – employment relations – and personal work profiles which involved multiple short-term personal work relations with many different employers or work-users.[20]

Indeed, this is in a way implicit in the very terminology which is used to identify personal work profiles which do not have the character of dependent employment. The terminologies of 'independent contractor' or 'self-employed worker' invoke the historical fact that the people in those personal work situations were viewed as working for many persons and therefore employed by or dependent on no one person. Only thus can we explain the otherwise very curious notion of

---

[20] On time as a determinant characteristic for different work relations cf the very perceptive V Bavaro, 'Tesi sullo Statuto Giuridico del Tempo nel Rapporto di Lavoro Subrdinato' in V Bavaro and B Veneziani (eds), *Le Dimensioni Giuridiche dei tempi del Lavoro* (Cacucci, 2009) 11. In *Wage Labour and Capital* Marx provides a rather vivid description of the importance of the temporal element in the provision of labour at the outset of the industrial revolution: 'The capitalist, it seems, therefore, *buys* their labour with money. They *sell* him their labour for money. But this is merely the appearance. In reality what they sell to the capitalist for money is their labour *power*. The capitalist buys this labour power for a day, a week, a month, etc . . . Labour power, therefore, is a commodity, neither more nor less than sugar. The former is measured by the clock, the latter by the scales.' K Marx, *Wage Labour and Capital* (Foreign Languages Press, 1978) 18–19.

'self-employment' itself. In the next section, we explore the implications of these critical analyses for the regulation of the legal construction of personal work relations.

E. Legal characterization as regulatory technique

In the two previous sections, we have in effect been concentrating on the taxonomical or classificatory aspect of the legal characterization of personal work relations. In this section, our attention turns to its regulatory aspect; we make the point that there are a number of different techniques for regulating personal work relations by means of legal characterization. These techniques of regulation by legal characterization can be used to respond to concerns which are identified by the critical analysis which we have advanced in the previous section. In this section, we seek to identify these techniques, and also to suggest an evaluative notion of 'personality in work' which might inform the use of these techniques.

Our main purpose in this discussion is to emphasize the width of variety of the techniques of regulation by legal characterization which are available. We believe that the whole discussion, of the activity which we are identifying as the legal characterization of personal work relations, has been impoverished by a tendency to assume that the arsenal of regulatory weapons is a very limited one. That is to say, the available techniques often seem to be envisaged as being limited to either (1) adjustment of the place at which to make the binary divide between contracts of employment and personal contracts for services, or (2) the introduction of a third intermediate contract type, or (3) the treatment of personal work relations as relationships rather than contracts as a way of opening out the contractual categories. These are very important techniques, but there are various other ones which should command our attention.

Among such further techniques we should count rules or doctrines of law which create presumptions in favour of one particular contractual or relationship analysis of any given personal work relation – for example, a rule or doctrine that a specified set of personal work relations shall be presumed to take the legal form of contracts of employment.[21] Equally, we should also count as such techniques rules or doctrines of law which authorize or require characterization of personal work relations in ways which override the formal characterizations which the participants have attached to those relations to fit into one category or avoid another category – for example, rules or doctrines which tackle 'disguised employment' or 'sham contracts'.[22] Such rules or doctrines may combine to create general notions of controlling the abusive adoption of legal forms with the purpose or effect of defeating the application of labour laws – that is to say that such notions may amount to anti-dodging measures to protect the integrity of labour laws.

---

[21] The paradigm in this sense remains the *présomption de salariat* contained in the recently renumbered Article L7313-1 of the French Labour Code, in spite of its important qualification by Article L7313-1 *bis*.

[22] ACL Davies, 'Sensible Thinking About Sham Transactions: *Protectacoat Firthglow v Szilagyi*' (2009) 38 Industrial Law Journal 318.

We suggest that one big further step can be taken in evolving the idea of 'legal characterization of personal work relations' as a larger, more dynamic way of thinking about the role of classification or taxonomy in the development of labour law. That big further step consists of recognizing and being alert to the ways in which the lawmakers and doctrinalists of labour or employment law are in fact constantly inventing or discovering novel forms of personal work contract or personal work relation. This continual process of invention or discovery takes place around or within the existing grand categories of employment or self-employment, but eventually disrupts or transforms those grand categories themselves.

Because, as labour lawyers, we live in the middle of these evolutions, we may fail to observe the full extent to which they are taking place. We may notice the emergence of novel forms or formulations of personal work contracts. This is a phenomenon which Simon Deakin encapsulated in the notion of the 'many futures of the contract of employment',[23] and which is instantiated by Anne Davies' articulation of the idea of the 'intermittent employment contract'.[24] But it may more easily escape our attention that new forms of personal work relation present themselves in ways which are even more subtly challenging to existing taxonomies. This is quite often because new kinds of personal work contract or personal work relation have in effect been created, but have not been endowed with a name which will secure conceptual recognition for them. This is the phenomenon of fully or partly innominate personal work contracts or personal work relations; it is of major significance in the evolution of labour or employment law.

Once one has accepted the possibility of this phenomenon, examples of it are to be found all about us. In English law, many such examples result from the implementation of EU Directives, themselves often modelled upon legal characterizations which it is difficult to reproduce directly within the particular conceptual framework of existing national employment law. In a sense, the largest and most striking example is the particular kind of transferable employment contract or relationship which is created by the Transfer of Undertakings (Protection of Employment) (TUPE) Regulations in implementation of the Acquired Rights Directive.[25] Another good example consists of the contract or relationship into which the fixed-term contract of employment is transformed in certain conditions by the Fixed-term Work Regulations, which implemented the Fixed-term Work Directive.[26] It will in our view turn out to be the case that another new personal

---

[23] S Deakin, 'The Many Futures of the Contract of Employment' in J Conaghan, RM Fischl, and K Clare (eds), *Labour Law in an Era of Globalization* (Oxford University Press, 2004) 177–96.

[24] ACL Davies, 'The Contract of Intermittent Employment' (2007) 36 Industrial Law Journal 102–18.

[25] The Transfer of Undertakings (Protection of Employment) Regulations 2006, SI 2006/246; Council Directive 2001/23/EC on the approximation of the laws of the Member States relating to the safeguarding of employees' rights in the event of transfers of undertakings, businesses or parts of undertakings or businesses, [2001] OJ L 82/16.

[26] The Fixed-term Employees (Prevention of Less Favourable Treatment) Regulations 2002, SI 2002/2034; Council Directive 1999/70/EC of 28 June 1999 concerning the framework agreement on fixed-term work concluded by ETUC, UNICE and CEEP, [1999] OJ L 43.

work relation has been ushered into existence by the Temporary Agency Work Regulations, which implement the Temporary Agency Work Directive.[27]

In an even more extended sense, we can observe the emergence of new and as yet innominate personal work relations from the legislation about 'flexible working' – the employment contract or relationship to which the provisions about 'flexible working' applies is distinctive in character from the employment contract or relationship to which those provisions do not apply. That is, incidentally, a legal characterization which is identified by reference to the personal work profile of the worker in question – where the personal work profile of the worker in question includes a qualifying work-related state as a carer, the primary employment contract or relationship is thereby transformed into this special kind of flexible work contract or relationship. European Union (EU) law is an increasingly fertile territory for the development and recognition of such complex personal work profile.

No less significantly, the inability of some EU national legal systems to encompass the idea that discrete but simultaneous personal work relations ought to be approached and regulated by reference to the overall personal work situation of the worker in question led, inter alia, to the collapse of the new Working Time Directive negotiations in 2009.[28] This is a dynamic which we can see as in stark contrast with the ones explored in the previous section, by reference to some more holistic readings operated by the Cour de Cassation and by the Corte Costituzionale.

Rather similarly, we believe that the implementation of the Employment Discrimination Framework Directive 2000/78 by the Employment Equality (Age) Regulations 2006[29] had effectively created a particular kind of employment contract or relationship with a 'default retirement age' attached to it, though – at the time of writing – this particular feature of UK employment law is effectively being 'retired' by the current Coalition Government.[30] We suggest and argue that these emergent new forms of personal work relation instantiate the idea of 'legal characterization' in its full and complex sense; that is to say, they are much more than simply emerging new taxonomies; they are also in and of themselves instruments of regulation. They are, indeed, very subtle instruments of regulation, capable of being highly tuned, in at least two dimensions. We proceed to display those two dimensions in the succeeding paragraphs.

First, these newly emerging types of personal work relation constitute complex regulatory instruments in that they represent new forms of regulation which, in various ways, fall between *jus cogens* and *jus dispositivum*. That is to say, they do not

---

[27] The Agency Workers Regulations 2010, SI 2010/93; Directive 2008/104/EC of the European Parliament and of the Council of 19 November 2008 on temporary agency work', [2008] OJ L 9.

[28] 'Finally, no substantive agreement could be reached on the issue of multiple contracts. For workers covered by more than one employment contract, Parliament considered that working time should be calculated per worker and not per contract', COD/2004/0209: 29/04/2009 – EP/Council: Conciliation committee, results.

[29] Council Directive 2000/78/EC establishing a general framework for equal treatment in employment and occupation, [2000] OJ L 303/16; Employment Equality (Age) Regulations 2006, SI 2006/1031, now Equality Act 2010.

[30] UK Department for Business, Innovation and Skills, 'Phasing Out the Default Retirement Age: Government Response to Consultation' (January 2011).

on the one hand represent mandatorily imposed terms and conditions for the making or conduct or termination of personal work relations; nor, on the other hand, do they represent mere default or optional terms and conditions for the making or conduct or termination of personal work relations. (In that sense, the 'default retirement age' is a misnomer.) Instead they represent complex instruments of control over the making, conduct or termination of personal work relations, imposing elaborate constraints often of a procedural kind (such as that a particular normative arrangement is allowable only if agreed according to certain individual or collective procedures).

Second, these newly emerging types of personal work relation constitute complex regulatory instruments in that they represent, in and of themselves, carefully nuanced positions on a 'flexicurity' spectrum. In this respect, they are rather unlike the traditional forms of labour law regulation, which consisted in a much more direct way of protective interventions in favour of defined sections of the workforce. The new generation of regulatory instruments, taking this form of novel legal characterizations, may as easily create models for the conduct of personal work relations which are retrogressive rather than progressive when measured against older patterns of legal intervention, and which would increase the processes of precarization of personal work relations.

One such example of retrogressive legal intervention may be provided by some reform proposals aimed, ostensibly, at re-unifying various forms of atypical work contracts through the introduction of a new, unifying, 'legal characterization', variably referred to as *contrat unique*,[31] *contratto unico*,[32] or *contrato único*.[33] These suggested reforms have the objective of replacing both 'atypical' and 'standard' contracts, and their distinctive regulations, with a new and unifying contractual structure which, while in principle of an indefinite duration, would derogate from standard employment protection legislation and provide for a progressive accrual of rights according to seniority and continuity in employment. There is substantial support from some European quarters for this third type of deregulatory approach, with the 2007 *Flexicurity Pathways* Report overtly suggesting that '[t]he flexibility of standard contracts and the security of non-standard contracts could be enhanced by having a system where certain entitlements (on top of the basics) and elements of protection are being built up gradually'.[34]

---

[31] P Cahuc and F Kramarz, *De la précarité à la mobilité: vers une Sécurité sociale professionnelle* (La Documentation française, 2004). On the basis of these proposals the UMP produced the report *Repenser le contrat de travail en instaurant un contrat de travail unique*, available at <http://www.u-m-p.org/site/index.php/ump/debattre/dossiers/economie_emploi/re-penser_le_contrat_de_travail_en_instaurant_un_contrat_de_travail_unique>.

[32] Disegno di Legge n 1481/2009, 'Disposizioni per il superamento del dualismo del mercato del lavoro, la promozione del lavoro stabile in strutture produttive flessibili e la garanzia di pari opportunità nel lavoro per le nuove generazioni'. See also T Boeri and P Garibaldi, *Un Nuovo Contratto per Tutti* (Chiarelettere, 2008).

[33] *Propuesta para la reactivación laboral en España*, available at <http://www.crisis09.es/propuesta/>. Also available in English at <http://www.crisis09.es/PDF/restart-the-labor-market.pdf>.

[34] European Expert Group on Flexicurity, *Flexicurity Pathways – Turning Hurdles into Stepping Stones* (June 2007) 12. See also explicit references at 32, 35.

A no less pertinent example of retrogressive legislation is offered to us by a *decreto delega legislativa*, adopted by the Italian Parliament in early 2010.[35] Among other things, this *decreto* sought to allow the parties to a contract for the provision of personal work to include terms specifying that, in case of grievances, they may bring the matter before ad hoc arbitration committees, whose decisions – unless the mandate given to arbitrator, or an applicable collective agreement, explicitly provides otherwise – may not be appealed before the ordinary jurisdiction of the *pretore del lavoro*.[36] This suggested reform was supposed to encourage alternative dispute resolution (ADR) mechanisms and reduce the backlog of cases pending before the notoriously log-jammed Italian courts. But, no doubt, its effects were to strengthen the *certificazione* procedures set up by Law 276/03,[37] by allowing the parties to *ex ante* 'certified' self-employment contracts to protect their choices over the nature and regulatory regime applying to their personal work relation – dare we say their very personal 'legal characterization' – from any unwelcome *ex post* judicial interference.

In this and the preceding sections, we have sought to demonstrate that there is a process or genre of legal taxonomy and legal regulation of personal work relations which it is useful to think about as the 'legal characterization' of those relations. We have also tried to develop a critical analysis of that process or genre, and to show that this process or genre plays a significant role in the development of labour or employment law. It follows from the arguments which we have advanced that this process or genre itself needs to be kept under careful strategic surveillance by those who are concerned with the evolution of labour or employment law. In our Conclusion, we consider how, within the European region, EU law might provide a basis or forum for that particular kind of strategic surveillance.

F. Conclusion

In the course of this chapter, we have argued for a certain way of thinking about the conceptual activity which is normally understood as the taxonomy of labour law or the establishing of the personal scope of labour law in general or particular labour laws. We have tried to reconceive that activity as a more complex one involving elements both of classification and regulation, and we have used the terminology of legal characterization to identify that more ambitious conception. We have suggested ways in which that activity might be undertaken, suggestions which have led us to articulate the notion of the 'personal work profile' and to identify a process of emergence of new, often innominate, types of personal work relation. These arguments have pointed towards the need for some quite fundamental stocktaking

---

[35] DDL 1167-B of 2010, available at <http://www.lavoro.gov.it/NR/rdonlyres/E4890E6F-EB00-4C3C-89C3-AAAD34DBD0DC/0/collegatolavoro.pdf>.

[36] Article 31(5). A provision that may well not withstand the scrutiny of the Italian Constitutional Court.

[37] Cf N Countouris, *The Changing Law of the Employment Relationship* (Ashgate, 2007) 68.

of the ways in which legal characterization is being done. In this Conclusion, we briefly consider the possibilities that some such stocktaking might usefully take place, so far as the European region is concerned, within the compass of EU labour or employment law.

We wish to suggest that some such stocktaking within the compass of EU labour or employment law would be desirable. It was, we believe, precisely this kind of stocktaking which the International Labour Organization (ILO) attempted to conduct at the level of international labour law, in the elaborate normative exercise which began with an unsuccessful attempt to enact a Convention on 'Contract Labour' and culminated,[38] many years later, in Recommendation 198 on the Employment Relationship.[39] This was, we dare to suggest, in fact, an exercise in trying to regulate the way in which the legal characterization of personal work relations is carried out in or by national labour law systems. In view of the enormous difficulty and complexity of such an exercise, it is not at all surprising that the ILO could take this no further than introducing what is, in effect, a rather loose Open Method of Coordination of the ways in which the legal characterization of the employment relationship is carried out at the national level.

One might hope that this kind of stocktaking could be taken further within the compass of EU employment law. The need for something at least as ambitious as this has been usefully identified by Jeffrey Kenner,[40] and in any event emerges from increasingly anxious debates about inconsistencies and ambiguities in the usage of the terminologies of 'employment contract' and 'employment relationship' in European national legal systems and in EU law itself. Indeed, there are quite strong reasons for regarding this as a matter of some urgency so far as the legal policy making of EU employment law is concerned. On the one hand, we suggest that the legal characterization of personal work relations is dominated, both in European national policy debates and at the EU level itself, by a conceptual apparatus and an ideology of 'flexicurity' which needs to be scrutinized and questioned. On the other hand, we also suggest, a powerful engine restatement of European private law, in the shape of the initiative for a Common Frame of Reference for European Private Law, which seems to be driving towards a new binary divide of personal work relations, in which 'employment contracts' are deemed to fall outside the realm of European private law but all other personal work contracts are deemed to fall outside the domain of labour law or employment law.

Detailed development of this set of arguments is beyond the scope of the present chapter. We confine ourselves to two concluding points. First, we suggest that, if the debate which we seek, about the legal characterization of personal work

---

[38] ILO, Contract labour – Fifth item on the agenda Report V (1) to the International Labour Conference 86th Session 1998 (ILO, 1997).

[39] ILO Recommendation R 198: Recommendation concerning the employment relationship (95th Conference Session, Geneva, 15 June 2006). Cf G Casale (ed), *The Employment Relationship – A Comparative Overview* (Hart Publishing, 2010).

[40] J Kenner, 'New Frontiers in EU Labour Law: From Flexicurity to Flex-Security' in M Dougan and S Currie, *50 Years of the European Treaties: Looking Back and Thinking Forward* (Hart Publishing, 2009) 279.

relations in European law, is to be a fully meaningful one, it requires the identification of the set of values or objectives which should inform the process of legal characterization of personal work relations. As we have indicated, we have some concerns about a state of affairs in which the notion of 'flexicurity' is seen as a conclusive identifier of that set of values or objectives. In further work which will follow on from this chapter, we will advance the suggestion of a different set of values or objectives with their own identifying notion. Our identifying notion is that of 'personality in work'; it embraces the objectives of promoting dignity, capability and stability in the arranging and conduct of personal work relations.

Our second and final point concerns the relation of our notion of legal characterization to the 'idea of labour law'. We are conscious of the need to establish the credentials of the notion of the legal characterization of personal work relations as coming within the 'idea of labour law'. We realize that doubts may be experienced on that score, as we sketch out a sphere of activity which consciously exceeds the traditional boundaries of labour law. We anticipate that those doubts may be intensified when we begin to frame an ideology – that of 'personality in work' – which, in its turn, may seem no less transgressive for those accustomed to an ideology of the redressing of the inequality of bargaining power within the compass of the contract for dependent employment. We hope that the notion of the 'legal characterization of personal work relations' may be robust enough to withstand such doubts – but we realize that we are in the hands of our readers in that respect.

13

Ideas of Labour Law – A View from the South

*Paul Benjamin**

A. Introduction: 1979

My first exposure to labour law was in 1979. As a final year law student at the University of Cape Town, I worked at the Workers Advice Bureau run by the Western Province General Workers Union, a trade union organizing largely African migrant workers in the Western Cape. While not illegal, the union was excluded from participation in statutory industrial relations because its members included workers classified as 'African'. The apartheid state used a range of techniques (including the security police) to persuade black workers to join plant-based works committees rather than trade unions.

On Saturday mornings we interviewed workers in the union's crowded offices in Athlone, a 'coloured' working-class area in Cape Town. Most were migrant workers from the Transkei for whom dismissal would probably mean removal from Cape Town under influx control legislation and a forced return to their Transkei 'homeland'. The Western Cape had the unique status under the apartheid mas-ter-plan of being a '"coloured" labour preference area' – African workers could only hold positions if neither white nor coloured workers were available.

In the afternoons, we would type letters of demand on the union's typewriter. The demands that we put in the post on behalf of dismissed workers were usually limited to claims for notice pay (usually a week's pay but in some industries as little as a day or even an hour), unpaid wages, leave pay, the return of illegal deductions, and to receive the Unemployment Insurance card. As African workers, they enjoyed a limited amalgam of common law contractual and statutory rights. Re-employment was not on the cards unless their co-workers came out on strike in their support.

In the same year, I studied labour law for the first time. We read Kahn-Freund and, with our experience in the Advice Bureau, needed no convincing that the employment relationship was one typified by submission and subordination.

---

* Professor of Law, University of Cape Town, and practising attorney.

1979 also saw the publication of the first volume of the report of the Wiehahn Commission into labour legislation. The Commission had been appointed in 1977 in response to the re-emergence of an independent trade union movement organizing black workers since 1973. In the two years that the Commission deliberated, the independent trade unions had grown from 70,000 to 200,000 members and by the end of the 1980s would have some 2 million members.

The Commission's recommendations were enacted into law marking the start of the modern era of labour law in South Africa. Racial job reservation was scrapped and trade unions with African members could by 1980 register under the then Industrial Conciliation Act which had regulated labour relations for 'non-black' workers since 1924. This watershed change was achieved by removing the words 'other than an African' from the statutory definition of an employee. In retrospect, this was the first major step towards dismantling the edifice of the apartheid state. Within a few years, the influx control legislation and the racial segregation of residential areas would also fall away.

The Commission confidently advised the Nationalist government that extending the right to register and participate in collective bargaining would take the political sting out of the emerging independent trade union movement who would henceforth spend their time looking after their member's economic (rather than their political) interests. A considerable portion of the trade union movement feared that the state could achieve this goal and argued against participation in the statutory system for fear of 'judicial deradicalization' and state interference in trade union democracy. For several years the unions were split by an acrimonious 'registration' debate but by 1984 this had been resolved; the union movement continued to grow rapidly throughout the 1980s using the legal space that flowed from participation in the system to advance their members' interests through collective bargaining while intensifying their opposition to the apartheid government.

The Commission had recommended the establishment of an Industrial Court with wide discretionary powers to rule on unfair labour practices. While the initial rationale for its establishment was to offer some protection for white workers who were losing the benefits of statutory job reservation,[1] it soon became the basis for unprecedented legal protections for all employees, significantly protection against unfair dismissal.

The workers who sought advice at the Advice Bureau have now had the protection of labour law for three decades. Falling in the middle of that period was the end of apartheid in 1994 – the evolution of a modern labour law in South Africa therefore spans the last decade and a half of the struggle against apartheid and the first decade and a half of the struggle to undo its deep-rooted legacy of inequality.

This chapter's focus is to assess the extent to which one of the key goals of employment law – protection against unfair and arbitrary dismissal – has been achieved for South African workers. Its approach is 'regulatory' – it seeks to

---

[1] See A van Niekerk, 'In Search of Justification: The Origins of Statutory Protection of Security of Employment in South Africa' (2004) 25 ILJ 853.

examine how successful legal techniques and institutions have been in translating this legal right into a real security in the lives of workers. At the same time two further themes are explored. The first is the issue of 'judicialization': what are the consequences of security of employment having been shifted from an organizational to a rights-based issue? In particular, to what extent have the nature of legal processes and the attitudes of the judiciary and the legal profession helped or hindered the achievement of this goal. The second theme involves locating the legislative project of enhancing security of employment within the wider context of changes in the composition of the labour market that South Africa has experienced along with economies worldwide.

B. Towards more secure employment

The organizing strategies of the independent trade union movement that re-emerged in apartheid South Africa in the 1970s centred on trade union recognition, wage negotiations, and protection against arbitrary dismissal. Dismissals, particularly of key union activists, led to frequent and widespread wild-cat strikes. In a hostile legal environment, greater security of employment was initially achieved on a plant-by-plant basis by including 'just cause' dismissal protections in hard-won collective agreements in terms of which contested dismissal disputes were resolved by private arbitrations.

From the early 1980s, protection against unfair dismissal was extended more broadly as the newly established industrial court ruled that a dismissal was an unfair labour practice unless the employer followed a fair procedure and had a valid reason. The court required employers to conduct an internal disciplinary inquiry before dismissing a worker for misconduct or incapacity and to consult trade unions before retrenching on account of their operational requirements. This approach drew on two key sources: international standards, in particular the ILO's Convention on Termination of Employment 158 of 1982, and the emerging practice of large corporations who were introducing formal disciplinary procedures to control the increasingly expensive knee-jerk tendency of managers and supervisors to fire on sight.

By the end of the apartheid era in 1994 the industrial court was dealing with 3,000 dismissal cases annually. A lack of resources meant that cases were taking up to three years to resolve, and considerably longer if there were appeals. Dismissals remained a significant cause of (generally wild-cat) strike action and the major trade unions and employers continued to make extensive use of arbitration to expedite adjudication.

While many of the initial precedents were established in cases involving individual (often white) employees, the newly registered trade unions used litigation strategies to advance their organizational drives. For instance, the National Union of Mineworkers which was established in 1982 had by 1985 won cases establishing the right of its members to conduct strike ballots on mine property, the right of shaft stewards to represent members at disciplinary inquiries and had obtained reinstatement orders for workers dismissed for refusing to work in dangerous conditions and for participating in lawful strike action.[2] These rights were achieved at a time when the trade union movement continued to face intense repression: in 1987 the headquarters of the largest trade union federation COSATU were blown up by the security police. The security police also funded rival (often violent) trade unions and 'front' labour consultancies which advised employers on anti-union strategies.

In 1988, the Nationalist Government enacted legislation to roll back many of the gains achieved through unfair labour practice litigation. This led to massive nation-wide stay-aways which persuaded organized business to withdraw its earlier support for this legislation. Negotiations between organized business and labour led eventually to the conclusion of a tri-partite agreement in 1990 between the apartheid state, organized business, and labour that future changes to labour law would not be introduced without negotiation. The 'social capital' forged in the intense battles over labour law in the last years of apartheid created the ethos in which the post-apartheid reform of labour laws were negotiated and enacted.

The transition to democracy was regulated by a 1993 Interim Constitution that entrenched a number of labour rights including protection against unfair labour practices, rights of freedom of association and collective bargaining, and rights to strike and lock-out. Protection against unfair labour practices was elevated to constitutional level to allay the fears of old order civil servants who anticipated mass dismissals at the hands of a democratic government.[3]

An innovative Labour Relations Act was enacted in late 1995, the first major legislative achievement of the new Parliament. It contained a reworking of unfair dismissal law that sought to reduce the time and costs involved in resolving dismissal disputes. The pre-1995 jurisprudence was codified and simplified. The new statute's core provisions were supplemented by a 'soft law' Code of Good Practice which sought to promote certainty while at the same time allowing for a flexible application of the law, permitting smaller businesses to adhere to less formalized procedures. The requirement to conduct an inquiry before dismissing was replaced by a less formal obligation to conduct an investigation and allow representations. Two new institutions for dispute resolution and adjudication were created: a para-statal Commission for Conciliation, Mediation and Arbitration (CCMA) and a specialist system of labour courts. The CCMA is governed by a tri-partite Governing Body and staffed by panels of full-time and part-time commissioners who conciliate and arbitrate disputes, many of whom were drawn from the ranks of the trade union movement.

The aim is to provide a system of industrial justice that is 'cheap, accessible, quick and informal'. There are simplified referral procedures and tight time-frames:

---

[2] C Thompson, 'Bending and Borrowing: the Development of South Africa's Unfair Labour Practice Jurisprudence' in R Blanpain and M Weiss (eds), *The Changing Face of Labour Law and Industrial Relations: Liber Amicorum for Clyde W Summers* (Nomos, 1993).

[3] H Cheadle, 'Labour Relations' in H Cheadle (ed), *South African Constitutional Law: The Bill of Rights* (Lexis-Nexis, 2010).

disputes must be referred within 30 days although late referrals can be condoned. The first conciliation meeting must be held within 30 days of the referral. Unresolved disputes about the most common categories of dismissals (misconduct and incapacity) may be referred to arbitrations in which the parties' right to legal representation is restricted.[4] Unless a party objects, the arbitration can start immediately after the failure of the conciliation process. The arbitrator's award must be delivered within 14 days of the end of the hearing and is not subject to appeal; in addition, the grounds on which the Labour Court can review arbitrator's awards are restricted to a narrow set of grounds typically applicable to consensual arbitrations. The Labour Court is the court of first instance for cases about dismissals for operational requirements, strike dismissals, and discrimination cases.

The Act articulates reinstatement as the primary remedy for employees dismissed without a valid reason. At the same time, the maximum compensation award is capped at 12 months (or 24 if the dismissal is automatically unfair).[5] The Act represents a trade-off: organized labour was attracted by the idea of quick arbitrations without the expense of lawyers and with a realistic possibility of reinstatement as a remedy. Employers saw their gains as the simplification of their obligations in respect of internal disciplinary inquiries, the short referral period, and the cap on compensation awards. At the same time, the line between disputes of right and interest was tightened and strike action over justiciable disputes was prohibited.

To what extent has the promise of greater security of employment been achieved? Access to dispute resolution has certainly been achieved: the number of dismissal cases has risen from an estimated 3,000 in the final years of the old system (1994–95) to approximately 120,000 per year a decade later in 2006–07.[6] Dismissal cases represent 80 per cent of the CCMA's case load and are the stock-in-trade of South African labour law. It is estimated that 4 per cent of the approximately 7 million employees in the private sector formal economy are dismissed each year and that one in two dismissed workers refer cases to the CCMA.[7] After a few years of operation, the CCMA appeared to be swamped under the weight of its enormous case load but increased funding and enhanced managerial and administrative efficiencies have allowed it to deliver substantially the initial vision of 'swift and cheap' dispute resolution.

Roughly 60 per cent of dismissal cases referred to it are settled through conciliation, generally within a month of the dispute being referred. The terms of these settlements are not known, but it is likely that the majority involve a financial settlement. Of the balance of cases that go on to arbitration, one-third of employees

---

[4] Other categories of disputes which must be referred to arbitration are those concerning trade union organizational rights, the interpretation of collective agreements, and certain individual unfair labour practices.

[5] The grounds which are classified as automatically unfair dismissals include dismissal where the reason is participation in a protected strike, the employee's pregnancy, unfair discrimination, and whistle-blowing.

[6] These numbers increased to 132,000 in 2007–08 and 140,000 in 2008–09 reflecting higher levels of retrenchment due to the recession.

[7] *Tokiso Review* 2009–10 at 21 (Juta). This publication is a review of labour dispute resolution published annually by a private dispute resolution agency.

succeed with a claim but less than 10 per cent of employees who win their cases (roughly 1,500 annually) receive a reinstatement award in their favour.[8] How many of those workers return to work is not known. This means that the vast majority of workers who are found to have been unfairly dismissed receive an award of financial compensation. The average award is equivalent to four months' pay. The low level of reinstatement is the result of a number of factors. It is not feasible for workers such as domestic workers and employees of very small businesses to be reinstated because of the personal nature of the relationship. However, many employees of larger employers do not seek reinstatement confining their claim to one for compensation only. Even where reinstatement is sought, many arbitrators are reluctant to order reinstatement and tend to accept uncritically the employer's opposition to reinstatement on the ground that the employment relationship has broken down.

On average, conciliations take 27 days and arbitrations are concluded within 39 days; the speed of dispute resolution is a considerable achievement compared to the standard of conventional litigation. However, if the employer resists the claim it can be several years before the worker sees any money or returns to work. At least one-third of those who receive an award in their favour are required to take further administrative steps to ensure payment. Employers are able to take advantage of judicial delays to put off the day of reckoning almost indefinitely which can result in workers receiving nothing or accepting a smaller sum in settlement. Ten per cent of arbitration awards are submitted to the Labour Court for judicial review although a significant proportion of these applications are not pursued to completion, indicating that they are more than anything else a delaying tactic. Where they are pursued to finality, a simple review takes an average of two years to be argued.[9]

The success of the 'rough justice' scheme in achieving access to adjudication can be contrasted with the fate of discrimination litigation. Although South Africa has explicitly prohibited discrimination and employees have been able to bring equal pay claims since 1998, no more than a handful of cases have been brought challenging wage discrimination on racial or gender grounds in this period despite clear evidence of the persistence of the 'apartheid' wage gap.[10] This contrasts with the UK where there are almost as many equal pay claims as there are unfair dismissal claims.[11]

C. Judicial responses

The successes and failures of the scheme illustrate many of the fault-lines along which labour law operates. Its design seeks to insulate the arbitration system from

---

[8] This assessment is based on information derived from the CCMA's electronic case management system. The CCMA's Annual Reports can be found at <http://www.ccma.org.za>.

[9] P Benjamin, 'Conciliation, Arbitration and Enforcement: the Achievements and Challenges of the CCMA' (2009) 30 Industrial Law Journal (SA) 26–48.

[10] P Benjamin, 'Different Routes to Equality and Empowerment' in O Dupper and C Garbers (eds), *Equality in the Workplace: Reflections from South Africa and Beyond* (Juta, 2010).

[11] These figures can be found in the Annual Reports of the Employment Tribunals.

many of the institutional practices and attitudes that load litigation in favour of employers as the stronger and better-resourced party and allow employers to utilize delay as a strategy to prevent workers enforcing their rights.

Chief among these has been the restriction on legal representation in arbitration hearings. This reform has certainly succeeded in reducing the costs of dismissal cases for employees, trade unions, and employers and levelling the playing field. While the legal profession has frequently threatened to challenge this incursion into its livelihood, the courts have accepted this restriction.[12]

It was envisaged that arbitrators would play an inquisitorial role in hearings thereby reducing the premium for legal representation. However, to a large extent this has not materialized, partly because of entrenched attitudes among the legal profession and the judiciary about the inherent superiority of adversarial proceedings. Many judges tended to see a more interventionist approach by an arbitrator as evidence of bias although more recently there has been a line of authority accepting the benefits of a more inquisitorial approach.

There have been a number of other areas of judicial 'resistance'. The most extreme judicial response was a ruling in the country's second highest court, the Supreme Court of Appeal, in 2006 that arbitrators should 'defer' to the reasons given by an employer for a dismissal decision and should be cautious about reversing an employer's decisions.[13] This approach drew its intellectual inspiration from the long-standing UK rule (articulated by Lord Denning) that employers should be allowed a 'band of reasonable responses' in dismissal cases.[14] This approach, which was without foundation in the text of the statute or its underlying policy, was the result of a perception that the ease with which employees could refer disputes to conciliation and arbitration was somehow unfair to employers. The decision was reversed by a unanimous decision of the country's highest court, the Constitutional Court, which pointed out that this had been an explicit policy decision of the legislature in order to prevent dismissals giving rise to industrial unrest.[15]

A similar tension can be seen in contrasting court decisions over the grounds for a judicial review of arbitrator's awards. While the law explicitly limited these grounds, judges during the first decade of the CCMA's life consistently expanded these to give themselves greater scope to set aside arbitral decisions. This made it easier for recalcitrant employers to use review proceedings as a delaying tactic. It took until 2007 for the Constitutional Court to restrict the permissible review grounds to those set out in the Act and remind the lower courts of the clear policy of the Act to limit the scope for judicial intervention in arbitral decisions.[16]

---

[12] *Netherburn Engineering CC t/a Netherburn Ceramics v Mudau NO and Another* [2008] ZALAC 13; (2009) 30 Industrial Law Journal 299 (Labour Appeal Court).

[13] P Benjamin, 'Friend or Foe? The impact of judicial decisions on the operation of the CCMA' (2007) 28 ILJ 1.

[14] *British Leyland UK v Swift* [1981] IRLR 91 (CA).

[15] *Sidumo & another v Rustenberg Platinum Mine (Pty) Ltd & others* (2007) 28 ILJ 2405 (Constitutional Court of South Africa).

[16] P Benjamin, 'Braamfontein versus Bloemfontein: The SCA and Constitutional Court's Approaches to Labour Law' (2009) 30 ILJ 776–90.

Another of the fault-lines along which unfair dismissal law operated has been the 'public–private' divide. This has thrown up two areas of potential duplication and controversy – the relationship between internal disciplinary inquiries and arbitrations and whether dismissals in the public service carry a public character that should allow for them to be subject to administrative review.

The right to challenge unfair dismissals extends to all employees, including public servants. However, due to the more bureaucratic disciplinary proceedings within the public service, this has resulted in a time-consuming duplication of internal and arbitration hearings, making dismissal procedures extremely cumbersome. In the transition period, existing disciplinary proceedings were often transformed into collective agreements which public sector trade unions are now reluctant to change. Civil servants facing dismissal for the more serious misconduct (in particular, corruption) are often suspended on full pay during internal hearings giving them a substantial incentive (with legal assistance) to drag out hearings while collecting their pay cheques. This has contributed to a widely held public perception that that labour law is undermining the state's capacity to deliver services.

In the 1980s, when black employees in the public service were rightless 'temporary' workers, liberal judges had extended administrative law protection to them, often in the context of mass strike dismissals. After 1995, these rights existed in parallel with new statutory rights with the result that public service employees had a choice of routes to attack a decision to dismiss. Again, it has taken the Constitutional Court's intervention in 2010 to confine employees challenging their dismissal to their labour law remedies. Up to this point, the state as employer had been in the anomalous position of having to comply with two (at times divergent) sets of rules. Within the legal community, this has been a bitterly contested dispute provoking unusually acrimonious exchanges in both judgments and academic writing. Ultimately, the argument for the special character of labour law has won out with the Constitutional Court ruling that the unfair dismissal protections in labour legislation 'ousted' employee access to administrative law protections, except in exceptional cases in which the dismissal has a 'public' effect.[17]

Ironically, at much the time that the administrative law–labour law dualism was being put to rest, the civil courts had a brief flirtation with granting employees across the spectrum an additional and parallel set of remedies under a constitutionally derived 'duty of fair dealing'. This would have allowed employees to challenge the fairness of a dismissal or any other labour practice in either the civil courts or the Labour Court. However, this development proved to be short-lived with a different panel of judges in the same court deciding that the statutory remedies were exclusive.[18]

Running through these controversies has been a tension between a 'rights'-oriented approach, which has sought to expand the remedies available to individual plaintiffs who have the resources to approach the superior civil courts, and the collective orientation of the statutory scheme, which gives a set of accessible although slightly restricted rights to all and ousts the jurisdiction of the courts.

---

[17] *Chirwa v Transnet Ltd & others* [2008] 2 BLLR 97 (Constitutional Court of South Africa).
[18] *Murray v Minister of Defence* (2008) 29 ILJ 1369 (Supreme Court of Appeal).

These judgments also reflect the reluctance of civil courts to give up any part of their general jurisdiction to specialist courts and tribunals. Although high court judges generally rely on the Constitution to expand individual rights, the Constitutional Court has consistently brought them back to the purposes of the Labour Relations Act and its promotion of effective dispute resolution.

From a trade union perspective, one of the potential pitfalls of 'judicialization' is that the right to litigate may be an ineffective replacement for industrial action. This issue has been most prominent in retrenchment (redundancy) cases where the specialist Labour Court has generally been reluctant to 'second guess' an employer's reasons for reducing its workforce. The wide definition of the term 'operational requirements' has allowed employers to use this route to restructure their businesses, including arrangements for outsourcing or externalizing work. Trade unions were prevented from using protected industrial action to challenge decisions to reduce workforces. This led to two changes to the law in 2002 for large-scale retrenchments: employers must refer proposed retrenchments to the CCMA for a facilitation process before deciding to dismiss and the union may elect to challenge the dismissals by either litigation or strike action. However, the weak bargaining power of trade unions at the time of mass lay-offs has meant that this provision is seldom used to take strike action against retrenchments.

D. Employer responses

The counter-narrative to the rise of collective bargaining and protective labour law (typified by unfair dismissal protection) has been the restructuring of businesses and the use of a range of strategies to disguise employment and break up bargaining units. In addition, fixed-term contracts have been increasingly used to restrict protection against unfair dismissal.

Since the mid-1980s, practices such as outsourcing and sub-contracting have been common. The 1995 Labour Relations Act does contain a 'transfer' provision based on the EU Directive and the UK Transfer of Undertakings (Protection of Employment) Regulations (TUPE), which facilitates business transfers by removing the requirement for individual consent while simultaneously seeking to prevent outsourcing and other business transfers being used to reduce conditions of employment. While these rules may prevent a reduction in terms and conditions at the time of transfer, trade unions generally have significantly less bargaining power after outsourcing has occurred.

Disguised employment by means of fraudulent 'independent contracting' became increasingly widespread in the 1990s, having initially been advocated in the last years of apartheid by an anti-union consultancy funded by the security police. However, by 2002, the transparently abusive nature of these practices led the courts to show a greater willingness to look beyond contractual labels and adopt a more substantive approach to identifying the employment relationship. That this transparent fraud was perpetuated for almost a decade was the result of the 'contractual fallacy' – that the courts required workers to prove their contract of employment even though this was not a requirement of the statutory definition of an employee. In 2002 the core labour legislation was amended to include a presumption of employment and the available evidence indicates that these changes led to a reduction in the use of 'independent contracting' as a vehicle for disguised employment.

Subsequently triangular employment has become the primary, and perhaps more pervasive, vehicle for labour law avoidance.[19] This has been possible because the legislative provisions recognizing triangular employment are not restricted to 'temporary employees'. Employees who are placed with a client (whether temporarily or indefinitely) by an agency are employees of the agency (rather than the client) if the employees' remuneration is routed through the agency. While the client can be held liable for the agency's non-compliance with statutory employment standards, this liability does not extend to unfair dismissal, leaving employees placed in this manner without any security of employment. Employees engaged in this manner also earn considerably less than 'direct' employees performing the same work. The vulnerability of low-paid employees to abuse by labour broking agencies is exacerbated by the absence of any framework for the registration and control of these agencies.

South African labour hire firms expanded their lucrative operations into the region, particularly Namibia. In 2007, Namibian legislators voted to prohibit labour hire on the basis that it resembled the labour contracting system used in Namibia under South African apartheid rule. The ban replaced proposals to regulate labour hire that had been enacted in 2004 but had not come into effect. The ban itself never came into effect and its constitutionality has been argued twice before the Namibian courts. It was initially held not to violate any provisions of Namibian Constitution by the county's High Court in a highly idiosyncratic decision which found that triangular employment was not recognized by the country's legal system, was akin to slavery and violated ILO norms because it turned labour into a commodity.

However, in December 2009 the country's highest court reversed the decision. The Supreme Court judgment describes the abuses associated with the apartheid era labour contracting at some length but points out that whatever the similarities of language used to describe these two phenomena, they are different and that agencies supplying temporary and specialized workers have a legitimate role in contemporary labour markets. The court struck down the prohibition as being unconstitutional because the abuses associated with agency work could in its view be dealt with through an appropriately designed regulatory regime.[20]

---

[19] An estimated 900,000 employees are placed through 'labour brokers' who are their employers. It is not known how many of these are working temporarily for the client and how many are working indefinitely.

[20] The following passage indicates the approach of the Namibian Supreme Court: 'If properly regulated within the ambit of the Constitution and Convention No 181, agency work would typically be temporary of nature; pose no real threat to standard employment relationships or unionisation and greatly contributes to flexibility in the labour market. It will enhance opportunities for the transition from education to work by workers entering the market for the first time and facilitate the shift from agency work to full-time employment.' *Africa Personnel Services v Government of the Republic of Namibia* (Supreme Court of Namibia, Case No SA 51 / 2008) at para [117].

Nevertheless, the 'populist' approach of the Namibian legislators and the High Court have influenced debates about triangular employment in South Africa, with the Minister of Labour, ruling party MPs and trade unions advocating a ban on triangular employment. At the time of writing, the issue remains unresolved with some sectors of government and the trade unions still favouring a ban.[21]

What is one to make of the 'populist' turn of events in debates about labour law? The emergence of labour broking and other forms of externalized and contingent work have reversed many of the gains achieved by the trade union movement. Bargaining units have been broken up and employment has become less secure. African workers who only gained protection against unfair dismissal and began to participate in pension and medical funds in the 1980s are being pushed back into greater insecurity.

In this context, the call for a ban is a response to the failure of labour law to offer a meaningful response to the rise of non-standard work and in particular the 'splitting' of the employer through techniques such as outsourcing, sub-contracting, and agency work. Proponents of a prohibition argue that a legal requirement compelling 'direct' employment by the party who supervises work will assist to reverse the decline of trade union bargaining power in the private sector and provide workers with more secure employment. In both South Africa and Namibia the intensity of the debate is exacerbated by the fact that negotiations to change the law have been going on for most of the last decade. While there are regulatory models which confine agency work to a limited range of 'true temp' activities, these proposals have not won the backing of either the unions or the employers yet.

The scale of the abuses associated with triangular employment has been exacerbated by regulatory failures, in particular the absence of a system for registering and controlling agencies. Inadequate enforcement also plays a significant role with vulnerable workers in both direct and indirect employment having great difficulty in enforcing claims for issues such as statutory minimum wages. The Department of Labour's inspectorate has been identified by an ILO-sponsored study as a significant 'Achilles heel' in terms of both monitoring and enforcement activities.[22] While post-apartheid labour legislation decriminalized labour regulation (with the exception of offences involving child labour and forced labour) inspectorates were not granted additional resources to take on new functions such as enforcing compliance orders through the court system. There has also been a very significant extension of the Department's jurisdiction to enforce minimum wages and other conditions of employment in a range of 'difficult' sectors including farmworkers and domestic workers. While the design and management of a dispute resolution institution such as the CCMA has been a significant area of institutional and legislative innovation, there has been no equivalent overhaul

---

[21] The ruling African National Congress' 2009 Election Manifesto states: 'In order to avoid exploitation of workers and ensure decent work for all workers as well as to protect the employment relationship, introduce laws to regulate contract work, subcontracting and out-sourcing, address the problem of labour broking and prohibit certain abusive practices.'

[22] C Fenwick, E Kalula, and I Landau, *Labour Law: A Southern African Perspective* (International Institute for Labour Studies, 2007) 26.

of the labour inspectorate. Ironically, the representatives of organized business and labour, in particular, who actively participate in the governance of the CCMA, have not pushed for enhanced performance capacity with the same vigour.

E. Conclusion

In South Africa, labour law operates within a context of extreme unemployment and inequality, and in which many of those who work received inferior schooling under apartheid's 'Bantu education' system which was designed to ensure that African workers remained 'hewers of wood and drawers of water'. The difficulties that have been encountered in turning around the education and training system means that the vast majority of new entrants in the labour market continue to lack the skills needed for employment. There continues to be an over-supply of low-skilled workers and a shortage of critical skills.

South Africa remains one of the most unequal societies in the world and income inequality increased between 1993 and 2008.[23] There has been an exponential increase in the incomes of the wealthy at the same time that the vast majority of the population are either earning minimum wages or are informally employed or unemployed.[24] The poorest sectors of society have benefited from the massive extension of social grants which are received by some 13 million individuals.[25] The earnings of those in the middle income brackets (lower white-collar and blue-collar workers) have decreased in real terms and the gap between this group and high-earners has increased, largely because of the premium paid for scarce skills. It is this group who perhaps most value protection against unfair and arbitrary dismissal. The value of their job is increased by the fact that many support members of their extended family who are without work

While South Africa's labour laws, including protections against dismissal, are not particularly onerous when compared to other middle-income countries, there is a widespread perception (among both the public and employers) that it is more difficult to dismiss than virtually anywhere else in the world. This perception (colloquially referred to as the 'hassle' factor) has had a major influence on the labour market behaviour of both local and international firms and has been a key driver of externalization.[26] While it can be expected that some employers will hold

---

[23] M Leibbrandt and others, 'Trends in South African Income Distribution and Poverty Since the Fall of Apartheid' (OECD Social, Employment and Migration Working Papers No 101).

[24] One measure of this growing inequality is that in 2005, adjustments in executive directors' packages was 278 times greater than that for minimum wage earners. (A Crotty and R Bonorchis, *Executive Pay in South Africa: Who gets what and why* (Double Story, 2006) 125–40.

[25] Expenditure on welfare and social assistance increased from R30.1 billion (3.2 per cent of GDP) in 2000/01 to R101.4 billion (4.4 per cent of GDP) in 2008/09. In April 2009, 13.4 million people were benefiting from social grants. Of these, 2.3 million were receiving old age pensions, 1.4 million were receiving disability grants and 9.1 million children were benefiting from Child Support Grants (Leibbrandt et al (n 23) 52).

[26] S Hayter, G Reinecke, and R Torres, *Studies on the Social Dimensions of Globalization South Africa* (ILO, 2001).

negative views on labour law, the gap between perceptions and reality appears to be higher in South Africa (and Namibia) than in any other country. Significantly, the perception has a fixed ideological character and changes in key areas of labour law do not lead to any change in perceptions.[27] The ease with which employers are able to lay off workers during the recent economic downturn is a further indication of the extent to which these claims are greatly exaggerated.

Employers have used triangular employment and other forms of non-standard work to escape the net of unfair dismissal protection. While there are very significant financial incentives for employers to employ unemployed workers through fixed-term learnerships, employers make limited use of these schemes. Proposals to promote the hiring of new employees, including introducing a qualifying period before workers qualify for full unfair dismissal protection as well subsidies for employing young first-time workers, have to date been rejected by the trade union movement who fear that these will be abused to displace their members.

Contemporary labour law debates tend to contrast 'narrow' conceptions of job security which focus on preventing employed workers losing their jobs unfairly with broader notions of labour market security. This notion underpins concepts of flexicurity in which a range of social protections are provided to workers through public unemployment and re-training programmes. This remains uncharted territory in South Africa.

To return to the workers who came to the Advice Bureau 30 years ago (or more likely their children). Many will have been laid off, a cruel reminder of the limits of labour law. For those in work, the existence of the CCMA, an institution of which they are aware and to which they (or their trade unions) can refer disputes without incurring any significant cost, is one of the most significant and real benefits that post-apartheid law has brought to them. While unfair dismissal law is highly unlikely to return dismissed employees to their previous jobs, it clearly serves as the guarantor of an approach to dismissal in which an employee's prospects of arbitrary exclusion from the workforce are significantly reduced. It has produced a more stable society and made the lives of the South African workforce considerably more stable and predictable than at any time previously. This has been achieved primarily through a series of legal reforms that emphasized access to justice as their primary concern. A traditional rights-based model in which rights were enforced

---

[27] This disjuncture between perception and labour market reality is borne out by the fact that in the World Economic Forum's Global Competitiveness Report which is based on the perceptions of groupings such as business executives, rates South Africa's hiring and firing rules as the fifth most restrictive in the world. On the other hand, the OECD concludes that South Africa's labour laws are relatively flexible and that of the OECD's 29 members only the United States has less restrictive laws on hiring and hours of work, and the dismissal protections are more flexible than the average for OECD countries; more flexible than countries such as Brazil, Chile, China, and India with which it is often compared. The World Bank's discredited *Doing Business* survey gives South Africa a mid-table ranking (102nd out of 182 countries), although it has been argued that if the relevant questions had been correctly answered the ranking would have been closer to 30. (See P Benjamin and J Theron, 'Costing, Comparing and Competing: The World Bank's *Doing Business* Survey and the Benchmarking of Labour Market Regulation' in H Corder (ed), *Global Administrative Law: Innovation and Development* (Juta, 2009) (also published as *Acta Juridica* 2009) 204–34).

through conventional litigation in the courts and parties had rights of legal representation would not have succeeded in entrenching these protections as successfully.

Employees are now unlikely to strike over the dismissal of a co-employee as they willingly did in the 1970s and 1980s. However, demands that employers do not use contingent workforces hired through labour brokers have in the last couple of years become increasingly common in collective bargaining and have given rise to several (generally successful) strikes. A declining proportion of employees now receive protection against unfair dismissal. At least 30 per cent of the employed workforce, while forming part of the supply and distribution chains of large formal sector businesses, can have their employment or supply of work terminated without any recourse to law and are excluded from benefits negotiated through collective bargaining. While these workers have political rights not enjoyed under apartheid, their working conditions are increasingly beginning to resemble those of the workers of an earlier era.

14

Informal Employment and the Challenges for Labour Law

*Kamala Sankaran**

The great sense of anticipation with which those in informal employment approach labour law is in striking contrast to the view of several observers of formal labour markets that labour law is well past its prime. It would perhaps not be overstating the case to say that the idea of labour law for 90 per cent of India's work force (running into hundreds of millions) is well summed up by the phrase '. . . the best is yet to be'.

The debates that have characterized the future of labour law and the role of regulation in the formal economy in countries such as India deal predictably enough with the view that there is too much law, unnecessary juridification of disputes, and an excessively interventionist role for the state than is good for the economy. What is striking is the magical quality that labour law seems to hold out for those in informal employment. Is this just a case of history repeating itself (hopefully, not as a farce) for the informal economy? Or does labour law itself need to transform if it is to address the questions confronting informality? Are there lessons to be learned as countries with huge informal economies begin legislating on a massive scale to include those previously outside the fold of labour law? This chapter examines some of the challenges that informal employment raises for labour law and policy.

A. From the contract of employment to informal employment

The binary of a 'worker' and an 'employer' mediated through a contract of employment was an important export of an industrializing Britain to its erstwhile colonies. Commentators have pointed out how the early law of master and servant had been pivotal in mobilizing labour supply for its colonies, public works, and, later, for private enterprise in plantations in Assam and Bengal.[1] Labour recruitment

---

* Associate Professor, Faculty of Law, University of Delhi, India.

[1] See, eg, MR Anderson, 'India 1858–1930:The Illusion of Free Labour' in D Hay and P Craven (eds), *Masters, Servants and Magistrates in Britain and the Empire, 1562–1955* (University of North Carolina Press, 2004); and MR Anderson, 'Work Construed: Ideological Origins of Labour Law in British India to 1918' in P Robb (ed), *Dalit Movements and the Meaning of Labour in India* (Oxford University Press, 1993).

mediated through intermediaries (sardars/khattedars) could make use of caste/kin links in order to provide labour to far-flung destinations. As a result, triangular relationships in employment, so central in today's discourse on employment relationships, have had a long history in much of South Asia. The central role of the intermediary not only in recruitment but also in ensuring labour discipline on the shop floor, introduced a rather distinctive feature to the received master–servant law in the South Asian context.

The gradual emergence of the contract of employment in some sectors of the economy required the emergence of the category of the free worker, the 'economic man', one capable of entering into such relationships. It also served as a strong counterpoint to the 'unfree labour', coerced by a variety of social and economic circumstances into performing work at the behest of the master. As many writers have pointed out, the central position accorded to the contract of employment has not only focused upon the full-time, male bread-winner model, but also privileged waged work as the only form of 'work' recognized by the market and law.[2]

Yet the contract of employment has never signified the sole or even predominant mode of employment in India. Informal employment in India characterizes the overwhelming numbers of work relationships today – 93 per cent of the workforce is in informal employment – and this proportion shows no signs of diminishing despite the emergence of a fast-growing economy. On the contrary, the sheer numbers of self-employed, who constitute more than *half* the workforce, the existence of bonded 'unfree' labour and the high presence of unpaid contributing family labour indicate that the employment contract cannot characterize most work relationships in countries such as India.[3] The continued presence of these forms of work indicates that labour law needs to take into account the forms of work dominant in economies such as India and address the challenges these pose to the dominant received notions of labour law. The growing interest in the informal economy and the greater visibility of the varied forms of work practices in countries of the 'South' has no doubt been brought about by changes in the global economy. These changes provide an opportunity for labour law to re-imagine and position itself in a manner that is relevant and inclusive of work and employment relationships across the world.

The category of informal employment, a category now current in both labour statistics and in labour law, points to forms of work and labour relationships that often go beyond 'classic' employment relationships. It is useful for labour law to study the categories used by labour statisticians since large-scale surveys map

---

[2] See, eg, A Supiot, *Beyond Employment: Changes in Work and the Future of Labour Law in Europe* (Oxford University Press, 2001); and K Rittich, 'Feminization and Contingency: Regulating the Stakes of Work for Women' in J Conaghan, RM Fischl, and K Klare (eds), *Labour Law in an Era of Globalization: Transformative Practices and Possibilities* (Oxford University Press, 2002).

[3] The question whether capitalism can work alongside earlier more 'feudal forms' of labour, without there being any natural progression to its contractual form, is well represented in the literature. See, eg, D Chakrabarty, *Rethinking Working-Class History: Bengal 1890–1940* (Princeton University Press, 1989); and J Lerche, 'A Global Alliance against Forced Labour? Unfree Labour, Neo-Liberal Globalization and the International Labour Organization' in J Breman, I Guérin, and A Prakash (eds), *India's Unfree Workforce: Of Bondage Old and New* (Oxford University Press, 2009).

various forms of working relationships and data are collected using categories generated by labour statistics. The classifications used and the numbers generated by labour force sample surveys and economic censuses are a kind of 'reality check' on the kinds and forms of labour found in the workforce. The reference to statistical categories also compels us to think through the relevance of the categories that labour law created in the course of its historical development that may now have outlived their utility.

Both labour statistics and labour law have traditionally used the firm/enterprise or industry as the starting point to determine the category of the worker and employer. Labour statistics, such as the UN System of National Accounts (SNA), have influenced the current definition adopted in India that defines the informal sector as consisting of all unincorporated private enterprises owned by individuals or households engaged in the sale and production of goods and services operated on a proprietary or partnership basis and with fewer than 10 workers.[4] One of the challenges in the informal enterprises, or the informal sector generally, is the disentangling of the income of the household enterprise from that of the individual members contributing to such income. This is particularly important since such household enterprises are not incorporated under any law, and nor do they have a separate legal identity from that of the members of the household. An informal 'enterprise' or 'sector' approach to define and measure informality ignores the informal nature of work or jobs performed by persons within such enterprises. For instance, those who are in casual self-employment may not get enumerated since they are not seen as regular enterprises engaged in work; nor are those households which employ domestic workers for providing services within the household identified as informal enterprises. More importantly, those with vulnerable, informal jobs in the formal sector get excluded since they do not fall within the sector or enterprise approach. As a result, current accounting practice takes a broader approach and includes even those persons in informal jobs within the formal sector as part of the category of informal employment.

Informal workers are now seen as consisting of those working in the informal sector or households, excluding regular workers with social security benefits provided by the employers and the workers in the formal sector without any employment and social security benefits provided by the employers.[5] The category of informal worker continues to locate the employer–employee relationship as central to labour and employment. Yet such an approach by implication excludes those who are self-employed, and also those who work but fall within the category of non-waged work: the unpaid family worker and those in a forced labour situation who work without receiving wages. (The category of unpaid family labour and forced labour could overlap. However, the International Labour Organization's (ILO's) understanding of 'forced labour' does not recognize patriarchal control over

---

[4] National Commission for Enterprises in the Unorganised Sector (NCEUS), *The Challenge of Employment* (Government of India, 2009) 3.
[5] Ibid.

women's unpaid work within the household as forms of forced labour[6] and as a result the two categories continue to be treated as distinct in the literature.)

Self-employed workers and unpaid family labour, who do not have access to any form of contributory social security cover, need also to be included within the category of those in informal employment. This broader category has now been recognized within labour statistics.

The following then emerge as instances of informal employment:

- own-account workers employed in their own informal enterprises
- employers employed in their own informal enterprises
- unpaid family workers, whether in the formal or informal sector
- employees in the formal and informal sectors classified as informal employees, if they do not enjoy specific employment security, work security, or social security.[7]

This understanding of informal employment[8] should not surprise us since the term 'informal employment' and the derivative term 'informal employee/worker' are used to describe the nature of the employment relationships which falls outside protection or regulation, in short, the *informality* of the nature of their work. What is constitutive of informality is not the manner of entering into employment or the employment contract, but the *vulnerability* of the informal worker which is caused by the absence of work/employment security and social protection.

The indicators developed by labour statistics to identify informal employment have an 'I know it when I see it' quality and have been used to collect data on the informal economy without addressing many of the definitional questions raised by labour lawyers and economists. In addition, the different categories of informal workers and their profound differences get swept aside when criteria are developed purely on vulnerability and static indicators of a decent work deficit. The indicators of informality often may not have the capacity to capture structural differences or causative factors of such vulnerability and therefore may lack the ability to guide policy prescriptions to deal with informality. However, the broad types of work falling within the category of informal employment reveal important insights into the kinds of working relationships covered and point to certain differences between the statistical and labour law approaches to understanding informality. I examine some important 'types' of informal employment below in order to understand how

---

[6] ILO Convention No 29 states that '*forced or compulsory labour* shall mean all work or service which is exacted from any person under the menace of any penalty and for which the said person has not offered himself voluntarily'. Patriarchal control would appear to fall outside the scope of the ILO conventions.

[7] For details see NCEUS, *Report on Definitional and Statistical Issues Relating to Informal Economy* (Government of India, 2008) 12–13. This report draws upon the definition of informal employment by the International Conference of Labour Statisticians and endorsed by the ILO. See ILO, Guidelines concerning a statistical definition of informal employment, available at <http://www.ilo.org/wcmsp5/groups/public/-dgreports/-integration/-stat/documents/normativeinstrument/wcms_087622.pdf>.

[8] I have used the expressions 'informal employment' and 'informality' interchangeably in this chapter.

labour law has dealt with or ignored such work situations, and what implications this has for the future of labour law.

B. Labour – from employment, to work, to activity?

The labour law of countries in the south Asian region, such as the Trade Unions Act 1926, modelled initially on the (British) Trade Disputes Act 1906, evolved in interesting ways to include the self-employed in the definition of a worker employed in an industry. Workers are defined to include not only persons 'employed' in an industry by an employer but also persons 'engaged' in a trade or industry.[9] This kind of early adaptation of the labour law may perhaps account for the relative lack of resistance, at the level of policy makers, trade unions, or industry, when some states in India, over three decades ago, legislated to create social security schemes for self-employed workers. Work, and not employment, was clearly the basis on which many of these state-run tripartite boards provided social security and welfare benefits.

In recent years the ILO has introduced a further broadening of the scope of 'labour' by adopting labour standards that do not deal with any form of 'work' howsoever broadly construed. Issues of forced labour and child labour offer us interesting examples of the kinds of issues that ILO is increasingly dealing with in its standard setting. The ILO takes the view that an activity need not be an economic activity for it to be a 'labour issue'. The ILO's position is striking: 'Similarly, an activity does not need to be recognized officially as an "economic activity" for it to constitute forced labour. For example, a child or adult beggar under coercion will be considered to be in forced labour.'[10] While elaborating on the convention dealing with the worst forms of child labour (Convention No 182) the ILO chose to include within this convention child prostitution and the use of child soldiers in armed conflict. The ILO terms child prostitution as a 'worst form' of child *labour*, and deals in a limited manner with child prostitution in this convention. However, several complex issues need to be settled before prostitution/sex work can be included in the usual ILO standard-setting process. The feminist movement has had a vibrant debate over the nature of sex work/prostitution, the agency of the commercial sex worker (or whether she is merely a victim or a dupe), and if such an activity constitutes work/labour. The ILO rationale for including forms of child prostitution in its standard setting is that it is a form of child 'abuse' and therefore a (worst) form of child labour. Such an approach acknowledges certain criminalized forms of activity as falling within the scope of its mandate, but it still falls short of declaring that such a person is a 'worker' under labour law and thus entitled to the protective mantle of labour law.

---

[9] Self-employed workers can register their trade unions under this law, a well-known example being the Self-Employed Women's Association (SEWA).

[10] ILO, *The Cost of Coercion*, Global Report under the follow-up to the ILO Declaration on Fundamental Principles and Rights at Work 2009, 6.

The ILO appears to take a nuanced position that while activity can be recognized as a labour issue, it does not follow that the person performing this activity is a worker. What needs to be underscored is that the ILO has indicated that an activity which may be a criminal one or which may have no economic value could yet be a labour issue. I examine the case of unpaid family workers to understand the implications of the extended ILO position on this point.

The matter of unpaid *domestic* work performed by members of a family is an instance of a work/activity, situated in the continuum between an employment relationship and an activity. The UN SNA excludes from within the boundary of national accounts, production of services provided by members of the household and consumed within the household. This would cover the cases of domestic and care work usually performed by women, and that is unpaid. This is an instance of an activity, traditionally considered a non-economic one for a variety of reasons.[11]

There is strong case made out by feminists for including women engaged in domestic and care work within the realm of national accounts, thereby attributing economic value, and hence, visibility and intra-household power to women doing this work.[12] It is not only women who perform unpaid work within households. Very often children, particularly girls, engage in long hours of unpaid *domestic* work. For instance, statistics on child labour often show a preponderance of boys rather than girls engaged in child labour. However, if unpaid activities are included under child labour, more girls than boys are engaged in child labour.[13] (According to India's National Sample Survey Organisation data, the incidence of child labour was 3.8 per cent in 1999–2000 whereas it was 5.1 per cent based on 1991 census data. However, based on time use surveys, 20 per cent of boys and girls in the age group of six to 14 years participate in economic activities. They are engaged in unpaid or subsistence activities such as animal grazing, collection of fuel and fodder, farming, and other services.)[14] Further, by the use of time-use surveys, labour statistics are moving in the direction of possible inclusion of domestic and care work, discussed earlier, within the scope of an economic activity.[15] The present definition of informal employment continues to make such unpaid domestic work invisible and does not recognize this as part of informal employment. Even where economic value is imputed to family members performing domestic and

---

[11] European Communities, International Monetary Fund, Organisation for Economic Co-operation and Development, United Nations and World Bank, *System of National Accounts 2008* (New York, 2009) paras 6.26–31 and para 25.24.

[12] The standard example used in classrooms is of the economist Alfred Marshall, who pointed that if he hired a woman as a domestic help the national economy would increase, but that if he married her it would go down.

[13] A Mata Greenwork, 'Gender Issues in Labour Statistics', in M Fetherholf Loutfi (ed), *Women, Gender and Work: What is Equality and How Do We Get There?* (Rawat Publications, 2002).

[14] S Mahendra Dev, 'Female Work Participation and Child Labour' (2004) 39 *Economic and Political Weekly* 741.

[15] For an analysis of how women's work is measured and its impact of their rights within the family and in matrimonial property see K Sankaran, 'Family, Work and Matrimonial Property: Implications for Women and Children' in A Parashar and A Dhanda (eds), *Towards an Inclusive Family Law* (Routledge, 2008).

subsistence level survival activities, the labour law continues to deny them a worker status.

The form of unpaid labour performed within households, and recognized by the SNA, which is considered an instance of informal employment, is unpaid *family* labour. Within self-employed households, there is unpaid labour performed by contributing family members in producing goods and services. Their contribution is recognized as an economic activity but these contributing family members are not paid since the income of the household accrues to the head of the household. The well-settled position of labour statistics has been to treat unpaid work performed by members of the household within the household enterprise as being economically productive since it has economic value for the household. Yet, contributing family members are not included within most labour law regimes as workers, and the 'head' of the household (usually the man) is the one counted as the main worker and the income earner. This is often the case where work performed by such informal workers is paid according to piece-rated wages. In the case of home-based workers, other family members, particularly women and children, contribute to increasing the daily output since it is only through a combined effort that a worker earns decent wages. (Piece rates are often fixed at relatively low levels requiring a person to work at least 10–12 hours to achieve an equivalent time-rated minimum wage.)

While the economic contribution of such unpaid family members is counted for the purposes of national income, their status as workers is not recognized. Contributing family members are engaged in *unpaid* economic activity, but are not given the status of a worker by the labour law.[16] In India, for instance, labour laws exclude unpaid family workers, usually women within a self-employed household, from their scope. Even the recent Unorganised Workers' Social Security Act 2008 excludes unpaid family workers from its scope. (As already mentioned, unpaid contributing family workers and their work is distinct from the domestic and care work usually performed by women due to the sexual division of labour within the household.)

The decent work agenda of the ILO and particularly the fundamental principles and rights at work relating to freedom from forced labour and child labour, have compelled the organization to look beyond the contract of employment to earlier and unfree forms of work. However, the ILO's manner of determining what constitutes a 'labour' issue is indicative, though not determinative of what normatively should be the main concern of labour law. In the 1990s, as the ILO moved closer to identifying core labour standards with issues relating to human dignity, development and human rights, egregious forms of abuse and exploitation were identified as labour issues in the core conventions of the ILO.[17] Yet as noticed above, such recognition by the ILO does not automatically grant a worker status to the person so affected, nor recognition under labour law to the work/

---

[16] Home-based workers may get enumerated as workers.
[17] Freedom from forced labour and child labour are identified by the ILO Declaration on Fundamental Principles and Rights at Work 1998.

activity performed. The choice of protecting such victims (say, child prostitutes) as workers under the labour law or instead regulating them by relying on criminal/ social welfare measures is one that the law has to make. As in the case of sex work, would conferring worker status legitimize such activities or grant agency to such victimized persons? The case of unpaid contributing family members can be distinguished from those like child prostitution or child soldiers identified by the ILO since the nature of the work performed in the former case is not usually subject to controversy. Granting such unpaid family members a worker status can be seen as challenging (and not legitimizing) patriarchy and leads to the redistribution of matrimonial property within the household. Clearly, economic activities can be included as a 'labour' issue and unless there are weighty reasons to the contrary, those who perform such work should enjoy a worker status under the labour law.

The limits of expansion of the scope of a 'worker' under present-day labour law appear to have been reached when considering the case of unpaid domestic/care work and unpaid contributing family labour. The variety of factors indicated above suggest that legislating for the informal economy could provide opportunities for labour law to confront some of its in-built limitations that flow from its adherence to the contract of employment as the central form of work.

C. Duality of an employer and employee

There is another instance where labour law may need to keep pace with the manner in which statistics determine the nature of work relationships. The category of the self-employed is a particularly large one for those countries where the informal economy accounts for over 80 per cent of the working population.

The SNA recognizes that self-employed enterprises may have several forms: those that are operated by an individual working alone or with the help of unpaid family members as a self-employed entrepreneur (own-account worker), while others may also engage paid workers.[18] The current classification treats persons who are engaged in their own farm or non-farm enterprises as self-employed.[19] Own-account workers are those self-employed persons who do not hire any workers on a regular basis; those who do so are employers. Own-account enterprises constitute the bulk of all enterprises in India, constituting 87.4 per cent of all enterprises in 1999–2000, while those establishments employing two to five workers are 10.9 per cent and those employing six to nine workers are 1.7 per cent.[20] In terms of numbers, 73 per cent of all workers were engaged in the work of own-account enterprises, signalling the sheer scale of the self-employed sector.

---

[18] European Communities, International Monetary Fund, Organisation for Economic Co-operation and Development, United Nations, and World Bank, *System of National Accounts 2008* (New York, 2009) para 25.9.

[19] Report available at: <http://mospi.gov.in/national_data_bank/pdf/516_final.pdf>.

[20] See NCEUS, *Report on Conditions of Work and Promotion of Livelihoods in the Unorganised Sector* (Government of India, 2007) 51.

Thus, those running such establishments could simultaneously be self-employed and employers, though the levels of earning may not differ greatly from the employer to the employee, and there could be a high degree of self-exploitation by the self-employed.

What is striking in the above classification is that 'self-employed *employers*' are also classified as part of the informal workforce. This approach is distinct from the understanding of the expression 'worker' as understood in traditional labour law which constructs the worker at the pole opposite to that of an employer. The autonomy and economic independence that characterizes the self-employed is what statisticians have identified as crucial to the self-employed status. Whether they are own-account or employers is secondary to their main identifiable characteristic as self-employed persons. In addition, the unincorporated nature of the household enterprise, its size, and the vulnerability of employers and workers alike within its fold is what has been crucial for labour statisticians to classify both own-account workers and self-employed employers to be in informal employment.

The blurring of the distinction between employers and workers for the purpose of the enumeration of the informal workforce in essence does away with the 'class divide' so central to labour law. The (nearly) shared levels of vulnerability between self-employed employers and their employees in the informal economy is an indication that many self-employed persons resort to self-employment as a survival activity. This is often because of lack of waged employment or to supplement their meagre wages obtained in waged employment. It is also an indicator of the reality that many in the informal economy often move between waged employment and self-employment seasonally or over their life cycles.

In the Discussion on Decent Work and the Informal Economy at the 2002 International Labour Conference, the distinction between employers and own-account workers among the informal self-employed was highlighted, particularly with regard to the groups among the self-employed persons who could be in the Workers Group in the ILO's tripartite system. The Resolution on Decent Work and the Informal Economy adopted at the 90th session of the ILO in 2002 stated: 'Workers in the informal economy include both wage workers and own-account workers.'[21] Clearly, the self-employed *employers* found no place in this formulation. The statistical approach focuses more upon the nature of the vulnerability whereas the discussion at the ILO focused far more upon the nature of the employment relationship, the locus of power in the relationship and the requirement of its tripartite structure that required drawing of clear lines of demarcation between an employer and a worker. Perhaps the idea of labour law based on the principle of human dignity could provide a way to reconcile these conflicting positions?[22]

The distinction between the notion of a worker from a statistical and the labour law point of view is one that continually arises and one that needs to be addressed

---

[21] See <http://www.ilo.org/public/english/standards/relm/ilc/ilc90/pdf/pr-25.pdf>, Conclusions, para 4.

[22] See, eg, the ILO Declarations of 1998 (referred to earlier) and the Declaration on Social Justice adopted in 2008.

UNIVERSITY OF WINCHESTER
LIBRARY

by labour law consciously guided by considerations of how broadly it wishes to confer benefits under labour law. Take for example the recently enacted (Indian) Unorganised Workers Social Security Act 2008 to provide social security for an estimated 420 million workers.[23] The definition of an unorganized worker[24] includes a self-employed worker[25] in the unorganized sector.[26] Reading all these definitions together, one could argue that the self-employed employer discussed above can also be included within the scope of the definition of an informal/ unorganized worker. It is unlikely that such an extension will go unchallenged once the new law becomes effective. However, if strengthening informal enterprises is seen as key to deal with the vulnerabilities of informal employment, excluding self-employed employers from the scope of social protection schemes may prove counter-productive.

Such a reading is possible only if the goal of labour law is seen as congruent with achieving equity at the workplace, and further, dealing with vulnerabilities and deprivation of all those who labour. The definition of a worker needs to include those whom the labour law, howsoever broadly construed, at present seems to exclude. Social protection, and not the contract of employment, then becomes the lens through which the scope of labour law gets determined. While the contract of employment and collective bargaining-centred approaches to labour law are greatly concerned with setting of ground rules for negotiations, an informal employment-centred approach appears more concerned with addressing deprivation and vulnerabilities. Fair outcomes are then as important as the means in order to ensure a level playing field.

D. Dealing with poverty and deprivation: is labour law the answer?

The presence of self-employment and the household enterprise as important forms of informal employment raises the question whether such forms of work are only a passing phase. For a long time informal employment was ignored by labour law on the premise that wage employment would emerge as the dominant form. Given that this is not the case (the reasons for this are many, and are not examined in this

---

[23] Indian law and policy documents usually use the expressions 'unorganized' or 'organized' rather than 'informal' or 'formal'.

[24] Section 2(m) states: '"unorganised worker" means a home-based worker, self-employed worker or a wage worker in the unorganised sector and includes a worker in the organised sector who is not covered by any of the Acts mentioned in Schedule II to this Act.'

[25] Section 2(k) states: '"Self-employed worker" means any person who is not employed by an employer, but engages himself or herself in any occupation in the unorganised sector subject to a monthly earning of an amount as may be notified by the Central Government or the State Government from time to time or holds cultivable land subject to such ceiling as may be notified by the State Government.'

[26] Section 2(l) states: '"unorganised sector" means an enterprise owned by individuals or self-employed workers and engaged in the production or sale of goods or providing service of any kind whatsoever, and where the enterprise employs workers, the number of such workers is less than ten.'

chapter), the categories of worker and employer need to lose their sharp differences to deal with forms of informality. Further, if protection against vulnerabilities becomes the chief goal of labour law, what is to distinguish labour law from human rights/constitutional/family laws, which may have the same goals? The overlap between general socio-economic rights of health care, old age pensions, or rights to subsidies available universally on the one hand, and social protection targeted at workers, is significant. Rights flowing from labour law seem to enjoy a greater legitimacy than do welfare rights/general socio-economic rights. As long as this is the case, there is value in identifying a set of social protection rights which a person obtains because she is a worker under labour law. Such an approach also allows us to keep the field of labour law distinct from a general constitutional law of citizenship that grants protection or socio-economic rights to all irrespective of whether they are engaged in economic activity, work, or employment. Labour law as a source of entitlements is then additional to and builds upon an initial bundle of citizenship rights.

The massive overlap between informality and poverty is a distinguishing feature of countries of the South. The choice of using general poverty reduction strategies or targeted labour policies to deal with vulnerabilities of the informal working poor constitutes a major challenge to policy makers. Often the choice is between one of universalizing socio-economic benefits by the state and partly financing social security benefits under labour law. Rights of citizenship often provide access to socio-economic rights for a wider group of persons than do social security benefits that are contingent upon the scope of a worker/employee under the labour law. There is a steady use of the constitutional courts to access socio-economic rights in many countries of the South where informal employment is massive. 'Constitutionalizing' of social protection rights/benefits often ensures universalizing of the benefits, and also delinks the source of financing of the benefits from contribution by the worker and/or the employer, and transfers the liability to the government or a broader tax base.

The challenge of legislating for the informal economy affords us a unique opportunity to look beyond traditional labour law and to capture forms of work and activity that currently fall through the cracks of labour law. It also allows us to focus on the goal of labour law in ensuring fair outcomes through directly addressing issues of deprivation and vulnerability. Social protection (as much as trade unions and collective bargaining) becomes a central vehicle through which labour law can create a level playing field. The possibilities this opens up for the future relevance of labour law and its 'transformative' capacity are critical. The creation of broad, inclusive legal categories and mechanisms that can suitably capture the many-layered qualities of the informal economy today may then reveal a multi-sided and richer nature of the law and labour law in particular.

15

The Impossibility of Work Law

Noah D Zatz*

A. Introduction

To maintain its vitality and its virtue, labour law must reach beyond its traditional domain of employment relationships and grasp the full range of relationships that organize productive work.[1] To that now-familiar call for 'work law', this chapter adds a decidedly pessimistic note. 'Work law' is indeed necessary, but it is also impossible. The very insights about the plasticity of work that make employment law look fatally narrow also imply that work law would be fatally shallow or, in avoiding that fate, would reproduce the narrowness it sought to escape. I reach these conclusions by considering how debates over the scope of the employment relationship, and the viability of broader and more complex categories, might be informed by consideration of nonmarket work.

B. Taking nonmarket work seriously

This section makes the case that labour law scholars, and policies regulating labour, need to include nonmarket work as an object of study and regulation. With the notable exception of the Supiot Report,[2] even expansive treatments of labour law 'beyond employment' typically substitute a conception of 'work law' that encompasses market labour but goes no further. There are two broad reasons to revisit this limitation.

First, the techniques traditionally used to distinguish employment from other market work also are losing their ability to differentiate it from nonmarket work.

* Professor of Law, University of California, Los Angeles School of Law. For helpful comments on prior drafts, I am grateful to Guy Davidov, Hiroshi Motomura, Viviana Zelier, and workshop participants at the 'Idea of Labour Law' conference and 2010 Labour Law Group meeting. Some passages below are reproduced from work previously published as ND Zatz, 'Prison Labor and the Paradox of Paid Nonmarket Work' in N Bandelj (ed), *Economic Sociology Of Work* (Emerald, 2009); ND Zatz, 'Working at the Boundaries of Markets' (2008) 61 Vand L Rev 857; and ND Zatz, 'Working Beyond the Reach or Grasp of Employment Law' in A Bernhardt and others (eds), *The Gloves-Off Economy* (Cornell University Press, 2008).

[1] Eg, G Standing, *Work After Globalization* (Edward Elgar, 2009) 268; and B Langille, this volume.
[2] A Supiot, *Beyond Employment* (Oxford University Press, 2001).

To show this, I distinguish two dimensions – control and exchange – along which a boundary has been erected between employment and other work, and I show the permeability of both.

Second, the primary reasons for expanding labour law's reach to other forms of market work are applicable to nonmarket work as well. These reasons are the *displacement* of protected employees by other unprotected workers and *exclusion* of these nonemployees from labour law's protections. Both dangers arise from the *relational flexibility of work*: quite different social arrangements can yield similar economic outputs.

1. Breaking down the boundaries of employment

When nonmarket work is considered, domestic housework and caretaking within families typically provides the principal example.[3] Using this site to conceptualize nonmarket activity as work and analyze its status within labour law risks confusion between two distinct ways to distinguish nonmarket work from employment.

First, family labour exists outside the supervisory structure of institutional control at the heart of conventional definitions of employment.[4] There is no obvious 'employer.' For related reasons, family labour lacks employment's temporal structure dividing 'personal' time from the 'work day.' Thus, along what I label the 'control dimension' of traditional tests for employee status, family labour seemingly falls far from the employee and close to the independent contractor.

Second, family labour occurs outside a conventional market relationship. There is no arm's-length contract focused on mutual pecuniary gain by tightly linking payment and services. Instead, the work is integrated into intimate, multidimensional relationships with particular family members, distinctive motivations, and context-specific forms of valuation. These considerations are quite distinct from those sounding in control. Instead, they cohere with those conventionally used to distinguish employees from volunteers and students or trainees, who either receive no compensation from an employer or produce nothing for one. I refer to this as the 'exchange dimension' of employee status.[5]

Figure 15.1 schematically presents four paradigmatic combinations of control and exchange considerations to clarify the two different modes of distinguishing employment from family labour.[6] To be sure, one also could characterize family labour in a way that converged with conventional employment,[7] translating traditional wifely duties into those of housekeeper, nurse, nanny, and prostitute. Here, I press in the opposite direction, starting with employment and making it look more like nonmarket work.

---

[3] Supiot, above n 2; Standing, above n 1; KB Silbaugh, 'Turning Labor Into Love' (1996) 91 Nw UL Rev p.

[4] G Davidov, 'The Reports of My Death Are Greatly Exaggerated' in G Davidov and B Langille (eds), *Boundaries and Frontiers of Labour Law* (Hart Publishing, 2006).

[5] ND Zatz, 'Working at the Boundaries of Markets' (2008) 61 *Vand L Rev* 857.

[6] Cf Chris Tilly and Charles Tilly, *Work under Capitalism* (Westview, 1998).

[7] P England and N Folbre, 'Gender and Economic Sociology' in NJ Smelser and R Swedberg (eds), *The Handbook of Economic Sociology* (Princeton University Press, 2005) 627.

	← Control dimension →	
	Employer control	**Independent work**
Paid/ market	Employment	Entrepreneurship
Unpaid/ nonmarket	Volunteering/ training	Family labour

Exchange dimension

Figure 15.1 Two dimensions of employment status

2. Following work across the market boundary

My research on prison labour in the United States reveals a class of cases in which, unlike family labour, any distinction from employment arises entirely along the exchange dimension. Inmate workers are as tightly supervised, controlled, and disciplined as one could imagine. Moreover, prison labour programmes often are designed to simulate the institutional arrangements typical of conventional employment.[8] Nonetheless, US courts conclude, or seriously contemplate, that inmate workers are not 'employees' for various statutory purposes, not due to inadequate control but because of 'a different boundary' to the employment relationship.[9] Thus, prison labour helps us isolate the exchange dimension and explore its contours.

When, as is typical, courts find no employment relationship, they do so on the theory that employment is necessarily an economic relationship. They reason that prison labour is *non*economic because it is thoroughly embedded in the social organization of imprisonment. The work is shaped by incarceration's coercive context[10] and by institutional goals that include matters of punishment, rehabilitation, and discipline. As one court explained, 'work at the prison was merely an incident of incarceration.'[11] In contrast, another reasoned, '[a] true employer–employee relationship' involves a 'bargained-for exchange of labour for mutual economic gain' between two free agents dealing 'at arm's length.'[12]

Courts thus invoke considerations characteristic of employment's exchange dimension in a context more challenging than that of volunteers or trainees. Unlike volunteers, inmates generally have been paid wages at a set rate, often hourly, tied

---

[8] ND Zatz, 'Working at the Boundaries of Markets' (2008) 61 Vand L Rev 857.

[9] *Vanskike v Peters*, 974 F 2d 806, 810 (7th Cir 1992) (USA).

[10] See also C Fenwick, 'Regulating Prisoners' Labour in Australia: A Preliminary View' (2003) 16 AJLL 284.

[11] *Morgan v MacDonald*, 41 F 3d 1291, 1293 (9th Cir 1994) (USA).

[12] *Harker v State Use Industries*, 990 F 2d 131, 133 (4th Cir 1993) (USA).

directly to time worked. And, unlike trainees, there is little doubt that they do useful work, though the form varies. Sometimes they produce goods and services contributing directly to prison or governmental operations – cooking meals in the prison cafeteria or fighting forest fires – and sometimes they produce for sale in wider markets, such as data entry of mail order catalog purchases or manufacturing of belt buckles.

Courts rely on classic separate spheres reasoning to distinguish inmate work that is 'merely an incident of incarceration' from employment's 'bargained-for exchange of labour for mutual gain.' Consistent with a worldview identifying the economy with the market and opposing it to other major social institutions, courts characterize prisoners as 'essentially taken out of the national economy' and placed into 'the separate world of the prison.'[13] The noneconomic sphere is the prison not the family, but the conceptual underpinnings are identical.

The prison labour cases provide a template for a much broader class.[14] Other examples include work performed by welfare recipients as a condition of receiving their benefits, by people with disabilities as part of rehabilitative programmes, by graduate students who provide teaching or research assistance, and so on. The easy distinctions that apply to family labour do not explain these situations involving productive work with a temporal and supervisory structure quite similar to conventional employment. Consequently, employment classification disputes focus on the exchange dimension, and putative employers characterize the activity as internal to some noneconomic social sphere – as crime, as punishment, as rehabilitation, as care.

As an alternative to separate spheres, feminist scholars in sociology and other disciplines have developed competing accounts of economic life. These fully incorporate activities associated with women and domestic households, ranging across subsistence agriculture, food preparation, clothing production, housecleaning, and child care. To characterize nonmarket activity as 'economic,' the family labour literature identifies three important phenomena: circulation, substitution, and incorporation.[15]

First, products of nonmarket activity *circulate* between nominally distinct institutional spheres. An industrial homeworker may sort beads or roll cigars at home to coordinate production with child care and mobilize familial relationships that enlist child or spouse in the work.[16] Notwithstanding this domestic embeddedness, the products subsequently circulate in conventional markets just like those produced in a factory. Similarly, familial housework and caregiving enable current and future wage-workers to work in labour markets.[17]

---

[13] *Vanskike v Peters*, above n 9, 810; see also *Hale v Arizona*, 993 F 2d 1387 (9th Cir 1993) (USA); and *Henthorn v Dept of Navy*, 29 F 3d 682 (DC Cir 1994) (USA).

[14] ND Zatz, 'Working at the Boundaries of Markets' (2008) 61 Vand L Rev 857–958; and J Krinsky, 'Constructing Workers' (2007) 30 Qualitative Sociology 343.

[15] ND Zatz, 'Prison Labor and the Paradox of Paid Nonmarket Work' in N Bandelj (ed), *Economic Sociology Of Work* (Emerald, 2009).

[16] E Boris, *Home to Work* (Cambridge University Press, 1994).

[17] R Rapp, 'Family and Class in Contemporary America' in B Thorne and M Yalom (eds), *Rethinking the Family* (Longman, 1982); N Folbre, *The Invisible Heart* (New Press, 2001); and J Fudge, this volume.

Second, work products may not circulate but still *substitute* for goods and services that otherwise would be obtained from conventional consumer markets. Subsistence agriculture substitutes for food purchases, home cooking for restaurants and take-out, parental child care for day care centers or nannies, and so on.[18]

Third, as Viviana Zelizer's work has demonstrated, nonmarket relationships ubiquitously *incorporate* quintessentially economic transactions that distribute valuable goods, services, money, or other 'media' of exchange.[19] Focusing specifically on family labour, Joan Williams interprets 'unpaid' housework and caregiving as components of a larger complex she labels 'domesticity.' Domesticity institutionalizes an intra-household gendered division of labour and structures (unequally) access *both* to the products of nonmarket work (by, paradigmatically, a wageworking husband and minor children) *and* wage income from market work.[20]

These tools easily can pick apart the notion that prison labour is noneconomic just because it is embedded in the prison. Economic circulation arises through prison labour's downstream effects on conventional markets, most obviously when inmates manufacture goods that are sold in competition with those produced by conventional employees. Additionally, inmate workers may directly substitute for ordinary hired employees. When the governor of Iowa threw a holiday party featuring cookies baked by state prisoners, he didn't have to hire a caterer.[21] A federal prison labour programme advertises its services as 'the best kept secret in outsourcing.'[22] Finally, conventionally 'economic' goods, services, and money are incorporated into the relationship between prison and inmate, most directly when the prison pays an hourly wage.

Based on such arguments, some courts take the view that because prison labour is productive work, the relationship is economic in character notwithstanding its penal nature. Accordingly, they classify prison labour as employment. One judge reasoned, albeit in dissent, that: 'The economic reality is that [the inmates] work. Their labour produces goods and services that are sold in the channels of commerce. And [the prison industry] pays them for their efforts. Common sense tells us this relationship is both penological *and* pecuniary.'[23]

Understood in these terms, nonmarket work can easily breach the boundaries of employment along its exchange dimension. At root, the point comes from the long tradition in economic sociology and anthropology harking back at least to Karl Polanyi: markets are simply one way to structure economic activity, understood as 'the production, distribution, exchange, and consumption of scarce goods and services.'[24]

---

[18] A Abbott, 'Sociology of Work and Occupations' in *The Handbook of Economic Sociology*, above n 7; J Boydston, *Home and Work* (Oxford University Press, 1990); and Folbre, above n 17.

[19] VA Zelizer, *The Purchase of Intimacy* (Princeton University Press, 2005).

[20] J Williams, 'From Difference to Dominance to Domesticity' (2001) 76 Chi-Kent L Rev 1441.

[21] W Petroski, 'Iowa Prison Inmates Bake Up Yuletide Cheer' *Des Moines Register* (Des Moines, 24 December 2006) 1B.

[22] Unicor Federal Prison Industries, Inc, 'A Community Service and A Valuable Employer Resource' (Contact Center webpage) <http://www.unicor.gov/services/contact_helpdesk/>.

[23] *Hale v Arizona*, above n 13, 1403 (Norris dissenting).

[24] NJ Smelser and R Swedberg, 'Introducing Economic Sociology' in *The Handbook of Economic Sociology*, above n 7, 3; accord K Polanyi, *The Great Transformation* (2nd edn, Beacon Press, 2001) 31–2.

3. Following work across the control boundary

Labour law scholars are busily developing conceptual frameworks that displace the traditional focus on a worker's place in a supervisory hierarchy within one organization. Doing so highlights aspects of work irreducible to the issues of control or subordination. These frameworks break down the boundary between employment and independent contracting. Stated in their relatively abstract forms, they do the same for employment's boundary with family labour along the control dimension. Despite this, scholars have assumed, implicitly or by stipulation, that the work lying 'beyond employment' remains work within labour markets.[25] Nonetheless, they imply that going beyond employment entails embracing all 'work.' In other words, they take for granted employment's boundary along the exchange dimension and fail to grapple with nonmarket work.

For instance, Guy Davidov distinguishes questions of supervisory subordination from those of economic dependence. The two together characterize employment, but the latter alone might justify certain protections associated with an intermediate category of 'worker' or 'dependent contractor.' 'Dependency on a specific relationship – especially economic dependency, but also dependency for the fulfillment of social and psychological needs – justifies various kinds of regulatory protections.'[26] This description seems to fit someone in an intensive caregiving relationship and for whom meeting economic needs depends on maintaining either that relationship (to the recipient of care) or to others who support it (for instance, a co-parent or a state social service programme). Indeed, Martha Fineman characterizes caretakers as facing 'derivative dependency.'[27] Davidov's dependency criterion certainly fits prisoners, students, and aid recipients whose access to income, goods, and services is tied to activities that take up much of their daily lives.

Judy Fudge calls for extending labour protections to all 'personal work arrangements.' She would jettison the bilateral model of employer/employee or user/contractor relationships and apply a flexible, multidimensional analysis of relationships between a worker and an 'enterprise.' An enterprise is 'an economic unity that brings together physical, technical, and human resources oriented toward the achievement of a productive goal, whether the production of goods or services.'[28] Labour law would regulate this relationship according to the principle that an 'entity that exercises control should be responsible for the risks and liabilities created' and that 'enterprises should share the risks inherent in socially useful activity.'[29] One might easily consider individual families, specific state

---

[25] For an exception addressing the continuity between informal employment and unpaid family labour, see K Sankaran, 'Informal Employment and the Challenges for Labour Law,' this volume.

[26] G Davidov, 'Who is a Worker?' (2005) 34 ILJ 57, 63.

[27] MA Fineman, *The Neutered Mother, the Sexual Family, and Other Twentieth Century Tragedies* (Routledge, 1995); see also E Feder Kittay, *Love's Labor* (Routledge, 1999); AL Alstott, *No Exit* (Oxford University Press, 2004); and Folbre, above n 17.

[28] J Fudge, 'Fragmenting Work and Fragmenting Organizations' (2006) 44 Osgoode Hall LJ 609, 638.

[29] Ibid 640.

programmes, or the broader complex of family–state interaction to be enterprises that achieve productive goals (the delivery of socially valuable caregiving) and in so doing create certain risks and vulnerabilities. More generally, the forms of paid nonmarket work described above all appear to take place within such enterprises. Nonetheless, Fudge restricts her analysis to 'workers who sell their capacity to work.'[30]

Mark Freedland offers a similarly capacious concept of the 'personal work nexus': 'the connection or connections, link or links, between a person providing service personally and the persons, organizations or enterprises who or which are involved in the arrangements for or incidental to the personal work in question.'[31] Again, family caretaking fruitfully could be conceptualized within this apparatus. For instance, Freedland's discussion of work's temporal structure suggests ways in which a given form of market work may be more similar to a given form of nonmarket work than to other instances of market work. In some respects, home-based self-employment may be closer to family caretaking than to an assembly-line job. To his credit, Freedland tentatively steps away from paradigmatic 'market' relationships by briefly considering public officeholders and volunteers in the course of introducing into his analysis matters of motivation or purpose, non-contractuality, and 'incidental' arrangements. Nonetheless, these remain quite marginal; there is no suggestion that his broadened conception of work would require tackling major social institutions generally thought to be outside the purview of either labour or commercial law.

4. What is at stake? Misclassification, displacement, or exclusion?

A core concern about the growth of independent contracting, subcontracting, triangular employment, informal employment, and related phenomena is the sense that work is *migrating* from employment into these forms and thereby escaping labour law's grasp. A common refrain is that labour law was designed around the 'old' workplace and needs to be updated to grasp 'new' forms of work.[32] On a certain naïve view, all the fuss is puzzling. After all, if labour law's raison d'être is to address problems specific to a particular relational form (employment), then the decline of that form and the growth of others is no cause for worry. The old problems continue to be addressed where they occur, and the new forms fail to present these problems. Three types of reason might explain why work outside traditional employment should provoke a shout rather than this yawn. In order of increasingly profound challenge to an employment-centered 'idea of labour law,' these are misclassification, displacement, and exclusion.

---

[30] Ibid 635.
[31] M Freedland, 'From the Contract of Employment to the Personal Work Nexus' (2006) 35 ILJ 1, 16.
[32] KVW Stone, *From Widgets to Digits* (Cambridge University Press, 2004).

a. Misclassification

The narrowest framework analyzes alternate work arrangements as simple mislabeling or *misclassification*.[33] Notwithstanding the presence of all essential features of employment, the employer dresses up the relationship as something else. On this view, employment is indeed the appropriate object of regulation, and the problem is simply one of clarifying and applying the appropriate definition of it. Some heroic efforts have been made to achieve this clarification,[34] but the balance of opinion appears to be that getting employment right is not enough; we must supplement it with additional categories[35] or altogether dislodge it from the center of labour regulation.[36]

b. Displacement

Diagnoses more capacious than misclassification see genuine variations in form, not mere window dressing, yet identify another type of regulatory evasion. Work that would have been organized as employment instead is structured otherwise, thereby escaping labour law's reach. At this point, we face a fork in the road. One worry about nonemployment work structures is that they threaten *displacement* of employees. Insofar as the nonemployment form offers advantages – including nonapplication of labour law – employees may be pushed aside, their shoes filled by others working under conditions favourable to would-be employers who now obtain labour through other means. This displacement can occur either within the firm (laying off employees and shifting work to contractors) or between firms (organizing work in an alternate form that drives employment-based firms out of business). More subtly, labour standards within employment relationships may face downward pressure from the threat of such displacement.

Concerns about displacement recur throughout treatments of prison labour and other nonmarket work. For many, the danger that prison labour competes with and undermines conventional employment itself becomes a reason to classify prison labour *as employment*, so as to remove the incentive for regulatory arbitrage. This rationale for inmate coverage facilitates denial of concern for the inmates themselves. Instead, such coverage is declared necessary to the protection of 'free labour', much as labour rights for unauthorized migrants have served as a proxy for protecting citizen workers.[37] Inversely, courts ruling against inmate coverage insist, often implausibly, that prisoners' work does not threaten ordinary employees because of various restrictions on its form.[38] In these ways, substitution and displacement are tightly linked, and the challenge they present is how to reconcile

---

[33] 'Working Beyond the Reach or Grasp of Employment Law', above n *.
[34] Eg G Davidov, 'The Three Axes of Employment Relationships' (2002) 52 UTLJ 357.
[35] Davidov, above n 4.
[36] Freedland, above n 31; Fudge, above n 28; and Standing, above n 1.
[37] H Motomura, 'The Rights of Others' (2010) 59 Duke LJ 1723.
[38] ND Zatz, 'Working at the Boundaries of Markets' (2008) 61 Vand L Rev 857.

seemingly significant differences between work relationships – including the social status of the workers – with the fungibility of work products.

On the surface, antidisplacement arguments keep employment central to labour regulation. Extending protections to nontraditional forms of work, perhaps even by labeling them 'employment,' protects traditional employees. But what about these traditional employees calls out for their defense, and what about these nontraditional workers makes them so threatening? One might have thought that competition from other forms of labour would be treated as just another factor in the competitive environment that affects labour market conditions. After all, employment levels and labour standards also are affected by commodity prices, consumer demand, trade regulation, the tax structure, and so on.[39]

Herein lies a difficulty in viewing labour law narrowly, or in antidisplacement rationales. If labour law simply remedies pathologies intrinsic to a specific relationship – employment – then it is difficult to understand why labour law should concern itself with threats to employees *above and beyond those threats directly regulated by labour law within employment relationships*. Antidisplacement reasoning treats employees as a favoured class, one with a protected interest not only in how they are treated if employed but also in remaining employed and, moreover, in being the ones who receive protections *as opposed to others*.

Unsurprisingly, antidisplacement rhetoric inevitably invokes a less technocratic conception of labour law, one that protects not merely people who happen to be employees but instead the state's paradigmatic political subjects: 'free labour,' 'hard-working, law-abiding citizens,' and so forth. Inversely, arguments *against* employment status for nonstandard workers routinely diminish their desert by highlighting personal characteristics differentiating them from the paradigmatic citizen-worker, casting them as foreign, as criminal, as irresponsible, as not having family responsibilities, as in need of supervision, as 'secondary workers.'[40]

Embracing a richer conception of whom labour law is for leaves open ample room for pragmatic debate: are the paradigmatic citizen-workers better protected, and honored, by sharply distinguishing them from potential interlopers, or must the latter receive protection precisely to make them unattractive as substitutes. For my purposes, however, what matters is that antidisplacement concerns open the door to analyzing the scope of labour protections in broader terms than internal features of an employee–employer relationship. By doing so, they beg deeper questions about why traditional employees are the proper subjects of labour citizenship and whether the criteria linking the two might properly apply beyond employment.

c. Exclusion

Misclassification and displacement provide reasons for labour law to concern itself with work that crosses, or at least confounds, the boundaries of employment, yet

---

[39] Howe, this volume.
[40] ND Zatz, 'Working at the Boundaries of Markets' (2008) 61 Vand L Rev 857.

these reasons remain grounded in the protection of employees. A quite different line of argument focuses on the putative nonemployees. As with misclassification, the problem is that these workers do not receive the protections or support they deserve. However, they deserve these not because they are really employees but because employment is underinclusive of the work relationships that merit protection or support. In other words, an employment-centered labour law unfairly excludes these workers because, despite working outside an employment relationship, they nonetheless share with employees whatever factors appropriately trigger labour law coverage.

Claims of exclusion need not apply uniformly across all aspects of labour law. Davidov, for instance, argues that some aspects of labour law attach to subordination and others to dependency; the latter could appropriately apply to work relationships lacking the control characteristic of employment.[41] By teasing out multiple features of the paradigm case of employment, scholars have reimagined labour law as concentric circles or related geometries.[42] These devices use a method of subtraction. They start with employment as the paradigm case and then conceptualize other forms of work as employment minus some crucial feature. The latter merit protection by the subset of labour law responsive to the remaining employment-like features.

A formally similar but broader perspective on exclusion focuses on labour law's place within the modern welfare state and on employment's relationship to citizenship within that state. TH Marshall famously interpreted economic inequality as a barrier to full and equal social citizenship, treating labour market differentiation as the source of inequality and participation in the consumer economy as the measure of belonging.[43] Labour law and social welfare policies together could reconcile egalitarian citizenship with market-generated inequalities.

Marshall's implicit assumption of universal labour market participation is, however, fatally flawed, and for reasons closely related to his failure to consider matters of economic relations within households. As feminist critics have long noted, modern welfare states tend to reflect and reinforce a family wage system, in which the normative household consists of a wage-earning man married to a woman who keeps house and cares for the couple's children. The male 'breadwinner's' market production brings resources into the household for consumption by his 'dependants.' Insofar as labour law and complementary social welfare policies aim to support the breadwinner's wage and facilitate dignified access to it, they attach social citizenship to the role reserved for men within the family wage system.[44]

Feminist critics of employment-based social policies have argued that privileging market over nonmarket work is arbitrary, because what matters to social citizenship

---

[41] Davidov, above n 26.

[42] Supiot, above n 2; and Davidov, above n 4.

[43] TH Marshall, 'Citizenship and Social Class' in *Citizenship and Social Class and Other Essays* (Cambridge University Press, 1950).

[44] T Skocpol, *Protecting Soldiers and Mothers* (Belknap, 1992); A Kessler-Harris, *In Pursuit of Equity* (Oxford University Press, 2001); L Gordon, *Pitied but Not Entitled* (Free Press, 1994); and N Fraser, 'After the Family Wage' in *Justice Interruptus* (Routledge, 1997) 41–68.

is the social contribution inherent in productive activity. In doing so they mimic standard formulations of labour's law rationale that invoke not merely internal features of employment relations but instead the dignity of the working person as a productive citizen.[45] This understanding of labour law echoes in its common gloss as the law of 'workers,' as if to call it merely the law of employment relations would miss much of the point. Picking up this ball and running with it, Fineman argues that: 'Taking care of someone such as a child while they are young, until they "become their own person," is work, represents a major contribution to the society, and should be explicitly recognized as such.'[46] Similar formulations are legion,[47] including variations that conceptualize childrearing as producing a 'public good' that economically benefits others[48] or as satisfying collective responsibilities for children's well-being and development.[49] At their most ambitious, such arguments lead toward a 'caregiver parity' model[50] in which nonmarket care equals market employment in affording access to social citizenship. Nancy Folbre once called for financial supports for caretakers 'equivalent to what he or she would receive at a well-paid job.'[51]

Here we see the pressure toward inclusion that arises when work-based regulation is understood to promote an egalitarianism among producers. Returning to the method of subtraction, the intuition is that what makes labour law special – and not merely a sector-specific elaboration of contract law – is its foundation in human work,[52] and *that* feature of employment is the one most widely shared. Observations of economic substitution highlight this point: if work is the medium of equal citizenship, then it is especially troubling when two people do 'the same work' but are treated differently.

C. Against homogeneous work regulation

Labour law cannot ignore nonmarket work, but what should it do once it starts paying attention? I offer nothing close to a full answer. Instead, this section argues that the same conceptual move that batters the market boundary of employment – appreciating the multiplicity of ways in which economic activity is woven into specific relationships and institutional arrangements – necessarily militates against

---

[45] JN Shklar, *American Citizenship* (Harvard University Press, 1991); V Schultz, 'Life's Work' (2000) 100 Colum L Rev 1881; WE Forbath, 'Caste, Class, and Equal Citizenship' (1999) 98 Mich L Rev 91; and Davidov and Langille, above n 4.

[46] Fineman, above n 27, 9.

[47] Folbre, above n 17; S White, 'Fair Reciprocity and Basic Income' in A Reeve and A Williams (eds), *Real Libertarianism Assessed* (Palgrave Macmillan, 2003) 136; and IM Young, 'Autonomy, Welfare Reform, and the Meaningful Work' in E Feder Kittay and EK Feder (eds), *The Subject of Care* (Rowman and Littlefield, 2002).

[48] N Folbre, 'Children as Public Goods' (1994) 84 Am Econ Rev 86.

[49] Alstott, above n 27; and Feder Kittay, above n 27.

[50] Fraser, above n 44.

[51] N Folbre, *Who Pays for the Kids?* (Routledge, 1994) 209.

[52] Langille, above n 1.

approaches that would purport to regulate work *qua* work, or workers *qua* workers, without regard to relational and institutional context. This point introduces the temptation to fall back to 'the labour market' as a unit of analysis that eliminates such contextual complexity, but that will not do either.

1. The social specificity of work and work regulation

Attacks on the market boundary of employment rely upon an important corollary to the point that markets are simply one way to organize work: establishing that a relationship or institution has some noneconomic purpose or function, or that it is structured by nonmarket norms or practices, tells us nothing about whether work is taking place. The converse is also true: establishing that a practice involves work tells us nothing about the other features of the relationship or institution in which it occurs. Simply knowing that work is involved leaves open who participates, what the time structure is, what authority relationships obtain, what other practices are systematically implicated, what it means to participants, and so on. The intensive, well-bounded labour of the industrial working day differs radically from the more fluid boundaries characteristic of both the freelancer and the family caregiver. Both actual and, most would say, appropriate authority relations vary as between parent and child, employer and employee, and prison warden and inmate.

In short, work is never just work. It always is a particular form of work. Similarly, one who works is never simply a 'worker.' It can be otherwise only if the designation 'worker' smuggles in far more specific content than it lets on with its invocation of work.

If work is never just work, then there cannot sensibly be a homogenous law of work. As applied, work law always regulates some specific form of work, and there is always more to that practice than its productive character. Furthermore, there are many different ways in which work is always more than only work. Therefore, labour law must in some combination (a) attempt a uniform regulation of work not predicated on any particular relational context, (b) regulate uniformly but based on relationally specific considerations drawn from a subset of work forms, or (c) proliferate into multiple variants responsive to particular forms of work.

Family caretaking and prison labour again illustrate the challenges of regulating diverse forms of work. Consider the 'commodification anxiety'[53] triggered by feminist proposals to recognize and restructure nonmarket work's economic character through such institutional changes as linking family caregiving to post-divorce entitlements, to qualification for social security benefits, or to contemporaneous income. The worry is that highlighting the economic character of nonmarket relationships will transform their meaning, experience, and social organization, disrupting or defiling them by imbuing them with market character.

Commodification critiques generally assume that intimate relationships possess a pastoral quality that will be undermined by integration with economic transactions,

---

[53] Williams, above n 20.

particularly monetary ones. This concern reflects both romanticism about family life and the 'hostile worlds' notion that intimate and economic relationships are intrinsically incompatible.[54] Treating family caregiving as an economic phenomenon implies interpreting and structuring it as a market bargain between the caregiver and somebody, whether a spouse, the state, or the recipient of care. In Zelizer's terms, the flip side of 'hostile worlds' is 'nothing but': identifying a relationship as economic (rather than intimate) fully specifies its essential nature because being economic entails a specific (market) relational form, and nothing else. By showing how a relationship's incorporation of economic transactions yields no intrinsic push toward market meanings and forms, Zelizer's work opens up a way out of the commodification critique. Indeed, she shows that such transactions may be constitutive of particular forms of intimacy.

This capacity to differentiate among relational forms – all of which involve work – blunts some of the prescriptive force of calling them 'work.' Both analytically and politically, the point of characterizing family caregiving or housework as 'nonmarket work' has been to identify their commonality with 'market work,' and thereby to cast doubt on practices that differentiate the two forms of work. Identifying this commonality, however, simply begs the question whether what matters for regulatory purposes is a shared status as 'work' or a divergent relationship to markets. Exclusions formerly justified by economic/noneconomic distinctions might simply be recharacterized to rest on market/nonmarket distinctions.

This difficulty dissolves if bare status as 'work' authorizes specific claims, regardless of relational context. Just such an argument often is made on behalf of nonmarket caretakers: those who receive benefits ('society') should not get 'something for nothing' but instead should share the economic benefits they receive from productive work (or, in what amounts to roughly the same thing, share its economic burdens).[55] Without such payments, caretakers 'subsidize' the rest of society.[56] Although caretaking remains his primary example of nonmarket work, Guy Standing explicitly generalizes the principle to advocate 'a floor of rights for everybody doing *all* types of work.'[57]

Social contribution theories of caretaker entitlements risk reverting to a 'nothing but' account of economic action. Not coincidentally, they often treat parental care for children in tandem with elder care, volunteering, political activism, and sometimes education. They do so by relying on the bare status as 'work.' With respect to the affirmative argument for economic entitlements, the distinctiveness of caretaking drops away, and we are left to recognize its 'economic' aspects in isolation. Consider one of the concluding passages to Nancy Folbre's wonderful recent book, offered in rebuttal to a variation on the commodification critique: 'Commitments to raising the next generation may be intrinsically satisfying. Economically, however,

---

[54] Zelizer, above n 19.

[55] Alstott, above n 27; and Folbre, below n 58.

[56] MA Fineman, 'Contract and Care' (2001) 76 Chicago-Kent L Rev 1403.

[57] Standing, above n 1, 268; see also IM Young, 'Autonomy, Welfare Reform, and the Meaningful Work' in E Feder Kittay and EK Feder (eds), *The Subject of Care* (Rowman and Littlefield Publishers, 2002).

they go largely unrewarded.'[58] This divide between intrinsic and economic rewards reintroduces a separate spheres analytic. But once we embrace the existence of myriad 'substantive varieties' of economic relationship,[59] why should we assume that their fairness can be evaluated by tallying up 'economic' gains and losses in isolation from other aspects of the relationship?

As stated, social contribution theories like Folbre's imply that those who benefit economically from others' productive work always wrong these workers if the beneficiaries do not reciprocate *in kind*. That view seems plainly overbroad. For instance, it would imply eliminating unpaid volunteer work and condemning children's household chores as intrinsically exploitative. These activities may well be 'productive,' but allowing that label to decide their employment status requires us to ignore everything else that might matter about them. Nor can the control dimension solve the problem, because the institutional integration and supervisory control that characterize employment may well be present. Any differentiation from employment – and minimum wage law – must occur along the exchange dimension. None of this denies that economic entitlements ought to be linked to caretaking or any other specific from of nonmarket work; it only denies that characterizing them as work goes far enough to justify such entitlements, even though it may get the ball rolling.

Similar difficulties can be seen in the regulation of authority. Standing argues that: 'All people doing all forms of work should have an equal right to freedom of association and freedom to bargain collectively.'[60] Consider inmate labour unions, once a major feature of prison activism in the United States. In *Jones v North Carolina Prisoners' Labor Union, Inc*,[61] the Supreme Court allowed North Carolina to suppress an inmate union on the ground that it would threaten prison discipline, especially through possible work stoppages. A strike's obvious economic significance cannot be hermetically sealed off from other aspects of imprisonment, in particular considerations of authority and discipline. Inmates might strike, for instance, over prison conditions outside the workshop. And even a strike over working conditions or wages could alter the dynamic between inmates and prison authorities by asserting prisoner power and fostering organization and solidarity.

Whether welcome or not, such shifts in authority relations would be inextricably intertwined with regulating prisoners' work. This is the core insight of opinions dismissing inmate employment claims for lack of a market character, opinions that often are concerned principally with employment regulation's impact on penal policy and administration. Those concerns may be misplaced, but simply reiterating the economic nature of inmate labour cannot tell us why. A substantive account of prisoner autonomy might well support union rights, but not just because they 'work.' The latter view also would imply unions of children who do household chores. Of course, there are legitimate concerns about use of power in parent–child

---

[58] N Folbre, *Valuing Children* (Harvard University Press, 2008) 191.
[59] N Bandelj, *From Communists to Foreign Capitalists* (Princeton University Press, 2008).
[60] Standing, above n 1, 269.
[61] 433 US 119 (1977).

relationships, too. But it is absurd to think that the same system of regulating authority over work would apply across all these relationships.

The difficulty, then, is that when labour law intervenes in an economic relationship, even with regard to its economic terms, it necessarily also intervenes in the relationship's noneconomic aspects. That conclusion is entirely of a piece with a perspective like Zelizer's that sees economic action as not merely coinciding with or being 'embedded in' various relationships but as a means of establishing and expressing their distinctive characters.[62] Therefore, the specific relational dynamics introduced by labour regulation will vary in their compatibility with different relationships that organize work.

2. Beyond economic organization

My argument suggests severe limits on the viability of any uniform system of work regulation. Different forms of work must be treated differently. Stated this way, my analysis has much in common with a number of recent attempts, introduced above, that grapple with the breadth of work that exists beyond employment, albeit largely within the labour market. There is much to be learned from these efforts, but I have misgivings.

Consider the method of subtraction, which recommends that work arrangements displaying a subset of employment's features should be subject to a corresponding subset of labour law. Proceeding by subtraction provides no affirmative account of the varying ways in which work is incorporated into relationships, of what shifts among forms might *add* as well as subtract. The reason to vary regulation from the employment paradigm may derive from the presence of some additional relational component, one incompatible with a standard regulatory device. For instance, by subtraction one might think that volunteers lack economic dependence on employers (or the economic responsibilities characteristic of employees), and that this justifies exclusion from regulations augmenting the economic returns to work. That may be true, but, additionally, there may be specific virtues of voluntary work – including gift-like structure – that would be undermined by direct linkage to immediate economic returns.[63] Or another: with regard to the subordination that arises from supervisory control, the method of subtraction might misapprehend the relevant comparison between conventional employment and prison labour. Plausibly, features of employment regulation designed to counter employee subordination are inappropriate to prison labour *not* because there is less subordination to counteract *but instead* because heightened subordination is appropriate to the relationship writ large.

Similar difficulties attend the more ambitious attempts to dislodge employment from the center of our maps of work. These efforts still appear thin when confronted with the *types* of variation among work practices that one sees in nonmarket work. How do we account for the linkages between the labour process

---

[62] See also GR Krippner, 'The Elusive Market' (2001) 30 Theory & Society 775.
[63] Cf MA Eisenberg, 'The World of Contract and the World of Gift' (1997) 85 CLR 821 (1997).

and 'non-economic' practices: the infliction of punishment, the relief of poverty, the treatment of disease, the formation of character, the construction of intimacy, and so on? Closely related, how do we account for the coexistence of multiple forms of interaction between workers and the individuals and institutions who make use of their labour? How do we account for the specific ways in which people enter into and exit from work relationships: by receiving a criminal sentence, by qualifying for aid, by receiving a medical diagnosis, by establishing a kinship tie? How do we account for the specific place that work practices occupy within the larger canvas of a worker's life: one component of daily and weekly time that complements and facilitates 'personal' time for family and consumption;[64] one facet of existence within a totalizing institution; one closely linked to a life stage understood as transitional or aberrant?

If even quite expansive, flexible frameworks fail to capture the full range of productive practices, where do we go next? Having started down this trail, one might press on, expanding our models' reach, adding new epicycles to capture variations in work, introducing yet more complexity. There certainly are good reasons to do so. Nonetheless, I have already suggested a basis for caution. It is not clear what makes this project hang together. Why is it that all practices involving 'work' belong in a single field, once we strip 'work' of all the baggage that ordinarily allows that simple word to stand in for a quite specific set of productive practices?

3. The futility of retreating to market boundaries

The preceding discussion invites a rebuttal: Stepping into the thicket of 'work law' is no end of trouble. We should stay out and settle for the good old law of market work. I demur for two distinct, though conceptually related, reasons. First, the embeddedness of work in specific social relationships irreducible to market transactions is omnipresent, even in relationships routinely characterized in market terms. Second, limiting labour law to the labour market assumes that 'the labour market' exists as a social phenomenon sufficiently well bounded that the application of labour law can track its perimeter. To the contrary, disputes over nonmarket work reveal that the boundaries of the market are themselves contestable, and one social mechanism for firming up these boundaries is the application (or not) of labour law itself. Under such circumstances, using the boundaries of the market to bound labour law is hopelessly circular.

a. Social specificity within 'the market'

The claim that work always is embedded in specific social relationships and institutions is not limited to 'nonmarket' work and workers. Market work is not a purely economic practice, devoid of other social characteristics, in contrast to nonmarket work which is work-plus-sociality. I mean this in a stronger sense than

---

[64] E Zaretsky, *Capitalism, The Family, and Personal Life* (HarperCollins, 1986).

the standard realist points about how markets are creatures of politics and law that dictate certain forms of security in person and property, define and enforce contracts, and so on. Beyond that lie specific socialities of market interactions.[65] There is an official public rhetoric of virtue and shame that not merely justifies but glorifies the hard bargain and marks those who walk away with less as suckers or fools. There is a hierarchy of legitimate ends that makes a virtue out of acquisitiveness and an embarrassment out of sentiment or solidarity. And of course there are the people thought best suited for markets, well-endowed with means–ends rationality, nicely ranked ordinal preferences, and no squeamishness about commensurability. This is no criticism of markets, merely insistence that they are social institutions among others, and that indeed this follows necessarily once we see the economic as a characteristic of the social, not an alternative to it.

Consider the labour law status of unauthorized migrants. The US Supreme Court recently limited their remedies if fired for union organizing.[66] The arguments for restriction were analogous to those against labour law coverage for prison labour and other 'non-market' work; this was so notwithstanding that the workplace in question was a paradigmatic factory where the other workers would have been treated as market employees without any hesitation. The court downplayed the economic relationship between employee and employer and gave precedence to matters of immigration policy, emphasizing the worker's possibly criminal conduct. Consistent with the highly racialized history of treating unauthorized workers, especially those from Mexico, as both a second-class labour force and a criminal menace, the social status of the workers appears to be driving the scope of employment protections.[67] As Catherine Fiske and Michael Wishnie have argued, the case turned on its framing as an 'immigration' rather than 'labour' case, reproducing the familiar separate spheres structure even when analyzing an institution ostensibly within 'the market.'

Such cases invite the kind of universalizing response that motivates 'work law.' Exclusions from employee status could be construed as *deviations* from the idealized, asocial market. In 'hostile worlds' fashion, these noneconomic considerations are sand in the gears. 'Workers are workers, and immigration enforcement should be a separate matter,' the argument goes.

The 'workers are workers' formulation of unauthorized workers' rights asserts an egalitarian claim as between citizen and migrant workers. But is it really grounded in the mere fact of work? I am skeptical. Far more likely, it cloaks in the language of the asocial market – in which all workers are fungible factors of production – a substantive egalitarian view about labour mobility and migration. Surely it is no coincidence that organizations structured around immigrant workers' rights find themselves drawn constantly to 'nonlabour' issues ranging from access to drivers' licenses to regularization of immigration status. It is difficult to see how one can

---

[65] Bandelj, above n 59; and P Bourdieu, 'Principles of an Economic Anthropology' in *The Handbook of Economic Sociology*, above n 7.
[66] *Hoffman Plastic Compounds, Inc v NLRB*, 535 US 137 (2002).
[67] MM Ngai, *Impossible Subjects* (Princeton University Press, 2004).

maintain that immigrants' rights are a labour issue yet immigration status is irrelevant to labour law.

None of this should be the least bit surprising given the robust tradition of framing labour rights in terms of access to full citizenship. In this tradition, labour law is not merely a species of market regulation, a full sibling of consumer protection, housing law, and so on. Instead, the founding intuition traces to the old rallying cry that labour is *not* a commodity. But if the imperative for and content of labour law derive not simply from tweaking the market *qua* market but also from workers' claims to community membership, then there is no avoiding the question whether particular workers are appropriate claimants to that membership. That question admits to many answers – including that 'work' itself provides the basis for inclusion. Some of these answers will put the migrant and formal citizen on equal footing, but not because the question of immigration status is irrelevant from the outset.

More generally, the historical record in the United States strongly supports the view that labour rights always have been intertwined with broader views of workers' place in society. To take just one example, the exclusion of women workers, especially women of color, from labour protections has never been a matter simply of the market/nonmarket divide. Instead, even among employment relationships, important exclusions hark back to the gendered work/family split. Many US statutes limit protection for domestic workers and personal care attendants, seemingly in part because this work is associated with the family domain. This 'nonmarket' character exists in synergy with the race and gender composition of the occupation, making these workers poor claimants to the mantle of 'free labour.'[68] This dynamic played out recently when the Supreme Court upheld a broadly exclusionary interpretation of the US wage and hour law as applied to home health workers.[69] The US Department of Labor's justification of that exclusion reeked of a stratified conception of citizenship, one linked, moreover, to ambiguities in the relationship between labour protections and the family wage system. Excluding home health aides from overtime protections purportedly addressed the 'special problems of working fathers and mothers who need a person to care for an elderly invalid in their home.'[70] Here, the gendered association of home care with nonwork follows the task even when market hiring substitutes for family caregiving and does so to enable market work by both adults in a prototypical middle-class household. The paradigmatic citizen in need of protection shifts from the worker to the employer, refigured as the 'working family' who ordinarily would be the protagonist of arguments favouring employment protections.

Now consider another example with a more complex political valence, one less easily explained away as a deviation from the ideal of egalitarianism among workers

---

[68] E Boris and J Klein, 'Laws of Care' [Fall 2007] Dissent 5; see also P Palmer, 'Outside the Law' (1995) 7 J Pol'y Hist 416; and S Mettler, *Dividing Citizens* (Cornell University Press, 1998).
[69] *Long Island Care at Home v Coke*, 551 US 158 (2007).
[70] US Department of Labor, 'Wage and Hour Advisory Memorandum No 2005-1' (1 December 2005) 2.

qua workers. California recently restructured publicly funded home health care to make home health aides public employees entitled to union representation. The campaign to do so relied on an alliance between organized labour and groups representing 'consumers,' namely senior citizens and people with disabilities. One point of tension involved the standard union contract provision requiring just cause for termination. The consumer groups were adamantly opposed, in part because of their specific conception of 'independent living' in which home health aides enabled consumers to achieve a level of personal and bodily autonomy taken for granted by the nondisabled. To require a process of justification, and to place consumers in the position of either forfeiting assistance or receiving it from someone not of their choosing, struck them as deeply corrosive of the independent living concept. The union allies gave way on this most basic of contract terms.[71]

Now, my point is not that giving up just-cause protection was the correct result. More modestly, I insist that even if one generally thinks of a just-cause termination rule as a basic protection, the home health context presents a serious question with which to grapple. That question does not arise because home health aides are less in need of job security than other employees. Instead, it arises because of a tension between job security provisions and arguably valuable features of the specific relationship that home health assistance helps bring into being, and the particular way that relationship interacts with the social project of civil rights for people with disabilities. Perhaps that tension should be resolved in favour of just-cause protections, but if so, it should be on reasoning more supple than 'workers are workers.'[72]

These last several examples point toward a broader claim. Not only does the method of subtraction fail to account for the affirmative value of the specific relationships of which work may be a part, but it risks obscuring the relational specificity of standard employment,[73] not merely its exceptions. The easiest way to see this is to consider the paradigmatic protagonist of labour law, the member of 'free labour.' This worker is not simply someone seeking to make a buck. Instead, 'free labour' links the receipt of wage payments to a broader, and specific, form of life involving the maintenance of an independent household (for which one seeks a 'family wage') that engages in market consumption.[74] Employment, in other words, is not just about making money, it is about 'earning a living,' and living a certain kind of life.

In this regard, we might build on but broaden Freedland and Kountouris' concept of the 'personal work profile,' which compiles over time one person's various forms of work and work-relative states like unemployment.[75] They rightly emphasize how analysis of one work arrangement might draw meaning from its

[71] L Delp and K Quan, 'Homecare Worker Organizing in California' (2002) 27 Labor Studies J 1.

[72] See also ND Zatz, 'Working at the Boundaries of Markets' (2008) 61 Vand L Rev 857 (discussing partial exceptions to labour law coverage for health care worker and religious organizations).

[73] M Crain, 'Arm's Length Intimacy: Employment as Relationship' (forthcoming 2011) 37 Wash U J Law & Policy.

[74] A Dru Stanley, *From Bondage to Contract* (Cambridge University Press, 1998); and L Cohen, *A Consumer's Republic* (Vintage Books, 2003).

[75] Freedland and Kountouris, this volume.

linkage to another, as when concern about overwork requires considering whether a worker holds multiple jobs. But analogous points apply to linkages between work and consumption patterns, family structure, immigration status, income level, health, incarceration, and so on.

b. Identifying market boundaries

The social character of market work suggests a more general problem with confining labour law to one side of the market/nonmarket boundary. We now have jettisoned both the idea that the economic resides exclusively in the market and that the social resides exclusively outside it. Once neither the presence of the economic nor the absence of the social distinguish market activity, how are we to identify it?

My contention is that law, including labour law, is partly constitutive of our designation of a practice as inside or outside the labour market. Legal and other practices institutionalize market/nonmarket boundaries, where that institutionalization is the result of contestatory 'boundary work'[76] or 'relational work'[77] by social actors, not simply reading off a preexisting map. Having argued this at length elsewhere,[78] I will add another somewhat speculative example here.

With respect to work by unauthorized migrants in the United States, two current trends are criminalization of work without proper documentation[79] and intensification of monitoring and identification regimes that reveal unauthorized status to employers.[80] Conceivably, these trends could largely eliminate the present-day phenomenon of unauthorized migrants regularly working side-by-side with authorized workers and, more generally, force work arrangements involving unauthorized migrants deep into the informal sector. How would we classify the resulting furtive exchanges of work and money? I suspect they decreasingly would be recognized as market employment and increasingly articulated as crime – not illegal employment, but instead not employment at all. That, after all, would be consistent with how prostitution and drug dealing are seen, notwithstanding ample basis for understanding them in market terms.[81]

D. Conclusion: channeling as a possible way forward

Labour law scholars are stuck with a dilemma. We must confront the diversity of work. Consistency and equality demand it, at least insofar as there is something

---

[76] TF Gieryn, 'Boundary-Work and the Demarcation of Science from Non-Science' (1983) 48 Am Soc Rev 781.

[77] Zelizer, above n 19.

[78] ND Zatz, 'Sex Work/Sex Act' (1997) 22 Signs 277; and ND Zatz, 'Working at the Boundaries of Markets' (2008) 61 Vand L Rev 857.

[79] H Motomura, 'Immigration Outside the Law' (2008) 108 CLR 2037.

[80] H Pham, 'The Private Enforcement of Immigration Laws' (2007–08) 96 Geo LJ 777.

[81] 'Sex Work/Sex Act', above n 78; P Bourgois, *In Search of Respect* (Cambridge University Press, 1995); and SA Venkatesh and SD Levitt, 'Are We a Family or a Business?' (2000) 29 Theory & Society 427.

special about productive action, and so do the practical problems generated by substitution among forms of work. Yet we are ill-equipped for this confrontation without a way to account for the relational specificity of work. Our best tools were designed to grapple with market work, but this specificity makes them both intrinsically self-limiting and vulnerable to the slipperiness of market boundaries.

Redrawing the line between protected and unprotected work is not the only way to relieve pressure on the boundaries of labour law. Another is what I call 'channeling,' borrowed from related usages in contract and family law. My earlier discussion of labour law's constitutive role implies that law channels productive activity into specific institutional forms and away from others. It shapes how work gets done, not just the legal implications that follow.

Channeling may act to suppress alternative work forms or to force greater differentiation from employment, as the identification and criminalization of unauthorized workers suggests. Responding to boundary pressure from displacement, one important channeling technique is to limit the substitutability among workers, including by limiting substitutability among their work products. In this fashion, rather than either *including* or *distinguishing* work at the margins of employment, channeling increases the difference between them.

The channeling mechanism with the most explicit relationship to substitution is an anti-displacement policy. Such policies permit nonstandard work relationships on condition that the workers do not displace conventional employees. For instance, current US welfare law bars 'workfare' programmes from using participants to fill vacancies created by another employee's 'layoff from the same or any substantially equivalent job' or by any termination designed to allow substitution of a workfare worker.[82] Similarly, certain prison labour programmes must 'not result in displacement of employed workers; be applied in skills, crafts, or trades in which there is a surplus of available gainful labor in the locality... significantly impair existing contracts,' or result in 'the inappropriate transfer of private sector job functions to inmates.'[83]

Another channeling mechanism prevents direct competition with conventional employment. For instance, there are broad prohibitions on the sale of inmate-produced goods, both in private commerce and as part of federal contracts.[84] Even when exceptions apply, priority often is given to producing goods and services with no alternative domestic source, thereby focusing any displacement on foreign workers.[85] Workfare programmes traditionally have barred placements with for-profit firms that might substitute workfare workers for regular employees.[86] And employer participation in guestworker programmes is conditioned (in theory) on the unavailability of a domestic workforce.

---

[82] 42 USC § 607(f) (2006).
[83] 64 CFR §§ 17,000, 17,010 (2009).
[84] 18 USC § 1761 (2006); 41 USC § 35(c) (2006).
[85] RP Weiss, '"Repatriating" Low-Wage Work' (2001) 39 Criminology 253.
[86] M Diller, 'Working Without a Job' (1998) 9 Stan L & Pol'y Rev 19.

On their face, these channeling mechanisms are meant to shepherd work toward conventional (domestic) labour markets.[87] Work that might otherwise have been assigned to inmates or welfare recipients instead gets directed to regular employees. But channeling rarely suppresses competing forms of work entirely. Instead, it marginalizes them and helps cast them as occurring outside the market, perhaps as something other than work at all.

In these ways, channeling rules overtly address and clarify the relationship between different forms of work. Rather than simply defining the scope of employment or prescribing separate rules for prison labour, channeling allocates between these fields both work itself and legal authority over it. For this reason, not only is channeling interesting and important in its own right, but it also offers a concrete place to begin formulating a legal analysis that grapples with the full range of work.

Notably, notwithstanding labour law scholars' limited attention to channeling between institutional domains, similar issues arise in two familiar regulatory contexts: international trade and immigration. Both feature efforts to police the boundaries of the domestic labour market, with major themes of steering work toward citizens and minor ones of concern for the labour conditions of workers abroad and migrants within.[88] This unabashed, though often fraught, linkage between work and citizenship resonates with theories of labour regulation grounded in notions of social solidarity, not merely recalibrating unequal bargaining power.

Likewise, the scope and content of citizenship presents the most difficult questions lurking beneath the dilemma I have outlined here. Is the combination of attaching labour protections to a subset of work and channeling work into that form an illegitimate form of privilege or, instead, perhaps in addition, the necessary foundation for egalitarian citizenship? The answers may well depend on who has access to that privileged zone and what the costs are of migrating into it.

---

[87] Channeling also occurs along the control dimension, for instance by pressuring organizations to hire workers as employees rather than independent contractors. SL Cummings and SA Boutcher, 'Mobilizing Local Government law for Low-Wage Workers' [2009] U Chi Legal F 187, 201, or even by creating new institutions that can serve as employers, 'Homecare Worker Organizing in California', above n 71.

[88] Howe, this volume.

16

Using Procurement Law to Enforce Labour Standards

Catherine Barnard*

Government has a key role to play in improving the lives and work prospects of our citizens. This means providing people with the opportunity to flourish as well as supporting those who are disadvantaged and ensuring that all have equal access to public services that meet the diverse needs of our communities.

With an annual spend of around £220 billion, public procurement can help towards achieving these social objectives through the way that Government buys public goods and services. By taking account of social benefits to society, Government can maximise value for money from its spending. (Office of Government Commerce, *Promoting social issues through procurement*[1])

A. Introduction

The issue of public procurement is becoming an increasingly sensitive one. During a recession, the purchasing power of the government becomes a major policy tool to get the economy back on its feet. And since, in the case of government purchasing, it is taxpayers' money that is being used, this raises the further question as to the extent to which governments can – both from a policy and a legal perspective – use their purchasing power to achieve social objectives, while at the same time securing value for money for the public purse.

Some academics have long realized the opportunities offered by public procurement to help improve labour standards.[2] However, for most of us it has taken the momentous decisions of the Court of Justice in *Laval*,[3] *Rüffert*,[4] and *Commission*

---

* I am grateful to Sjoerd Feenstra, Vassilis Hatzopoulos, Claire Kilpatrick, Louise Merrett, Oke Odudu, and Phil Syrpis for interesting discussions about the issues raised here.

[1] <http://www.ogc.gov.uk/delivering_policy_aims_through_public_procurement_social_issues. asp>.

[2] Most notably C McCrudden, *Buying Social Justice. Equality, Government Procurement, and Legal Change* (Oxford University Press, 2007); and S Arrowsmith and P Kunzlik, *Social and Environmental Policies in EC Procurement Law* (Cambridge University Press, 2009).

[3] Case C–341/05 *Laval un Partneri Ltd v Svenska Byggnadsarbetareförbundet* [2007] ECR I–11767.

[4] Case C–346/06 *Rüffert v Land Niedersachsen* [2008] ECR I–1989.

v Germany (occupational pensions)[5] to bring this potential to our attention. I have written elsewhere about the use of public procurement law to realize employment objectives.[6] This chapter looks at the scope for governments and other public bodies – within the framework of European Union (EU) and World Trade Organization (WTO) law – to impose requirements on those tendering for contracts to respect not only minimum terms and conditions of employment for their staff (such as the minimum wage) but also terms above the minimum (such as the London Living Wage).

We shall begin by examining the public procurement regime and how it might affect a contracting authority's ability to require a successful bidder to respect certain terms and conditions of employment (section B). We then consider the decision in *Commission v Germany* and its implications for opening up public procurement to social considerations (section C). Section D considers the *Laval* and *Rüffert* line of case law, examining in particular the extent to which a contracting authority can, in the light of the Posted Workers Directive 96/71,[7] require compliance with host state labour standards by an out-of-state service provider. Section E then examines the possibility of public and private actors encouraging tenderers to comply voluntarily with labour standards above the minimum, looking particularly at the living wage campaign in the United Kingdom. Section F concludes.

B. Labour law and the public procurement rules

1. Introduction

Under both EU law and international law, namely the WTO's Agreement on Government Procurement (GPA), public sector procurement must follow transparent, open procedures ensuring fair conditions of competition for suppliers.[8] Much public procurement in the EU is covered by the EU Public Procurement Directives, which were streamlined in 2004 with the adoption of the procurement package (the Utilities Directive 2004/17/EC,[9] the General Directive 2004/18/EC,[10] and the Remedies Directives[11]). For the sake of brevity I will consider the position under the General Directive 2004/18 only.

---

[5] Case C–271/08 *Commission v Germany* [2010] ECR I–000.
[6] C Barnard, '"British Jobs for British Workers": The Lindsey Oil Refinery Dispute and the Future of Local Labour Clauses in an Integrated EU Market' (2009) 38 Industrial Law Journal 245.
[7] [1997] OJ L 18/1.
[8] Full details can be found at <http://ec.europa.eu/internal_market/publicprocurement/index_en.htm>.
[9] [2004] OJ L 134/1.
[10] Directive 2004/18 on the award of public works contracts, public supply contracts, and public service contracts [2004] OJ L 134/114.
[11] Directive 2007/66/EC [2007] OJ L 335/31 amending Council Directives 89/665/EEC [1989] OJ L 395/33 and 92/13/EEC [1992] OJ L 76/14.

The General Directive provides that, where the value of a tender exceeds a prescribed minimum, it must be publicly advertised in accordance with the Directive. Where the thresholds laid down in the Directive are not satisfied, the procurement regime must nevertheless still respect the Treaty principles of equal treatment, mutual recognition, and proportionality.[12] In the discussion that follows I consider how a tendering procedure might be used to specify certain labour standards, specifically in the British context, focusing in particular on tenders to which the Directive applies.[13]

2. The territorial application of labour law

The starting point of any analysis is the territorial application of labour law. Domestic labour law certainly applies to the employees of domestic bidders. Domestic labour law also applies to bidders from other Member States who are established in the host state under Article 49 of the Treaty on the Functioning of the European Union (TFEU). The reason why employees of domestic bidders and established bidders from other Member States are in the same position is because, under *EU* law, namely Article 8(2) of the Rome I Regulation, the law which prima facie applies is the law of the country where people work.[14] Furthermore, under *British* law (Employment Rights Act (ERA) 1996), employment rights apply to those employed in the United Kingdom, irrespective of their nationality and the duration of their employment. ERA 1996, section 204(1) provides: 'For the purposes of this Act it is immaterial whether the law which (apart from this Act) governs any person's employment is the law of the United Kingdom, or of a part of the United Kingdom.' This wording resembles the provisions on *mandatory rules* under Article 8(2) of the Rome I Regulation ('Nothing in this Convention shall restrict the application of the rules of the law of the forum in a situation where they are mandatory irrespective of the law otherwise applicable to the contract'). The effect of ERA 1996, section 204(1) is that the UK considers the whole of ERA 1996 to be a mandatory rule[15] and so its provisions will apply to anyone working in the UK.[16]

The territorial application of labour law is also implicit in the rather weak provision in Article 27 of Directive 2004/18: contracting authorities must request that tenderers 'indicate that they have *taken into account*, when drawing up their tender, of the obligations relating to employment protection provisions and the working conditions which are in force in the place' where the works/services are to be performed. By contrast, the Commission's 2001 interpretative communication is more explicit about the application of the labour law rules of the place where the

---

[12] See, eg, Case C–264/03 *Commission v France* [2005] ECR I–8831, para 33; and Case C–6/05 *Medipac-Kazantzidis AE v Venizelio-Pananio (PE.S.Y KRITIS)* [2007] ECR I–4557, paras 32–33.

[13] The Directive also applies to domestic tenderers: Case C–243/89 *Commission v Denmark (Storebaelt)* [1993] ECR I–3396.

[14] Reg 593/2008 [2008] OJ L177/6.

[15] *Dicey and Morris on the Conflict of Laws* (14th edn, Sweet & Maxwell, 2006) para 33-090. The same reasoning is likely to apply to other pieces of UK employment legislation.

[16] See further L Merrett, 'The Extra-Territorial Reach of Employment Legislation' (2010) 39 Industrial Law Journal 355.

tender is performed: 'even if the public procurement directives do not contain a specific provision to this effect, all [Union], international and national regulations, rules and provisions which are applicable in the social field shall apply fully during the performance of a public procurement contract following award of the contract'.[17]

The question then is what scope is there in Directive 2004/18 for contracting authorities to require tenderers to offer terms and conditions over and above the national minima ('improved' labour standards). Before we consider this point (section 3 below) it is important to note that the position is different in respect of a foreign service provider which has won a tender but intends not to establish itself in the host state but merely to provide services there under Article 56 TFEU, using its own (posted) workers (the situation in *Laval* and *Rüffert*). Under Article 8(2) of the Rome I Regulation, in particular the second sentence, the law of the country from which the posted workers come will govern their terms and conditions (that is the *home*, not the host, state law), subject to the provisions of the Posted Workers Directive (PWD). The question in respect of these posted workers is whether, apart from the areas listed in Article 3(1) PWD, the public procurement rules can be used to require the service provider to respect *any* of the host state's labour standards, let alone improved labour standards. This is considered in section D below. First, we examine the possibility of using public procurement to impose improved labour standards in the non-posted worker cases.

3. The basic procurement regime

There are five main stages in a procurement regime under the Directive: (1) the pre-procurement stage where the contracting authorities identify whether and what to purchase, and which procedure to apply; (2) the specification stage where the contracting authorities set out technical specifications in the contract documentation;[18] (3) the identification of suitable potential suppliers stage; (4) the contract award stage; and (5) the performance stage. Stages (3)–(5) offer the most potential for requiring tenderers to adopt improved terms and conditions and we shall examine these three stages in turn.

a. Supplier selection stage

Directive 2004/18 prescribes a list of criteria for the selection of contractors permitted to submit a tender.[19] These are:

---

[17] Commission Interpretative Communication, COM(2001) 566, 18. See also p 19. In addition, see Art 3 of ILO Convention No 94: 'Where appropriate provisions relating to the health, safety and welfare of workers engaged in the execution of contracts are not already applicable in virtue of national laws or regulations, collective agreement or arbitration award, the competent authority shall take adequate measures to ensure fair and reasonable conditions of health, safety and welfare for the workers concerned.'

[18] Art 23.

[19] Case C–94/99 *ARGE* [2000] ECR I–11037, para 27.

- the personal situation of the candidate or tenderer[20]
- their suitability to pursue a professional activity (for example, their membership of a professional organization)[21]
- their economic and financial standing (for example, are they financially sound based on their annual accounts?)[22]
- their technical capacity (for example, are they adequately equipped to do the job and do they have a good track record?).[23]

On their face, it does not seem as though these provisions provide much scope for social matters to be taken into account. However, one of the discretionary grounds on which a tenderer can be excluded, under the first heading 'personal situation', is that the tenderer has been found 'guilty of grave professional misconduct'. According to the Recitals,[24] this includes non-compliance with the obligations under the Posted Workers Directive 96/71, the Equality Framework Directive 2000/78,[25] and the Equal Treatment Directive 76/207[26] (now Directive 2006/54[27]).

What about excluding the tenderer by reference to non-respect of terms and conditions of employment more generally? According to the orthodoxy, the Directive lists exhaustively the grounds capable of justifying the exclusion of a contractor from participation in a tender.[28] And since there is no reference to non-compliance with terms and conditions of employment in the Recitals it would appear that a contractor could not be excluded on this basis. However, in *Michaniki*[29] the Court said that 'in addition to the grounds for exclusion based on objective considerations of professional quality, which are listed exhaustively' a Member State is entitled, subject to the principle of proportionality, 'to provide for exclusionary measures designed to ensure observance, in procedures for the award of public contracts, of the principles of equal treatment of all tenderers and of transparency'.[30] So an exhaustive list is less exhaustive than would first appear. This might open the way for contracting authorities to exclude, on the grounds of equal treatment, tenderers who refuse to comply with a certain number of specified terms and conditions of employment. *Commission v Germany* (considered in section C below) might provide further support for this as a possibility.

---

[20] Art 45.
[21] Art 46.
[22] Art 47.
[23] Arts 46–48.
[24] Recitals 34 and 43.
[25] [2000] OJ L 303/16.
[26] [1976] OJ L 39/40. See also to this effect Office of Government Commerce (OGC), *Social Issues in Purchasing*, (February 2006).
[27] [2006] OJ L 204/23.
[28] Case 31/87 *Beentjes v State of the Netherlands* [1988] ECR 4635, para 28 (contracting authorities could not add other grounds for exclusion such as a condition relating to the hiring of the long-term unemployed).
[29] Case C–213/07 *Michaniki v Ethniko Simvoulio Radiotileorasis* [2008] ECR I–9999.
[30] Para 47.

b. The contract award stage

i. MEAT and social clauses

The next stage in the procurement process is the award of the contract. According to Article 53, contracts can be awarded on one of two bases: (1) the lowest price; or (2) the most economically advantageous tender (MEAT). The former offers no room for contracting authorities to take into account additional factors and so is rarely used in British public procurement. The latter basis, MEAT, might offer space for social factors to be taken into account but the precise scope is more unclear.

According to the 1993 version of the public procurement directive:

... the most economically advantageous tender, [involves] various criteria depending on the contract in question, such as: delivery or completion date, running costs, cost-effectiveness, quality, aesthetic and functional characteristics, technical merit, after-sales service and technical assistance, commitments with regard to spare parts, security of supplies and price.[31]

While the purists had argued that this provision provided no scope for non-economic matters to be taken into account by contract-awarding bodies, in *Nord-Pas-de-Calais*[32] the Court disagreed: 'that provision does not preclude all possibility for the contracting authorities to use as a criterion a condition linked to the campaign against unemployment provided that that condition is consistent with all the fundamental principles of [Union] law, in particular the principle of non-discrimination . . . '[33] However, the Court added that such an award criterion had to be expressly mentioned in the contract notice 'so that contractors may become aware of its existence'.[34]

In *Concordia Bus Finland*[35] the Court added a further limitation on the use of social clauses. It said: 'Since a tender necessarily relates to the subject matter of the contract, it follows that the award criteria which may be applied in accordance with that provision must themselves also be linked to the subject matter of the contract.'[36] This conclusion indirectly made it harder for contracting authorities to include social criteria in their tenders because the link between social criteria and the specific nature of the product/service can be tenuous.[37] This problem is exacerbated by the revisions made in the 2004 public procurement directives (key revisions in italics). Article 53(1)(a) now provides:

... when the award is made to the tender most economically advantageous *from the point of view of the contracting authority*, various criteria *linked to the subject-matter of the public*

---

[31] This is taken from Art 34 of the Utilities Directive 93/98.
[32] Case C–225/98 *Commission v France* [2000] ECR I–7445.
[33] Para 50.
[34] Para 51.
[35] Case C–513/99 [2002] ECR I–7213.
[36] Para 59. See also Case C–448/01 *EVN v Republik Österreich* [2003] ECR I–14527, para 33; and Case C–331/04 *ATI EAC Srl e Viaggi di Maio Snc v ACTV Venzia SpA* [2005] ECR I–10109, para 21.
[37] P Charro, Case note (2003) 40 CMLR 179, 187.

contract in question, for example, quality, price, technical merit, aesthetic and functional characteristics, *environmental characteristics*, running costs, cost effectiveness, aftersales service and technical assistance, delivery date and delivery period or period of completion [can be taken into account].

As can be seen, not only must the criteria now be linked to the subject-matter of the contract but the tender must be the most economically advantageous from the point of view of the contracting authority, the point the Commission had lost in *Concordia* but had already included as an accurate statement of the law in its 2001 Interpretative Communication.[38] It is hard to argue that a condition relating to the specification of improved terms and conditions of employment is economically advantageous from the point of view of the contracting authority, apart from in the most general terms that improving labour standards ultimately improves productivity. Moreover, the failure to refer to social matters is exacerbated by the fact that environmental characteristics are listed for the first time in Article 53.[39]

Why did the 2004 version of the directive not reflect the case law more closely?[40] Although the European Parliament pushed for greater recognition of social matters, the Commission (DG Internal Market) and the Council were opposed. The compromise was to move a number of the social clauses from the body of the Directive to the Preamble. Contrast, for example, Article 53(1)(a) of the Directive (set out above) with Recital 46, which does offer some space for social matters to be taken into account in determining the MEAT:

. . . a contracting authority may use criteria aiming to meet social requirements, in response in particular to the needs – defined in the specifications of the contract – of particularly disadvantaged groups of people to which those receiving/using the works, supplies or services which are the object of the contract belong.[41]

This is still a long way removed from requiring tenderers to take into account improved terms and conditions of employment. Here again *Commission v Germany* (considered in section C below) might provide further openings, especially if read in the light of the Commission's 2001 Interpretative Communication which says that working conditions 'more favourable to workers may, however, also be applied (and must then also be complied with), provided they are compatible with [Union] law'.[42]

---

[38] Commission, *Interpretative Communication on the Community law applicable to public procurement and the possibilities for integrating social considerations into public procurement*, COM(2001) 566, 13.

[39] Although cf the first Recital, which says that the 2004 Directive is 'based on the Court of Justice case law, in particular the case law on award criteria, which clarifies the possibilities for the contracting authorities to meet the needs of the public concerned, including in the environmental and/or social area'.

[40] See further C Kilpatrick, 'Internal Market Architecture and the Accommodation of Labour Rights: Posting of Workers, Public Procurement and the Court of Justice', on file with the author.

[41] Recent case law shows the extent to which the Court is now prepared to refer to Preambles: see, eg, Case C–307/05 *Del Cerro Alonso v Osakidetza-Servicio Vasco de Salud* [2007] ECR I–7109, para 36. However, recitals have only interpretative value and cannot be used to contradict express provisions in a Directive: Case C–267/06 *Maruko v Versorgungsanstalt der deutschen Bühnen* [2008] ECR I–1757, para 60.

[42] Commission, above n 38, 20.

ii. Abnormally low tenders

There is one other area, in the context of the award, where social matters can be taken into account: where the bid appears abnormally low, the contracting authority must request the details of the constituent elements of the tender including 'compliance with the provisions relating to employment protection and working conditions in force at the place where the work, service or supply is to be performed'. This might indicate that only minimum terms and conditions can be requested but the vagueness of the phrase 'place where the work...is to be performed' might be broad enough to include improved terms and conditions in that particular workplace.

c. The performance stage

From the public authority's point of view, including social clauses is best considered as a condition at the performance stage of the contract. Here the Directive appears to offer greater flexibility to the contracting authority since, as with the pre-procurement stage, it is the area least regulated by the Directive. Article 26 of the Directive merely says:

Contracting authorities may lay down special conditions relating to the performance of a contract, provided that these are compatible with [Union] law and are indicated in the contract notice or in the specifications. The conditions governing the performance of a contract may, in particular, concern *social and environmental considerations*. [Emphasis added.]

Most of the situations envisaged by the Preamble to the Directive concern local hiring.[43] However, the Preamble adds that 'mention may be made, amongst other things of the requirements – applicable during performance of the contract... to comply in substance with the provisions of the basic International Labour Organization (ILO) Conventions, assuming that such provisions have not been implemented in national laws'. This view is now reinforced by the Commission's 2010 Staff Working Document, *Buying Social: A Guide to Taking Account of Social Criteria in Public Procurement*,[44] which says that: 'Sustainability criteria (including social criteria) may also be incorporated in the contract performance condition, provided they are linked to performance of the contract in question (eg minimum salary and decent labour conditions for the workers involved in the performance of the contract).'

This suggests that it would be possible, at least at performance stage, to include requirements for tenderers to take into account minimum terms and conditions of employment and possibly improved terms and conditions, a view now given further support by *Commission v Germany*, provided those social conditions are 'not

---

[43] Recital 33. See also the Commission's Interpretative Communication, above n 38, 17.
[44] SEC(2010) 1258 final, 34 and 51. Requirements under the Transfer of Undertakings Directive 2001/23 could be incorporated here.

directly or indirectly discriminatory and are indicated in the contract notice or in the contract documents'.[45]

So what then does the Grand Chamber say in *Commission v Germany?*

C. The implications of *Commission v Germany* (*occupational pensions*) for social clauses

1. Public Procurement

a. *Position under the Directive*

In *Commission v Germany* a number of local authorities entered into a collective agreement with the trade unions concerning the conversion of earnings into pension savings. The collective agreement identified a limited list of pension providers entrusted with implementing the salary conversion measure. Given the existence of this collective agreement, the local authorities did not issue a call for tenders, as required by Directive 2004/18, with the result that other pension providers were denied the chance to offer their services.

The case therefore pitted the fundamental social right to engage in collective bargaining against the fundamental economic freedoms, freedom of establishment and free movement of services, as enshrined in the Public Procurement Directive. The Court noted the need for balance between the competing interests[46] but found that this balance had not been struck on the facts because the effect of the collective agreement was 'to disapply the public procurement rules completely, and for an indefinite period, in the field of local authority employees' pension saving'.[47] It rejected the German government's argument that the public procurement directives should not be applied because: (1) they did not provide room for worker participation; and (2) the collective agreement was a manifestation of the principle of solidarity (with good risks offsetting the bad). However, it did say at paragraph 56 that the 'application of the procurement procedures [do not] preclude the call for tenders from imposing upon interested tenderers conditions reflecting the interests of the workers concerned'. It also said that the directives do not prevent 'a local authority employer from specifying, in the terms of the call for tenders, the conditions to be complied with by tenderers in order to prevent, or place limits on, workers interested in salary conversion being selected on the basis of medical grounds'.[48] It added that the preservation of 'elements of solidarity is not inherently irreconcilable with the application of a procurement procedure'.[49]

From a single market perspective the outcome of this case is not surprising: earlier case law had already rejected attempts to ring-fence sensitive matters from

---

[45] First sentence of Recital 33.
[46] Paras 44 and 52.
[47] Para 53.
[48] Para 58.
[49] Ibid.

the scope of the procurement directives.[50] However, from a practical perspective the implications of subjecting pensions arrangements negotiated collectively to the full rigours of the public procurement directives[51] are serious and have caused consternation in some states, particularly in Scandinavia. The procurement rules are bureaucratic and burdensome for local authorities without necessarily resulting in actually attracting tenders from other Member States. This is particularly so in respect of pension provision in Germany, a highly specialized and localized field.[52]

A more positive note, from the perspective of labour law, is the fact that in paragraph 56 of *Commission v Germany* the Court appears to countenance significantly more space for social matters in the tendering process. Further, unlike its previous decisions on social clauses in procurement, the Court is not prescriptive at which stage the social factors can be included (albeit, unlike its earlier case law on social clauses, the complaint concerned a total failure to tender, rather than a criticism of the terms included in the tender document or controls on the actual performance of the contract). In this way, the Court gives some backbone to Article 27 of Directive 2004/18 (considered in section B.2 above) and possibly paves the way for the inclusion of improved labour standards as a requirement in the contract documentation.

b. Position under the Treaties

Commission v Germany will also be relevant for tenders which fall below the thresholds of the Directive. It will be recalled that even these tenders must still respect the Treaty requirements of equal treatment, advertising and proportionality. If it is argued that a requirement by tenderers to take social factors into account interferes with, say, the freedom of establishment, following the traditional 'market access'/restrictions approach,[53] the contracting authority could justify the requirement on the basis of worker protection, provided the steps taken are proportionate.[54] The problem with the market access approach is that it inevitably prioritizes the economic freedom over the social interest[55] because once a rule is found to be a restriction it is presumptively unlawful unless justified and proportionate. This appears the antithesis of balancing, a balance now mandated by Article 3(3) of the Treaty on European Union.[56] There are some signs in

---

[50] Eg Case C–160/08 *Commission v Germany (ambulance)* [2010] ECR I–000, paras 125–131. More recently, see Case C–45/09 *Rosenbladt* [2010] ECR I–000, para 52 (collective agreements not exempt from review under the equality legislation).

[51] These are Annex IIA services to which the full procedure applies, not Annex IIB.

[52] Cf Case C–507/03 *Commission v Ireland (An Post)* [2007] ECR I–9777, para 34 where, in a case that involved a tender which was not subject to the full rules of the Directive, the Court found that the contract lacked cross-border interest and so EU law did not apply. See further COM (2011) 15.

[53] Case C–55/94 *Gebhard* [1995] ECR I–4165. See also C Barnard, 'Restricting Restrictions: Lessons for the EU from the US?' (2009) 58 Cambridge Law Journal 575.

[54] See also, by analogy, Case C–438/05 *Viking* [2007] ECR I–10779.

[55] See AG Trstenjak in *Commission v Germany*, para 185.

[56] Art 3(3) Treaty on European Union identifies, as one of the objectives of the Union, 'a highly competitive social market economy'. For a discussion of this term, see C Joerges and F Rödl, '"Social Market Economy" as Europe's Social Model?' EUI Working Paper Law No 2004/8. According to

Commission v Germany that the Court wished to engage in a more genuine attempt at balancing when it said:

Exercise of the fundamental right to bargain collectively must therefore be reconciled with the requirements stemming from the freedoms protected by the FEU Treaty, which in the present instance Directives 92/50 and 2004/18 are intended to implement, and be in accordance with the principle of proportionality . . .[57]

The Court said that reconciling the competing interests entails verification as to whether, when establishing the content of the collective agreement, 'a fair balance was struck in the account taken of the respective interests involved, namely enhancement of the level of the retirement pensions of the workers concerned, on the one hand, and attainment of freedom of establishment and of the freedom to provide services, and opening up to competition at EU level, on the other'.[58] It concluded, as we saw above, that a balance on the facts of this case had not been struck (because no procurement process had been undertaken at all) but then outlined a way for a better balance (opening up the tendering process but providing more space for contracting authorities to specify social conditions).[59]

What is striking about the case is that the reference to balance is not diluted by any express mention of the market access approach nor by the presumption underpinning *Laval* that requiring respect for social standards is unlawful unless justified. Although *Commission v Germany* concerned an interpretation of the public procurement directive and not the Treaties, the Treaty context is evident.[60] It seems that in *Commission v Germany* the Court may be moving towards accepting that the economic and social interests are of equal weight and need to be reconciled through the principle of proportionality.[61]

Returning to the subject of this chapter, the result of *Commission v Germany* suggests that, in respect of procurement which falls outside the Directive, the host state can now, with confidence, insist on applying its labour standards to out-of-state tenderers, except services providers under Article 56 TFEU (see section D below). However, what remains unclear is whether the application of the proportionality principle might result in the application of only minimum, not improved, labour standards.

Working Group XI on Social Europe (CONV 516/1/03 REV 1), para 17, the objectives of the Union should refer to the concept of the 'social market economy' in order to underline the link between the economic and social development and efforts made to ensure greater coherence between economic and social policies. See further the monti Report 'A new strategy for the simple market', 9 May 2010, 68.

[57] Para 44.

[58] Para 52.

[59] See by analogy Case C–160/08 *Commission v Germany (ambulance)* [2010] ECR I–000, paras 125–31, where the Court refused to exempt services of general economic interest (the provision of ambulance services) from the obligations under the public procurement directives.

[60] Eg para 47. See also the Advocate General's opinion, especially paras 183–4. This is discussed further by P Syrpis, Case note (2011) 40 Industrial Law Journal forthcoming.

[61] In this respect the Court's approach appears to show some signs of convergence with the EU's post-2000 Social Agenda: rather than viewing social policies as a burden on the economy, they are in fact one of the keys to its success: COM(2000) 379 and COM(2001) 313, 17.

D. Public procurement, the Posted Workers Directive, and labour standards

So far, we have concentrated on the public procurement regime to see what scope it provides for mandating both minimum and improved labour standards. It has been argued that, particularly following *Commission v Germany*, it may be possible for contracting authorities to require more of contractors by way of specified terms and conditions of employment. However, in *Laval* and, more importantly for our purposes, *Rüffert*, the space for contracting authorities to impose even minimum labour standards on a successful tenderer from another Member State has been reduced when the work is being performed by posted workers. This is because under Article 3(1) PWD, as interpreted in *Laval*,[62] only those host state rules listed in Article 3(1) (for example, rules on working time, health and safety, equality and minimum rates of pay, but not other key aspects of labour law such as protection against unfair dismissal and redundancy) can be applied by the host state to posted workers. All other matters are governed by the law of the home state. So Latvian posted workers working on a contract in the UK will enjoy the benefit of UK rules in respect of the matters listed in Article 3(1) PWD but Latvian law in respect of all other matters. The potential 'get out' clauses for host states (the so-called minimum standards clause in Article 3(7) and the Article 3(10) public policy provision) have effectively been neutered by the Court in *Laval*, *Rüffert*, and *Luxembourg*, thereby curtailing the possibility for host states (the UK) to require contractors to respect its terms and conditions in areas outside those listed in Article 3(1).[63] And even if it wants contractors to respect its legislation in areas listed in Article 3(1), the host state must comply to the letter with the detailed provisions in both Article 3(1) and Article 3(8) (which specifies the circumstances when terms laid down in a collective agreement should apply to a posted worker) before its rules can be applied to contractors. The PWD therefore seems to apply – and possibly take precedence over – matters covered by the Public Procurement Directives. This can be seen in *Rüffert*.

The case concerned the Law of Lower Saxony on the award of public contracts, introduced to counteract 'distortions of competition which arise in the field of construction'. This law provided that public (but not private) contracting authorities could award contracts for building works but only to undertakings and subcontractors which paid the wage laid down in the collective agreements at the place where the service was provided. Following a public invitation to tender, Lower Saxony awarded Objekt und Bauregie (O&B) a contract for the structural work in the building of a prison. The contract contained a declaration regarding compliance with certain collective agreements and, more specifically, with the collective agreement regarding payment to employees employed on the building site of at least the minimum wage in force at the place where those services were to

---

[62] *Laval*, above n 3, para 70.
[63] For further detail, see C Barnard, 'The UK and Posted Workers: The effect of *Commission v Luxembourg*' (2009) 38 Industrial Law Journal 122.

be performed. However, when it was discovered that O&B's Polish sub-contractor employed workers on the site at a wage well below that provided for in the collective agreement the *Land* terminated the contract with O&B.

By requiring respect for the German collective agreement by both domestic and foreign tenderer, Lower Saxony was complying with the key principle of equal treatment, expressly articulated in Article 2 of Directive 2004/18. This point was noted by the Advocate General,[64] who added that while the aim of public procurement was to meet an identified administrative need for works, services, or supplies, 'the award of public contracts also authorises the attainment of other public interest requirements, such as environmental policy or, as in the present case, social objectives'.

However, the Court adopted a different approach. It found that the German law contravened the PWD because the German authorities had failed to comply with the detailed provisions of Article 3(8). In particular, they had failed to declare the collectively agreed pay in the building industry to be universally applicable[65] with the result that the collectively agreed rules on pay rates could not be applied to the posted workers.[66] The Court added that by requiring undertakings performing public works contracts and, indirectly, their subcontractors to apply the minimum wage laid down by the collective agreement, the German law could impose on undertakings established in another Member State where minimum rates of pay are lower 'an additional economic burden' that is 'capable of constituting a restriction within the meaning of Article [56 TFEU]'.[67] In other words, the application of social provisions constituted a restriction on market access and was presumptively unlawful. Even more striking in this regard was the Court's reference to the procurement context but its failure to mention the public procurement directives.

The divergence between the Court and its Advocate General highlights the fundamental problem at the core of the decision: should the *Land* insist on an equal treatment approach (as the Advocate General would suggest) or a single market perspective (as the Court would suggest). The effect of the Advocate General's approach would be to allow contracting authorities to impose on contractors all labour standards justified in the name of equal treatment. The effect of the Court's approach is that the imposition of the host state's labour standards on the staff of temporary service providers – with the exception of those areas listed in Article 3(1) PWD – is an impediment to market access. The Court's stance therefore significantly restricts the extent to which even minimum terms and conditions can be imposed on posted workers through any procurement regime.

Yet, in reaching this conclusion the Court created its own (reverse) discrimination: domestic service providers and established service providers exercising their rights under Article 49 will be subject to all the employment conditions of the procuring state (for example, the UK), to the extent this is compatible with the

---

[64] Para 131.
[65] Ibid, para 26.
[66] Ibid, para 31.
[67] Ibid, para 37.

public procurement regime. By contrast, out-of-state (for example, Latvian) service providers will not be subject to host state (UK) laws except in the areas listed in Article 3(1) PWD. Could the domestic/established service providers claim that they have been subject to unequal treatment contrary to Article 2 of Directive 2004/18? If they can, does this mean that the domestic/established service providers can demand a 'levelling down' (at least from a labour law perspective) of requirements,[68] resulting in their being subject to UK laws only in those areas listed in Article 3(1)? If this argument were accepted, it would have three unexpected consequences.

First, it would mean that the effect of applying EU law would be to reduce the level of terms and conditions for the employees of domestic/established service providers, contrary to Article 151(1) TFEU which identifies 'improved living and working conditions' as one of the objectives of the Union. Second, in areas outside those listed in Article 3(1) PWD the employees of domestic/established service providers no longer enjoy the protection of national laws, contrary to Article 8(2) of the Rome I Regulation. Third, the Latvian service provider would now itself be subject to discrimination: its employees will be subject to two sets of rules (UK law in respect of matters listed in Article 3(1) PWD and Latvian law in respect of all other employment-related issues), whereas domestic/established service providers would have to respect one set of rules only (the UK's) and a reduced set of rules at that. This could be resolved only by applying Latvian law to the employees of domestic/established service providers. This would mean the extra-territorial application of Latvian labour law not just to Latvian workers (which is envisaged by Article 8(2) of the Rome I Regulation when they carry their home state laws to the place where they are temporarily working) but to UK workers (which is not).

The only apparent way out of this conundrum is to say that, in respect of working conditions at least, the situation of domestic/established service providers is not comparable with that of (Latvian) service providers and so the principle of equal treatment in Article 2 of the General Directive is not engaged. Nevertheless, the practical effect of this is that the Treaty provisions on free movement of services trump those of the principle of equal treatment found in the Directive.

E. Procurement outside the scope of the General Directive

1. Non-public authorities

As we have already seen, where a *public* sector contract falls outside the scope of the public procurement directives, the contracting authorities are still subject to the principles of the Treaties. Do these Treaty principles also apply to private sector

---

[68] A 'levelling up' (ie, service providers being treated in the same way as domestic providers) would not be permissible because, according to well-established case law, by making the provision of services in a state's territory subject to compliance with all the conditions required for freedom of establishment would undermine the Treaty provision on services: Case 33/74 *Van Binsbergen* [1974] ECR 1299, para 11; and Case 205/84 *Commission v Germany (the insurance cases)* [1986] ECR 3755, para 26.

companies when engaged in a tendering process? Much turns on the question of the horizontal direct effect of the Treaty provisions. It is far from clear that Articles 49 and 56 TFEU have full horizontal direct effect.[69] If they do not, then private contracting authorities will not need to respect EU law when putting work out to tender. If they do have to comply with the Treaties, then their position will be the same as for public bodies: subject to *Commission v Germany*, any requirement to respect certain labour standards would amount to a restriction on free movement but could be justified on the grounds of worker protection and, at least in the area of minimum standards, the requirement is likely to be proportionate. In respect of improved standards, private contracting authorities might also argue that a requirement to respect host state labour standards reflects a commitment to corporate social responsibility (CSR),[70] a policy that the EU has also recognized.[71]

2. Voluntary compliance

So far we have focused on using public procurement to secure mandatory compliance with improved terms and conditions. However, the British Office of Government Commerce notes that: 'There may be opportunities post-award for contracting authorities to work outside the formal procurement process, *on a voluntary basis*, to promote the importance of social issues such as equality and adult skills to their suppliers and supply chain. This can be an effective means of influencing suppliers' culture, and helping to ensure that it fits with the contracting authority's own set of values and needs' (emphasis added). It then gives as an example the London Living Wage:

---

[69] Case 36/74 *Walrave and Koch* [1974] ECR 1405 suggested that there might be horizontal direct effect: 'the rule on non-discrimination applies in judging all legal relationships in so far as these relationships, by reason either of the place they are entered into or the place where they take effect, can be located within the territory of the Community'. Subsequent cases have concerned action taken by public authorities (Case 41/74 *Van Duyn* [1975] ECR 1337) or professional regulatory bodies, such as the Bar Council (Case 71/76 *Thieffry* [1977] ECR 765), and the Italian football association (Case 13/76 *Dona v Mantero* [1976] ECR 1333). Cf Case C–281/98 *Angonese v Cassa di Risparmio di Bolzano* [2000] ECR I–4139, paras 35–36 where the Court said that since Art 45 TFEU was designed to ensure that there was no discrimination on the labour market it applied to private persons as well as public authorities. However, in respect of Arts 49 and 56 TFEU, the Court has merely said that they applied to trade unions when acting in a collective capacity. Case C–438/05 *Viking* [2007] ECR I–10779; and Case C–341/05 *Laval* [2007] ECR I–11767.

[70] CSR is 'a concept whereby companies integrate social and environmental concerns in their business operations and in their interactions with stakeholders on a voluntary basis': Commission Communication, 'Implementing the Partnership for Growth and Jobs: Making Europe a Pole of Excellence on Corporate Social Responsibility' COM(2006) 136, 2.

[71] Presidency Conclusions Lisbon European Council, Presidency Conclusions, 23–24 March 2000, para 39. According to the Commission's Green Paper on CSR (COM(2001) 366, para 43): 'Corporate social responsibility is also about the integration of companies in their local setting, whether this be in Europe or world-wide. Companies contribute to their communities, especially to local communities, by providing jobs, wages and benefits, and tax revenues. On the other hand companies depend on the health, stability, and prosperity of the communities in which they operate. For example, they recruit the majority of their employees from the local labour markets, and therefore have a direct interest in the local availability of the skills they need . . . The reputation of a company at its location, its image as an employer and producer, but also as an actor in the local scene, certainly influences its competitiveness.'

Authority K worked with suppliers on a voluntary basis, to bring workers on the authority's existing contracts where appropriate, into line with the London Living Wage. Many of the industries where workers are paid below the Living Wage level employ significant numbers of women and BAME groups.

The London Living Wage (currently £7.85) is set at more than £2.00 above the national minimum wage to reflect the higher cost of living in London. It has assumed a new importance given the commitment made in September 2010 by Ed Miliband, the newly elected Labour party leader, that the living wage should be the foundation of the economy.[72] The following day the provost of University College London (UCL) agreed to 'work towards implementing the London living wage pay rates in contracts with outsourced suppliers as they fall due for review in the next couple of years, in common with some other higher education institutions in London'.[73] In 2008 Boris Johnson, the Mayor of London, committed the Greater London Authority (GLA) to paying it. Around 100 other companies, including Barclays, HSBC, KPMG, Clifford Chance, and Standard Chartered have also adopted the London Living Wage.[74]

Rhetorical commitment is one thing, application in practice is another,[75] as the controversy surrounding the contracts for the London 2012 Olympics has shown. The London Mayor and Lord Coe, Chairman of London 2012, signed an 'Ethical contract' in 2005 with London citizens before winning the Olympics.[76] This promised a living wage for everyone involved. However, it seems this has not been delivered in practice. Lord Coe told the London Assembly that 'any of the issues about a living wage is a consideration, not a condition'.[77] In October 2010 the *London Evening Standard* reported that: 'Almost one in five Olympic site workers says he or she is being paid less than the Mayor's suggested £7.60-an-hour London living wage, official statistics show.'[78]

F. Conclusions

Using public procurement to achieve social goals is increasingly seen as an alternative way of trying to impose improved labour standards on employers who might

---

[72] <http://www.bbc.co.uk/news/uk-politics-11426411>.

[73] D Cohen, 'University to pay cleaners living wage . . . thanks to the Standard', *Evening Standard*, 29 September 2010, 18–19. See generally, 'Becoming a Living Wage Borough: A Guide for Local Authorities', 2010.

[74] Ibid, <http://www.thisislondon.co.uk/standard/article-23883079-university-to-pay-cleaners-living-wage-thanks-to-the-standard.do>.

[75] See, eg, <http://www.glalibdems.org.uk/news/000443/olympic_games_must_secure_a_living_wage_for_all_londoners__doocey.html>. See also <http://www.guardian.co.uk/uk/davehillblog/2010/mar/25/boris-johns0n-london-citizens-living-wage-campaign>.

[76] <http://www.london2012.com/press/media-releases/post-bid-2005/london-2012-and-london-citizens-sign-agreement.php> (last accessed 25 October 2010).

[77] <http://www.spectacle.co.uk/spectacleblog/tag/living-wage/> (last accessed 4 February 2010).

[78] M Beard, 'London Recruits Paid Less than London Living Wage',<http://www.thisislondon.co.uk/standard/article-23888727-olympic-recruits-paid-less-than-london-living-wage.do> (last accessed 20 October 2010).

not otherwise be willing to apply them. As the Olympics example shows, social clauses in contracts are probably more effective than relying on voluntary standards however much this may chime with the CSR agenda. And herein lies a paradox. Traditionally, higher standards of employment conditions are expected of public bodies in their capacity as role models (the 'good employer' model) with the private sector (reluctantly) following in their wake. Yet, the Commission and Council's approach to the public procurement regime is generally to constrain public authorities from using their money and influence to shape employment relations[79] while at the same time encouraging private sector employers to do just that through CSR.

[79] Implicit criticism of the 'good employer' model can also be found in the Court's rejection in *Rüffert* of the distinction drawn by the Lower Saxony law between public and private contracts.

17

Labor Activism in Local Politics:
From CBAs to 'CBAs'

*Katherine Stone and Scott Cummings**

A. Introduction

In the past, when labor unions were a respected aspect of American life and when labor law was a thriving academic field, there was no question about what a 'CBA' was. A 'CBA' was a collective bargaining agreement, a contract negotiated by a union and an employer that set terms and conditions of work for a given workplace for a given period of time. Labor law scholars had heated debates about whether a 'CBA' was an ordinary contract or whether it was a code of governance, whether it created vested rights for individual workers or whether unions could vary its terms to the detriment of individuals, whether a 'CBA' imposed duties on unions as well as on employers, and who could enforce it and against whom.[1] But at the most literal level, the basic concept was clear.

In contemporary labor parlance, however, 'CBA' may not refer to a collective bargaining agreement at all, but to another type of contract: a community benefits agreement. These new 'CBAs' are agreements negotiated by labor and community groups to leverage benefits – including labor-related provisions such as living wage, local hiring, and card check neutrality requirements – from developers, typically in connection with publicly subsidized projects.[2] And CBAs are only one of the tools that labor and community groups have developed to secure worker protections that operate outside the framework of federal labor law.[3] Other local legislation designed

---

* Katherine Stone is Arjay and Frances Miller Professor of Law, UCLA School of Law; Scott Cummings is Professor of Law, UCLA School of Law.

[1] See Katherine VW Stone, 'The Steelworkers' Trilogy: The Evolution of Labor Arbitration' in LJ Cooper and CL Fisk (eds), *Labor Law Stories* (Foundation Press, 2005) 149, 150–6 (summarizing debates over essential nature of collective bargaining agreement).

[2] See SL Cummings, 'Mobilization Lawyering: Community Economic Development in the Figueroa Corridor' in A Sarat and S Scheingold (eds), *Cause Lawyers and Social Movements* (Stanford Law and Politics, 2006) 302; see also J Gross with G LeRoy and M Janis-Aparicio, *Community Benefit Agreements: Making Development Projects Accountable* (Good Jobs First, 2005); and RC Schragger, 'Mobile Capital, Local Economic Regulation, and the Democratic City' (2009) 123 Harv L Rev 483, 509.

[3] See SL Cummings and SA Boutcher, 'Mobilizing Local Government Law for Low-Wage Workers' (2009) Univ of Chicago Legal Forum 187.

to enhance labor protections for private sector employees, such as living wage and big-box retail ordinances, have proliferated in the past decade.

The new 'CBAs' and other local initiatives have emerged in the vacuum where labor law has failed. Labor unions in the United States have suffered a drastic decline in their numbers over the past two decades, particularly in the private sector, contributing to a decay in their political clout at the national level. The standard diagnosis for this decline is that federal labor law, codified in the National Labor Relations Act, has failed to protect the rights of workers by excluding from coverage categories of workers who play important roles in the contemporary workplace,[4] erecting a structure to govern union elections that tilts decisively in favor of employers,[5] and limiting the ability of unions to play an effective role in protecting jobs.[6] In response, unions have looked outside the NLRA framework to advance organizing goals,[7] yet many of these efforts are still primarily directed to achieving old-style 'CBAs' – collective bargaining agreements.

Alongside campaigns to advance traditional unionism, labor groups have also promoted a distinct set of local initiatives – the new 'CBAs' and, beyond them, a range of other labor-related measures – that seek to influence labor conditions outside of the traditional collective bargaining framework.[8] Unions and their community allies in some cities have had success in securing benefits traditionally achieved through collective bargaining. What is striking is that all of these achievements have been built on a new legal foundation: local government law. Labor–community alliances have leveraged different facets of local government power – contracting power, land use power, and general regulatory power – to wages create programs and policies that serve multiple labor-related ends such as imposing minimum wages, creating training programs and pathways to higher-paying jobs, and facilitating worker collective action.

This chapter describes some of the ways in which these alliances have exercised power at the local level. After situating labor's turn to the local in the broader economic and political context, we focus on Los Angeles as a case study of the robust use of local governmental levers to further labor objectives. We then turn to the question of whether, and to what extent, local labor initiatives can provide an adequate substitute for, or enhancement of, labor power at the national level. In addressing this question, we discuss the legal challenges facing local labor activism, including the enforceability of private agreements and the preemption of local laws by national law. We also examine practical challenges that stem from the dependence of local strategies on jobs in industries that are not likely to relocate. We conclude by exploring the question of whether labor-community alliances are an embryonic form of a new type of unionism.

---

[4] See KVW Stone, *From Widgets to Digits: Employment Regulation for the Changing Workplace* (Cambridge University Press, 2004).

[5] BI Sachs, 'Employment Law as Labor Law' (2008) 29 Cardozo L Rev 2685, 2694–95.

[6] KVW Stone, 'Labor and the Corporate Structure' (1988) 55 Chicago L Rev 73.

[7] BI Sachs, 'Labor Law Renewal' (2007) 1 Harv L & Pol'y Rev 375, 376–77.

[8] Cummings and Boutcher, above note 3, 189.

B. The local as an alternative site of labor activism

Two factors have generated a profound change in the power of unions in the past two decades: the globalization of economic life and the flexibilization of work. With increased global trade, firms can resist union demands and even avoid unions altogether by threatening, and sometimes actually shifting, production to low-wage areas of the world. Routine manufacturing jobs and many types of service work that used to be performed in the United States by unionized workers are now performed in Asia, South America, and Eastern Europe.[9] Even the threat of globalization diminishes labor's bargaining power. Companies with a realistic option to move overseas are able to resist union demands and force concessions. As a result, unions in mobile firms have become reluctant to make demands out of fear of triggering business flight, thereby reinforcing a perception that they are ineffective.

Jobs in the large-scale manufacturing industries that comprised the core of the unionized sectors in the United States for much of the 20th century have been the ones most vulnerable to transnational capital flight. The automobile industry, steel industry, electrical goods industry, and other heavy manufacture firms now pro-duce large portions of their inventory in facilities all over the world.[10] Their departure from the United States has left a large hole in the US labor market in a space that unions used to occupy. Since the 1980s, job losses to plant closings have cost unions massive membership losses.[11]

The other trend that has undermined unions has been the changing nature of work. Firms have moved away from utilizing long-term employment relationships within well-regulated internal labor markets, and instead have adopted flexible forms of employment. These new forms of employment include the increased use of temporary workers, independent contractors, and project workers – workers who have no assurance of long-term employment.[12] The flexibilization of employment has also meant a change in the employment relationships of 'regular' employees, who no longer enjoy tacit or explicit job security and no longer have reliable pay trajectories, paths for promotion, or fixed job definitions. Firms now move workers between departments and job tasks, making numerous adjustments to job defini-tions on an on-going basis. They utilize flexible compensation systems in which a large portion of pay is based on performance measures rather than set rates.[13]

---

[9] Eg a new study by the Economic Policy Institute found that all 50 states in the United States have lost a considerable number of jobs to China since 2000.

[10] See, eg, B Bluestone and B Harrison, *The De-Industrialization of America: Plant Closings, Community Abandonment, and the Dismantling of Basic Industry* (Basic Books, 1984).

[11] See, eg, K Bronbrenner and T Juravich, 'The Evolution of Stategic and Coordinated Bargaining Campaigns in the 1990s: The Steelworkers' Experience' in L Turner, H Katz, and R Hurd (eds), *Rekindling the Movement: Labor's Quest for Relevance in the 21st Century* (Cornell-ILR Press, 2001) 211, 214–15.

[12] Stone, above n 4.

[13] Ibid.

The new flexible practices are located primarily in the private, manufacturing and non-place-based service sectors. They are also more prevalent in large urban areas than small isolated areas because in big cities employers have more opportunities to churn their labour forces to suit current production and demand conditions, and employees have more competing opportunities and thus have higher quit rates.[14]

The new employment practices are fundamentally antithetical to unionism.[15] Employers today want discretion and flexibility and thus eschew unions with their insistence on regular procedures and rigidly defined practices. Nonunion firms resist unions more adamantly than ever, and firms with unions demand concessions to give them the operational freedom they feel they need. As a result, unions have had a harder time than ever getting in and staying in private-sector, manufacturing, and non-place-based service-sector workplaces. Further, the high turnover that characterizes flexible production is not conducive to unionization because, under current US labor law, workers must take great personal risks to form a union, yet they stand to lose whatever benefits and rights they obtain by doing so once they leave their bargaining unit.

The result of these trends has been precipitous union decline. Unions now represent less than 7 per cent of the US private-sector workforce. And with membership decline has come a decline in union resources to organize or service existing members effectively. Also, having fewer members translates into diminished political clout at the national level. One indication of organized labor's political weakness is that, despite having spent millions of dollars to elect a Democratic President and Congress in 2008, they were not able to get their sole legislative priority on the national agenda: the Employee Free Choice Act, a statute that would have made it easier for labor to organize and achieve first contracts.

In the face of the challenges to traditional unionism, labor leaders have turned away from the traditional paradigm of federally supervised union organizing and toward an alternative model emphasizing local coalition building and policy reform designed to increase union density in targeted industries. This turn to localism responds to three central features of the contemporary field of labor activism. First, it targets non-exportable industries tied to local economies – industries that either offer inherently immobile services, have fiscal ties to local governments, or gain economic benefits through association with larger regional economies.[16] Second, it has sought to take strategic advantage of the spatial configuration of political power, de-emphasizing advocacy at the federal level and instead building political alliances with progressive big-city politicians who possess the political will to advance

---

[14] M Storper and AJ Scott, 'Work Organization and Local Labour Markets in an Era of Flexible Production' (1990) 129 Int'l Labour Rev 573, 581–82.

[15] KVW Stone, *From Widgets to Digits*, above n 4, 198–216; C Heckscher, 'Living With Flexibility' in Turner et al (eds), *Rekindling the Movement*, above n 11, 59, 64–5. See also TA Kochan, HC Katz, and RB McKersie, *The Transformation of American Industrial Relations* (Basic Books, 1986) 93–108 (nonunion firms have been increasingly moving to flexible employment practices rather than rigid hierarchical job structures since the 1960s).

[16] See KVW Stone, 'Flexibilization, Globalization, and Privatization: Three Challenges to Labour Rights in Our Time', (2006) 44 Osgoode Hall LJ 77, 96–103.

regulation on behalf of workers. Finally, labor's local strategy has provided it with important new legal levers for advancing labor rights.

C. Local labor initiatives: the Los Angeles experience

Los Angeles has been at the center of the development of this local approach. It is the site of a dynamic labor movement, propelled forward over the past decade by the dominance of Change to Win unions whose historical focus on organizing by occupation has made them well-positioned to respond to the challenges of deindustrialization.[17] The work of these unions has been supported and extended by an innovative coalition of community groups. In addition, Los Angeles is home to the largest concentration of immigrant workers in the United States, who have proven strong supporters of unionism in low-wage sectors.[18] These factors have coalesced to make Los Angeles 'a center of labor movement resurgence'[19]

1. Labor–community activism and the turn to sticky industries

Labor resurgence in LA had its roots in the creation of innovative groups that reached across the traditional labor–community divide to promote new alliances and implement alternative forms of worker collective action. A catalyst was a campaign by a coalition of activists, trade unionists, and progressive University of California, Los Angeles (UCLA) academics to stop General Motors from closing its auto plant in Van Nuys in the early 1980s. This coalition, which formed the basis for what became the Labor/Community Strategy Center, organized demonstrations and provided research support for efforts by local unions and community activists to keep the plant open.[20] Although their efforts were successful for a few years, the plant cut back production throughout the 1980s and eventually closed altogether in 1991.[21]

Another precursor of LA's labor–community movement occurred in the early 1990s when the city proposed to raise fares and cut service to finance light rail lines. The Labor/Community Strategy Center formed an alliance with the Korean Immigrant Workers Advocates and the Southern Christian Leadership Conference to resist the fare increases and pressure the city to expand affordable bus service to the city's transit-dependent population. The alliance, known as the Bus Riders' Union (BRU), brought a civil rights lawsuit in 1994 alleging that the city was creating a 'two-tier' mass transit system – a new, efficient light rail system for the more affluent, and 'a dilapidated, overcrowded bus system for 400,000

---

[17] R Milkman, *LA Story: Immigrant Workers and the Future of the US Labor Movement* (Russell Sage Foundation Press, 2006) 4–5, 23.

[18] Ibid 9.

[19] Ibid 6.

[20] See E Mann, 'Radical Social Movements and the Responsibility of Progressive Intellectuals' (1999) 32 Loy LA L Rev 761.

[21] Ibid.

UNIVERSITY OF WINCHESTER
LIBRARY

overwhelmingly Latino, Black, and Asian/Pacific Islander bus riders.'[22] After the California state court temporarily enjoined the city from raising fares and eliminating discounted monthly passes, the city and the BRU entered into a consent decree, in which the city agreed to upgrade the quality of service, end overcrowding, and limit fare increases on lines that served the transit-dependent populations.

The decree withstood subsequent legal challenge, marking the first major victory of the embryonic labor–community alliance in Los Angeles. By addressing the interests of low-income minority communities in obtaining access to jobs, the BRU bridged the divide between classic community organizing and labor issues – thus providing the platform on which subsequent Los Angeles activists built.[23]

The fate of the plant closing campaign of the Labor/Community Strategy Center's convinced some community-labor activists that to succeed they needed to target 'sticky' industries – like tourism – that were not likely to leave the city.[24] Labor leaders from the Hotel Employees and Restaurant Union (HERE) Local 11 formed the Tourism Industry Development Council (TIDC) to assist low-wage workers and to promote accountability for firms in the tourism industry that received subsidies from the city.[25] In 1993, the TIDC changed its name to Los Angeles Alliance for the New Economy (LAANE), which emerged as a powerful force in the new sticky industry strategy.

2. Local government levers of labor reform

To advance this strategy, LAANE and other groups have repeatedly leveraged the traditional tools of local government – its contracting, land use, and regulatory powers.

a. Government contracting

i. City contracts and the Worker Retention Ordinance
In the 1990s, many operations at Los Angeles Airport (LAX) were privatized and there was high turnover in city-hired contractors. Each time a new contractor was retained, it fired the previous contractor's work force and hired new workers at lower wages. LAANE and other community groups combined with HERE and Service Employees International Union (SEIU) locals to press for limitations on the ability of LAX contractors to fire workers and cut wages. In 1995, LAANE succeeded in getting the LA City Council to enact a landmark worker retention ordinance. The ordinance required new city service contractors to retain long-term workers for 90 days and to provide continuing employment to those who met performance standards. This victory prevented new airport restaurant

---

[22] See Bus Riders' Union, Consent Decree Compliance Campaign, <http://oldbru.thestrategycenter.org/engli/Campaigns/consentdecree/consentdecreehistory.htm>.

[23] EW Soja, *Seeking Spatial Justice (Globalization and Community)* (University of Minnesota Press, 2010).

[24] Ibid.

[25] H Khalil and S Hinson, 'The Los Angeles Living Wage Campaign' in *Public Subsidies, Public Accountability: Holding Corporations to Labor and Community Standards* (Grassroots Policy Project 1998) 18, 19.

concessionaires like McDonald's from firing long-term workers and paying new workers lower wages.[26] Although the Worker Retention Ordinance initially applied only to contractors at LAX, it was later extended city-wide. A crucial community–labor alliance was thus born, with LAANE taking the lead; over time, other important groups entered the field, including the UCLA Downtown Labor Center, and immigrant worker groups, such as Sweatshop Watch and the National Day Labor Organizing Network (NDLON).

ii. Contracting out services: living wage

Two years after LAANE's successful campaign for the Worker Retention Ordinance, it spearheaded a city-wide living wage campaign that resulted, in 1997, in an ordinance that required private companies providing services to the city or receiving certain levels of city subsidies to pay their workers at wage rates set above the state and federal minimums.[27] In 1998, the LA Living Wage Ordinance was amended to extend coverage to all entities with a lease or license of city property.[28] The Worker Retention Ordinance and the Living Wage Ordinance showed the power of community–labor alliances to enact work policy that indirectly promoted unionism (by protecting public unions from outsourcing), while providing benefits to workers beyond the union fold.[29]

iii. Contracting Out Goods: Sweat-Free Procurement Ordinance

Just after the Living Wage Ordinance was enacted, LA labor reporter Harold Meyerson predicted that it 'was just LAANE's opening salvo.'[30]

Over the past year, [LAANE] has been finding a way to collectively bargain for low-wage workers who aren't in unions, doing more to upgrade low-income jobs than anyone else in town. At the same time, it has embarked upon the conversion of LA's growth coalition (long the exclusive province of business lobbies, building-trades unions and politicians in their sway) into a growth-with-equity coalition ...[31]

In accord with the prediction, LAANE not only led the way in the succeeding decade, but also influenced other groups to achieve other gains for workers.

One example in the garment industry demonstrated how the city's contracting power could be used to promote higher wages among not merely service contractors, but goods contractors as well. In 2004, after a decade-long litigation campaign to stop abuse in LA's garment industry (which was the nation's largest), a coalition of groups that included Sweatshop Watch, the Garment Worker Center (GWC), and the Union of Needle Trades, Industrial and Textile Employees (UNITE), persuaded the city council to enact the Sweat-Free Procurement Ordinance.[32]

---

[26] Ibid 20.
[27] Khalil and Hinson, above n 25, 26.
[28] Cummings and Boutcher, above n 3, 7.
[29] Khalil and Hinson, above n 25, 18.
[30] H Meyerson, 'No Justice, No Growth', *LA Weekly* (July 23, 1998).
[31] Ibid.
[32] Cummings and Boutcher, above n 3, 198.

The ordinance requires all city contractors to sign a 'Contractor Code of Conduct' in which they agree to comply with all applicable employment, labor, and environmental laws, and all 'human and labor rights ... obligations that are imposed by treaty or law on the country in which the equipment, supplies, goods or materials are made or assembled.'[33] For contracts involving the procurement of apparel, contractors are bound to ensure that workers are paid a 'procurement living wage' equal to the federal poverty threshold for a family of three plus an additional 20 per cent, paid as hourly wages or health benefits.[34]

iv. City concessions to private entities: Clean Trucks Program

Community-labor activists have also focused on the city's power to award concessions to private companies as a tool to promote unionization. The campaign to create a Clean Trucks Program at the Port of Los Angeles is particularly notable because it links labor and environmental goals. The Port of Los Angeles is the largest in the nation in terms of the volume of container cargo. It is governed by a public entity, the Los Angeles Harbor Commission (whose members are appointed by the mayor), which hires a terminal operator to oversee port activity. The terminal operator, in turn, enters contracts – called concession agreements – with shipping and trucking companies, under which they pay tariffs for the privilege of accessing the port facilities.[35]

Since the 1980s, the trucking companies that service the port have been gradually converting their employee-drivers into 'independent operators' in order to prevent unionization and avoid labor law obligations. One consequence has been to shift the costs of truck maintenance to workers – whose meager income prevents them from investing in maintenance and upgrade. As a result, the trucking fleet is old and dirty, contributing to high levels of air pollution at the Los Angeles-Long Beach ports complex.[36]

In 2007, LAANE together with over 40 environmental, public health, and labor groups formed the Coalition for Clean and Safe Ports to address both the working conditions of the drivers and the air pollution caused by poorly maintained trucks.[37] In 2008, the coalition convinced the Los Angeles City Council to enact an ordinance authorizing the Harbor Commission to rewrite the port's concession agreements. Under the new agreements, trucking companies seeking to access the ports are required to convert all of their drivers from independent contractors to employees by December 31, 2013, and to retrofit or replace all trucks to meet specific environmental standards.[38] The city council justified the employee provision on the grounds that '[s]erious and long-standing safety problems ... exist as a consequence of unsafe, negligent or reckless driving of trucks on the Port or on

[33] LA Administrative Code § 10.43.3A and B.
[34] Ibid 10.43.3.D.
[35] Cummings and Boutcher, above n 3, 200.
[36] Los Angeles Alliance for a New Economy, 'The Road to Shared Prosperity: The Regional Economic Benefits of the San Pedro Bay Ports' *Clean Trucks Program*' 23 (August 2007), available at <http://www.laane.org/>.
[37] Cummings and Boutcher, above n 3, 201.
[38] Drayage Services Concession Agreement for Access to the Port of Los Angeles 2–4.

public roads and highways accessing the Port.'[39] It also justified the shift on the grounds that having a few employers responsible for the trucks would make it easier to enforce safety and environmental standards.[40]

The Clean Trucks Program attempts to achieve a crucial objective of organized labor – facilitating unionization – while also forging an alliance with environmental groups.[41] The Teamsters' Union, which has been heavily involved in the campaign, stands to benefit from the ordinance because if the trucking companies use employees rather than independent contractors, their workers can be unionized. And by progressively eliminating or upgrading approximately 17,000 diesel trucks, the program would significantly reduce the emission of diesel particulates. The Clean Trucks Program thus represents a seminal alliance of labor and environmental groups.[42]

The Program's implementation has been delayed by legal challenges from the trucking industry. In July 2008, the American Trucking Association (ATA) brought suit challenging the program as preempted by federal law. On an application for a preliminary injunction, the Ninth Circuit Court of Appeals ruled that crucial aspects of the program – including the employee and maintenance provisions – were likely to be preempted by the Federal Aviation Administrative Authorization Act (FAAA), a statute that governs the 'price, route, or service' of motor carriers engaged in interstate commerce.[43] However, after a full trial, the district court reversed course and, in a sweeping victory for the campaign, upheld the program's key terms against preemption, ruling that the port acted appropriately as a market participant in authorizing the employee provision.

b. Land use power

Perhaps the most innovative adaptations of local government law have occurred around city land use authority, which is at the heart of local power. Virtually every business requires some sort of land use permit to operate, which opens the door to community intervention to prevent or delay permitting for objectionable businesses. Community–labour coalitions in Los Angeles, again led by LAANE, have used these openings to pressure developers to be more responsive to worker and low-income community demands, while also pushing for new land use policies that create greater community input in the approval of certain types of projects, namely, big-box retail stores.

i. Redevelopment: community benefits agreements
In the white-hot real estate market of the late 1990s and early 2000s, private development boomed in Los Angeles, gentrifying low-income neighborhoods and often displacing poor residents. The city participated in this process by providing public subsidies and approving land use entitlements. Unions generally supported

---

[39] Los Angeles Ordinance No 179981 (June 26, 2008).
[40] *American Trucking Ass'n v City of Los Angeles*, 559 F 3d 1046, 1050 (9th Cir 2009) (quoting Los Angeles Board Resolution 6522).
[41] Cummings and Boutcher, above n 3, 202.
[42] Ibid 199–293.
[43] 49 USC § 14501(c)(1) (2006).

these projects at the outset because they provided large numbers of unionized construction jobs. Yet, once built, unions were dissatisfied because the developments often leased space to nonunion retail establishments. In addition, community groups began insisting that development subsidies be conditioned on benefits for all segments of the community. Out of this alignment of labor and community interests, the 'accountable development' movement was born whose goal was to ensure the equitable distribution of the benefits of the development boom.[44] Its primary tool was a new type of development contract, the 'community benefits agreement,' in which a developer would agree to provide designated benefits in exchange for community support for the project.

The seed of 'CBAs' was planted in 1998 when a private developer sought approval for an entertainment and retail complex in Hollywood.[45] On learning of the plan, LAANE persuaded the city to require the developer to provide benefits to the community as part of the land use and subsidy approval process. In exchange for approvals, the developer promised the city that it would pay living wages on the construction jobs, engage in local hiring, provide job training, and remain neutral and agree to card check certification if the employees wanted to unionize.

Although the Hollywood community benefits package was a major achievement, it was an agreement between developer and the city redevelopment authority so that only the city had the right to enforce it. LAANE was concerned that once the agency's attention shifted elsewhere, it might not be enforced. Thus LAANE decided to explore the possibility of negotiating agreements directly between developers and community organizations in order to give those organizations enforcement rights.

The first such CBA was negotiated by the Figueroa Corridor Coalition for Economic Justice, led by Strategic Actions for a Just Economy (SAJE), along with groups active in the living wage and antisweatshop movements: LAANE, ACORN, AGENDA, Esperanza Community Housing Corporation, the Coalition for Humane Immigrant Rights of Los Angeles (CHIRLA), HERE Local 11, and SEIU Local 1877.[46] The coalition gained bargaining leverage by threatening to hold up the land use approvals for a project called LA Live, a $1 billion sports and entertainment complex to be built adjacent to the Staples Center. The coalition succeeded in using leverage to negotiate a CBA with the project developer, under which the coalition released its right to oppose the development project (for example, through litigation) and also agreed to provide affirmative support in press statements and public hearings. In exchange, the developer agreed to a substantial community benefits program, including $1 million for a park, $25,000 per year for five years to create a residential parking permit program, a commitment by employers to hire local residents, and an agreement to produce a substantial number of affordable housing units.[47] The developer also promised to 'make all reasonable efforts to maximize the number of living wage jobs' in the project and agreed to a 70 per cent living wage goal for the anticipated 5,500 jobs.[48]

[44] See Cummings, 'Mobilization Lawyering', above n 2.
[45] Ibid 319.
[46] Ibid 317.
[47] Ibid 322.
[48] Ibid.

Two major CBAs were subsequently negotiated in Los Angeles. The first was between community groups and LAX, which provided nearly $500 million environmental retrofitting and job training in connection with the LAX modernization. The second was negotiated around the proposed $2 billion Grand Avenue mega-development project to build 400,000 square feet of retail space, a high-end hotel, housing, and a park near the Disney Hall Music Center in downtown Los Angeles. That CBA included provisions that echo the LA Live terms, including a 20 per cent inclusionary affordable housing provision, $50 million for the development of a public park, local hiring and job training requirements, and an agreement to require all permanent jobs to pay the living wage rate.

ii. Conditional use permits: Superstores Ordinance

Under the conditional use permit (CUP) process, a property owner may obtain permission for a land use not otherwise allowed under zoning law. Traditionally, the CUP process has been used to regulate noxious or incompatible land uses in order to preserve the character of a community. But community-labor groups have succeeded in some cases in extending its reach to address negative economic impacts of some types of development.

LAANE's campaign against Wal-Mart big-box retail stores provides an important illustration of this approach.[49] In 2002, Wal-Mart announced plans to develop Supercenters in the Los Angeles area, including one in the separately incorporated and historically African American city of Inglewood. The plan posed a significant threat to unionized grocery stores because Supercenters combine consumer merchandise with grocery departments under one nonunionized roof. The announcement triggered the largest supermarket strike in Southern California history, which ended in a bitter defeat for the unions. Although the strike failed, the United Food and Commercial Workers union (UFCW) and LAANE waged a simultaneous legislative battle against Wal-Mart's plan. They successfully pressured the Inglewood City Council for an ordinance banning big-box stores – those larger than 155,000 square feet. Soon thereafter, Wal-Mart threatened to sue, so the City Council repealed the ordinance. In response, the UFCW helped elect new city council members opposed to the development.

Wal-Mart countered by establishing a front group called the Citizens Committee to Welcome Wal-Mart to Inglewood, and began to collect signatures for a ballot initiative that would have enabled Wal-Mart to bypass all of the standard approvals in authorizing the development of its Supercenter. LAANE, the UFCW, Clergy and Laity United for Economic Justice (CLUE), ACORN, Inglewood residents, and other community groups embarked on a voter turnout campaign to defeat Wal-Mart's initiative. Ultimately, the Inglewood residents voted down Wal-Mart's initiative.

In the wake of the ballot measure's defeat, LAANE and the UFCW moved to enact policies that would prevent the unrestricted entry of big-box stores into Los Angeles. Because outright big-box bans invited risky and expensive litigation, the

---

[49] See SL Cummings, 'Law in the Labor Movement's Challenge to Wal-Mart: A Case Study of the Inglewood Site Fight' (2007) 95 Cal L Rev 1927, 1955–1978.

coalition took another tack. LAANE advocated for a city-wide ordinance requiring retailers to submit to an 'economic impact analysis,' demonstrating the absence of adverse economic impacts, prior to the issuance of a CUP. The LA Council adopted LAANE's idea and enacted a Superstores Ordinance in 2004. Two years later a similar ordinance was passed in Inglewood.

The superstore ordinances require developers of proposed big-box stores in designated low-income communities to submit a report specifying whether the store would 'have an adverse impact or economic benefit on grocery or retail shopping centers,' 'result in the physical displacement of any businesses,' 'require the demolition of housing,' destroy park space, displace jobs, impact city revenue, and create other 'materially adverse or positive economic impacts or blight.'[50] In order for a CUP to issue, the developer must describe any mitigation measures and the city must conclude that no irremediable adverse impacts exist.

The CUP requirement not only gives city planning authorities a basis for rejecting big-box store applications, it also gives community groups another point of leverage to obtain other community benefits. That is, by promising not to oppose the CUP community groups can exact a return promise from a developer to take remedial steps such as the promise of living wage jobs, local hiring and training, and card check neutrality. Thus far, Wal-Mart has declined to test this process, and has instead moved its Supercenters to the suburban periphery. Some jurisdictions have followed the Los Angeles model and adopted ordinances that provide for economic impact analyses rather than impose bans.

c. Direct regulation

In addition to using its contracting and land use planning powers to affect the labor market, Los Angeles, like other cities, has drawn upon its fundamental police power to directly impose regulations designed to promote labor rights.

Most prominently, in 2008 the Los Angeles City Council passed a new living wage law that mandates that all hotels operating in the vicinity of LAX pay workers at the living wage rate.[51] The ordinance broke new ground as the first living wage law in the country to apply to private employers (as opposed to only those with city contracts). It was the product of another LAANE-led campaign that began in 2006, with the creation of a coalition that included the Los Angeles County Federation of Labor, UNITE-HERE (the then-combined hotel and garment workers' union), and CLUE. Their goal was to expand the existing living wage ordinance to hotel workers along Century Boulevard, the main thoroughfare leading into LAX, which is lined with large hotels catering to travelers.

The coalition argued that the hotels should be required to pay a living wage because the city invested in the airport and the hotels situated near it 'derive significant and unique business benefits from their close proximity to LAX,' and

[50] LA Municipal Code § 12.24(U)(14)(d)(2)(i)–(ix) (2004).
[51] LA Municipal Code §§ 104.101–104.115.

thus should meet city-imposed wage standards.[52] The city council agreed, and in late 2006 enacted an ordinance that required businesses in the airport zone to pay a minimum of $9.39 per hour to workers who received health benefits, and $10.64 to workers who did not. The hotels immediately filed lawsuits in state and federal court, which they ultimately lost. The ordinance is expected to cover up to 3,500 hotel workers.[53]

D. Local labor activism beyond Los Angeles

As the innovative nature of the LAX living wage ordinance underscores, Los Angeles provides a leading example of what can be accomplished when organized labor acts in concert with other community groups around shared objectives.[54] Some other cities have had some similar experiences. The living wage movement has been one of the most successful national movements promoting labor standards. Since 1994, over 140 cities have enacted living wage ordinances that apply to firms that contract with the city.[55] Some of these not only specify wage rates, but also require city contractors to offer their employees health insurance, vacations, sick pay, and job security.[56] In addition, San Francisco enacted an ordinance that requires hotels for which the city is landlord, lender, or loan-guarantor – a large portion of the hotels in San Fransisco's tourism areas – to remain neutral when unions attempt to secure representation rights by collecting a majority of authorization cards.[57]

There have also been community benefit agreements negotiated in nearly 30 cities.[58] These include CBAs in connection with the development of a sports arena in Pittsburgh, a mixed-use housing project in Seattle, the Hunters Point Shipyard Development Project in San Francisco, a new cancer treatment center in New Haven, and the Ballpark Village Project in San Diego.

Another example of an initiative that relies on the local police power to raise standards is the San Francisco Health Care Security Ordinance, passed in 2006, that requires employers to provide health insurance regardless of employment and immigration status. The Health Access Program provides coverage to all uninsured residents with fees paid through a combination of city funding and individual contributions based on an income sliding scale.[59]

---

[52] LA Municipal Code, § 104.101.

[53] See Cummings and Boutcher, above n 3, 221.

[54] See Milkman, above n 17.

[55] H Holzer, 'Living Wages: How Much Do (Can) They Matter?', Brookings Discussion Paper, December 2008.

[56] MJ Wells, 'When Urban Policy Becomes Labor Policy' (2002) 31 Theory and Society 115, 140.

[57] Ibid 131.

[58] See PE Salkin and A Lavine, 'Negotiating for Social Justice and the Promise of Community Benefits Agreements: Case Studies of Current and Development Agreements' (Fall 2007/Winter 2008) 17 J Affordable Housing & Community Dev L 113.

[59] SF Admin Code §§ 14.1(7), 14.3(a). The ordinance was upheld against a challenge by a business trade association on the ground of ERISA preemption. See *Golden Gate Restaurant Association v City and County of San Francisco*, 546 F 3d 639 (9th Cir 2008). The case is on appeal to the Supreme Court.

E. Is local labor activism the new front of labor law?

The emergence of local labor initiatives constitutes an important development in efforts to reconstruct the field of labor law. Their proliferation raises important questions about the scope of local governmental power to promote labor rights and the degree to which local initiatives can constitute an effective and enduring mechanism for workers to protect their interests in the face of declining national union power and the threats posed by globalized labor markets. Another important issue is whether labor–community coalitions will become sustainable and effective advocates for labor rights. Or will they devolve into special interest groups that foster sweetheart deals between developers and a small sector of a community?[60]

1. Legal challenges

There are two types of local labor initiatives that raise distinct legal questions. The first involve the enforceability of community benefits agreements. The second type involve the power of localities to enact local ordinances on issues that might arguably be preempted by by federal law.

a. *Enforcement*

Systematic studies of CBA enforcement do not exist largely because, as of yet, few if any CBA-related developments have been fully completed. This makes it difficult to assess their impact or evaluate any enforcement issues that may arise. However, there are some enforcement issues that may be anticipated. Here, we highlight enforcement issues related to: (1) the potential for parties to come and go, or to change interests; (2) the aspirational nature of some CBA provisions; and (3) the difficulty monitoring and enforcing different types of CBA provisions.

There could be questions as to which parties have standing to enforce CBAs, and which parties' actions may trigger possible breaches. In one recent example, the Yankees baseball team and local government officials signed a CBA in connection with plans for a new stadium that was not signed by any community group at all – raising the question of whether any group had the power to enforce it and whether it was a legally binding contract at all.[61]

There is also a question about what happens when community groups and developers that sign a CBA later cease to exist. Community organizations often have shifting leadership, amorphous membership, and occasionally changing names and missions. Whether the organizations that sign the agreement are the only ones

---

[60] See V Been, 'Community Benefits Agreements: A New Local Government Tool or Another Variation of the Exactions Theme?' (2010) 77 Univ of Chicago L Rev 5 (suggesting that some New York community benefits agreements coopted local community groups).

[61] See J Gross, 'Community Benefits Agreements: Definitions, Values, and Legal Enforceability' (Fall 2007/Winter 2008) 17 J of Affordable Housing and Comm Dev L 35, 42.

that can enforce it, or whether individuals or other groups in the community have standing to enforce them as third-party beneficiaries is an open question that may have to be confronted. On the other side, what happens to hard-won benefits when development stalls, is scaled back, sold to another party, or scuttled? Some coalitions are attempting to negotiate provisions that are recorded in the project's chain of title so that CBA beneficiaries have claims to development assets in a bankruptcy proceeding or against subsequent purchasers.

Enforcement concerns also arise in situations where organizations in the coalition develop a split amongst themselves about priorities in enforcement. If one of the signatory groups withdraws its support for the project, a developer might argue that it is a contract repudiation so that all obligations of the developer would be discharged. In the LA Live CBA, there was language that went even further, suggesting that opposition by certain non-signatories' community groups would relieve the developer of its obligation to provide community benefits. Hence organizations in CBA coalitions will likely need to work together on an on-going way, avoid internal dissension, and police each other if the agreements are to stand.

Another enforcement issue is that many important provisions in the CBAs are merely aspirational. In one example, a provision of the Bronx Terminal Market CBA states that the developer 'commits to working with the Coalition to use every commercially reasonable effort to strongly encourage Employers of the Development to use good faith efforts to employ or cause to be employed Bronx residents and to use Bronx-based [women and minority] contractors.'[62] Similarly, the LA Live CBA has aspirational language stating that the developer 'shall make all reasonable efforts to maximize the number of living wage jobs.' As written, it would seem that failure to comply with these types of aspirational goals might not breach the agreements.

Some of these problems are not unique to CBAs, but are a more general problem of enforcement of multi-party contracts. Courts have often had difficulty determining which terms apply to which parties in a multi-party contract, and whether a default by one party of one term amounts to a cancellation or repudiation of the obligations of all the other parties.[63] One solution for the drafters of CBAs would be to include an alternative dispute resolution mechanism such as arbitration that would establish a forum to decide the issue of shifting group membership and compliance with aspirational norms in a way that would build up, over time, a normative framework that would inform all parties of their rights and obligations.

It may also prove to be the case that some CBA provisions are harder to enforce than others. To the extent that CBA affordable housing provisions require developers to either build a specified portion of units or pay into an affordable housing fund, they may be enforceable because the developers' obligations are clearly

---

[62] Bronx Terminal Market CBA, § VI.B.3.g, available at <http://www.bronxgateway.com/documents/copy_of_community_benefits_agreement/Signed_CBA_2_1_06.pdf>.

[63] See, eg, *Flippo v F & L Land Co*, 241 Va 15, 400 SE 2d 156 (Va,1991) (multiparty contract to purchase real estate); and *Indianapolis-Marion County Public Library v Charlier Clark & Linard*, 929 NE 2d 722 (Ind, 2010) (multiparty construction contracts).

defined. In contrast, jobs provisions may be more difficult to enforce over time, since they continue throughout the project, posing challenges of ongoing monitoring.

b. Preemption

As the litigation over the Clean Trucks Program demonstrates, sometimes courts will not enforce local labor ordinances on the ground that they cover matters already addressed in federal legislation. Preemption is a function of the Supremacy Clause of the US Constitution, which provides that when state law conflicts with federal law, the federal law takes precedence.[64] Preemption is implicated whenever localities engage in private-sector labor regulation, such as by providing organizing rights to private sector workers whose rights to unionize are specified in the National Labor Relations Act.[65] State law is also preempted when it conflicts with other explicit federal statutes, such as the FAA Act, which the ATA argued preempts the Clean Truck Program at the Port of Los Angeles.

There have been numerous preemption challenges to local labor ordinances in the past decade, and the courts have been divided. For example, the DC Circuit upheld a District of Columbia ordinance requiring that contractors retain employees of their predecessors for a period of time.[66] On the other hand, the Seventh Circuit recently invalidated a state law that required hotels in Chicago to give their room attendant employees one day of rest in every seven-day period.[67]

To date, some living wage ordinances and some other labor-related ordinances have escaped preemption because they are designed to further the state's interests as a market actor, rather than its role as a regulator. Thus, for example, in the case of the San Francisco card check and neutrality ordinance, the city argued that, as owner and/or lessor of the hotels in the downtown area, it enacted the ordinance to protect its proprietary interests in avoiding labor unrest, not to make labor market regulation.[68] So far the court has not ruled on this issue. However, as cities enact more extensive labor ordinances, there will be more preemption challenges ahead.

---

[64] There are several different types of preemption in the labor area, of which the most relevant here are *Garmon* and *Machinists* preemption. In *San Diego Building Trades Council v Garmon*, the Supreme Court held that any activity that is actually or arguably protected by Section 7 or actually or arguably prohibited by Section 8 of the National Labor Relations Act is preempted – 359 US 236 (1959). In *Machinists v Wisconsin Employment Relations Commission*, the Court held that states cannot regulate in labor relations matters which Congress intended to leave unregulated and subject to the free play of economic forces – 427 US 132 (1975).

[65] Eg, in a recent case, *Machinists* preemption was used to nullify a California law that prohibited employers who received certain types of state funds from using those funds to deter union organizing – *Chamber of Commerce v Brown*, 128 S Ct 2408 (2008).

[66] *Washington Service Contractors v District of Columbia*, 54 F 3d 811 (1995).

[67] *520 South Michigan Ave v Shannon*, 549 F 3d 1119 (2009).

[68] Wells, above n 56.

2. Practical challenges

a. Measuring impact

The criteria for assessing the impact of local labor initiatives depend on the way in which their goals are understood. Where the initiative's goal is to increase wages, impact is amenable to direct measurement. According to a study of the Los Angeles Living Wage Ordinance, nearly 9,600 workers received pay increases as a result of the ordinance, mostly in jobs at the Los Angeles or Ontario airports.[69] Of these, approximately 7,700 received mandatory raises that averaged $2,600 per year, for a total aggregate pay increase of roughly $20 million.[70] An estimated 1,900 workers also received 'indirect' wage increases (to maintain wage differentials at their firms) that averaged $1,300, for a total aggregate increase of nearly $2.5 million.[71] The study found that covered employers did not significantly cut jobs in response to the higher wage requirement, estimating that only 112 jobs were lost as a result of the ordinance.[72] There is, more broadly, a large literature on the impact of living wage laws on overall city income distribution and welfare, but the results are ambiguous and the experts are divided.[73] Some contend that living wage ordinances raise wages for some, but also diminish job opportunities. Others have found an overall positive impact on the wages of those in the lower half of the income distribution without significant negative impact on employment or municipal budgets.[74]

Another way to measure impact is to look at the consequences of a local initiative on unionization. For example, LAANE contends that one result of the LAX Enhancement Zone Ordinance was that four of the area's 13 hotels have been unionized, thereby raising the wages of approximately 1,000 workers by over $12 million through 2012.[75] The Superstores Ordinance prevented Wal-Mart from opening a Supercenter in Los Angeles – a fact that has been credited with allowing the grocery unions to negotiate better terms in their most recent round of contract negotiations.

Many of the local labor initiatives are tied to the development process – and thus are subject to uncertainty based on fluctuations in development cycles. This is most obvious with respect to CBAs, which in Los Angeles have been differentially affected by economic conditions based on when the development was approved.

---

[69] D Fairris et al, 'Examining the Evidence: The Impact of the Los Angeles Living Wage Ordinance on Workers and Businesses', Policy Report prepared for Los Angeles Alliance for the New Economy (2005), 2, 'available at <http://www.laane.org/downloads/Examining_the_Evidence.pdf>.

[70] Ibid 43.

[71] Ibid 45.

[72] Ibid 2.

[73] See, generally, HJ Holzer, 'Living Wage Laws: How Much Do (Can) They Matter?', Brookings Institute Discussion Paper, December 2008.

[74] For an overview of this research, see J Chapman and J Thompson, 'The Economic Impact of Local Living Wages', Economic Policy Institute Brief Paper 170, February 15, 2006, available at <http://www.epi.org/publications/entry/bp170/>.

[75] Cummings and Boutcher, above n 3.

For example, the nation's first CBA – in connection with LA Live – was signed in 2001 but still hasn't yet been fully completed. The project officially opened in 2007 and completion of the final phase of development is scheduled for 2011. According to the developer, all of the jobs in Phase One – the construction of a 7,100-seat theater – met the living wage requirements of the CBA and half of the jobs were held by local residents in compliance with the local hiring requirement.[76] Furthermore, a 2006 Status Update found that a job training program was established in August 2003 and that the developer had provided $62,000 in seed funding to support the program.[77] There is no information yet available on CBA compliance for Phase Two, which includes restaurants and other entertainment venues, where one would expect most low-wage jobs to be produced.

On the other hand, the LA Grand Avenue CBA received final project approval in 2007, but the recession has prevented any development to date. When established, the Grand Avenue CBA was forecast to create 29,000 construction jobs, approximately 30 per cent of which (8,700) would go to local residents and at-risk individuals under the local hiring provisions.[78] The CBA was also forecast to create 5,900 permanent living wage jobs, of which approximately 30 per cent would go to local residents.[79] However, because no development has yet commenced, there are no job gains to report.

b. Can local labor initiatives respond to mobile and flexible jobs?

One concern created by local labor initiatives is that the more that unions and community groups impose labor standards on corporations, the more likely it becomes that corporations will relocate. This is the well-known danger of a race to the bottom. Absent some particular reason for remaining in a particular locale, corporations will tend to move to locations that have the lowest labor costs.[80]

While corporations often race to the bottom or at least away from the top, there are some reasons to believe that the types of local initiatives described above may not be as dangerous as some would suggest. As the LA examples demonstrate, most of the initiatives to date concern jobs that cannot leave the city – jobs of municipal workers, hotel employees, truck drivers, and others whose jobs must be done locally. And according to the operation of labor markets, it is reasonable to believe that once a significant number of a locality's workers obtain higher wages and more job protections, there will be an upward pressure placed on other employers to raise wages as well. Such an upward spiral is precisely what local labor and community

---

[76] Telephone Interview with Martha Saucedo, Vice President of Community Affairs, AEG World-wide (August 26, 2009).

[77] LA Live, Community Benefits Program, Status Update (March 2006), available at <http://www.edf.org/documents/5196_LALive_CBAupdate.pdf>.

[78] Grand Avenue Project, 'Summary of Community Benefits', Attachment H at 1, available at <http://www.edf.org/documents/5196_LALive_CBAupdate.pdf>.

[79] Ibid.

[80] See KVW Stone, 'To the Yukon and Beyond: Local Laborers in a Global Labor Market' (1999) 3 J of Small & Emerg Bus Law 93, 96–8; and KVW Stone, 'Labor and the Global Economy', (1995) 16 Mich J of Int'l Law 987, 992–4.

coalitions hope to generate. On the other hand, though, a city that was known as a high-wage haven could have difficulties persuading new capital to come in.

However, the danger of capital flight and capital avoidance is not always present, even in areas with high labor standards. This is because sometimes corporations want to take advantage of a specifically trained labor force, or be near particular markets or raw materials.[81] In today's world, often corporations want to be near others that produce in their field to take advantage of what economists call 'agglomeration economies.' Certain localities develop workforces that specialize in certain types of skills, and these generate enormous value for the corresponding firms that locate there. Numerous studies have confirmed the existence of localized agglomeration economies that play a powerful role in the locational choices of firms.[82] One well-known example is Annalee Saxenian's description of the dramatic effects of agglomeration in the Silicon Valley computer industry.[83] When location-al choices of firms are influenced by the prospects of valuable agglomeration effects, those firms will be less likely to move overseas, or across the country, to escape rising labor costs. Indeed, some of the measures for which labor community coalitions have mobilized – training, job stability, educational institutions – are measures which could enhance the value of the region's human capital, and thus increase the value of agglomeration.[84]

F. Concluding observations

Activism by labor and community coalitions at the local level is redefining labor law in the United States. Such alliances have marshaled the powers of local govern-ments to impose living wage requirements, local hiring preferences, sweat-free procurement obligations, training requirements, and even health benefits for work-ers in their territorial jurisdictions. In addition, labor–community coalitions have managed to pressure private-sector actors to provide benefits to workers and communities through negotiated community benefit agreements. While these efforts are dynamic and promising, there are several challenges they face in promot-ing labor revival in the United States.

First, unlike unions, the coalitions do not provide representation to workers on an on-going basis. Nor do they provide workers with sustained assistance on work-related problems. There are some other new organizations emerging, such as worker centers for immigrant, contingent, and other vulnerable workers – that

---

[81] See Stone, above n 80, 97–8.

[82] See, eg MP Drennan, 'National Structural Change and Metropolitan Specialization in the United States' (1999) 78 Regional Science 297, 314–15 (empirical study finding agglomeration economy in information-intensive industries in urban areas). See, generally, EL Glaeser, 'Are Cities Dying?' (1998) J of Econ Perspectives 139, 148–50 (citing studies).

[83] A Saxenian, *Regional Advantage: Culture and Competition in Silicon Valley and Route 128* (Harvard University Press, 1994).

[84] See, generally, KVW Stone, 'A Labor Law for the Digital Era: The Future of Labor and Employment Law in the United States' in K Dau-Schmidt, S Harris, and O Lobel (eds), *Labor and Employment Law and Economics* (Edward Elgar, 2009) 689, 709–11.

do provide such services and that might fill a role that unions have performed.[85] However, neither the worker centers nor the coalitions provide representation at the workplace itself.

Second, there is a question about solidarity. Because these new labor–community coalitions are not workplace based, they are not built upon the kinds of social bonds that usually sustain worker organizations over time. Unions serve not merely as economic and political organizations – they are also a source of social ties for members of a shared workplace or a shared craft. Without those types of organic, on-going connections, it is unclear whether these new forms of organizations will generate the loyalty and cohesiveness necessary for a sustained and engaged membership.

Third, the local initiatives depend on having a friendly local government and auspicious local economic conditions. CBAs only exist when there are major development projects contemplated. Local living wage and procurement ordinances must be enacted and enforced by local government officials. As in other political arenas, these conditions can change. Hostile mayors and legislators can make it more difficult for alliances to form and undermine their efforts. And the current economic turndown has slowed the spread of CBAs.

Despite these challenges, local labor initiatives may hold promise not only for new worker organizations and improved labor protections in the United States, they may also serve as an inspiration for similar initiatives in other countries.

---

[85] See, eg, J Fine, *Worker Centers, Organizing Communities at the Edge of the Dream* (Cornell University ILR Press, 2006); and J Gordon, *Suburban Sweatshops: The Fight for Immigrant Rights* (Harvard University Press, 2005).

PART IV

NEW LABOUR LAW IDEAS: RETHINKING EXISTING BOUNDARIES

18

The Broad Idea of Labour Law: Industrial Policy, Labour Market Regulation, and Decent Work

John Howe*

The 'old' Protection had contented itself with making good wages possible.
The 'new' Protection seeks to make them actual.[1]

A. Introduction

The traditional 'idea' of labour law is a combination of subject matter and purpose. According to Kahn-Freund's famous articulation of labour law, it is generally considered to be the law which regulates the employment relationship with the goal of correcting an imbalance in bargaining power between employer and employee in order to secure a more just working relationship for the worker.[2]

In Australian labour law, the so-called *Harvester* case[3] from 1907 is perhaps the most iconic court decision in the history of the field. In that case, the second President of the Australian Court of Conciliation and Arbitration, Justice HB Higgins, made observations which could be considered a forerunner to Kahn-Freund's later and more internationally recognized articulation of the protective

* Centre for Employment and Labour Relations Law, Melbourne Law School, University of Melbourne. I thank participants in the 'Idea of Labour Law' workshop held at Cambridge University, 8–9 April 2010, in particular the organizers, Guy Davidov and Brian Langille, and my colleagues Sean Cooney, Beth Gaze, Tess Hardy, Richard Mitchell, and Joo-Cheong Tham for their comments on an earlier version of this chapter.

[1] *Explanatory Memorandum in Regard to New Protection*, Commonwealth Parliamentary Papers, vol 2, 1907–1908, pp 1887–9.

[2] 'The main object of labour law has always been, and I venture to say will always be, to be a countervailing force to counteract the inequality of bargaining power which is inherent and must be inherent in the employment relationship. Most of what we call protective legislation . . . and indeed most labour legislation altogether must be seen in this context': O Kahn-Freund, *Labour and the Law* (Stevens, 1972) 8.

[3] *Ex Parte HV McKay (Harvester* case) (1907) 2 CAR 1. HV McKay was the owner of the Sunshine Harvester Works in Melbourne, Australia, a manufacturer of combine harvesters and other agricultural machinery.

purpose of labour law. Higgins observed that the provision for 'fair and reasonable remuneration' in the relevant legislation 'must be meant to secure to [employees] something which they cannot get by the ordinary system of individual bargaining with employers', which Higgins referred to as '"the higgling of the market" for labour'. Instead, fair and reasonable remuneration must have as its starting point 'the cost of living as a civilised being'.[4]

The *Harvester* case is therefore famous for setting a precedent that legal minimum wages in Australia were to be a 'living wage', and confirming that the underlying purpose of Australian labour law is the protection of employees. However, this decision was not made under the Conciliation and Arbitration Act 1904, at that time the still-nascent federal industrial relations legislation in Australia (although subsequently Higgins' concept of the fair and reasonable wage came to be applied under that Act). Instead, the case had been chosen as the first implementation of the policy and legislation package known as the 'New Protection',[5] which linked tariff protection with protection of wages, and the decision was actually made under the Excise Tariff Act 1906 (Cth). Under that legislation, in return for exemption from an excise tax (thereby gaining an advantage over foreign competitors), Australian manufacturers of agricultural machinery were required to demonstrate that they paid their workers fair and reasonable remuneration. At the time of the decision, then, the determination of a living wage for many workers was inextricably tied up with industrial policy in the form of tariff protection legislation. To all intents and purposes, the tariff legislation was labour law – but we would not normally think of tariff protection as being within the scope of labour law, or having a social protection function.

The overarching goal of this chapter is to re-state the case for a broader interpretation of the traditional subject matter and purpose of labour law, and to locate industrial policies such as tariff protection, industry assistance and other economic development initiatives within that broader perspective. Over recent years, for reasons which are explored later in the chapter, there has been considerable support in labour law scholarship for the reformulation of labour law around a wider, labour market perspective of the subject (the LMR perspective).[6] Efforts to develop the LMR perspective have been particularly strong in Australia.[7] On this view, labour law

---

[4] Ibid 3–4.

[5] J Rickard, *The Rebel as Judge* (George Allen & Unwin, 1984) 171.

[6] See, eg, R Mitchell (ed), *Redefining Labour Law: New Perspectives on the Future of Teaching and Research* (CELRL, University of Melbourne, 1995); M d'Antona, 'Labour Law at Century's End: An Identity Crisis?' in J Conaghan, RM Fischl, and K Klare, *Labour Law in the Era of Globalisation* (Oxford University Press, 2002); J Conaghan, 'Labour Law and the New Economy Discourse' (2003) 16 Australian Journal of Labour Law 9; S Sciarra, 'The "Making" of EU Labour Law and the "Future" of Labour Lawyers' in C Barnard, S Deakin, and G Morris (eds), *The Future of Labour Law* (Hart Publishing, 2004); P Davies, KD Ewing, and M Freedland, 'General Editors' Preface' to S Deakin and F Wilkinson, *The Law of the Labour Market* (Oxford University Press, 2005); O Lobel, 'The Four Pillars of Work Law' (2006) 104 Michigan Law Review 1539; and R Mitchell and C Arup, 'Labour Law and Labour Market Regulation' in C Arup, P Gahan, J Howe, R Johnstone, R Mitchell, and A O'Donnell (eds), *Labour Law and Labour Market Regulation: Essays on the Construction, Constitution and Regulation of Labour Markets and Work Relationships* (Federation Press, 2006).

[7] An excellent overview of Australian developments can be found in A Frazer, 'Reconceiving Labour Law: The Labour Market Regulation Project' (2008) 8 Macquarie Law Journal 21.

encompasses various forms of labour market regulation in addition to employment regulation, including social security law, active labour market policy, and, as I argue in this chapter, industrial policy. The chapter will use the example of the implementation of the New Protection during the early beginnings of federal labour regulation in Australia to explore both the historical contingency of traditional labour law and to illustrate the importance of industrial policy settings to the subject matter and goals of traditional labour law in both industrialized and developing country contexts. I will also consider the advantages of including industrial policy within the idea of labour law to both scholarship and labour policymaking and practice.

B. Time and place: the historical and cultural contingency of traditional labour law

The starting point for a discussion of the importance of a broader perspective on labour law is with the limitations of the traditional perspective. Heeding Mitchell and Arup's call for labour lawyers to 'remain alive to the historically contingent nature of labour law and be prepared to revise our present understanding of the field by reference to its historical legacy',[8] it is first necessary to recognize that what is considered to be the traditional subject matter of labour law is historically and culturally contingent. Labour law scholarship only emerged as a distinct field of endeavour in industrialized countries during the 1950s, a time when the employment relationship took hold as the most common work arrangement in the conditions of full employment that these countries enjoyed in the 1950s and 1960s.[9]

There are a number of reasons why the traditional discourse has since lost traction and deprived labour law of what Mitchell and Arup describe as 'its descriptive and normative capacity'.[10] Most of these have been well canvassed by others, and include: changing labour market practices, both within the enterprise and beyond it (such as the increase in non-standard employment arrangements) rendering traditional labour law prone to avoidance; the globalization of capital and the subsequent challenge to the capacity and willingness of national governments to maintain social protection; the rise to prominence of new economic theories of the labour market, especially neoliberal perspectives (which have impacted on the policy goals behind labour regulation); the decline in union membership and the rise of more sophisticated human resource practices; and wider changes in the structure of society, such as changes in the working patterns of women, so that the typical household is no longer a male wage-earner supporting his spouse and children.[11]

---

[8] Mitchell and Arup, above n 6, 7.
[9] For an eloquent discussion of the conditions under which traditional labour law evolved, see B Langille, 'What is International Employment Law For?' (2009) 3 Law and Ethics of Human Rights 47, 57–8.
[10] Mitchell and Arup, above n 6, 6.
[11] R Mitchell, 'Where Are We Going in Labour Law? Some Thoughts on a Field of Scholarship and Policy in Process of Change', Monash University Workplace and Corporate Law Research Group, Working Paper No 16, 2010; Mitchell and Arup, above n 6, 6; and S Deakin, 'A New Paradigm for

The latter category includes social and economic changes in developing countries, where we are seeing a growing interest in labour law, especially in fast-industrializing nations such as China and India, but also in countries struggling to generate sustainable economic growth and to reduce poverty. Traditional labour law, while it is important to development, does not necessarily capture all of the issues presently confronting workers in those economies, where unemployment, or employment in the informal economy, leaves those workers outside the scope of labour law with little hope of protection in the absence of economic growth and formalization.[12]

Labour law is therefore under pressure to cope with factors relating to the realms of both time and place. The issue here is that the concerns of workers will depend on the pressing matters of the time in their local economic, political, and social context. In the present climate, economic development policies, including industrial policy, are crucial to the interests of many workers in both industrialized and developing countries.

There is no better illustration of this than the global financial crisis (GFC) of 2008 and its effect on maintenance of social protection through traditional labour law. For example, in the United States, where the GFC has had a significant negative impact on the economy, the main concern of many American workers at present is the high rate of unemployment and the availability of paid work, pushing much-needed reform of a traditional labour law subject – reform of collective bargaining laws in the form of the Employee Free Choice Bill – to the back pages.

The GFC has also impacted on jobs and economic growth in developing countries. The International Labour Organization (ILO) called for a Global Jobs Pact in the wake of the crisis, emphasizing (among other things) the need for 'coordinated global policy options' to protect and increase jobs through 'sustainable enterprises' as well as building and maintaining social protection systems.[13] The Jobs Pact continues the ILO's campaign to make the availability of employment a more important issue in global labour regulation debates, especially in relation to developing countries. Under the 'Decent Work' framework, the ILO set itself the goal of securing decent work for men and women throughout the world. Importantly, the objective of decent work is intended to promote the creation of not just any type of job, but 'the creation of jobs of an acceptable quality'.[14] The Decent

Labour Law' (2007) 31 Melbourne University Law Review 1161 at 1162. See also Langille, above n 9; and H Arthurs, 'What Immortal Hand or Eye? – Who Will Redraw the Boundaries of Labour Law' in G Davidov and B Langille, *Boundaries and Frontiers of Labour Law: Goals and Means in the Regulation of Work* (Hart Publishing, 2006).

[12] Sankaran, this volume; K Sankaran, 'Protecting the Worker in the Informal Economy: The Role of Labour Law' in Davidov and Langille, ibid; C Fenwick, J Howe, I Landau, and S Marshall, *Labour and Labour-Related Laws in Micro and Small Enterprises*, SEED Working Paper No 81 (ILO, 2007); and T Teklé (ed), *Labour Law and Worker Protection in Developing Countries* (Hart Publishing, 2010).

[13] ILO, *Recovering from the Crisis: A Global Jobs Pact*, Adopted by the International Labour Conference, 98th Session, June 2009.

[14] J Somavia, 'Employment-Intensive Growth in the Context of Globalization', speech by the Director-General of the ILO to a public meeting on the Social Summit+5, organized by the Swiss Agency for Development and Cooperation (SDC) in Bern, 11 May 2000. Available at: <http://www.ilo.org/public/english/bureau/dgo/speeches/somavia/2000/bern.htm> (visited 11 March 2010). See also ILO, 'Decent Work' Report of the Director-General to the 87th Session of the International Labour Conference (ILO, 1999).

Work agenda has shifted the focus of the ILO from goals to outcomes, and has helped to emphasize that economic and social policies are development policies serving a common purpose: 'improving people's economic and social well-being through economic development'.[15]

This brief discussion of the importance that has been placed on generating employment and economic development in recent times serves to emphasize that the debate over regulation of working conditions has, both historically and in contemporary debates, moved on from one that is confined to regulation of working relationships as a means of protecting workers. There is a growing interest in the *impact* of a number of forms of labour market regulation on working conditions, the availability of paid work, poverty, and social inequality.[16] The LMR perspective is well placed to take account of this change in what matters, and what is happening, in terms of law and policy affecting working conditions and social equality over time and space.

Under the LMR perspective, in place of a focus on protecting *employees*, the scope of labour law should encompass the concerns of those people who are dependent on their labour to earn a living[17] (that is, who are not owners of capital), whether they are in employment, are engaged in other forms of working arrangements, or are 'out in the labour market'.[18] The new subject of labour law is the 'worker' or 'active labour market participant': 'not the full-time employee pursuing a specific "job for life", but a person moving between periods of employment [and unemployment], other forms of paid work, unpaid work, training and so on over the course of a lifetime'.[19]

Based on this perspective, labour lawyers can legitimately be interested in regulation which constitutes and shapes labour markets, including regulation which impacts on the demand and supply of labour in the external labour market, as well as that which is constitutive of the labour market at the level of the firm, the internal labour market.[20] The LMR perspective is also based on a pluralist conception of regulation, whereby it is recognized that a variety of regulatory approaches might operate in achievement of substantive goals, including legislation, but extending to other regulatory mechanisms, such as 'soft law' and the financial incentives which are a feature of many industrial policies.[21]

---

[15] GS Fields, 'Decent Work and Development Policies' (2003) 142 International Labour Review 239, 240.

[16] See Deakin, this volume. See also S Deakin and P Sarkar, 'Assessing the Long-run Economic Impact of Labour Law Systems: A Theoretical Appraisal and Analysis of New Time Series Data' (2008) 39 Industrial Relations Journal 453.

[17] C Arup, J Howe, R Mitchell, A O'Donnell, and J Tham, 'Employment Protection and Employment Creation: The Contested Terrain of Australian Labour Law' in M Biagi (ed), *Job Creation and Labour Law* (Kluwer, 2000).

[18] C Arup, 'Labour Law as Regulation: Promises and Pitfalls' (2001) 14 Australian Journal of Labour Law 229, 233.

[19] R Mitchell, J Murray, and A O'Donnell, 'Labour Law and a New Social Settlement', Growth 49 (Committee for the Economic Development of Australia, 2001) 73. See also R Owens, 'Reproducing Law's Worker: Regulatory Tensions in the Pursuit of Population, Participation and Productivity' in Arup et al, above n 6.

[20] J Howe, R Johnstone and R Mitchell, 'Constituting and Regulating the Labour Market for Social and Economic Purposes' in Arup et al, above n 6.

[21] P Gahan and P Brosnan, 'The Repertoires of Labour Market Regulation' in Arup et al, above n 6.

In recent years, in response to the challenges to traditional labour law outlined earlier in the chapter, labour law scholars have explored the role of legal and policy fields such as social security law, employment policy, training and education, and immigration in constituting and regulating labour markets. In particular, a number of commentators have investigated how regulation which impacts on the unemployed, such as conditional income support, or job creation policies and other active labour market programs, help to constitute the nature of the 'employed' section of the labour market and regulate access to the means for subsistence.[22]

However, beyond these labour market programs, the fallout from the GFC illustrates that in any economy, government policies and regulation designed to stimulate 'industry demand' will be crucial to the demand for labour in the labour market. In this chapter, I adopt Rodrik's definition of industrial policy as 'policies that stimulate specific economic activities and promote structural change'.[23] Today, we might use a broader definition of 'industry' than was common in the *Harvester* days. International competition is as likely to occur in services such as call centres as it is in manufacturing. Indeed, Rodrik's definition is not limited to industry at all, and can include subsidies to agricultural activities. It encompasses a number of state policies designed to foster economic growth. Thus, tariff protection might be considered industrial policy, as might trade liberalization and adjustment assistance to alleviate the effects of trade liberalization, expenditure on infrastructure development, public procurement, and financial incentives to attract investment, business, or to stimulate economic growth.[24]

As noted earlier with regard to tariff protection, labour lawyers would not normally consider industrial policy as within the scope of labour law. Labour lawyers might agree that the industrialization strategies and policies of a particular government form part of the broader *context* in which labour law operates, but resist the argument that industrial policies form part of the law of labour market regulation. In my view, the adoption of a broader view of what constitutes labour law is crucial to the future health and vitality of labour law scholarship. Adopting an LMR perspective, labour lawyers should be interested in the role and impact of a range of industrial policies, including tariffs, industry support schemes, as 'regulation which affects the distribution of labour between sectors of the economy and

---

[22] See, eg, P Davies and M Freedland, *Labour Law: Text and Materials* (2nd edn, Weidenfeld & Nicolson, 1984) ch 1; A O'Donnell and C Arup, 'Social Security and Labour Law: Constructing the Labour Market Subject', Working Paper No 24, Centre for Employment and Labour Relations Law (Melbourne, 2001); T Carney, G Ramia, and A Chapman, 'Which Law is Laggard? Regulation and the Gaps Between Labour Law and Social Security Law' in Arup et al, above n 6; and J Howe, *Regulating for Job Creation* (Federation Press, 2008).

[23] D Rodrik, 'Normalizing Industrial Policy', Working Paper No 3, Commission on Growth and Development, 2008. Aiginger describes such a definition as 'middle of the road', somewhere between narrow and broad definitions. For discussion of narrower and broader definitions, see K Aiginger, 'Industrial Policy: A Dying Breed or Re-Emerging Phoenix?' (2007) 7 Journal of Industry, Competition and Trade 297, 299–300.

[24] For consideration of the latter within a labour law paradigm, see J Howe and I Landau, 'Do Investment Attraction Incentives Create Decent Jobs? A Study of Labour Conditions in Industry Assistance Contracts' (2009) 19(3) Labour and Industry 97–136.

different industries',[25] and indeed between nations. As the *Harvester* case example illustrates, the versatility and mobility of capital and its capacity to seek out labour markets with lower labour standards and costs is one of the longstanding challenges to the effectiveness of the social protection function of labour law.[26] Industrial policy is a state response to capital mobility which is often justified by its capacity to create or retain jobs. The New Protection was explicitly intended to protect jobs *and* the living standards which those jobs deliver. More recently, industrial policy and strategies in the form of trade liberalization – an industrialization strategy that has often been associated with lower labour standards – has been more popular than trade protection. In either guise, industrial policy is an important aspect of state constitution and regulation of a labour market, and a crucial factor in the effectiveness of traditional labour law in achieving its goals.

For reasons I outline below, this argument is consistent with the call made by a number of scholars for a longer term time-frame for labour law analysis.[27] The broader conception will also take into account differences in what forms of labour regulation matter to workers not only over time, but also according to place: across different countries and regions.[28]

Indeed, in some developing countries, notwithstanding their inheritance of the traditional labour law model, greater attention has been paid to broader labour market issues in domestic labour law over time. As Cooney et al note in their book on labour law and labour market regulation in East Asia:

It is an interesting characteristic of labour law in many East Asian states that there has been less of an estrangement between the formal 'traditional' model of employee protection and the broader labour market dimensions of state policymaking and intervention.[29]

Moreover, a number of studies by labour law and industrial relations scholars have noted that the industrial policy (or industrialization strategy) adopted by developing countries has had a significant impact on the form of that country's industrial relations and human resources policies and outcomes.[30]

---

[25] 'Project Outline: Law and Regulation of the Labour Market', Appendix to C Arup, 'Labour Market Regulation as a Focus for a Labour Law Discipline' in Mitchell, *Redefining Labour Law*, above n 6.

[26] C Arup, 'Labour Market Regulation as a Focus for a Labour Law Discipline' in Mitchell, above n 6, 31–3; and K Klare, 'The Horizons of Transformative Labour and Employment Law' in Conaghan, Fischl, and Klare, above n 6, 7.

[27] Mitchell and Arup, above n 6; S Deakin, 'The Comparative Evolution of the Employment Relationship' in G Davidov and B Langille, *Boundaries and Frontiers of Labour Law: Goals and Means in the Regulation of Work* (Hart Publishing, 2006); and Deakin and Wilkinson, above n 6.

[28] J-C Javillier, 'The Employer and the Worker: the Need for a Comparative and International Perspective' in Davidov and Langille, ibid.

[29] Footnote omitted. The authors cite the example of the Philippines. S Cooney, T Lindsay, R Mitchell, and Y Zhu, 'Labour Law and Labour Market Regulation in East Asia States: Problems and Issues for Comparative Inquiry' in S Cooney, T Lindsay, R Mitchell, and Y Zhu (eds), *Law and Labour Market Regulation in East Asia* (Routledge, 2002) 2.

[30] Ibid; C Fenwick and E Kalula, 'Law and Labour Market Regulation in East Asia and Southern Africa: Comparative Perspectives' (2005) 21(2) International Journal of Comparative Labour Law and Industrial Relations 193, 205–6; S Kuruvilla, 'Linkages between Industrialisation Strategies and Industrial Relations/Human Resources Policies: Singapore, Malaysia, the Philippines and India' (1996) 49 Industrial and Labor Relations Review 635; and VB Coutinho, 'Economic Liberalisation

I will return to these matters later in the chapter, but at this stage there would therefore seem to be significant grounds for adopting a broader LMR perspective on labour law which includes industrial policy. There are two key advantages to the LMR perspective. First, it provides greater clarity on changes in the purpose and nature of labour regulation and the changing problems and issues confronting workers over time, taking account of variations across different jurisdictions. As Mitchell has recently argued, it is important to know more about the 'reality' of labour law:

... there is always labour law in some shape or form according to different stages of economic development and different systems of production. Labour law is simply part of the political economy . . . Those approaching labour law from this perspective think there is value (and formative value) in trying to understand the complexity of this regulation, and to provide an analysis of how it operates and what impact it has.[31]

Javillier has also emphasized the importance of finding out more about what is happening in labour law and practice 'around the world', and 'to avoid developing new theories or conclusions, which are linked mainly or only to one specific context such as, for example, developing countries and the post-industrial relations system'.[32]

However, the comparative perspective outlined above illustrates that the LMR perspective can also be used to advance a normative view, one that is more likely to capture current issues in labour regulation which impact on social inequality. The adoption of a broader LMR perspective does not signify an abandonment of concern for justice or egalitarian redistribution.[33] It is instead an acknowledgement that achieving such goals is not always simply a matter of addressing the imbalance in bargaining power between employers and employees. Imbalance in power can occur across the labour market, often by reason of unemployment or underemployment, and this type of imbalance can itself lead to widespread inequality and poverty. It also recognizes that from time to time, regulation of the employment relationship has been conducted for a range of purposes, including the advancement of micro-economic efficiency, national competitiveness, and macro-economic regulation (such as when incomes and employment policies have been pursued through labour law).[34]

What follows is a modest contribution to the broad idea of labour law I have just charted. To illustrate the important role that industrial policy has played (and might come to play) in labour market regulation and the achievement of decent work in both an industrialized and a developing economy context, the next section

---

and the Task of Implementing Strict Standards of Occupational Health and Safety in Asian Countries' in R Mitchell and J Min Aun Wu, *Facing the Challenge in the Asia-Pacific Region: Contemporary Themes and Issues in Labour Law* (CELRL, 1997).

[31] Mitchell, above n 11.

[32] Javillier, above n 28. See also Mitchell, above n 11.

[33] Klare argues that 'a commitment to egalitarian redistribution and the empowerment of subordinated groups should inform legal work, in practice and in scholarship': Klare, 'The Horizons of Transformative Labour and Employment Law' in Conaghan, Fischl, and Klare, above n 6, 4.

[34] See, eg, H Collins, 'Regulating the Employment Relation for Competitiveness' (2001) 30 Industrial Law Journal 17; Arup et al, above n 17; and Mitchell and Arup, above n 6, 10–11.

of the chapter examines the introduction of tariff protection and the adoption of conciliation and arbitration in Australia at the beginning of the 20th century.

C. Labour law as labour market regulation and the role of industrial policy: 'new protection' and the foundations of Australian labour law

Taking up the challenge of revising our understanding of labour law with reference to its historical legacy, this section discusses the Australian government's adoption of the New Protection policy at the time of the establishment of the Australian conciliation and arbitration system. The aim is to illustrate the value of a perspective which recognizes that the subject of labour regulation is historically and culturally contingent, and to emphasize that an LMR perspective is necessary in order to encompass a number of issues which may be of interest to working people at any given point in time and space.

Although Arup and Mitchell identified industry assistance as an area of interest within the labour market perspective, there is very little scholarship on the role of industrial policy as labour market regulation in Australia.[35] This is somewhat surprising given that, as noted earlier, industrial policy in the form of tariff protection was crucial to the introduction of a new labour relations system.

At the beginning of the 20th century, the newly established Commonwealth of Australia implemented a number of innovative economic and social policies. Of most interest to labour lawyers was the enactment of the Conciliation and Arbitration Act 1904, which established a labour tribunal that was empowered to settle interstate industrial disputes between employers and trade unions.[36] However, other key initiatives during the first few years of the federation included the adoption of the White Australia immigration policy, and in 1906, the New Protection tariff policy.

Australian journalist Paul Kelly has described the combination of racially based immigration controls, tariff protection and conciliation and arbitration as a uniquely 'Australian Settlement' which defined Australian politics and society until the 1980s.[37] Although that term has subsequently been criticized,[38] commentators agree that by design or otherwise these different policies were complementary to the

---

[35] An exception is P Smyth, 'Closing the Gap? The Role of Wage, Welfare and Industry Policy in Promoting Social Inclusion' (2007) 50(4) Journal of Industrial Relations 647. See also D Plowman, 'Protectionism and Labour Regulation', Proceedings of the HR Nicholls Society Meeting, Adelaide, November 1992, available at <http://www.hrnicholls.com.au/archives/vol13/vol13-4.php> (last visited 24 August 2010).

[36] For an historical account of the enactment of this legislation, see S Macintyre and R Mitchell (eds), *Foundations of Arbitration: The Origins and Effects of State Compulsory Arbitration 1890–1914* (Oxford University Press, 1989).

[37] P Kelly, *The End of Certainty: the Story of the 1980s* (Allen & Unwin, 1992).

[38] P Smyth and B Cass (eds), *Contesting the Australian Way: States, Markets and Civil Society* (Cambridge University Press, 1998).

establishment of high living standards for workers in the Australian context.[39] A racist immigration policy prevented cheap labour from the Asia-Pacific region undercutting local wages and conditions,[40] tariff policy soothed business concerns that conciliation and arbitration would increase labour costs by offering protection from overseas competition, which in turn delivered domestic business prosperity. Conciliation and arbitration, in theory, ensured an equitable distribution of that prosperity.

The use of tariffs to encourage and sustain local industries by imposing a tax on imported goods was a carryover from the colonial period, and had often been justified on the grounds that it helped safeguard employment. It was also an important source of revenue for colonial governments. After Federation, there was concern that Australia was too reliant on primary industry and exports for economic growth, and as a result tariffs were favoured as a mechanism to secure a more self-sufficient model of growth through the promotion of secondary industry.[41]

To what extent was tariff protection a 'labour issue' at the time, as distinct from a purely business concern on the part of domestic Australian industrialists? It is important to note that at the beginning of the 20th century, the Australian economy was in the midst of a transition from a largely agrarian base to one with more developed secondary industry. It had experienced a depression in the early 1890s, from which it was only just recovering, with the result that unemployment and industrial unrest had been a significant issue for over a decade. Although the Australian economy had acquired many of the structural characteristics of urban industrial societies in Europe and North America, such as a strong primary industry sector (agriculture and mining), and a developing services sector, its manufacturing sector was still relatively small.[42] As a result, while wages were a major focus of the labour movement and of the public at this time, tariffs and the creation of industrial employment were also key concerns.[43]

It should be noted that the politics of the newly formed Australian Parliament were complex. There were three key factions in the first decade of the Australian Parliament: Labour, Liberal Protectionists, and the more conservative 'Free Traders'. Each grouping struggled to form a majority in Parliament in their own right, so was dependent on attracting one of the other factions to its agenda. One of the Labour caucus' key goals was the passage of legislation to protect union activity and working conditions in the form of arbitration legislation. However, the Conciliation and Arbitration Act was only passed with the support of non-Labour Liberals,

[39] See, eg, S Macintyre, *The Labour Experiment* (McPhee Gribble, 1989); K Hancock and S Richardson, 'Economic and Social Effects' in J Isaac and S Macintyre (eds), *'The New Province of Law and Order: 100 Years of Conciliation and Arbitration* (Cambridge University Press, 2004).

[40] A O'Donnell and R Mitchell, 'Immigrant Labour in Australia: the Regulatory Framework' (2001) 14 Australian Journal of Labour Law 269; and M Crock and L Friedman, 'Immigration Control and the Shaping of Australia's Labour Market: Conflicting Ideologies or Historical Imperatives' in Arup et al (eds), above n 6.

[41] Macintyre, above n 39, 21.

[42] R Maddock and IW McLean, 'The Australian Economy in the Very Long Run' in R Maddock and IW McLean (eds), *The Australian Economy in the Long Run* (Cambridge University Press, 1987) 19.

[43] F Crowley, '1901–14' in F Crowley (ed), *A New History of Australia* (Heinemann, 1974) 278.

some of whom had played an important role in the advancement of this particular form of labour regulation.[44]

The Liberal Protectionists favoured tariff protection as a means by which to protect business and provide room for social development, but the first federal tariff set in 1902 (or 'old' protection) was widely regarded as a temporary measure that was only weakly protective. However, Labour parliamentarians were soon convinced that tariffs could be used to improve workers' standard of living, and joined Liberal Protectionists in pursuing a more comprehensive tariff policy which became known as the 'New Protection'. In 1906, Liberal Protectionists and Labour parliamentarians formed an alliance which allowed the Deakin government to pass the New Protection into federal law. There is some disagreement among historians about whether the New Protection was designed by Liberals to attract the support of the Labour party and defeat the opposition of the Liberals' more conservative Free Trade opponents, or whether it was forced upon the Liberals by Labour as a condition of their support in Parliament.[45] Whatever the correct version of events, there was disagreement within the Labour ranks in the late 19th and early 20th century about the merits of protective tariffs as a policy that would benefit working people. In Parliament, there were Labour 'Free Traders' who were concerned that tariffs would increase the prices of necessities, thereby increasing the cost of living for working people (a concern shared with conservative Free Traders).[46] On the other hand, Labour 'Protectionists' believed the tariff would keep unemployment down and facilitate the payment of higher wages.[47] Eventually the Labour Party formally adopted New Protection as part of its policy platform at its Inter-State Labour Conference in 1908.[48]

The New Protection was an explicitly labourist form of tariff protection. To address Labour's concern that domestic businesses would not automatically share the gains from a higher level of protection with their workers, the New Protection sought to link trade protection with working conditions by requiring the beneficiaries of tariff protection to provide 'fair and reasonable' wages and working conditions for their employees.[49] The New Protection was a suite of legislation that combined import tariffs, excise duties and industrial tribunals. So, for example, the Customs Tariff Act 1906 (Cth) provided protection to agricultural implement manufacturers by imposing duties on imported machinery, while the Excise Tariff (Agricultural Machinery) Act 1906 imposed an excise on Australian manufactured agricultural machinery of approximately 50 per cent of the customs tariff.[50]

---

[44] S Macintyre, 'Neither Capital Nor Labour' in Macintyre and Mitchell, above n 36, 189.

[45] See JA La Nauze, *Alfred Deakin: A Biography* (1965) 410 and fn 8, 658.

[46] PG McCarthy, 'Employers, the Tariff, and Legal Wage Regulation in Australia – 1890–1910' (1970) 12 Journal of Industrial Relations 182, 184. See also Crowley, above n 43, 268.

[47] J Hagan, 'The Australian Labour Movement: Context and Perspective, 1850–1987' in W Ford and D Plowman (eds), *Australian Unions: an Industrial Relations Perspective* (Macmillan, 1989) 19–22.

[48] La Nauze, above n 45, 436. See also Crowley, above n 43, 285.

[49] La Nauze, above n 45, 410.

[50] For further consideration, and discussion of other legislation enacted before 1908 which was consistent with the New Protection policy, see Plowman, 'Protectionism and Labour Regulation', above n 35, 1–2.

As noted earlier in relation to the *Harvester* decision, the Excise Tariff Act then declared that the excise would not be payable by manufacturers whose employees were paid a 'fair and reasonable' wage, to be assessed by industrial tribunals such as the Court of Conciliation and Arbitration.

This goal of ensuring that the benefits of protection were distributed between capital and labour is apparent in the quote at the beginning of this chapter, from the Explanatory Memorandum to the New Protection policy. The practice of connecting social protection legislation and the tariffs can be traced back to at least the 1890s, when the Victorian government established a system of Wages Boards to regulate working conditions in protected industries under the Factories and Shops Act 1896 (Vic).[51] Like that initiative, the New Protection had a number of express labour market objectives, including the promotion of demand for labour, and 'to render stable the conditions of labour and to prevent the standard of living of the employes [sic] in [protected industries] from being depressed to the level of foreign standards'.[52] Indeed, part of the impetus for the implementation for the New Protection came from the threat that international manufacturers of agricultural implements posed to the local industry (including HV McKay) which at that time employed almost 3,000 workers.[53]

Tariff protection was therefore very much part of the Australian labour movement's agenda in the early part of the 20th century. It is important to observe here that the Australian labour movement had followed a different trajectory from its US and European counterparts when it came to involvement in the political system, in that it saw the state as something over which it could exercise control in order to bring about positive change.[54] Moreover, the concerns of the labour movement at the turn of the century were distinctly 'labourist' (as opposed to socialist) and reflected the pressing issues faced by workers at this point in Australian history. Some of these concerned job security and wage rates; however, given the still-recent experience of mass unemployment in the 1890s 'and against a continuing background of seasonal unemployment, it [the working class] wanted to ensure that jobs were available to all'.[55]

The New Protection was relatively short lived. Only two years after its implementation, as a result of employer legal challenges, the legislation implementing the policy was declared unconstitutional by the High Court of Australia, and the minimum wage requirements of the New Protection were struck down.[56] However, tariff protection for domestic industry continued, although it was just one element of Australian industrial policy at this time. The federal government also

---

[51] Alfred Deakin, Prime Minister in 1906, had also been instrumental in the development and passage of the Victorian Factories legislation as a member of the Victorian government. See La Nauze, above n 45, 411.

[52] *Explanatory Memorandum in Regard to New Protection*, above n 1, 1887–9.

[53] La Nauze, above n 45, 413; Tariff Commission, *Report on the Agricultural Implements Industry*, 1906.

[54] Macintyre, *The Labour Experiment*, above n 39, 11.

[55] Ibid 19.

[56] *R v Barger* [1908] HCA 43; (1908) 6 CLR 41. On the employers' campaign against both the New Protection and the Conciliation and Arbitration Act, see D Plowman, 'Forced March: the Employers and Arbitration' in Macintyre and Mitchell, above n 36.

provided other forms of domestic industry assistance, as well as infrastructure spending, and the establishment of public enterprises to compete with private capital in certain sectors, such as banking.[57] For example, financial subsidies were a more attractive form of assistance for those industries which were less susceptible to competition, such as the iron and steel industries.[58] Moreover, there were clear connections between industrial policy and a broader agenda of social protection among both labour and liberal political activists. Smyth has argued that what was distinctive about Australia's industrial policy compared to other industrialized countries at the same time was not that it was protectionist, but that the state had played such an important role in ensuring that the gains from protection were spent on infrastructure and social investment, including education and health.[59] This, then, was the 'high road' to economic development – the use of tariff protection as part of an industrial development strategy to achieve 'a higher-wage economy with a broader, more diverse structure of opportunities available to its citizens'.[60]

In the first two decades of the 20th century, traditional labour law was therefore only one piece of a complex policy puzzle that delivered high living standards to many Australian workers. Although Higgins' concept of the 'fair and reasonable wage' from the *Harvester* case was applied in federal award determinations under the Conciliation and Arbitration Act, in the first two decades of the legislation's operation it had limited impact. Only a small number of workers were covered by federal awards, with many working in non-standard work arrangements and thus outside the scope of the system, and the living wage principles were not applied consistently until the 1920s.[61] A Committee of eminent economists appointed to review the Australian tariff in the late 1920s (the Brigden Committee) argued that the success of the tariff policy in decreasing Australia's dependence on agricultural and pastoral polices and fostering the development of the manufacturing sector may have had had a greater impact on living standards than minimum wage levels in awards.[62] The maintenance of protection ensured the growth of secondary industry, thereby increasing employment opportunities and facilitating population growth. The Brigden Committee further argued that the tariff had a distributional function in that it raised the prices of local products, redirecting income from landholders in primary industry to workers in retail and manufacturing sectors.[63]

---

[57] J Pincus, 'Evolution and Political Economy of Australian Trade Policies' in R Pomfret (ed), *Australia's Trade Policies* (Oxford University Press, 1995) 62; and Macintyre, *The Labour Experiment*, above n 39.

[58] Pincus, above n 57, 62.

[59] Smyth, above n 35.

[60] Ibid 653. For further consideration of the concept of the high-road approach to economic development, see S Deakin and F Wilkinson, 'Rights vs Efficiency? The Economic Case for Transnational Labour Standards' (1994) 23 Industrial Law Journal 289.

[61] Smyth, above n 35, 651; see also S Macintyre, 'Arbitration in Action' in Isaac and Macintyre, above n 39; on the extent of non-standard work arrangements, see O'Donnell and Arup, above n 22.

[62] Hancock and Richardson, above n 39, 186–7, referencing the Brigden Committee Report on tariff protection in the first three decades after Federation: JB Brigden, DB Coplan, EC Dyason, LF Giblin, and CH Wickins, *The Australian Tariff: an Economic Inquiry* (Melbourne University Press, 1929).

[63] Brigden Committee, above n 62, 96.

This distributional function was supported by the conciliation and arbitration system, in that the standard of wage regulation adopted by the Conciliation and Arbitration Court reflected the overall average income generated by the tariff, and ensured that employers were not tempted to undercut average wage levels.[64]

It is not intended that the preceding discussion of the New Protection suggest that the emergence and development of arbitration was dependent upon protectionist trade policy. Instead, this discussion of the early years of Australian labour regulation shows that arbitration and protection (as a form of industrial policy) were closely related, and that it is difficult to consider the effectiveness of one in the achievement of better labour standards without the other. Although Australia's industrial policy settings changed over time, industrial policy continued to be an important form of labour market regulation over the remainder of the 20th century, and is still important in present-day political debates. The question of just how important industrial policy has been as an instrument of labour market regulation in recent decades is a matter for further research. However, for present purposes, it remains to draw some conclusions about the implications of this discussion for the inclusion of industrial policy within a broader, LMR perspective of labour law.

D. The new industrial policy as labour law

In the previous section, it was shown that industrial policy was a key factor in the social protection of workers in early 20th-century Australia. It is arguable that under the Australian Settlement, the adoption of tariff protection along with immigration restrictions was crucial to the establishment of a legal system regulating labour relations for the benefit of employees.

Independently of this, the New Protection itself explicitly connected industrial policy (in the form of tariff protection) with labour standards (in the form of minimum wage requirements). Indeed, supporters of the New Protection, whether Liberal or Labour, were for the most part as much concerned with social protection and investment as they were with the profits of protected businesses. This once again confirms that labour regulation can have both economic and social justifications.

The New Protection also played a significant role in the constitution of Australia's labour market by stimulating labour demand within Australia. By encouraging labour demand through industrial development, the policy influenced the *pattern* of employment, the types of jobs that would be available in the Australian economy. Under the New Protection, the government was privileging manufacturing jobs over employment in agriculture (Australia's farmers faced lower prices for their exports, and higher costs in getting their produce to market).

The preference for industry over agriculture, and the insulation of industry from international competition, in turn had some influence on maintenance of wage

---

[64] Ibid. See also Hancock and Richardson, above n 39, 187; and Plowman, above n 35, 3.

levels and the quality of life of workers and their families over the first two decades of the 20th century. To that extent, tariff protection was inseparable from traditional labour law's protective function.

I have argued that the broader, LMR perspective on labour law is better suited to investigating the nature and impact of labour regulation across time and place. While it is difficult to be sure without further research into the role of industrial policy in other jurisdictions, parallels can be drawn between the relevance of industrial policy settings to working conditions in Australia in the early 20th century and current debates about the role of industrial policy in both industrialized and developing countries in the 21st century.

Australia was not alone in employing a protectionist industrial policy to buttress capitalist economic development during key phases of its industrialization. There is evidence that the UK, USA, Germany, Sweden, and Japan used active tariff and non-tariff measures to promote industrial development in the late 19th and early 20th centuries.[65] Moreover, industrialized countries continued their tariff protections until the 1980s, in part enabling them to maintain social protection systems including traditional labour law.[66] Industrialized countries have also made extensive use of government procurement, another form of industrial policy, to regulate labour standards of employees of firms benefiting from government contracts.[67] It is at least possible to speculate that industrial policy may have had something to do with labour law and labour market developments in those countries.

There is also evidence that some developing countries have from time to time made use of industrial policies to foster economic development and job growth. However, these initiatives began later, and since the 1980s have been curtailed by the so-called 'Washington consensus' around the approach which nation states should adopt in the pursuit of economic development. To simplify, it has been strongly argued that the path to development and poverty alleviation must be based on trade liberalization strategies and labour market deregulation – in other words, that developing nations should adopt free trade and laissez-faire industrial policy, and introduce greater flexibility into employment regulation, to lower the cost of hiring and firing workers, in order to achieve economic growth.[68] This has been

---

[65] A useful overview can be found in H-J Chang, 'Kicking Away the Ladder: Infant Industry Promotion in Historical Perspective' (2003) 31(1) Oxford Development Studies 21, 24–7.

[66] A Blackett, 'Trade Liberalisation, Labour Law and Development' in Teklé, above n 12, 100.

[67] See Barnard, this volume; C McCrudden, *Buying Social Justice: equality, Government Procurement and Legal Change* (Oxford University Press, 2007); and J Howe, 'The Regulatory Impact of Using Public Procurement to Promote Better Labour Standards in Corporate Supply Chains' in K Macdonald and S Marshall, *Fair Trade, Corporate Accountability and Beyond: Experiments in Globalizing Justice* (Ashgate, 2010).

[68] Eg, for a number of years the World Bank has been disseminating its 'Employing Workers' index (EW Index) as part of its annual 'Doing Business' report. The report rates countries against a range of indices that measure the theoretical 'ease' of doing business under particular legal and institutional models. The EW Index is a composite indicator which reports on matters such as the ease of 'hiring and firing workers', and appears to be included on the assumption that higher formal labour standards in the organized sector lead to an increase in informal employment, and therefore lower growth. See J Berg and S Cazes, 'Policymaking Gone Awry: The Labor Market Regulations of the Doing Business Indicators' (2008) 29(4) Comparative Labor Law and Policy Journal; and S Lee, D McCann, and

characterized as the 'low road' to economic development, which can be contrasted with the 'high road' referenced earlier, where development is pursued by stimulating economic growth through the creation of quality jobs in sustainable industry.[69]

While those in favour of free trade might paint industrialization strategies involving more active state promotion of economic activity as detrimental to economic growth,[70] another view is that active industrial policies were key to the economic development and high living standards of industrialized countries. As one commentator has suggested, the dominance of trade liberalization as an industrialization strategy means that developing countries have not had the 'privilege of cushioning the adverse domestic effects of market exposure'.[71] In other words, historically industrialized countries experienced development in very different circumstances to those facing developing countries, and certainly not under conditions of 'free trade' and in the absence of industrial policy.[72]

Trade liberalization is just one of a number of industrialization strategies that developing countries might pursue. In recent years there has been some reaction against trade liberalization by many developing countries in the absence of a greater commitment by industrialized countries to winding back tariff protections and other subsidies. It is also apparent that notwithstanding the apparent consensus around trade liberalization and abstinence from active industrial policy, industrialized and developing countries continue to pursue economic policies involving active promotion of innovation and industry.[73] However, the practice and analysis of industrial policy has also become more sophisticated. In relation to encouragement of industrial development, what has been described as the 'new industrial policy' is less focused on tariff protection and 'picking winners', that is, government selecting particular industries which it sees as being more sustainable and a better fit with local labour market conditions and business expertise than others. New industrial policy is more directed through horizontal measures which encourage 'innovation' and competitiveness across particular regions or across an economy rather than being confined to particular sectors.[74]

Much of the debate about the role of industrial policy in both industrialized and developing countries at present is connected to the debate about the appropriate path to economic development. There is evidence to suggest that the strong

---

N Torm, 'The World Bank's "Employing Workers" Index: Findings and Critiques – A Review of Recent Evidence' (2008) 147 International Labour Review 416–32.

[69] P Mattera: Good Jobs First, 'High Road or Low Road? Job Quality in the New Green Economy' (2009).

[70] See, eg, H Pack and K Saggi, 'Is There a Case for Industrial Policy? A Critical Survey' (2006) 21 (2) The World Bank Research Observer 267–97.

[71] J Ruggie, *Taking Embedded Liberalism Global: The Corporate Connection*, New York University School of Law, Institute for International Law and Justice Working Paper, New York 11, quoted in Blackett, above n 66, 100.

[72] Chang, above n 65.

[73] In relation to industrialized countries such as the USA, see F Block, 'Swimming Against the Current: The Rise of the Hidden Developmental State in the United States' (2008) 36 Politics & Society 169. In relation to developing countries, see, eg, Rodrik, above n 23.

[74] See, eg, Aiginger, above n 23.

connection between industrialization strategy, industrial policy, and traditional labour law that was apparent in Australia's New Protection policy is also apparent in relation to industrialization strategies pursued by developing countries. As noted earlier, comparative studies of labour market regulation in East Asia and Southern Africa have observed that states will endeavour to shape their industrial relations regulation to fit the industrialization strategy they pursue. For example, in the East Asian context, a number of studies have observed that 'East Asian states have progressed through stages of industrialization, from import-substitution to export-oriented and then to higher-value export oriented; and that industrial relations strategies change accordingly to reflect those different strategies'.[75] For example, Kuravilla notes that export-oriented strategies have often relied on exporting labour-intensive goods where low costs of labour and production are the chief source of competitive advantage.[76] States which have followed a more inward-focused industrialization strategy have been more willing to maintain stronger labour protections.[77] There are many variations within these simplified categories, and it is not possible to conclude simply that export-oriented strategies are more likely to be associated with lower labour standards and downward pressure on labour protections than more inward-looking policies. However, it is apparent that there are connections between industrial policy and labour law settings which are a legitimate subject for inquiry from a LMR perspective.

What is the relevance of these findings to contemporary debates over the idea of labour law? I have argued that the inclusion of industrial policy within an LMR perspective on labour law is important to the legitimacy of the field across time and space. Industrial policy contributes to both the constitution and regulation of labour markets through its impact on the supply and demand of labour, as well as the conditions of those in work. Moreover, as my discussion of industrial policy in Australia at the turn of the 20th century demonstrates, from a normative perspective, industrial policy settings can be very important to economic development, and hence social protection and quality of life. There is often a relation between labour law and industrial policy which cannot be ignored. Moreover, the broad approach, I have argued, is useful for comparing jurisdictions and exploring the intersection between international trade regulation and domestic labour regulation settings.

However, mindful of the concern that the broad idea of labour law should not become too broad, therefore undermining the coherence of the field, it will be worthwhile to conclude with some remarks about what aspects of industrial policy and industrialization strategies should be included within the LMR perspective on labour law. In other words, what topics would be of relevance when examining industrial policy as labour market regulation?

---

[75] See, eg, Cooney et al, above n 29, 6; and Kuruvilla, above n 30, 636–7.
[76] Kuruvilla, above n 75, 637.
[77] Eg India: ibid; see also PV Dutta, 'Trade Protection and Industry Wages in India' (2007) 60(2) Industrial and Labor Relations Review 268.

First, the LMR perspective enables examination of a number of topics which do not necessarily assume the existence of a particular economic system, or variety of capitalism.[78] For example, one might consider the question of public versus private *ownership of capital* as a relevant concern. One possible industrial policy open to nation states is government delivery of goods and services, whether by way of a monopoly or as a competitor with private capital. Given that public sector employment in capitalist economies is often assumed to offer better and more secure employment than many private sector employers, one might at least speculate that a high rate of public ownership of capital would have implications for working conditions across an economy. With respect to private sector employers, it is arguable that different varieties of capitalism exist with implications for labour law and its application in each country context. There has already been extensive consideration of the variation in labour management practices across different national capitalist systems. One approach offers two categories of the latter, the liberal market model and the coordinated market model, with some scholarship suggesting that coordinated market economies have historically been more supportive of cooperative labour market institutions than liberal market systems.[79]

Second, we should include regulation which affects *industrial structure and the stability of industry*. Here, labour law scholars should be interested in policies which are designed to maintain existing structures or facilitate structural adjustment through industry assistance, or which open up new industries by attracting new investment and industry and encouraging innovation. Reacting against the hegemony of trade liberalization strategies and associated downward pressure on labour costs in recent years, there has been an increase in interest from labour regulation scholars in economic development strategies which are consistent with the creation of decent work.[80] Arguably, such a topic is of much interest to workers in developing nations who are employed in the informal economy, with little hope of enjoying the legal minimum working conditions.

Third, regulation which impacts on the geographic *location of industry* within a country would also be of key importance to the LMR perspective. This category would include public procurement with 'local content' requirements along with other policies which encourage industry to move to, or commence in, regions with high unemployment rather than locating in areas with stronger labour demand.[81] It might also address competition between regional governments for investment and

---

[78] P Hall and D Soskice (eds), *Varieties of Capitalism: The Institutional Foundations of Comparative Advantage* (Oxford University Press, 2001); H Gospel and A Pendleton (eds), *Corporate Governance and Labour Management: An International* Comparison (Oxford University Press, 2005); and S Marshall, R Mitchell, and I Ramsay (eds), *Varieties of Capitalism, Corporate Governance and Employees* (Melbourne University Press, 2008).

[79] For a critique of this dual characterization of national capitalist systems, see N Wailes, J Kitay, and RD Lansbury, 'Varieties of Capitalism, Corporate Governance and Employment Relations Under Globalisation', in Marshall, Mitchell, and Ramsay (eds), above n 78.

[80] As evidenced by the formation of the Regulating for Decent Work Network in 2008. The RDW Network held its first conference at the ILO in 2009: <http://www.ilo.org/travail/whatwedo/projects/lang–en/WCMS_122341/index.htm>. See also Fenwick et al, above n 12.

[81] See, eg, McCrudden, above n 67.

industry, and the extent to which states use their high or low labour standards as a bargaining chip in that competition.

Of course, consideration of this subject matter necessarily brings the labour lawyer with a broad LMR perspective into contact with the field of trade regulation, usually regarded as an aspect of economic policy, but also defined by legal regulation. The dominance of trade liberalization as an industrialization strategy, implemented through bilateral and multilateral trade agreements, means that industrialization strategies which depart from the trade liberalization model may come into conflict with free trade rules. Yet the intersection (or conflict) between labour law and trade law is one with which labour lawyers have become increasingly comfortable over the last decade.[82]

In relation to all of these categories, it will be possible to ask questions which can be derived from traditional labour law scholarship. From a normative perspective, including industrial policy within a LMR perspective would not signify an abandonment of interest in the protective function of labour law. One of the rationales for including industrial policy in the study of labour law is that it will provide more information about why traditional labour law – protection of working conditions – is or is not effective. Industrial policy, which can be equated with economic development strategy, will have significant implications for the achievement of decent work for all, and social and economic equality. This approach will enhance empirical scholarship in labour law which takes as its main concern the *impact* of labour law and labour market regulation.

Moreover, it will be possible to inquire as to whether industrial policy is determined by the state, or is conducted through a process which provides workers or representative organizations with a role in determining appropriate strategies. To what extent has Sinzheimer's idea of industrial councils seen the light of day in one context or another?[83] The labour lawyer's interest in legal standards and their content can also be maintained through the study of industrial policies as labour market regulation. Some studies have already sought to examine whether, like the New Protection, states not only set targets for the number of jobs that are to be created by financial assistance to industry, but also set minimum labour standards through public procurement and/or industry assistance contracts.[84]

E. Conclusion

This chapter has argued in favour of a broad, labour market perspective in labour law. Including industrial policy within the scope of labour law would have a number of benefits for both scholarship and policymaking in this field. The LMR

---

[82] See, eg, B Hepple, *Labor Laws and Global Trade* (Hart Publishing, 2005); VA Leary and D Warner (eds), *Social Issues, Globalisation and International Institutions: Labour Rights and the EU, ILO, OECD and WTO* (Martinus Nijhoff, 2006); and Blackett, above n 66.

[83] See R Dukes, 'Constitutionalizing Employment Relations: Sinzheimer, Kahn-Freund, and the Role of Labour Law' (2008) 35 Journal of Law and Society 341, 349.

[84] Howe, above n 67; and Howe and Landau, above n 24.

perspective view reinforces that markets and labour markets are not autonomous and self-generating, by showing the importance of state policy in constituting and regulating those markets. Industrial policy helps to shape labour demand, which is not only important in the constitution of labour markets, but in turn impacts on what sort of labour standards can be achieved. The broader perspective assists in conducting more complete, long-term analysis of regulation which pertains to the person dependent upon their labour for subsistence. It is less prone to crises related to avoidance of traditional labour law and changing work relationships, because the subject matter is not tied to a particular form of work relationship, and allows for analysis of variation in working arrangements by industry. Finally, it facilitates comparative study as findings will foster greater understanding of how different countries at different stages of development, and with different economic systems, have regulated labour.

I suggest that the inclusion of at least some aspects of industrial policy within labour law is essential because not only does it give us a better understanding of how labour markets are constituted and regulated across different jurisdictions, it also helps in understanding why traditional labour laws are effective or ineffective in achieving greater social equality and reducing poverty. This in turn suggests that the broader LMR perspective can also be helpful in a normative sense – for the achievement of socially just working conditions which are accessible to all those who are dependent on their labour for a living.

19

The Third Function of Labour Law: Distributing Labour Market Opportunities among Workers

*Guy Mundlak**

A. Introducing two functions of labour law, and then a third

An 'empty' functional definition of labour law would suggest that labour law includes all the norms that concern the labour market. This is merely a classification principle.[1] When functions are sought in a thicker sense, there is an attempt to identify a telos of labour law.[2] This can be identified at the descriptive level, a way of comprehending a complex reality. Alternatively, it can be identified at the normative level, prescribing a desirable state of affairs. The scholarship on labour law encompasses both levels.

Two functions are commonly attributed to labour law, recognized as a distinct corpus of law.[3] The first is that labour law determines where norms that govern work are written, who their authors are, and by which process they come about.[4] This function stems from the fact that labour law governs all interactions in the labour market and within the firm that concern the activity of work. To a varying extent, distinct ideological and political views adhere to the idea that labour is not a commodity, or, at least, is different from other commodities. If labour law were to be reduced solely to the law of contracts, then nothing distinct would remain of this body of law. Similarly, in a non-market regime, labour law would collapse into administrative law. The importance of labour law as a distinct area of law lies in its

---

* Faculty of Law and the Department of Labour Studies, Tel-Aviv University.

[1] This function merits the critique of functionalism: B Tamanaha, *A General Jurisprudence of Law and Society* (Oxford University Press, 2001).

[2] H Collins, 'Labour Law as a Vocation' (1989) 105 LQR 468; and K Ewing, 'The Death of Labour Law?' (1988) 8(2) OJLS 293.

[3] The three functions were originally presented in G Mundlak, *Fading Corporatism* (Cornell University Press, 2007) ch 8.

[4] Cf S Deakin and F Wilkinson, *The Law of the Labour Market* (Oxford University Press, 2005). Their emphasis on the evolution of law is more than a methodological comment on the study of labour law, but also a substantive point on the importance of the processes in which law comes about and how it affects the agents thereafter.

attempt to draw the lines between public regulation, private ordering, and various forms of collective and autonomous self-regulation. Labour law prescribes a 'division of labour' between different forms of governance and the method of interests' representation in each.

Vertically beneath the first function is the second common function, which holds labour law to be the brokerage of power that is distributed between labour and capital.[5] In economic terms, labour law regulates the distribution of economic rent between labour and capital and therefore influences labour's share in firms' profits. Protection of rights at work has similar, albeit indirect effects on the distribution of economic gains. Otherwise stated, labour law's second function can also be identified in terms of distributing property rights and their derivative – namely, the managerial rights – between labour and capital. The importance of the second function is that scholars and political agents cannot ignore the way labour law has developed against the backdrop of social and economic developments. Traditionally, this function of labour law has been strongly correlated with the oft-repeated claims that workers are 'weak' while employers are 'strong'; the former are 'contract takers', while the latter are 'contract makers'. Labour law seeks to redress this imbalance. Currently, some dispute the strong/weak dichotomy, or the assumption that labour law, by its nature, must protect the workers.[6] Nevertheless, whether or not it has a pro-labour tilt, labour law has an intrinsic distributive function that must take into consideration the economic and social consequences of the labour market's asymmetries.

The two functions of labour law share similar premises in the sense that they do not assume a simple market (or administrative) mechanism for the distribution of power and economic resources. They recognize the unique historical and socio-economic nature of labour–capital relations, market imperfections, and distributive goals. The first function emphasizes process, the second, substance. They complement each other, and leave much leeway for debates – both moral ('who deserves what') and strategic ('how to accommodate the deserving').

This is the basic structure in reliance on which I want to establish the third function. I assume that the characterization of the first two functions can be contested. However, I believe the third function that follows can also be inter-twined into alternative basic propositions regarding the idea of labour law as well.[7]

---

[5] On the notion of labour law as the brokerage of power between labour and capital, see, eg O Kahn-Freund, *Labour and the Law* (Stevens, 1972); KVW Stone, 'The Legacy of Industrial Pluralism: The Tension Between Individual Employment Rights and the new Deal Collective Bargaining System' (1992) 59 U Chi L Rev 575; and O Lobel, 'Four Pillars of Work Law' (2006) 104 Mich LR 1539.

[6] Cf R Mitchell and C Arup, 'Introduction: Labour Law and Labour Market Regulation' in C Arup et al (eds), *Labour Law and Labour Market Regulation* (Federation Press, 2008) 3–20.

[7] Eg some emphasize that labour law functions as a regulatory institution that is intended to correct market failures. Cf A Hyde, 'What Is Labour Law?' in G Davidov and B Langille (eds), *Boundaries and Frontiers of Labour Law: Goals and Means in the Regulation of work* (Hart Publishing, 2006) 37–61. Such an approach may need the so-called 'third function' to accept that information asymmetries are not limited to the asymmetry between workers and employers, but there are also asymmetries between the workers themselves; that workers and employers may reach agreements that have a negative externality on other workers that they do not capture and need to bear, unless labour law intervenes and imposes the cost; that monopoly power can increase when agreements are reached by a vast

Like the second function, the third seeks to describe and prescribe the substance of labour law. However, I propose that labour law seeks not only to influence the distribution of rents, power, rights, resources, and economic risks among labour and capital, *but also between workers* (broadly defined to include all people of employment age, hence those who can work). The third function is therefore horizontally aligned with the second, and both are distinct from the first, in that they observe substance and simultaneously interact with process.

By implication, recognizing the third function means downgrading the centrality of the labour–capital cleavage in accounting for the social and economic organization of society and in intra-firm interactions. It throws light on another dimension that can explain preferences and norms and be used to draw attention to possible normative tradeoffs. The relevance of the third function is particularly easy to demonstrate when there is a blunt distinction (for example, two-tiered collective bargaining) or competition (for example, affirmative action in promotions) between different groups of workers. However, I argue that the third function is much more pervasively relevant in the governance of work, and diverse appearances of this cleavage can be identified throughout the whole panoply of labour market institutions.

The following discussion is organized in two parts. Part B links the third function with the second and justifies the need to treat the intra-labour cleavages as a distinct distributive axis, rather than a by-product of the more familiar labour-capital axis. Part C links the third function of labour law with the first, and discusses the effects of the third function on structures of interests' representation and processes for authoring the norms that govern the labour market.

B. The problem of intra-labour distribution

The common narrative of labour law is that labour and capital are not on equal grounds and therefore law should even the playing field. In this narrative, labour and capital are held to be like two 'black boxes', monolithic in their interests, and the objective is centred on how to bring them on par. However, the literature in political economy emphasizes the divergence of interests *within* each side of the labour–capital cleavage. This may imply one of two things. First, it can be argued that if both sides are not monolithic, it is necessary to equally unpack each of them. Second, it can be argued that despite the divergence, tensions within labour or capital are merely instrumental to the fundamental cleavage between the two. The proposed ('third') function rejects both of these claims. It holds that the labour side must be treated differently from the capital side, and that conflicts within labour's side must be discussed separately from the labour-capital conflict.

---

majority of the employers *and* a trade union that represents most workers, hence leaving no resort to the few who are excluded from coverage (this last example was elaborated on in *Fading Corporatism*, above n 3, ch 7).

A similar adaptation can be made when looking at labour law from the point of view of human rights, dignity, and liberty.

1. Claus Offe's political economy of the employment relationship

Several accounts have tried to grasp the nature of the labour market. Claus Offe's analysis is a particularly useful and important example of such attempts.[8] According to Offe, the labour market differs from other commodity markets, and he lays emphasis on the fact that the strategies available to supply (labour) and demand (capital) comprise the difference.[9] These differences aid in highlighting the labour–capital cleavage (and, hence, the second function described above). Capital is more liquid, and the owners of capital can better control the demand side. The labour side cannot diversify its portfolio, is constrained by the need for adequate subsistence, and cannot easily control the number of 'suppliers', which is governed by demography. In this general description, Offe highlights the nature of labour's strategies, individual and collective alike, for affecting the price. These strategies include attempts at the exclusion of some from the labour market, demarcating occupations to a limited group of providers, and individual attempts at enhancing one's chances in the labour market vis-à-vis those of others.[10]

Consequently, a shortage on the supply side can be addressed by the state and capital by means of training, geographical relocation, raising prices for consumers, and other strategies that can be individually deployed or collectively coordinated. On the other hand, a shortage in demand requires either coordinated political pressure on the state to invest in job creation, or the expedient of 'bumping' some workers from the labour market. Aside from individual strategies (for example, individuals who seek better education to improve their competitive position in the market), structural changes require collective or coordinated action. This can take the form of trade union representation, but also of political action and coordination by professional guilds. In Offe's analysis of the difference between collective action on labour's and capital's respective sides, this point is further developed.[11] The nature of labour and its attachment to the person marks collective action as political by nature. Moreover, coordinated policies can be distinguished according to the extent to which they pool the workforce together or split it into competing groups.

Offe provides an institutional analysis that goes beyond the caricature of 'labour is weak and capital is strong'. It indicates that labour's strategies are intrinsically collective and political, and they entail competition among workers, rather than merely between labour and capital. To the extent that labour is 'weak', it is because the strategies available to labour are limited compared to those which are available to capital (and not because individuals or groups on labour's side are always devoid of power).

Admittedly, capital's side can also rely on collective strategies and the potential for conflicts within capital's camp also exists. However, the differences between

---

[8] C Offe, *Disorganized Capitalism: Contemporary Transformations of Work and Politics* (MIT Press, 1985).
[9] Ibid 10–51.
[10] Ibid 30–51.
[11] Ibid, 'Two Logics of Collective Action' (170–220).

capital and labour remain. They are partially a matter of degree, because the above-mentioned strategies of capital provide a greater power of exit to individual employers. Furthermore, some of the collective strategies of capital are not in the domain of labour law but in the field of antitrust and commerce. A cartel of large companies that is intended to exclude smaller rival producers may have implications on labour, although it is situated in the commercial sphere. The regulation of commercial activity by antitrust law (as well as trade law) is governed by different considerations than the exclusion of workers by other workers. The common exemption of labour relations from antitrust legislation is symptomatic of the way in which labour law demarcates its own territory, distinct from the general commercial sphere.[12] Nevertheless, occasional rivalry between employers remain in the field of labour law.[13] From a socio-historical perspective, the problems associated with intra-capital rivalry are less common from those of intra-labour confrontation, and therefore do not animate the field to the same extent.

2. Collective strategies – inclusion and exclusion

The factional nature of labour's strategy is further developed in writings that describe the tendency towards an uneven distribution of labour market privileges among groups of workers and the unemployed. The literature on trade unions highlights the fact that trade unions' strategy is shaped by multiple objectives: some are ideological, others instrumental, such as increasing membership and members' contributions and support.[14] For example, with regard to wage bargaining, higher wage premiums may increase the employer's hostility towards association and also result in layoffs to adjust the demand to the wage level imposed by the trade union.[15] The larger the membership and the stronger the trade union, the greater is the likelihood of such a response on the employer's side. There are various strategies that can ameliorate this problem. In brief, a trade union may level down its demanded wage premium, albeit at the risk of losing the support of incumbent membership. Conversely, it may uphold its wage demands as long as it continues to enjoy the membership's support, even when some members are laid off. The trade union may also concede to a tradeoff whereby higher wages will be offset by increasing peripheral contracting or two-tiered (second-generation) bargaining.[16]

---

[12] A Cox,' Labour and Antitrust Laws – A Preliminary Analysis' (1955) 104 U Penn L Rev 252.

[13] F Traxler, 'Business Associations and Labor Unions in Comparison: Theoretical Perspectives and Empirical Findings on Social Class, Collective Action and Associational Organizability' (1993) 44(4) British Journal of Sociology 673.

[14] A Booth, *Economics of Trade Unions* (Cambridge University Press 1995) ch 4; A Clark and A Oswald, 'Trade Union Utility Functions' (1993) 32(3) Industrial Relations 391–411; J Pencavel, *Labour Markets Under Trade Unionism: Employment, Wages and Hours* (Basil Blackwell, 1991); and R Freeman and J Medoff, *What Do Unions Do?* (Basic Books, 1984).

[15] D Belman and PB Voos, 'Union Wages and Union Decline: Evidence from the Construction Industry' (2006) 60(1) Indus & Lab Rel Rev 67–87; and BT Hirsch and EJ Schumacher, 'Private Sector Union Density and Wage Premium: Past, Present and Future?' (2001) 22(3) Journal of Labour Research 487–518.

[16] *Economics of Trade Unions*, above n 14, ch 5.

Each of these strategies has different consequences for the distribution of benefits within the labour side. Theoretically, the employer can be agnostic to the three options, as all of them may result in a similar package for the membership as a whole, although in some strategies the gains and losses will be spread over a large group, whereas in others the losses will target a small group for the benefit of the others.

To further complicate the effects of collective action, there are considerable differences in trade union strategies, contingent on the political economy of the specific industrial relations system. Corporatist structures ensure more encompassing bargaining domains, and therefore accommodate trade union attempts at distributing goods for a larger group of workers. By contrast, pluralist structures direct bargaining to the enterprise level, exacerbating the distinction between those who benefit from the union wage premium and those who don't.[17] Legal recognition and encouragement of sector- and national-level bargaining therefore accommodates different distributive patterns (which are mediated by different trade union strategies) than those that prevail in countries where law and norms provide only for enterprise bargaining and smaller domains (or bargaining units).

3. Endogenizing the choice of legal arrangements

The importance of the legal background should not be understated. However, the legal norm must be endogenized as well. Law not only constitutes the available distributive strategies that are open to the trade unions, but is also an outcome of different interactions in the electorate body and of various interest groups that influence the writing of the legal norm. Studies of political strategies for impacting resources and employment policy similarly indicate that labour does not necessarily favour comprehensive inclusion. While it might be assumed that trade unions and left-wing political parties would always endorse egalitarian policies in the area of labour and social welfare, it has been found that such is not always the case.[18] The strategies chosen by political agents are dependent on their electorate. A greater degree of homogeneity among the workforce and universal benefits elicit stronger support for inclusive policies. By contrast, greater stratification between primary and secondary labour markets or other groups within the working population (for example, on the basis of ethnic differences), and the prevalence of targeted and selective benefits, may elicit political patterns that strengthen the resources available to some over others.[19]

---

[17] For a comparison of the corporatist/pluralist institutions and their effects on insiders and outsiders, see C Teulings and J Hartog, *Corporatism or Competition?* (Cambridge University Press, 1998).

[18] D Rueda, *Social Democracy Inside Out: Partisanship & Labour Market Policy in Industrialized Democracies* (Oxford University Press, 2009).

[19] G Lester, 'Can Joe the Plumber Support Redistribution? Law, Social Preferences, and Sustainable Policy Design' (2011) 64 Texas L Rev (forthcoming).

4. Unpacking labour – demographic cleavages in the labour market

Collective strategies are therefore affected by and concomitantly affect labour market and legal institutions, and consequently affect the distribution of resources among workers and between workers and the unemployed. These processes can be observed with reference not only to the state and the social partners, but also to other groups. For example, with regard to labour market stratification, there are supply-side theories that emphasize that stratification is the result not only of the demand side's preferences, but also of the supply side's strategies. This observation is particularly visible in processes of discrimination whereby one group of workers has incentives to improve their lot by excluding others.[20] Some forms of exclusion are informal (exclusionary networking in recruitment, preferences for hiring 'people like me', and the like). At other times more formal means are used: negotiating hiring criteria or a list of necessary qualifications in collective agreements, upholding employment policies with disparate impact, advancing the cause of some discriminated groups over others (for example, preferences for eliminating the glass ceiling over the sticky floors), imposing and contesting exclusive rights (for example, in affirmative action programs), accepting some groups as worthy of anti-discrimination policies while denying recognition to others, and the like. In all of these examples, the motivations for exclusionary practices are not only those of employers, but also those of the workers themselves.

Problems of exclusion within labour's side seem to pervade the whole gamut of labour market institutions. Selective or categorical recognition in labour and welfare law usually has the effect of unevenly distributing benefits. Similarly, equal application of labour norms, without taking into consideration intrinsic differences, has an uneven impact.[21] For example, differences in pay between hourly and salaried workers can be used to subtly differentiate in wages between groups. At the same time, seemingly universal minimum wage arrangements can disregard the disparate conditions of those who are paid on the basis of the time worked and those who are compensated for performance. When assessing the political negotiations that lead to such arrangements and the way individuals and collective agents draw on such arrangements, it is clear that tendencies toward segmentation are pervasive.

To summarize thus far, the distribution of goods, power and resources among workers, broadly defined, appears in many contexts. It sheds light on a host of labour market institutions over which labour scholars and practitioners are debating. Among those that were mentioned, or hinted at, thus far are minimum standards (such as work-time arrangements and minimum wage), occupational closure, provisions for the unemployed, the representativeness of trade unions, two-tiered collective agreements, equal opportunities and affirmative action, and transnational distribution of employment opportunities. But this list, expansive as it is, does not exhaust the dilemmas of distribution. Arguably, most, if not all,

---

[20] E Bonacich, 'A Theory of Antagonism: A Split Labour Market' (1972) 37 Am Soc Rev 547–59.
[21] This argument expands on Mark Freedland's discussion of false duality and false unity, in M Freedland, *The Personal Employment Contract* (Oxford University Press, 2003).

labour market institutions give rise to such dilemmas. Offe's analysis suggests that such dilemmas are intrinsic to interactions in the labour market, and are the result of its particular nature.

5. Why a distinct function?

Nevertheless, it can be argued that these dilemmas are merely a by-product of the dominant cleavage between capital and labour, and therefore do not merit recognition as a separate function of labour law. If labour law included only the free-market regime, or conversely only an administrative regime, the proposed function of labour law would seem to be of diminished importance. This clearly does not imply that a wholly free market or administrative systems of governance are better options or that they produce a fairer distribution of resources (or that such systems can actually exist). However, it is the emergence of labour market institutions that seek to regulate the distribution of rents, power and resources, which creates the leeway for measures that protect some rather than others. Each protective measure should be scrutinized with regard to the question 'who does it protect and who does it neglect?' Because workers are intrinsically similar and at the same time necessarily different, each institution covers some and leaves out others. Because labour market institutions are the outcome of various forms of bargaining – economic or political – groups of workers will endorse those arrangements that best advance their cause. Because labour market institutions are always somehow category-based, they include some and leave out others. The category might be 'incumbent workers in the firm', 'workers in the state', 'workers with particular training and education', 'women/men', 'domestic or migrant', and 'parent/single'. Yet even universal institutions usually fall short of their intended span of protection. Universal rights that are extended to the entire labour market by extension orders may still be denied to migrant workers, or to workers who labour abroad. Collective bargaining no longer covers the whole span of the labour market, which has become globalized. Global rights, such as the prohibition of child labour, do not affect all families and children evenly, because not all families and children are similarly situated. The partial coverage is therefore intrinsic to the operations of all labour market institutions. Consequently, the distribution of goods among categories of workers is an intrinsic function of labour law.

According to these assumptions, it is neither possible nor desirable to collapse the third function (distribution of rents, power and resources among workers) into the second (distribution between labour and capital). There is no reason to assume a priori that capital insists on one category or institution at the expense of another. Capital can adjust its demand on the basis of the given minimum wage, while maintaining its level of profit. Otherwise stated, capital can react with different strategies that constitute its indifference curve. For example, in a stylized model, capital can be indifferent to an across-the-board wage cut and a second-tier collective agreement, and even to layoffs to avoid a wage cut altogether. Capital sticks to the simple utility function of expanding its shareholders' value (or household income for a small employer). How the labour costs are divided may be of only secondary importance.

Admittedly, the stylized model ignores long-term and structural preferences. For example, two-tiered bargaining is associated with a fall in stock prices, while an across-the-border reduction of wages may signal managerial strength.[22] On occasion, capital can gain from playing groups of workers against each other. For example, playing the supporters of one trade union against those of the others, or deploying strategies of 'divide and conquer', can help an employer get rid of all trade unions.[23] Supporting the closure of one group at the expense of another can aid in achieving a stronger degree of worker commitment (in gratitude for the employer's aid or for fear of having the employer switch its support). Yet these examples indicate that employers' strategies can emerge from the distribution within the labour side. It is therefore wrong to assume that the labour–capital cleavage is lexically prior to the labour–labour cleavage.

To generalize, the labour–capital cleavage is focused mostly on the distribution of economic rents and determining labour's share. In this, there are two forces in play – increasing the profit (expanding the pie) and distributing the profit (slicing the pie). The interaction between the two reflects a duality in the relationship of labour and capital, whereby they have a joint interest in maximizing the profit and at the same time an enduring conflict over its distribution.[24] The third function of labour law indicates that within labour's side there is a joint interest in maximizing labour's profit, but at the same time an enduring conflict between workers (and job-seekers) with regard to its distribution. Labour's side is therefore swayed by multiple interests and forces that can either pull workers together or break them apart.

6. The relationship between the second and third functions of labour law

The second and third functions are not lexically ordered. For example, legal arrangements that limit the employment of migrant workers may be considered first and foremost as a means of limiting capital in its choice of workers, infringing on its managerial prerogative, and denying arrangements that make low wages possible (de jure or de facto). At the same time, such limitations are often supported by trade unions and political representatives of labour, because they are concerned with the undercutting effect of migrant workers.[25] Similarly, employers may hold different views on policies that extend working age and delay retirement. However, the major arguments highlighting the vices and virtues of such policies are

---

[22] S Thomas and M Kleiner, 'The Effects of Two Tier Collective Bargaining Agreements on Shareholders' Equity' (1992) 45(2) Indus & Lab Rel Rev 339.

[23] J Rogers, 'Divide and Conquer: Further Reflections on the Distinctive Character of American Labour Laws' [1990] Wis L Rev 57–9.

[24] R Freeman and E Lazear, 'Economic Analysis of Works Councils' in J Rogers and W Streeck (eds), *Works Councils: Consultation, Representation and Cooperation in Industrial Relations* (Chicago University Press, 1995) 27–52.

[25] J Watts, *Immigration Policy and the Challenge of Globalization: Unions and Employers in Unlikely Alliance* (Cornell University Press, 2002); and R Penninx and J Roosblad (eds), *Trade Unions, Immigration, and Immigrants in Europe, 1960–1993: A Comparative Study of the Attitudes and Actions of Trade Unions in Seven West European Countries* (Berghahn Books, 2000).

UNIVERSITY OF WINCHESTER
LIBRARY

concerned with distribution within labour's side: stabilizing pension schemes (particularly with regard to pay-as-you-go pensions), 'vacating' the labour market of those who have already received an opportunity in favour of those who seek to enter a crowded market, or allowing older workers to continue their work in light of longer life expectancy and effective years of work.[26]

As long as labour law is explained by reference to the relationship between labour and capital, only some aspects of labour law's problematics are highlighted. It is therefore essential to recognize the third function of labour law. In speculative fashion, I would like to suggest that the third function has often been concealed by labour's side. Recognizing the distributive impact of labour law within labour's side has often been left to free-market advocates. For example, staunch critics of minimum wage tend to highlight the potential of minimum wage arrangements for sending some workers into unemployment.[27] Critics of antidiscrimination law argue that oftentimes such legislation only causes more damage to the group of workers it seeks to protect.[28] Advocates of trade union democracy on the right wing of the map present their arguments in terms of concern for some workers' freedom of choice and the need to protect them from union coercion.[29] More generally, the simplistic insiders–outsiders argument holds that labour market institutions distort the mechanism of the free market.[30]

Recognizing the third function may risk an unwarranted ideological tilt. To be clear, recognition of the third function does not endorse, a priori, any of these claims. There are sufficient evidence and alternative economic models that doubt the empirical claims of the insiders–outsiders caricature.[31] The assumption that the unfettered market provides the ideal baseline to which the outcomes of labour market institutions should be compared is merely a claim, not a matter of truism. The question of whether such ideal unfettered markets actually exist should be contested. Similarly, there is no intrinsic moral worth that should be attributed to allegedly unfettered markets and the distributive outcomes they produce. The absence of labour market institutions has distributive implications for inter-group rivalry, just as the institutions themselves. The normative implications of the distributive effects within labour's side are far more complicated than simply assuming that labour market institutions should be removed.

---

[26] ECJ, Case C–341/08 *Domnica Petersen v Berufungsausschuss für Zahnärzte für den Bezirk Westfalen-Lippe* (12.1.2010) OJ C 179/4.

[27] This view can be traced back to the model presented by G Stigler, 'The Economics of Minimum Wage Legislation' (1946) 36 American Economic Review 358.

[28] R Epstein, *Forbidden Grounds: The Case Against Employment Discrimination Laws* (Harvard University Press, 1992).

[29] See, eg, the conservative advocacy of union democracy in the UK – C Howell, *Trade Unions and the State: The Construction of Industrial Relations Institutions in Britain, 1890–2000* (Princeton University Press, 2007) ch 5; the claim for extending choices in the Australian labour reform – J Murray, 'Work Choices and the Radical Revision of the Public Realm of Australian Statutory Labour Law' (2006) 35(4) Industrial Law Journal 343; and the rhetoric of free choice in right to work laws in the United States – National Labour Relations Act 14(b), 29 USC 164.

[30] A Lindbeck and D Snower, *The Insider-Outsider Theory of Employment and Unemployment* (MIT Press, 1989).

[31] S Lee and D McCann (eds), *Regulating for Decent Work* (forthcoming 2011).

At the same time, the third function should not be resisted by the advocates of labour market institutions. Empirical claims need to be measured and assessed, not simply dismissed. Recognizing tradeoffs and prices does not suggest in itself that labour market institutions should be removed. Accepting the persistence of the third function accommodates a critical quest for those who pay the price to the benefit of others. It is important to bear in mind that labour's unity is intrinsically a simplification of more complex interests.

C. Who speaks for 'labour'?

Recognizing the third function implies that labour law cannot look merely at the relationship between labour and capital, but must also comprehend the groups and individuals on labour's side as a distinct system of distribution. This affects the first function of labour law, which determines who authors labour law, the process by which it is written, and how labour market institutions are developed.

The primacy of the labour–capital cleavage has resulted in a governance scheme that is tailored to address and remedy the imbalance between capital and labour. The ILO, for example, is designed on a tripartite basis. Labour courts in many countries place representatives of labour and capital alongside the professional judge. States accord a distinct status of partnership to labour and capital's representatives. Social partners are formally acknowledged by the European Union. These structures of representation rarely provide for the institutionalization of conflict *within* labour's side. Recognizing the proposed third function of labour law as horizontally equal to the second function requires us to take a step backward and ask how the coexistence of the two functions should affect structures of interests' representation in the labour market's governance scheme.

The recognition of the third function of labour law should be considered as a diachronic evolution of the field. The integration of labour's voice into the system of governance was the outcome of the industrial revolution and accompanied the development of industrial relations as a field of theory and practice. Acknowledgment of the labour–capital cleavage resulted in a unitary voice that was accorded to labour by means of collective bargaining and political representation through labour and social-democratic parties. The unitary representation of labour continued well into the 20th century with the evolution of labour law and the welfare state. But towards the end of that century, various factors highlighted the weakness of labour's unitary voice.

Some factors were a result of changes in the nature of the labour market. Globalization highlighted the problem of distributing work across borders, with much resentment on labour's side at the disappearance of jobs to other countries where lower labour costs prevailed.[32] Technological changes also had an effect on the perception of jobs' distribution. A greater cleavage was riven between manual

---

[32] B Langille, 'Labour Law is Not a Commodity' (1998) 19 Indus LJ (RSA) 1002.

blue-collar workers and highly skilled and high-tech workers.[33] Moreover, it was argued that technology will gradually substitute the need for manual work, leading to a jobless future.[34] A declining political commitment to full employment, Keynesian measures of state intervention and a growing demand to deregulate labour markets were associated with growing unemployment, with a particular focus on long-term structural unemployment.[35] The entry of women into the labour market as deserving selves, rather than merely as substitutes for male workers in wartime, underscored the recognition of gender differences and similarities that rendered the traditional labouristic model a male-dominated benchmark.[36] The human rights revolution highlighted the fact that various social institutions enjoyed a stability that came at the price of excluding all who did not conform to the institutional benchmark (women, minorities, the old, migrants, the disabled, to name just a few).[37] A phenomenal growth in critical academic studies that mainstreamed discourses of colonialism, patriarchy, ageism, ableism, and intersectionality between the various groups, further accentuated the false unity of many social and political institutions, including labour's unitary voice.[38]

The diachronic evolution described here is not meant to suggest that labour used to de facto act in concert against capital. In part, labour was more successful in the past at asserting a unitary and universal claim. This success has been undermined by structural changes such as globalization, whereby labour markets no longer overlap the scope and coverage of governance schemes. In part, labour was successful in the past in concealing the fact that some paid the price of arrangements that were advocated by what only appeared to be a unitary voice. This was made possible by simplified structures of interests' representation that clustered labour as a unitary agent, despite its intrinsic fragmentation.

A growingly critical look at labour's unitary appearance and the decline of universal rights, benefits, and collective arrangements leads to the development of the third function of labour law as an equal to the second. This turn of events in the critical study of labour market institutions should also be reflected in the institutions themselves. However, institutions are known to be sticky and tend to adapt very slowly to changing circumstances. This is partially because the traditional partners, which enjoyed the myth of a unitary voice and the regulatory power that was associated with the recognition of *the* 'workers' voice', are reluctant to give access to multiple voices. At the same time, new voices are fighting the hegemonic position of the old unitary voice and are blind to its achievements.[39] The state

---

[33] S Zuboff, *In the Age of the Smart Machine* (Basic Books, 1984).

[34] S Aronowitz and W Difazio, *The Jobless Future. Sci-Tech and the Dogma of Work* (University of Minnesota Press, 1994).

[35] G Standing, *Global Labour Flexibility* (Macmillan Press, 1999).

[36] J Rubery, 'Equal Opportunities and Employment Policy' in P Auer (ed), *Changing Labour Markets in Europe* (ILO, 2001) 116–83.

[37] K Kolben, 'Labour Rights as Human Rights?' (2010) 50 Va J Int'l L 449–84.

[38] Cf J Conaghan, M Fischl, and K Klare (eds), *Labour Law in an Era of Globalization* (Oxford University Press, 2001).

[39] Cf G Mundlak, 'Addressing the Legitimacy Gap in the Israeli Corporatist Revival' (2009) 47(4) British J of Industrial Relations 765–87.

and employers are similarly reluctant to admit multiple voices. As long as labour's voice was played out by a limited number of institutions, bargaining may have been difficult, but it was easier to identify joint interests and reach compromises. The disparity of voices and their conflicting goals and aims within the labour camp make any kind of an institutionalized compromise more difficult to legitimize and stabilize. A possible response is to adhere to the old tradition of representation, or to simply give up on deliberative solutions and opt for market solutions that respond to individual preferences rather than collective goals.

The discrepancy between the unitary system of representation and the growingly disparate interests within the labour camp can be identified in many contexts. At the international level, the tripartite nature of the ILO is being questioned.[40] The voice of disadvantaged workers surfaces in the debates over the legitimacy of the WTO as a venue for indirectly governing labour and social matters.[41] The growingly disparate conditions of the workforce in the European Union is a matter that raises concerns regarding the appropriate relationship between the individual states and the union's objectives, with controversies surrounding who gains and who loses from protective legislation on the one hand and the free movement of services and workers on the other hand.[42]

At the state level, similar concerns are identifiable. States with a corporatist heritage face pressures to give voice to competing trade unions and non-labour movements that assert the interests of factions. At the regional level there is a drive to provide effective representation to the unemployed and to recipients of welfare benefits, as it is no longer assumed that the traditional social partners and labour parties provide adequate representation to the interests of marginalized groups.

The ongoing contestation of the old forms of representation touches on many aspects of labour law.[43] These are particularly acute with regard to collective labour law. For example, to what extent should collective agreements be immune to contestation by groups of workers who are not satisfied with the labour–capital compromise? To what extent should methods of exclusive representation be compromised to allow rival trade unions and non-union forms of representation to voice the interests of dissenters? Should alternative means of collective representation be recognized, for example – by means of class action law suits?

---

[40] S Cooney, 'Testing Times for the ILO: Institutional Reform for the New International Political Economy' (1999) 20 Comp Lab L & Pol'y J 365; and G Nolte and S Lagodinsky, 'The Role of Non-Governmental Organizations in the International Labour Organization' in E Benvenisti and G Nolte (eds), *The Welfare State, Globalization, and International Law* (Springer-Verlag Berlin, Heidelberg, 2004) 321, 336.

[41] S Charnovitz, 'Opening the WTO to Nongovernmental Interests' (2000–01) 24 Fordham Int'l LJ 173.

[42] A Reale, 'Representation of Interests, Participatory Democracy and Lawmaking in the European Union: Which Role and Which Rules for the Social Partners?' (2003) Jean Monnet Working Paper No 15/03 20–21 <http://centers.law.nyu.edu/jeanmonnet/papers/03/031501.html>; and S Smismans, 'The European Social Dialogue, Between Constitutional and Labour Law' (2007) 32 Eur L Rev 341, 358; F Milman-Sivan, 'Representativity, Civil Society, and the EU Social Dialogue: Lessons from the International Labour Organization' (2009) 16(1) Ind J Global Legal Studies 311–37.

[43] Fading Corporatism, above n 3, ch 8.

D. Conclusion – 'Proletarier aller Länder, vereinigt euch!'[44]

Well, the idea that all workers of the world (should) unite made sense, but it is miles apart from the current reality of an ever-growing fragmentation of the workforce. If the workers of the world could *all* unite, it may be assumed that there is a mechanism, preferably a democratic one, which could justly bring the interests of all workers into coalescence and justly distribute the goods, resources and power among them. Short of universal association, however, the heterogeneous interests of labour and recognition of the political nature of labour's association inevitably require a more complex system of interests' representation. 'Workers of the (single) land unite', 'workers covered by collective agreements unite', 'full-time workers unite', 'workers of a multinational unite' – these are all options that demarcate borders of inclusion and exclusion. It could not be clearer that any belief that prevailed in the past regarding common interests of solidarity was somewhat a mirage.

The ever-growing heterogeneity of interests makes it necessary to admit that the idea that the labour–capital cleavage is the single most important institution that animates the development of labour market institutions can no longer be adhered to. Instead of concealing other cleavages, it is important to admit them and to make labour law accountable to the distributive impact it bears.

If workers of the world could unite and their voice could be cartelized, then labour's power as a group might increase. Fragmentation of voice and internal disputes over the distribution of resources and power potentially weaken labour's united front and its contestation of shareholders' profits and the managerial prerogative. As noted, there are three considerations that operate at the same time – increasing the joint gain, distributing the gain between capital and labour, and distributing labour's share among the workers. At the descriptive level, labour law's third function is to determine the latter. At the normative level, it must strike a balance between the three axes. A welfarist argument would seek to toggle labour market institutions to increase the joint gain. Other normative views might demonstrate a preference for one type of distribution over another (benefit the least well-off, benefit those who contribute most, benefit all to the level that accommodates self-development and progressive realization of basic human capacities). I doubt that labour law should be identified by any single choice on these matters. I do argue, however, that all labour law systems, at both the descriptive and the normative level, must at present identify and address the tradeoffs between these questions. Consequently, the question labour scholars and practitioners often ask – who gains from any particular arrangement, employers or workers? – must be complemented by its counterpart – which workers gain and which lose? Sacrificing the interests of some workers for the benefit of 'labour' as a group is but one option, but clearly not the only one, nor necessarily the most redeeming, even if recognizing the gains and losses of some groups risks the size of the aggregate gain, or labour's gain.

---

[44] Workers of all lands unite – as inscribed on Karl Marx's tombstone.

20

Beyond Collective Bargaining: Modern Unions as Agents of Social Solidarity

*Gillian Lester**

Trade unions in both North America and Europe have long embraced – at least rhetorically, but often manifestly – participation in the civic and political spheres as part of their mission. This chapter, as part of this collection's exploration of the 'idea of labor law,' revisits the fundamental question of whether and how trade unions ought to participate in the civic sphere. Should unions focus on bread-and-butter private bargaining concerns and eschew broader civic engagement? Function as an interest group that lobbies for legislation and spending favorable to the interests of organized labor? Serve as agents for working people as a whole, pressing for policies that redistribute opportunities and resources from capital to labor or from the well-off to less well-off? Or, perhaps, unions ought to be agents of some broader vision of social integration.

Unions' role can and does change over time as social conditions evolve. With union density in decline, and growing alienation of the mass citizenry from the idea and value of organized labor, unions are seeking paths to revitalization. One way they might be able to do this, I argue, is to galvanize public sentiment around an issue of universal concern to contemporary workers: the need for a strong social safety net. The changed nature of jobs, increased volatility of family income, and high levels of unemployment have heightened workers' interest in policies designed to mitigate social risks. Rather than focusing exclusively on job security and high wages, workers are turning their sights to policies designed to help bridge gaps when employment is no longer sufficient for economic security: public health insurance, sick leave, unemployment protection, retirement security, training, work–family policies.

Mobilization of mass preferences to strengthen social legislation requires solidarity, and yet the mechanisms for inculcating such solidarity can remain elusive. Unions, for their part, possess the technology of mobilization, but have often (and

* Associate Dean and Professor of Law, Berkeley Law School. The author wishes to thank Guy Davidov and Brian Langille for organizing the conference that led to this volume, as well as conference participants, Jack Jackson and Matthew Dimick for comments and assistance with earlier drafts of this chapter.

not unreasonably) focused their resources on grassroots organizing and local bargaining strategies. If unions are to speak to the concerns and values of the contemporary workforce, a dialogue of social and distributive justice may resonate more broadly than a strict focus on organizing and bargaining tactics.

Advocacy in the realm of social legislation has not been ignored by organized labor. At various points in history, unions have played a vital role in advancing universal social policies. Part A explores the role of unions in the civic sphere during the past century, with particular attention to the United States. In recent years, union leadership in the civic arena has been less visible and unions have come to be seen by many, rightly or wrongly, as pursuing their own 'special interests.' Part B examines organizing strategies that have succeeded as unions have fought to stem declining density. What they have in common is their efforts to relocate the locus of solidarity formation. The first relocates the locus of solidarity formation from class to other aspects of identity. The second leverages statutory and social welfare rights in the service of organizing. I bring the insights from each of these developments to bear in the final part of the chapter, where I argue that unions may benefit from taking leadership in generating broader social solidarity, in particular by pursuing improvements in the American social safety net.

A. Unions and the civic sphere

Scholars who have analyzed the core function of unions commonly acknowledge that unions can, do, and should function at least partly in the political sphere. Richard Hyman's conceptualization of a 'triple tension' at the heart of union identity and purpose is illuminating.[1] All unions are market intermediaries, concerned with regulating the wage–labor relationship (the market function); they are also inescapably agents of class as organizations whose collective identity divides them from employers (the class function); and they also by necessity operate within a social framework that they may aspire to change but that constrains their current choices (the society function).[2] Trade unions, in essence, are a complex amalgam of multiple objectives and potentialities, but political action and engagement is clearly one of them. The balance among these factors varies among nations and unions, with legal, historical, social, and economic forces influencing the particularities of any given movement.

No singular normative claim informs the question of union engagement in the civic sphere. Catholic social doctrine has long emphasized the moral imperative of unions to advance the interests of workers as a class and social welfare broadly conceived.[3] Secular communitarian morality, rather than religious ethic, animated

---

[1] R Hyman, *Understanding European Trade Unionism: Between Market, Class and Society* (Sage, 2001) 4.
[2] Ibid 3–4.
[3] Ibid 3. See also Catholic Scholars for Social Justice, 'Catholic Social Doctrine and Worker Justice: A Call to Common Good' <http://www.catholicscholarsforworkerjustice.org> (CSWS Foundational Statement), ('in Catholic teaching . . . all organizations exist not only for themselves, but also to serve the common good . . . Unions have an essential role to play in education, in public matters, and in the political arena').

British social theorists Beatrice and Sidney Webb's argument that trade unions should in significant part serve as a vehicle for workers' participation in the political sphere to secure legal enactment of general work regulations.[4] A defense from public choice theory is that in a polity governed significantly through the rival bidding of interest groups, unions must claim a place at the table alongside corporations and wealthy individuals in order to give voice to those who would otherwise not be heard.[5] Another view focuses less on unions' direct engagement in political and civic activities than on unions' role as 'schools for democracy' that facilitate the development of civic virtues among the citizenry.[6]

In Europe, unions have played, and continue to play, a significant role in the civic sphere. In the post-war years, the desire to mobilize European economies, provide soldiers with opportunities, and ward off the threat of socialist revolution gave rise to the widespread acceptance of collective bargaining and, in many European social democracies, the ascendance of unions to the role of a quasi-public authority.[7] The 'golden age of capitalism' was characterized by sustained union involvement in the development of national regulation and standardization of the employment relationship.[8] This collaboration between unions and national governments was denoted as 'social partnership.'[9] Social partnership focused in part on collective bargaining and features of the broader economic environment that would be favorable to bargaining success, but also very significantly on more universal social policy objectives. Despite a dénouement over the past quarter century from the heyday of European social partnership,[10] the normative frame of cooperative partnership remains influential in Europe and has established norms that differ in deep and fundamental ways from the experience of North American unions.

In the United States, unions' role in the civic sphere has been complex and at times contradictory. A familiar characterization of American trade unions, particularly when compared to European unions, emphasizes voluntarism (private collective bargaining) and 'business unionism' (a focus on union wages and working conditions).

---

[4] Hyman, above n 1, 2; and B Webb, *The Co-operative Movement in Great Britain* (Swan Sonnenschein & Co, 1891) 225–6.

[5] See, eg, P Levine, 'The Legitimacy of Labor Unions' (2001) 18 Hofstra L Emp L J 527, 554, 560–5.

[6] Ibid 565–7; and TC Kohler, 'Civic Virtue at Work: Unions as Seedbeds of Civic Virtues' (1994–5) 36 BCL Rev 279, 297–302.

[7] W Streeck, 'Labor Unions' in N Smesler and P Baltes (eds), *International Encyclopedia of the Social and Behavioral Sciences* (Elsevier, 2001) 8215; and W Streeck, 'The Sociology of Labor Markets and Trade Unions' in NJ Smelser and R Swedberg (eds), *The Handbook of Economic Sociology* (2nd edn, Princeton University Press, 2005) 273.

[8] Streeck, 'Labor Unions', above n 7, 8216.

[9] Hyman, above n 1, 55.

[10] Ibid 51 (describing the weakening, starting in the late 1980s, of government deference to unions' economic and social policy agenda and 'corporatist' deals of the previous era); and G Taylor and A Mathers, 'Social Partner or Social Movement? European Integration and Trade Union Renewal in Europe' (2002) 27 Lab Stud J 93, 95, 98 (expressing pessimistic view that increasingly, 'an underlying logic of labor market exclusion is legitimated through the language of partnership and dialogue').

This view is perhaps most strongly associated with the founding ideology of the American Federation of Labor (AFL) under the leadership of Samuel Gompers. In its early years at the turn of the 20th century, the AFL took as its central mandate the use of collective bargaining as a means to advance the economic interests of organized workers.[11] It eschewed mobilization around passage of universal workers' compensation, unemployment, and health care legislation, and refrained from political activity except where it would specifically benefit its members or strengthen its bargaining power.[12] Gompers believed, in part, that to do otherwise would run afoul of the liberal and upwardly mobile middle-class aspirations of the American working class.[13] He also believed that it would undermine trade union power to pursue labor regulations that offered a public alternative for regulating the conditions of work.[14] Finally, constitutional invalidation of social legislation that had been championed by unions, as well as police and military violence against unions that engaged in sympathy strikes and other forms of general protest, inhibited the development of forms of union activity conducive to mass solidarity, channeling unions instead towards perfecting contractual bargaining strategies and focusing their public role on political lobbying.[15]

Aside from judicial invalidation of social legislation, the labor laws themselves dampened unions' ability to catalyze social solidarity over matters of broad public concern. Statutory and jurisprudential development of key labor law doctrines de-emphasized or flatly prohibited the use of organizing and strike activity in the service of broadly collectivist goals.[16] The crabbed interpretation of the right to strike has in myriad ways inhibited unions' capacity to mobilize in the service of citizen solidarity: absent a strong showing of immediate self-interest, collective action falls outside the ambit of the National Labor Relations Act's protection for concerted activities, and the NLRA's ban on secondary boycotts has been construed broadly to include 'political' as well as 'economic' boycotts.[17]

---

[11] DC Bok and JT Dunlop, *Labor and the American Community* (Simon & Schuster, 1970) 386.

[12] Ibid.

[13] Ibid 389. See also D Moss, *When All Else Fails: Government as the Ultimate Risk Manager* (Harvard University Press, 2002) 153 (describing Gompers' opposition to compulsory unemployment and health insurance as grounded in the belief that they were antithetical to voluntarism and personal liberty). Note that Gompers' view was not universally shared by American labor leaders of the time. Moss, ibid 177; and C Fisk, '"Still Learning Something of Legislation": The Judiciary in the History of Labor Law' (1994) 19 L & Soc Inq 151, 180–1.

[14] Moss, above n 13, 176.

[15] R Archer, *Why is There no Labor Party in the United States?* (Princeton University Press, 2007) 128–30 (arguing that military and police repression of incipient industry-wide unions delegitimized broad-scale union activity); and WE Forbath, *Law and the Shaping of the American Labor Movement* (Harvard University Press, 1991) 3, 54–8, 95–7 (tracing the role of the late 19th and early 20th century courts, legal doctrine, and state exercise of violence in shaping the American labor movement).

[16] J Gray Pope, 'How American Workers Lost the Right to Strike, and Other Tales' (2004) 103 Mich L Rev 518, 524; and Christopher L Tomlins, *The State and the Unions: Labor Relations, Law, and the Organized Labor Movement in America, 1880–1960* (Cambridge University Press, 1985) 277 (arguing that the Taft-Hartley Act reflected post-war conservative antipathy towards New Deal 'collectivism').

[17] Pope, above n 16, 544–5; and S Kupferberg, 'Political Strikes, Labor Law, and Democratic Rights' (1985) 71 Virg L Rev 685, 688 (tracing the development of the NLRA section 7 right to engage in concerted activity for mutual aid or protection through the specific lens of the status of political strikes).

Notwithstanding these obstacles, unions played a critical role in the advancement of several cornerstones of the American welfare state. As millions of people lost their jobs during the Great Depression, the unwillingness of the AFL to support unemployment legislation seemed out of step with the times.[18] The new Congress of Industrial Organization (CIO) began by the 1930s to organize unskilled and semi-skilled workers, many from disadvantaged and poorer groups, and many of whom were adherents of the progressive-leaning Democratic party.[19] Social policy in the domain of old-age pensions, unemployment insurance, and minimum wage laws garnered support among the working classes and gave organized labor a new awareness of the benefits – or necessity – of appealing to a potentially very large constituency through advocacy of social legislation that spread risks on a broad scale and instituted basic minimum workplace standards.[20] In the aftermath of the Second World War, buoyed by the public's support of Keynesian demand stabilization policies, unions had an accepted role to play in pushing wages upward and spearheading a broad progressive coalition in support of social legislation.[21] Unions' mobilizing efforts eclipsed what could reasonably be considered the narrow interests of organized labor.[22] Federal, state, and local government legislation on minimum wages, overtime, unemployment insurance, old age pensions and medical insurance, disability and injury protection, safety and health laws, and employment discrimination laws all were advanced and defended in significant part by unions.[23]

As much as it is misleading to ignore American unions' history of engagement in the civic sphere, it is also misleading to suggest that American unions were entirely transformed in their mix of objectives after the war, nor even that issues of broad social policy were their dominant priority.[24] Post-war American unions continued to devote considerable time and resources to securing the support of legislators and other government officials for the direct interests of their membership through lobbying, member education, contributions, and endorsements. Despite its support for racial equality and civil rights legislation in the 1960s, organized labor often sought exemptions for unions in order to preserve, for example, the

---

[18] Bok and Dunlop, above n 11, 390.

[19] Ibid.

[20] Ibid 391.

[21] Ibid 391–6. See also MJ Piore, 'Can the American Labor Movement Survive Re-Gomperization?' (1983) Proceedings of the 35th Annual Meeting of the Industrial Relations Research Association 32–3.

[22] Piore, above n 21, 34.

[23] Bok and Dunlop, above n 11, 424; JT Bennett and JE Taylor, 'Labor Unions: Victims of their Political Success?' (2001) 22 J Lab Res 261 (identifying union influence over various forms of American social and workplace legislation); and RB Freeman and JL Medoff, *What Do Unions Do?* (Basic Books, 1984) 206 (empirical study finding that between 1947 and 1982, American unions supported not only 'special interest' legislation, but also general 'social' legislation that benefited lower-income persons and workers in general).

[24] Nor do I intend to suggest that the social legislation unions advanced was always universal in its benefits. For example, the original Social Security Act of 1935 excluded agricultural labor and domestic workers. This exclusion, which was racially neutral in form, in fact excluded most African-American workers from coverage, particularly in the American South. JS Quadagno, 'Welfare Capitalism and The Social Security Act of 1935' (1984) 49 Am Sociol Rev 634.

'seniority system.'[25] Over time, as the civil rights era came into full flower, the progressive coalition that had pressed for legislative gains in the immediate post-war period found itself struggling with internal conflict.[26] Unions' pursuit of broad coalition-building and general social legislation began to recede, and in its place, the 'interest group' facet of unions' public role returned to prominence, hardening contemporary American perceptions of organized labor.[27]

There is a cynical vein in American public opinion that American unions' political engagement has been an instrument of crass self-interest, serving overwhelmingly to advance the interests of their membership to the exclusion and disadvantage of other workers and citizens.[28] The story of American labor's civic engagement is a complicated one, and I do not intend to elide that complexity. But the central observation remains: American labor unions have been vital to passing important pieces of social welfare legislation that have provided protection and support to a broad swath of the populace beyond the borders of any union contract.

B. The crisis of labor and the idea of social solidarity

Over the past quarter century, as labor unions have lost membership and influence on a global scale, a robust field of inquiry has emerged on the causes, consequences, and solutions to unions' decline. Explanations for the decline include increased global competition, the neoliberal turn in politics, demographic change, the rise in informal, part-time, and sub-contracted work, structural change, especially towards service industries, technological change, complacency and corruption of unions, aggressive anti-union tactics, the rise of corporate human resources practices, affluence, and changing social attitudes towards unions.[29] Rather than analyze causal factors in detail, or seek to identify a dominant cause, I am interested in one aspect of the story, related to unions' role in the civic sphere.

As noted, unions are often treated with skepticism by the American public – seen as looking out for their own interests and not responding to the contemporary tastes or needs of working people.[30] This skepticism is not limited to conservatives

---

[25] Paul Frymer, *Black and Blue: African-Americans, the Labor Movement, and the Decline of the Democratic Party* (Princeton University Press, 2008).

[26] Piore, above n 21, 37.

[27] Ibid 37–8.

[28] M Reynolds, 'A Critique of What Do Unions Do?' (1989) 2 Rev Austrian Econ 259, 267 (arguing that even when it appears that unions are advancing general social welfare, they are acting in their own interests, eg, lobbying for public transit redounds to the benefit of bus drivers' unions); and A Thieblot, 'Unions, The Rule of Law, and Political Rent Seeking' (2010) 30 Cato J 23, 38–45 ('Unions are deemed to remain the presumptive spokesman for the working man even while seeking political rents for themselves, and they are excused from the accusations of selfish motivation that routinely are charged to, say, an AT & T or a National Rifle Association') (41).

[29] This is a very large literature and I do not attempt to survey it here. For a good overview of explanations of unions' decline, see GN Chaison and JB Rose, 'The Macrodeterminants of Union Growth and Decline' in George Strauss et al (eds), *The State of the Unions* (Industrial Relations Research Association Press, 1991) 3–45.

[30] See, eg, Kohler, above n 6, 283 (noting that unions do not fare well in the popular mind – even the minds of working people – with Archie-Bunker stereotypes and caricatured stereotypes of corrupt

who have deep ideological disagreement with the concept of unions. Overall public approval of unions had declined since the New Deal era.[31] While the determinants of public opinion are complex, appeals to 'working class status' or 'union solidarity' may no longer resonate with the working public.[32]

One way for unions to restore their vitality is to reclaim and reinvigorate their role as agents of social solidarity. The concept of social solidarity can be elusive.[33] At its most general level, solidarity is 'a form of social bond founded on a feeling of common membership in a group united by some commonality.'[34] Social movements are enabled, in part, by these social bonds because they generate reciprocity grounded partly in kindliness towards others who are part of the same group.[35] Most members of the group can be motivated to contribute even if they will not receive any direct material gain or recognition, provided they perceive similar attitudes in the others.[36] This group identity, in essence, is what enables social movements to overcome problems of collective action that would otherwise thwart their survival.

What levers do unions have to spark *broad* social solidarity as opposed to the solidarity required to succeed in a local organizing drive? In the remainder of this Part, I explore some recent analyses of union renewal. I explore two recent trends: the use of identity-based organizing, and union enforcement of employment law and labor standards as a means to catalyze solidarity. What these two accounts have in common is that they relocate the locus of solidarity formation. These analyses open the way to my ultimate inquiry: the possibilities for *expanding* the locus of solidarity formation.

1. Identity rivals class

There is a growing literature contending that status and cultural affiliation have come to rival – some would say replace – class as a locus of identity.[37]

leaders pursuing self-interested ends). Cf S Rabin-Margalioth, 'The Significance of Worker Attitudes: Individualism as a Cause for Labor's Decline' (1998–9) 16 Hofstra Lab & Emp L J 133, 152–60 (arguing that a general diminution of the social impulse towards collectivization helps explain declining union density in the United States).

[31] P Jarley and S Kuruvilla, 'American Trade Unions and Public Approval: Can Unions Please All of the People All of the Time?' (1994) 15 J Lab Res 97, 100–2.

[32] A Hyde, 'New Institutions for Worker Representation in the United States: Theoretical Issues' (2005–06) 50 NYL Sch L Rev 385, 411. See also Rabin-Margalioth, above n 30, 158 (arguing that unions are no longer perceived as representing the common interests of working people and attributing this to the rise of expressive individualism).

[33] C Barnard, 'Solidarity and the Commission's "Renewed Social Agenda"' in M Ross and Y Borgmann-Prebil (eds), *Promoting Solidarity in the European Union* (Oxford University Press, 2010) 74, 105.

[34] L Mayhew, 'The Differentiation of the Solidary Public' in JC Alexander and P Colomy (eds), *Differentiation Theory: Problems and Prospects* (Columbia University Press, 1990) 298.

[35] O Widegren, 'Social Solidarity and Social Exchange' (1997) 31 Sociol 755, 759, 763.

[36] AE Komter, *Social Solidarity and the Gift* (Cambridge University Press, 2005) 119 (arguing that reciprocal 'gift' exchange, which combines altruistic and self-interested elements, is a central aspect of social solidarity).

[37] M Hechter, 'From Class to Culture' (2004) 110 AJS 412–14; and K Moody, *Workers in a Lean World: Unions in the International Economy* (Verso Books, 1997) 143–7.

Ethnicity, immigration status, race, gender, sexual orientation, religion, environmentalism, and other personal, intimate, and endangered ways of life, rather than trade, industry, or class position within the capitalist social order, increasingly serve as the basis for social networks, friendships, and intimate and family relations.[38] These status-based affiliations, in turn, become the 'axes' around which political mobilization, solidarity, and resistance can take shape.[39]

Scholars have chronicled organizing successes in low-wage industries, often characterized by part-time and contracted work, when mobilization is structured around appeals to gender or ethnic identity rather than exclusively to class.[40] Examples include custodial work, landscaping, care work (especially home health care, elder care, and child care), and low-wage sectors of the construction, clerical work, and meat processing industries.[41] A key element of the campaigns has been the use of 'identity-based' community mobilization in the style of 1960s civil rights activism, using street marches and organizing at neighborhood churches, community centers or other cultural meeting places.[42]

The rise of these alternative social movements as agents of worker mobilization has led some to argue that unions must, in order to adapt and survive, not only use identity-based techniques to organize groups of workers traditionally excluded from unions, but also actively construct coalitions with other progressive social movements.[43] In the campaigns discussed, identity has operated as a non-traditional lever of solidarity, but with traditional objectives – collective bargaining agreements that establish regional patterns.[44] Ironically, the use of identity as a lever of solidarity may impose limitations borne of the very cultural forces that made it work in the first place: fragmentation, localism, and limitations on capacity for catalyzing broad social change. Although on balance most scholars voice enthusiasm for tapping ethnic, community, and cultural identity as organizing tools, some worry that identity movements may fail to sustain strong organizational commitments, as they are vulnerable to shifting self-definitions and shifting alliances that destabilize their core.[45]

---

[38] Hechter, above n 37.

[39] MJ Piore and S Stafford, 'Changing Regimes of Workplace Governance, Shifting Axes of Social Mobilization, and the Challenge to Industrial Relations Theory' (2006) 45 Indus Rel 299, 310–11. See also B Klandermans, 'How Group Identity Helps to Overcome the Dilemma of Collective Action' (2002) 45 Am Behav Scientist 887.

[40] See, generally, R Milkman (ed), *Organizing Immigrants: The Challenge for Unions in Contemporary California* (ILR Press Books, 2000).

[41] K Klare, 'Toward New Strategies for Low-Wage Workers' (1995) 4 BU Pub Int LJ 245, 270–3; and H Wial, 'The Emerging Organizational Structure of Unionism in Low-Wage Services' (1993) 45 Rutg L Rev 671, 693–8.

[42] Klare, above n 41, 271–2; ML Ontiveras, 'A New Course for Labor Unions: Identity-Based Organizing as a Response to Globalization' in J Conaghan et al (eds), *Labor Law in an Era of Globalization: Transformative Practices and Possibilities* (Oxford University Press, 2002) 417.

[43] See, eg, Moody, above n 37, 7275–6; and P Waterman, 'The New Social Unionism: A New Union Model for a New World Order' in R Munck and P Waterman (eds), *Labour Worldwide in the Era of Globalization: Alternative Union Models in the New World Order* (Palgrave, 1998) 247–64, 260–1 (advocating 'social movement unionism').

[44] G Chaison, 'The Changing Role of Unions: A Review Essay' (2006) 27 J Lab Res 424, 426.

[45] Hyde, above n 32, 410–14 (discussing these claims but skeptical that identity-based organizations have unique collective action problems).

Another possibility is that unions are superfluous. Identity can operate as a mechanism of solidarity for organizations that pursue advocacy on behalf of a particular community or identity-based constituency but are not themselves labor unions. Alan Hyde offers examples of campaigns, having varying degrees of success, on behalf of employees of greengrocers, drugstore and supermarket deliverymen, and domestic workers in New York City, in which unions played only a passive or partial role alongside legal advocacy groups, ethnic or immigrant advocacy groups, and public entities such as the offices of elected officials.[46] Here, worker mobilizations occurred because of the efforts of other social movements and in some cases despite of the *lack of* traditional union affiliation or involvement. This brings us back to the core question of the role, if any, that unions can or ought to play as agents of broad social solidarity.

2. Statutory rights and solidarity formation

In addition to collaboration with social movements outside of traditional union structures, another phenomenon is the strategic deployment by unions of *laws* outside of traditional labor law. A familiar analytic claim counterpoises the relevance and success of trade unions against the strength of social legislation and welfare state provision. Individual employment rights and welfare state provision should, in theory, reduce the need for class-based organizations such as trade unions and thereby undermine collective identity around class.[47] American scholars in particular have theorized a tension between statutory rights and collective bargaining.[48]

At the same time, there is a growing number of examples of the *strategic deployment* of employment standards and antidiscrimination laws in the service of organizing. This is distinct from a defense of unions as vital in helping workers to enforce their statutory rights.[49] Karl Klare's description of the successful Justice

[46] A Hyde, 'Who Speaks for the Working Poor? A Preliminary Look at the Emerging Tetralogy of Representation of Low-Wage Service Workers' (2003–04) 13 Cornell J L & Pub Pol'y 599.

[47] Eg, Hechter, above n 37, 429; and P Manow, 'Welfare State Building and Coordinated Capitalism in Japan and Germany' in W Streeck and K Yamamura (eds), *The Origins of Nonliberal Capitalism: Germany and Japan in Comparison* (Cornell Studies in Political Economy, Cornell Press, 2001) 94–120 (giving the example of the German Bismarck offering workers social insurance during the 1880s as a way to sever the ties of workers with socialist leaders).

[48] Eg, S Bacharach, P Bamberger, and WJ Sonnenstuhl, *Mutual Aid and Union Renewal: Cycles of Logics of Action* (Cornell University Press, 2001) 42–3; J Brudney, 'The Changing Workplace: Reflections on Group Action and the Law of the Workplace' (1996) 74 Tex L Rev 1563; C Estlund, 'Rebuilding the Law of the Workplace in an Era of Self-Regulation' (2005) 105 Colum L Rev 319, 329; and KVW Stone, 'The Legacy of Industrial Pluralism: The Tension Between Individual Employment Rights and the New Deal Collective Bargaining System' (1992) 59 U Chi L Rev 575, 593. See, generally, B Sachs, 'Employment Law as Labor Law' (2008) 29 Cardozo L Rev 2685, 2701–06.

[49] T Hardy and J Howe, 'Partners in Enforcement, The New Balance Between Government and Trade Union Enforcement of Employment Standards in Australia' (2009) 22 Australian J Lab L 312–14 (describing the importance of the regulatory role, often overlooked, that Australian unions have played as enforcers of minimum employment standards); and D Weil, 'Individual Agents and Collective Agents: The Role of Old and New Workplace Institutions in the Regulation of Labor Markets' (2001) National Bureau of Economic Research Working Paper No 9565 (Boston).

for Janitors campaign emphasizes the use of statutory rights enforcement as an ancillary organizing strategy.[50] In Klare's view, the litigation was not the most important organizing tool, but by aiding in the enforcement of wage and hour, child labor, safety, immigration, and discrimination laws, the union was able to demonstrate to workers its ability to provide them with concrete benefits.[51] Richard Michael Fischl has similarly argued that statutory law enforcement can be deployed strategically, as a way to generate additional pressures on employers through negative publicity and threatened liability, while simultaneously demonstrating the utility of union representation to the employees in question.[52] Klare and Fischl's arguments stress the instrumental use of statutory enforcement as a demonstration to unorganized workers of the value of the union, ultimately as a means to the end of organizing.[53]

Benjamin Sachs presses the argument a further link up the chain in arguing that employment laws such as discrimination and wage and hour laws have, in significant ways, come to *replace* labor laws as traditional legal channels for organizing.[54] Professor Sachs offers illustrations of non-unionized garment workers who, with the assistance of an immigrant workers' advocacy organization called We Make the Road by Walking (MRBW), successfully campaigned for enforcement of their federal wage and hour rights, and a group of unorganized Mexican immigrant construction workers who, with some assistance from organizers for the Carpenters' Union, mobilized around the enforcement of their federal statutory rights against discrimination.[55]

Professor Sachs emphasizes a different aspect of the utility of employment standards enforcement for worker organizing: rather than merely demonstrating to unorganized workers the virtues of unions, the very process of galvanizing efforts around enforcement of statutory employment laws is generative of solidarity. As workers come to recognize their common experience of statutory rights deprivation, they form an identity around their shared possession of a right against low wages or discrimination and the injustice collectively suffered.[56] This is related to, but nevertheless distinct from their racial or ethnic identity: it is their status as *statutory rights-holders* that catalyzes solidarity.[57] Sachs goes on to argue that this

---

[50] Klare, above n 41, 272.

[51] Ibid.

[52] RM Fischl, 'Rethinking American Work Law' (2007) 28 Berk J Emp & Lab L 163, 212.

[53] Neither Prof Klare nor Prof Fischl would deny the role of unions in securing and defending social legislation (see, eg, Fischl, ibid, and n 171), but they both suggest that this is a lesser function.

[54] Sachs, above n 48, 2721. Fischl, above n 52, 208–9 also makes this argument in part (noting that the inefficiency of agency-conducted secret-ballot elections, vulnerable to post-election appeals and illegal employer interference, have led unions to engage in 'labor law avoidance' strategies).

[55] Sachs, above n 48, 2708–21. See also J Gordon, 'We Make the Road By Walking: Immigrant Workers, the Workplace Project, and the Struggle for Social Change' (1995) 30 Harv CR – CL L Rev 407 (describing her experiences working as an attorney with MRBW).

[56] Sachs, above n 48, 2728–9.

[57] Cf Piore and Stafford, above n 39, 305 (arguing that identity groups gave rise to statutory employment laws such as discrimination, living wage, and family leave laws, and that these laws, in turn, have led to the consolidation and reinforcement of identity-based associations pressing for enforcement of their rights and benefits under those laws). Similar ideas are advanced by Katherine

solidarity-formation moment can serve as the first step in a nascent organizing campaign, and may be better insulated from employer interference than a traditional organizing campaign.[58]

3. Modern unions as agents of social solidarity

In this final section, I advance an idea that has not been widely explored in recent debates. The economic forces that have changed the nature of work, eroding traditional forms of workplace security and stable wage employment, have also intensified the need for a well-functioning social welfare state. Working people – and by this I mean not only the traditional 'working class' (however that may be defined), but also the working poor and the increasingly precarious 'middle class' – share a deepening anxiety about personal and family economic security. If unions can tap into this shared feeling of anxiety about the 'gaps' in the safety net when a job ends, health crisis strikes, child is born, or pension fund shrinks, they might increase the resonance of their message and relevance for American workers. The universalizing theme of the need for a dependable social safety net may serve as common ground within which solidarity can take root.

Social institutions that spread the risks of common life-cycle events might themselves become instruments of identity-creation and social solidarity, operating as an institutional 'frame' within which citizens find common cause with other citizens in collectivizing the risks of the vicissitudes of life.[59]

American unions have, in recent years, appealed successfully to universalizing themes. In the 1997 strike at United Parcel Service (UPS), this was an important part of the success of the campaign.[60] The main issue of the strike was fairness to workers and the ability to make a living wage in a consumer economy. Well-paid, full-time UPS workers went on strike in order to secure benefits for their fellow UPS workers who were part-time and low-paid.[61] Fighting for full-time jobs that can support a family struck a chord with Americans across the country, who were disturbed by the trend of downsizing and the replacement of full-time family wage jobs by lower-paid jobs with no benefits and little security.[62] Another example of

Stone, who identifies emerging forms of 'citizen unionism', locality-based organizations (that may or may not be formally recognized as unions) that operate by enlisting employees in a locality to pressure employers to provide labor market and other protections to workers – not only workplace protections, but issues of concern to working people more generally, such as training, national health policy, family policies, and the like. Stone argues for reform of labor laws to facilitate the formal recognition of citizen unions and increase their potency in both bargaining and political spheres. KVW Stone, *From Widgets to Digits: Employment Regulation for the Changing Workplace* (Cambridge University Press, 2004) 227–31, 233–9.

[58] Sachs, above n 48, 2734–43.
[59] Elsewhere, I develop this argument in depth, although without considering the possible role of unions. G Lester, 'Can Joe the Plumber Support Redistribution? Law, Social Preferences, and Sustainable Policy Design' (forthcoming, 2011) 64 Tax L Rev.
[60] CR Martin, 'The 1997 United Parcel Service Strike: Framing the Story for Popular Consumption' (2003) 27 J Communication Inq 190, 200.
[61] Ibid 201.
[62] Ibid.

the potency of universalizing themes is the bargaining program advanced by the Canadian Auto Workers in 1996, which culminated in a strike at General Motors.[63] The union's demands were aggressive and yet won support because they were oriented explicitly around increasing employment levels in the industry and in communities, rather than just increasing union jobs. The union was able to rally support among working people who felt a collective sense of anxiety about systemic loss of jobs and the attendant erosion of community life.[64]

To be sure, the UPS strike must be recognized for what it was: a successful campaign by the UPS organizers, not naïve to the importance of public opinion, nor naïve to the threat of proliferation of part-time jobs in their ranks, to increase the well-being of UPS workers. Part-time and temporary workers elsewhere in America were left to their own devices, as much as they may have enjoyed a boost of public awareness of their plight. And the CAW would not, presumably, have mobilized around community jobs but for the fact that General Motors was a massive employer of local union workers. My point, for the moment, is that themes tapping into the mounting insecurity of working people in a post-globalization economy struck deep chords and garnered the attention and sympathy of a broader cross-section of the public.

But are unions essential to this effort? Why not mobilize social solidarity around collective social risk and responsibility through the vehicle of advocacy groups on behalf of the poor, the elderly, the disabled, or women? The answer is probably that unions are *not* essential. But if unions want to remain relevant, perhaps they should *make* themselves essential. Unions that can effectively frame advocacy around risks that are common across identity and income groups – for example, vulnerability to job loss in a bad economy, risk of unexpected illness, or the difficulty of balancing work and family care – might not only spearhead progressive social change, but also reduce the perception that unions are a 'special interest group' that lobbies and operates to increase wages for their membership to the exclusion of other workers' and citizens' concerns.

Furthermore, unions may have the institutional tools to sustain themselves more effectively than other social movements. Organized labour is a core mediating institution that has the capacity to mobilize public opinion around progressive social policies, the creation and sustenance of which will feed back into public consciousness. Union investment in garnering public support for social legislation, framing public debates, and serving as a trustworthy 'agent' to educate and lead opinion is a critical social function. Unions have valuable technologies for mobilizing mass publics: they can arrange meetings with legislators, register voters, produce slick advertisements and mailings, and target get-out-the-vote drives.[65]

An example is the recent aggressive involvement of organized labor in mobilizing the American public to support reform of federal health care towards a more

---

[63] Moody, above n 37, 278.

[64] Ibid.

[65] MF Masters and JT Delaney, 'Organized Labor's Political Scorecard' in JT Bennett and BE Kaufman (eds), *What Do Unions Do? A Twenty-Year Perspective* (Transaction Publishers, 2004).

universal form of provision with greater state involvement. The AFL-CIO, Teamsters, Service Employees International, and other major unions launched aggressive public education campaigns leading into the 2008 elections in which health-care reform was a key issue.[66] They used websites, grassroots education efforts, mailings, and other techniques to influence public opinion.[67] This represented a sustained investment by organized labor in mobilizing public support around an expansion of broad social legislation, rather than a program that would target benefits towards unionized workers or bread-and-butter bargaining issues.

The AFL-CIO later passed a resolution, following a unanimous vote at their national convention, to support a 'single-payer' model of health insurance.[68] The health care legislation that ultimately passed was not single-payer, but organized labor's endorsement of the social insurance model was significant. It was the first time in two decades that the AFL-CIO had publicly supported a social insurance model of health care.[69] Unionized workers have historically enjoyed some of the best health care coverage in the United States, and are more likely than non-union workers to receive private health insurance coverage through their employer.[70] A federal program of health insurance would reduce the relative advantage of unions in health-care benefits.[71] Yet unions took a strong position favoring universal, redistributive, national health insurance, educating citizens who stood to benefit from reform but had difficulty in understanding the complex design features and long-term implications of reform, and played a critical leadership role within a national debate characterized by political brinksmanship and sometimes virulent rhetoric and misinformation.

There remains a classic conundrum. Unions' core base has historically been relatively stable wage-earning employees, often to the exclusion of low-wage workers whose need for social welfare protection is perhaps most acute. If social benefits accrue to a population broader than unionized workers, there is a potential

---

[66] M Andrews, 'Do Unions Still Shape the Healthcare Debate?' US News & World Report (Washington, 27 March 2008) (praising organized labor for taking a collaborative rather than confrontational role on the issue of universal health care).

[67] As just one example, see AFL-CIO Working Families e-Activist Network, 'Support Real Healthcare Reform' <http://www.unionvoice.org/campaign/healthinsreform2> (accessed 26 September 2010) (containing a form that users can fill out urging Congress to pass health care reform with a strong public health insurance option).

[68] 'AFL-CIO Convention Endorses Single-Payer' (16 September 2009) <http://www.medicalnewstoday.com/articles/164072.php>.

[69] Ibid.

[70] Bennett and Taylor, above n 23, 269–70.

[71] Negative media coverage of labor's opposition to a so-called 'Cadillac tax' (a tax on the most generous employer-sponsored health plans, which would have included many union health plans) in a proposed bill leading up to reform was misleading in suggesting that organized labor was willing to jeopardize prospects for health reform for self-serving reasons. The unions did not simply oppose the 'Cadillac tax,' they favored an alternative bill that contained a far more progressive funding mechanism, a tax on couples earning $1 million or more annually. To be sure, union members would be better off with the tax on high earners. But its benefits would accrue mainly to non-union workers. K Jacobs et al, 'Who Benefits from the Proposed Amendment to the Senate Excise Tax on Employer Health Premiums?' University of California, Berkeley Center for Labor Research and Education Issue Brief (February 2010) 6.

free-rider problem: unions invest time and money in promoting social legislation, and for whom? The reward they reap, diluted by its general application, may be insufficient to sustain membership and motivation. Worse, the very existence of the social legislation may make unions superfluous. Workers may decide that the benefits of joining a union are insignificant if union-like benefits are provided by the government.[72] Perhaps unions – whose density is as threatened as it has ever been – would be better off focusing on grassroots organizing, not the integrative aims of social legislation.

At the heart of this dilemma is an empirical question, to which I cannot offer a decisive answer. What I can say, however, based on existing research, is that unions are likely to have greater success in the legislative arena if they pursue broad rather than narrow issues, that the championing of a strengthened social safety net is likely to enhance their public appeal, and that legislative successes will not inevitably undermine unions' viability. Freeman and Medoff, in their study of 40 years' worth of union legislative activity, found that unions were more likely to be successful when the goal was 'social' legislation than when it was special interest legislation designed to increase unions' monopoly power.[73] Twenty years later, based on a meta-analysis of studies between 1984 and 2004, Masters and Delaney found that Freeman and Medoff's observation still held true.[74] Efforts by organized labor to secure pro-organized labor legislation continued to fail, while efforts to advance legislation promoting the general welfare and social justice, such as raising the minimum wage, or defending such legislation against retrenchment, more often succeeded.[75]

Moreover, it is not at all clear that unions lose in the end when the government strengthens social legislation. Neumann and Rissman's well-known empirical study finding a negative correlation between government social welfare spending and union density between 1904 and 1980 provoked much subsequent research and refinement of the 'government-for-union substitution hypothesis.'[76] Follow-up research using more refined methods has, on balance, failed to generate robust support for the hypothesis.[77]

I do not mean to be naïve about the need for unions to continue in their efforts to build union membership. In a world of scarce resources, there is some tension between developing innovating organizing strategies and focusing outward, on

---

[72] Bennett and Taylor, above n 23, 262, 271.

[73] Freeman and Medoff, above n 23, 206. In addition, public approval of unions declines when there is a large wage gap between union and non-union workers. Jarley and Kuruvilla, above n 31, 110. This is consistent with the idea that unions are less popular when they are seen as pursuing their own interests to the exclusion of others.

[74] Masters and Delaney, above n 65, 368.

[75] Ibid 503.

[76] See GR Neumann and ER Rissman, 'Where Have All the Union Members Gone?' (1984) 2 J Lab Econ 175.

[77] WJ Moore et al, 'Welfare Expenditure and the Decline of Unions' (1989) 71 Rev Econ & Stat 538 (finding only mixed support); Chaison and Rose, above n 29 (finding no support); and LP Stepina and J Fiorito, 'Toward a Comprehensive Theory of Union Growth and Decline' (1986) 25 Indus Rel 248, 253, 261 (finding no support).

large-scale legislative activity. A critical thrust of my argument, however, is that there can be synergies between the two endeavors. It seems likely that the relationship between inward and outward labor strategies is iterative, where too sustained a focus on any one strategy to the exclusion of the other may weaken the project of organized labor as a whole. The returns to reinvigoration of unions' political engagement with progressive social reform, far from alienating workers from unions, could be part of a process by which social cohesion in the general society would spark a renewed sense of the mission and vitality of unions.

21

From Conflict to Regulation: The Transformative Function of Labour Law

Julia López, Consuelo Chacartegui, and César G Cantón[*]

A. Conflict and regulation: the transformation of labour law through conflict

The history of labour law poses important questions for the future construction of labour rights for vulnerable members of societies. Especially important for labour rights in the context of globalization is the issue of how *divergences* – to borrow a term from social theorist Georg Simmel – can be integrated or resolved in ways that promote positive transformations. Following Simmel's claim that 'there probably exists no social unit in which convergent and divergent currents among its members are not inseparably interwoven',[1] we see the divergence of interests and approaches as a natural part of the social system. But despite the wide acceptance of the proposition that conflict is present in social relations, it is uncommon to study debates on labour regulation through a framework emphasizing conflict and ways in which divergences are manifested. In this chapter we seek to do precisely that, making the case for understanding labour law through the prism provided by strikes and other forms of conflict.

Most approaches to labour law currently treat conflict more as a *problem* than a value in itself, promoting ongoing transformations – both in labour law and other outcomes. We suggest that a holistic perspective on contemporary developments entails an optimistic and realistic[2] approach toward strikes or protest, and their legal recognition, instead of the 'commonsense' view of conflict as disruptive and destructive,[3] which may be seen in part as a reaction to the political component that strikes introduce into the industrial relations system.[4]

[*] Julia López, Professor of Labour Law, Pompeu Fabra University; Consuelo Chacartegui, Associate Professor of Labour Law, Pompeu Fabra University; and César G Cantón, Visiting Professor of Labour Law, Pompeu Fabra University.

[1] G Simmel, *Conflict and the Web of Group-Affiliations* (The Free Press, 1955) 15.

[2] L Turner and D Cornfield (eds), *Labor in the New Urban Battlegrounds. Local Solidarity in a Global Economy* (Cornell University Press, 2007), vii.

[3] R Hyman, *Strikes* (Fontana-Collins, 1984) 74.

[4] E Shorter and C Tilly, *Strikes in France, 1830–1968* (Cambridge University Press, 1974); and D Snyder, 'Institutional Setting and Industrial Conflict: Comparative Analyses of France, Italy and the United States' (1975) 40/3 ASR 259–78.

Conflict is a dynamic process which, born in divergence, continues with the emergence of discontent and can then be resolved by different means. The emergence and expression of divergences is, we argue, healthy for societies, and opens pathways for possible solutions to underlying problems. Regulation plays a crucial role in this process; social regulations entitle workers to use certain rights – such as the freedom of association, the right to strike, and the freedom of expression – to express divergences.[5] The right to strike or protest occupies a vital role in the list of ways to externalize divergences.

The right to strike has been identified in existing scholarship with two elements: (1) the cessation of work; and (2) concerted action by workers, both of these ingredients connected with the essence of the legal system's treatment of labour. Strikes and the political handling of the freedom, or right, to strike have been interacting with labour law since the birth of labour regulation.[6] In this interaction two different but complementary functions have been crucial: the integrative and the transformative role of the right on which we focus. The study of the strike and protest must first take up the integration function, which guarantees a certain control of social conflict between firms and workers, and second the role of this right in those transformations involving the capacity of actors to change the relations power, not only within firms, but also through legislative power and the reshaping of regulation. It is clear that these two functions of strikes introduce a strong element of politics inside labour law which cannot be fully understood with an exclusively economic approach.

The strike, and other forms of protest in resistance to public and private policies, has been present since the origins of labour law. The evolution of labour law, permitting one to define labour law as a process, as a historical branch of the legal system, is manifested in the development of the right to strike. Labour law was born as a combination of contract and collective rights. Labour law and collective rights have been walking together in the last century with a changing equilibrium in their connection. Yet due to a predominant culture which views bargaining and arbitration as the principal basis of industrial relations, current debates generally fail to incorporate the right to strike in their construction of the essence of labour law. The right to strike – and the exercise of that right – contribute significantly to the embryonic or germinal capacity to historically shape the changing regulation of social relationships and adaptations.

The right to strike in the contemporary context shares with the overall body of labour law the challenges and complexities imposed by a changing reality. Some of those important challenges or questions from the perspective of the right to strike can help to illustrate the need for labour law scholars to incorporate the discourse and regulation of conflict inside their understanding of labour law's transformation.

---

[5] These rights and freedoms constitute important components of the quality of democracy. See G O'Donell et al (eds), *The Quality of Democracy. Theory and Applications* (University of Notre Dame Press, 2004).

[6] O Kahn-Freund and B Hepple, *Laws against strikes* (Fabian Society, 1972).

One fundamental question for labour law scholars concerns the notion of the worker and how to maintain the identity of labour law as a countervailing instrument connected deeply with welfare state systems.[7] Labour law faces the challenge of how this part of the legal system can integrate diversity – including that provided by racial, gender, sexual orientation, and religious differences as well as work status issues such as that of precarious workers – and of whether it is possible for labour law to organize alone, without other legal branches, the protection of the vulnerable.

Analyzing the notion of the worker, which includes a broad variety of sub-themes, raises important issues involving the definition and regulation of strikers. This right may be understood to encompass all actors who are workers, including independent workers, the unemployed, retired workers, immigrant workers in an illegal situation, etc. The right to strike may imply, now more than ever with the economic crisis, the challenge to compose networks of solidarity among broad groups with disparate race, gender, and labour market situations including retirees or young people with different interests and demands. In this sense, the right to strike is located inside the political sphere of society. The right has been constrained to adapt to new realities in the relations between workers and employer but – in a cyclical process – it is also becoming more and more a way to defend the most vulnerable in society. This increases the political component of the right which emerges as an important way to show discontent, not only with the firm, but also with government. The networking of solidarities between strikers and others implies that the right to strike creates a constellation of related rights – such as freedom of expression – to protect the rights, not only of workers, but also of other groups to protest. Thus the right to strike includes forms of protest not generating labour contract effects. One such case would be general strikes against government policies.

A second challenge for labour law facing the future is related to the increasing complexity of firms and the new technological society. The complexity of firms as corporations is produced because, on the one hand, there is an intense movement of networks created among firms while, on the other hand, there is a significant process of decentralization within firms oriented to reducing the number of workers in each workplace. The right to strike, in order to maintain its effectiveness, has to transform its provisions for the exteriorization of conflict in ways taking account of the new organization of firms. This means that in the current scenario workers and other protestors define the territory for demonstrations in a flexible way as exemplified by the evolution from national strikes to euro-strikes. The networking of solidarity has created a flexible structure of collective actions connecting the global with the local in an interactive relation.[8]

On the other hand, the use of the right to strike has also tried to adapt and take advantage of new technologies, working within new ways to organize production, developing new forms of action connected with technology such as the cyber-strike.

---

[7] M Freedland, 'From the Contract of Employment to the Personal Work Nexus' (2006) 35/1 Ind Law J 1–29.

[8] RM Fishman, *Democracy's Voices: Social Ties and the Quality of Public Life in Spain* (Cornell University Press, 2004).

This permits strikers to gain more influence and publicity quickly without the cost in salaries that other forms of strike imply. The right to strike, in the context of this new reality, signifies that strikers have to know who the employer is.

A third point of reference in the contemporary debate is on sources of regulation for labour rights. This debate examines a series of questions such as the role of international and regional law, the construction of rights by law and collective bargaining, the role of self-regulation instruments and the hybridization of legal systems, making use of combinations of hard and soft law. Strikes – and the constellation of rights that guarantees the emergence of discontent – are connected with the debate on a flexible framework of national and multinational labour rights involving new techniques regulatory of rights.

The undervaluation of the role played by the right to strike is unfortunate for many reasons. Societies often refuse to face conflict and thus promote its invisibility as a way to deny it. One of the main points in this debate is the connection between forms of protest and unionism.

One of the most important transformations in labour relations in recent decades follows from strategies that unions have developed in order to face globalization. Workers' organizations, attempting to become more international in scope, re-founded the international labour network, creating the International Trade Union Confederation (2006) which includes 175 million workers and a very large number of national unions, 311, from 155 countries and regions. Unions are remodelling themselves in order to participate more effectively in the global level of labour market regulation. On the other hand, unions in some countries are more involved than ever in politics, sometimes with successful results, as in the Obama campaign in the USA. Unions are a major actor in politics in many countries and they have an important role transforming societies with the complicity of other actors, a phenomenon that is for some authors a crucial element of rebuilding unions in the future.[9]

Labour scholars have to put more attention on the role that union and other actors have played, using the right to strike as both a political and social instrument for transformation of labour law – and other relevant outcomes. This means that it is not sufficient to study the right to strike in the law in a static way. It is important to consider the strike as an instrument of equilibrium not only for the legal systems but also for democracy in a broader sense. In a related vein, collective bargaining should not be seen as the only basis for integrating conflict. The predominant model of industrial relations based exclusively on bargaining, and on the idea of social dialogue as the sole reference for regulation, is a failure. The denial or weakening of non-consensual instruments of transformation such as the strike pushes workers to find other ways to express collective conflict, some of them more tragic for themselves and others. The denial of workplace rights and dignity for workers exploded in a violent way in cases such as France Telecom, as we will examine later.

---

[9] KVW Stone, *From Widgets to Digits: Employment Regulation for the Changing Workplace* (Cambridge University Press, 2004).

The undervaluing or ignoring of strikes and protest as manifestations of divergences is connected with a model of industrial relations – and of scholarly debate – reflecting basically an economic perspective instead of a holistic approach. Incorporating protest as a very vital form of activism into the normal debates on labour transformations is not only a 'realist' recognition of elements of solidarity present in the system as a result of collective action, but also a means to treat labour law as a serious part of the political debate on how to construct a society and communities that attend to the most vulnerable social groups. Thus, the approach presented here locates the debate on labour law inside a broad perspective connected with the analysis of welfare state systems.

B. Invisibility of rights (in international instruments of regulation) and the invisibility of conflict at the national level

In order to transform the regulation of labour rights, conflict has to be a process with *visibility* for societies. The transformative capacity of conflict depends partially on the visibility of divergences and proposed or realized solutions. Visibility is thus one of the crucial elements for promoting the transformative capacity of labour and related issues of regulation. Critical studies of the news media show that media coverage is mediated by ideological beliefs and power relations.[10] What media analysts call hard news, which encompasses coverage of politics and the economy, typically has not included political information on strikes and protest as part of a strategy to offer neutral information. Furthermore, soft news which includes stories on celebrities and social events occupies a large part of the information offered by the media. Such outcomes have been shaped by a kind of homogenization of journalist cultures.[11] The relative invisibility of conflict in the media is also the result of the impact that the regulative framework has exerted on the social position of strikes and protest.

The first reference in the invisibility of the right to strike from a multilevel perspective lies in the indifference toward direct recognition of this right in most of the international instruments emanating from the International Labour Organization (ILO). Indeed, the right to strike is not expressly mentioned in any convention of the ILO. However, the absence of explicit ILO standards should not lead to the conclusion that the Organization disregards the right to strike or abstains from providing a protective framework within which it may be exercised.[12] The ILO's

---

[10] S Graig, 'Framing Protest: News Media Frame of the Million Man March' (March 2001) 18/1 Crit Stud Mass Comm 83–101.

[11] F Plasser, 'From Hard to Soft News Standards? How Political Journalists in Different Media Systems Evaluate the Shifting of News' (2006) 10/2 Harv Int J Press-Pol 47–68.

[12] B Gernigon et al, *ILO Principles Concerning the Right to Strike* (International Labour Office, 1998) 7. The ILO Convention 87, Art 3, lays down the right to association. This states that 'workers' and employers' organisations shall have the right to draw up their constitutions and rules, to elect their representatives in full freedom, to organise their administration and activities and to formulate their programmes'.

Freedom of Association Committee through ongoing rulings established principles on the right to strike. Thus, the ILO Committee on Freedom of Association and other ILO bodies have interpreted all core ILO conventions as protecting the right to strike as an essential element of the freedom of association. The ILO has ruled that 'the right to strike is an intrinsic corollary of the right of association protected by Convention no. 87', although this right may be restricted in essential services under particular circumstances.[13] Thus for the ILO the right to strike constitutes a corollary of other rights.

The right to strike is not explicitly recognized in the Universal Declaration of Human Rights 1948, but this Declaration states that: 'Everyone has the right to form and to join trade unions for the protection of his interests' (Article 23). Like the ILO convention, this formulation includes the implication that trade unions have the right to strike. Nevertheless, the right to strike has been the subject of regulation under some of the conventions of human social rights,[14] and we can locate the direct application of the international regulation in some countries.[15]

An explicit recognition of the right to strike took place in one European instrument of programmatic social principles in 1961. The Council of Europe in that year agreed upon the European Social Charter, committing Member States to a series of fundamental rights. Compliance with the Charter is monitored but not legally enforceable. The European Social Charter, signed in Turin on 18 October 1961, expressly protects the right to strike.[16]

---

[13] According to the ILO, the right to strike derives from the right of workers' organizations to formulate their programmes of activities to further and defend the economic and social interests of their members. However, the right to strike is not absolute. It may be subject to certain legal conditions or restrictions, and may even be prohibited in exceptional circumstances (Freedom of Association and Protection of the Right to Organise Convention (1948) No 87, Art 3; General Survey on Freedom of Association and Collective Bargaining, ILO, 'Labour Legislation Guidelines. Substantive Provisions of Labour Legislation: The Right to Strike', ch V (2004) para 15. <http://www.ilo.org/public/english/dialogue/ifpdial/llg/noframes/ch5.htm>).

[14] Thus, the right to strike is also recognized in international and regional instruments, including the International Covenant on Economic, Social and Cultural Rights of 1966 (Art 8(1)(d)), the Inter-American Charter of Social Guarantees of 1948 (Art 27) and the Additional Protocol to the American Convention on Human Rights in the Area of Economic, Social and Cultural Rights of 1988 (Art 8(1)(b)).

[15] One interesting case is the Netherlands. In this country, the relevant source of regulation of the right to strike is the European Social Charter. Dutch law does not contain any positive statutory regulation of the right to strike. However, since 1872, when a prohibition was abolished, industrial action has been regulated by case law. An important decision by the Supreme Court in 1986 recognized the right to engage in and take collective action on the basis of Art 6(4) of the Council of Europe Social Charter. This decision of the Dutch Supreme Court, which states that the Charter prevails if inconsistent with national legislation, recognized forms of industrial action other than purely political strikes.

[16] Article 6 states that, with a view to ensuring the effective exercise of the right to bargain collectively, the Contracting Parties undertake the right of workers and employers to collective action, including the right to strike, in cases of conflicts of interest subject to obligations that might arise out of collective agreements previously entered into.

This suggests that any restrictions should be voluntary and agreed upon. Like the International Covenant on Economic, Social and Cultural Rights, the Social Charter of 1961 permits each signatory country to abridge the right to strike. However, the Appendix to the Charter carries the provision that the right to strike can be restricted if this can be justified as necessary in a democratic society for the protection of the rights and freedoms of others or for the protection of public interest, national security, public health, or morals.

At the national level, the undervaluation of conflict presents a different profile that in the international sphere because the denial of conflict and its invisibility are manifested in socio-political practice but not in regulation. Indeed, the main mechanism through which legal systems entitle workers to the right to strike is located at the domestic sovereign state level and is created through hard law instruments. This gives the right stability which can withstand changes of circumstance rooted in historical process.

The techniques employed in regulating strikes through concrete rules vary from one country to another. This pattern of difference can be organized into, at least, three groups of countries. There is a first block of countries in which the constitution has explicitly recognized the right to strike for the defence of the worker's interests. In a second group of countries, the right to strike is not explicit but is instead implied by other rights (such as freedom of association or collective bargaining). In a third category of countries, it is not possible to speak of a right, but only of a freedom to strike. The visibility of conflict appears in legal regulation at different levels.

Thus, the response of national laws to the collective action of workers substantially varies. The right to strike is, in most European countries, guaranteed in the Constitution. In these cases the right to strike has been judged sufficiently fundamental so as to warrant insertion into the Constitution and the nature of the right is therefore more than a mere freedom to strike.[17] This is the case in France, Italy, Greece, Portugal, and Spain, where the right to strike is recognized as a fundamental human right exercised within the framework of the laws, with consequences for the contract of employment – which is considered suspended for the duration of a strike. Thus, the right to strike is recognized 'within the framework of the laws that regulate it' (French Constitution of 1958), which in practice leaves further provisions to case law. However, in these countries the Constitution only guarantees the right to strike, rarely any other form of industrial action.[18]

Also in South Africa the right to strike has been crystallized as a constitutional right, adopted by the Constitutional Assembly on 11 October 1996. The South African Constitution recognizes that there are potent lessons to be learned not only from the country's apartheid past, but also from the experience of other countries.[19] It is

---

[17] T Novitz, *International and European Protection of the Right to Strike* (Oxford University Press, 2003) 2.

[18] According to Aaltonen (J Aaltonen, *International Secondary Action in the EU Member States* (Metalli (Finnish Metalworker Union), 1999) 206), a strike has been considered to be a common complete cessation of work by some or all employees of an enterprise in promotion of demands concerning employment conditions. A strike means to exercise the right to strike irrespective of whether it is carried out as a circulating strike, a selective strike or a spot strike. Still, for example, go-slows, blacking of products, boycotts and Italian (sic) strikes remain outside the scope of the strike definition.

[19] The right to strike is recognized in section 23(c), which provides that 'every worker has the right to form and join a trade union, to participate in the activities and programmes of a trade union and to strike', although strike statistics show a significant decline in levels of industrial action since the Commission for Conciliation, Mediation and Arbitration (CCMA) was established as a new dispute resolution body in November 1995. P Benjamin and C Gruen, 'The Regulatory Efficiency of the CCMA: A Statistical Analysis of the CCMA's CMS Database' (2006) DPRU Working Paper

important to stress that the history of labour rights in South Africa is intrinsically linked to the history of the workers and the citizens' movements. Exploitation of workers was a feature of life in this country for a long time, under conditions of poverty and the oppressive laws of apartheid, and trade unions were an important source of resistance. Labour rights were part of a wider struggle for democracy linked to the growth of the labour movement.[20] The case of South Africa is a very clear example of connection between conflict and social transformation.

In a second group of countries the strike is legally seen as a corollary of collective bargaining and as equivalent to an industrial sanction.[21] It is conceived as a 'negative liberty' based on principles of statutory immunity.[22] This is the case in the United Kingdom, Ireland, and the United States. When the right of strike is not guaranteed in the Constitution, it usually provokes the effect of substantial instability in its legal regulation, with changes of the political party in power generating shifts in the regulation of strikes. This situation has been criticized by the Council of Europe's Committee of Independent Experts.[23]

The instability of the right implies an important role for judges in the process. Interesting cases are found in the United Kingdom, where the right to strike is constantly subject to reshaping by the courts and Parliament.[24] Since the election of Margaret Thatcher in 1979, the number of cases of industrial conflict that must be resolved by the Advisory, Conciliation and Arbitration Service (ACAS) – the main body involved in conciliation and arbitration in the United Kingdom – has increased considerably.[25] In the United States, the right to strike is guaranteed in

No 06/110 <http://papers.ssrn.com/sol3/papers.cfm?abstract_id=943999>, accessed 20 September 2010.

[20] B Nkabinde, 'The Right to Strike, an Essential Component of Workplace Democracy: Its Scope and Global Economy' (2009) 24 Md J Int'l L & Trade 274.

[21] O Kahn-Freund and B Hepple, *Laws Against Strikes* (Fabian Society, 1972) 9.

[22] Novitz stresses that: 'within some states there is a "positive" entitlement or right to take industrial action guaranteed as a constitutional right or as a key feature of labour legislation. Within others, this is phrased as a "negative" liberty such that workers and organizers are immune from what would otherwise be the legal consequences of industrial action'. T Novitz, *International and European Protection of the Right to Strike* (Oxford University Press, 2003).

[23] Novitz, above n 22.

[24] Successive governments pursued a legislative programme that placed legal restrictions on trade unions' ability to engage in industrial action. A Conservative government, led by Prime Minister Margaret Thatcher, was elected in 1979 on an anti-trade union and neo-liberal platform. Since then, the number of cases of industrial conflict that must be resolved by the Advisory, Conciliation and Arbitration Service (ACAS) – the main body involved in conciliation and arbitration in the United Kingdom – has increased considerably: B Montgomery, 'The European Community's Draft Fifth Directive: British Resistance and Community Procedures' (1989) 10 Comp Lab L 438.

[25] In India, the right to strike is not a fundamental right but a legal one, to which statutory restriction is attached in the Industrial Dispute Act of 1947. Nevertheless, the right to protest is a fundamental right under Art 19 of the Constitution of India. In this legal context, the right to strike is organically linked with the right to collective bargaining, following the historical tradition of the United Kingdom. In India, the strike may be justified or unjustified depending upon several factors such as the nature of the demands of the workers, the cause leading to the strike, the urgency of the cause or demands of the workers and the reasons for not resorting to the dispute-resolving machinery provided by the Act or the contract of employment. The Supreme Court of India held that a strike may be illegal if it contravenes the provisions of the Industrial Dispute Act or of any other law or the terms of employment, depending upon the facts of each case (*Syndicate Bank v K Umesh Nayak* [19 March

the National Labour Relations Act of 1935, which tries to avoid the denial by some employers of the right to organize and the refusal of some employers to accept collective bargaining as well as strikes and other forms of collective action based on the solidarity of workers.[26] The right to strike has been significantly limited by the Supreme Court, which defined the sit-down strike as 'an illegal seizure of the buildings in order to prevent their use by their employer in a lawful manner',[27] criminalizing many labour strikes as trespassing.[28]

Another interesting type of regulation is found in Sweden,[29] Belgium, Austria, Finland, and Germany. In these countries, the right to strike is based on collective agreements, thus carrying a duty to maintain industrial peace.[30] In Germany, the Constitution of 1949 made no reference to industrial action but only to the protection of freedom of association. Although there is no specific law on strikes in Germany, the basic right to take industrial action is based on the guarantee of freedom of association in the Basic Law (*Grundgesetz*). Nevertheless, the Federal Labour Court (*Bundesarbeitsgericht*) in 1955 placed a restrictive interpretation on this. The *Bundesarbeitsgericht* has created several restrictions on the possibilities to take industrial action. To be valid, a strike must be conducted by a trade union, and must pursue an aim that can be regulated by collective agreement.[31]

According to Hepple, these consequences are very undesirable for workers. Taking part in an industrial action may lead a worker to be dismissed or to be

1994] SCC). This is a conditional or qualified right only available after certain preconditions are fulfilled, which involves an important element of legal uncertainty. R Anand, *The Right to Strike* (National Law University, 2009).

[26] S Lynd and D Gross, *Labour Law for the Rank and Filer* (PM Press, 2008) 73.

[27] In *National Labor Relations Board v Mackay Radio & Telegraph Co* (1938) and in *National Labor Relations Board v Fansteel Metallurgical Corp* (1939), it allowed the permanent replacement of economic strikers.

[28] J Hilgert, 'Mapping the Boundaries of Human Rights at Work. Questioning How the ILO Defines Labor Rights and Social Justice' (2009) 34/1 Labour Studies Journal 29.

[29] The 1928 Collective Agreement Act deals with collective labour agreements between employers or employers' associations and trade unions. It specifies in particular the legal effects of such agreements. According to a resolution of the European Court of Human Rights in 1976, the right to strike in Sweden is not an absolute right. Thus, 'the Swedish State has in fact selected collective bargaining, the concluding of collective agreements and the recognition of the right to strike as three of the means making possible the conduct and development of action by trade unions in both the public and private sector': *Schmidt and Dahlström v Sweden*, ECHR, 6 February 1976.

[30] The Belgian industrial relations system is characterized by a complex web of negotiation and consultation. This structure is important for the determination of the substantive as well as the procedural elements and limitations of the right to strike. The Superior Court of Belgium in 1981 ruled that individuals have the right to strike, but employers have also successfully sought legal backing to restrict these rights. The result is that since 1987 fines have been imposed on some workers attending strike meetings, or involved in strikes and related actions (Etui-Rehs, *Strike Rules in the EU 27 and Beyond. A Comparative Overview* (European Trade Union Institute for Research, Education and Health and Safety, 2007); and P Fairbrother et al, *The Right to Strike in the Electricity Sector in the European Union Countries* (Public Services International Research Unit, University of Greenwich, 2002).

[31] Eurofound, 'German Strike Legislation Does Not Fulfil Standards of the European Social Charter' (1998) <http://www.eurofound.europa.eu/eiro/1998/02/inbrief/de9802253n.htm>.

disqualified for the jobseeker's allowance or other benefits.[32] The Federal German Court decided that in order to be legal a strike action had to be complementary to collective bargaining – and thus is protected only insofar as its purpose is the achievement of a collective agreement – and that the action had to be 'socially adequate' or proportionate.

An important way to repress or restrict conflict is to regulate a strict number of motivations for legal strikes and to create a complex process of formalities to declare a strike. Comparison between countries in their treatment of strike motivations is difficult due to the absence of a single legal concept of the strike. The only characteristic that is common across countries is the understanding that a strike is an action of solidarity manifested though a deliberate stoppage undertaken in order to put pressure on the employer to accede to demands. Given this lack of greater specificity, case law is of crucial importance in delineating the limits of the regulation of the right to strike, particularly by domestic courts. The limits that are commonly not identified by case law have traditionally been divided into external limits, such as those deriving from the presence of other constitutionally protected rights, and internal limits, those inherent to the intrinsic structure and notion of the strike.[33]

Indeed, whether a particular strike is judged to be legally justified or not is a question of fact, assessed in the light of circumstances of each case. This introduces an important element of legal uncertainty. According to Stewart and Bell, in the European Union countries it is possible to identify three distinctive blocks of strikes: political strikes, solidarity strikes, and picketing. Political strikes are illegal in most of the Member States. Solidarity strikes are legal in most of the states. Picketing is legal in practically all Member States.[34]

One common trend that we can see is that the manifest motivation for a strike affects its legality. Under certain circumstances, a solidarity strike can be lawful. In most countries, when a sympathy strike is organized there are some legal requirements, varying by country. There must be a justified collective interest at stake for strikers (Spain, France, Italy), or it is necessary to consider if a solidarity strike is included in the union's freedom of activity as guaranteed in the Constitution (Germany).

According to Hyman, the simple assumption that the causes of a specific strike must be either economic or non-economic poses a false dichotomy, given that few strikes have a single immediate cause, whereas many strikes take place due to a multiplicity of immediate issues.[35] The difficulty arises from the fact that it is often impossible to distinguish in practice between the political and occupational aspects of a strike, since a policy adopted by a government frequently has immediate repercussions for workers or

---

[32] B Hepple, 'The Right to Strike in an International Context', Symposium: Is There a Constitutional Right to Strike in Canada? (University of Toronto, 5 December 2009) <http://www.law.utoronto.ca/documents/conferences2/StrikeSymposium09_Hepple.pdf>.

[33] Eurofound, 'German Strike Legislation Does Not Fulfil Standards of the European Social Charter' (1998) <http://www.eurofound.europa.eu/eiro/1998/02/inbrief/de9802253n.htm>.

[34] A Stewart and M Bell (eds), *The Right to Strike: A Comparative Perspective. A Study of National Law in Six EU States* (The Institute of Employment Rights, 2009).

[35] R Hyman, *Strikes* (Fontana-Collins, 1984).

employers; this is the case, for example, with a general wage and price freeze.[36] On the other hand, in its General Survey of 1983, the Committee of Experts on the Application of Conventions and Recommendations of the ILO defined sympathy strikes ('where workers come out in support of another strike') and determined that a general prohibition of sympathy strikes could lead to abuse and that workers should be able to take such action provided that the initial strike they are supporting is itself lawful (ILO, 1983b, paragraph 217).

Although one cannot overlook the special characteristics and legal and social traditions of each country, it is also important to establish fairly uniform criteria in order to examine the compatibility of legislation with the provisions of Convention No 87. For example, in 2007 the Supreme Court of Canada[37] made it clear that the different instruments of human social rights that the Court mentioned[38] are intended to provide at least as good a level of protection as is to be found in international labour and human rights instruments that Canada has ratified.[39] According to the Court, the application of these international instruments means that these documents reflect not only international consensus, but also principles that Canada has committed itself to uphold.

One clear example of this kind of limitation can be seen in the Turkish regulation. Turkish law establishes serious limitations to the right to strike. Solidarity strikes, general strikes, go-slows, and workplace occupations continue to be banned. Severe penalties, including imprisonment, are possible for participation in strikes. Any strike that is not called by a trade union executive body is banned. Strikes over the non-observance of collective labour agreements are forbidden. We can see an example of this limitation through the resolution of the European Court of Human Rights in *Enerji Yapi-Yol Sen v Turkey* (2009). In this case, the European Court of Human Rights delivered a ruling concerning a Circular published by the Prime Minister's office to all public employees prohibiting participation in a national one-day strike. The Court resolved that this constituted a violation of the rights of a trade union in relation to Article 11.

The European Court of Human Rights accepted that the right to strike was not absolute and could be subject to certain conditions such as action by civil servants exercising the functions of the authority of the State. But a blanket prohibition, of the sort issued in Turkey, could not be justified under Article 11(2). Such restriction represents a democratic deficit that also serves as an obstacle to Turkish accession to the European Union, according to the Report of the European Commissioner responsible for enlargement, which emphasizes the urgency of

---

[36] B Gernigon et al, *ILO Principles Concerning the Right to Strike* (International Labour Office, 1998) 15.

[37] *Bargaining Assn v British Columbia* [2007] 2 SCR 391, 2007 SCC 27.

[38] The International Covenant on Economic, Social and Cultural Rights, the International Covenant on Civil and Political Rights, and the International Labour Organization's (ILO's) Convention (No 87) Concerning Freedom of Association and Protection of the Right to Organize ('Convention No 87'). Canada has endorsed all three of these documents, ratifying Convention No 87 in 1972.

[39] Hepple, above n 32.

Turkey's need to undertake judicial and constitutional reforms to reach European standards in some regulation fields, such as the right to strike.[40]

C. Self-regulation instruments: a corporate culture of denial of conflict

The current ascendancy of self-regulation instruments is a feature of the general shift from a conflict model of labour relations to one progressively emphasizing social dialogue and worker–employer negotiation. Among other things, this implies that freedom of association and the right to collective bargaining are increasingly stressed over the right to strike, which fades out almost to the point of invisibility. Thus we expect not to see the right to strike mentioned in the Codes,[41] either in those issued by companies themselves or in those elaborated by other entities from the outside. Instead, we expect a general recognition of the other two rights, that is, freedom of association and collective bargaining as in the ILO model. The trend toward self-regulation and the broader tendencies to which it is linked establish for us the importance of studying hybridization of soft and hard law from the perspective of the right to strike. A complementary task undertaken in this chapter is the identification of conflict arbitration channels in the documents examined.

This phenomenon is reinforced by companies' – and above all transnational companies' (TNCs') – consideration of their brand image as an asset to leverage within a general framework of cost–benefit analysis. Image promotion brings companies to pursue legitimacy for their socially responsible efforts by seeking a backdrop for their own Code in well-established external documents. Insofar as external Codes do not mention the right to strike, this is not likely to be found in corporate Codes either. It is useful to adopt a typology of codes of conduct (hereafter CoC), which may be classified in a number of ways. In order to bring clarity to our analysis, and following a review of existing scholarship, we adopt a primary classification based upon the Code's source, distinguishing between (1) corporate Codes and (2) types of multi-company Codes.[42] The first group encompasses those Codes issued

---

[40] Dr Olli Rehn, as the European Commissioner responsible for enlargement, puts the accent on this circumstance: 'Now the EU is eagerly awaiting a revitalisation of Turkey's long-awaited reforms, to accelerate the country's democratic transformation and bring it closer to meeting the criteria for joining the Union...Another example is the law on trade unions, presently before the Turkish Grand National Assembly. This law will align Turkey's legislation with EU standards and ILO conventions on important issues, such as the right to organise, the right to strike and the right to bargain collectively'. O Rehn, 'Time to Revitalise Turkey's EU Progress', *Milliyet* (25 August 2008) <http://www.abhaber.com/english/haber.php?id=4144>.

[41] By multi-company Codes is meant also Guidelines and Principles, and under corporate Codes also understood are sustainability reports, codes of ethics, employees policies, and similar documents.

[42] For this classification, see B Burkett et al, 'Corporate Social Responsibility and Codes of Conduct: The Privatization of International Labour Law', Proceedings of the 33rd Annual Conference of the Canadian Council on International Law (Ottawa, 14–16 October 2004); and C McCrudden, 'Human Rights Codes for Transnational Corporations: What Can the Sullivan and MacBride Principles Tell Us?' (1999) 19/2 OJLS 167–201.

by companies themselves, whereas multi-company Codes of different sorts are proposed to the companies from the outside and are intended to perform a model role. Here a sub-division is to be found:

- Trade Association Codes: These instruments may be adopted by associations of firms in a particular industry, as in the case of the International Council of Toy Industries, or offered to companies by country governments, such as the Bangladesh Garment Manufacturers and Exporters Association Code and the Kenya Flower Council Code.

- In relation with Multi-Stakeholder Codes, these codes are adopted as a result of negotiations between several stakeholders, including firms or their industry representatives, NGOs and/or trade unions. Governments may also be involved in the development of such codes. The UK's Ethical Trade Initiative (ETI) Base Code is an example of such a multi-stakeholder approach, as are the Fair Labour Association (FLA) or the Global Reporting Initiative (GRI).

- On the other hand, Intergovernmental Codes are negotiated at an international level by national governments. They date back to the 1970s, when both the OECD Guidelines for Multinational Enterprises and the ILO's Tripartite Declaration of Principles concerning Multinational Enterprises were adopted. Other intergovernmental codes are the EU Code of Conduct, the UN Norms of Responsibilities of Transnational Corporations and other Business Enterprises with Regard to Human Rights, and the UN Global Compact.

- The last reference includes Other Actors Codes devised to provide a benchmark of what a particular organization regards as good practice. These organizations may range from international trade unions (such as the ICFTU's Basic Code of Labour Practice) to certificating agencies (such as Social Accountability International), through NGOs (such as Amnesty International's Human Rights Guidelines for Companies). They are intended as a guide for companies and trade associations that are contemplating adoption of voluntary measures.

The selection of corporate and multi-company Codes for our discussion is based on a number of substantive criteria (different for each group), such as standard-setting role, cross-culturality, extent of rights covered (for multi-company Codes); and size and brand value of the company, sector, and membership of organizations that promote ethical business standards.[43] An exhaustive review of Codes is beyond

---

[43] Together with these substantive criteria a procedural one has been added, namely, information availability. This factor has determined to a substantial extent the number and type of Codes examined in our study. Intensive use of the outstanding 'Compendium of Ethic Codes and Instruments of Corporate Responsibility' has been made (K McKague and W Cragg, *Compendium of Ethics Codes and Instruments of Corporate Responsibility. A Collection of Influential Ethics Codes, Principles, Guidelines, Standards, and Other Instruments of Corporate Social Responsibility in Global Markets* (York University, Toronto, 2007) <http://www.yorku.ca/csr/_files/file.php?fileid=fileCDOICwJiei&filename=file_Codes_Compendium_Jan_2007.pdf>). Also data provided by more than 60 organizations have been used, including Worldwide Responsible Accredited Production (WRAP, www.wrapcompliance.com), Asia Monitor Resource Center (AMRC, http://www.amrc.org.hk/), and the Business & Human Rights Resource Center (www.business-humanrights.org).

the objective of this work. Here we only intend to extract a sense of self-regulation's trends as by examination of CoC. Keeping this in mind, a sample as broad and representative as possible is offered.

Careful application of the selection criteria have yielded a total of 25 multi-company Codes, and 55 corporate Codes (38 TNCs and 17 domestic companies), including those Codes combining as many respective selection criteria as possible. Our examination of these codes confirms our basic hypothesis, namely that current labour relations models prioritize social dialogue and negotiation over conflict, having as a side-effect the invisibility of the right to strike. The findings can be summarized as follows.

Scarcely any multi-company Code (ie, the Codes serving as models for Corporate Codes) includes the right to strike. Of the Codes examined, no inter-governmental Code includes it – not even the UN Global Compact – nor does any trade association Code, other actors Code or multi-stakeholder Code.[44] Most striking is the fact that even some international unions do not mention it.[45] They universally, however, place emphasis on honouring the rights of association and collective bargaining.[46] At the company level, few companies include the right to strike in their Code of Conduct. Apparently companies do not go beyond the principles covered in multi-company Codes. Therefore, corporate Codes typically include only freedom of association and the right to collective bargaining. Some companies' codes may be said to discourage striking or even some of the other rights, as in the case of The Coca-Cola Company, BP plc, and Levi Strauss Co, that speak of 'strike aversion'.

Some forerunner companies explicitly cover the right to strike in their documents, such as Nike, Inc and Adidas-Salomon. Significantly, they are strongly image-concerned enterprises and belong to the apparel industry, heavily hit by sweatshop scandals in the late 1990s. It can also be argued that some firms offer an implicit commitment to respect the right to strike by reason of their membership of organizations that mention it in their Codes, such as the Amnesty Business Group or the Fair Labor Association (FLA).

In respect of the other two rights, companies are mostly accustomed to express their will to open dialogue with employees and to promote the necessary means to ensure workers' participation wherever that is not supported, or prohibited, by domestic laws. Many firms have implemented – or more frequently trusted to external parties – some kind of monitoring system and certification process to make sure their suppliers respect basic rights, among them labour rights. This might

---

[44] There are few exceptions to this pattern. In regard to other actors' Codes, they are the Amnesty International Human Rights Principles for Companies, or the International Trade Union Confederation (ITUC) for multi-stakeholder Codes, the Fair Labor Association Workplace Code of Conduct, and for trade associations, the Australian-Asian Pacific Mining Network: Principles for the Conduct of Company Operations.

[45] Instances of that are the international trade union ICFTU's Code, or the Codes of Conduct presented as appendix to the 'Agreement between IKEA and the union International Federation of Building and Wood Workers' (IFBWW).

[46] However, an exception is the International Council on Mining and Metals (ICMM).

indirectly account for some conflict arbitration systems in place. Nike, Inc, H&M, Gap, Inc, Rio Tinto, and Sasol (with its 'joint forums between trade unions and management') are examples of companies that explicitly address the need for managers to sort out labour problems through dialogue and workers' participation. In some cases, the codes go so far as to detailing specific measures for the case of conflict outbursts – that is, strikes. That is the case of Adidas-Salomon's 'Improving Worker–Management Communication' chart. This example apart, most companies apparently do not consider it important to set out conflict-handling measures in their Codes. Summarizing, the general invisibility of the right to strike both in multi-company and corporate Codes is evident.

Employer culture promotes arbitration systems to resolve divergences but conflict is not understood as a dynamic reality with the possibility to build new industrial relations relationships.

D. Transforming the regulation of social rights through conflict as a manifestation of solidarity

In examining labour law in transformation, it is important to incorporate within a broadened debate the role played by conflict as a natural instrument not only of integration of social divergences but also of transformation of labour regulation. The role that conflictual activism plays in changing social relations of power is undeniable and encompasses a multilevel scenario extending from eurostrikes to local activism. Although the critical public voice of workers – and other actors such as the unemployed, public servants, and the self-employed – may often be ignored by the media, such expressions of criticism hold an ability to transform social rights. Union-based conflict is often linked with allied social movements which have become significant.

The metamorphosis that unions have undergone, responding to globalization by acting simultaneously nationally and internationally – an approach some scholars have called the new transnational activism[47] – and subsequent changes within this transnational activism,[48] have to be analysed within the framework of the dynamics of contention which permit actors such as labour to play a role in the regulation of social conditions essential to developing democracy.[49] Strikes, and the way they are regulated legally, are intrinsic to this process. Some examples of how the right to strike can play a transformative role will be introduced below along with a brief examination of tragic results of the non-integration of conflict in the workplace.

As we have suggested above, the strike and protest form part of a broader set of ways to externalize social conflict, but more and more the right to strike has come to encompass political (or partially political) protest which includes broader groups of strikers than workers. Strikes reflective of this political component may be

---

[47] S Tarrow, *The New Transnational Activism* (Cambridge University Press, 2005).
[48] J Smith, *Social Movements for Global Democracy* (John Hopkins University Press, 2008) 128.
[49] D McAdam et al *Dynamics of Contention* (Cambridge University Press, 2001).

organized not only to defend labour law outcomes but also to shape a broader policy agenda. Several cases serve to illustrate this point.

France provides us with an example of a regulatory system shaped by strikes and protests as well a long tradition of conflictual activism. This national case could be integrated in a first group of protests or strikes intended to influence state regulations in what we may think of as 'blocking' strikes and protest which seek to *prevent* approval of newly proposed regulations. In France in 2006, Prime Minister Villepin proposed a reform of labour contracts for young people called the Contract for First Employment. These proposed contracts were intended to increase the possibilities of young people to enter the labour market. France's major unions called for a general strike to protest against this policy, which introduced a more precarious labour situation for young workers. The regulation was initially approved by the National Assembly but never applied. As a consequence of the pressure generated by strikes, the French legislature approved a new regulation replacing the precarious new contracts for young workers. In this case, the impact of the protesters went directly to parliamentary power, in the sense that the strikes and protest achieved their goal of rescinding a regulation. This type of activism obligates political powers to eliminate regulations which reduce labour rights. Here the main actors were not only workers but also young students. The French combination of protests and strikes introduced new actors into the regulatory process with important consequences, transforming macro-level policies. The impact of strikes was transformative.

A second case of transformation by conflict oriented toward regulatory powers took place in Spain. In that country a major general strike attempted to reverse a policy which had been put into effect. In 2002 the government introduced a regulation (Real Decreto-ley 5/2002, de 24 de mayo) reducing rights for the unemployed. The principal unions offered a strong response and organized a general strike against the policy. The strike was very successful and the government withdrew some of the most controversial articles in the regulation. In this case the main actors were the unions but just as in the French case, students also participated in large numbers. The Spanish regulation was modified by the government following the protesters' effort to reorient the political powers. Additionally, the Spanish Constitutional Court resolved a case-law action posed by the unions and declared there was no urgent situation justifying the use of decree power by the government to introduce the new restrictive regulation.

The Spanish and French cases, both instances in which the goal was to reverse new policies which made work more precarious, provide evidence of the political ingredient of strikes and protest. In the French case this is characterized by the macro policy goal, to transform labour market policy protecting unemployment and in this sense the transformation was located at the macro level. One of the differences with the Spanish case is that in this second instance after the protest unions bargained with the Minister of Labour agreeing to the elimination of some regulations in the Law.

These two examples illustrate the effect that strikes can have interacting with legislative and judicial powers and that strikes can modify the initial equilibrium of forces. These are cases of political activism which mobilizes against the macro-politics of proposed regulations. In these two instances, the law permitted the right to strike and protest for political ends. We can view the conflict as holding significant visibility in the shape ultimately taken by legislation but nonetheless not to the same extent in the media which tried to minimize the number of protesters reported in its coverage. In these cases, strikes converged with massive protest in the streets and ended in a general strike. Such campaigns typically hold a greater capacity to interact with political powers than more limited strike actions, reflected by recent conflicts in China.

An important recent case took place in China in 2010, when protest and strikes were initially directed against two multinational firms, Honda and Toyota. As the Chinese case shows, the spill-over of these micro level cases can have a contagious effect, provoking a series of similar strikes and protests in other multinationals. The protest was not called by the unions, but instead by rank-and-file workers fighting for a wage increase during a 10-day strike against Honda. This initial effort produced important consequences. The *New York Times* reports the protest on 30 May 2010 and 'wonders if rapidly rising industrial wages in China may disrupt supply lines to companies around the world and discourage future investment by Chinese and global alike'. The striking workers accused the Chinese unions including the All-China Federation of Trade Unions (ACFTU) of corruption. Many intellectuals supported the workers, emphasizing their poor labour conditions. Although strikes are illegal in China, the government feared that the conflict could spread through a spill-over effect generating more protest against other multinationals. The ACFTU placed on their web page a proposal for a collective bargaining salary system. Honda offered some increase in salaries. The workers' efforts made an impact.

This Chinese case was an initially micro-level strike which ultimately exerted an important spill-over effect on unions, government, and multinationals. The media took notice but their coverage heavily emphasized the strictly economic impact of the protest. *Businessweek* announced on 22 July 2010: 'Honda strike in China ends pay hike.' *The Guardian*, 17 June 2010, said: 'Strikes in China signal end to era of low cost labour and cheap exports'; and *The Independent*, 19 June 2010, announced: 'Strikes threaten China's status as the factory of the world.' The workers' action occupied a very important part of the hard news, but not as politics or as a positively transformative event. The coverage centred on the strike's economic relevance.

The impact of conflict transforms societies and regulation, creating a dynamic interaction among social actors and increasing political participation. But can we assume that conflict is always channelled in a positive direction or that it always takes the form of strikes? What could happen in the absence of an industrial relations system within the firm that recognizes the dignity of workers? It is possible to extract some lessons from the France Telecom case.

Between the beginning of January 2008 and 2010, 34 workers of France Telecom committed suicide. France Telecom faced a scandalous situation in which 32 workers ended their lives as a result of the firm's human resources policy.

Each of these workers left a letter explaining the reason for this dramatic decision. The letters coincided in their declaration of a motivation, with some of them writing: 'I commit suicide because I work in France Telecom.' The workers also linked their suicides with one another, each one indicating: 'I am number . . .' The workers connected their suicides to one another as a macabre collective action protesting against the inhuman policy which the firm had introduced in response to the economic crisis.

The impact of these suicides resulted in the French government's intervention pushing the firm to change its policies. Recent information related with the case confirms that the company's new salary policy, in order to create better relations in the workplace, reduces the salaries of managers.

The interesting question about this case is how the workers constructed collective action connecting the different suicides by communicating in writing the motivation for their decision and by elaborating a line enumerating all the workers who died. There is another reported case of several workers suicides which took place in China. Foxconn Technology Group is a multinational with its main plant in China. It is the largest manufacturer of electronics in the world. In 2010 some of the workers, pressured by the firm's stress-inducing security system, committed suicide – after being subject to interrogation by the Central Security Division. Apple has confirmed these suicides. The suicides in both the French case and the Chinese case have been reported by the media.

Despite the tendency of the media to limit information on strikes and protest, the hard news has reported the impact of activism on economies. This opens a new perspective on the media visibility of protest; economic information appears to constitute the core of hard news. One other avenue leading to the reporting of conflict is the discussion in the soft news of suicides, which are seen as information that will attract an audience.

Labour law is a dynamic process involving different actors who interact in a framework of complex instruments of regulation and as such, 'has a contribution to make to the real and large problems of the world'.[50] Conflict has its place in this process as part of the overall strategy that workers and employees make use of to improve labour and social conditions within democratic societies. Trying to achieve these goals, workers need alliances with other groups and a dialectic relation with collective bargaining. Only a complete and interactive puzzle can provide labour law with the conceptual and empirical ingredients needed to work successfully.

It is crucial to underscore the capacity of workers to organize, to bargain (with power) and to strike, and to assert the view that labour scholars have to be more conscious of these multiple capacities.[51] Labour law as a scholarly field should not be contaminated with the invisibility and the denial of social conflict which often predominate in the larger society. Conflict exists even if scholars

---

[50] B Langille, 'Labour Law's Back Pages' in G Davidov and B Langille (eds), *Boundaries and Frontiers of Labour Law* (Hart Publishing, 2006) 33.
[51] G Davidov, 'The Reports of my Death are Greatly Exaggerated: "Employee" as a Viable (Though Over-Used) Legal Concept' in Davidov and Langille (eds), above n 50, 138.

UNIVERSITY OF WINCHESTER
LIBRARY

minimize its significance. Pressures from below and worker solidarity help to configure the terrain of industrial relations and, more broadly, of democracy. The right to strike has a crucial place in the future of labour law, channelling and at times reducing conflict and transforming societies in ways that may limit injustice and promote equality.[52] Legal systems have to be more permeable to new forms of activism, eliminating the prohibition on political strikes which has a negative effect constraining the creation of solidarities. Labour law scholars have to be aware of the significance of strikes and conflict, and to integrate it as a point of reference in the general debates on the transformation of labour law. We have to *hear* workers in the academic arena, not only when they are sitting in a collective bargaining session, but also when they are in movement, because this is the way for fresh air to enter in the construction of labour law.

---

[52] A Hyde, 'What is Labour Law?' in Davidov and Langille (eds), above n 50.

PART V

NEW IDEAS OF LABOUR LAW FROM AN INTERNATIONAL PERSPECTIVE

22

Out of the Shadows? The Non-Binding Multilateral Framework on Migration (2006) and Prospects for Using International Labour Regulation to Forge Global Labour Market Membership

Leah F Vosko[*]

Around the turn of the 21st century, the International Labour Organization (ILO) embarked on efforts to remake itself in response to challenges to the boundaries of labour law and policy, on the one hand, and its role vis-à-vis other international organizations related to migration, trade, and development, on the other hand. It did so partly by adopting 'constitutionally significant'[1] declarations on Fundamental Principles and Rights at Work (1998) and Social Justice and Fair Globalization (2008) and partly by renewing normative instruments in targeted areas.

A growing body of scholarship examining the foregoing declarations critically assesses which principles and rights these instruments cast as fundamental and with what effects.[2] However, there has been limited attention to the visions of membership

---

[*] Professor and Canada Research Chair in the Political Economy of Gender and Work, York University, Toronto. I thank the Social Sciences and Humanities Research Council of Canada (Standard Grants Program) for funding the research undertaken for this chapter, Melissa Sharpe and John Grundy for their research assistance, and Gerald Kernerman, Christina Gabriel, and participants at the workshop 'The Idea of Labour Law' (Cambridge University, April 2010), especially Guy Davidov and Brian Langille, for their comments on earlier versions of the text.

[1] B Langille, 'The ILO and the New Economy: Recent Developments' (1999) 15(3) International Journal of Comparative Labour Law & Industrial Relations 229.

[2] Upon its adoption in 1998, a number of scholars argued that the Declaration of Fundamental Principles and Rights at Work threatened to erode the large corpus of international labour regulations by making adherence to only a limited set of conventions a constitutional obligation among ILO Member States (See, for instance, L Compa, 'The ILO Core Standards Declaration: Changing the Climate for Changing the Law' (2003) Perspectives on Work 24; and P Alston and J Heenan, 'Shrinking the International Labour Code' (2004) 36 NYU Journal of International Law and Politics 221. Tacitly acknowledging the validity of these early concerns, in a more recent intervention the ILO's legal advisor suggests that the subsequent Declaration on Social Justice and Fair Globalization resolves such concerns by calling for social justice and fair globalization through decent work and adopting an integrated approach (F Maupain, 'New Foundation or New Façade? The ILO and the 2008 Declaration on Social Justice for a Fair Globalization' (2009) 20(3) European Journal of International Law 823).

poised to underpin normative international labour regulations of the future – that is, to the question of *who* is assumed to belong to the group of workers entitled to, and able to access without undue risk or hardship, the full range of labour protections?[3] This question is nevertheless critical to international labour regulations responding to changes in the global economy such as shifts in the balance between permanent and temporary international migration for employment and in patterns of labour force participation among women and men.

Responding to this gap, this chapter analyzes how and to what effect one such instrument approaches the question of membership for workers hitherto excluded or partially excluded on the basis of citizenship – the Non-Binding Multilateral Framework on Migration (2006). Through a review of historical and contemporary international labour regulations on migration, pursued on the assumption that migration laws and policies represent the main hurdle to citizenship,[4] I show that the Multilateral Framework on Migration (MFM) brings issues fundamental to migrant workers' protection out of the shadows. At the same time, membership norms underlying this newest normative ILO instrument on migration continue to reflect familiar tensions between nation states' preoccupation with preserving their sovereignty in the migration policy field and the objective of improving labour protection for migrant workers, presumed to require collective action at the international scale. Although this outcome is predictable in light of historical patterns and tendencies, it underlines a fundamental political limit to using international labour regulation to reshape labour law and policy with respect to citizenship in an inclusive direction. The overarching logic of the MFM highlights the need for an alternative approach fostering what I label global labour market membership – a notion I elaborate towards the conclusion of the chapter that entails freeing key labour protections from the domain of the nation state.

Before proceeding, two framing comments are in order: first, in this chapter, I use membership to refer to participation norms surrounding who labour protections aim to serve by design, application, and enforcement. An emphasis on membership permits exploring a variety of axes of differentiation and exclusion from labour protection. It allows for probing, for example, how form of employment (eg, part-time or full-time, temporary or permanent) relates to the scope of coverage of labour laws and policies,[5] how gender relations impinge on divisions of paid and unpaid

---

[3] In this chapter, consistent with the terms of the MFM and its precursors, I adopt a broad definition of labour protection, encompassing mechanisms (collective and individual) providing for fair and just terms and conditions of work and employment as well as social security.

[4] C Dauvergne, 'Citizenship with a Vengeance' (2007) 8(2) Theoretical Inquiries in Law 489; see also C Dauvergne, *Making People Illegal: What Globalization Means for Migration and Law* (Cambridge University Press, 2008).

[5] See, eg, W Clement, *The Struggle to Organize: Resistance in Canada's Fishery* (McClelland & Stewart, 1986); LF Vosko, *Temporary Work: The Gendered Rise of a Precarious Employment Relationship* (University of Toronto Press, 2000); G Davidov, 'The Three Axes of Employment Relationships: A Characterization of Workers in Need of Protection' (2002) 52 University of Toronto Law Journal 357; J Fudge et al, *The Legal Concept of Employment: Marginalizing Workers* (Law Commission of Canada, 2002); J Fudge et al, 'Employee or Independent Contractor? Charting the Legal Significance of the Distinction in Canada' (2003) 10(2) Canadian Journal of Labour and Employment Law 193; and J Fudge et al, 'Changing Boundaries of Employment: Developing a New Platform for Labour Law' (2003) 10(3) Canadian Journal of Labour and Employment Law 361.

labour shaping men's and women's labour force status (e.g., employed, unemployed, or discouraged) and, among the employed, scheduling and work arrangements,[6] as well as how age, especially the youth and retirement phases of life, affects perceptions of labour force attachment.[7] It also supports investigations of how citizenship boundaries mediate conditions of work and employment through entry category (ie, citizens, temporary migrant workers, and non-status workers are often accorded differential labour protection) – a central preoccupation of this chapter.[8]

Second, international labour regulations are the chosen focus since certain patterns and tendencies in the regulation of migration for employment are uniquely visible at this scale.[9] Because by definition international migration for employment is a trans-border process and thus laws and policies governing migrant work, while developed and applied predominantly within nation states, hinge on inter-state dynamics, international labour regulations offer an instructive window through which to explore the tension between states' concern to preserve their sovereignty in the migration policy field and the need for collective action to protect migrant workers. More than international labour regulations addressing other policy fields, those on migration come up against national sovereignty: namely, the ability to define populations that can make claims on the state in contrast to those, within and outside a given national territory, who cannot.[10] They thereby have the capacity to reveal the 'institution of citizenship, tying particular persons to particular states . . . as a powerful instrument of social closure.'[11] Through this angle, the management of populations covered by the inter-state system comes uniquely into view.[12] The MFM is, moreover, especially instructive to analyze through this lens since, as

[6] See, eg, P and H Armstrong, *The Double Ghetto: Canadian Women and their Segregated Work* (McClelland and Stewart, 3rd edn, 1994); and A Nyberg et al, 'Sweden: Precarious Work and Precarious Unemployment' in LF Vosko, M MacDonald, and I Campbell (eds), *Gender and the Contours of Precarious Employment* (Routledge, 2009).
[7] See, eg, P Anisef and P Axelrod (eds), *Transitions: Schooling and Employment in Canada* (Thompson Education Publications, 1993).
[8] See, eg, R Lister, *Citizenship: Feminist Perspectives* (Macmillan, 1997); LS Bosniak, *The Citizen and the Alien: Dilemmas of Contemporary Membership* (Princeton University Press, 2002); and D Sainsbury, 'Immigrants' Social Rights in Comparative Perspective: Welfare Regimes, Forms of Immigration and Immigration Policy Regimes' (2003) 16(3) Journal of European Social Policy 229.
[9] They are the focus due to their framing role, specifically, the frameworks for adaptation in multiple contexts that they offer. As I argue elsewhere, although international labour regulations are undeniably limited in their direct effects, their terms reflect the negotiation of key tensions between workers and employers as well as state and non-state actors since they are constructed through cumulative processes of exchange between interconnected sources of regulation (LF Vosko, *Managing the Margins: Gender, Citizenship and the International Regulation of Precarious Employment* (Oxford University Press, 2010)).
[10] S Hall and D Held, 'Citizens and Citizenship' in S Hall and M Jacques (eds), *New Times: The Changing Face of Politics in the 1990s* (Verso, 1990) 173, 176; J Brodie, 'Three Stories of Canadian Citizenship' in R Adamoski, DE Chunn, and R Menzies (eds), *Contesting Canadian Citizenship: Historical Readings* (Broadview Press, 2002) 43, 44; and DK Stasiulis and AB Bakan, *Negotiating Citizenship: Migrant Women in Canada and the Global System* (University of Toronto Press, 2005) 16.
[11] R Brubaker, 'Are Immigration Control Efforts Really Failing?' in W Cornelius, P Martin, and J Hollifield (eds), *Controlling Immigration: A Global Perspective* (Stanford, Stanford University Press, 1994) 227, 230; see also Bosniak, above n 8.
[12] B Hindess, 'Citizenship in the International Management of Populations' (2000) 43(9) American Behavioural Scientist 1486.

opposed to its constitutional counterparts, as a normative regulation it represents a 'tool through which the ILO provides guidance to its members about the steps recommended to implement its objectives'.[13]

As such, in considering justifications and means for broadening labour law's focus from employment relations to work or labour market relations, one of this volume's central themes, this chapter might also be read as a reflection on the 'methodological nationalism' of international labour regulation – its tendency to take 'the nation/state/society [a]s the natural social political form of the modern world' or to equate society and the nation state.[14] Scholars analyzing its prevalence in academic inquiry point to two intersecting modes of methodological nationalism in particular: naturalization, that is, taking national discourses, agendas, and logics for granted, contributing to a 'container model of society that encompasses a culture, a polity, an economy, and a bounded social group';[15] and, territorial limitation[16] (or what some label the territorialization of the imaginary[17]), that is, the reduction of analytic focus to boundaries of nation states, with the effect of making a category of practice (the nation state) *the* category of analysis, leading to the treatment of nation states as domains of identity in which 'the people' share common origins and of states as sovereign systems of government identified with particular territories.[18]

The notion of methodological nationalism has developed principally as a critique of scholarship in the social sciences. In its focus on tensions surrounding national sovereignty and the objective of improving labour protection for migrant workers characterizing the MFM, this chapter, in contrast, explores the methodological nationalism of this instrument itself. At the same time, its findings suggest that scholars studying international labour regulation, and labour law and policy more broadly, could benefit from interrogating the methodologically nationalist bases of their own practices.

A. Citizenship boundaries in international labour regulations on migration for employment: an historical perspective[19]

To comprehend fully the membership norms underpinning the MFM, it is necessary to situate them in their historical context. This process entails considering, in particular, axes of differentiation and exclusion from labour protection on the basis of citizenship. For this reason, the remainder of the chapter focuses on

---

[13] See Maupain, above n 2, at 831.
[14] A Wimmer and N Glick Schiller, 'Methodological Nationalism and Beyond: Nation-State Building, Migration and the Social Sciences' (2002) 2(4) Global Networks 301; and U Beck and N Sznaider, 'Unpacking Cosmopolitanism for the Social Sciences: A Research Agenda' (2006) 57(1) British Journal of Sociology 1, 3.
[15] A Wimmer and N Glick Schiller, 'Methodological Nationalism, the Social Sciences and the Study of Migration: An Essay in Historical Epistemology' (2003) 37(3) International Migration Review 579.
[16] Ibid, 581.
[17] Wimmer and Glick Schiller, above n 14.
[18] Beck and Sznaider, above n 14, 3–4.
[19] Elements of this section draw on historical research undertaken for my book *Managing the Margins*; see Vosko, above n 9.

membership norms along this axis even though I illustrate elsewhere that in the international labour code citizenship boundaries have always been intimately intertwined with gender relations, age, form of employment, etc. International labour regulations related to migration for employment fall into three categories – those of general application,[20] those of relevance to migrant workers, and those addressed to migrant workers specifically. Substantively, they tend to focus on social security and problems confronting migrant workers.[21] Considering international labour regulations in all three categories, conceptions of membership with respect to citizenship evolved in four phases from the inception of the ILO to the adoption of the MFM. Each phase was shaped by the tension between nation states' concern to preserve their sovereignty in the migration field and the recognized need for international cooperation in protecting migrant workers. Yet at different historical moments, approaches to mediating this tension, and thus to citizenship boundaries, varied in form and intensity.

1. Phase I: National worker-citizenship: subjecting membership to reciprocity

In the first phase, full membership extended exclusively to national citizens. ILO constituents sought to improve conditions of labour internationally. At the same time, in defense of national sovereignty, they distinguished sharply between labour protections for national citizens and migrant workers. In this phase, the approach was to make the terms of international labour regulations then under development subject to reciprocity, specifically to reciprocal agreements between nation states (bilateral or multilateral) governing the protection of covered migrant workers in their respective territories.

This initial phase began with the Treaty of Versailles creating the ILO, which stated that 'the standard set by law in each country with respect to conditions of labour should have due regard to equitable economic treatment of all workers *lawfully present*.'[22] Shortly thereafter, similar sentiments were expressed in the preamble to the ILO Constitution (1919), which characterized the 'protection of the interests of workers when employed in countries other than their own' as vital to improving the conditions of labour internationally.[23] The latter thereby sought to foster the observance of basic labour rights internationally and the former gestured towards non-discrimination, albeit qualified to encompass 'lawfully present' migrant workers only.

---

[20] Analyses published by the International Labour Office often note that all conventions and recommendations adopted by the International Labour Conference are of general application even if they do not contain provisions dealing with migrants; substantiating this claim, the ILO Committee of Experts on the Application of Standards refers explicitly to the situation of migrant workers in supervising the application of many such instruments. For a list of instruments referenced by this Committee in recent years, see ILO, *Committee of Experts on the Application of Standards* (87th International Labour Conference, Geneva, June 1999) para 38.

[21] Ibid para 34.

[22] League of Nations, Treaty of Versailles: Treaty of Peace between the Allied and Associated Powers and Germany (1919) Art 427, italics added.

[23] ILO, *Constitution of the ILO* (1919) Preamble, para 2.

Despite the inclusive tenor of these constitutionally significant instruments, many standards of relevance to or addressed explicitly to migrant workers were motivated by different aims. The Unemployment Convention (1919), for example, obliged ratifying countries with systems of unemployment insurance to make arrangements to provide the same rates of benefits to migrant workers as national citizens; however, rather than promoting inclusivity, the goal of this provision was preventing unfair competition within nations, specifically the concern that the limited duration of many migrant workers' stay would undermine the sustainability of social security provision for national citizens.[24] This dynamic took sharper expression in the Reciprocity of Treatment of Foreign Workers Recommendation (1919), the first international labour regulation addressed specifically to the situation of migrant workers, which called for equality of treatment, on the condition of reciprocity, between citizen and migrant workers regarding a broader set of social protections that included unemployment relief as well as freedom of association. Together with the Unemployment Convention, this recommendation worked to shape the subsequent Equality of Treatment (Accident Compensation) Convention (1925), addressing migrant workers' conditions of employment. Contrasting with previous tendencies, the Equality of Treatment (Accident Compensation) Convention provided for extending to migrant workers and their families equality of treatment in terms of workers' compensation subject neither to reciprocity nor to any condition of residence. However, accident compensation for decades remained the only area in which no such conditions were to apply, an exception justified by the consensus that national compensation systems addressing occupational injury and disease for all workers are integral to improving labour conditions everywhere.[25]

Of the instruments focusing specifically on migrant workers adopted early in ILO history,[26] foremost was the Migration for Employment Convention (1939) aimed at limiting abuses, such as misleading propaganda, and improving the supply of information and the provision of services to migrant workers. To foster the observance of basic human rights, this convention called for agreements between countries, setting out terms for recruitment, placement, and conditions of employment. In addition, it provided a framework for applying 'to foreigners treatment no less favourable than that which it applies to its own nationals', with respect to remuneration, the right to belong to a trade union, employment taxes, dues or contributions, and legal proceedings related to contracts of employment.[27]

---

[24] Ibid Art 3; ILO, 'The International Emigration Commission' (1921) 4(3) International Labour Review 537, 551–2. Furthermore, as Hasenau has shown, 'concern about the competitive repercussions of advanced social security schemes' influenced early ILO regulations encouraging countries to negotiate bilateral agreements to provide select provisions for equality of treatment between national and migrant workers (M Hasenau, 'ILO Standards on Migrant Workers: The Fundamentals of the UN Convention and their Genesis' (1991) 25(4) International Migration Review 687).

[25] H Creutz, 'The ILO and Social Security for Foreign and Migrant Workers' (1968) 97(4) International Labour Review 351.

[26] For instance, the ILO Inspection of Emigrants Convention (No 21) (1926) and Migration (Protection of Females at Sea) Recommendation (No 26) (1926).

[27] ILO, Migration for Employment Convention (No 66) (25th International Labour Conference, Geneva, June 1939) Arts 6.1 and 6.2.

Such provisions could also be made subject to reciprocity. Even so, the convention never came into force because it did not achieve a sufficient level of ratification: nation states' objections to including the principle of equal treatment between national citizens and lawfully present migrant workers in a normative instrument, even strictly qualified, thwarted its implementation.

2. Phase II: Graduated worker-citizenship: an international consensus on preferential treatment for national citizens and permanent residents

In the second phase, which commenced with the end of the Second World War, a graduated conception of membership took shape in international labour regulations. The concern to accommodate populations displaced by war and to support the creation of welfare states, particularly of the Keynesian variety in advanced capitalist countries, shaped efforts to mediate familiar tensions. To this end, the Philadelphia Declaration (1944) singled out the problems faced by migrant workers. It strengthened the obligation of the ILO to support nations in developing 'facilities for training and the transfer of labour, including migration for employment and settlement.'[28] Shortly thereafter, a Migration for Employment Convention (1949) was finally adopted that came into force. This convention required any state that ratified it to give 'immigrants lawfully within its territory treatment no less favourable than that which it applies to its own nationals' on matters relating to remuneration, family allowances, and, where applicable, hours of work, overtime arrangements, holidays with pay, membership of trade unions, and the benefits of collective bargaining and social security.[29] Yet in these and other areas the notion of treatment no less favourable than nationals was qualified even further than in its 1939 precursor.[30] Although its provisions were to apply 'without discrimination in respect of nationality, race, religion or sex', the terms of the convention extended most fully to workers entering with authorization to settle permanently and ultimately to obtain citizenship in a receiving country.[31] The convention's provision for preferential treatment of immigrants took particular expression in Article 11.1, permitting exclusions from the definition of 'migrant for employment,' including 'short-term entry of members of

---

[28] ILO, Declaration Concerning the Aims and Purposes of the International Labour Organization (Philadelphia Declaration) Part III c.

[29] ILO, Migration for Employment (Revised) Convention (No 97) (32nd International Labour Conference, Geneva, June 1949) Art 6.1.

[30] Eg, social security provision was subject to arrangements, set out by receiving countries, for the acquisition of rights; the convention also permitted receiving countries to 'prescribe special arrangements concerning benefits or portions of benefits which are payable wholly out of public funds' (ibid Art 6.1b.i–ii).

[31] Ibid Art 6.1. To foster this outcome, a Model Agreement on Temporary and Permanent Migration for Employment appended to the associated recommendation included a provision calling on authorities in the country of immigration to 'facilitate the procedure of naturalisation' for those destined for permanent migration (ILO, Migration for Employment Recommendation (No 86) (32nd International Labour Conference, Geneva, June 1949) Annex Art 14).

liberal professions and artists.' To facilitate ratification, the convention also included a section of universally applicable general provisions, as well as three optional annexes, which governments could include or exclude in any combination.

The formulation of this convention, as well as provisions permitting preferential treatment for immigrants, introduced yet another fundamental distinction or boundary linked to membership that would later become entrenched in ILO regulations, and developed further in a subsequent UN convention – the division between migrant workers authorized to reside on a temporary basis and immigrants destined for permanent residency. Only immigrants were to benefit, as far as possible, from the full range of labour protections. In this way, the first ILO standard on migrant work entering into force provided for inferior rights and entitlements for employed workers lacking national citizenship in the countries in which they worked.

Adopted a decade later, the Discrimination (Employment and Occupation) Convention (1958) reinforced this approach. Although in crafting this standard of general application, in response to collective struggles among women and people of colour in particular, constituents included sex, race, colour, religion, political opinion, and national extraction as grounds for non-discrimination, but they omitted nationality.[32] Negotiations towards the convention pronounced that restrictions on employment based on nationality are 'expected, non-discriminatory and a natural outcome of the migration contract.'[33] There were some attempts to compensate for this omission through the adoption of international labour regulations geared specifically to migrants.[34] There were also efforts to develop further an international social security system.[35] However, they were limited.

Almost two decades later, marking the apex of this second phase, the Migrant Work (Supplementary Provisions) Convention (1975) entrenched this graduated framework. This convention was motivated by concerns to address abuse as well as to extend provisions for equality of opportunity and treatment for migrant workers but without undermining the terms of a convention on discrimination excluding nationality as a ground for non-discrimination. Advancing the latter aim was, however, complicated by the growth of guest worker programs in Western Europe, North America, and Australia resorting to migrant workers under time-limited arrangements. Drafters of the 1975 convention thus divided it into two parts, either of which ratifying states could exclude. The outcome: discrimination on the basis of workers' national citizenship, and hence differentiation by entry categories, then becoming more numerous, remained permissible.

[32] ILO, Fourth Item on the Agenda: Discrimination in the Field of Employment and Occupation (Report IV) (42nd International Labour Conference, Geneva, June 1958).
[33] ILO, Discrimination in the Field of Employment and Occupation, Report VII (1) (39th International Labour Conference, Geneva, June 1956) paras 17–18.
[34] Chief examples include the Protection of Migrant Workers (Underdeveloped Countries) Recommendation (No 100) (1955) and the Plantations Convention and Recommendation (Nos 110 and 101) (1958).
[35] Two examples include the Equality of Treatment Social Security Convention (No 118) (1962) and the Social Policy (Basic Aims and Standards) Convention (No 117) (1962).

Part I of the convention committed states to respect the basic human rights of all migrant workers and to limit their 'illegal movements'. Nation states' concerns to address the abuse of migrant workers, such as the 'dubious recruitment practices' of agents recognized since the adoption of the Unemployment Convention in 1919, while preserving their autonomy in the arena of immigration policy, shaped this section.[36] Part II, in contrast, obliged ratifying states to promote 'equality of opportunity and treatment in respect of employment and occupation, of social security, of trade union and cultural rights and of individual and collective freedoms' for migrant workers and their families.[37] Despite this compromise two-part formulation, states such as Australia and the United States opposed the passage of the convention, fearing that the free choice of employment provided for in Part II would undermine their guest worker programmes. Furthermore, of the few Western states that subsequently ratified the convention, many opted to exclude Part II.

3. Phase III: Multi-tiered worker-citizenship: differential treatment on the basis of (expanding) entry categories through a human rights-based approach

For decades after the adoption of the Migrant Work (Supplementary Provisions) Convention, there were no new ILO regulations addressing migrant workers specifically. However, in 1990, initiating a third phase in international labour regulation, motivated by the failure of the ILO's tripartite model to foster modifications of old and/or the creation of new instruments on migrant work, a UN Convention on the Protection of the Rights of All Migrant Workers and Members of their Families sought to mediate the mounting tensions between the need for collective action to improve migrant workers' protection, now scarcely questioned by states and non-state actors, and nation states' continued reticence to reduce their sovereignty in the migration policy field. It did so by furthering a multi-tiered conception of worker-citizenship involving a degree of territorial limitation; that is, it introduced a framework, guided partly by a human rights-approach,[38] in which national citizenship remained a central factor mediating access to labour protections for many non-citizen workers while providing for other mediating factors unrelated to citizenship, such as non-citizen workers' socially recognized skill level.[39]

---

[36] WR Böhning, 'The ILO and Contemporary International Economic Migration' (1976) 10(2) International Migration Review 147.

[37] ILO, Migrant Work (Supplementary Provisions) Convention (No 143) (60th International Labour Conference, Geneva, June 1975) Part I, Art 6.1 and Part II, Art 10.

[38] A 'human rights-based approach' refers to UN agencies' efforts to mainstream human rights principles underpinning the Universal Declaration of Human Rights and other international instruments, specifically universality and inalienability, indivisibility, interdependence and interrelatedness, non-discrimination and equality, participation and inclusion, accountability and the rule of law. See UN, 'The Human Rights-Based Approach: Statement of Common Understanding (Annex B)' (2003) Inter-Agency Workshop on a human rights-based approach in the context of UN reform.

[39] To be clear, as it is defined in scholarship on methodological nationalism, territorial limitation entails focusing exclusively on the boundaries of nation states. However, the multi-tiered conception of worker-citizenship fostered by the UN convention permits factors beyond an exclusive focus on

Elaborating a longstanding tiering process, this convention divided migrant workers into 'irregular' workers or persons that are 'undocumented' and 'regular' workers or persons 'lawfully' employed within the territory of the receiving country. Under its terms, regular workers were further subdivided into those admitted on a permanent basis (or immigrants eligible ultimately for citizenship or residency in their country of employment) and those admitted on finite bases (ie, migrant workers).[40]

The first tier of the convention, designed to be universally applicable, enumerated civil and political rights as well as economic, social, and cultural rights delineated elsewhere while naming those of particular importance to migrant workers, such as freedom of exit and the right to stay in one's country of origin. It also articulated a series of new rights and protections for all migrant workers, including protection from arbitrary expulsion.[41] Applicable to workers in a regular (ie legalized) situation, the second tier provided for access to education and social services. It also called for the extension of 'treatment no less favourable than' that which applies to nationals to so-called regular workers in a variety of areas (eg, remuneration, hours of work, safety, etc).[42] The third tier, in turn, extended additional rights applicable to 'particular categories' of workers in a regular situation and their families regardless of the terms of their stay, such as a general right to freedom of movement within a state of employment and the right to be temporarily absent from that state.[43] To promote ratification among countries that might otherwise reject the terms of the convention due to concerns that they would undermine their guest worker programs, several provisions of this tier permitted receiving states to limit regular migrant workers' free choice of employment and to set other conditions tied to their terms of employment.[44] Carrying this logic further, the fourth tier provided for a range of exclusions from rights delineated in the third tier for certain subcategories of regular workers, such as migrant

---

nationality to shape access to labour protections and rights, such as the skill level of workers. Specifically, as illustrated below, the various tiers of worker-citizenship introduced under the UN convention provide a framework for countries to provide migrant workers deemed to hold specialized skills pathways to full citizenship while preserving mechanisms for excluding migrant workers deemed to be low-skill. The framework of the convention thus facilitated the consolidation of temporary migration programs for low-skilled migrant workers in countries such as Canada. For a concise review of such programs, see, eg, J Fudge and F McPhail, 'The Temporary Foreign Worker Program In Canada: Low-Skilled Workers As An Extreme Form Of Flexible Labour' (2009) 31(5) Comparative Labor Law and Policy Journal 5.

[40] UN, Convention on the Protection of the Rights of All Migrant Workers and Members of their Families (1990) Arts 5a and 5b.

[41] Ibid Arts 22 and 56.

[42] Ibid Part IV and Art 25.

[43] Ibid Arts 40–2.

[44] Ibid Art 52.2a–b.

Eg, marking an early movement to codify requirements linked to duration of territorial presence, already in place in many national contexts, at an international level states were permitted to make certain rights conditional on the fact that the so-called regular worker has 'resided lawfully in its territory' for employment purposes for a prescribed period of no more than two years (ibid Arts 52.2a–b and 52.3).

seasonal, itinerant, and project-tied workers.[45] Through this multi-tiered conception, characterized by qualifications at each level, this UN convention provided for extensive protections, equivalent to full membership, to workers that are citizens of the countries in which they are employed, fewer protections to those that are not, especially those permitted only to reside temporarily, and still fewer protections for those that are undocumented.

4. Phase IV: Problems of exclusion

The multi-tiered conception of worker-citizenship established in the UN convention of 1990 continued through to negotiations towards the ILO's MFM, inaugurating the fourth phase, during which many ILO-level discussions on migration highlighted the need to update normative ILO instruments. Influenced by its UN precursor's human rights-based approach, some such discussions addressed issues of discrimination whereas others focussed on changing patterns and conditions of migration in an era of globalization, and the vulnerabilities they engender. Examples of the former included a 1991 inquiry into 'Combating Discrimination Against Migrants,' focusing on forms of discrimination covered in the Discrimination (Employment and Occupation) Convention. They also included a noteworthy 'Special Survey on the Discrimination (Employment and Occupation) Convention', which recommended the creation of a supplemental protocol to this convention to insert additional grounds upon which discrimination would be forbidden, including nationality, although it was rejected ultimately.[46] Examples of the latter were more numerous. Foremost was a 1997 investigation into the 'Future of ILO Activities in the Field of Migration,' conducted by a tripartite committee of experts, documenting, and recommending remedies for,

---

[45] Eg, seasonal workers were to be entitled only to rights that are 'compatible with their status as seasonal workers, taking into account that they are present in that State for only part of the year' and the rights of itinerant workers were similarly constrained (ibid Arts 59 and 60).

The convention also introduced the category 'specified-employment workers' and provided for excluding this group from a variety of protections to be extended, in principle, to regular workers. Under the convention, specified-employment workers included: migrant workers sent by their employers for restricted periods to a State of employment to undertake a specific assignment or duty; migrant workers engaging for finite periods in work that requires professional, commercial, technical, or other highly specialized skills; and, migrant workers who, at the request of their employers, engage for finite periods in work whose nature is transitory or brief and who are required to depart at the expiration of their authorized periods of stay.

The creation of this category, and terms applicable it, emanated from a debate between European delegations and Australia and the United States. The former took the position that 'a migrant worker whose labor input contributes to the economic performance of the State of employment would eventually earn a right to stay permanently in that State after a number of years' (J Lonnroth, 'The International Convention on the Rights of All Migrant Workers and Members of their Families in the Context of International Migration Policies: An Analysis of Ten Years of Negotiation' (1991) 25(4) International Migration Review 710, 722). Australia and the United States opposed this position in an attempt to preserve admissions schemes permitting certain categories of migrant workers to enter for a specific type of work for a finite period, and to renew work permits for that purpose. Specifically, they objected to extending the right to the free choice of employment to such workers. The compromise reached ultimately was the addition of the 'specified-employment worker' category.

[46] ILO, *General Survey: Equality in Employment and Occupation*, Report III (Committee of Experts) (84th International Labour Conference, Geneva, June 1996); and ILO, *Committee of Experts on the Application of Standards* (87th International Labour Conference, Geneva, June 1999).

problems confronting migrant workers in time-bound activities and recruited by private employment agents, naming women workers as particularly vulnerable to exploitation. Through this exercise, experts charted gaps in national laws and regulations and international labour regulations regarding migrant workers in time-bound activities[47] and problems associated with the operation of private employment agencies. Accordingly, an annex attached to the experts' final report stated forcefully that 'special measures are needed to protect such persons . . . [who] incur risks, deprivations and vulnerabilities' and offered guidelines for the 'type of treatment which should be envisaged for . . . workers whose legal situation is regular as regards to entry, residence, employment or economic activity' but for whom differential treatment on the basis of nationality continued to be sanctioned under the Discrimination (Employment and Occupation) Convention.[48]

The 1998 Declaration of Fundamental Principles and Rights at Work and Decent Work, first introduced as an organizational agenda of the ILO in 1999, came on the heels of these developments, and they heightened a definitive paradox: on the one hand, the decent work agenda identified people at the margins of the labour force, for whom normal measures for labour and social protection are particularly difficult to apply, as requiring greater attention, naming migrant workers specifically. Its purpose was to improve the conditions of all workers, waged and unwaged, through the expansion of labour and social protections, objectives codified subsequently through the Declaration on Social Justice and Fair Globalization, which recognized that globalization, defined as increasing 'economic cooperation and integration,' led certain countries to 'benefit from economic growth and employment creation' while at the same time 'caus[ing] many countries and sectors to face major challenges,' including 'the growth of unprotected work.'[49] On the other hand, the Declaration of Fundamental Principles and Rights at Work, introduced partly to respond to the failure to include social clauses in international trade agreements, enumerated a set of fundamental labour rights, cast their promotion via a set of 'core' conventions as a constitutional obligation of ILO membership, and established a mechanism for monitoring adherence among member countries. Flowing from the renewed commitment to the elimination of discrimination in respect of employment and occupation, one such convention was the unmodified Discrimination (Employment and Occupation) Convention. Thus, despite the mounting concern with the treatment of migrant workers, expressed, for example, by the World Commission on Globalization at that time, there were few openings for modifying normative international labour regulations subject to ratification to shift membership norms in an expansive direction. The result: in 2004, ILO constituents called for a 'fair deal' for migrant workers through a resolution recognizing both 'the sovereignty of States

---

[47] The report included seasonal workers, protect-tied workers, special-purpose workers, cross-border service-providers, and students and trainees who are permitted to work as migrants under time-bound arrangements.

[48] ILO, *Future of ILO Activities in the Field of Migration* (Report) (1997).

[49] ILO, Declaration of Fundamental Principles and Rights at Work (86th International Labour Conference, Geneva, June 1998).

in determining their own migration policy' and 'the need for international cooperation on migration, and in particular labour migration, among government and other stakeholders' and casting a multilateral framework as an appropriate means of advancing such aims.[50] Introduced in 2006, the MFM was the answer to this call.

B. The Multilateral Framework on Migration: expanding citizenship boundaries through international labour regulation?

Developed by a tripartite group of experts, the MFM is a unique normative ILO instrument. It is a non-binding framework consisting of principles and guidelines organized around the themes of decent work, means for international cooperation on labour migration, a global knowledge base, effective management of labour migration, protection of migrant workers, prevention of and protection against abusive migration practices, the migration process, social integration and inclusion, and migration and development. It also includes a follow-up mechanism and annex of best practices. The result is an instrument including principles and guidelines exceeding central tenets of its ILO and UN precursors subject to ratification as well as extending beyond their ambit. However, entrenching familiar tensions, the overarching logic of the MFM undermines its inclusive features, illustrating the political limit to using international labour regulation to reshape labour law and policy with respect to citizenship.

1. Principles and guidelines exceeding international labour regulations subject to ratification

Through the principles and guidelines it articulates, the MFM makes two key moves exceeding central tenets of its forerunners.

First, it actively pursues non-discrimination in an attempt to limit the proliferation of rules, justified on the basis that nationality is a legitimate ground for discrimination, permitting differential labour protections for citizen- and migrant-workers, as well as among migrant workers themselves, on the basis of entry category. To this end, under the theme of 'the protection of migrant workers,' the MFM advances the linked principles that 'all international labour regulations apply to migrant workers, unless otherwise stated,' that national laws and regulations pertinent to labour migration and migrant workers' protection should be informed by relevant international labour standards, and that migrant workers' protection requires a foundation in international law; in connection with these pronouncements, the MFM names as central existing ILO and UN instruments 'concerning equality of treatment between nationals and migrant workers in a regular situation and minimum standards of protection for all migrant workers.'[51]

Several guidelines attached to this set of principles surpass terms of the ILO Discrimination (Employment and Occupation) Convention and its omission of nationality as an unacceptable ground for discrimination. One guideline, for example, calls for the adoption, implementation, and enforcement of legislation

---

[50] ILO, *Towards a Fair Deal for Migrant Workers in the Global Economy* (Report) (92nd International Labour Conference, Geneva, June 2004).

[51] ILO, *Multilateral Framework on Migration* (2006) Principles 9a–c.

and policies 'eliminat[ing] all forms of discrimination against migrant workers in employment and occupation' without qualification.[52] Another supports measures ensuring that migrant workers in 'regular situations,' a definitive qualification, receive equal treatment with nationals with regard to safety and health protection and occupational risk as well as with regard to employment and training opportunities after a reasonable period of employment.[53]

The second move involves addressing the human rights of workers' during the migration journey, a trans-border process over which individual nation states lack considerable control. Here, the MFM stretches the terms of preexisting ILO instruments by stating that governments in countries of origin and destination should 'give due consideration to licensing and supervising recruitment and placement services for migrant workers.'[54] In so doing, it refers to the ILO Private Employment Agencies Convention (1997). Its associated guidelines also carry forward proposals advanced by the 1997 Committee of Experts on 'Future of ILO Activities in the Field of Migration.' They call for policies standardizing systems of licensing and certification for recruitment and placement services and ensuring that entities providing such services respect migrant workers' human rights, provide them with understandable and enforceable contracts, and 'do not recruit, place or employ workers in jobs which involve unacceptable hazards or risks or abusive or discriminatory treatment of any kind.'[55] And they recommend, in turn, policies ensuring that fees for recruitment and placement are not borne directly by migrant workers, compensating migrant workers for financial losses resulting from failures of recruitment or contracting agencies, and providing for the suspension of agents' licenses when they behave unethically or violate the law.[56]

In addition to exceeding existing terms of ILO and UN instruments subject to ratification in the foregoing ways, the MFM includes a number of principles and especially guidelines addressing previously neglected issues central to migrant workers' protection. Some such moves fall under the preceding themes; for example, under the theme of 'the protection of migrant workers', to address specific challenges facing women migrant workers, it calls for 'national labour legislation and social laws and regulations cover[ing] all male and female migrant workers, including domestic workers and other vulnerable groups' and emphasizes the need for coverage in, among others, the area of maternity protection.[57] It also pursues goals long-omitted from normative international labour regulations. For example, on the subject of 'migration and development,' the MFM articulates the principle that 'the contribution of labour migration to . . . the alleviation of poverty . . . should be maximized for the benefit of origin and destination countries.'[58] Guidelines that follow, moreover, call for national policies providing 'incentives to

---

[52] Ibid Guideline 8.4.4.
[53] Ibid Guidelines 9.4 and 9.12.
[54] Ibid Principle 13.
[55] Ibid Guidelines 13.1–13.5.
[56] Ibid Guideline 13.5–13.7.
[57] Ibid Guideline 9.8.
[58] Ibid Principle 15.

promote the productive investment of remittances in the countries of origin' as well as for 'reducing the costs of remittance transfers,' naming 'accessible financial services' and 'reducing transaction fees' as priorities.[59] They recommend, in addition, measures mitigating the loss of workers with skills critical to countries of origin, including the establishment of rules for ethical recruitment.[60] Complementing such principles and guidelines, under the theme of social 'integration and inclusion,' the MFM states that governments, workers, and unions should take measures 'preventing discrimination against migrant workers' and 'combat[ing] racism and xenophobia.'[61] And associated guidelines call, for example, for policies and practices 'ensuring that the children of migrant workers born in destination countries have the right to birth registration and to a nationality,' integrating the children of migrants into educational systems in receiving countries, and providing language courses to migrants of all ages.[62] They also propose measures approximating denizenship fostering migrant workers' participation in economic, social, and political life after a period of legal residence in the country, including support for migrant workers' associations as a means of improving their representation.[63]

2. Persisting tensions

Through its principles and guidelines pursuing non-discrimination and human rights more forcefully than in pre-existing international labour regulations and addressing long-neglected subjects, the MFM articulates key aspects of an inclusive vision of membership with respect to citizenship. However, the tension between nation states' concern to preserve national sovereignty in the migration field and the need for concerted international action to protect migrant workers continues to limit this vision at every level of the instrument. Even though the MFM is non-binding, its preamble calls for principles and practices taking into account ' . . . the sovereign right of all nations to determine their own migration policies . . . '[64] A further indication of the persistent tension is also found in the body of the framework under the theme of 'effective management of migration.' Here, the MFM confers the following double-edged principle that: on the one hand, '[a]ll States have the sovereign right to develop their own policies to manage labour migration' and, on the other hand, 'international labour standards and other international instruments, as well as guidelines, as appropriate, should play an important role to make these policies coherent, effective and fair.'[65]

Upon the adoption of the MFM, reservations expressed by representatives from highly industrialized countries reinforced this dynamic. Even as they approved the consensus text, representatives from Australia, Canada, Japan, and the UK cast the

---

[59] Ibid Guidelines 15.6 and 15.6.
[60] Ibid Guideline 15.7.
[61] Ibid Principle 14.
[62] Ibid Guidelines 14.11, 14.12, and 14.7.
[63] Ibid Guidelines 14.6 and 14.8.
[64] Ibid Preamble Para 8.
[65] Ibid Principle 4.

instrument as a whole as overly prescriptive.[66] The representative speaking for Canada objected, for example, to 'promoting coherence [in labour migration policy] at an international level,' comments echoed by the US representative.[67] Such representatives also expressed their disapproval of the principles and guidelines articulated specifically under the protection theme; to this end, the UK representative described guidelines regarding equality of rights as 'rais[ing] unrealistic expectations in regard to rights of migrant workers in irregular status.'[68] Effectively affirming the exclusion of nationality as a ground for non-discrimination in the Convention on Discrimination (Employment and Occupation) (1958), the representative of the US stated further that such provisions 'failed to acknowledge that the applicable international conventions recognized that *migratory status may be a lawful basis for differential treatment.*'[69] Additionally, this grouping of states criticized the scope of the MFM. Those from Australia and the US indicated that 'development and remittances' were 'beyond the scope and mandate of the ILO.'[70] Concurring with the representative of Japan, the US representative added, more broadly, that 'the Framework highlighted receiving country obligations and responsibilities, but ignored the obligations of source countries in the creation of decent work.'[71]

Such positions are in many ways predictable in light of historical patterns and tendencies in the negotiation of citizenship boundaries in international labour regulations. However, the overriding concern of such states to preserve their national sovereignty, even while acknowledging the need to improve labour protection for migrant workers, reduces significantly the force of the MFM's expansive gestures, that is, its attempts to move migrant workers out of the shadows of international labour regulation.

C. Fostering global labour market membership

Tensions underpinning the MFM, and the dynamics of international labour regulation they reflect, highlight the need for an alternative vision of membership norms. They call for global labour market membership, a notion that entails, in part, freeing key labour protections from the exclusive domain of nation states. As I conceptualize it elsewhere in connection with the development of a new imaginary, global labour market membership aims to address processes central to workers' social reproduction and thereby to limit differentiation and exclusion from labour protection on the basis of citizenship, gender relations, form of employment,

---

[66] ILO, 'Synthesis of Observations Submitted by Experts and Observers on the Draft ILO Multilateral Framework on Labour Migration: Non-Binding Principles and Guidelines for a Rights-Based Approach to Labour Migration Adopted by the Tripartite Meeting of Experts,' *Tripartite Meeting of Experts* (2005) B.1.
[67] Ibid B.2 and B.6.
[68] Ibid B.4.
[69] Ibid B.4, italics added.
[70] Ibid B.3.
[71] Ibid B.5.

age, etc. However, consistent with the foregoing analysis, my elaboration of this alternative vision in this concluding section concentrates on transcending citizenship boundaries and hence rejecting central tenets of methodological nationalism, especially naturalization and territorialization.[72]

An initial step in this direction entails sketching principles and mechanisms drawing interdisciplinary social science research into dialogue with scholarship working to re-conceptualize labour law and policy. In recent years, scholars studying alternatives to national citizenship, working at the intersection of citizenship and migration studies, labour studies, and women's studies, have developed notions such as 'inclusive citizenship'[73] and 'social connection'[74] in imagining possibilities for limiting exclusions and partial exclusions flowing from external as well as internal citizenship boundaries (eg, those related to social relations of gender and race).[75] Such theorizations shape, and are shaped by, conceptions developed by legal scholars, such as Bosniak's notion of 'the citizenship of alienage'[76] and Macklin's idea of 'the heft of citizenship.'[77] Taken together, these complementary scholarly strains point to five principles for fostering global labour market membership; several such principles are already reflected in existing or proposed measures, including, paradoxically, in a number of those listed as 'Examples of Best Practices' attached to the MFM, although these measures by no means represent a panacea.

The first principle is parity,[78] or providing for labour protections attentive to the diverse needs of migrant workers holding different citizenship statuses, specifically, for the elimination of rules permitting exclusions from or different levels of labour protections on the basis of entry category and for minimizing the significance of the duration of territorial presence in their acquisition.[79] Interventions working towards this end often take the shape of agreements between sending and receiving states providing for the extension of work- and employment-related social security

---

[72] For a fuller discussion of my evolving conception of global labour market membership, see Vosko, above n 9.

[73] R Lister, above n 8; and R Lister, 'Inclusive Citizenship: Realizing the Potential' (2007) 11(1) Citizenship Studies 49.

[74] IM Young, 'Responsibility and Global Justice: A Social Connection Model' (2006) Social Philosophy and Policy 102.

[75] See, eg, E Nakano-Glenn, *Unequal Freedom: How Race and Gender Shaped American Citizenship and Labor* (Harvard University Press, 2002); and Stasiulis and Bakan, above n 10.

[76] Bosniak, above n 8.

[77] A Macklin, 'Who is the Citizen's Other? Considering the Heft of Citizenship' (2007) 8(2) Theoretical Inquiries in Law 476.

[78] This principle builds on my previous sole and co-authored work on developing mechanisms (procedural and substantive) for improving protections for workers in precarious forms of employment such as self-employed work and various types of part-time and temporary paid employment and seeks to extend it by embracing Fraser's notion of 'participatory parity,' which she identifies with the political dimension of justice and identifies broadly with 'social arrangements that permit all [individuals affected] to participate as peers in social life.' See LF Vosko, above n 5 and n 9; J Fudge and LF Vosko, 'By Whose Standards? Re-regulating the Canadian Labour Market' (2001) 22(3) Economic and Industrial Democracy 327; C Cranford et al, *Self-Employed Workers Organize: Law, Policy and Unions* (McGill-Queen's University Press, 2005); and N Fraser, *Scales of Justice: Reimagining Political Space in a Globalizing World* (New York: Columbia University Press 2010) 16–17.

[79] Lister, above n 8; and LS Bosniak, 'Being Here: Ethical Territoriality and the Rights of Immigrants' (2007) 8(2) Theoretical Inquiries in Law 389.

benefits beyond national borders. Presently, for example, mainly migrant workers from highly industrialized countries, especially those migrating to other highly industrialized countries, have access to and portability of pension and medical benefits through such bilateral or multilateral agreements, a group representing just 23 per cent of all migrants worldwide.[80] However, measures for extending portable and especially exportable benefits to migrant workers from low-income countries and world regions are surfacing gradually and more are necessary.[81]

The second principle involves casting human rights and labour rights as insepa-rable.[82] One concrete strategy adopted by sending countries is the establishment of overseas offices in receiving countries, whose role is to support their nationals in securing labour rights and entitlements in the country of employment. An example, identified as a 'best practice' in the MFM, is the 43 Mexican consulates in the US providing legal assistance for Mexican migrants experiencing human rights viola-tions.[83] Another example is the Philippine Overseas Labour Office, which works, through various means, with national and sub-national labour ministries to pro-mote adherence to labour standards.[84]

The third principle is the autonomous legal status for migrants regardless of gender and marital status[85] and the nature of work in which they engage. Existing initiatives congruent with this principle are limited. However, one localized exam-ple gesturing in this direction, and also named as a 'best practice' in the MFM, was a Spanish regularization program carried out in 2005. This program permitted undocumented migrant workers who had registered with local governments for at

---

[80] J Avato et al, *Definitions, Good Practices, and Global Estimates on the Status of Social Protection for International Migrants* (Washington, Social Protection and Labor Division, The World Bank, SP Discussion Paper No 0909, 2009) 4.

[81] For instance, temporary foreign workers who pay premiums recently gained access to provisions for maternity and parental benefits provided under Canada's Employment Insurance Act (1996) even upon return to a sending country. For other examples, see N Yeates, 'The General Agreement on Trade in Services (GATS): What's in it for Social Security?' (2005) 58(1) International Social Security Review 3; Avato, above n 80; B MacLaren and L Lapointe, *Making a Case for Reform: Non-Access to Social Security Measure for Migrant Workers* (Policy Monograph, FOCAL, Ottawa, 2009); and W Van Ginneken, 'Social Security and the Global Socio-Economic Floor' (2009) 9(2) Global Social Policy 228.

[82] G Mundlak, 'Industrial Citizenship, Social Citizenship, Corporate Citizenship: I Just Want My Wages' (2007) 8(2) Theoretical Inquiries in Law 718.

[83] ILO, above n 51, Best Practice 55.

[84] This office initiates and monitors non-binding bilateral agreements between labour departments in the sending and receiving country governing migrant workers' terms and conditions of employment. One example, applicable to migrant health care workers, is an agreement between the province of Manitoba, Canada, and the Philippine Overseas Labour Office covering exchange of information concerning employers and sending agencies; recruitment and selection of workers; cost of recruitment of workers; offers of employment and labour contracts; protection of workers; and human resource development. Terms of this agreement aim to prevent workers from being charged direct and indirect fees incurred in the hiring process, to mandate providing workers copies of their employment contracts, to empower the Philippine Overseas Labour Office to ensure the protection of migrant workers under applicable federal and provincial laws, and to contribute to sustaining health and human resource development in the Philippines (Department of Labour and Employment, The Philippines and Government of Manitoba Canada, online: <http://www.dole.gov.ph/>).

[85] Lister, above n 8; see also S Hassim, 'Global Constraints on Gender Equality in Care Work' (2008) 36(3) Politics & Society 388.

least six months to regularize their status, and explicitly included domestic workers as eligible applicants.[86]

The fourth principle is internationalism, emphasizing especially, as Lister articulated in a formative intervention on this notion, highly industrialized countries' obligations to migrants from economically disadvantaged world regions and efforts to limit global economic polarization more broadly.[87] Proposals for taxes on receiving countries linked to trade and migration and aimed at improving social and physical infrastructure in sending economies are a chief example.

The fifth and final principle is transculturalism conceived here as the affirmation of multiple means of belonging in an era of globalization, a principle complementing both Beck's proposal for replacing methodological nationalism with 'methodological cosmopolitanism' and Glick Schiller's call for embracing a global perspective on migration rejecting the divide between nation state and migrants including scalar perspectives on locality, addressing transnational fields of power, and assuming multiple entry points and pathways of local and transnational incorporation.[88] The practical proposal for 'transnational labour citizenship' advanced by Gordon goes some distance towards this principle. To address the lack of protection among especially Mexican migrant workers in the US, Gordon calls for 'a new [binational] immigration status...entitl[ing] the holder to come and go freely between the sending country and the [receiving country]...and to work...without restriction' based on membership in a transnational workers' organization instead of ties with a particular employer.[89] Drawing inspiration from innovative provisions of bi-national collective agreements, Gordon envisages using such membership to shift the enforcement of basic labour standards into 'the arena of labour solidarity.'[90] Although there are fundamental limits to her model,[91] building on

---

[86] ILO, above n 51, Best Practice 44.

[87] Lister, above n 8; see also F Williams, 'Theorising Migration and Home-based Care in European Welfare States,' Annual Conference of the Canadian Political Science Association, 4–6 June, 2008, University of British Columbia in Vancouver.

[88] On transculturalism, see N Yuval-Davis and P Werbner, *Women, Citizenship and Difference* (Zed Books, 1999); and R Lister, above n 8. On the complementary strategies of methodological cosmopolitanism and a global perspective on migration respective, see U Beck, 'The Cosmopolitan Condition: Why Methodological Nationalism Fails' (2007) 24 Theory, Culture & Society 7–8; and N Glick Schiller, 'Beyond the Nation-State and its Units of Analysis: Towards a New Research Agenda for Migration Studies' in K Schittenhelm (ed), Concepts and Methods in Migration Research: Conference Reader (2007) 39, available at <http://www.cultural-capital.net>.

[89] J Gordon, 'Transnational Labor Citizenship' (2009) 80(3) Southern California Law Review 503, 263.

[90] Ibid 509.

[91] Three limits of transnational labour citizenship are particularly noteworthy: first, its closed-shop approach simply replaces national citizenship with compulsory membership in a union of paid workers, and thereby risks perpetuating another set of exclusions. Second, as McNevin illustrates, this compulsory membership creates 'a problematic citizenship boundary of its own by tying rights recognition to one's status as worker...[with] obvious gendered implications for migrants whose work in caring roles is not recognized within the scope of the formal economy' (A McNevin, 'Contesting Citizenship: Irregular Migrants and Strategic Possibilities for Political Belonging' (2009) 31(2) New Political Science 163). Third, as Gordon herself acknowledges, transnational labour citizenship is an interim strategy; a long-term solution also fostering the principle of internationalism would focus not only on developing new entry categories but on global redistribution (see also Hassim, above n 85; and Williams, above n 87).

this new-found solidarity, her aim is to use transnational labour citizenship to limit competition between migrant workers and national citizen-workers in receiving countries and ultimately raise the floor of conditions of work and employment for all workers regardless of immigration status.

As evidenced by the measures (proposed or existing) fostering their realization, none of these principles either assumes or prescribes a particular scale of intervention. Rather, directed as they are at global labour market membership and thus dispensing with methodological nationalism, each principle could be realized, in practice, at multiple scales, minimizing the tension between nation states' desire to maintain their sovereignty and the objective of improving labour protection for migrant workers, presumed to require coordinated international action, long characterizing international labour regulations on migration for employment. These are but a few practical routes towards global labour market membership.

23

Flexible Bureaucracies in Labor Market Regulation

*Michael J Piore**

A. The problem: the need for flexibility in a regulatory framework

This chapter addresses the problem of labor market flexibility. The problem arises most immediately in the context of the revival of labor market regulation and a renewed effort to enforce labor standards which have been allowed to atrophy over the course of time. The revival is part of a broader reaction against the neo-liberal agenda and the Washington Consensus, an approach to public policy which places almost exclusive reliance on the competitive market and simulated market mechanisms. The reaction is especially intense in Latin America, but it is actually very widespread. And the skepticism about market-based solutions has been reinforced by the current crisis which has drawn even the United States, the intellectual fountainhead of the old Consensus, into active intervention not only to limit and control the impact of the market, but actually to guide its operation. Even before the crisis, however, virtually every major country – with the notable exceptions of Mexico and the United States – had increased the resources and personnel devoted to labor inspection in the course of the last five years. In labor market policy, however, the reaction is taking place without addressing the basic problem to which the Washington Consensus was itself a response: the inflexibility and rigidity of governmental regulations and the way in which these led to inefficiencies in production and the allocation of resources, and which stifled economic development.

But while my initial concern is derivative of my colleagues' preoccupation with the impact of regulation adjustment within a market economy, it arises in a different way in the context of globalization, where rigidification (or the lack of flexibility) grows out of the pressures for standardization. In this sense, it appears to be inherent in the attempt to create a single global trading system out of national systems with different institutional traditions. The pressure for standardization comes from both the adherents of free trade and the competitive market and

* David W Skinner Professor of Political Economy, Department of Economics, Massachusetts Institute of Technology. The argument here was developed in collaboration with Andrew Schrank.

from its critics. For the former, it derives from their belief that one can define in a clear and meaningful way competitive market capitalism and the institutions associated with it, and that anything that does not fit this definition gives an unfair trading advantage and is thus an impediment to free trade. For the critics, trade standardization, particularly in labor standards, is an attempt to forestall competitive pressures and, with them, a race to the bottom. Against these pressures for standardization is the sense that institutional differences reflect differences in culture and history which a global regime must respect and accommodate, and a fear of the institutional imperialism of the dominant economic powers, particularly the United States. This has been reinforced from a different direction by the tendency of international economic agencies to impose a single policy regime on all countries seeking their aid and support and the evident failure of that approach to produce neither economic stabilization nor growth and prosperity in the developing world. The basic argument of this chapter is that the conflict between labor market regulation (and indeed regulation more broadly) and flexibility, in each of these domains in which it seems to arise, is in large measure artificial. It emerges because we have conceived of the problem in terms of a model of labor market regulation that is prevalent in the United States. The system of labor market regulation in Southern Europe and Latin America is fundamentally different and provides much greater opportunity to address these issues of flexibility. This chapter is concerned with:

(1) fleshing out the difference between the two models;

(2) suggesting the advantages of the latter for addressing the problems of flexibility and adjustment, but also some of the limitations of this form of regulation, at least as presently practiced; and

(3) identifying some of the conceptual and institutional problems which need to be addressed to realize these advantages.

While the bulk of the argument here is directed at the economic debate about labor market flexibility, the last section of the chapter turns specifically to the issues posed by globalization.

B. A note about analytical ambition

The argument here is, however, not simply an attempt to move beyond US institutions as a model of regulation but to move beyond the competitive market model in terms of which not only US institutions but economic institutions in general have come to be conceived. The ambition is to build a conceptual framework in which approaches to public policy involving active government can, first, compete alongside the competitive market framework and the structures which build off of it and are promoted by it (whether deregulation, privatization, or simulated market mechanisms) and, second, which works, as competitive pressures are *supposed* to work, toward increasing efficiency or effectiveness. To do so, the chapter seeks to go beyond the conventional economic focus on individual motivation and competitive pressures and to draw upon sociological and anthropological understandings of human motivation and behavior which stress the social context in which the economic actors operate. For these purposes, it attempts to recover a literature anchored in these understandings that has been eclipsed in the last 25 years by scholarly work grounded in economics and in the so-called new public management.

The moment is opportune, at least in the US, because the economic crisis has gone a long way toward discrediting the competitive market as an efficient, effective model of social organization, and the expansion of government in response to the crisis has limited the resources available to manage through monetary incentives even as it has increased the pressure for management of some kind. One might note, however, that the Obama Administration has been slow to take advantage of this opportunity and that so far its policies, and the way it has presented them to the country, have departed very little from the prescriptions of conventional economics.[1]

A second note of caution about the analytical framework is important here. The study of labor market regulation in Latin America has historically been the province of lawyers and has stressed legal texts in which the regulations are embedded.[2] The argument which is developed here is that the texts themselves are a misleading guide to how labor market regulation actually works. This is probably true in general but it is especially true with respect to labor market regulation in Europe and Latin America because the very nature of the institutions which govern the regulatory process place enormous power in the hands of the inspectors to *interpret* the law as they administer it: The inspectors on the line decide where and under what circumstances to apply the law. Hence, in order to understand the regulatory process and assess its impact, actual and potential, upon the economy, one has to focus upon and attempt to understand not the letter of the law but actual practice in the field, on the ground. This is a lesson that is important not only for analysts of the Franco-Latin system but for commentators and critics in the United States as well; it upends the conventional distinction between common law and civil law which in recent years has been particularly prominent in the writings of American economists. The conventional belief is that civil law regimes like those of Southern Europe and Latin America apply legal doctrine much more strictly and interpret it more literally than common law countries such as the United States.[3] But in labor market regulation, the opposite is much closer to capturing the differences between the two regimes.

---

[1] J Alter, *The Promise: President Obama, Year One* (Simon & Schuster, 2010).

[2] See, eg: Universidad Nacional Autoínoma de Meíxico, *Revista Latinoamericana de Derecho Social: La inspección del trabajo*, Número 6 *Enero-Junio* (Universidad Nacional Autoínoma de Meíxico, Instituto de Investigaciones Juriídicas, Meíxico DF 2008).

[3] M Van der Veen and W Korthals Altes, 'Strategic City Projects, Legal Systems and Professional Effectiveness' [2005] Mimeo, Paper for 45th Congress of the European Regional Science Association, Amsterdam.

C. Two models of labor market regulation

Our starting point here is the contrast between the US and the Franco-Latin systems of labor market regulation.

The US system is specialized and sanctioning. Regulatory responsibility is divided among nearly a dozen different Federal agencies, each with a relatively narrow jurisdiction (Wages and Hours Division of the Department of Labor, Occupational Safety and Health Administration, Employee Retirement Income Security Act, Equal Employment Opportunity Commission, National Labor Relations Board, the Federal Mediation Service, the Justice Department, the State Department [immigration visas and work permits], etc). Many of these agencies also have counterparts at the state level and occasionally at the local level as well. Each agency is then supposed to identify violations of the laws in the narrow domain for which it is responsible and to impose penalties for those violations.

The Franco-Latin model is, by contrast, a general or unified system and is focused upon conciliation and/or remediation. The whole of the labor code is in this model administered by a single agency, the *Inspeccion de Trabajo* or *Inspection du Travail*. In principle, a single inspector has responsibility for overseeing all aspects of the legislation. The inspector can impose sanctions (or initiate a process which leads to sanctions), but the responsibilities of the employer cannot be discharged through penalties. The enterprise is expected to come into compliance with the law, and the responsibility of the inspector is to see that it does so. Toward this end, he or she is empowered to work out a plan which brings the enterprise into compliance over time, often by giving technical advice on how to make the requisite adjustments or pointing to consultants who can help to do so.

These characteristics give the labor inspectors an enormous margin of discretion as to which provisions of the law they will enforce and under what circumstances, and with what degree of stringency. Because the inspectors cannot possibly inspect for every provision of the code, they are effectively in a position to pick and choose which provisions they will look at, where to focus their attention. They can weigh the different aspects of law, and in effect the different goals of legislation, against each other and against the viability of the enterprise, adjusting the regulations to the particularities of each establishment and to the economic and social environment in which it operates. Their ability to work out the process through which the enterprise comes into compliance gives them further latitude to adjust the code. Thus, for example, they might enforce health and safety standards more stringently and allow less time to come into compliance in a tight labor market where unemployment is low and jobs are plentiful than in a recession, when imposing the costs of compliance risks driving the firm out of business and destroying jobs. This presents a sharp contrast to the US system, where the jurisdiction of each agency is so narrow that there is very little scope to pick and choose among which provisions of the code to enforce; and because the focus is on sanctions and deterrence, virtually no scope to focus on how compliance is to be achieved or over what time period. Nowhere in the system is the total burden which all these different agencies impose on the enterprises, and the associated costs, assessed and weighed against the value of the jobs which are at stake. In principle, the regulatory burden is assessed by the legislature when the provisions of the law are considered, but in fact even at this level the focus is generally on one provision at time, and very often new legislation is provoked by a dramatic event (such as a major industrial accident or a scandal concerning child labor or clandestine immigrant shops), which narrows the focus and limits deliberation ever further.

Of course there are exceptions here, but they are particular and generally viewed as a perverse reaction. For example, responsibility for enforcing provisions mandating equal pay for women was placed in the Wages and Hours Division of the Labor Department, which had jurisdiction over minimum wage and overtime pay, without a corresponding increase in budgetary resources. The Division responded by diverting resources from minimum wage enforcement to equal pay provisions.

Whether the flexibility inherent in the Franco-Latin system works in fact to address the problems we have outlined initially depends upon how it is used and whether it can be managed and directed to address the problem of reconciling regulation with growth and efficiency. On this score, we have two kinds of insights. One is a series of interviews with the inspectors themselves on how they manage their roles in practice. The second is a series of insights drawn from social science theory and from studies of other organizations with similar types of discretion.

In both of these respects we have drawn heavily on a literature for which we will use the shorthand term: street-level bureaucracy.

D. Managing the Franco-Latin model: work inspectors as street-level bureaucrats

Street-level bureaucracies are organizations in which the line officers have substantial decision-making authority. The canonical street level bureaucrats are policemen on the beat.[4] While nominally charged with enforcing the law, their actual role is to maintain social order; they use the law as an instrument toward this end and invoke it situationally, depending on circumstances. Thus, for example, laws against prostitution are enforced in suburban residential neighborhoods but, although formally just as illegal in urban 'adult entertainment' districts, there prostitution is typically tolerated. Thus, to take a particular example, when a policeman is called in a domestic dispute, literal application of the law would require him to make an arrest for disorderly conduct or threatened violence, but typically he will do so only if he cannot otherwise calm the situation and restore order. The police are probably the most studied class of street-level bureaucrats, but such organizations are

---

[4] J Wilson, *Varieties of Police Behavior: The Management of Law and Order in Eight Communities* (Harvard University Press, 1968); and J Van Maanen, *Working the Street: A Developmental View of Police Behavior* (MIT, 1973).

pervasive throughout the public service sector. Other typical street-level bureaucrats include classroom teachers, social workers, and forest rangers.[5]

These types of organizations were an active area of research in the immediate postwar decades but were eclipsed after 1980 by the emphasis on privatization and simulated market mechanisms in what became known as the *new public management*.[6] The older literature is now being resurrected and expanded by a generation of younger scholars, many of whom are students at MIT.[7] The lessons of that literature, as well as very recent material gathered in interviews conducted in France and in different Latin American countries, are discussed in several articles which Andrew Shrank and I have written separately and together.[8]

Several key lessons emerge from this literature. The first and most important of these is that while there is a substantial idiosyncratic component to the way line officers (in our case, labor inspectors) make their decisions, there is nonetheless a core of tacit rules and procedures that govern their work and give it a certain consistency to the way the rules are enforced from one inspector to another and across time. We will argue that these tacit rules and their evolution in time must be the focus of public sector management. But before turning to this issue, it is important to address the question of idiosyncratic behavior, which tends to be stressed when these organizations are viewed through the lens of the individual maximizing behavior assumed in conventional economic theory. Typical of the kind which emerged in interviews was a labor inspector who told about discovering that he had a reputation in his district as a 'firebug'. It was known that he always looked first at fire safety provisions when he visited a plant. Upon reflection, trying to understand his own behavior about which he had not been conscious and that at first he found difficult to believe, he came to attribute it to his experience working in Sao Paolo the year just before he entered the inspectorate. The day he arrived, there was a fire in one of the large skyscrapers; the construction of the building created an inferno in which large numbers of people were trapped and suffered particularly horrific deaths; the newspapers reported on this in extensive detail throughout the following week. Other examples of idiosyncratic behavior which

---

[5] M Lipsky, *Street-Level Bureaucracy: Dilemmas of the Individual in Public Services* (Russell Sage, 1980); and H Kaufman, *The Forest Ranger: A Study in Administrative Behavior* (Johns Hopkins Press, 1960).

[6] For a flavor of the older literature, see, eg: K Hawkins, *Law as Last Resort Prosecution Decision-Making in a Regulatory Agency* (Oxford University Press, 2001); Kaufman, above n 5; and S Kelman, *Regulating America, Regulating Sweden: A Comparative Study of Occupational Safety and Health Policy* (MIT Press, 1981).

[7] SS Silbey, R Huising, and V Salo Coslovsky, 'The Sociological Citizen: Relational Interdependence in Law and Organizations' (2009) 59(1) L'Année Sociologique 201; and R Pires, 'Promoting Sustainable Compliance: Styles of Labour Inspection and Compliance Outcomes in Brazil' (2008) 147 International Labour Review 199.

[8] M Piore and A Schrank, 'Trading Up: An Embryonic Model for Easing the Human Costs of Free Markets' (2006) 31(5) Boston Review 11; M Piore and A Schrank, 'Toward Managed Flexibility: The Revival of Labor Inspection in the Latin World' (2008) 147 Indus & Lab Rel Rev 1; A Schrank and M Piore, 'Norms, Regulations, and Labor Standards in Central America' (2007) 77 CEPAL – Serie Estudios y Perspectivas 1; and MJ Piore, 'Sociology, Street-Level Bureaucracy, and the Management of the Public Sector' (mimeo 2009), MIT.

emerged in interviews were political, although not of the kind which have generally been attributed to inspectors by the employer associations who see them as out to undermine the capitalist system. Several inspectors in France, for example, said they never enforced immigration laws against individual workers (although they sometimes did against employers). Corruption, which is among the very first topics raised when one discusses the discretion of inspectors in Latin America, was seldom actually mentioned in interviews with people who had firsthand contact with the system: In most countries, the inspectors themselves cannot impose monetary penalties and the process of imposing sanctions is considered so arduous and time-consuming that the inspectors generally reported it is not usually worth initiating, especially if problems can be handled in other ways (a similar finding emerges in studies of the police and their use of formal arrest and prosecution[9]). For the most part, however, the street-level bureaucrats in general (and work inspectors in particular) explain their decisions in interviews in terms of a set of general standards and operating procedures which they share with their colleagues. It is in this sense that one can speak of the tacit codes which govern their behavior.

These rules, and the way in which they evolve over time, can be managed so as to minimize the idiosyncrasies of individual inspectors and increase the responsiveness of the organization to the social goals which in principle it should be designed to serve. The key here is the recognition that the tacit rules and procedures are embedded in the culture of the organization, and evolve as that culture evolves over time through contact with the environment in which it operates. The line agents adhere to that culture because they are basically professionals whose identity and self-conception are bound up with the roles which they play within the organization and the judgments of their colleagues about their performance in these roles. The culture itself is passed on from one generation of inspectors to another through the process of training and socialization when new inspectors enter the service. It is reinforced and refined through the continual discussions, both formal and informal, among the inspectors about particular cases in the course of the work day, and in war stories told in social gatherings after work. And it evolves over time, influenced in part by ideas and attitudes which new members of the corps bring with them from the outside and as the inspectors encounter new situations and try to figure out how to mold existing practice to accommodate them.[10]

Such organizations are difficult to manage by fiat, or through monetary incentives, almost by definition because to do so is to reduce the flexibility in the application of the rules.[11] It is possible, however, to manage the culture and the

---

[9] Wilson, above n 4.
[10] Piore, above n 8; and, more generally, J Van Maanen, 'Pathways to Membership: Socialization to Work' (1979) MIT Sloan School of Management Working Paper 1082–79; E Schein, *The Corporate Culture Survival Guide: Sense and Nonsense about Culture Change* (Jossey-Bass, 1999); and G Kunda, *Engineering Culture: Control and Commitment in a High-Tech Corporation* (Temple University Press, 1992).
[11] This is conventionally illustrated in police work by the example of traffic tickets. This is the one aspect of the work which can be easily controlled by issuing quotas. But the role of the police is actually to ensure the smooth flow of traffic, and quotas tend to lead the police to block traffic in the attempt to issue enough tickets to meet their quota: Wilson, above n 4.

commitment of the agents to it. In terms of managing the culture itself, there are basically three points of entry for managerial control. First, management has control over the recruitment and selection of new members of the organization and hence, over the background – the education, skills and attitudes – which they bring into the organization from the outside. In Morocco, for example, entry requirements for new inspectors were raised in one shot from high school degrees to a master's degree in Human Resource Management, creating a cleavage between the new inspectors and the old, and a professional rapport not only among the new inspectors themselves, but also between the inspections and the large, multinational firms which the country was seeking to attract as part of its development process. Second, management controls the process of training and socialization which prepares members for organizational membership. Here the ability to actually change the culture once it is established is limited by the role of apprenticeship in the training process; it is difficult to imagine sending new inspectors cold into the field without some prior experience working with experienced agents. In the course of that experience, the new agents are bound to pick up much of the approach and attitudes which the older inspectors bring to their work. Management does, however, control the classroom component of the training process and, moreover, can adjust its importance to counteract the impact of apprenticeship. Third, management can enter into and try to guide and direct the ongoing discussion within the organization as the agents review their work and confront novel situations. The discussion of ongoing practice can take place on a variety of levels. Among the inspectors themselves, without outside management and structure, the discussion is very much rooted in practice. The discussion which ought to take place with the professional hierarchy and with the political leadership is the relationship between practice and the different, and often conflicting, goals of the organization. For example, how should the inspectors view the enforcement of various regulations which can involve substantial cost to the enterprise against the value of the jobs which might be lost if the enterprise were forced by these costs to curtail employment.

The organization which seems to be most adept at doing this is the *Inspeccion de Trabajo* in the Dominican Republic. The ministry officials meet with the rank-and-file inspectors several times a year and develop through these discussions the government's priorities and plans for implementing them. To be effective, however, these meetings require rapport and mutual confidence between the inspection corps and their bureaucratic and political superiors. This exists in the Dominican Republic because the corps as it now operates is the product of a major administrative and legal reform conceived and implemented by the Minister of Labor, who subsequently became Vice President, and the current corps of inspectors along with their bureaucratic and political supervisors lived through these reforms together and are essentially the product of them.[12] This rapport, however, is unusual. In other countries, the management of the inspectors has been clumsy and created a distance between the inspectorate and the ministry which has later

---

[12] A Schrank, 'Strengthening Labor Inspection in the Dominican Republic' (mimeo 2008), University of New Mexico.

proven to be difficult or impossible to overcome. One of the worst countries in this regard is France, where one would have expected a particularly deft and enlightened management of the public sector, but where instead the neoliberal discourse of the political class had already created enormous resentment and suspicion on the part of the inspectors, which was then aggravated by the failure of the government to condemn swiftly the killing of two young inspectors by an irate peasant whose farm they were attempting to inspect. (The contrast to the way that Nicolas Sarkozy secured the loyalty of the police when he was Minister of Justice by going to the hospital to visit the men who were shot by rioters in the slums is particularly striking.) In Morocco, the government missed a similar chance to gain the loyalty and respect required to lead the inspection corps when it failed to support one of the newly recruited business school graduates who was sued, and then convicted and jailed, for false arrest by a company he had found to be in willful violation of the statutes.

The ultimate goal, however, is not simply to enter into the process through which the tacit rules and procedures evolve but to actually surface the rules which govern the inspectors' decisions, make them explicit and subject them to systematic evaluation, and then in the light of that evaluation, to revision. An example of how this might be done is provided in the medical care industry by an effort to promote more consistent approaches to patient care and management in a large hospital.[13] The doctors in a hospital setting are essentially street-level bureaucrats. They nominally work under the supervision of the hospital but they retain complete control over the treatment of the patients under their care. Patients are diagnosed when they enter the hospital and assigned, on that basis, to a specialist who manages the case. In an attempt to standardize treatment, the doctors in each specialty were asked to develop a list of the most frequently treated conditions. For each condition, they then developed a standard protocol for treatment. The protocol was circulated among all of the doctors in the specialty for comment and amendment, and the amended protocol was then adopted by the group. Once adopted, doctors were expected to refer to the protocol when managing the patient. They were not required in any sense to adhere to the protocol, but when they departed from it, they were expected to explain the reasons for the departure. In this way, each group built up a file of exceptional cases which was then used periodically to revise and amend the protocol. The use of protocols never went further in this particular example, but one could imagine using them as the basis for the evaluation of various treatments and as a basis for evaluating and compensating doctors as well.

Work inspection differs from medical practice in two important respects. First, there is no standard list of 'conditions' which place enterprises in violation of the law comparable to the standard medical specialties and the conditions which they treat. Second, the goals of work inspection are a good deal more complicated than those of medical practice and the weights placed upon different goals more fluid. Thus, medical practice is generally concerned with curing the patient. To be sure,

---

[13] P Adler et al, 'Performance Improvement Capability: Keys to Accelerating Improvement to Hospitals' (2003) 45(2) California Management Review 12.

the doctor is also concerned with the quality of life during and after treatment, and with the cost of treatment; but generally these are secondary concerns. Work inspectors, in contrast, must weigh the value of the employment opportunities which the enterprise offers the community and the income which it generates against a long list of working conditions including not only health and safety, but also industrial peace, wages and hours, the rights of national workers and immigrants, equal employment opportunity, etc. The relative importance of these different goals will vary over the business cycle with the level of economic development and with the social relations in the community. The weights will also vary depending on the political party in power. The supposition in the street-level bureaucracy literature, which is essentially confirmed by the inspectors themselves in interviews, is that there is an underlying pattern to the way these issues are understood and the conflicting goals weighted by the inspectors; that the pattern, like the pattern in medical practice, can be surfaced and made the subject of explicit review and discussion, and that through discussion we can obtain both more consistency in the way in which the regulatory process treats different enterprises and reduce the conflict among various regulatory objectives. But it is not clear that it can be reduced to a set of standard protocols.

Nonetheless, the medical example and its limits when applied to labor inspection does help to clarify some of the issues in the distinction between specialized labor inspection as it is practiced in the United States and the general inspection model in Latin America. First, it suggests that it is not so much the division of labor standards regulation into specialties which makes the US model so rigid, but the way in which the specialties are defined. The divisions within the US administrative system appear to be only loosely related to the factors causing labor standards violations, and it is thus not very useful in either diagnosing problems or fashioning solutions. The Latin American model does in fact recognize certain specialties, but they are not based upon the standards themselves. Thus, for example, a number of countries have services specialized in particular industries, typically agriculture, mining, and transportation. France, among others, makes a distinction between large and small enterprises, and has specialized agents (the contrôleurs) who inspect enterprises with fewer than 50 employees. In Guatemala, there is a separate small unit of inspectors that deals exclusively with maquilas. A number of countries have units which specialize in child labor.

A second point that emerges in pursuing the medical analogy is that the underlying rationale here is the division of knowledge, and this may or may not be reflected in the actual organization of the work itself or the separation of organizational units. We can, in other words, make a distinction between the specialization of knowledge and the specialization in its application. One of the advantages of keeping even the specialized units within a single organizational entity is that one can take advantage of the specialized knowledge and adjust national priorities in the administration of the law. One might thus want to vary the enforcement of standards in small enterprises with the level of economic development, nationally or in the region. Typically, Latin (and French) labor; inspectorates have staff units specialized in labor law, engineering, and industrial medicine which the line inspectors can call upon for advice. Some actually assign general inspectors with different backgrounds to local offices (France and Brazil do this, for example) so that the inspectors can turn informally to their colleagues for advice.

Nonetheless – and this is the third general point – one would still like not only to codify the knowledge upon which the inspectors' judgments are built but also to examine it in a form which enables it to grow and improve over time. Can we, in other words, go beyond the rules and procedures implicit in the decisions of the inspectors themselves and subject them to systematic evaluation and improvement, making them more consistent with the shifting values of the society as a whole, or the weights placed on different values as these shift with economic and social conditions, by actually reducing the conflict between the standards and the economic goals of efficiency and development? We turn to the scholarly literature for clues as to how we might do so.

E. A scientific foundation for labor inspection

Two bodies of scholarly literature appear particularly relevant, especially in developing countries, for organizing knowledge about labor standards and for the endeavor of surfacing the tacit knowledge of the inspectors themselves, formalizing it and subjecting it to evaluation. The first of these literatures concerns the relationship between labor standards and business practice. The second concerns the relationship between business practice and the normative system governing the workplace. We will discuss them sequentially.

1. Labor standards and business practice

The literature on production systems and business strategies is extremely dispersed over time and over different fields of study. But its import can be illustrated by four strands. The most basic of these in the context of the still-developing countries of Latin America is Max Weber's classic observation that the key to industrial development is the creation of a realm where activity is evaluated rationally, in terms of economic efficiency, separate and distinct from the affective, personalistic or charismatic standards which typically govern relationships in the household, the family, or in political life.[14] This observation is particularly germane in the traditional industries (textiles, clothing, shoes, furniture, and the like) which have been the subject of my own research in Italy, Mexico, and Central America.[15] Production in these industries typically takes place in the household and in

---

[14] M Weber, *The Protestant Ethic and the Spirit of Capitalism* (Scribner, 1958); and M Weber, *Economy and Society: An Outline of Interpretive Sociology*, 2 vols (G Roth and C Wittich (eds), E Fischoff et al (trs), University of California Press, 1978).
[15] MJ Piore, 'Rethinking International Labor Standards' in W Milberg (ed), *Labor and the Globalization of Production: Causes and Consequences of Industrial Upgrading* (Palgrave Macmillan, 2004) 249–65.

outbuildings once used for agriculture, and the layout and flow of production is dictated not by economic efficiency and the standards of quality demanded by the marketplace but rather by the original uses for which the structures were built and the need to accommodate ongoing household activity or residual agriculture. Children are pervasive in these shops, sometimes actually engaged in production or learning about production (informal apprenticeship) but often they are simply *there* because that is where they live, perpetually underfoot and a distraction from the production process in which their parents and older siblings are engaged. The household finances are intertwined with those of the business, defying rational accounting, precluding cost analysis, and placing working capital hostage to household emergencies. Business transport doubles for the household as well, and the delivery of supplies to the shop and finished goods to clients is frequently delayed by household chores.

The organization of these shops invariably entails violations of a long list of formal labor standards ranging from elementary health and safety regulations to those governing wages and hours, and, of course, child labor. But the separation of the business from the household is a prerequisite for determining what these are, let alone for bringing the enterprise into compliance on anything more than a momentary basis. Thus, for example, so long as the shop is in the family's living quarters it is really hard to tell whether the children there are working or simply being kept close to their parents' watchful eye and maybe being entertained by participating in a piece of the production process. Without separate business accounts, it is hard to say what people are being paid, indeed if they are being paid at all. A separation of the household from the business would, of course, also promote economic development and a more efficient flow of production and quality – a prerequisite for participation in the global marketplace which requires compliance with a set of standards associated with statistical quality control, on-time delivery and the like. There is a sense in which the integration of the business and the household makes it difficult to adhere not just to labor standards but to any standards at all. The alternative to the reorganization of the business in this way is the development of a separate set of standards for the traditional sector, a point to which we turn below.

A second strand of the literature on production processes suggests that it may be possible to induce some of these changes without engaging in the reorganization of production directly. Labor standards in the garment industry are a laundry list of separate regulations concerning child labor, health and safety standards, wages and hours, etc. They seem to have grown up piecemeal, in reaction to particularly dramatic events which moved public opinion such as the Triangle Fire in New York City in the early 20th century. But they are actually all related to each other as distinct aspects of a single production system, the *sweatshop*. The sweatshop in turn appears to be characteristic of an extremely labor-intensive industry in which wages are paid by the piece. The piece rate system equalizes the cost to the employer of virtually all types of labor (skilled and unskilled, children and adults); all labor costs become variable costs that are directly proportional to output. When production takes place in the factory setting, the major fixed cost, virtually the only cost which is not directly proportional to output, is the cost of space, that is, rent. As a result, the employer has an incentive to crowd as much work into a given space as possible. The crowding may reduce labor productivity but that cost is born by the workers under the piece rate system. The crowding also leads to major health and safety risks, especially that of fire, and the dangers of fatalities in case of fire are magnified by aisles clogged with materials and blocked exits, a further attempt to conserve real estate. The piece rate system also encourages child labor since the employer is indifferent to the low productivity of children or the fact that the children distract the adults and slow down the pace of the work overall. Ultimately, it also encourages industrial home work and the integration of the factory and the household about which Weber was concerned, since by moving production into the household the employer escapes even the fixed cost of space. But by the same token, the whole system of production, and the complex of associated standards violations, can be rectified by imposing a minimum hourly wage rate and enforcing it strictly.[16]

A third more contemporary literature relating labor standards to production systems grows out of the adjustment to the pressures of international competition among industrial countries, particularly the emergence of Japan as a major competitive threat in the 1980s. The literature is built around a distinction between the 'high' road and the 'low' road to industrial adjustment. The low road involves adjustment by draconian cost cutting; especially by squeezing the labor force through lower wages, longer hours, the use of untrained and/or temporary workers (who have a higher propensity for industrial accidents), as well as the crowding of more workers into limited space, which are characteristics of sweatshops. The high road involves a more deliberate attempt to change production practices, typically in a way which enables the firm to move up-market and to manage more flexibly with lower inventories. In work practices, it involves a broadening of job responsibilities, so that each worker is responsible for a wider range of tasks (or operations), and a decentralization of power and authority within the enterprise in a way which encourages more self-supervision but also more cooperation among the line workers. It typically increases efficiency and product quality and can facilitate compliance with wage standards, hours regulations, and health and safety standards. But the new work practices have also been accompanied by an increased use of temporary employees and a blurring of the line between supervisory and production workers, and more work at home in ways which make compliance with formal labor regulations problematic and have fed a debate about whether traditional standards, most of which date from the time when the economy was dominated by manufacturing, are consistent with modern technology.

There is now a literature developing these alternatives and comparing the high and low roads in a number of specific industries.[17] The literature does not

---

[16] MJ Piore, 'Labor Standards and Business Strategies' in S Herzenberg and J Perez Lopez (eds), *Labor Standards and Development in the Global Economy* (US Department of Labor, Bureau of International Labor Affairs, 1990).

[17] P Osterman, 'How Common is Workplace Transformation and Who Adopts It?' (1994) 47 Indus & Lab Rel Rev 173; P Osterman, 'Work Reorganization in the Era of Restructuring: Trends in Diffusion and Effects on Employee Welfare' (2000) 53 Indus & Lab Rel Rev 179;

specifically focus on labor standards but it is explicitly concerned with work practices and hence could easily be extended to standards. And it should be possible to link the inspectors' own observations to this literature as well.

Finally, closely related to the high road/low road are separate literatures on supply chains and industrial districts. These literatures often focus on traditional industries as well, but on sectors within them which are competitive in, and integrated into, the global marketplace. Industrial districts and supply chains are often discussed together, although in fact they are quite distinct. The supply chain literature emphasizes the hierarchical relationship among firms which are tightly integrated but located at different stages of the production process, and typically cross establishment and national boundaries.[18] The industrial district literature, in contrast, emphasizes flexible relationships among essentially equal partners in a well-defined and delineated geographic region.[19] Both literatures are concerned with how the institutional configuration is related to business strategy and economic welfare. They were not initially focused on labor standards but there is work in each literature related to standards, and both lend themselves to extension in that direction.

The supply chain in particular has been the focus of efforts emanating from NGOs in advanced industrial countries to monitor and upgrade labor standards in those parts of the chain located in developing countries. These efforts play upon a characteristic which receives particular emphasis in the literature: That power and authority in a given chain typically reside at one stage of the production process (such as retailers in apparel, assemblers in automobiles) and hence the exercise of economic pressure at this point, even from afar, can police the whole chain. This contention has proven to be disappointing on several grounds, but a few very prominent brand names have been forced by consumer boycotts to monitor labor conditions in their suppliers' shops. The data collected in this process – which is now being analyzed by a research group under the direction of Richard Locke at MIT – provides a potential source for a detailed understanding of the determinants

P Osterman, 'The Wage Effects of High Performance Work Organization in Manufacturing' (2006) 59 Indus & Lab Rel Rev 187; E Appelbaum and R Batt, *The New American Workplace: Transforming Work Systems in the United States* (ILR Press, 1994); in cars: TA Kochan and SA Rubinstein, 'Toward a Stakeholder Theory of the Firm: The Saturn Partnership' (2000) 11 Organization Science 367; J-P MacDuffie, 'Human Resource Bundles and Manufacturing Performance: Organizational Logic and Flexible Production Systems in the World Automobile Industry' (1995) 48 Indus & Lab Rel Rev 197; in steel: C Ichniowski, K Shaw, and G Prennushi, 'The Effects of Human Resource Management Practices on Productivity: A Study of Steel Finishing Lines' (1997) 87 American Economic Review 291; and in restaurants: A Bernhardt, S McGrath, and J DeFilippis, 'Unregulated Work in the Global City: Employment and Labor Law Violations in New York City' (2007) Research Report, Brennen Center for Justice, New York University School of Law.

[18] G Gereffi and M Korseniewicz, *Commodity Chains and Global Capitalism* (Praeger, 1994).

[19] F Pyke, G Becattini, and W Sengenberger (eds), *Industrial Districts and Interfirm Cooperation in Italy* (International Institute for Labour Studies, 1990); H Schmitz and K Nadvi, 'Clustering and Industrialization: Introduction' (1999) 27 World Development 1503; and A Saxenian, *Regional Advantage: Culture and Competition in Silicon Valley and Route 128* (Harvard University Press, 1994).

of labor conditions.[20] Three results stand out from initial studies. First, there is substantial variation in labor standards across firms at similar positions in the supply chain, working for the same buyers, and hence with cost structures that are apparently competitive with each other. The research has not established what the differences among these firms are, but presumably it could be extended to do so and integrated with a typology abstracted from interviews with labor inspectors. Second, a major factor in the ability of subcontractors to adhere to labor standards, in terms of hours and the pace of work, are the business practices of the retailers, and particularly the lead time they allow between placing and filling orders. This, in turn, depends on the business practices *within* the retail firm, especially the coordination among designers and sales reps, on the one hand, and the procurement department and the department responsible for monitoring the subcontractors, on the other. The third finding of this research is that the power in the supply chain is actually more diffuse than the literature suggests. Rather than being concentrated in the retailers with brand names who are subject to consumer pressure, it sometimes lies with the suppliers, some of whom are themselves large international companies who work for enough different clients that they are able to resist pressure exerted by any one of them (but might at the same time make them more responsive to regulatory efforts exerted by their own governments or those at their production locations – as opposed to pressures emanating from consumer boycotts and exerted through brand-name retailers).

2. Les économies de la grandeur

A last scholarly literature which is relevant in providing a framework for the systematization and evaluation of the judgments of labor inspectors is a literature on moral judgment growing out of the conventionalist school of economics and sociology.[21] The central tenet here is that rather than applying a single system of moral standards, people judge economic relations – and in fact social relations generally – in terms of a series of distinct and different moral systems. Each of these systems entails its own set of values, its own system through which people are evaluated and ranked, its own set of procedures or tests for making that evaluation, etc. In a sense, this is an extension of Max Weber's argument, discussed above, of economic development involving the creation of a realm separate and distinct from the family with its own standards of judgment and evaluation. But the conventionalists identify five such realms, which they call *cites*. In addition to the family or domestic realm, they identify an inspirational realm, a civic realm, an industrial realm and a market realm. The industrial realm roughly corresponds

---

[20] R Locke and M Romis, 'Beyond Corporate Codes of Conduct: Work Organization and Labor Standards in Two Mexican Garment Factories' (2006) MIT Sloan Working Paper 4617–06; Harvard University Corporate Social Responsibility Initiative Working Paper 26; and R Locke et al, 'Beyond Corporate Codes of Conduct: Work Organization and Labour Standards at Nike's Suppliers' (2007) 146 International Labour Review 21.

[21] L Boltanski and L Thévenot, *Les Economies de la Grandeur* (Presses Universitaires de France, 1987).

to the bureaucratic systems of large corporate enterprises; the civic realm to the relationships among skilled workers in a craft or profession. The realms involve different authority relationships and different standards of worth, and hence presumably different rules for compensation, promotion, job allocation, etc. The norms governing the workplace will thus vary from one realm to another, and one can imagine that just as the police in a large city apply the law differentially depending on the neighborhood in which they are working, the labor inspector is sensitive to the type of workplace he or she is controlling and picks different parts of the labor code to inspect for and enforce. The conventionalist literature will then help to clarify what the different moral realms are, which particular rules are appropriate in each, and how one should decide whether to accept the standards prevailing there or, as we implied in discussing traditional family firms above, whether to encourage them to adopt a different approach to work and in effect alter the norms which govern work relations.

F. The moral foundations of labor standards

The conventionalist typology points toward the broader question of the underlying legitimacy of labor standards. The centrality of that question has been obscured by the deterrence model through which the emphasis on economic incentives has taught us to think about government regulation. But, in the case of labor standards at least, a close examination of the implications of that way of thinking points toward its limits as well. Compliance in that model is understood as a business decision. Each enterprise weighs the cost of compliance against the cost of non-compliance and adheres to the regulation (in this case the labor standard) only if the former outweighs the latter. The cost of noncompliance reflects the chances of being inspected and hence getting caught. A back-of-the-envelope calculation dividing the number of enterprises by the number of inspectors reveals, however, that even in countries with the largest relative inspection corps the chances of getting caught are minimal, too small to make deterrence in this sense a credible enforcement mechanism. Evidently other forces come into play.

There is actually not a single analytical framework which captures those 'other' forces. But two modifications in the standard economic model point toward what these are likely to be. First, the standard model is one of the rational man maximizing his material wellbeing on all margins of the endeavors in which he is engaged. Even the most rational actor does not and cannot operate on all margins at once, however. Business managers, in particular, typically focus on a few particular points in the business process which they judge key to success in the market. A good deal of what is done in the rest of the operation is dictated by standard routines or practices borrowed from somewhere else in the system or inherited from the past.[22] The role of labor inspection in this view is thus one of policing those

---

[22] This is a central point of the economic models of RR Nelson and SG Winter, *An Evolutionary Theory of Economic Change* (Belknap Press of Harvard University Press, 1982); or of HA Simon, *Models*

routines, making sure that they are consistent with prevailing labor standards and held in place. Violations develop when that policing function fails.

The key processes here are illustrated by the case of the New York State investigation of minimum wage violations at grocery stores in Manhattan. Such groceries are located on virtually every corner in the city, and for at least the last 10 years virtually all of these groceries have been owned and operated by Korean immigrants. The state agency discovered that all or nearly all of the groceries were paying wages below the statutory minimum. In the investigation of how this had happened, they learned that the owners all belonged to a single association; the association provided a list to their members of the laws and regulations with which they were expected to comply (health standards, building codes, taxes, etc). Nowhere on this list were labor market regulations. The labor code was simply not a standard which self-respecting Korean groceries were expected to uphold. The process through which labor standards fell off this list (or failed to get on it in the first place) then becomes key to understanding compliance. To explore this story completely would require more space than is available in a chapter of this kind. But we know from other studies that Korean businessmen are extremely sensitive to their prestige and moral standing both in the Korean community and the larger American society, and see the role of their business associations as furthering their position in this regard.[23] This suggests that one needs to look to the way in which labor standards violations have come to be viewed in the society at large to understand the lack of attention devoted to them by the association from which the grocers took their clues.

The second set of amendments to the standard economic model which appears helpful in understanding labor standards enforcement are those which we drew upon earlier in understanding the behavior of the labor inspectors themselves. Entrepreneurs and managers, like inspectors, live in a broader community composed of their colleagues and fellow business executives, but also of civil society more broadly. The communities have a set of expectations about how people should behave in their business roles, and their identity and self-respect is dependent on how their behavior is evaluated in the light of these expectations. Because they value the opinions of their colleagues, those opinions operate to modify the behavioral patterns promoted by the pursuit of narrow material wellbeing. One can call these community expectations a set of moral or normative values, although these are very general terms for a complex set of factors.

Morality here must operate on at least two levels (or perhaps one could say with respect to two communities). One is at the grass roots: Do the people whom these standards directly affect, and the employers and managers who are responsible for

---

of Man: Social and Rational (Wiley, 1957). The sociologist's concept of institutional isomorphism captures part of this process as well in PJ DiMaggio and WW Powell, 'The Iron Cage Revisited: Institutional Isomorphism and Collective Rationality in Organizational Fields' (1983) 48 American Sociological Review 147.

[23] E Lee, 'Why Did They Comply While Others Did Not? Environmental Compliance of Small Firms and Implications for Regulation' (DPhil thesis, MIT, 2005).

UNIVERSITY OF WINCHESTER
LIBRARY

adherence to them, think of the standards as fair and violations as wrong? Are the standards, in other words, consistent with the *felt* sense of justice? Here there are at least two separate issues: One is whether the regulations are just; the second is whether they are fairly administered. For the first of these questions, the normative distinctions which form the basis of conventionalist's *cite*, which we have just discussed, should be critical, and the ability of the inspectors in the Latin system to adjust enforcement to different normative standards would seem to enhance their legitimacy. It follows that any systematic reflection within the corps of the inspectorate which strengthens their capacity to do this effectively will strengthen the adherence. The second issue, that of administration, underscores the importance of the processes which we discussed in the first part of the chapter, which operate to maintain a sense of consistency in the treatment of cases.

But the felt sense of justice is only one level at which morality operates. Labor market regulation has also been buttressed historically by a higher level of morality which justified the intervention of the state into this domain as being in the interest of the society as a whole, irrespective of the way in which the specific codes were viewed in the shops and offices to which they applied. It is this broader moral justification which was undermined by the neoliberal ideology. That ideology, moreover, has done so not simply on the intellectual and ideological level but in the way in which it has permeated the rhetoric and symbolism of politics. This is no doubt how the Korean grocers' association came to neglect labor regulations in its list of standards to which it felt its members were obliged to adhere. But the way in which this has operated is most vividly illustrated from an interview in France where the inspectors have a strong sense of being caught between the high rhetoric of the political class (on the left as well as the right) and the pressures from the rank-and-file workers for protection by the inspectors as the agents of the State. Thus, one of our interviews occurred the day after the president of the Michelin Tire Company had died in a boating accident. The President of the Republic went on television that night to express the condolence of the nation to the family. One of the inspectors in the interview bitterly pointed out the contrast to the death of the two inspectors shot in the back by a peasant whose farm they were inspecting; it took several weeks before government officials made any comment at all.

This brings us back to a question raised in the introduction. The neoliberal ideology has clearly collapsed and this is the proximate cause of the rise of labor standards. But is it enough to sustain that revival of labor standards? Is there not a need for a positive ideological justification? And, if so, where would such an ideology come from? This, is it should be said, is not simply a question of labor market regulations in the abstract, but – an issue which we have not thus far discussed – the justification of the particular standards which are currently enforced. That justification has been undermined considerably by the notion of a post-industrial society and the idea which it implies that the standards currently on the books are the product of some earlier moment in industrial history which new technologies and associated modes of organization have rendered obsolete.

These issues may actually be more relevant to the advanced industrial societies of the United States, Western Europe, and Japan than to the still-developing world.

Take, for example, the North and South of the Western Hemisphere. Post-industrial society in the North has entailed the movement of traditional manufacturing abroad and led in Mexico, Central America, and the Caribbean to economies which more closely resemble those in which traditional labor standards were relevant. This is probably less true in the more southern countries of Latin America, but even there transition has been less dramatic than in the advanced industrial countries. By the same token, the historic pressures for state intervention to protect workers against market pressures remain much stronger in Latin America. Thus, while the decline of the Soviet Union and the communist parties has reduced the threat of class warfare and revolution, civil unrest and class conflict still are very real concerns in much of Latin America, and have been powerful forces promoting the revival of labor market regulation, most notably in Chile and central America (for example, Guatemala), but in much of the rest of the continent as well. Similarly, Catholic ideology remains an important factor, perhaps most interestingly in Mexico where it was the guiding ideology of reforms in the Ministry of Labor under the Partido Acción Nacional, albeit not enough to overcome the generally *laissez faire* bias of that regime.

Still the technical case for labor inspection as part of a broader economic policy would provide a new justification for labor standards. That case would be strengthened by a more deliberate approach to the management of labor inspection, by a greater emphasis on the pedagogical and entrepreneurial functions of the service, and by drawing upon and extending the scholarly literature on the relationship between production processes, business practices, and labor standards which we reviewed in a preceding section.

G. Conclusions: globalization

While the focus here has been primarily upon the implications of the flexibility of the Franco-Latin model of labor market regulation for economic adjustment and efficiency, I would like to conclude with a brief discussion about the implications of that model for institutional standardization in a global trading regime. The major effort to address this issue historically has been through the ILO, where the emphasis had been upon a set of norms or standards adopted by the governing body of that organization to which member nations are then expected, in their turn, to subscribe. It is an approach in which individual standards are considered in isolation from each other, and which fits readily with the US system of regulations rather than the Franco-Latin model. These norms have accumulated over the years into a substantial body of regulations, and in recent years have come under severe criticism, in part as part of the neoliberal critique of labor market regulation in general. The norms have also been criticized as increasingly obsolete in the context of the changes in economic organization and in technology. One of the problems in addressing the question of global norms has been the difficulty of separating out these two types of criticism. In so far as the ILO has responded to these criticisms, however, it has been largely by retreating from the elaborate list of standards which have accumulated over the years to an abbreviated list of core standards. But the core standards continue an approach to standardization which requires the international community to adopt a common set of very specific regulations with no flexibility to adapt to differences in economic conditions or levels of economic development, let alone to the peculiarities of history and culture which differentiate national institutions.

The Franco-Latin model suggests a more organic approach to standardization which focuses not on the norms themselves but instead upon the evolution of culture, both of business culture and the culture of regulatory institutions. Presumably, trade itself promotes a degree of cultural convergence, particularly in business and consumer cultures. An international organization like the ILO could seek to influence the evolution of the regulatory cultures of different national contexts so as to bring them into harmony with each other in much the same way that management seeks to gain influence over the culture of a street-level bureaucracy. Of the several instruments for doing so which we noted earlier (recruitment, selection, training and socialization, etc), the one which seems to lend itself most readily to this would be training. One might, for example, create an international institution in which work inspectors from different countries were trained together at a single location using a common curriculum. New recruits could be brought together before they went into the field in their own country, but both new recruits and experienced inspectors could also serve apprenticeships in other countries. An international organization could also bring experienced inspectors together on a regular basis to discuss specific cases and/or to conduct research along the lines suggested earlier about the relationship among labor standards, production systems, and business practices and their impact upon economic development and social welfare.

What this approach does not address is the fundamental incommensurability of the Franco-Latin model of labor market regulation and that of the United States, and here I have no obvious solution to propose.

24

Collective Exit Strategies: New Ideas in Transnational Labour Law

*Silvana Sciarra**

A. A short preface on transnational juridification

This chapter discusses new ideas related to labour law, its functions, and its consistency as a legal discipline, in the framework of European and transnational developments. A shift in the emphasis put in previous comparative research is required. After elaborating on the autonomy of labour law, its 'boundaries and frontiers',[1] attention is now concentrated on how labour law captures new transnational demands. Labour law's embedding in national legal systems is put into question by an accentuated mobility of companies and labour. Furthermore, labour law is influenced by the effects of an unprecedented economic and financial crisis. In responding to new emergencies, national and supranational institutions should not be left with contingent and temporary answers. They should rather elaborate on long-term trends, in order to forge new ideas in labour law.

The question to be asked is whether, because of a dominant transnational dimension, emphasized by the need to address the crisis and its impact at a global level, long-established labour law measures are at risk of marginalization. This may be for various reasons. The very high number of jobs lost as a consequence of the crisis threatens recognized regulatory techniques and gives rise to dissimilar regimes of solidarity. As a result of economic uncertainties, standardized guarantees are broken into multiple systems of norms, running parallel to each other and addressed to different groups of workers, each of them driven by different expectations.

National governments should refrain from taking independent initiatives, whenever major sectors of productive activities are hit by the crisis, yet the temptation to act in a protectionist mood may be real. Thus, supranational institutions – both political and financial – become crucial in establishing objective and transparent criteria. Non-state actors become involved in considerable ways in the interstices of institutional dialogues, either on their own initiative, or when solicited by

---

* Jean Monnet Chair, European Labour and Social Law, University of Florence.
[1] G Davidov and B Langille (eds), *Boundaries and Frontiers of Labour Law* (Hart Publishing, 2006).

other actors. Their role is viewed as a quasi-institutional one, because they deal with matters relevant in the public sphere and, not least, because they put into effect their own normative power. Scholarship in international relations takes an interest in this process of 'constitutionalization', occurring whenever acknowledgment is made of the evolving 'social power' in the international system.[2] Legitimacy beyond the state thus becomes a goal to be achieved, in parallel with the recognition of new sources characterized by a transnational scope.

Furthermore, mobility of companies and labour gives rise to potential conflicts of law and to the enforceability of variable standards. Protectionist answers emerging from national legal systems are counterintuitive to the expansion of global markets. Nonetheless, they may be originated by the fear that internal balances of rights be destroyed and national social partners be disempowered. The danger perceived at national level has to do with the progressive weakening of organized groups participating in the law-making process. The perception of such deep and unsettling changes is mainly oriented towards collective bargaining, by tradition a source of cooperative knowledge and a creator of consensus within national legal orders. A 'network failure'[3] of this kind could end up breaking robust chains of obligations and promises, well designed for the functioning of domestic legal systems and yet capable, if necessary, to release the pressure put by external actors and establish links with them.

In this unstable scenario hierarchies of sources are dismantled into multiple systems of norm-setting, even beyond national borders. Hybridization of state and voluntary sources occurs without experiencing a prior clarification on powers and legitimacy of the organized groups, active in managing the consequences of the crisis. On the one hand collective uncertainties may engender protectionist behaviour, leaving cross-border solidarities outside the scope of collective actions. On the other hand, lack of resources and losses of jobs may provoke asymmetric collective answers, tailored around urgent – and at times temporary – prospects, for both management and labour.

It is argued in this chapter that collective labour law can still provide 'exit strategies' to all actors dealing with the effects of the crisis, somehow re-inventing the scope of what used to be a self-inclusive national legal discipline. It is also suggested that a deeper understanding of changes taking place at national and supranational level should foster new theoretical definitions of existing hybrid systems of norms.

Processes of transnational standard-setting could progressively disentangle labour law from its national roots and weaken the authority of legal points of view. Therefore, states could feel the urgency to regain their role as regulators and support transnational private orders, so to enhance new dimensions of social justice. Since the collective interests in question are supranational and so are the targets to be

---

[2] J Steffek, 'Sources of Legitimacy Beyond the State: A View from International Relations' in C Joerges et al (eds), *Transnational Governance and Constitutionalism* (Hart Publishing, 2004) 81 and 101.

[3] G Teubner, '"And if I Beelzebub cast out Devils . . .": an Essay on the Diabolics of Network Failure' (2009) 10 German Law Journal 395.

reached, states are forced to proceed within a network of obligations towards and among other states. At the same time, states feel compelled to defend essential parts of their sovereignty on key policy issues, particularly when priorities must be set in managing national budgets.

Against this articulate background, labour lawyers should undertake a new comparative evaluation of what I suggest to describe as 'transnational juridification'.[4] Broad transnational trends in the evolution of labour law should engender new ideas and shake existing hierarchies of sources. Transnational juridification in labour law is characterized by a tendency to connect with different regimes of fundamental rights. The European Union sets a good example for this ongoing process, when it creates links among national constitutional traditions and supranational rights and principles.[5] Furthermore, transnational juridification interferes with sub-systems of norms in the social spheres, most significantly with groups representing employers and labour. As we shall see further on in this chapter, these autonomous social spheres are now, more noticeably than in the past, torn between national and supranational goals. They seek independency from national labour law systems, in order to establish themselves as authoritative sources of supranational regulation in the global sphere. However, they continue to be related to national legal orders and must return to their constituencies whenever they need to build up legitimacy and report back to their members.

Labour law's patterns of regulation are coherent with recent theoretical investigations on open processes of juridification. They imply the interaction of national and transnational systems of norms. For example, fundamental social rights exercised collectively – right to bargain, right to information and consultation – are part of the yet unfinished process of constitutionalization within the EU, giving rise to 're-institutionalization'.[6] Traditional deliberative bodies within the framework of collective bargaining are re-institutionalized through juridification of their collective behaviour, namely by setting new, widely recognized transnational goals and by creating new bonds of representation.

In formulating constitutional questions, theories on fundamental rights and principles, typically embedded in national labour law, need to be re-framed within evolving trends of transnational juridification. The concept of 'societal constitutionalism' takes into account the fact that there is no global state behind the construction of a global constitution. Hence, attention must be paid to the evolution of all actors contributing to the de-nationalization of deliberative

---

[4] Seminal comparative research in labour law is presented in G Teubner (ed), *Juridification of Social Spheres* (de Gruyter, 1987).
[5] Art 6 TEU recognizes the 'same legal value as the Treaties' to the Charter of Fundamental Rights of the EU. It also provides for the EU's accession to the ECHR. Fundamental rights, as guaranteed by the ECHR and as they result from the constitutional traditions common to the Member States 'shall constitute general principles of the Union's law'.
[6] F Snyder, 'The Unfinished Constitution of the European Union: Principles, Processes and Culture' in JHH Weiler and M Wind (eds), *European Constitutionalism Beyond the State* (Cambridge University Press, 2003) 65.

processes, taking place in the 'peripheries of law, at the boundaries with other sectors of world society, and no longer in the existing centres of law-making'.[7]

In the following pages some examples will be offered in order to prove that new ideas in labour law go into the direction of re-formulating institutional balances of power and re-designing theories of democratic representation within an incomplete world legal order.

B. A war of messages and measures

'Exit strategy' is an expression borrowed from military jargon, utilized as a metaphor in discussing possible ways to react to the economic and financial crisis. Arguments adopted in wars, as well as in economic and financial downturns, indicate that, whenever there is a need to act, at least one option must be left open, so to abandon the battle field. It is remarkable how often this expression penetrates current European discourses, both in circles of independent policy making and in official documents produced by European institutions.

Research carried on in a Brussels-based independent think tank shows that emergencies may lead to abuses in government interventions. Exit strategies are thus evoked to deal with macroeconomic issues, such as fiscal and monetary policies, to allow for better competition and diminish state control on institutions of the financial market.[8]

In analysing the early stage of the Greek crisis, exit strategies were foreseen, suggesting that the International Monetary Fund (IMF) should be involved and act jointly with EU institutions. A reform of Article 143 of the Lisbon Treaty (TFEU) was also envisaged, arguing for loans to be granted to euro-area Member States, as well as to those with a 'derogation', namely those staying outside of the euro area. Market integration must, whenever possible, pursue inclusion, rather than exclusion of states undergoing economic difficulties. The lack of effective sanctions to be enforced against Member States not complying with economic policy guidelines suggests, therefore, that the European Commission should act for preventing imbalances, through better surveillance mechanisms.[9] These arguments are coherent with theoretical definitions of 'legitimate governance beyond the state' and indicate rational ways of achieving consensus around shared values within the EU.[10]

In the above-mentioned policy analysis attention is paid to governments' capacities to monitor their own internal competitiveness, for example through wage guidelines and buffer funds. Experiments carried on in Belgium and Finland in the

---

[7] G Teubner, 'Societal Constitutionalism: Alternatives to State-Centred Constitutional Theory?' in C Joerges et al (eds), *Transnational Governance and Constitutionalism* (Hart Publishing, 2004) 17.

[8] N Veron, 'Will Governments Overreach in Their Crisis Interventions?,' <http://www.breugel.org/uploads/tx_btbbruegel/op-ed_nvdecember.pdf> (2009).

[9] B Marzinotto et al, 'Two Crises, Two Responses', <http://www.bruegel.org> (December 2009).

[10] See above, n 2.

1990s are recalled for their significant contribution to coordination of wage policies, with a view to preventing negative impacts in the adoption of the single currency. These examples are relevant to the arguments developed in this chapter, inasmuch as they prove the efficiency of collective measures in dealing with the effects of the crisis.

Policy-makers have also gone as far as suggesting that a 'social stability pact' should be the new regulatory tool in the attempt to overcome problems of competing welfare states, in the absence of a European-level coordination. This analysis relies on collective bargaining or on legislation to set minimum wages, linked to economic productivity and measured on a percentage of national average wage levels.[11]

Mention of exit strategies has been made in recent European Council meetings. Under the Swedish presidency measures were encouraged, while waiting for the implementation of 'sustainable recovery', through economic reforms, affecting the financial sector and employment. The implications of exit strategies were all related to the most vulnerable individuals hit by the crisis.[12]

The recent 'EU 2020 strategy', launched by the Commission as a follow up to the Lisbon strategy, has similar contingent characteristics.[13] As a response to the failure of the Lisbon agenda, aggravated by the current crisis, the Commission seeks the collaboration of national governments in setting common priorities. There is a sign of repetitiveness in announcing knowledge as one key factor in the upsurge of growth and recovery. There is some novelty in indicating the green economy as a connecting factor for revitalizing several sectors of production, as well as education and research. Along these lines, the European Council recommends exit strategies in its integrated guidelines for the economic policies, arguing for 'smart', 'sustainable', and 'inclusive' growth.[14]

After the launch of a renewed Lisbon agenda, during the first Barroso presidency of the Commission, principles of flexicurity were incorporated into the Guidelines for growth and jobs. Financial support to the Lisbon strategy was first envisaged in the work of groups of experts and is now materializing in specific proposals.[15] Structural funds thus become a significant support for weaker economies and

---

[11] B Hacker, 'Discussion Paper: A European Social Stability Pact' (Friedrich Ebert Foundation, International Policy analysis, <http://www.fes.de.pa>, Berlin, December 2008).

[12] EU Presidency Conclusions 1 December 2009, sections 27–28, <http://www.consilium.europa.eu/uedocs/cms_data/docs/pressdata/en/ec/110889.pdf>.

[13] Communication from the Commission, *Europe 2020. A Strategy for Smart, Sustainable and Inclusive Growth*, 3 May 2010, COM(2010) 2020, 3.3.2010. The European Council adopted 'Europe 2020' in the session held on 25–26 March 2010, <http://register.consilium.europa.eu/pdf/en/10/st00/st00007.en10.pdf>.

[14] Council Recommendation of 27 April 2010 on broad guidelines for the economic policies of the Member States and of the Union, Part I of the Europe 2020 Integrated Guidelines, SEC(2010) 488 final, sections 7–10. Member States seem so far reluctant to accept supranational targets, even when it comes to setting aside 3 per cent of GNP for research and development.

[15] M Heidenreich, 'The Open Method of Coordination' in M Eidenreich and J Zeitlin (eds), *Changing European Employment and Welfare Regimes* (Routledge, 2009), referring to the European taskforce on employment, chaired by W Kok, who produced the Report 'Jobs, Jobs, Jobs. Creating More Employment in Europe' (November 2003).

should transform the whole process of coordinating employment policies into a more pragmatic exercise, supporting innovative legislation and finalizing financial help towards most efficient outcomes. Monitoring of all such practices still remains a difficult exercise, in particular with regard to the implementation of the agreed measures. However, a virtuous circle of praising good performances could be started. Whenever financial resources are offered to support labour law measures, new collective exit strategies should consist in practising good governance of the resources. The setting up of independent internal monitoring too should be part of a new auxiliary kind of legislation which keeps the state active in exercising control.

A new path in employment policies must be considered with some attention, since it could prompt new ideas in labour law. The visible decline in soft law coordination, the way it had been conceived during the early days of the Lisbon employment strategy, is a critical issue, aggravated by the crisis. Unsatisfactory results of that method lead policy-makers towards new exit strategies, based on selective incentives. The availability of resources may change the overall scenario and even shape new collective interests, thus empowering again collective actors.

The recurring metaphor of exit strategies can also be applied to the closing down of business, followed by mass dismissals. Governments announcing exceptional measures, when the crisis spreads globally, inevitably need to link up domestic financial support with broader strategies of recovery.

One of the latest examples is offered in the automotive industry. The announcement that Opel would close down the Antwerp plant in Belgium followed the indications of the US parent company General Motors to cut down jobs in Europe. The point to underline in this case is that a 'collective exit strategy' is pursued by the so-called European Employee Forum, made out of the European Metalworkers' Federation and General Motors Europe's works councils. The alternative solution to closing down is to find a new investor for the Antwerp plant, while, at the same time, drafting a 'social plan' for workers, which offers early retirement schemes and individual pay outs. All these solutions, put to the vote of the majority of Belgian unions' membership at plant level, were agreed in April 2010. Meanwhile, the Flemish regional government backed the so-called 'conversion group' in the search for new investors.[16]

As one can see from this example, a worldwide strategy practised by a multinational finds its outcome in a deliberation endorsed by a national government. Representatives of management and labour face the challenge of enforcing the collective rights to information and to bargain collectively, pursuing democratic accountability. A national political decision should follow in a convergent way, so to accompany the collective deliberation taken at plant level. Hybridization of

---

[16] V Telljohann, 'General Motors Announces Europe-Wide Restructuring Plans' (Eironline, 24 May 2010); and M Carley, 'Opel/Vauxhall Reaches Europe-Wide Restructuring Agreement' (European Employment Review, June 2010). The closure of the Fiat plant at Termini Imerese was announced in late 2009. On 16 February 2011, an agreement was reached among the Sicilian region, national government, and seven new investors – two of which in the automotive industry – to develop new productions, when Fiat leaves at the end of 2011. A short list of new investors, sponsored by the Sicilian regional authorities, should have been evaluated by the Italian government in September 2010. In November 2010, new investments were announced by the Region with the intention of continuing the manufacturing of cars.

sources is a visible product of all such messages and measures. The good functioning of national private orders and the democratic accountability of the same are preconditions for constitutionalizing collective rights. Collective exit strategies are contingent and yet functional to the construction of a supranational network of obligations among private and public actors.

Many similar examples in the automotive industry can be quoted. Innovative collective agreements dealing with workers in more than one country range over solutions aimed at 'spreading the load' of job losses throughout Europe (General Motors); guaranteeing hiring priorities within companies of the same manufacturer (Ford); granting training for 'reconversion and reclassification' of workers within the group (Renault).[17] All this confirms a widespread scope of transnational negotiations, leading either to decentralized agreements at company level, or to shared commitments among several employers, enforceable according to varying market demands. It also makes the metaphor of collective exit strategies even more powerful and yet dramatic, whenever the strategy materializes in the reduction of jobs.

A gateway to support workers hit by such events is provided by the European globalization adjustment fund. First entered into force in 2006, the Fund has been updated in 2009. In order to be eligible, in a highly formal and competitive procedure, Member States applying to the Fund must put forward 'a reasoned analysis of the link between the redundancies and major structural changes in world trade patterns or the financial and economic crisis, a demonstration of the number of redundancies, and an explanation of the unforeseen nature of those redundancies'.[18] It also recommends emergency measures to provide immediate help to workers who have lost their jobs as a 'direct result of the global financial and economic crisis'.[19]

The underpinning rationale in the Regulation is that selective support can be granted to EU workers, whenever a causal bond can be established between global market outcomes and the exercise of managerial prerogatives. Different notions of solidarity can thus be envisaged, shaped around uncertain circumstances.[20] Solutions to such inextricable problems all depend on exit strategies, planned to overcome the effects of global trade or the consequences of the economic and financial crisis.

On a different and yet interrelated level, increasing attention is paid to the training of workers whose employment is at risk. Field research shows that skill needs prompted by the green economy should be framed within an 'holistic' paradigm, implying a more multidisciplinary combination of professionals coming

---

[17] References to the agreements in P Loire, J-J Paris, T Ward, and C Weis, *Comprehensive Analysis of the Evolution of the Automotive Sector in Europe*, Alpha Metrics Report, April 2008.
[18] Regulation 546/2009 of the European Parliament and of the Council of 18 June 2009, amending Regulation 1927/2006 on establishing the European Globalisation Adjustment Fund, Art 1.4, replacing Art 5(2)(a), ([2009] OJ L 167/26).
[19] Regulation 546/2009, above n 18, Art 1.1.
[20] S Sciarra, 'Notions of Solidarity in Times of Economic Uncertainty' (2010) 39 Industrial Law Journal.

from different backgrounds. The specific skills required will not be so different from the previous ones and yet they will need to be adapted to new productions.[21]

Collective exit strategies in this case can be twofold. Social dialogue may provide the perfect set-up for the definition of new training schemes and for their export-ability to different environments. It is even suggested that 'energy assessors' should certify these new requirements in education. At EU level a compensation fund for 'going green', similar to the previously mentioned Globalisation Fund, should provide financial assistance to those who loose their jobs.[22]

In this latter example, intentionally chosen to expand the metaphor of exit strategies, the suggestion is that selective support is the foreseeable outcome in innovative forms of standard setting. Instead of following traditional negotiating patterns, embedded in national collective bargaining, it is argued that new criteria for the description and evaluation of skills are more efficiently defined at a transnational level. The aim is to make them recognizable across national borders, therefore 'portable' for potentially mobile workers, who will thus become employable all through the green economy. The new envisaged Fund should enforce selective criteria in choosing the addressees of financial support. The selection of weaker workers, most in need of support, should take place against the background of markets' transnational interdependence. The challenge here consists in converting into transnational skilled labour those who lost their jobs because of restructuring.

Both the language and the ideas emerging from this recent policy document have strong resemblances with the outcomes of comparative work on varieties of capitalism. General skills – as opposed to firm-specific and industry-specific skills – allow better mobility of the workforce and should enhance better investments. On the contrary, specific skills are protected by collective bargaining within the productive sectors in which they are needed. Wage guarantees incrementally reinforce employment protection and call for a strong coordination of collective bargaining.[23] This circle of reciprocal benefits – firms with specific needs and workers with specific skills – is corroborated by the idea that workers should stay as long as possible in that particular employment, enjoying well established rights, both individual and collective.

The other side of the coin is to enhance portable skills, which will favour responsiveness and dynamism in investments and make innovative productions possible. This theory puts an emphasis on the active role of firms, rather than on welfare states. It also presupposes a significant change in the horizon of political choices and a redistribution of power towards actors different from the strong collective organizations of management and labour. In other words, there is an indication that national systems of collective bargaining gain strength from political systems, thus perpetuating institutions and policies.[24]

---

[21] Cedefop Research Paper, 'Future Skill Needs for the Green Economy' (Publications Office of the EU, 2009) 91.

[22] Ibid 92.

[23] P Hall and D Soskice, *Varieties of Capitalism: the Institutional Foundation of Comparative Advantage* (Oxford University Press, 2001) 150–3.

[24] Ibid 182–3.

In his very articulate criticism of neo-institutionalism, Crouch argued for a more diversified analysis, so to prove that actors are not kept in 'an iron cage of institutions, which they cannot change'. Changes occur whenever actors are exposed to a variety of institutions and strategies.[25]

It is submitted here that changes of this kind are under way in transnational collective bargaining, up to the point of breaking institutional cages. Changes are such to require a new understanding of means and ends in collective processes of standard setting. Private orders operating as regulators in the elaboration and in the enforcement of standards are re-establishing their own autonomous role, while keeping their dialogue open with state institutions.

Collective exit strategies prove indispensable even in the re-definition of skills requirements. The hybridization of labour law sources in this case is the consequence of widespread market demands, counterbalanced by different functions assigned to national and supranational private orders. National social partners take on board the re-drafting of professional qualifications resulting from a world re-distribution of productions. We shall see in the next section how collective answers are formulated to counteract other worldwide productive strategies. Even when based on apparently frail procedural machineries, apt to producing non-normative standards, private orders occupy a significant role between states and supranational institutions. They set examples for theoretical definitions of collective learning and for clarifications of 'reflexive governance beyond the State', particularly when it comes to conceiving new forms of non-state regulations.[26]

C. Beyond the state: consensual strategies at a global level

Crouch's critique of approaches that are too deterministic brought about in neo-institutionalism is relevant to the present analysis, insofar as its constructive proposal assigns importance to institutional innovations. The metaphor of collective exit strategies focuses on alternative solutions and consequently on new ideas in labour law, arguing that 'institutional heterogeneity' facilitates novelties.[27]

In the European tradition employers and labour organizations are mostly inclined to bring in innovative solutions and to force institutions towards new outcomes. They generate dynamic systems of collective bargaining, the expansion of which typically prompts interconnections with statute law. Hence, mutual hybridization of legal and voluntary sources has constant implications in determining the normative function of private sources.

This synergy among labour law regulatory techniques cannot be taken for granted at a transnational level. Whenever exposed to transnational strategies and to new ways of

---

[25] C Crouch, *Capitalist Diversity and Change* (Oxford University Press, 2005) 2–3.
[26] C Scott, 'Reflexive Governance, Regulation and Meta-Regulation: Control or Learning?' in O De Schutter and J Lenoble (eds), *Reflexive Governance. Redefining the Public Interest in a Pluralistic World* (Hart Publishing, 2010) 54, 59.
[27] Crouch, above n 25, 126.

representing collective interests, collective bargaining operates beyond state sovereignty. To do so, it often takes advantage of domestic legitimizing processes for reaching
external purposes. Transnational collective bargaining also generates new empowering
mechanisms for the negotiators, mixing together different actors – supranational,
national, or company representatives – within the bargaining delegation.

Employers and labour organizations, acting as collective regulators within
well-defined private orders – be they national or transnational – facilitate major
transformations of the state. They may contribute to 'denationalization of political
authority' whenever they gain spaces of legitimacy for their own autonomous interventions. However, even in pursuing their autonomy, they continue to trust states as
centres of authority, confirming the prevailing function of political and democratic
institutions.[28] Whereas international organizations may not always be able to provide
for full participation of individuals and for transparency in decision making, states
cannot abandon these tasks. This is why, in the end, the spreading of transnational
non-state actors confirms a return to states as 'managers of political authority'.[29]

In the ongoing interaction among new transnational actors and states we observe
profound changes taking place within national legal orders. Transnational organized
groups open up to demands generated beyond the state, while still providing support
to their national membership, exposed to the uncertainties of not yet fully typified
collective behaviour. They also raise new expectations towards states, pressed to
intervene actively and take in hand the consequences of transnational competition.

For example, codes of conduct or labelling adopted by transnational non-state
actors lack the enforceability of state sources. Consequently, they are assisted by
transnational monitoring, outside traditional judicial control. In all these cases,
occurring even outside of the EU, notions of independence and power in admin-
istering justice are called into question.[30] This is yet another example of a latent
marginalization of strictly legal points of view, giving way to rule-making within
private orders and consequently to the issuing of private sanctions.

In European companies organized into subcontracting networks a new generation
of codes of conduct is implemented, whereby labour standards are extended by the hub
company towards all other companies affected by the main economic activity. Problems of legitimacy are raised with regard to monitoring, since subcontractors are
forced to comply with unilaterally extended sources.[31] The European Parliament, too,

---

[28] P Genschel and B Zangl, *Transformations of the State – From Monopolist to Manager of Political
Authority* (TranState WP 76, Universität Bremen, <http://www.staatlichkeit.uni-bremen.de> (2008) 6).

[29] Ibid 15–16. For a similar point of view in labour law scholarship see A Baylos, 'Un instrumento
de regulación: Empresas transnacionales y acuerdos marco globales' (2009) 27 Quaderno de Relaciones
Laborales 108.

[30] M Barenberg, *Sustaining Workers' Bargaining Power in an Age of Globalization* (EPI Briefing Paper,
Washington DC, 2009); H Arthurs, 'Private Ordering and Workers' Rights in the Global Economy:
Corporate Codes of Conduct as a Regime of Labour Market Regulation' in J Conaghan, K Klare, and M
Fischl (eds), *Transformative Labour Law in the Era of Globalization* (Oxford University Press, 2001) 47.

[31] A Sobczak, 'Codes of Conduct in Subcontracting Networks. A Labour Law Perspective' (2003)
Journal of Business Ethics 225. It is worth mentioning in this regard a recent agreement signed on 16
September 2009 by employers' organizations and trade unions, involving the network of Tuscan
subcontractors within the Gucci group, with the aim of 'supporting' Italian know-how and avoiding
reduction in employment, through the enforcement of common quality standards.

has recommended ways of raising awareness in production chains, establishing principles of liability to increase transparency for socially responsible sub-contracting.[32]

Other examples of transnational consensus building within the EU have to do with regime competition. LO Sweden and LBAS (Free trade union Confederation of Latvia) signed an agreement on cooperation on 13 October 2005 for the prevention of social dumping. As a consequence, the Latvian Construction Workers' Union should refuse to work at lower wages for the company Laval's Swedish Layers. This example is viewed by commentators as an opportunity to improve and strengthen communication among unions in different countries and to search solutions which can anticipate and avoid conflict.[33] Reciprocity here is to be interpreted as a moral sanction, as well as a social norm of cooperation, in the attempt to avoid potentially negative consequences and introduce new regulatory functions.[34]

On 14 January 2010 an agreement on 'Draft rules of procedure for the European sectoral social dialogue committee in the sector of the metal engineering and technology based industries' was signed by the relevant collective organizations on both sides of industry. This document is significant for its procedural scope, since it enables other collective parties to sign agreements at EU level, with special attention being paid to measures for workers hit by the crisis, ranging at around 10 million in the sector. Here again, rather than relying on normative standards, consensus is built around expectations, in the search for solutions alternative to dismissals. Once more a supranational private order is sending signals to other decentralized negotiators, dealing with differentiated regimes of non-normative standard-setting.

In February 2010 a worldwide agreement was reached at GDF Suez, a multinational in the energy and utilities sector, setting broad guidelines on health and safety for the prevention of risks and introducing measures for monitoring and training. These are all examples of procedural rules, consistently enforceable at a global level through private monitoring mechanisms.[35]

A Europe-wide agreement is also part of the deal. Its main scope is the safeguarding of employment, through career development schemes and mobility within the group. 'Anticipating changes' is the expression adopted, whenever measures are agreed in view of expected negative outcomes, such as reduction of the workforce. The technique described as 'forward-looking management' of jobs and skills is put in practice via social dialogue, rather than through unilateral actions. Attention is paid to trade unions and employee representatives, with a view to promoting consensual solutions and dialogue at each company level, even

---

[32] EP Resolution 26 March 2009, Social Responsibility of Subcontracting Undertakings in Production Chains (2008/224 (INI)).

[33] K Gajewska, *Transnational Labour Solidarity* (Routledge, 2009) 69–70.

[34] Ibid 156–7. With regard to the construction and the metalworkers' unions, a consensual approach towards wage coordination since the 1990s is reported by R Erne, *European Unions. Labor's Quest for a Transnational Democracy* (Cornell University Press, 2008) 86–95.

[35] M Carley, International: Post-merger EWC agreed at GDF Suez, EER 425, 18 June 2009.

when it is established that the European Works Council (EWC) is the interlocutor of the general management.

The European agreement at GDF Suez has been praised for providing the best enforcement of the new principles enshrined in the recast Directive on EWCs.[36] Part of the renewed Lisbon agenda, the Directive occupies a significant place in transnational juridification processes, in particular for its implications with transnational agreements on company restructuring. In compliance with Article 27 of the Charter of Fundamental Rights of the European Union, it is a relevant source in constitutionalizing rights to information and consultation.

The revised Directive aims at improving the effectiveness of such rights, putting forward criteria that are mainly procedural. EWCs give an opinion to the undertaking in a 'timely fashion' and make sure that information and consultation take place 'at the relevant level of management and representation, according to the subject under discussion' (recital 14 and 15). The transnational 'potential effects' of managerial decisions must be considered by EWCs, fulfilling their duty to report back to the employees they represent (recital 33).

Article 10.1 refers to a collective representation of the employees' interests, 'without prejudice to the competence of other bodies or organisations'. It is also specified that EWCs have a duty to inform 'the representatives of the employees of the establishments or of the undertakings' and, in their absence, 'the workforce as a whole' (Article 10.2). The importance attached to this crucial passage is also confirmed by other detailed provisions, such as access to training without any loss of wages, for both members of the negotiating body and the EWC, whenever this is deemed 'necessary for the exercise of their representative duties in an international environment' (Article 10.4).

A most relevant innovation, despite its potentially difficult enforcement, rests on the idea that EWCs should adapt to 'significant' changes in the structure of the undertaking or group of undertakings. The GDF Suez agreement deals with this issue providing for information and consultation on transnational matters, namely those affecting the group as a whole or at least two of its undertakings located in two different countries covered by the agreement. Decisions having a potential impact on the European workforce are also considered. Furthermore, the agreement covers companies in which GDF Suez has a controlling interest, holding more than 50 per cent of the shares, or having a special dominating position for strategic reasons.

Transnational juridification is well exemplified by looking at the EWC recast Directive and by reading the first transnational agreements inspired by the same. European secondary law is, in this case, supportive of increasingly widespread social systems materializing into transnational collective agreements. Although the Directive does not specifically mention bargaining powers as part of the

---

[36] Directive 2009/38/EC of the European Parliament and of the Council of 6 May 2009 on the establishment of a European Works Council or a procedure in Community-scale undertakings and Community-scale groups of undertakings for the purposes of informing and consulting employees, OJ L 122/28, 16 May 2009.

EWC's entitlements, they are in practice becoming a prerogative of such bodies, whenever transnational matters come to the fore.

The Commission is not unaware of all this, as it appears from its survey, listing 147 'joint transnational texts' in 89 companies since 2000.[37] The breadth of this phenomenon calls into question the compatibility of national – both legal and voluntary – sources, whenever the transnational scope of these new operations needs to be addressed. The question to be asked when private collective actors enter transnational agreements of this sort is how they are empowered and what their aim is in designing the coverage of the texts they draw. In fact, when economic uncertainties are foreseen, it is not straightforward nor intuitive to reach a balance of powers in norm-setting. It may be necessary to rethink bargaining powers and reconsider forms of democratic accountability within organized groups. The acquisition of transnational legitimacy should become a prerequisite for the bargaining agents, whenever collective agreements cross national frontiers.

The most interesting examples of transnational procedures oriented towards consensus building can thus be found in a de facto expansion of EWCs' negotiating powers. A majority of agreements are signed in the automotive industry, characterized by strict interdependence of products and markets. At Chrysler, ever since 1998 a transnational trade union network has been active. It paved the way to the establishment in 2002 of a World Works Council, in addition to the one provided for by the European Directive. At Volkswagen a similar tradition goes back to the 1960s, although a World Works Council only saw the light in 1999.

In some cases international trade unions appear on the negotiating scene. In the technology sector the Thales agreement, signed in June 2009, saw the European metalworkers union determined to negotiate on skills development, arguing for workers' international mobility within the group, particularly for highly skilled workers. In other cases negotiators prefer to build up a 'global employee forum', as in the Norway-based multinational DNV, where the existing EWC continues to operate within European companies. The DNV forum, set up in 2009, has seven employee representatives, two from Norway, two from EWCs outside of Norway, two representing the Asia-Pacific region, and one the Americas and Africa.

Even a US-based multinational, such as RR Donnelley, a world provider of print and other related services, signed an agreement in May 2009, establishing an EWC in line with the recast Directive. Here the number of representatives from different countries follows the percentage of the workforce employed. At AXA, a France-based multinational providing financial services, the agreement on EWCs revised in June 2009 relies entirely on EU law, rather than on French law, and also provides for the enforcement of international standards throughout its European undertakings.

All these examples are taken from the world of facts. They confirm the spreading of a new transnational law in action which is mainly customary, albeit attached to an auxiliary legal measure, if we consider that transnational or world agreements,

---

[37] European Commission Staff Working Document, *The Role of Transnational Company Agreements in the Context of Increasing International Integration* (Brussels, 2 July 2008, SEC (2008) 2155).

such as the ones previously mentioned, are indirectly originated by an expanded scope attributed by the negotiators to the EWC Directive.

The notion of auxiliary legislation, part of a widely acknowledged European legal scholarship,[38] was thought of as a means to the end of strengthening the autonomy of collective bargaining and enhancing 'collective *laissez faire*'. It can now be revisited and adapted to new ideas in labour law if we name it 'transnational auxiliary legislation'. In this new facet, auxiliary measures should serve the purpose of re-empowering national systems of standard-setting and open them up to a worldwide scenario. Even when non-normative agreements are produced and merely procedural machineries are operated, new forms of guarantees emerge for labour. This can be said for transnational collective agreements and for employment policies, when supranational support is intertwined with specific national measures, be they oriented towards training, the planning of skills' requirements, company restructuring, or other alternative solutions to the loss of jobs.

Financial support granted from European institutions on selective grounds and on a temporary basis could represent a novelty in shaping transnational auxiliary measures which offer concrete answers to otherwise unclear expectations.

D. Concluding remarks

New ideas in labour law elaborated in this chapter rotate around an open process of transnational juridification in which non-state collective actors occupy a significant place. Such ideas should help building bridges among private and state sources, ascertaining that the primacy of legal points of view is not completely lost.

Transnational juridification is confronted with untraditional structural coupling between politics and labour law. In absorbing different regimes of standard-setting within its own web of rules, it enhances synergies among them. However, this process is imperfect as well as being incomplete, since it still lacks specific and efficient sanctions. The active and even dominant role gained by private actors may imperil the functions of welfare states. Not only the latter are distressed by economic deficits; they are also at constant risk of losing political accountability, when they are unable to fulfil expected redistributive policies.

Voices of weaker and marginal groups may not be heard, if traditional channels of social protest are progressively dried out. However, recourse to conventional forms of industrial action may prove less accessible than in the past and even less efficient, whenever collective interests to represent are fragmented and even dispersed across national boundaries. Because of the unsettled performances of welfare states and the absence of a supranational level of coordination, transnational juridification may insinuate perverse consequences and even facilitate imbalances in the exercise of collective social rights, facing the expansion of economic freedoms.

---

[38] O Kahn-Freund, *Labour and the Law*, 2nd edn (Stevens & Sons, 1977) 46–7.

For all these reasons, issues of legitimacy beyond the State are persistently raised within national legal systems. There are no meaningful answers to such queries, because the nation state's regulatory crisis calls into question traditional notions of efficiency in the enforcement of legislation. Labour law measures, challenged by the urgency to meet supranational targets, cannot be based on exclusively national parameters. Yet the choice to compete on the transnational scene and to adopt the necessary means towards this end is national and structurally coupled with politics.

Arguments developed in this chapter signify that whereas in the last century national welfare states had a dominant role in shaping innovative labour law, transnational social systems are now the bearers of new ideas.[39] Collective labour law should thus empower a variety of collective actors and deal with fragmented notions of collective interests, taking on board phenomena related to an increased mobility of business and labour. It should also re-consider balances between economic freedoms and collective social rights, particularly when it comes to acknowledging the lack of traditional legal sanctions in the new worldwide scenario of private ordering.

In discussing the interrelation and mutual hybridization among labour law's regulatory techniques, it can be argued that discourses on governance in the EU prompted a redefinition of the role played by law-makers, leading, in the long run, to the weakening of 'internal' legal points of view.[40] Closer links with civil society, advocated as a sign of openness and transparency of the supranational legal order, may generate ambiguous solutions on the transnational scene, when legitimacy of social sub-systems becomes an essential prerequisite. It is submitted in this chapter that this tendency be counterbalanced by strengthening 'external' legal points of view, characterized by transnational scopes.

Such authoritative legal points of view should lead to rediscovering the function of transnationally binding legal principles and to ascertaining the effectiveness of legal sanctions. New forms of legitimacy beyond the State and transparency in standard-setting, operating at a transnational level, should prepare the ground for overcoming potential conflicts of law and facilitating the interpretation of transnational sources.

---

[39] An authoritative point of view on this is J Habermas, *The Postnational Constellation. Political Essays* (Polity Press, 2001) 57 ff.

[40] A recent documented analysis is MR Ferrarese, *La governance tra politica e diritto* (il Mulino Bologna, 2010) 36 ff.

25

Emancipation in the Idea of Labour Law

*Adelle Blackett**

A. Introduction

Brian Langille ends his chapter with the language of emancipation,[1] a crucial starting point for the idea of labour law. The language evokes historical, structural inequality – forms of unfreedom. It suggests that mere amelioration of conditions is insufficient. Emancipation demands structural unshackling from a status that is the basis of subjugation, disenfranchisement, commoditization. While it can be individually conferred, emancipation is profoundly collective. It includes the agency of those who claim nothing less than their freedom,[2] which is not just proclaimed, but claimed. Emancipation embraces a re-constructionist, transformative ethos.

This chapter explores emancipation as continuity, alongside disjuncture, in the idea of labour law. The language evokes economic regulation of labour and responses to it beyond the narrow confines of the Industrial Revolution, recalling the relationship between earlier forms of capital accumulation via slavery and forced labour regimes, and the construction of the varieties of mature capitalism upon which contemporary labour regulation rests. Without claiming that human labour regulation over time and in 'peripheral' geopolitical spaces like Africa and its diaspora approximates or credibly emulates 'labour law' governing the standard employment relationship in industrialized market economies, Part B nonetheless reflects a commitment to constructing an idea of labour law that takes its normative core beyond the industrialized North.

This chapter similarly hints at labour traditionally considered beyond – indeed invisible to, but contemporaneous with – the market: care work in the household.

* Associate Professor and William Dawson Scholar, Faculty of Law, McGill University. This research has been supported by Canada's Social Sciences and Humanities Research Council and McGill University. I am grateful to Guy Davidov, Brian Langille, Harry Arthurs, and Cambridge workshop participants as well as Bill Alford, Lucie White and students at the Harvard International Law Workshop for helpful comments. I thank Mélyssa Rinaldo for her research assistance. Any errors are my own.

[1] Langille, this volume, references Hugo Sinzheimer, whose theorization of labour law has been defining of the field. It is meaningful that the account in this chapter, deliberately situated outside of the traditional 'boundaries and frontiers' of labour law, resonates with the justifying rationale of Sinzheimer's account of emancipation. See Dukes, this volume.

[2] See E Williams, *Capitalism and Slavery* (University of North Carolina Press, 1944, 1994) 197–8.

It rejects stark characterizations of the metaphorical market, rigidly demarcated from reproductive household labour emphasizes that care work is market enabling. It builds on the experiences of workers who have remained outside of the story of the paradigmatic worker,[3] to identify a different, transcendent starting point for the idea of labour law: emancipation. Acknowledging historical legal forms may nonetheless constitution provide an important foundation for broadening the base of labour law's hegemonic narrative.[4]

In between the two is the resolutely domestic (that is, state-centred) conceptualization of the idea of labour law, which seals out distributional consequences past national borders. I posit that the ability to imagine a labour law 'beyond' the (domestic) market offers a valuable way to think about the idea of labour law, particularly at a time of profound global market restructuring in which the idea itself is called into question.

The argument developed in Part C of this chapter is that labour law's specificity is rooted in resistance to the commoditization of the factor of production that is labour. This story is about workers' agency, but also about workers' capabilities and empowerment. To evoke the concept of 'emancipation' and to tell labour law's story in workers' 'resistance'[5] to commoditization through the inherently redistributive, recognition-based and representational claims for 'citizenship at work' is to reaffirm the pluralist character of labour law. Any reconstruction of labour law's narrative should look across time, space, and place.

B. Commoditization

1. Commoditization 'before' the market?

> The gap between a vision of future social organization and the practice of labor was even wider in French Africa than in British ... Unlike its leftist predecessors, Vichy was uninhibited by suppositions that Africans would not – or could not be made to – work. Some of Vichy's leading economic minds thought that the corporatist ideas being applied to French workers should be applied to Africans as well: they should face an 'obligation to work,' but should be guaranteed decent wages, working conditions, and a family life at the place of work. Yet such ideas were pure fantasy, part of a grand vision of a disciplined French empire, rationally organized and productive ... what the development effort actually meant was a more vigorous and more overt recruitment of forced labour.[6]

---

[3] See A Blackett and C Sheppard, 'Collective Bargaining and Equality: Making Connections' (2003) 142 ILR 419, 422–7.

[4] A helpful starting point is to acknowledge the impact of earlier legal forms on the formation of the contract of employment. See S Deakin and F Wilkinson, *The Law of the Labour Market: Industrialization, Employment, and Legal Evolution* (Oxford University Press, 2005) 41–51, who contend within the British context that 'the model of the contract of employment which we are familiar with today is the result of a process of accumulation and adaptation of earlier juridical models' (Deakin and Wilkinson, 44, 24).

[5] See, eg, B Hepple and B Veneziana (eds), *The Transformation of Labour Law in Europe: A Comparative Study of 15 Countries, 1945–2004* (Hart Publishing, 2009) 23, 28.

[6] F Cooper, *Decolonization and African Society: The Labor Question in French and British Africa* (Cambridge University Press, 1996) 141–2.

Although accounts of commoditization tend to invoke the Industrial Revolution, an important part of Karl Polanyi's theorization of the embedding of social relations in the economic is the relationship to colonial modes of production within non-metropolitan territories, where local African labour was forcibly commoditized.[7] Likewise, as suggested above, the labour commoditization of slavery is increasingly understood by economic and social historians to have accelerated economic development; rather than considering the destruction slavery as 'a necessary precondition for capitalism's emergence'[8] they emphasize 'capitalism's systemic dependence on these multiple, simultaneous, and overlapping forms of inequality'.[9]

Eric Williams' authoritative account of British commerce and the triangular trade recalls that: 'England – France and Colonial America equally supplied the exports and the ships; Africa the human merchandise; the plantations the colonial raw material.'[10] Although Williams repeats the common affirmation that '[t]he seventeenth and eighteenth centuries were the centuries of trade, as the nineteenth century was the century of production',[11] this is ultimately from the perspective of the British metropole.[12] Williams quickly recalls that under mercantile capitalism, the production was by the slaves 'whose labor supplied Britain with all plantation produce'.[13] The nuance is that the slaves' production was not considered to be

---

[7] K Polanyi, *The Great Transformation* (Beacon Press, 1944, 2001). See also K Polanyi, *Dahomey and the Slave Trade: An Analysis of an Archaic Economy* (University of Washington Press, 1966); and W Rodney, *How Europe Underdeveloped Africa* (Howard University Press, 1972, 1981 rev edn) 149 ff (arguing that the surplus value and raw materials helped fuel European economic development). In his study of Unilever's colonial production, Rodney argues also that non-colonizing industrialized economies who did not hold African colonies benefited from colonialism through factories established in Switzerland, New Zealand, Canada, and the United States (190–1). The US role grew to include post Second World War Marshall Plan funding extended through the Economic Commission for Africa to Western European and US mineral interests in Africa through 1960 (194–5).

[8] See S Rockman, *Scraping By: Wage Labor, Slavery, and Survival in Early Baltimore* (Johns Hopkins University Press, 2009) 7. This short discussion relies on an eclectic, invariably limited, mix of sources on slavery.

[9] Ibid 10. In light of the discussion that follows, it is important to underscore that Williams also asserts that mature capitalism compelled the end of slavery. His is largely a critique of monopoly capitalism in the wake of the American Revolution and the opportunity of technical revolution for industrial production in England. Williams, above n 2, 120–36. See also CA Palmer, 'Introduction', in Williams, xv (recalling that Williams insisted that his book was a book about British capitalism, the model for other forms of capitalism, not a book about slavery in the West Indies). But see MV Tushnet, *Slave Law in the American South* (University Press Kansas, 2003) 124 (contending that '[Williams'] argument was never entirely plausible in connection with slavery in the United States, where slavery remained profitable throughout its existence').

[10] Williams, above n 2, 51. Williams' thesis has been the subject of significant academic debate since it was first published, in particular his contention that mature capitalism destroyed slavery. See Palmer, above n 9, xx. (contending that Williams' 'central contentions have not been vanquished intellectually'.) See also BL Solow and SL Engerman (eds), *British Capitalism and Caribbean Slavery: The Legacy of Eric Williams* (Cambridge University Press, 1987/2004) 6 (carefully reviewing the contemporary debates, resisting easy causal relationships but offering distinct scholarly support for the claim that plantation economies were important 'in explaining the spurt in British industrial output of the late eighteenth century').

[11] Williams, above n 2, 51.

[12] This assumption is made explicit at 105. See also Cooper, above n 6, 33 (noting in reference to the work of visionaries of the 1920s and 1930s on decolonization in African society, that 'Africa appeared in this genre of colonial literature as space, not people, and certainly not as society').

[13] Williams, above n 2, 52.

industrial;[14] moreover, trade of the product of the slave's labour was subject to colonial monopoly.[15] Indeed, sugar refining was not done on the plantations in the West Indies, but in England, for colonial policy reasons having 'nothing to do with the skill of labor or the presence of natural resources'.[16] For contemporary historian Nuala Zahedieh, the triangular trade 'provided labour for the plantations, without draining the mother country's population, and provided profitable manufacturing employment at home'.[17] Although Williams' conclusion that the profits from the triangular trade constituted one of the 'main streams of... accumulation of capital in England which financed the Industrial Revolution'[18] is now generally considered an overstatement, his broad thesis emphasizing that slavery increased investment in the Empire, which in turn increased income in England, stands.[19]

In the story of capitalist development, enslavement and free waged labour have tended to be severely dichotomized, with slavery understood at one extreme end of a spectrum, anathema to capitalism and democracy,[20] and that rare species of 'entirely of free, self-owned, and legally equal workers'[21] at the other end, central to the virtuous rise of capitalism and democracy. Yet Williams notes the difficulty that defenders of the West Indian monopoly faced in making their case for sugar grown with free labour rather than slave labour, because the distinction 'was not so clear that it could be drawn with uniform and absolute precision'.[22] Contemporary historians of labour and capital studying the juxtaposition of older and newer forms in the US are increasingly following the tradition of leading Caribbean intellectuals[23] to suggest

---

[14] See J Jones, *American Work: Four Centuries of Black and White Labor* (Norton, 1998) 194–5, 242.

[15] Williams, above n 2, 57 (noting that '[t]hose who, in 1840, were loudest in their opposition to free trade, were, in 1660, the most fervent advocates of free trade' (56, 136–42) and that 'protection' by 1846 was deemed 'necessary to safeguard the experiment of free labor' (141)).

[16] Williams, above n 2, 75, 107.

[17] N Zahedieh, *The Capital and the Colonies: London and the Atlantic Economy, 1660–1700* (Cambridge University Press, 2010) 248. See also Williams, above n 2, 106.

[18] Williams, above n 2, 52; 62, 106–7 (similarly contending that capital accumulation was deeply intertwined with the slave trade through the development of shipping in ports like Liverpool, which then significantly increased the local population that stimulated the manufactures of Manchester). See also D Mouafo, 'Espace géographique et enjeux économiques: Une lecture du *Code noir*' in A Kom and L Ngoué (eds), *Le Code noir et l'Afrique* (Nouvelles du sud, 1991) 120, 131–2 (similar argument on the French triangular trade; and Solow and Engerman, above n 10, 10 (challenging Williams' claim of a direct relationship between plantation profits and the technological changes of the Industrial Revolution, but contending that 'if the technical change of the Industrial Revolution is put into the context of an increasingly rich, commercial, manufacturing society, then the connection holds').

[19] Solow and Engerman, above n 10, 8. See also G Wright, 'Capitalism and Slavery on the Islands: A Lesson from the Mainland' in Solow and Engleman, above n 10, 283, 295–6 (noting that Williams' thesis could have been strengthened in the US given the accepted link between New England manufacturing capital and merchants who had only recently participated in the slave trade or related commerce).

[20] See S Rockman, 'The Unfree Origins of American Capitalism' in C Matson (ed), *The Economy of Early America: Historical Perspectives and New Directions* (Pennsylvania State University Press, 2006) 335 (divorcing the emergence of capitalism in the United States from democracy and freedom).

[21] Rockman, above n 8, 6.

[22] Williams, above n 2, 142.

[23] H McD Beckles, '"The Williams Effect": Eric Williams's *Capitalism and Slavery* and the Growth of West Indian Political Economy' in Solow and Engleman, above n 10, 303, 308 ('[i]t was not particularly difficult to illustrate that with market-determined legalistic emancipation in the English West Indies in 1838, the central structural features of the slave-plantation economy and society were

that labour at the advent of capitalism entailed 'blurred boundaries between categories of labor, assuring the interchangeability of different workers along a continuum of slaves-for-life to transient day laborers – with term slaves, rented slaves, self-hiring slaves, indentured servants, redemptioners, apprentices, prisoners, children, and paupers occupying the space in between'.[24] Slave labour also included the urban, and in some of the large plantations showed significant job specialization; according to Jones, '[t]hese plantations resembled proto-industrial, self-contained villages'.[25] Jones contrasts the diversity of occupations held by blacks during slavery with the menial jobs that were 'reserved' for them, without any guaranteed exclusivity during economic downturn, after emancipation.[26] For Rockman, 'the market could serve to entrench slavery as readily as to undermine it'.[27]

To consider the interaction of slavery alongside other forms of de facto unfreedom is not to underestimate the inherently dehumanizing nature of a legal system that constituted the slave to be a commodity alongside the products slave labour produced.[28] Yet it is more than the personal relationship of owned to owner that captures slavery's depersonalization; as Meillasoux argues, it is the relationship of the slave to the market, the exclusion of kinship through the capture of the capacity to be bought and sold that renders the slave a commodity. Historically, reproduction and transfer ensured that 'production could increase independently of the productivity of labour through the mere addition of other producers'.[29]

---

further entrenched, rather than undermined; and that the emergent use of money wages was essentially a minor adjustment in the relations between capital and labor').

[24] Rockman, above n 8, 7: employers constantly adjusted their workforces, shifting between and combining laborers who were enslaved, indentured, and free; black and white; male and female; young and old; native born and immigrant. The simultaneous sale of laborers' time *and* laborers' bodies brought employers the power to choose whom to buy, hire, rent, or recapture in order to find exactly the worker they sought at any given moment. See also RJ Steinfeld, *Coercion, Contract, and Free Labor in the Nineteenth Century* (Cambridge University Press, 2001); Jones, above n 14, 223, 210–11 (establishing the importance of urban slavery, and the changing social division of labour in the South, which saw legal prohibitions on hiring blacks in urban jobs); and C Tomlins, *Freedom Bound: Law, Labor and Civic Indentity in Colonizing English America, 1580–1865* (Cambridge University Press, 2010) 232–3, 276 (insisting on the variety of rules and experiences of oppression, as well as age, gender, and race as limiting conditions on 'free' labour).

[25] Jones, above n 14, 195.

[26] Jones, above n 14, 242.

[27] Rockman, above n 8, 240. See also Palmer, above n 9, xx; Jones, above n 14, 222–32.

[28] League of Nations, Slavery Convention, Geneva, 25 September 1926, Art 1; Supplementary Convention on the Abolition of Slavery, the Slave Trade, and Institutions and Practices Similar to Slavery, Geneva, 7 September 1956, UNTS, vol 266, 3. J Pope Melish, *Disowning Slavery: Gradual Emancipation and 'Race' in New England, 1780–1860* (Cornell University Press, 1998) 24–5 ('slaves are permanent strangers in a given society; the nature of that estrangement lies in depersonalization – their reduction to the status of chattels or things'). Cf L Sala-Molins, *Le Code noir ou le calvaire de Canaan* (PUF, 1987) 73; and Tomlins, above n 24, 9–11 (re-examining the existence of a 'default culture of generic unfreedom', accepting that 'the variegated legal culture of work and labor that empirical research exposes does not correspond to consistent conceptual polarities of free and unfree', but insisting upon differentiation of distinct legal categories, notably that of chattel slavery); and J Allain, 'The Definition of Slavery in International Law' (2008–09) 52 Howard LJ 239 (defining de jure and de facto slavery).

[29] C Meillasoux, *The Anthropology of Slavery* (Atlone Press & University of Chicago Press, 1991) 93, 24–5, 95. See also Solow and Engerman, above n 10, 19. M Craton, 'What and Who to Whom and What: The Significance of Slave Resistance' in Solow and Engerman, above n 10, 281–2.

The transformation characteristic of the depersonalization is a 'legal' one.[30] The affirmation in 1835 by a Baltimore newspaperman that 'labour is a commodity, and persons may dispose of, or purchase it, at discretion the same as bread and meat'[31] was not referring to slavery, but to wage labour absent a protective labour law framework limiting notably the amount of time per day the labour could be bought and sold, that is, working time.[32] Both forms of labour are part of the emerging, unromantic labour history, which 'has vastly enlarged the scope of "who counts" as a worker... [and] clearly complicates labor history's preference for the citizen worker'.[33]

Yet 'protection' alone is not the key distinction. In some colonial jurisdictions legislative 'protection' of labour conditions not only helped to legitimize the commodification of the slave and slave labour, but 'preceded constraints concerning the use of free labour and the conditions of transport of free migration'.[34] The French law of slavery was codified in the form of 'Codes noir', initially decreed by King Louis XIV in 1685.[35] The objects were the slaves.[36]

Article 6 of the 1685 Code Noir made Sunday and other Roman Catholic holidays rest days, establishing both fines and confiscation of sugar and slaves found working[37] or sold at slave markets on rest days.[38] Freedom of association was

---

[30] Pope Melish, above n 28; Allain, above n 28, 263 (listing legal criteria for the exercise of any or all of the powers attached to the right of ownership).

[31] H Niles, quoted in Rockman, above n 8, 241.

[32] Rockman, above n 8, 241–4; and Allain, above n 28, 263–4.

[33] Rockman, above n 8, 10.

[34] See SL Engerman, *Slavery, Emancipation & Freedom: Comparative Perspectives* (Louisiana State University Press, 2007) 90 (adding that '[l]egislation on slave working conditions, including the various amelioration codes, often preceded the introduction of these labor standards for free workers'). See also Sala-Molins, above n 28, 77 (ironizing the 'distributive' justice character of the provisions); and Tomlins, above n 24, 428–508 (discussing the origins and diversity of slave law in the United States).

[35] There were a number of legislative modifications to the Code Noir, and a revised Code Noir was promulgated for Louisiana in 1724. The full text of the 1685 Code Noir on which this analysis is mainly based is available at <http://www.liceolocarno.ch/Liceo_di_Locarno/materie/biologia/martinica/code_noir.html>. The Code Noir was formally abolished five years after the French Revolution, in 1794, but the measures were never implemented; it was re-established by Napoleon in 1802. It remained in place until 1848, when slavery was abolished in the French colonies. See Sala-Molins, above n 28, 13–18. See also P Titi Nwel, 'L'émancipation des Noirs et les principes de la Révolution française' in Kom and Ngoué (eds), above n 18, 15, 16. It bears noting that the later colonial period in Africa gave rise to a Code de l'Indigénat, meant to cover those persons indigenous to the colonies; although the colonies are French territory, the natives are not French citizens. See D Abwa, 'Code noir et Code de l'indigent, ou la permanence d'une attitude' in Kom and Ngoué (eds), above n 18, 52, 54. Moreover, the League of Nations' Slavery Convention was passed only in 1926, and in a context that still questioned whether free labour in colonial Africa was 'practicable'; Cooper, above n 6, 28. Often overlooked is the anti-semitism in the first Article of the Code Noir, which categorically banned Jewish people from the territory. See Sala-Molins, above n 28, 92–3.

[36] See A Mbembe, *On the Postcolony* (University of California Press, 2001) 29 (despite the French Revolution, 'the principles of equality before the law, freedoms, and property rights that emerged... were thwarted by the continued existence of a slave mode of exploitation'); and S Ambiana, 'Statuts semiotiques du Noir dans deux discourse juridiques: Le Code noir et la Déclaration des droits de l'homme et du citoyen' in Kom and Ngoué, above n 18, 141.

[37] Art 6. Sala-Molins observed that rather than encouraging piousness in slaves, the Sunday rest provided space to organize and plan resistance. It was subsequently weakened: above n 28, 102–4.

[38] Art 7. The paradox of regulating labour conditions while acknowledging the slave's commoditization through the 'market' is blatantly embodied in this provision.

prohibited under Article 16; violation of the provision was sanctioned by corporal punishment or judicially pronounced capital punishment for repeated violation. Slave masters convicted of permitting or tolerating assemblies would be held personally responsible to repair damages suffered by neighbours.[39]

Status was strictly policed: slaves born of slaves were deemed slaves;[40] they were property and could not be the owners of property.[41] Slave masters were required to provide food and subsistence to their slaves in closely regulated portions.[42] Masters had a responsibility to take care of (*entretenir*) sick or elderly slaves.[43] While a master could free his slaves,[44] fugitive slaves were subject to specific forms of corporal punishment and branding with the sign of the fleur de lys, and on the third occasion, to death.[45] The egregious labour market rules of the Code Noir coexisted with – indeed depended upon – the characterization of the slave as a commodity.[46] For Pope Melish, the Code Noir is an example of legislative 'wrestl[ing] with the fiction of depersonalization' that was so much a part of the very definition of the oxymoronic notion of 'human slavery'.[47] For labour law, it raises the vexing paradox of

---

[39] Art 17. See Sala-Molins, above n 28, 124. Vicarious liability of the slave master for the actions of the slave was also foreseen in Arts 29 and 37.

[40] Art 12. In Art 9, fines were foreseen for free, married men who had one or more child with a slave, as well as the denial of any ability for the slave to be emancipated. Note that a different term was used to refer to freed slaves – *les hommes libres* compared with *les affranchis*; this ambiguity was subsequently clarified to prevent marriage between 'white subjects' and to exclude from the application of this provision 'black men, enfranchised or free'. See also Art 13 (freedom following the matrilineal line; and Art 47 banning the separate sale of the husband, wife and pre-pubescent children if all belonged to the same master).

[41] Art 18; see also Art 30. An 'attenuation' of this particularity of slavery was Art 47's restriction on the separation through sale of pre-pubescent children from their parents if owned by the same master. See W Johnson, *Soul by Soul: Life inside the Antebellum Slave Market* (Harvard University Press, 1999) 122–3 (cautioning that the effects of this provision should hardly be overemphasized, given that it essentially gave 'legal credence' to the transactional logic that the slave trade either obeyed, or could easily circumvent).

[42] Arts 18–26. The provisions were barely observed, and were the source of complaint by masters. Enlightened self-interest was not the norm; rather, the tendency in the French sugar islands was to exact hard labour in exchange for insufficient food and miserable conditions. Art 26's 'free' procedure through the attorney-general's office for slaves against masters who did not meet their food and subsistence requirements to be either an act of extreme cynicism or idiocy as the slave's testimony is of no legal value (Art 30), and to expect any ex officio action by the magistrate from pure compassion would be to expose his or her family to vengeance and corporal punishment. Sala-Molins, above n 28, 134–5, 142–3.

[43] Art 27. Nothing like a hospital referred to in Art 27 existed in the islands before 1780. See Sala-Molins, above n 28, 144–5.

[44] Art 55. Slaves, particularly domestic slaves, were enfranchised more frequently before the Code Noir than after, and the provision became stricter over time, notably by increasing the minimum age for masters who could grant enfranchisement. Sala-Molins, above n 28, 192–3.

[45] Art 38. See Sala-Molins, above n 28, 166–7.

[46] Art 44. The (further) distinction made by this provision was that slaves were no longer immovable property, upon which a hypothec can be placed, but rather movable property permitting in particular the separation of slaves belonging to the same master. See Sala-Molins, above n 28, 178–9. Cf M Tanger, *Les juridictions coloniales devant la Cour de cassation (1828–1848)* (Economica, 2007) 33–42 (citing judicial attenuation of the principle notably through the recognition of the personality of the slave).

[47] Pope Melish, above n 28, 25–6.

legally sanctioning the abject commoditization of labour, while palliating it with ambiguous, 'enlightened' profit maximizing protections.

2. Contemporary commoditization 'after' the domestic market?

There is continuity between the discussion of commoditization under the triangular trade in the development of capitalism, and the market-enabling impact of multilateral trade in a post-industrial market economy comprises varieties of capitalism. Certainly at a most basic level, contemporary multilateral trade law refuses the enslaved commoditization of labour power.[48] The troubling reality is that trade liberalization proceeds, nonetheless, alongside conditions of abject human exploitation. While contemporary trade relations are widely understood as a solution to poverty alleviation, their ability to coexist with forced labour, the worst forms of child labour, and conditions of deeply racialized and gendered inequality makes the loose historical parallel worth closer scrutiny.[49]

The full implications of dealing with labour as a factor of production are overlooked, moreover, in mainstream discussions of multilateral trade, and this despite a proliferation of linkage claims. Labour law remains resolutely domestic, despite experimentalist attempts to integrate incentives-based trade measures into continuous improvements in domestic law.[50] The terms of market access are established through rules of comparative advantage across state borders, emphasizing the freedom of exchange by market access irrespective of the processes (including labour conditions) under which production has taken place, alongside robust investor protections.[51] As Brian Langille aptly captured over a decade ago, by crossing the line into trade in subsidies, trade regulation post-Uruguay Round lost its 'intellectually sustainable stopping point'.[52]

Roberto Unger further contends that the theory of comparative advantage is 'only half of the theory that we need'[53] in that it fails to capture regulatory diversity,

[48] See Hepple, below n 53; see also A Blackett, 'Mapping the Equilibrium Line: Fundamental Principles and Rights at Work and the Interpretive Universe of the World Trade Organization' (2002) 65 Sask L Rev 369.

[49] See, eg, K Bales, *Disposable People: New Slavery in the Global Economy* (University of California Press, 2000). The closer scrutiny is of course beyond the scope of this short chapter.

[50] See, eg, K Kolben, 'Integrative Linkage: Combining Public and Private Regulatory Approaches in the Design of Trade and Labor Regimes' (2007) 48 Harvard Int'l LJ 203.

[51] On the historical legacy, see A Anghie, *Imperialism, Sovereignty and the Making of International Law* (Cambridge University Press, 2004) 252.

[52] B Langille, 'General Reflections on the Relationship of Trade and Labour (Or: Fair Trade is Free Trade's Destiny)' in J Bhagwati and R Hudec (eds), *Free Trade and Harmonization* (MIT, Boston, 1996) 231; and JG Ruggie, 'International Regimes, Transactions, and Change: Embedded Liberalism in the Postwar Economic Order' (1983) 36 International Organization 379 (trade and financial liberalization were constructed on shared understandings of the need to establish a division between internationally regulated matters and domestically regulated matters).

[53] R Mangabeira Unger, *Free Trade Reimagined: The World Division of Labour and the Method of Economics* (Princeton University Press, 2007) ('the political division of humanity is both the premise of trade theory and a fact to whose significance, transmutations, and possible functional equivalents – from the standpoint of the interest in diversity of stuff – the theory is, and has always been, blind') (ibid 51). Cf B Hepple, *Labour Laws and Global Trade* (Hart Publishing, 2005) (applying Hall and Soskice's

and in relation to that, a sustainable allocation of productive capacity across economic units structured through states. Moreover, it fails to capture market freedom for the factor of production, labour, to 'work at will anywhere in the world'.[54] If market structuring through multilateral trade is built on an incomplete theorization, affecting asymmetrical production patterns, labour mobility, and distributional consequences, what are the implications for regulatory efforts to prevent the commoditization of labour?

Labour relations in industrialized market economies have relied on controlled borders and commodity flows as well as a gendered/racialized division of labour to sustain an embedded liberal compromise in the North and to allow the domestic regulation of social security frameworks.[55] For example, heavily protected sectors such as agriculture have been retained in an attempt to ensure that workers who are citizens of industrialized market economies in Europe and the US retain decent work conditions that provide them with a stable livelihood, some leisure and access to social security mechanisms that are characteristic of what Max Corden refers to as the 'conservative social welfare function'.[56] This has rightly been understood as a form of resistance to the commoditization of labour in the North, although it very much speaks to the distributive function of labour law as between workers. Yet labour law has acted to seal out the South, or worse, to sustain citizens' privilege through asymmetrical policies, namely the colonial and neo-colonial division of labour ensuring privileged access to primary commodities in the process of industrial transformation,[57] and the dependence in many industrialized market economies on foreign, irregular workers to perform a broad range of critical forms of work beyond the shadow of labour law, including in the agricultural sector. In this regard, the idea of labour law (in the implicit North) looks rather different when we think about the impact of industrial and trade policies that sustain it in relation to the South, and the 'South in the North'.[58] Moreover, the standard employment relationship ceases to appear so standard once the closed borders of the current trade bargain are scrutinized. Despite labour law's internationalist, universalist claims, could it be that labour law rejects the commoditization of some, but at least tolerates the commoditization of 'other others'? Looking 'past' the domestic market in discussions of the idea of labour law puts squarely into focus the broader geopolitical asymmetries.

---

analysis of comparative institutional advantage to the division of labour in trade and the potential role of labour law).

[54] Unger, above n 53, 49; see also Hepple, above n 53.

[55] A Blackett, 'Labour Law, Trade and Development: A Contextualization' in T Teklè (ed), *Labour Law and Worker Protection in Developing Countries* (Hart Publishing, 2010) 93.

[56] See WM Corden, *Trade Policy and Economic Welfare* (Clarendon, 1974/1997) 74–7.

[57] S Amin, 'Africa: Living on the Fringe' (2002) 53 Monthly Review 41.

[58] A Blackett, 'Situated Reflections on International Labour Law, Capabilities, and Decent Work: The Case of *Centre Maraicher Eugène Guinois*' (2007) (hors série) RQDI 223.

3. Commoditization in the domestic household, 'beyond' the market?

Third, the continuity of certain forms of work across pre-capitalist, industrial, and new economy contexts provides a further site for understanding the ways in which labour is commoditized. The form to which I have turned most of my research attention is domestic work, or care within the household.[59] A similar form of historical and conceptual exclusion operated to exclude domestic labour. Arguably more contemporary mileage has been made on feminist labour law analyses than on the 'post-colonial'[60] rethinking of labour law. The analyses have build upon scholarly work that situates labour history's constructive narrative beyond highly influential scholarship pioneered by EP Thompson[61] centring the rise of working class consciousness from the vocal, organized, but ultimately limited category traditional craft workshop.[62] Accounts increasingly re-situate the paradigmatic worker within the household[63] and theorize the importance of the enabling relationship of reproduction to production in the construction and maintenance of capitalism.[64]

There is heterogeneity in domestic work, but the classic master–servant relationship reflects the confluence of traditional employment relationships with prevalent labour market informality.[65] Although there is a theoretical continuation of the care economy between unpaid care and care that has been marketized,[66] it is also true that domestic work as a status ('slave', 'servant', foreign/racialized/'illegal' other), sits alongside persistent ideologies (domestic workers as 'one of the family'; the household as a private place to which labour law should not venture; and

---

[59] A Blackett, 'Promoting Domestic Workers' Human Dignity through Specific Regulation' in A Fauve-Chamoux (ed), *Domestic Work as a Factor of European Identity: Understanding the Globalization of Domestic Work, 16th – 21st Centuries* (Peter Lang SA, 2005) 211; see also ILO, Report IV(1) Decent Work for Domestic Workers, International Labour Conference, Geneva, 2009.

[60] This reference is to a tradition of scholarship, rather than to a precise historical period.

[61] EP Thompson, *The Making of the English Working Class* (Penguin, 1963/1991).

[62] Rockman, above n 8, 9 ('[t]he craft workshop could hardly have provided the experiential basis for working-class formation for the simple reason that most workers labored outside it').

[63] See notably C Steedman, *Master and Servant: Love and Labour in the English Industrial Age* (Cambridge University Press, 2007).

[64] Pope Melish, above n 28, 19–20. See also Rockman, above n 8, 10 (noting that the politics of class change when the paradigmatic worker becomes a woman, or an African American, or an immigrant).

[65] B Guha-Khasnobis et al, 'Beyond Formality and Informality' in *Linking the Formal and Informal Economy: Concepts and Policies* (Oxford University Press, 2006) 1 at 16 (considering formality and informality as part of a 'continuum of the reach of official intervention in different economic activities and resisting a characterization of the formal economy as "unstructured" and "chaotic"'; instead acknowledging the plurality of informal norms and regulating in a manner that takes them into account' (ibid 10). MA Chen, 'Rethinking the Informal Economy: Linkages with the Formal Economy and the Formal Regulatory Environment' in Guha-Khasnobis et al (ed), 75, 77, and 81 (the informal economy should be understood as a basic component of the economy, not an aberration, and linked to the formal economy, rather than a separate entity).

[66] M Fineman, *The Autonomy Myth: A Theory of Dependency* (The New Press, 2004); M Fineman, *The Neutered Mother, the Sexual Family and Other Twentieth Century Tragedies* (Routledge, 1995); and M Fineman and T Dougherty (ed), *Feminism Confronts Homo Economicus: Gender, Law, and Society* (Cornell University Press, 2005).

perhaps most importantly for this discussion, the work as other than market activity that is legitimately conceptualized as such to ensure that 'the family' is not commoditized).[67] This remains despite the crucial historical work re-establishing the economic significance of domestic work, including in slavery, where virtually all of the household labour was performed by slaves.[68] The value could be understood both 'per se but also ... [because] it released white males to engage in new professional, artisan, and entrepreneurial activities, thus increasing productivity and easing the transition from a household-based to a market-based economy'.[69] In the new economy, it is the level of constructed precariousness under temporary migration schemes, limited community market access rules, or quite simply through channels of perpetual irregularity that sustains the care economy in the North. This too is a form of trade in services, in which women's choices are so narrowly constructed that their exercise of agency is to leave their own children behind in unstable care arrangements of the South, to migrate within or beyond their countries to work in someone else's home in the North,[70] only to face ready unemployment and deportation in the event of financial crisis. This hyper labour mobility too often unmediated by labour law but heavily policed by 'protective' immigration law[71] becomes an ultimate re-presentation of contemporary labour market commoditization.

While analyses of unpaid care work critically shift the analytical frame of traditional labour law accounts,[72] focusing on paid care centres the work performed by historically disenfranchised women who have always also worked outside of their own home, and are held responsible for multiple forms and sites of care.[73] The re-centring should unavoidably yield an analysis that engages the intersection of class, patriarchy, racialization, and national asymmetries: that is, the borders where the market for reproductive 'care' work is regulated.

To conclude this part, one simple point emerges from the three canvassed examples: labour market regulation alone as the core idea of labour law offers a

---

[67] See generally 'Regulating Decent Work for Domestic Workers' (forthcoming 2011) 23(1) Special Issue, Canadian Journal of Women and the Law; J Henshall Momsen, *Gender, Migration and Domestic Service* (Routledge, 1999); and MK Zimmerman et al (eds), *Global Dimensions of Gender and Carework* (Stanford University Press, 2006).

[68] See, eg, Pope Melish in relation to New England, above n 28, 14; and Johnson in relation to Louisiana, above n 41, 89–100.

[69] Pope Melish, above n 28, 8, 17–18, 23 (affirming that this claim contributes to the 'debate between social historians and market historians over the timing and nature of the transition of the New England economy to capitalism').

[70] See R Salazar Parreñas, *Children of Global Migration: Transnational Families and Gendered Woes* (Stanford University Press, 2005).

[71] See Blackett, above n 59, 211.

[72] See notably Judy Fudge's contribution to this volume. See also S Razavi and S Staab, 'Underpaid and Overburdened: A Cross-National Perspective on Care Workers' (2010) ILR 149.

[73] Historical accounts of white women during slavery who performed limited unpaid care beyond physical reproduction, relegating all of the remaining unpaid care to their domestic slaves, underscores the relevance of focusing on historically marginalized women. See notably Johnson, above n 41; and J Jones, *Labor of Love, Labor of Sorrow: Black Women, Work and the Family, from Slavery to the Present* (Basic Books, 2010).

dangerously thin conceptual starting point. Another is that a context-dependent interpretation of what makes work 'decent' may similarly be perilously unstable. The normative core of labour law must surely entail more than worker protection. To the extent that labour law helps to resist commoditization,[74] its regulatory response should not only be protection, but emancipation. In other words, it recognizes resistance and creates/preserves space (capabilities)[75] for the effective exercise of agency. The space is claimed by workers, and may be enabled and preserved by the state; it becomes the site for workers' empowered exercise of workplace self-governance in the labour market.[76] Both protective and agency-creating purposes of labour entail distributive justice and recognition dimensions, but the latter purpose leaves room for representation.[77]

C. Emancipation

> In 1833 . . . the alternatives were clear: emancipation from above, or emancipation from below. But EMANCIPATION. Economic change, the decline of the monopolists, the development of capitalism, the humanitarian agitation in British churches, contending peroration in the halls of Parliament, had now reached their completion in the determination of the slaves themselves to be free.[78]

1. Resistance 'before' the market

Resistance to enslavement and forced colonial labour, and insistence upon the emancipatory power not of 'decent' working conditions as defined by colonial authorities, but of freedom and what may be referred to as citizenship at work, are central to labour law's core, humanizing narrative. Resistance may be tragic, as with slaves who killed their own children to save them from a life of slavery, or as in the case of Angélique, an enslaved domestic who as an act of resistance to the refusal to grant her promised emancipation burned her master's house down and in the

---

[74] The environment is also considered by Polanyi in *The Great Transformation* to be a 'fictive' commodity, above n 7; much of the discourse surrounding the need for 'protection' of labour applies also to the natural environment and evokes the case for sustainable development. See also Tomlins, above n 24, 402 ('With the transformation of land had come the transformation of social relations on the land ... In the grand scheme of *keeping*, commoditization of labor was no less essential than commoditization of land.')

[75] See A Sen, *Development as Freedom* (Oxford University Press, 1999); and MC Nussbaum, *Women and Human Development: The Capabilities Approach* (Cambridge University Press, 2000).

[76] A Blackett, 'Global Governance, Legal Pluralism and the Decentered State: A Labor Law Critique of Codes of Corporate Conduct' (2001) 8 Indiana J Glob Leg Stud 401, 418.

[77] See N Fraser, *Scales of Justice* (Columbia University Press, 2009) (arguing for a transnational politic of representation); G Mundlak, this volume (explicitly referencing distribution amongst workers); and B Hepple, 'Equality and Empowerment for Decent Work' (2001) ILR 140 (discussing vertical and horizontal equality in labour law). See also JE Roemer et al, *Racism, Xenophobia and Distribution: Multi-Issue Politics in Advanced Democracies* (Harvard University Press, 2007).

[78] Williams, above n 2, 208.

process set much of Old Montreal on fire.[79] And it may be heroic, as in the case of William and Ellen Craft's brilliant escape from slavery in the US southern state of Georgia[80] or Furcy's 27-year-long legal battle claiming judicial emancipation from France.[81] Mostly resistance was unspoken, woven into the everyday acts of discomfort, defiance and affirmation designed to hold onto human dignity through survival, until freedom called.

Resistance necessarily entails the exercise of agency. Yet the agency to turn resistance into emancipation requires the capability to yield transformation. In this sense, it is usually collective,[82] as witnessed by revolution in the sugar island of San Domingo, the first republic of slaves to emancipate themselves.[83] Similarly in the colonial context, trade unionists often fought first for an end to forced labour regimes, and then carried their struggles forward for political independence.[84] Yet with the value of hindsight after the bittersweet 50-year anniversary of independence of many post-colonial states, it may be more compelling to focus on the continued resistance to the plantation economy by Caribbean workers in the post-colonial period, as those who remained in agriculture repeatedly insisted on working in small, cooperative-based structures that offer living wages, decent working conditions, and local autonomy.[85] Ultimately emancipation requires more than protection ('rights') and more than an abstract notion of resistance ('agency'). Emancipation from slavery with few material resources meets the familiar story of labour law without the state: 'subject to the vagaries of the marketplace . . . "free" to be hired at the lowest wages, and "free" to be fired at a moment's notice'.[86]

The importance of resistance to emancipation helps to decentre, while preserving an important role for, the state. In other words, labour 'law' was not simply the

---

[79] A Cooper, *The Hanging of Angélique: The Untold Story of Canadian Slavery and the Burning of Old Montréal* (Harper Collins, 2006).

[80] Ellen Craft proclaimed: 'I had so much rather starve in England, a free woman . . . than be a slave of the best man that ever breathed upon the American Continent.' RJM Blackett, 'The Odyssey of William and Ellen Craft', Bibliographical Essay published in W Craft, *Running a Thousand Miles for Freedom: The Escape of William and Ellen Craft from Slavery* (Louisiana State University Press, 1999) 71; see also 74, 81.

[81] See M Aïssaoui, *L'affaire de l'esclave Furcy* (Gallimard, 2010). See also RM Cover, *Justice Accused: Antislavery and the Judicial Process* (Yale University Press, 1975).

[82] See Pope Melish's account of the backlash seeking to 'reverse the tide of black bodies brought into North America' through gradual emancipation, above n 28, 163–08.

[83] See CLR James, *The Black Jacobins: Toussaint L'Ouverture and the San Domingo Revolution* (Random House, 1963/1989); and Craton, above n 29, 281 ('Haitian slaves achieved a revolutionary overthrow of the industrializing process' while most other revolutions and resistances lost their transformative thrust, and the claimed 'free wage labor' that 'was the "part peasant – part proletarian" lifestyle that was . . . substituted for slavery in most of the British West Indian colonies after 1938, though the terms of relationships remained resolutely in favour of the landowner/employer master class').

[84] See, eg, Rodney, above n 7, 276. This was a form of resistance ultimately sanctioned by colonialism, that is 'mild nationalism'. See B Rajagopal, *International Law from Below: Development, Social Movements and Third World Resistance* (Cambridge University Press, 2003) 9.

[85] See K Levitt, *Reclaiming Development: Independent Thought and Caribbean Community* (Ian Randle, 2005); see also GL Beckford, *Persistent Poverty: Underdevelopment in Plantation Economies of the Third World* (University of the West Indies Press, 1972) (theorizing the specificity of the pluralist plantation economy, which impedes development).

[86] Jones, above n 14, 19.

triumph of the French Overseas Labour Code of 1952 over colonialism's Code Noir equivalent, the Code de l'Indigénat. The Overseas Labour Code of 1952 was adopted in response to strikes, representations, growing international pressure by the ILO in its work on non-metropolitan territories and comparisons of how colonial powers were rethinking the regulation of the 'native' who increasingly embraced the status of 'worker', and increasingly destabilized colonialism itself.[87]

2. Resistance in the domestic household

A similar contemporary story of resistance can be told of domestic workers beyond the 'productive' economy: domestic workers in India have engaged in hunger strikes to change the public perception of their status and to claim their place as workers like any others,[88] and in places as diverse as Hong Kong, Colombia, South Africa, France, Trinidad and Tobago, Canada, and Namibia, have organized in trade unions or workers' associations whenever they have had the chance. They have lobbied for legislative change, and taken collective strike action.[89] Moreover, sociological studies of domestic work are replete with accounts of everyday resistance,[90] which the workers have relied upon despite power differentials to shape the pluralist law that governs the home-workplace.

Critiques of regulatory approaches that emphasize 'protection' for domestic workers rightly challenge both patriarchal understandings of the work, and state paternalism as the goal of labour regulation for this category of workers.[91] Leah Briones, building on Martha Nussbaum and Amartya Sen, argues for an approach that recognizes the interdependency of agency and capabilities, or capability as the freedom both to do, and to be.[92] A robust citizenship at work has to be understood as no less a claim of domestic workers than of any other workers.[93]

3. Resistance in the new economy

Resistance in the new economy witnesses and responds to the unravelling of industrial citizenship through collective bargaining rights claimed during the Industrial Revolution. Within a tightly demarcated framework, workers and employers were allowed to create the law that applied to them.[94] As Arthurs explains:

---

[87] See Cooper, above n 6; and Craton, above n 29, 281.

[88] See, eg, N Cunningham Armacost, 'Domestic Workers in India: A Case for Legislative Action' (1994) 36(1) Journal of the Indian Law Institute 53, 56–7.

[89] See ILO, Decent Work for Domestic Workers, above n 59.

[90] Cf S Ally, *From Servants to Workers: South African Domestic Workers and the Democratic State* (Cornell ILR Press, 2009) (offering an important critique of the limits of everyday resistance as a transformative strategy).

[91] Ally, above n 90; and E Hill, *Worker Identity, Agency and Economic Development: Women's empowerment in the Indian informal economy* (Routledge, 2010) 135.

[92] L Briones, *Empowering Migrant Women: Why Agency and Rights are not Enough* (Ashgate, 2009) 166.

[93] See Blackett, above n 59.

[94] See O Kahn-Freund, *Labour and the Law* (Hamlyn Trust, 1972).

In various societies, at various times, collective bargaining has been tolerated, encouraged, licensed, regulated, or co-opted by the state. But the most distinctive feature of collective bargaining is not its nexus with the state; rather it is that collective bargaining relies upon employers and workers to generate and enforce the norms which govern workplace behaviour.[95]

The decline of traditional forms of industrial citizenship has not necessarily led to a decline in resistance. Indeed, from the margins of migrant construction, farm and domestic workers deprived of permanent residence status, workers in export processing zones and other forms of offshore production, and small local farmers dispossessed of their ability to make a livelihood from their lands, resistances to a particular form of neo-liberal globalization disconnected from decent livelihoods have sprung up to infuse claims for a 'fair' globalization with a fundamentally more transformative core.[96] In other words, it may not be from the standard employment relationship that a transformative politic has most prominently emerged,[97] but from those at the margins whose claim for 'citizenship at work' challenges the very notion of the idea of a labour law dependent on exclusions 'before' and 'beyond' the market. Citizenship at work is reframed at the intersection of labour law and human rights law; it plays out across the movement of persons and labour as a factor of production in international trade law; it calls into question some of the boundary drawing between labour law and family law; it pulls at the core of labour law as development. Citizenship at work shakes the unacknowledged distributive justice consequences of 'decent work for all' out onto 'labour law's back pages'.[98]

Yet pluralist accounts of labour law are usefully resisted when they leave insufficient space for analyses of power. To start this chapter with the virtually absolute character of slavery and the undisciplined authority to use violence to extract labour from colonial peoples is to support the need for vigilance. Not unlike the discussion of commoditization before, the pluralism of labour law recognizes the difference between it and a *lex mercatoria* developed by multinational corporations in the new economy as in times past to govern their own relationships between transnational and national legal space.[99] De Sousa Santos understands this as the space between global governance and global hegemony, or where counter-hegemonic spaces unveil 'power struggles and alliances between and within legal elites in the North and the South through which the hegemony of transnational capital and Northern

---

[95] See H Arthurs, 'Labour Law Without the State?' (1996) 46 U Tor LJ 1. See also J-M Fecteau, 'Du droit d'association au droit social: Essai sur la crise du droit libéral et l'émergence d'une alternative pluraliste à la norme étatique, 1850–1930' (1997) 12 Can JL & Soc 143; and J Fudge and E Tucker, *Labour Before the Law: The Regulation of Workers' Collective Action in Canada, 1900–1948* (Oxford University Press, 2001).

[96] See S George, *Another World is Possible If...* (Verso, 2004).

[97] See LF Vosko, *Managing the Margins: Gender, Citizenship, and the International Regulation of Precarious Employment* (Oxford University Press, 2010).

[98] Cf B Langille, 'Labour Law's Back Pages' in G Davidov and B Langille (eds), *The Boundaries and Frontiers of Labour Law* (Hart Publishing, 2006).

[99] G Teubner, '"Global Bukowina": Legal Pluralism in the World Society' in G Teubner (ed), *Global Law Without a State* (Dartmouth, 1997) 1; and J-P Robé, 'Multinational Enterprises: The Constitution of a Pluralistic Legal Order' in Teubner ibid, 45, 49.

states is reproduced'.[100] Whether, for example, a code of corporate conduct as a form of labour market regulation meets the normative ideals of labour law requires an assessment both of its protective value, as well as its representative character and ability to foster agency. The pluralism of labour law is alive to the manner in which one party to the relationship may consolidate control over the means of production and exercise it transnationally. Legal orders may coexist, conflict and challenge each other and state law is both recognized as a site of repression,[101] but also called upon – domestically and internationally, some States differently and more effectively than others – to mediate, reconstitute, and counterbalance the power that transnational actors may exercise over workers. Similarly, new forms of coexistence between state law and pluralist norms are the result of resistance, struggle, and experimentation.[102] They entail the active maintenance of counter-hegemonic space for engagement with social movements of the South and the South in the North. Understanding capabilities and empowerment[103] is crucial to a labour law that acknowledges continuity in calling for emancipation from above while claiming it from below.

D. Conclusion

As it turns out, in the context of neoliberal globalization, the most desperate and marginalized – those living in poverty and excluded from the benefits of social citizenship due to class, gender, racial or ethnic oppression – account for the immense majority of the world population. The challenge of institutional imagination, therefore, cannot be met but by privileging the excluded as actors and beneficiaries of new forms of global politics and legality. This is the strategy of counter-hegemonic globalization and its legal counterpart, subaltern cosmopolitan legality.[104]

This is a deliberately simple chapter, which ultimately reflects my conviction that the idea of labour law should be simple too.[105] Labour law resists the commoditization of the factor of production that is labour; the resistance entails both a protective role for the state but also an enabling role for actors.

---

[100] B de Sousa Santos and CA Rodrìguez-Garavito, 'Law, Politics, and the Subaltern in Counter-Hegemonic Globalization' in *Law and Globalization from Below: Towards a Cosmopolitan Legality* (Cambridge University Press, 2005).

[101] See, eg, Rajagopal, above n 84, 255.

[102] See, eg, DJ Doorey, 'In Defence of Transnational Domestic Labor Regulations' (2010) Comparative Research in Law & Political Economy Research Paper vol 6 no 1.

[103] See A Trebilcock, 'Using Development Approaches to Address the Challenge of the Informal Economy for Labour Law' in Davidov and Langille, above n 98, 63.

[104] De Sousa Santos and Rodrìguez-Garavito, above n 100, 1, 9.

[105] While there are important distributive justice implications, this short chapter merely hints that the original post-war embedded liberal bargain so central to the story of modern labour law was suspect from the perspectives of those in the South. For a fuller discussion limited to regional integration, see A Blackett and C Lévesque, 'Introduction' in *Social Regionalism in the Global Economy* (Routledge, 2011) 1, 9.

The nation state is part of the story of labour law, but only part. The discipline of labour law will remain, not because we deem it a separate field of study, and not even because the market needs it, but because people will continue to insist on exercising agency over the terms under which they exchange their labour power, within and across territorial borders. A project for labour 'lawyers', then, is to decide whether to engage with the transformative potential of labour law, as it affects both productive and 're-productive' capacity, and across multiple borders – one of which is the deeply permeable notion of the 'market'. This may well be a part of the project Polanyi understood as preventing a market economy from also becoming a market society.[106] Or it may be as basic as retaining our humanity, which post-colonial scholars like Frantz Fanon urged should never be confined within a nationalist paradigm.[107]

---

[106] F Cunningham, 'Market Economies and Market Societies' (2005) 36 J Social Philosophy 129, 137 (claiming that our focus should be to remove fear from markets).

[107] F Fanon, *The Wretched of the Earth* (Grove Press, 1963/2004).

Index

ACAS *see* Advisory, Conciliation and Arbitration Service
ACFTU *see* All-China Federation of Trade Unions
Acquired Rights Directive 203
activism 246, 336, 348, 358–62
  labour activism *see* Chapter 17
  transnational activism 358
ADR *see* alternative dispute resolution
AFL *see* American Federation of Labor
Advisory, Conciliation and Arbitration Service 351
agency work 35, 46–7, 204, 218–19
Agreement on Government Procurement 257
All-China Federation of Trade Unions 370
alternative dispute resolution 206, 287
America *see* United States
American Federation of Labor 332–3, 341
American Law Institute 183
American Trucking Association 281, 288
anti-discrimination legislation 35, 39–40, 199, 370–78
apartheid 163, 209–14, 217–22, 350
arbitrary dismissal 15, 210–11, 220
Argentina 169
Assam 223
Atlanta 197
Australia 165, 295, 297, 303–14, 372–3, 379–80
Austria 39, 352
autonomy 61, 70, 75, 79, 133, 135, 151–2, 179, 191, 231
autonomus labour law 60, 405

bargaining power
  inequality of 34, 44–9, 86, 105–18, 122–5, 180, 208, 295, 302
  trade union 217–19, 275, 416–17
  see also collective bargaining
Belgium 39, 197–8, 352, 408, 410
Bengal 224
Bolivia 169
boycott 17, 28, 55, 332, 398–9
Brandeis, Louis 89
Brazil 169–70, 395
Britain *see* United Kingdom
Brook, Peter 96
Bus Riders' Union 277–8

Canada 112–13, 122–3, 379–80, 433
  Supreme Court 20–21, 354

capitalism 40–41, 50–52, 57, 138, 165, 309, 336, 371, 386, 391, Chapter 25
  golden age 331
  North American 24–8
Carter, Jimmy 91
CCMA *see* Commission for Conciliation, Mediation and Arbitration
change in labour law
  content 14–15, 43–4, 73–4, 90, 122, 124, 223–30, Chapter 17, 326
  purpose 31, 89, 116
  reality 45–8, 58, 135, 181, 240, 297–8, 334
  work definition and status 275–6
Charter of Fundamental Rights of the European Union 50, 416
Central America 395–6, 403
child labour 125, 143, 227–9, 322, 396, 427
China 163, 298, 360–61
Chile 169, 403
CHIRLA *see* Coalition for Humane Immigrant Rights of Los Angeles
CIO *see* Congress of Industrial Organization
circulation 237
CLUE *see* Clergy and Laity United for Economic Justice
Clergy and Laity United for Economic Justice 283–4
Coalition for Humane Immigrant Rights of Los Angeles 282
code of conduct 25, 54–5, 280, 355–7, 414
coercion 121, 130, 137, 145, 227, 324
collective bargaining 15–17, Chapter 10, 217, 222, Chapter 17, 322, Chapter 20, 347, 351
  achievements 31
  agreement 74, 273–4, 336
  common interests 52–4
  empowerment 106–10, 122–4
  legislation 20–21, 39, 45, 127, 138, 180, 186, 298
  purpose 137
  right 31–9, 50, 63, 111, 127, 131, 210–12, 264, 352–7, 371, 406–13, 433
  social 28
  state intervention 61
collective organization 37–8, 40, 134, 140, 143, 412
  see also trade union
Colombia 433
Commission for Conciliation, Mediation and Arbitration 212–15, 217, 219–21

Commodity, labour as 44–6, 64, 68, Chapter 7, Chapter 8, 151, 251, 316
community benefits agreement 273, 281–3, 285–7
competition
  global 36–8, 83, 143, 154, 266, 300, 308–9, 334, 397
  market failure 33
  regulator 138, 167, 254, 370
  workers 238, 304, 318, 384
  see also race to the bottom
conditional use permit 283–4
Congress of Industrial Organization 333, 341
corporate social responsibility 270, 272, 355–6
constitutionalism 37, Chapter 4, 140, 233, 406–7
Contracts
  fixed-term 47, 204, 217
  indefinite 47
Convention on Termination of Employment 211
Council of Europe 50, 53, 349, 351
Covenant of Economic, Social and Cultural Rights 141
CSR *see* corporate social responsibility
CUP *see* conditional use permit

Davies, Paul 105, 123
Declaration of Philadelphia 64, 71
Declaration on Fundamental Principles and Rights at Work 52
Deliège, Christelle 197–8
democratic deficits 180, 183, 185, 188
Denmark 31, 167
dependency 44, 70, 75, 85–7, 119, 126, 180, 183–9, 239, 243, 433
dependent contractors 186
deregulation 33, 38, Chapter 10, 309, 386
disability protection 333
discrimination 321
displacement 241–2
divergences 344–5, 348, 358
domestic
  work 131, 199, 228, 238, 429–30, 433
  workers 214, 219, 225, 251, 254, 378, 383, 434
  see also family labour
Dominican Republic 392

ECHR *see* European Convention on Human Rights
ECJ *see* European Court of Justice
economic crisis 23, 40, 51, 298, 300, 346, 361, 387, 411
economic subordination *see* subordination
ECtHR *see* European Court of Human Rights
ETI *see* Ethical Trade Initiative
employee-like 186
  see also dependent contractors
employee status 182, 184, 235, 250

employment at will 215
Employment Discrimination Framework Directive 204
employee involvement in management 51
equality 31–2, 34, 111, 204
  legal 119, 132–6, 370–72, 380
  opportunity 41, 148–9
  pay 31–3, 141–3, 149, 173, 214, 313–14, 389
  political 60
  racial 333
  social 299
Ethical Trade Initiative 356
EU *see* European Union
European Comparative Labour Law group 30
European Convention on Human Rights 34, 50, 199
European Court of Justice 66, 197
European Court of Human Rights 50, 354
European Social Charter 53, 349
European Union 83, 138
  directives 50, 203
  legislative activities 45, 204, 325–7, 407
  strike 352–4
EWC *see* European Works Council
exclusion 242–3
exit strategy 405–19

FAAA *see* Federal Aviation Administrative Authorization Act
fair distribution 137
Fair Labour Association 356–7
fair pay 34, 142
family labour 224–6, 229–30, 235–9
Federal Aviation Administrative Authorization Act 281
feminism 39–40, 129, 134, 227–9, 236–8, 243–5, 429
financial crisis *see* economic crisis
Fineman, Martha 239, 244
Finland 352, 408–9
Fixed-term Work Directive 203
Fixed-term Work Regulations 203
FLA *see* Fair Labour Association
flexibility 33, 38–41, 67, 73–7, 84, 169, 275–6, 290–91, Chapter 23
  flexicurity 49, 73, 76–8, 167, 205, 208, 221, 409
  regulations 124–6, 309
foreign workers 254, 370
Framework Agreements 53–4
France 38–40, 91, 194, 350, 359–61, 390–95, 402, 417, 422, 432–3
freedom of association 30, 103, 119, 141, 143, 150, 173, 212, 247, 349–57, 426
free labour 252, 423–4
freelance 77, 185, 245
free market 41, 65–6, 118–19, 137, 179–81, 322–4

Garment Worker Center 279
GDP *see* gross domestic product
General Directive 257–8, 269
Germany 31–2, 38–40, 44–8, 51, 58, 63–5, 89–91, 164, Chapter 16, 309, 352–3
global financial crisis *see* economic crisis
gross domestic product 25, 112, 116, 169, 173
globalization 22, 33, 39, 41, 45–6, 52, 61–2, 66, 92, 143, 154, 275, 297, 325–6, 344, 347, 358, 365, 375–6, 383–6, 403, 411, 434–5
Global Reporting Initiative 356
good faith 287
GPA *see* Agreement on Government Procurement
Great Depression 23, 40, 333
Greater London Authority 271
Greece 39, 350
GRI *see* Global Reporting Initiative
gross domestic product 25
Guatemala 394

HDI *see* Human Development Index
HERE *see* Hotel Employees and Restaurant Union
hierarchy of norms 63
high-performance work systems 25–6
high transaction costs 125
see also market failures
Hong Kong 433
Hotel Employees and Restaurant Union 278, 282, 284
human capital 24–6, 112–14, 125, 180, 291
Human Development Index 173
human dignity 44–6, 50, 141, 174, 180, 229–31, 432
human rights 23–4, 28–30, 122–4, 140–45, 153–4, 157, 229, 354, Chapter 22, 434

ILO *see* International Labour Organization
IMF *see* International Monetary Fund
India 163, 223–9, 298, 423, 433
independent contractors 185–9, 275, 280
see also freelance
individualization 34, 39, 124
Industrial Court 210–11
industrialization 32, 45, 157, 164–9, 174, 300–01, 309–11, 313
  deindustrialization 277
  industrial revolution 14, 36, 112, 325, 420, 422–3, 433
  post-industrialization 45
informal employment 223–33, 240
information asymmetry 125
see also market failures
injury protection 333
internationalism 383

International Labour Organization 52–5, 67–71, 156–7, 218–20, 224–31, 298–9, 312–13, 325–7, 348–9, 354–6, Chapter 22, 403–4
International Monetary Fund 408
international regulation 74, 349
Ireland 351
Italy 38–40, 91, 350, 353, 395

Japan 41
job security 160, 171, 221, 252, 275, 306, 329
job tenure 15, 25, 169
joint employers 187
just cause dismissal 180, 211, 252

Kahn-Freund, Otto 32, 37, 105, 119, 123, 209, 295
Keynes, Maynard 12
Keynesianism 15, 38, 40, 326, 333, 371
  see also Keynes, Maynard
Klare, Karl 31, 337–8

Labour flexibility *see* flexibility
Labour Relations Act 212, 217
Labour-social alliance 277–83
labour solidarity 20–22, 383
Latin America Chapter 5, 162–70, 385–6, 390–91, 394–5, 403
Lisbon Treaty 50, 408
living wage 28, 271, 279–92, 296, 307, 339
London Living Wage 270–71
Los Angeles
  Alliance for the New Economy 278–84, 289
  airport 278–9, 283–5, 289

market failures 125, 137, 160–61, 166, 180
Marx, Karl 64
marxism 316, 323
MEAT *see* most economically advantageous tender
media 348
medical insurance 333
Mexico 250, 382, 386, 395, 403
MFM *see* Multilateral Framework on Migration
migrant workers 48, 143, 209, 250, 277, 322–3, 338, 346, Chapter 22
minimum wage 159–69, 180, 219–20, 267–71, 296, 306, 321–2, 333, 389, 401
misclassification 241
Mitchell, Richard 18, 125
MNE *see* multinational enterprise
morality 400–03
Morocco 392–3
most economically advantageous tender 261–2
Multilateral Framework on Migration 365–9, 375, 377–80, 382
multinational enterprise 52–5
multiple employers 187–8, 218–21, 240

Namibia 218–19, 433
National Day Labour Organizing Network 279
nationalism 368, 381–4
neoclassical approaches 80–82, 125–8, 158–61, 171, 175
Netherlands 39, 58, 91
new forms of work *see* change in labour law
new institutionalist approaches 159–62
New Zealand 165
NGO *see* non-governmental organization
non-governmental organization 55–6, 67–8, 356, 398
non-standard employment 21, 297
    see also change in labour law
North America 16–17, 21, 25–7, 164–5, 168–72, 329–31
North Carolina 247
Nussbaum, Martha 171–2, 433

OECD *see* Organisation for Economic Co-operation and Development
Offe, Claus 318–19, 322
Organisation for Economic Co-operation and Development 54–5, 356
outsourcing 22, 83, 217–18, 238
overtime 251, 333, 371, 389

Peck, Jamie 121
pension 25, 169–70, 185, 219, 264–6, 324, 382
personal work contract 35, 79, 191, 198, 201–3, 207
Philadelphia Convention 122
picketing 17, 353
pluralism 16, 37, 434, 435
Poland 170–71
Polanyi, Karl 64, 121, 127, 130, 165, 175, 238, 422, 436
Portugal 39, 350
Posted Workers Directive 257–60, 267–9
prerogative 60, 123, 146, 323, 328, 411, 417
primary goods 146–50, 154
prison labour 236–8, 241, 245, 248, 254–5
privacy 46, 50, 147, 150
privatization 38, 170, 278, 390
public procurement Chapter 16, 300, 312–13
purposive analysis 183
PWT *see* Posted Workers Directive

Quadrangular employment *see* multiple employers

race to the bottom 44, 104, 290, Chapter 19, 386
redistribution 57, 115–16, 124, 133–5, 152, 179, 230, 302, 412
regulatory theory 32–3
Restatement of Employment Law 183
Rodgers, Daniel 23

Scandinavia 265
Scharpf, Fritz 66
SEIU *see* Service Employees International Union
self-employed 21, 46–8, 165, 191, 202, 224–32, 358
self-regulation 34, 44, 47, 105, 121, 316, 347, 355–8
Sen, Amartya 76, 79, 92, 111–12, 126–7, 171, 433
Service Employees International Union 95, 278
Simmel, Georg 344
Sinzheimer, Hugo 32, 44, 49–50, Chapter 4, 89, 104, 119, 122, 313
Slavery 141, 218, 422–7, 430–32
social clause 261–7, 272, 376
social insurance 59, 163–71, 174, 341
social law 18
social norms 127, 130, 135
social rights 24, 50, 66, 82, 126–8, 153, 163, 349, 354, 358–62, 407, 418
social security 31, 38, 41, 44, 49, 76–7, 86, 141, 149, 163, 167, 169–70, 172–3, 200, 225–7, 229, 232–3, 245, 297, 300, 369–73, 381, 428
social status 19, 242, 250
soft law 55–6, 74, 85, 212, 299, 347, 410
South Africa 163, 210–14, 218–21, 350–51, 433
Soviet Union 403
Spain 39, 194–5, 350, 353, 359
strike Chapter 2, Chapter 6, Chapter 13, 247, 283, 339–40, Chapter 21, 433
    cyber-strike 346–7
    political strikes 353, 359, 362
    right 173, 344–62
    solidarity strikes 332, 353–4
subordination 32, 35–7, 45–6, 59–60, 75–9, 85–6, 186–7, 209, 239, 243, 248
sub-contracting 217, 219, 415
substitution 238
Summers, Clyde 90
Supiot, Alain 113, 126, 200
Sweden 91, 167, 309, 352, 415
systemic approaches 162

temporal structure 235, 240
temporary agency
    regulations 204
    work 47
    worker 46
Teubner, Gunther 24, 67
theory of justice Chapter 7, 144–5, 155
TNCs *see* transnational corporations
Tobago 433
trade union 32–5, 39–40, 62, 173, 319–20, Chapter 20, 351
    decline of 47, 217, 274, 319, 323, 334
    exclusive representation 327

international 54–5, 356, 417, 432
legality 64, 127, 141, 150, 217, 349, 370
North American 17
Trade Unions Act 227
Transfer of Undertakings (Protection of Employment) Regulations 35, 203, 217
transnational
corporations 40, 67–8, 355–7
juridification 405–8
Treaties of Rome 66
triangular employment *see* multiple employers
Trinidad 433
TUPE *see* Transfer of Undertakings (Protection of Employment) Regulations
Turkey 354–5

UN *see* United Nations
unemployment 158–9, 167–70, 175, 220–21, 298, 302–4, 312–13, 326, 359
insurance 333, 370
unfair dismissal *see* wrongful dismissal
United Kingdom 19, 37–40, 63–4, 138, 258, 309, 351, 422–3
United Nations 54
United States 17, 28, 43, 94, 122–3, 138, 236, 247, 251–3, 274–7, 291–2, 330–31, 341, 351, 385–6, 394, 402–4
Universal Declaration of Human Rights 140, 142–3, 349
University of Cape Town 209
unjust dismissal *see* wrongful dismissal
Unorganised Workers' Social Security Act 229

Uruguay 169, 427

Veneziani, Bruno 122
Versailles Treaty 143

Wagner Act 17
Walker, Neil 62
Washington consensus 156, 171, 173–4, 309, 385
Webb, Beatrice 63
Webb, Sidney 63
Weber, Max 395–9
Weimar
constitution 32, 58, 62
Republic 37, 58
welfare state 36–41, 153, 170–71, 243, 337–9, 346, 371, 418
anti-welfare state 121
We Make the Road by Walking 338
Western Europe 26, 73, 91, 122, 158, 164–5, 170–74, 372, 402
Williams, Joan 238
work councils 27, 31, 51, 58–9, 62–3, 67, 89, 410
Works Councils Act 59
European Works Council 54, 415–18
work inspector 389–94, 404
World Trade Organization 257
wrongful dismissal 18, 35, 148–9, 155, 160–61, 210–22
WTO *see* World Trade Organization

Zelizer, Viviana 238, 246, 248

UNIVERSITY OF WINCHESTER
LIBRARY